NOVELS
for Students

Advisors

NOVELS

for Students

**Presenting Analysis, Context, and Criticism
on Commonly Studied Novels**

VOLUME 35

Sara Constantakis, Project Editor

Foreword by Anne Devereaux Jordan

GALE
CENGAGE Learning·

Detroit • New York • San Francisco • New Haven, Conn • Waterville, Maine • London

Novels for Students, Volume 35

Project Editor: Sara Constantakis

Rights Acquisition and Management: Margaret Chamberlain-Gaston, Leitha Etheridge-Sims, Kelly Quin, Aja Perales

Composition: Evi Abou-El-Seoud

Manufacturing: Drew Kalasky

Imaging: John Watkins

Product Design: Pamela A. E. Galbreath, Jennifer Wahi

Content Conversion: Katrina Coach

Product Manager: Meggin Condino

For product information and technology assistance, contact us at
Gale Customer Support, 1-800-877-4253.
For permission to use material from this text or product, submit all requests online at **www.cengage.com/permissions.**
Further permissions questions can be emailed to
permissionrequest@cengage.com

Gale
27500 Drake Rd.
Farmington Hills, MI, 48331-3535

ISBN-13: 978-1-4144-6698-9
ISBN-10: 1-4144-6698-6

ISSN 1094-3552

This title is also available as an e-book.
ISBN-13: 978-1-4144-7364-2
ISBN-10: 1-4144-7364-8
Contact your Gale, a part of Cengage Learning sales representative for ordering information.

Printed in the United States of America
1 2 3 4 5 6 7 14 13 12 11 10

Table of Contents

The Informed Dialogue: Interacting with Literature

When we pick up a book, we usually do so with the anticipation of pleasure. We hope that by entering the time and place of the novel and sharing the thoughts and actions of the characters, we will find enjoyment. Unfortunately, this is often not the case; we are disappointed. But we should ask, has the author failed us, or have we failed the author?

We establish a dialogue with the author, the book, and with ourselves when we read. Consciously and unconsciously, we ask questions: "Why did the author write this book?" "Why did the author choose that time, place, or character?" "How did the author achieve that effect?" "Why did the character act that way?" "Would I act in the same way?" The answers we receive depend upon how much information about literature in general and about that book specifically we ourselves bring to our reading.

Young children have limited life and literary experiences. Being young, children frequently do not know how to go about exploring a book, nor sometimes, even know the questions to ask of a book. The books they read help them answer questions, the author often coming right out and *telling* young readers the things they are learning or are expected to learn. The perennial classic, *The Little Engine That Could, tells* its readers that, among other things, it is good to help others and brings happiness:

"Hurray, hurray," cried the funny little clown and all the dolls and toys. "The good little boys and girls in the city will be happy because you helped us, kind, Little Blue Engine."

In picture books, messages are often blatant and simple, the dialogue between the author and reader one-sided. Young children are concerned with the end result of a book—the enjoyment gained, the lesson learned—rather than with how that result was obtained. As we grow older and read further, however, we question more. We come to expect that the world within the book will closely mirror the concerns of our world, and that the author will *show* these through the events, descriptions, and conversations within the story, rather than *telling* of them. We are now expected to do the interpreting, carry on our share of the dialogue with the book and author, and glean not only the author's message, but comprehend how that message and the overall affect of the book were achieved. Sometimes, however, we need help to do these things. *Novels for Students* provides that help.

A novel is made up of many parts interacting to create a coherent whole. In reading a novel, the more obvious features can be easily spotted—theme, characters, plot—but we may overlook the more subtle elements that greatly influence how the novel is perceived by the reader: viewpoint, mood and tone, symbolism, or the use of humor. By focusing on both the obvious and more subtle literary elements within a novel,

Novels for Students aids readers in both analyzing for message and in determining how and why that message is communicated. In the discussion on Harper Lee's *To Kill a Mockingbird* (Vol. 2), for example, the mockingbird as a symbol of innocence is dealt with, among other things, as is the importance of Lee's use of humor which "enlivens a serious plot, adds depth to the characterization, and creates a sense of familiarity and universality." The reader comes to understand the internal elements of each novel discussed—as well as the external influences that help shape it.

"The desire to write greatly," Harold Bloom of Yale University says, "is the desire to be elsewhere, in a time and place of one's own, in an originality that must compound with inheritance, with an anxiety of influence." A writer seeks to create a unique world within a story, but although it is unique, it is not disconnected from our own world. It speaks to us *because* of what the writer brings to the writing from our world: how he or she was raised and educated; his or her likes and dislikes; the events occurring in the real world at the time of the writing, and while the author was growing up. When we know what an author has brought to his or her work, we gain a greater insight into both the "originality" (the world of the book), and the things that "compound" it. This insight enables us to question that created world and find answers more readily. By informing ourselves, we are able to establish a more effective dialogue with both book and author.

Novels for Students, in addition to providing a plot summary and descriptive list of characters—to remind readers of what they have read—also explores the external influences that shaped each book. Each entry includes a discussion of the author's background, and the historical context in which the novel was written. It is vital to know, for instance, that when Ray Bradbury was writing *Fahrenheit 451* (Vol. 1), the threat of Nazi domination had recently ended in Europe, and the McCarthy hearings were taking place in Washington, D.C. This information goes far in answering the question, "Why did he write a story of oppressive government control and book burning?" Similarly, it is important to know that Harper Lee, author of *To Kill a Mockingbird,* was

born and raised in Monroeville, Alabama, and that her father was a lawyer. Readers can now see why she chose the south as a setting for her novel—it is the place with which she was most familiar—and start to comprehend her characters and their actions.

Novels for Students helps readers find the answers they seek when they establish a dialogue with a particular novel. It also aids in the posing of questions by providing the opinions and interpretations of various critics and reviewers, broadening that dialogue. Some reviewers of *To Kill A Mockingbird,* for example, "faulted the novel's climax as melodramatic." This statement leads readers to ask, "Is it, indeed, melodramatic?" "If not, why did some reviewers see it as such?" "If it is, why did Lee choose to make it melodramatic?" "Is melodrama ever justified?" By being spurred to ask these questions, readers not only learn more about the book and its writer, but about the nature of writing itself.

The literature included for discussion in *Novels for Students* has been chosen because it has something vital to say to us. *Of Mice and Men, Catch-22, The Joy Luck Club, My Antonia, A Separate Peace* and the other novels here speak of life and modern sensibility. In addition to their individual, specific messages of prejudice, power, love or hate, living and dying, however, they and all great literature also share a common intent. They force us to *think*—about life, literature, and about others, not just about ourselves. They pry us from the narrow confines of our minds and thrust us outward to confront the world of books and the larger, real world we all share. *Novels for Students* helps us in this confrontation by providing the means of enriching our conversation with literature and the world, by creating an *informed* dialogue, one that brings true pleasure to the personal act of reading.

Sources

Harold Bloom, *The Western Canon, The Books and School of the Ages,* Riverhead Books, 1994.

Watty Piper, *The Little Engine That Could,* Platt & Munk, 1930.

Anne Devereaux Jordan
Senior Editor, TALL (Teaching and Learning Literature)

Introduction

Purpose of the Book

The purpose of *Novels for Students* (*NfS*) is to provide readers with a guide to understanding, enjoying, and studying novels by giving them easy access to information about the work. Part of Gale's "For Students" Literature line, *NfS* is specifically designed to meet the curricular needs of high school and undergraduate college students and their teachers, as well as the interests of general readers and researchers considering specific novels. While each volume contains entries on "classic" novels frequently studied in classrooms, there are also entries containing hard-to-find information on contemporary novels, including works by multicultural, international, and women novelists. Entries profiling film versions of novels not only diversify the study of novels but support alternate learning styles, media literacy, and film studies curricula as well.

The information covered in each entry includes an introduction to the novel and the novel's author; a plot summary, to help readers unravel and understand the events in a novel; descriptions of important characters, including explanation of a given character's role in the novel as well as discussion about that character's relationship to other characters in the novel; analysis of important themes in the novel; and an explanation of important literary techniques and movements as they are demonstrated in the novel.

In addition to this material, which helps the readers analyze the novel itself, students are also provided with important information on the literary and historical background informing each work. This includes a historical context essay, a box comparing the time or place the novel was written to modern Western culture, a critical essay, and excerpts from critical essays on the novel. A unique feature of *NfS* is a specially commissioned critical essay on each novel, targeted toward the student reader.

The "literature to film" entries on novels vary slightly in form, providing background on film technique and comparison to the original, literary version of the work. These entries open with an introduction to the film, which leads directly into the plot summary. The summary highlights plot changes from the novel, key cinematic moments, and/or examples of key film techniques. As in standard entries, there are character profiles (noting omissions or additions, and identifying the actors), analysis of themes and how they are illustrated in the film, and an explanation of the cinematic style and structure of the film. A cultural context section notes any time period or setting differences from that of the original work, as well as cultural differences between the time in which the original work was written and the time in which the film adaptation was made. A film entry concludes with a critical overview and critical essays on the film.

To further help today's student in studying and enjoying each novel or film, information on media adaptations is provided (if available), as well as suggestions for works of fiction, nonfiction, or film on similar themes and topics. Classroom aids include ideas for research papers and lists of critical and reference sources that provide additional material on the novel. Film entries also highlight signature film techniques demonstrated, and suggest media literacy activities and prompts to use during or after viewing a film.

Selection Criteria

The titles for each volume of *NfS* are selected by surveying numerous sources on notable literary works and analyzing course curricula for various schools, school districts, and states. Some of the sources surveyed include: high school and undergraduate literature anthologies and textbooks; lists of award-winners, and recommended titles, including the Young Adult Library Services Association (YALSA) list of best books for young adults. Films are selected both for the literary importance of the original work and the merits of the adaptation (including official awards and widespread public recognition).

Input solicited from our expert advisory board—consisting of educators and librarians—guides us to maintain a mix of "classic" and contemporary literary works, a mix of challenging and engaging works (including genre titles that are commonly studied) appropriate for different age levels, and a mix of international, multicultural and women authors. These advisors also consult on each volume's entry list, advising on which titles are most studied, most appropriate, and meet the broadest interests across secondary (grades 7–12) curricula and undergraduate literature studies.

How Each Entry Is Organized

Each entry, or chapter, in *NfS* focuses on one novel. Each entry heading lists the full name of the novel, the author's name, and the date of the novel's publication. The following elements are contained in each entry:

Introduction: a brief overview of the novel which provides information about its first appearance, its literary standing, any controversies surrounding the work, and major conflicts or themes within the work. Film entries identify the original novel and provide understanding of the film's reception and reputation, along with that of the director.

Author Biography: in novel entries, this section includes basic facts about the author's life, and focuses on events and times in the author's life that inspired the novel in question.

Plot Summary: a factual description of the major events in the novel. Lengthy summaries are broken down with subheads. Plot summaries of films are used to uncover plot differences from the original novel, and to note the use of certain film angles or other techniques.

Characters: an alphabetical listing of major characters in the novel. Each character name is followed by a brief to an extensive description of the character's role in the novel, as well as discussion of the character's actions, relationships, and possible motivation. In film entries, omissions or changes to the cast of characters of the film adaptation are mentioned here, and the actors' names—and any awards they may have received—are also included.

Characters are listed alphabetically by last name. If a character is unnamed—for instance, the narrator in *Invisible Man*—the character is listed as "The Narrator" and alphabetized as "Narrator." If a character's first name is the only one given, the name will appear alphabetically by that name.

Variant names are also included for each character. Thus, the full name "Jean Louise Finch" would head the listing for the narrator of *To Kill a Mockingbird*, but listed in a separate cross-reference would be the nickname "Scout Finch."

Themes: a thorough overview of how the major topics, themes, and issues are addressed within the novel. Each theme discussed appears in a separate subhead. While the key themes often remain the same or similar when a novel is adapted into a film, film entries demonstrate how the themes are conveyed cinematically, along with any changes in the portrayal of the themes.

Style: this section addresses important style elements of the novel, such as setting, point of view, and narration; important literary devices used, such as imagery, foreshadowing, symbolism; and, if applicable, genres to which the work might have belonged, such as Gothicism or Romanticism. Literary terms are explained within the entry but can also be found in the Glossary. Film entries cover how the director conveyed the meaning, message, and mood of the work using film in comparison to the author's use of language, literary device, etc., in the original work.

Historical Context: in novel entries, this section outlines the social, political, and cultural climate in which the author lived and the novel was created. This section may include descriptions of related historical events, pertinent aspects of daily life in the culture, and the artistic and literary sensibilities of the time in which the work was written. If the novel is a historical work, information regarding the time in which the novel is set is also included. Each section is broken down with helpful subheads. Film entries contain a similar Cultural Context section because the film adaptation might explore an entirely different time period or culture than the original work, and may also be influenced by the traditions and views of a time period much different than that of the original author.

Critical Overview: this section provides background on the critical reputation of the novel or film, including bannings or any other public controversies surrounding the work. For older works, this section includes a history of how the novel or film was first received and how perceptions of it may have changed over the years; for more recent novels, direct quotes from early reviews may also be included.

Criticism: an essay commissioned by *NfS* which specifically deals with the novel or film and is written specifically for the student audience, as well as excerpts from previously published criticism on the work (if available).

Sources: an alphabetical list of critical material used in compiling the entry, with full bibliographical information.

Further Reading: an alphabetical list of other critical sources which may prove useful for the student. It includes full bibliographical information and a brief annotation.

Suggested Search Terms: a list of search terms and phrases to jumpstart students' further information seeking. Terms include not just titles and author names but also terms and topics related to the historical and literary context of the works.

In addition, each novel entry contains the following highlighted sections, set apart from the main text as sidebars:

Media Adaptations: if available, a list of audiobooks and important film and television adaptations of the novel, including source information. The list also includes stage adaptations, musical adaptations, etc.

Topics for Further Study: a list of potential study questions or research topics dealing with the novel. This section includes questions related to other disciplines the student may be studying, such as American history, world history, science, math, government, business, geography, economics, psychology, etc.

Compare and Contrast: an "at-a-glance" comparison of the cultural and historical differences between the author's time and culture and late twentieth century or early twenty-first century Western culture. This box includes pertinent parallels between the major scientific, political, and cultural movements of the time or place the novel was written, the time or place the novel was set (if a historical work), and modern Western culture. Works written after the mid-1970s may not have this box.

What Do I Read Next?: a list of works that might give a reader points of entry into a classic work (e.g., YA or multicultural titles) and/ or complement the featured novel or serve as a contrast to it. This includes works by the same author and others, works from various genres, YA works, and works from various cultures and eras.

The film entries provide sidebars more targeted to the study of film, including:

Film Technique: a listing and explanation of four to six key techniques used in the film, including shot styles, use of transitions, lighting, sound or music, etc.

Read, Watch, Write: media literacy prompts and/or suggestions for viewing log prompts.

What Do I See Next?: a list of films based on the same or similar works or of films similar in directing style, technique, etc.

Other Features

NfS includes "The Informed Dialogue: Interacting with Literature," a foreword by Anne Devereaux Jordan, Senior Editor for *Teaching and Learning Literature* (*TALL*), and a founder of the Children's Literature Association. This essay provides an enlightening look at how readers interact with literature and how *Novels for Students* can help teachers show students how to enrich their own reading experiences.

A Cumulative Author/Title Index lists the authors and titles covered in each volume of the *NfS* series.

A Cumulative Nationality/Ethnicity Index breaks down the authors and titles covered in each volume of the *NfS* series by nationality and ethnicity.

A Subject/Theme Index, specific to each volume, provides easy reference for users who may be studying a particular subject or theme rather than a single work. Significant subjects, from events to broad themes, are included.

Each entry may include illustrations, including photo of the author, stills from film adaptations, maps, and/or photos of key historical events, if available.

Citing Novels for Students

When writing papers, students who quote directly from any volume of *NfS* may use the following general forms. These examples are based on MLA style; teachers may request that students adhere to a different style, so the following examples may be adapted as needed.

When citing text from *NfS* that is not attributed to a particular author (i.e., the Themes, Style, Historical Context sections, etc.), the following format should be used in the bibliography section:

> "*Night.*" *Novels for Students*. Ed. Marie Rose Napierkowski. Vol. 4. Detroit: Gale, 1998. 234–35.

When quoting the specially commissioned essay from *NfS* (usually the first piece under the "Criticism" subhead), the following format should be used:

Miller, Tyrus. Critical Essay on "*Winesburg, Ohio.*" *Novels for Students*. Ed. Marie Rose Napierkowski. Vol. 4. Detroit: Gale, 1998. 335–39.

When quoting a journal or newspaper essay that is reprinted in a volume of *NfS*, the following form may be used:

> Malak, Amin. "Margaret Atwood's *The Handmaid's Tale* and the Dystopian Tradition." *Canadian Literature* 112 (Spring 1987): 9–16. Excerpted and reprinted in *Novels for Students*. Vol. 4. Ed. Marie Rose Napierkowski. Detroit: Gale, 1998. 133–36.

When quoting material reprinted from a book that appears in a volume of *NfS*, the following form may be used:

> Adams, Timothy Dow. "Richard Wright: 'Wearing the Mask.'" In *Telling Lies in Modern American Autobiography*. University of North Carolina Press, 1990. 69–83. Excerpted and reprinted in *Novels for Students*. Vol. 1. Ed. Diane Telgen. Detroit: Gale, 1997. 59–61.

We Welcome Your Suggestions

The editorial staff of *Novels for Students* welcomes your comments and ideas. Readers who wish to suggest novels to appear in future volumes, or who have other suggestions, are cordially invited to contact the editor. You may contact the editor via e-mail at: **ForStudentsEditors@cengage.com.** Or write to the editor at:

Editor, *Novels for Students*
Gale
27500 Drake Road
Farmington Hills, MI 48331-3535

Literary Chronology

1640: Aphra Behn is born in Canterbury, England.

1688: Aphra Behn's novel *Oroonoko; or, The Royal Slave: A True History* is published in *Three Histories: Oroonoko, The Fair Jilt, Agnes de Castro*.

1689: Aphra Behn dies on April 16 in London, England.

1874: William Somerset Maugham is born on January 25 in Paris, France.

1876: Jack London is born on January 12 in San Francisco, California.

1904: Jack London's novel *The Sea-Wolf* is published.

1914: Howard Fast is born on November 11 in New York City.

1915: William Somerset Maugham's novel *Of Human Bondage* is published.

1916: Jack London dies of uremia and other factors on November 22 in Glen Ellen, California.

1937: Virginia Euwer Wolff is born on August 27 in Portland, Oregon.

1938: Robert Lipsyte is born on January 16 in New York, New York.

1945: Suzanne Fisher Staples is born on August 27 in Philadelphia, Pennsylvania.

1948: Art Spiegelman is born on February 15 in Stockholm, Sweden.

1950: S. E. (Susan Eloise) Hinton is born on July 22 in Tulsa, Oklahoma.

1952: Amy Tan is born on February 19 in Oakland, California.

1954: Gregory Maguire is born on June 9 in Albany, New York.

1954: Kazuo Ishiguro is born on November 8 in Nagasaki, Japan.

1961: Howard Fast's novel *April Morning* is published.

1961: Laurie Halse Anderson is born on October 23 in Potsdam, New York.

1965: William Somerset Maugham dies on December 15 in Nice, France.

1966: Chris Abani is born on December 27 in Afikpo, Nigeria.

1967: Robert Lipsyte's novel *The Contender* is published.

1967: S. E. Hinton's novel *The Outsiders* is published.

1983: Director Francis Ford Coppola's film *The Outsiders* is released.

1986: The first volume of Art Spiegelman's graphic novel *Maus: A Survivor's Tale*, subtitled *My Father Bleeds History*, is published.

1989: Amy Tan's novel *The Joy Luck Club* is published.

1989: Suzanne Fisher Staples's novel *Shabanu: Daughter of the Wind* is published.

1990: Kazuo Ishiguro is awarded the Booker Prize for *The Remains of the Day*.

1991: The second volume of Art Spiegelman's graphic novel *Maus: A Survivor's Tale*, subtitled *And Here My Troubles Began*, is published.

1992: Art Spiegelman is awarded the Pulitzer Prize in the special awards and citations—letters category for *Maus: A Survivor's Tale*.

1993: Director Wayne Wang's film *The Joy Luck Club* is released.

1993: Virginia Euwer Wolff's novel *Make Lemonade* is published.

1995: Gregory Maguire's novel Wicked: The Life and Times of the Wicked Witch of the West is published.

2000: Laurie Halse Anderson's novel *Fever 1793* is published.

2003: Howard Fast dies on March 12 in Old Greenwich, Connecticut.

2004: Chris Abani's novel *GraceLand* is published.

2005: Kazuo Ishiguro's novel *Never Let Me Go* is published.

Acknowledgments

The editors wish to thank the copyright holders of the excerpted criticism included in this volume and the permissions managers of many book and magazine publishing companies for assisting us in securing reproduction rights. We are also grateful to the staffs of the Detroit Public Library, the Library of Congress, the University of Detroit Mercy Library, Wayne State University Purdy/Kresge Library Complex, and the University of Michigan Libraries for making their resources available to us. Following is a list of the copyright holders who have granted us permission to reproduce material in this volume of *NfS*. Every effort has been made to trace copyright, but if omissions have been made, please let us know.

COPYRIGHTED EXCERPTS IN *NfS*, VOLUME 35, WERE REPRODUCED FROM THE FOLLOWING PERIODICALS:

America, v. 191, August 2, 2009. Copyright © 2009 www.americamagazine.org. All rights reserved. Reproduced by permission of America Press. For subscription information, visit www.americamagazine.org.—*American Literature*, v. 70, June, 1998. Copyright © 1998 Duke University Press. All rights reserved. Used by permission of the publisher.—*ANQ*, v. 16, Summer, 2003. Copyright © 2003 by Helen Dwight Reid Educational Foundation. Reproduced with permission of the Helen Dwight Reid Educational Foundation, published by Heldref Publications, 1319 18th Street, NW, Washington, DC 20036-1802.—*ARIEL*, v. 39, October, 2008 for "Riffing on Resistance: Music in Chris Abani's 'Graceland'" by Stefan Sereda. Copyright © 2008 The Board of Governors, The University of Calgary. Reproduced by permission of the publisher and the author.—*BOMB*, v. 96, Summer, 2006. Copyright © *BOMB* Magazine, New Art Publications, Inc., and its Contributors. All rights reserved. Reproduced by permission.—*Bookbird*, v. 35, Fall, 1997. Copyright © 1997 by Bookbird, Inc. Reproduced by permission.—*Booklist*, v. 90, March 1, 1994; v. 101, April 15, 2005. Copyright © 1994, 2005 by the American Library Association. Both reproduced by permission.—*Business Wire*, June 13, 2005. Copyright © 2005 Business Wire Inc. All rights reserved. Reproduced by permission.—*Clio*, v. 28, Fall, 1998. Copyright © 1998 by Purdue Research Foundation. Reproduced by permission.—*Commonweal*, v. 132, July 15, 2005. Copyright © 2005 Commonweal Publishing Co., Inc. Reproduced by permission of Commonweal Foundation.—*Daily News* (New York), November 7, 2002. © 2002 New York News, L.P. Used with permission.—*Essays In Literature*, v. 4, Fall, 1977. Copyright © 1977 by Western Illinois University. Reproduced by permission.—*The Globe and Mail* (Toronto), January 19, 1978. Copyright © 1978 Globe Interactive, a division of Bell Globemedia Publishing, Inc. Reproduced by permission.—*The Horn Book Magazine*, v. 76, September, 2000; v. 77, May, 2001. Copyright 2000, 2001 by The Horn Book, Inc., Boston, MA, www.hbook.com. All rights reserved. Both reproduced by permission.—*Journal of Youth Services in Libraries*, v. 14, Summer, 2001. Copyright © 2001 by the American Library Association. Reproduced by permission.—*Lancet*, v. 365, April 9-15, 2005. Copyright © 2005 Elsevier Limited. All rights reserved. Reproduced by permission.—*Literature/Film Quarterly*, v. 24, 1996; v. 27, 1999. Copyright © 1996, 1999 Salisbury State College. Both reproduced by permission.—*The Midwest Quarterly*, v. 43, Summer, 2002. Copyright © 2002 by *The Midwest Quarterly*, Pittsburgh State University. Reproduced by permission.—*The Nation*, v. 280, May 16, 2005. Copyright © 2005 by *The Nation* Magazine/The Nation Company, Inc. Reproduced by permission.—*National Post* (Canada), March 30, 2004. © 2004 The National Post Company. All rights reserved. Material reprinted with the express permission of The National Post Company, a Canwest Partnership.—*National Review*, v. 45, November 15, 1993; v. 55, April 7, 2003. Copyright © 1993, 2003 by National Review, Inc., 215 Lexington Avenue, New York, NY 10016. Both reproduced by permission.—*Negro American Literature Forum*, v. 9, Summer, 1975. Reproduced by permission.—*The New Advocate*, v. 6, Summer, 1993 for "A Discussion with Suzanne Fisher Staples: The Author as Writer and Cultural Observer" by Walter E. Sawyer and Jean C. Sawyer. Reproduced by permission of the publisher and the authors.—*The New Leader*, v. 87, January-February, 2004; v. 88, March-April, 2005. Copyright © 2004, 2005 by The American Labor Conference on International Affairs, Inc. All rights reserved. Both reproduced by permission.—*New Statesman*, v. 18, March 7, 2005. Copyright © 2005 New Statesman, Ltd. Reproduced by permission.—*The Ottawa Citizen*, January 15, 2000 for "Sea Wolf a Swede? Not on Your Life: Rough and Ready Cape Bretoner Was Real Inspiration in Jack London's Best-seller" by Pat MacAdam. Copyright © 2000 CanWest Interactive Inc. and CanWest Publishing Inc. All rights reserved. Reproduced by permission of the author.—*The Progressive*, v. 69, January, 2005. Copyright © 2005 by The Progressive, Inc. Reproduced by permission of *The Progressive*, 409 East Main Street, Madison, WI 53703, www.progressive.org.—*Publishers Weekly*, v. 247, February 14, 2000; v. 247, December 18, 2000 v. 252; January 31, 2005. Copyright © 2000, 2005 by Reed Publishing USA. All reproduced from *Publishers Weekly*, published by the Bowker Magazine Group of Cahners Publishing Co., a division of Reed Publishing USA, by permission.—*School Library Journal*, v. 47, May, 2001; v. 47, June, 2001; v. 48, February, 2002; v. 55, June, 2009. Copyright © 2001, 2002, 2009. All reproduced from *School Library Journal*, a Cahners/R. R. Bowker Publication, by permission.—*Solander*, v. 13, spring, 2003 for "Hope for the Heart and Food for the Soul: Historical Fiction in the Life of Howard Fast" by Sarah Cuthbertson. © 2009 Historical Novel Society. All Rights Reserved. Reproduced by permission of the author.—*The Spectator*, v. 297, February 26, 2005. Copyright © 2005 by *The Spectator*. Reproduced by permission of *The Spectator*.—*Studies in English Literature, 1500-1900*, v. 47, summer, 2007. Copyright © William Marsh Rice University, 2007. Reproduced by permission.—*Studies in Short Fiction*, v. 34, winter, 1997. Copyright © 1997 by *Studies in Short Fiction*. Reproduced by permission.—*Studies in the Novel*, v. 39, spring, 2007. Copyright © 2007 by the University of North Texas. Reproduced by permission.—*Teaching Pre K-8*, v. 24, March, 1994. Reproduced with permission of the publisher, *Teaching K-8*, Norwalk, CT 06854.—*Top of the News*, v. 39, 1983. Copyright © 1983 by the American Library Association. Reproduced by permission.—*Video Business*, v. 25, September 5, 2005. Copyright © 2005 Reed Business Information, a division of Reed Elsevier Inc. All rights reserved. Reproduced by permission.—*Virginia English Bulletin*, v. 36, Winter, 1986 for "*April Morning*: Coming of Age, All in a Few Hours" by Ken Donelson. Copyright © 1986 by the Virginia Association of Teachers of English. Reproduced by permission of the author.—*The Virginian-Pilot*, May 11, 2009. Copyright © 2009 The Virginian-Pilot News. Reproduced by permission.—*Voice of Youth Advocates*, v. 23, December, 2000. Reproduced by permission.—*The Washington Post*, March 25, 1983 for "Greasy Kids' Stuff" by Gary Arnold. Copyright © 1983, *The Washington Post*. Reprinted with permission of the author.—*Weekly Standard*, v. 10, July 4-11, 2005. Copyright © 2005, News Corporation, *Weekly Standard*. All rights reserved. Reproduced by permission.

COPYRIGHTED EXCERPTS IN *NfS*, **VOL-UME 35, WERE REPRODUCED FROM THE FOLLOWING BOOKS:**

Burt, Forrest D. From *W. Somerset Maugham*. Twayne Publishers, 1986. Copyright © 1985 by G. K. Hall & Company. Reproduced by permission of Gale, a part of Cengage Learning.—Loss, Archie K. From *"Of Human Bondage": Coming of Age in the Novel*. Twayne Publishers, 1990. Copyright © 1990 by G. K. Hall & Co. Reproduced by permission of Gale, a part of Cengage Learning.— Reesman, Jeanne Campbell. From "The Critics: Carl A. Sandburg," in *Jack London: A Study of the Short Fiction*. Edited by Gary Scharnhorst and Eric Haralson. Twayne Publishers, 1999. Copyright © 1999 by Twayne Publishers. Reproduced by permission of Gale, a part of Cengage Learning.

Contributors

Bryan Aubrey: Aubrey holds a Ph.D. in English. Entries on *GraceLand* and *Never Let Me Go*. Original essays on *GraceLand* and *Never Let Me Go*.

Cynthia A. Bily: Bily is an instructor in English and literature. Entry on *The Sea-Wolf*. Original essay on *The Sea-Wolf*.

Catherine Dominic: Dominic is a novelist and a freelance writer and editor. Entries on *Of Human Bondage* and *Oroonoko; or, The Royal Slave: A True History*. Original essays on *Of Human Bondage* and *Oroonoko; or, The Royal Slave: A True History*.

Charlotte M. Freeman: Freeman is a freelance writer and former academic who lives in Montana. Entries on *Fever 1793* and *Wicked: The Life and Times of the Wicked Witch of the West*. Original essays on *Fever 1793* and *Wicked: The Life and Times of the Wicked Witch of the West*.

Joyce Hart: Hart is a published author and creative writing teacher. Entries on *April Morning* and *The Contender*. Original essays on *April Morning* and *The Contender*.

David Kelly: Kelly is a writer and an instructor of creative writing and literature at two colleges. Entries on *The Joy Luck Club* and *The Outsiders*. Original essays on *The Joy Luck Club* and *The Outsiders*.

Kathy Wilson Peacock: Wilson Peacock is a nonfiction writer who specializes in literature and history. Entry on *Maus: A Survivor's Tale*. Original essay on *Maus: A Survivor's Tale*.

Bradley A. Skeen: Skeen is a classics professor. Entry on *Shabanu: Daughter of the Wind*. Original essay on *Shabanu: Daughter of the Wind*.

Rebecca Valentine: Valentine is a writer with extensive background in literary theory and analysis. Entry on *Make Lemonade*. Original essay on *Make Lemonade*.

April Morning

HOWARD FAST

1961

Howard Fast's young-adult novel *April Morning* is more than a story of war. It is the story of a fifteen-year-old boy finding himself and becoming an adult in the middle of a revolution. When the story begins, Adam Cooper is a typical teen, living in eighteenth-century rural Massachusetts. As he does his morning chores, he grumbles about his parents not taking him seriously and treating him as if he were still a child, but everything in Adam's life is about to change. In just a little over twenty-four hours, he will be looked upon as a man—a successful soldier who is considered mature enough to marry and to become the new head of his family's household.

Fast is well known for taking stories from history books and turning them into gripping tales as seen through the eyes of common folk. Rather than narrating this novel, for example, through the experience of the high-ranking officers whose names appear frequently in the historical accounts, Fast creates a fictional character who witnesses all the same events but from a different and more personal point of view. In this novel, readers feel both the pride and the fear of the teenage protagonist who wants to be respected as an adult. Then, when he is suddenly given the chance, he questions why he wanted to grow up so fast.

April Morning was published in 1961, a transitional period for young-adult novels, which were finally coming into their own. Authors of stories

Howard Fast (Michael Smith / Time & Life Pictures / Getty Images)

written for teens were developing more serious subjects and were writing in a more literary form than had been used for young-adult books in previous decades. Fast's *April Morning* was considered one of the first to take on these new elements. J. Donald Adams, writing a review for the *New York Times*, predicted back in the 1960s that this novel would "some day reach the standing of an American classic."

AUTHOR BIOGRAPHY

Fast was born in New York City on November 11, 1914. His father held various positions as a manual laborer. Because his father earned only a meager wage, when Fast was twelve, he sold newspapers to provide more income for the family. After graduating from high school, Fast left home and traveled across the country by hopping free rides on railroad cars, mingling with train hobos along the way. It was during this time that Fast wrote his first novel, a historical romance called *Two Valleys* (1933), which enjoyed moderate success. His second

book, *Conceived in Liberty, A Novel of Valley Forge* (1939), brought him more fame as well as more money. It was with his second novel that Fast developed an interest in the American Revolution, a theme he would continue to pursue in his 1961 novel *April Morning*.

As his career as a writer progressed, Fast soon discovered his love of retelling history. For example, his 1941 novel *The Last Frontier* tells the little-known story of a Cheyenne uprising that took place in 1878, and his best-selling 1944 novel *Freedom Road* relates the story of the Reconstruction Era after the Civil War from the experience of a former slave. In another popular novel, *Citizen Tom Paine* (1943), Fast recounts the life of the man who spoke for the common man as Paine urged the colonies to go to war against Britain in the American Revolutionary War.

Fast became embroiled in politics in the 1950s. He had joined the Communist Party and was subpoenaed by the U.S. Congress to appear before the House Un-American Activities Committee. While facing the committee, Fast was asked to name his fellow members in the U.S. Communist Party. However, Fast refused and for this was sent to prison. This did not stop him from writing, though. While in jail, Fast produced one of his more famous novels, *Spartacus* (1951), which nine years later was adapted to film. However, once word spread that Fast was a communist, his books were taken off library shelves, and publishers were not as enthusiastic about publishing his new works, so he chose a pen name, E. V. Cunningham. Under this name, he wrote detective stories, such as *Sylvia* (1960) and *Alice* (1963). It was during this time that Fast moved to Los Angeles, California. He continued writing novels but also wrote plays and scripts. In 1975, Fast won an Emmy Award for outstanding writing in a drama series for his television script "The Ambassadors" (1963), which was part of the series *Benjamin Franklin*.

Fast produced more than eighty novels before his death on March 12, 2003, at the age of eighty-eight. He had returned to the East Coast in 1980 and lived in Connecticut with his wife, Bette, until she died in 1994. Fast was survived by his second wife, Mercedes, his daughter, Rachel, his son, Jonathan, and several stepchildren and grandchildren.

MEDIA ADAPTATIONS

- Delbert Mann directed the film version of *April Morning*, starring Tommy Lee Jones as Moses Cooper and Chad Lowe as Adam. The film was released in 1988 and was shown on television by Hallmark Hall of Fame Productions.

- Recorded Books offers a 1988 audio presentation of Fast's *April Morning* in both CD and audiocassette forms. Jamie Hanes is the reader.

PLOT SUMMARY

The Afternoon

April Morning opens on the afternoon of April 18, 1775, in the town of Lexington, Massachusetts. Adam Cooper, the fifteen-year-old protagonist, is doing chores while grumbling about how his father, Moses, under-appreciates him. Moses appears to be a stern father who does not waste his words but is quick to throw out a proverb, such as "slow to start and quick to finish," in his appraisal of his son's work ethics. When Moses tells Adam to draw water from their well, the boy recites the words of a spell. His eleven-year-old brother, Levi, overhears this and tells their father. Later that night at the dinner table, Moses reprimands Adam. First, he states that although Adam is tall enough to be a man he is not acting like a man. This is exactly what has been bothering Adam lately. He senses that he is approaching manhood, but no matter what he does, his father will not acknowledge that Adam is growing beyond childhood. Repeating the spell over the water is something Moses has declared superstitious and thus childish.

Granny Cooper, Moses's mother and Adam and Levi's grandmother, chastises her son for making a big fuss about Adam's reciting the spell. Though Adam's grandmother sometimes reprimands him for talking too freely about controversial topics, she enjoys Adam's conversations and often stands up for him. Granny Cooper also has a tendency to continue to speak to her son, Moses, as if he were still a child.

Joseph Simmons, Adam's cousin, comes to talk to Moses about a speech he has been asked to make on the universal rights of men. Joseph and Moses are going to an important committee meeting after dinner. Adam asks if he can also attend. Moses again challenges Adam, questioning whether he is ready to be a man. He tells Adam that the proof of manhood is found in his "will to work and the ability to use his mind and his judgment." Adam backs down, concerned that he does not yet have such proof. After his father leaves, Adam asks his mother and grandmother why his father disapproves of him. His father always finds fault with him, Adam tells them. They answer that that is just the way Moses is. Granny Cooper adds that Moses finds fault with everyone.

The Evening

Adam overhears his father talking to his mother about what happened at the meeting. Moses dislikes the committee's attention on weaponry, preferring arbitration. Adam says his father "deeply believed that if you could win an argument, you could win a war."

Adam visits Ruth Simmons, with whom he has been friends for most of his life. Ruth appears to have her mind set on eventually marrying Adam. However, Adam is not quite prepared to even think that far into the future. He notices, though, that Ruth is changing—she is turning into a woman. When Adam talks about possibly joining his Uncle Ishmael and sailing to the Indies, Ruth says that would make her very lonely. It pleases Adam that Ruth would miss him.

When Adam returns home, he finds Levi cleaning Adam's gun. Though he is still angry with Levi for telling their father about the water spell, Adam eventually softens and thanks Levi for the good job he has done. Levi has fantasies about being a soldier. He and his friends play games that entail killing imaginary redcoats.

After Adam goes to bed, he overhears his parents. His mother suggests that Moses find some way to show Adam that he loves him. At first, Moses rebels against this idea, stating that he is raising his son in the same way his father raised him. However, Moses relents and says he will think the matter over.

The Night
In the middle of the night, Levi runs to Adam to tell him about a nightmare he had about his own death. Adam takes Levi to the window and tries to calm him down. While standing there, Levi hears horse hooves beating against the road, an unusual occurrence in the middle of the night. Moses comes into the room and the boys tell him what they have heard. They also heard someone shouting. Moses is concerned. He suspects it is a messenger from Cambridge, Massachusetts, and he leaves the house to find out what is happening. Adam follows his father. A crowd has gathered around the rider, who tells them that a large troop of British soldiers is marching toward Lexington. Their destination is Concord, where they plan to destroy military supplies.

Jonas Parker wants to immediately call up the militia. Some people, including Sam Hodley, do not believe the British Army is really coming. The Reverend asks how they could fight this army, if it really is coming. Lexington has, at most, only seventy or eighty men who could fight, whereas the British might number nearly a thousand. Opposing the Reverend is Moses, who is against fighting but who is also an intellectual who likes to argue with the Reverend. Moses gives one of his rousing speeches, and by the time he stops talking, he has convinced the people that it is their moral obligation to stand up to the British and fight for their

rights. Adam is proud of his father's speech and follows the men to sign the muster book, a form of enlisting in the military. When Cousin Simmons sees Adam, he says to him: "A boy went to bed and a man awakened."

When Adam returns home, he overhears his mother telling Moses she is angry that he allowed Adam to sign up. "He's just a boy," Sarah says. Then Moses says, "Yesterday, he was a boy.... Tonight, he's not."

The Morning
Later, as Moses and Adam return to the village center, Moses puts his arm around his son's shoulders. This is the first sign of affection that Adam can remember receiving from his father. Moses then says: "I have found that when adversity confronts them, the Cooper men stand firmly." This is Moses's way of telling Adam that he has proven that he is now a man.

When they arrive at the common, a group of men is there with their guns. The coming of the British Army has been confirmed. However, the Reverend and Moses recommend that the men not be too eager to shoot. They hope the British are willing to negotiate. If the British refuse to talk, the Lexington men should let the British pass by. The British outnumber them, so there is no way of stopping them. When shots are heard in the distance, the men grow silent. Moses, Jonas Parker, and the Reverend stand at the front. The road is filled with redcoats—British soldiers—"so that they appeared to be an endless force and an endless number."

The British major, Pitcairn, commands his troops to line up opposite the Lexington militia. At this point, Adam says: "I realized, and I believed that everyone else around me realized, that this was not to be an exercise or a parade or an argument, but something undreamed of and unimagined." The Reverend attempts to speak to Major Pitcairn, but he does not listen and instead orders the Lexington men to put down their weapons.

The younger men want to comply, but Jonas Parker tells them to hold their positions. Then a shot is heard. Immediately afterward, a British soldier aims his gun at Moses. Adam sees his father fall. Filled with fear, Adam runs. As he does, he sees men lying on the ground, wounded or dead. Samuel Hodley has a hole in his neck. Jonas Parker is bleeding from his belly. Adam sees a British soldier run a bayonet through Parker's back. When he comes to a storage hut, Adam crawls in and hides. While he sits there shaking, Adam reexamines what he has just been through. It is then that the death of his father finally hits him. His father "would never come home again," Adam tells himself.

The Forenoon

Moses hides in the shed until he thinks the British soldiers have left. He sneaks out and runs for a meadow. He runs fast and hard, barely noticing what is up ahead of him. When he reaches a stone wall, he collapses on it and into a pair of strong arms. He fights to get free but is stopped by Solomon Chandler, who is part of the Massachusetts militia. Chandler makes Adam turn around to see the two soldiers he was running from and who are standing on the other side of the field. They are no longer chasing him.

Chandler, an older man, shares his lunch with Adam and gives him insights about the British soldiers. Adam tells Chandler about the events in Lexington, and Chandler commiserates with Adam's sadness over the loss of his father. Adam confesses he feels he acted cowardly in running away. However, Chandler tells him that that is exactly the proper tactic in dealing with the British. The colonists cannot defeat the British by using the same military tactics as the redcoats. The colonists will inflict the most damage by continually shooting at the British and then running away.

Chandler thinks the Concord militia will meet the British at North Bridge. The militia's plan is not to stop the British as the Lexington men had tried but rather to kill as many as they can, shooting at them from the sides of the road. When they reach a meeting place, Asley's Pasture, Adam is reunited with Cousin Simmons and the Reverend, whom Adam had worried might have been killed in Lexington.

The Midday

As men gather from the surrounding towns, Adam learns there are several meeting points along the main road where committee members have gathered. One of the bigger groups is poised at North Bridge, outside Concord. Adam, upon hearing this information, is proud of his father and his role in organizing the communities in eastern Massachusetts, in preparation for them to confront the British.

As the men wait for the British to turn around at Concord and march back to Boston, Cousin Simmons talks to Adam about Moses's death.

Simmons insinuates there is a chance that he might die in the war and asks Adam to look after his family, especially his daughter Ruth. As Simmons is talking, they hear gunshots in the distance. Chandler tells everyone to break up into small groups along the sides of the road. They should hide themselves as best they can, shoot, and then run quickly out of the reach of the British gunshots. Adam is with Cousin Simmons and the Reverend. Chandler tells Adam not to shoot his gun until he can count the buttons on the British soldiers' coats; his gun can have an effect only at very close range. When Chandler says they are fighting "in God's cause," the Reverend disputes this point: "Isn't it enough to kill in freedom's name? No one kills in God's cause. He can only ask God's forgiveness."

As the British soldiers approach, Adam notices how many are wounded. Blood is everywhere on their uniforms. They looked tired, angry, and full of fear. After Adam takes his first shot, he freezes in the spot. Cousin Simmons saves him by grabbing Adam by the arm and pulling him away. Later, as the fighting continues, Cousin Simmons explains to Adam that though he does not believe in fighting or war, their actions are now necessary because they are fighting for their freedom and their land. On the other hand, Simmons tells Adam that Chandler fights out of revenge. Adam observes some of the men around him, including Chandler. He hears them boasting of how many British they have killed. Adam is disgusted with their talk. He has seen young boys his own age mortally wounded. He saw a soldier's head blown off. He has had enough of the war.

The Afternoon

Adam is ready to forget all about fighting, but Cousin Simmons tells him this is just the beginning. The war could last years. Chandler confirms this as he rallies the men to follow him to where they can ambush the British. Chandler wants to clear the British out of their towns.

Adam is so worn out that he falls asleep in the middle of a battle. While he sleeps, Cousin Simmons and the Reverend look for him, praying that Adam has not been killed. As they search, they mention how proud they are of him. As they approach the place where Adam has fallen asleep, Adam hears their conversation, which makes him feel good. When Simmons and the Reverend find him, they greet him almost as if he were their own son, they are so pleased that Adam is alive. Cousin Simmons tells Adam it is time to go home. The

British have been driven away from Lexington. New committeemen have taken over the pursuit.

Near his home, Adam is greeted by his brother. Levi had heard that Adam was dead and can hardly believe that he is actually alive. When Adam enters his home, he finds his mother and grandmother are surrounded by neighbor women, who are there to prepare for Moses's funeral. Adam is led to his father's room to pay his respects. Adam is too numb from all the death he has seen that day to mourn for his father. He will remember him later, he states, not as a corpse but as he had lived. Adam returns downstairs and talks to Levi. He makes his younger brother realize that the two of them must now take on their father's responsibilities. They must take care of their mother. Levi tells Adam about the British soldiers that stormed their town while Adam was away, stealing food and crops, burning houses, and taking away horses and wagons. Then Adam's mother comes to him. She is crying and has no idea how they are going to survive without Moses. Adam attempts to soothe her, telling her everything will work out. Cousin Simmons then arrives and, with several other men, carries Moses's casket to the meetinghouse.

The Evening

Ruth accompanies Adam as he takes candles to the meetinghouse. His mother wants to make sure Moses's body will not be left in the dark. As Adam bemoans his surprisingly quick passage from childhood to manhood, he looks at Ruth and realizes she looks different to him, more beautiful than ever before. Ruth wraps her arms around him and kisses him. She tells him that when she heard the news that he was dead, everything died within her. She tells him she loves him and is not ashamed of saying so. Adam feels the same. He realizes there could not be another woman for him. Ruth knows so much about him and accepts him for who he is. It would take forever for another woman to learn as much about him.

Ruth asks whether Adam killed anyone. Adam does not think so; he says he did not hate anyone enough to kill him. When Ruth asks whether the British will return, Adam says no. Nothing will ever be the same. The Americans have now committed to fighting the British so they can gain their freedom. They will become better at fighting the British, Adam tells her.

The Reverend sees them and tells Adam that the Committeemen have called a muster. Ruth

does not want Adam to sign it. Adam says he has not made up his mind yet, but when Adam goes home, his grandmother knows better. She tells Adam that sooner or later he will once again leave. Adam tries to deny this but cannot. When he goes to bed, he gives thanks that the day is finally over. Before falling asleep, he says farewell to his childhood.

CHARACTERS

Solomon Chandler

Adam meets Solomon Chandler when Adam is running away from the British soldiers. Adam describes Chandler as a skinny but strong man, with a long face and yellow teeth. At first, Adam admires Solomon's strength, wisdom about war, and generosity. However, after hanging around him for several hours during that day of war, Adam comes to resent Solomon. Adam believes that Solomon, who has fought in many wars, enjoys killing.

Adam Cooper

Adam is the fifteen-year-old protagonist of this novel. The story is told from his perspective. Though he is considered a boy in the first section of this book, as he witnesses war, sees his father die, and shoots at British soldiers, he is quickly accepted as a man.

Manhood comes to Adam at a high cost. He is terrorized by the killing and brutality that he witnesses, especially the murder of his father. Though the experiences of the war force him into maturity, becoming a man is not as much fun as he once thought it might be. He must take on the responsibilities at home. He must watch over his mother, his grandmother, and his brother, Levi. He also contemplates marriage to Ruth, something he had thought would not occur for a long time into the future. The war has changed him, though. He must say good-bye to his childhood, for there is no turning back.

According to Cousin Simmons and the Reverend, as well Solomon Chandler, Adam has matured in a very honorable way. He has handled himself well in the midst of battle. He has not complained about the lack of sleep, the fear that nearly overwhelmed him, or any of the challenges that he has been forced to face. Though he is saddened by the loss of his father, he has not been distracted by his sorrow.

Granny Cooper

Granny Cooper, the mother of Moses Cooper, is a widow whose other children all died before the start of the novel. Granny lives with Moses, his wife, and their two children. Though her relationship with Levi is never portrayed, she is obviously close to Adam. She enjoys his company. Though Adam sometimes shocks her with some of his radical thoughts, she appreciates that he thinks deeply about things. Granny often sticks up for Adam when Moses reprimands, disagrees with, or criticizes him. Granny is not afraid to speak up to her son, though she is living in his house and is the head of the household. She often talks to Moses as if he were still her juvenile son.

Levi Cooper

Levi is Adam's eleven-year-old brother, the son of Moses and Sarah. The author uses Levi to compare the boy's rather immature thoughts about war with Adam's real experience with death on the battlefield. Levi lives in a fantasy world; he believes war might be fun. Though Levi gets Adam in trouble by reporting that he recited a spell, it is obvious that the young boy admires and loves his older brother. It is through Levi that Adam can see how much he has changed. When Adam returns home after the battle with the British soldiers, he understands so much more about life and war than Levi can comprehend. Levi still lives in his fantasies of the adult world, whereas Adam has witnessed the realities of war and the challenges of growing up.

Moses Cooper

Moses is Adam and Levi's father, Granny Cooper's son, and Sarah Cooper's husband. As captain of the Lexington Committee and with his flair for elegant rhetoric, Moses is viewed as one of the most prominent men of Lexington. People look up to him, and they are often roused by his eloquent and rational judgments. Although he is very capable in the public realm, Moses is not always quite as eloquent at home. He can be very critical of Adam, which makes Moses appear harsh and cold-hearted.

Moses insists that he does not want to go to war with the British, but when British soldiers march into Lexington, Moses wants them to know that he does not approve of their presence. He wants to demand his right to freedom from British rule. Moses is the first of the Lexington men who are shot down. However, before he dies, Moses confesses to Adam how proud he is of him for stepping up and taking on the responsibility of

defending their town. Moses finally acknowledges that Adam has become a man.

Sarah Cooper

Sarah is Adam and Levi's mother and Moses's wife. She is the peacemaker at home, especially between Moses and Adam. She is a good cook and supportive mother. Her character as an independent person, however, is not very well developed. Sarah is shown mostly in a supportive role, attending to the men in her family. When Moses is killed, Sarah leans on Adam, whom she is hoping will step up to the task of taking on many of the duties for which his father was once responsible.

Joshua Dover

Joshua is Adam's cousin. Along with Solomon Chandler, he helps to organize the committeemen and the militia as they gather in the fields after the killing in Lexington. Cousin Dover, as Adam calls him, attempts to keep a record of the events of every battle as they happen.

Samuel Hodley

Samuel was one of the Lexington villagers who did not believe the British were coming. Adam sees Samuel mortally wounded with a hole in his neck after the British march through his town.

Grandfather Isaac

Isaac, a sea captain, was Sarah Cooper's grandfather. He was a topic of gossip in the family because he had two wives. He kept them separate, with one living in Boston and the other in Philadelphia. His Philadelphia wife was part Shawnee. When Isaac died, he left Sarah a large amount of money, which Moses believed absolved the grandfather from all the wrongdoings he had done during his lifetime.

Ishmael Jamison

Ishmael Jamison is Adam's uncle on his mother's side. He is a ship captain and had wanted Adam to join him for a voyage to the Indies. Ruth refers to Ishmael as a smuggler. Adam defends his uncle, blaming the British for taking away his uncle's legal trade. His uncle, Adam proclaims, is merely making a living as best he can.

Jonas Parker

Jonas was elected captain of the Lexington militia. Moses Cooper often argues with Jonas about who is the top commander of the town. Moses is the head of the committee and believes in arbitration.

Jonas, as head of the militia, believes in using force, if necessary, against the British. Adam sees a British soldier push a bayonet through Jonas, which makes Adam realize he must run for his life.

Isaiah Peterkin

Isaiah is a deacon in the Lexington church. Adam refers to Isaiah as being "mean and wicked and two-faced." Granny Cooper chastises Adam for calling Isaiah names. However, Adam states that he is merely telling a truth that everyone else already knows.

Major Pitcairn

Major Pitcairn is the head of the British forces that march through Lexington. He is unwilling to negotiate with the Lexington men and nearly runs down the Reverend and Moses with his horse when they try to talk to him.

The Reverend

The Reverend is the religious leader and second-best debater in Lexington. He and Moses often argue over political and religious issues. After Moses is killed, the Reverend looks after Adam as if he were his own son. He also helps Adam work through his emotions of having lost his father.

Rider

An unnamed rider arrives in the middle of the night with news of the British troops heading for Lexington. Though he is not identified in this novel, there is a good chance that the author modeled him on Paul Revere, who rode through the night to warn the colonists of the British Army's approach.

Joseph Simmons

Joseph is described as a big man who loves food. Joseph is Adam's cousin and Ruth's father and lives close to the Cooper house. He is a blacksmith. Joseph's five brothers had shared a financial interest in a slave ship because this was extremely profitable. This caused Joseph to break away from his brothers and never speak to them again.

Cousin Simmons, as Adam refers to him, watches over Adam after Moses dies. He feels responsible for Adam's safety. However, before he and Adam face a second encounter with the British soldiers, Cousin Simmons fears for his own life. He asks Adam, if something should happen to him, to look after his family, especially his daughter Ruth.

Rebecca Simmons

Rebecca is Joseph Simmons's wife and Ruth's mother. Rebecca plays a very minor role in this story, merely holding the position of mother and wife with very little to say. She offers Adam some pie when he comes to visit Ruth. She is also at Adam's house, helping Adam's mother with the funeral of Moses.

Ruth Simmons

Ruth is Adam's second cousin and Joseph Simmons's daughter. She is three months younger than Adam and is strong willed but has a sympathetic heart. Adam likes talking to her, pressing his new ideas on her and relying on her to help him sort his thoughts. It is obvious that Ruth likes Adam, as she is the one who initiates the few kisses that they share. However, after Adam comes home from the battles with the British, Ruth tells Adam that she loves him. Ruth is the only woman Adam can imagine marrying.

Susan Simmons

Susan Simmons is the widowed sister of Rebecca Simmons. Susan lives with Rebecca and her family. Once when Adam comes to the Simmons's house looking for Ruth, Susan asks Adam to read a passage from the Bible.

THEMES

Coming of Age

April Morning begins with the fifteen-year-old protagonist, Adam, wishing that his parents would take him seriously. He is tired of being treated like a child. He wants his father, in particular, to see him as a man, but his father refuses. Thus, Fast sets up a major theme in his story: Adam's coming of age. A novel with a coming-of-age theme usually presents a young teen, male or female, who is on the cusp of becoming an adult. The protagonist finds himself or herself caught between the two worlds of childhood and adulthood. In this novel, Adam is said to be the physical size of an adult, but he does not work hard enough to be considered one, or at least, this is how Adam's father puts it. Adam is slow to finish his chores, and he continues to do childish things, such as reciting a superstitious chant over the family's drinking water. Moses, Adam's father, uses this as the measuring stick by which

TOPICS FOR FURTHER STUDY

- The names of towns and nearby villages are mentioned throughout *April Morning*. Create a map, either on paper or in a three-dimensional medium such as papier-mâché, of the countryside of Massachusetts as it was in 1775. Trace the progress of the British forces as they marched from Boston to Concord. Also map out the points at which the British met the colonists both on the way to Concord and on the way back to Boston. Match the details found in the novel with information you find in a reference book about the first encounters with the British on that day. Share your map with your class.

- Choose one of the characters in this novel and draw a portrait of that person. The author provides a few clues as to how the characters might have looked, so use them as a guideline, but also research the type of clothing they might have worn to keep your sketches authentic with the times. Share the portrait with your class, allowing them to guess which character it might be before you tell them.

- Create a diary, writing as Ruth Simmons. Express her feelings for Adam Cooper before the confrontation with the British, while Adam was away fighting, and upon his return. Keep her character as written by the author in mind. Remember that she is a strong-willed young woman who has confessed her love for Adam. Also be mindful of the time she was living in. Otherwise, use your imagination in trying to guess what emotions she was having at critical moments in this story. Read the diary to your class.

- There are several Web sites that are used to promote modern towns and cities. Investigate a few of them to give you an idea of how they are set up and what information they provide. Then choose either Concord or Lexington and research the details of what these towns looked like and what they might have offered a visitor in colonial times (such as the early 1700s). Create a Web site using this information and photos from history books or online publications. Provide a brief history of the town and descriptions of the natural environment. Make up activities that you think tourists might have enjoyed back then, such as canoeing at a nearby river, hunting, or fishing. Where might visitors have gone to eat? What were the names of inns where they might have slept? Provide the Web address to your class and invite them to investigate your Web site.

- Read the young-adult novel *The Fighting Ground* by Avi Wortiz. Create a chart that compares and contrasts the experiences of Jonathan in *The Fighting Ground* with those of Adam, the protagonist in *April Morning*.

---

to judge whether Adam has indeed reached adulthood. By that measure, Adam has failed.

As the story progresses, though, Adam is thrown into the world of adult responsibilities. There, Adam faces the challenges and passes with honors into the adult world. He is praised by his father when he signs the muster book and commits himself to defending his village and standing up for the human rights his father has proposed. Later, Cousin Simmons and the Reverend praise Adam for his mature acceptance of his father's death and facing the hardships of war without complaining. When he returns home, Adam's mother leans on her son as if he had left the house a child but returned as a man.

Wars

A minor theme that runs through this novel is that of antiwar sentiment, set in the context of the American Revolutionary War. As the men in Lexington wait for the British Army to arrive, they argue about how they are going to confront the

British Revolutionary War soldiers (*Image copyright egd, 2010. Used under license from Shutterstock.com*)

soldiers. Moses Cooper does not believe in war. He thinks that all conflicts should be solved through negotiation. Moses has a good mind for a logical argument and is used to winning the debates that he engages in. The Reverend, though he often likes to argue with Moses on other topics, agrees with Moses when it comes to the issue of war. He makes a strong stand against Solomon Chandler when Chandler suggests that God takes sides in a war. The Reverend believes that God is also against war and would take no one's side in a battle.

Adam also expresses his antiwar feelings. He is excited at first when he is allowed to sign the muster book. This makes him feel like a man. However, after he sees the horrors that war can bring, Adam does not understand why anyone ever uses the excuse of a war to kill someone. It is through these characters and their expressions that the author makes his own antiwar sentiment apparent.

Freedom

There are two overarching themes of freedom or independence in this novel. The most obvious is the war that the colonists are willing to fight to rid their land of British dominance. The colonists have grown tired of paying the taxes that the British have imposed on them. They also want to make their own rules. They have come to the point where they believe they can stand on their own as a nation, so they want to make their declaration of freedom known. According to this novel, the majority of men in Lexington want to tell the British what they want. When the British do not listen, the colonists are willing to fight for their independence.

On another level, Adam, the protagonist, is also fighting for his freedom. He is tired of being looked upon as a child. He wants to be able to do what adults do. He wants to attend important meetings. He wants to do what he wants without limitations, whether this is to ship out with his uncle to the Indies or to court his neighbor, Ruth. When Adam finally wins his independence, though, it is met with some sadness. For example, he must say good-bye to his childhood. He also realizes that with his independence comes bigger responsibilities.

STYLE

Journal Writing

April Morning is written in a style that is similar to actual journal writing. It is as if the narrator, Adam, were keeping a diary. The style makes the reader feel like the story is being read while looking over Adam's shoulder as he records the details and events of his days. Adam either directly experiences what he records or he overhears someone else describe an event that he did not personally witness.

The shortcoming of a novel written in this way is that the reader receives only Adam's interpretations. The reader sees and feels what Adam sees and feels. No one knows how Ruth feels, for example, except through Adam's reactions to her. The same is true for all the other characters. Readers experience the story from the viewpoint of a male teenager. A female point of view is never provided, nor an adult interpretation. The strength of this journal type writing is that the author can go deep within the protagonist's mind, giving insight into Adam's emotions and his reflections. The war, for example, is described through Adam's fears as well as his lack of military prowess.

Historical Setting

By placing this fictional work in a historical setting, the author accomplishes two things. First, he tells a story of a young eighteenth-century boy. Second, he also enhances the details of a historical event. Most readers might be familiar with the general context of the battles that took place in Lexington and Concord, but through this fictional account, readers are invited to share the incident on a personal level. It is as if one were there at the battle of Lexington, rather than merely reading historical data about the beginning of the Revolutionary War.

Much like the modern-day tactic of embedding reporters with a military troop in Iraq or Afghanistan so that people at home can read about the activities of the soldiers, this novel, set in the past, transports readers to the battlefield. In this way, readers can imagine what it might have been like to be involved in the colonists' fight for independence.

HISTORICAL CONTEXT

The Beginning of the Revolutionary War

The battle at Lexington, Massachusetts, as Fast recounts in his novel *April Morning*, was the first military conflict between the colonists and the British forces in 1775. This event would begin what was called the Revolutionary War, as the colonists fought for their independence from British rule. However, the tension between the British and the colonists started several years prior to this event.

In order to command control of the colonists and to make a profit, the British issued a series of taxes. They enforced taxes on sugar, printed materials, and paints. There was also a law that demanded that the colonists feed and house the British troops without compensation. In 1768, as tension rose, mostly in Boston, the governor of Massachusetts, Thomas Hutchinson, asked for and received an additional four thousand British soldiers to help preserve the peace. This action did not deter those who protested the British laws, and on March 5, 1770, a skirmish occurred in which five colonists were killed. This event was later referred to as the Boston Massacre; it increased the tensions between the colonists and the British forces.

In 1773, when the British Parliament passed a tax on tea, the colonists revolted by tossing a shipload of tea into the Boston Harbor. This came to be known at the Boston Tea Party. In retaliation, the British closed Boston Harbor to all ship traffic. This meant that the colonists could not receive or ship out any goods. A year later, the colonists formed the First Continental Congress, during which time they appealed to the British king, George III, to repeal all the punishing acts. If the British did not respond favorably, the colonist stated that they were ready to refuse to buy all British goods sent to colonies.

It was under these conditions that that fateful march took place, with the British Army moving toward Concord via Lexington. The British were aware that the colonists were agitated and had heard rumors that they might take some kind of rebellious military action, so when they learned that the colonists were storing supplies at Concord, the British decided to plan what they thought would be a covert maneuver. In the middle of the night, they set out from Boston, hoping the darkness would hide them. Their mission was to learn the truth of these rumors of stored goods and to destroy whatever they found.

There were reportedly between 640 and 900 British soldiers involved. They crossed the Charles River and were heading to Concord, less than twenty miles from Boston. In charge of the troops were Lt. Colonel Francis Smith and Major John Pitcairn. The British had witnessed very little

COMPARE
&
CONTRAST

- **1770s:** Colonial soldiers go to war with the British to gain their independence and to create the country of the United States of America.

  1960s: American soldiers go to war in Vietnam in an attempt to stop the communist takeover of South Vietnam.

  2000s: American soldiers go to war against terrorists who threaten their country's security.

- **1770s:** War is fought mostly on the ground with men face to face with their enemies, using rifles with attached bayonets.

  1960s: Bombs dropped from airplanes flying a thousand feet in the air destroy villages and kill masses of people without the pilots coming in contact with them.

  2000s: Destructive missiles can be launched from hundreds of miles away, with the soldiers never seeing their targeted victims.

- **1770s:** Messengers, such as Paul Revere, ride on horseback to deliver messages during the Revolutionary War.

  1960s: For the first time, images from the battlefields are televised, sending coverage of the war from Vietnam to homes in the United States.

  2000s: Soldiers can send messages via the Internet to families at home.

---

military resistance by colonists up to this point and expected none to occur that day.

The colonists, in the meantime, organized by John Parker, waited in Lexington with guns in their hands. Upon arriving there, Pitcairn gave orders for his British troops to disarm the local militia. It was then that a shot rang out. To this day, no one is sure which side fired that first shot. Upon hearing the single gunshot, the British opened fired on the colonists, killing eight of the men and wounding ten others before the colonists retreated to the nearby woods. These actions thus became the first battle of many more to follow and would be later collectively known as the Revolutionary War.

The Minutemen

Outside Boston, most of the adult male population of the surrounding areas of Massachusetts were farmers. Though they might also have been blacksmiths, furniture makers, and merchants, primarily the men worked the land to provide food for their families. In times of trouble, though, many of these men came to their town's call, with guns in hand, ready to protect their families and their economic interests. Out of this group of militia, a few men were chosen to become Minutemen. The name of this group of men reflected the fact that they were trained to be ready with only a minute's warning.

The Minutemen were often younger than the general population of the militia. They were around twenty-five years old and in good physical shape, and they were trained more vigorously than the older men. In 1775, the town of Concord was the first to create a group of Minutemen. It was the Minutemen of the surrounding area who met the British forces at North Bridge just outside Concord and gave the redcoats their first show of military opposition. Unfortunately, although the Minutemen were well trained, they lacked a unified leadership, so when various companies of Minutemen came together to fight the British, no one leader was in charge and confusion often reigned.

CRITICAL OVERVIEW

In a tribute to Fast, written for *Booklist*, Brad Hooper states: "The bottom line is that when it comes to reading Howard Fast, we continue to understand and appreciate that simply, he could tell a darn good story." From reviews of Fast's

Betsy Ross's flag, a symbol of the new nation (*Image copyright Christoff, 2010. Used under license from Shutterstock.com*)

books, whether written in the 1960s or twenty years later, most reviewers have the same sentiment. For historical novels, Fast is one of the best storytellers.

In 1961, when *April Morning* was first published, Kenneth Fearing reviewed it for the *New York Times*. Fearing writes that in this novel, "events move swiftly along in a nimbus of historic color and detail." He adds: "Howard Fast has admirably recaptured the sights and sound, the religious and political idioms, the simple military tactics and strategies of that day." In another review from the same time period, J. Donald Adams, also writing for the *New York Times*, states that *April Morning* was one of those rare books that he could not put down. "Another kind of book of the same length," Adams writes, "might well have taken me longer, but this was one of compelling narrative power, of unflagging interest."

In another tribute to Fast, Dennis McLellan, writing for the *Los Angeles Times*, calls Fast "one of the most widely read authors of the 20th century." In the *Guardian*, Eric Homberger refers to Fast as a "literary phenomenon" as well as a "champion of the progressive novel in the United States."

CRITICISM

Joyce Hart

Hart is a published writer and creative writing teacher. In this essay, she examines the loss of innocence as portrayed in April Morning.

Howard Fast has incorporated many different themes in his novel *April Morning*. Some of these themes are very powerful as well as very obvious, such as the fight for independence. However, the story also presents some much more subtle themes. One of the more potent of these minor themes is that of the loss of innocence. Whereas the fight for independence, both on an individual and a community level, dominates much of the story line, the theme of the loss of innocence is very quiet. The fight for independence is out in the open, rousing a public outcry and leading the characters into a war, but the loss of innocence is more personal and secretive. It can sneak up on a character without him or her recognizing it or being aware that it is present. There are no public allusions to this particular theme, as there are for the fight for independence. None of the characters offers a speech with the concept of the loss of innocence as the main topic. However, almost every character in

WHAT DO I READ NEXT?

- Fast's fictionalized biography of the American Revolution, *Citizen Tom Paine* (1943), tells the story of the newly arrived patriot who woke the colonial citizenry with calls for "Common Sense." The novel weaves in the important figures of the revolutionary period while telling the story of Paine.

- James Lincoln Collier's *My Brother Sam Is Dead* (2005) tells the story of a family torn apart by the Revolutionary War, as the protagonist, Tim Meeker, must choose which side to fight on. In this young-adult novel, the author portrays both sides, the British and the revolutionaries, on equal terms as they wage war against each other. No matter which side Tim supports, he will end up fighting against one of his family members, his father or his older brother.

- In Ann Rinaldi's young-adult novel from 2004, *Cast Two Shadows: The American Revolution in the South*, the Revolutionary War is witnessed by fourteen-year-old Caroline Whitaker. The young teen loses her father when he refuses to support the British, and she watches as a friend is brutally murdered. Caroline also learns that her real mother is not the woman who has raised her but a former slave who used to work for the family. The mother and daughter are reunited as they share a mission to save Caroline's brother, who has been court-martialed.

- There is mention of slave ships in Fast's novel. The novel *Amistad* (1997), written by David

Pesci and based on true events that occurred many years after the Revolution, is a fictional rendition of a real slave rebellion on one of those ships. The revolt occurred in 1839 and was ultimately unsuccessful. However, the incident brought the issue of slavery to the forefront of public debate.

- *Red, White, and Black: The Peoples of Early North America* (2005), written by Gary B. Nash, describes for readers the interconnectedness among Native Americans, African Americans, and European Americans during the colonial and revolutionary eras as they shared the land that would later become the United States.

- For a different look at early Americans about a hundred years after the Revolutionary War, Fast has written a series of books about immigrants. His first, *The Immigrant* (1977), follows a poor couple from Europe as they land in the United States and then travel from the East Coast to California looking for a new home and new life. Dan, their son, is born in a boxcar on a train and grows up determined to evade the poverty of his youth. The second book of the series, *Second Generation* (1978), is about Dan's daughter, Barbara, who grows up rejecting her father's wealth. The third novel is called *Establishment* (1979) and is set at the end of World War II. As Fast did in real life, Barbara must face the House Un-American Activities Committee.

---

this story is influenced by this loss. In contrast to the theme of independence, the author has artfully embedded the loss of innocence theme deep within the story. Fast appears to have woven this loss of innocence theme into his story almost in the same way that it affects his characters—silently and unobtrusively, sneaking it in without much fanfare.

One of the most accessible constructs of the loss of innocence theme can be seen especially clearly when readers compare the characters of the Cooper brothers, Adam and Levi. The difference between the ages of these two boys is only four years. If both of them were adults, this expanse of four years would not make much difference, but Adam is fifteen years old and Levi is

> FAST APPEARS TO HAVE WOVEN THIS LOSS OF INNOCENCE THEME INTO HIS STORY ALMOST IN THE SAME WAY THAT IT AFFECTS HIS CHARACTERS—SILENTLY AND UNOBTRUSIVELY, SNEAKING IT IN WITHOUT MUCH FANFARE."

eleven, which puts Adam at the edge of maturity whereas Levi has yet to reach adolescence. Whereas Adam strains for independence, Levi is still lost in childlike innocence, with fantasies filling the holes created by his lack of experiences in the world. For example, Levi spends much of his day pretending to be at war with the British. He and his friends probably use sticks for imaginary guns as they shoot at one another, and they may pretend to be dead. Fast uses Levi to represent the world of children. Levi's pretend wars do not hurt, either physically or mentally. His wounds do not bleed. After his war games are over, Levi and his friends return home, eat a hearty meal, and go to bed. They do not suffer from any trauma from war.

In contrast to this child, the author provides the teenage protagonist. Adam has grown tired of childhood. He wants to be accepted into the world of adults. He is anxious to join this new, more mature group, but as the story begins, he does not fully understand what membership in this group will cost him. He eagerly wants to attend committee meetings with the men in his community. He is distracted by his desire for his father to honor him as a man. It is not until right before the Lexington battle, which will be Adam's first experience of war, that he senses the grave consequences of what he has asked for. He perceives that something that he has never imagined is about to happen to him.

It takes Adam several hours to realize what that something is. Though he reflects on the terror he has gone through as he heads home after the battles, he is not able to fully clarify its effect on him. However, when the author reunites the brothers, readers can more easily see the differences between them. On one hand, Adam has seen their father shot. He has witnessed British soldiers' heads blown off. He has heard men and boys crying out from the pain of their wounds.

Significantly, he has faced his own death, knowing how close he came to dying when the British soldiers pursued him. The war, for Adam, was real, not imagined. It was not a game that has left him unchanged. Adam has come home almost completely transformed. This is not to say that Levi has not also been changed. He, too, saw his father's dead body, and he was frightened by the British soldiers who took over the village, so Levi has also experienced a loss of innocence. Adam's loss, however, is greater. It is Adam who needs to explain to Levi that they will have to take on more responsibilities at home now that their father is gone. It is also Adam who understands that though Levi can go back to playing soldier, he has no pathway to such a return. For Adam, childhood is gone forever. It is Adam who must say goodbye to his childish fantasies.

Other characters in this story also experience the loss of innocence, but in different ways. The Reverend, for instance, a man who has devoted his life to interpreting the words of his Bible and preaching peace, finds himself in the middle of a deadly battle. The Reverend states that it is his opinion that God does not partake in wars, and yet here is the Reverend, a man of God, in the middle of combat, fighting for his and his people's right to make their own laws. The Reverend, like Moses Cooper and Joseph Simmons, once believed that all disagreements could be resolved through arbitration. They were pacifists, believing in the wisdom, open-mindedness, and rationality of all humankind to solve their problems without killing one another. The war has also robbed the Reverend of his innocence. By partaking in killing, the Reverend can no longer say that all disagreements can be worked out verbally and therefore peacefully. He cannot uphold one of the Biblical commandments: Thou shalt not kill. He may continue to preach the power of peace but not in the same way that he taught that message before he picked up a gun. As Adam cannot return to his youth, the Reverend cannot regain his innocence.

Another character who suffers a loss of innocence is Adam's mother, Sarah. When the story begins, Sarah's only concern seems to be to get food on the table for her family. She does worry a little about Adam's relationship with his father, but all else appears to be running smoothly in Sarah's life. For the times, her life might be considered ideal. She is happily married and well provided for. Her only complaint is that her mother-in-law is sometimes pushy; Granny Cooper often talks to

British soldiers in a Revolutionary War battle reenactment (*Image copyright J.T. Lewis, 2010. Used under license from Shutterstock.com*)

her son, Moses, as if he were still a child. Other than that, Sarah leads a secure and substantial existence. She does not lack for anything.

This all changes, of course, once the colonists begin battling the British. First, Moses is killed. He was not only one of the more powerful leaders of the community, thus providing the family with status, but he was also the one who brought home the food, did the heavy chores around the house, and otherwise offered the family security. Sarah is shaken by Moses's death, not just because she misses his presence but because she is uncertain who will take care of her. With Moses gone, Sarah becomes more aware of the world around her and of her vulnerability in relation to it. She must think about survival, something she might not have had to consider prior to Moses's death. Her innocence in terms of worldly necessities has come to an end.

Like the Reverend, Sarah also has lost her innocence in terms of peace. Moses gave her peace in many ways. Her community also offered her a sense of tranquility, which no longer exists now that the war has begun. The British soldiers

have been there once. They could come again. Added to this is her fear of the war taking her sons away from her. Adam has already fought and is likely to fight again. If the war lasts several years, Levi would be the next one to enlist.

Although war can, in some ways, lead to greater things, such as independence, the author seems to say that there are dire consequences. Some of these consequences are severe and immediately observable, such as death, but there are more subtle costs too. Though the loss of innocence does not result in a visible wound, it does leave its mark, changing people forever.

Source: Joyce Hart, Critical Essay on *April Morning*, in *Novels for Students*, Gale, Cengage Learning, 2011.

Willam F. Buckley

In the following essay, Buckley reflects at the time of Fast's death on the connection between his membership in the communist party and his blacklisting in the 1950s.

Some years ago the caller identified himself as Howard Fast. We are representatives, he said, you and I, of different faiths, and I would like to dine with you. We did this, and some weeks later he joined the editors for dinner. The friendship did not blossom—we were indeed apostles of different faiths. I was candid enough to tell him at lunch that if he hadn't left the Communist party I would not have shared dinner with him, inasmuch as the faith I belonged to demurred at social consort with active Communists. He smiled, nodded his head, and told me about when he had resigned.

The famous author of best-selling historical fiction including *Citizen Tom Paine* and *Spartacus* had been, no less, the managing editor of the Communist *Daily Worker*. His work for the party was recognized by, among others, Josef Stalin, who awarded him the Stalin International Peace Prize the very year that Stalin died.

Fast's engrossing story was that when Khrushchev gave his famous 20th Congress speech in 1956, renouncing Stalin and his works, a copy of that speech reached the *Daily Worker* immediately before the CIA got hold of it. It was released to the press, which would give this revolutionary speech, or perhaps better, this counterrevolutionary speech, front-page attention, even as the historians have done. "There was a dispute in the *Daily Worker* on whether we should publish a report of Khrushchev's speech," Fast said. "The editor complained that if the *Worker* went with it, the Communist party of America would lose 10 percent of its membership. I corrected him. We'll lose 90 percent, I predicted.

"And I was right."

Howard Fast too left the Communist party. But when he died on March 12, the long obituary in the *New York Times* referred (Paragraph #1) to "the blacklisting of the 1950s," to his proclivity for unpopular causes (Paragraph #4), to the interruption in his writing caused "by the blacklisting he endured in the 1950s, after it became known that he had been a member of the Communist party and then refused to cooperate with the House Un-American Activities Committee." It was finally (Paragraph #9) noted that he had joined the party in 1943 "because of the poverty he experienced as a child growing up in Upper Manhattan," and that he had left it in 1956.

Paragraph #18 recounts that "because of the blacklist," Fast's book *Spartacus* was turned down by various publishers, but that (Paragraph #19) "the stigma of the blacklist gradually faded after Mr. Fast's repudiation of Communism."

The lesson here is that obituary writers for the *New York Times* proceed on the cultural assumption that blacklists were undeserved, and that what is worth writing about in the Howard Fast situation isn't what poison Mr. Fast encouraged, during his years of servitude to the criminality of Stalin, but the blacklisting of him. Until, that is, Khrushchev enlightened him that Stalin was a terrible man who brought death to 20 million Russians and decades of servitude to the captive nations, which lived on in captivity because Stalin's reach greatly outlived his own death.

A suitable lead for Howard Fast's obituary might have read, "Howard Fast, best-selling historical novelist, brought on his blacklisting when the public sought to draw attention to his activities as a prominent advocate of Stalin. Mr. Fast went on to write many best sellers...."

If a writer who had been an activist pro-Nazi until ten years after the Nuremberg trials were to die tomorrow, that part of his life would merit some attention, and would get it.

I liked Howard Fast, and hope that he will rest in not entirely untroubled peace.

Source: Willam F. Buckley, "Howard Fast, R. I. P.," in *National Review*, Vol. 55, No. 6, April 7, 2003, pp. 14, 16.

Sarah Cuthbertson

In the following excerpt, Cuthbertson connects Fast's theme of the human need for freedom with the author's early life.

Howard Fast probably owed his highly successful career as a writer of politically, socially, and morally committed historical fiction to a crush he had at age seventeen on an older woman whose later criticism of his first published novel stung him into finding his true *métier*. More on this story later, as TV news anchors are so fond of saying.

In his long life, Howard Fast wrote over eighty works of book-length fiction and non-fiction, as well as short stories, plays, journalism, screenplays and essays. His novels include both crime and science fiction, but it is for his historical fiction that he will be best remembered. Nevertheless, in "History and Fiction," a 1944 article for the left-wing magazine *New Masses*, Fast rejected the term *historical fiction* for his novels, "as of late—that is during the 1930s—it was familiarly used to describe a massive, carelessly written, escapist tome." Yet in *Current Biography* (H.W. Wilson, 1943) he declared that

"

BY THE 1960'S, HIS BOOKS ONCE AGAIN
TAKEN UP BY MAINSTREAM PUBLISHERS, FAST HAD
REACHED MIDDLE AGE, LEAVING BEHIND THE
PASSIONATE ENGAGEMENT OF HIS EARLIER
NOVELS, AS WE HAVE SEEN, FOR A MORE
REFLECTIVE AND LOW-KEY TYPE OF FICTION."

he was "going to try a one-man reformation of
the historical novel."

If I dwell long on Howard Fast's youth, this is
not only because it formed him as a novelist, but
also because his young life represents the American Dream writ large. It is only later that we see
how the dream—temporarily—turned into a
nightmare for this gifted author who, as a young
man, raised himself out of the ghetto by his writing, and lived his life with the same passionate
commitment that he brought to his historical
novels.

Howard Fast was born in 1914 in the slums of
Lower East Side Manhattan, the third child and
second son of poor Jewish immigrants. His father,
Barney, arriving in New York in 1878 aged nine,
was given the surname Fast from his hometown of
Fastov in the Ukraine. His Lithuanian-Jewish
mother, Ida, who came to America via London,
died when Howard was eight, leaving Barney with
a nineteen-year-old daughter and three young sons.
He never remarried. To avoid being tied down as
second mother to her three brothers, the daughter
soon left home, while the youngest son was farmed
out to relatives. Barney, often depressed and either
unemployed, on strike, or exhausted from working
long hours at poorly-paid physical labour, was
never an adequate father to Jerome and Howard,
who by the time they were ten and eleven were
themselves working outside school hours to help
make ends meet. And when that was not enough,
they were reduced to scavenging and even, at one
stage, stealing from grocery deliveries left on richer
people's doorsteps. In many ways, they were the
father to Barney's child. (In his memoir, *Being Red*,
Fast describes his father as "a good, decent dreamer
of a man who always had both feet planted firmly
in midair" p. 38).

Eventually, with its combined earnings, the
family was able to move out of the Lower East
Side Jewish ghetto to a better apartment in a better
neighbourhood. But it was an Irish-Italian district,
and Howard came up hard against gang warfare,
racism and anti-Semitism. He had not been raised
as a practising Jew and bewildered by accusations
of "Christ-killing," it was here that he began to take
an interest in his cultural and religious heritage. It
was here, too, in the struggle to make a decent life
amid poverty, bigotry and street-fighting, that he
witnessed the lynching of a thirteen-year-old black
youth by a white gang. Later he turned this into a
story that caused the issue of the magazine in
which it was published to be banned in Boston.

Relief from gruelling poverty, hunger and brutality came during working summer vacations
spent with relatives in the Catskills. These vacations
were often marred by family tensions (the rural
branch had worked its way out of the ghetto and
looked down on the poorer one still trapped there).
But as well as satisfying the city boy's yearning for
wide open spaces, these summers gave Fast a lifelong love of nature and the countryside which adds
atmosphere to so many of his novels.

But always he had to return to the city slums,
and things got worse with the stock market crash
of 1929 and the ensuing Depression. The company
Barney worked for folded and he rarely found
steady employment again, though the boys carried
on working.

In *Being Red*, Fast describes himself as a "not
a quiet or contemplative kid, but one of those
irritating, impossible, doubting, questioning mav-
ericks, full of anger and invention and wild
notions, accepting nothing, driving my peers to
bitter arguments and driving my elders to annoy-
ance, rage, and despair" (p. 48). And significantly,
in view of his circumstances, he saw himself as
innocent enough to be free of hate.

He hung on to his job at the Harlem branch of
the New York Public Library, working as a page
boy for six hours after school and five on Satur-
days, with overtime. Here he had discovered
books. In what little spare time he had, he read
voraciously, if indiscriminately, absorbing the
world of literature and ideas: "I loved working in
the library. The walls of books gave me a sense of
history, of order, of meaning in this strange world"
(*Being Red*, p. 41). But above all, books taught
him how to think: "I had seen my father on strike;
I had seen him locked out, his head bloodied on
the picket line. I had seen the economy of my

country collapse...; I did not have to be instructed about poverty or hunger. I had fought and been beaten innumerable times... because I was Jewish; and all of it worked together to create in my mind a simple plea, that somewhere, somehow, there was in this world an explanation that made sense" (*Being Red*, p. 42).

Two of the books that most influenced him at this time were Jack London's *The Iron Heel* and *The Intelligent Woman's Guide to Socialism and Capitalism* by George Bernard Shaw. *The Iron Heel* presciently portrays an underground socialist struggle against fascism, while Shaw's book provided this sixteen-year-old "with a new way of thinking about poverty, inequality and injustice" (*Being Red*, p. 46). It didn't take him long to realize that the power of books and writing, along with his thorough if rigid education in the New York public schools, were the tools he needed to understand the trap he was in, and the means by which he could extricate himself from it.

Even before graduating from George Washington High School and enrolling in the National Academy to study art, Howard had made the decision to become a writer. He had already written two novels and now began to submit handwritten short stories to magazines, meeting with no success until one of the Harlem librarians told him no magazine would consider a hand-written manuscript. The family agreed to rent a typewriter and three months later *Amazing Stories* accepted his science fiction tale, "The Wrath of the Purple," for the handsome fee of $37, equivalent to a month's library pay.

Quitting the library after three years, Howard went to work at a hat-maker's for better wages. It was impossible to do this physically demanding job as well as write and attend college so, the job and the writing being for their different reasons necessary to him, he chose to drop out of the Academy.

At about this time, he became more involved with communism. He abandoned *Das Kapital* after 200 pages but found *The Communist Manifesto* and *Ten Days That Shook the World* more to his liking. Through his elder brother Jerome, he met Sarah Kunitz, a Communist Party member who had visited the Soviet Union. She was clever and wise and seven years his senior; he fell in love with her instantly. Though fond of him, she didn't requite his ardour. She introduced him to other left-wing intellectuals, but talked him out of joining the party at such a young age (he was seventeen). Later, criticizing his first two published novels as escapist

fairy tales and betrayals of his working-class background, she would be instrumental in setting him on the road to writing the politically-grounded historical fiction which is his lasting legacy.

In 1933, needing to get away from New York, he set off for the South with a friend who was also an aspiring writer. Hitching rides and sleeping rough (often moved on more or less forcibly by the local police) from Philadelphia to Miami, the two refought the Civil War with local boys and generally absorbed the nature and atmosphere of the Deep South, all of which would stand Fast in good stead when he came to write his Reconstruction novel, *Freedom Road*. But he also felt (like "a prolonged electric shock") that he had "journeyed through a society in disintegration" and "began to understand that society could be planned and function in another way, called socialism" (*Being Red*, p. 61).

He returned to factory work, and that same year his novel *Two Valleys* was published. A historical romance set in Colonial West Virginia, it was the sixth he had written. He was not yet nineteen. He published two more novels, in 1934 and 1937. Then, spurred by Sarah Kunitz's scorn, he wrote a novella-length story, *The Children*, based on his own life as a slum boy (and featuring the above-mentioned lynching), but found it such a painful experience that he returned to researching the American Revolution, a rich vein from which he was to produce some of his finest work.

Soon after marrying art student Bette Cohen, he gave up factory labour to write stories for various magazines, including *The Saturday Evening Post* and *The Ladies' Home Companion*. During a trip to Valley Forge, he got the idea for his next novel, *Conceived in Liberty* (1939), which was written in the style of *All Quiet on the Western Front*, the first time the Revolutionary War had been dealt with in the realist manner. It was his breakthrough novel.

With a little money behind them, he and Bette went to Oklahoma to research the tragic story of the Cheyenne Indians who had fought a running battle with the U.S. Army in 1878-9 while attempting to return to the Wyoming homeland from which they had been forcibly exiled. Originally written from the viewpoint of the Cheyenne chief Little Wolf, it was rejected. Fast's former editor, Sam Sloan, advised him to rewrite it from the white perspective, having realized the impossibility of a white author getting inside the head of a Cheyenne and rendering his speech into English.

Fast agreed to a rewrite and Sloan accepted the novel for the publishing house he had recently set up. It was a popular and critical success, and signalled the end of financial insecurity for the Fasts.

The following year, Duell, Sloan, and Pearce published *The Unvanquished*, a novel about the Continental Army in defeat and retreat which was described by *Time* magazine as "the best book about World War II." It is also notable for a fine character study of George Washington.

While waiting to be drafted for World War II, Fast worked in the Office of War Information, writing scripts for Voice of America news broadcasts to occupied Europe. The retrospective irony of a communist sympathizer with party connections as mouthpiece of the U.S. government and armed forces no doubt wasn't lost on Fast, although he maintained at the time that his sympathy merely took the form of compassion for the Soviet struggle against Nazism and a refusal to condemn communism. He never was drafted, due to defective sight in one eye, but the OWI would have insisted on keeping him, even in uniform, valuing the clarity of his prose, his historical perspective and his idealistic patriotism. Although troubled by the necessity of watching unedited battlefield footage as part of his job, this harrowing experience was invaluable for his novels, lending a horrifying clarity and realism to the scenes of war depicted in many of them. It also helped make him a pacifist.

During his time on Voice of America, he published *Citizen Tom Paine*, a fictional biography of the rabble-rousing 18th-century revolutionist whose writings were an inspiration for the American Revolution, and *Freedom Road*, the story of an ex-slave who rises to become a state senator in post-Civil War South Carolina, only to be betrayed when Reconstruction fails. These novels offer evocations of their respective periods that are both passionate and intellectually serious. As well as becoming an enduring bestseller, *Freedom Road* was acclaimed by such luminaries as Eleanor Roosevelt and W. E. B. du Bois and won its author the Schomburg Race Relations Award for 1944.

The same year, Fast's application for a Voice of America post in North Africa was turned down. It transpired that the State Department, on FBI "advice," would have refused him a passport because of his communist sympathies and communist party connections. Angrily, he resigned from the OWI, but after much hustling,

he was commissioned by *Coronet* magazine (on a limited passport) as a war correspondent in Burma and India. By this time, the war was almost over but Fast, ever the observant writer, found much material in this adventure that would help shape future novels. En route to the Far East, he flew low over the Negev Desert, Sinai and Palestine, collecting images that would enhance his Biblical-era novels, *Moses, Prince of Egypt* (1958), *Agrippa's Daughter* (1964), and *My Glorious Brothers*, the story of the Maccabees who fought to free Judaea from its Graeco-Syrian oppressors. This novel, published in 1948, was soon taken to the heart of newly-born—or reborn—Israel.

In India, Fast met the British, who always come off badly in his writing, perhaps understandably in the Revolutionary War novels, where they are usually portrayed as effete snobs, decadent, boorish and stupid. As an American and a socialist, Fast loathed colonialism and criticized the British in India for their refusal to acknowledge the humanity of their subjects. A vivid example of this was his description of two British army officers maintaining complete indifference to the Indian servants towelling down their genitals after a shower. He uses this vignette in at least two novels, *The Pledge* (1988) and his last Revolutionary War novel, *Seven Days in June* (1994). Incidentally, much of *The Pledge* was inspired by his experiences in India, including meetings with Indian communists, and a major famine that he and others controversially accused the British of engineering in order to weaken the native population and prevent them giving support to the Japanese.

Before Fast went to India, he and Bette—after much deliberation—had joined the American Communist Party (CPUSA), having come to "the conclusion that if the anti-fascist struggle was the most important fact of our lives, then we owed it to our conscience to join the group that best knew how to conduct it" (*Being Red*, p. 83). This, Fast points out, was at a time when the Soviet Union was an ally, having defeated a monstrous Nazi enemy at unimaginable human cost and thereby "restoring hope to mankind." Stalin's atrocities, the gulags and show trials, were ignored or rejected.

In his memoir, Fast traces the origins of the American socialist movement to the seventeenth-century English Levellers who fled to America to escape Cromwell's persecution of them for their belief in total political and economic equality. In the CPUSA, Fast met many idealistic intellectuals, most of whom kept their membership secret, but the majority of members were working-class. The party was active in fighting for workers' rights throughout the Thirties and Forties but its membership was depleted by post-war repression.

Returning to America armed with his journalistic experiences in the Far East, Fast wrote for the Communist *New Masses* magazine and *Daily Worker* newspaper, usually without pay and at his own expense, as when the *Daily Worker* sent him to cover the Chicago labour strikes. To do this, he temporarily put aside *The American*, a novel he was writing about John Peter Altgeld, the late nineteenth-century reforming Governor of Illinois who controversially pardoned three men convicted on the flimsiest evidence of involvement in the 1886 Chicago Haymarket bombing which took place during a workers' protest meeting. *The American* was published in 1947.

By this time Fast had fallen foul of the U.S. government's growing intolerance of the Left and of Communists in particular, which resulted in the House Un-American Activities Committee and the McCarthy Senate hearings. President Truman's executive order requiring federal employees to take a loyalty oath, swearing that they were not and had never been members of the Communist Party, soon spread to state governments, schools, universities, hospitals, and eventually to the film and publishing industries. If a party member took the oath he risked a perjury conviction; refusal was effectively an admission of party membership. The penalties were dismissal from one's job, and blacklisting, which carried the very real possibility of never being able to work in one's profession again.

In 1946 Fast, already the subject of an extensive and expensive FBI investigation, received a subpoena to appear with others before HUAC to testify about his support for the Spanish Refugee Appeal. Under the auspices of the Joint Anti-Fascist Refugee Committee, this appeal was raising funds to finance a hospital for Spanish Republicans who had fled to France at the end of the Spanish Civil War. Fast was later recalled to answer a trumped-up charge that appeal money had been used to help the Yugoslav Communist partisan leader, Tito. He reacted angrily and with characteristic intemperance, calling the HUAC chairman, among other things, "a contemptible and disgusting little man, an enemy of not only human rights but of human decency" (*Being Red*, p. 152). Finally, in 1947, he was convicted of

contempt of Congress for refusing to disclose the names of contributors to the Spanish appeal. His three-month prison sentence was delayed by appeals until 1950.

None of this did his writing career any good. Already, President Truman's special counsel, hauled up before a congressional committee for giving copies of *Citizen Tom Paine* to fifty friends, had pleaded that he didn't know the book was Communist propaganda. But worse was to come. Fast's literary agent informed him that she could no longer sell his work under his real name, and a group of librarians told him that the FBI had ordered his books to be taken off public library shelves and destroyed (but they had hidden them to restore once the madness had passed). Meanwhile, *The American*, a bestseller and Literary Guild selection, began to be vilified in the press. While praising it, the scholar and journalist H. L. Mencken had taken Fast to task for recently helping found the left-liberal, Communist-inspired Progressive Party: "These clowns will destroy you as surely as the sun rises and sets" (*Being Red*, p. 193). And *My Glorious Brothers*, lauded in Israel, was ignored by U.S. reviewers, but managed to attract venom from both the Left (for "Jewish nationalism") and the Right (criticized by the FBI, the Jewish Book Council of America removed all reference to the award it had given Fast for the novel). Many bookshops declined to stock it.

Ever the activist, Fast accepted an invitation to a left-wing peace meeting at Peekskill in rural New York State which was to feature a concert by Paul Robeson. When the meeting was threatened by gangs of right-wing hooligans, Fast organized a small force to hold off their attacks. This was a perfect metaphor-in-action for a major theme of his historical fiction—a brotherhood fighting oppression against the odds.

In 1950, all appeals having failed, Fast finally served his three-month sentence for contempt of Congress at a "prison without walls" in rural West Virginia. In one of his court appearances, an accuser had become so exasperated at his lengthy diatribes that he had told Fast to "go write a book." It was in Mill Point Prison that he began to do just that. The book was *Spartacus*, an innovative fictional rendering of the great Roman slave revolt of 73-71 BCE which Fast completed in 1951, after his release. Perhaps he wasn't entirely surprised to find that no publisher would touch the novel, or indeed anything written by him. His name had entered the blacklist.

Angus Cameron, a well-respected reader at Little, Brown, which in 1950 had published Fast's Revolutionary War story, *The Proud and the Free*, gave *Spartacus* his highest praise, but the FBI leaned menacingly on Little, Brown and on every other publisher Fast approached. Eventually the author set up his own small press to print and distribute *Spartacus*. His faith in the novel was vindicated by sales of more than 40,000 in the first three months after publication. When the Communist witch hunts were over, *Spartacus* went on to be a major bestseller, and in 1960 it was turned into a blockbuster Hollywood movie ("an intelligent epic") starring Kirk Douglas, Laurence Olivier, Charles Laughton and Peter Ustinov. Its screenplay was written by another blacklisted writer, Dalton Trumbo.

Other self-published books followed—*The Passion of Sacco and Vanzetti* (1953), based on the true story of two Italian-American anarchists executed in the 1920s for a crime they didn't commit, and two novels based on his own recent experiences of the Red Scare, *Silas Timberman* and *The Story of Lola Gregg* (both 1954). Fast's fiction wasn't published commercially again until *Moses, Prince of Egypt* in 1958.

He considered exile abroad to get away from the Red-baiting. The family—he and Bette now had two small children—spent some months in Mexico, but returned to live quietly in New Jersey, managing on the steady flow of royalties from abroad where his novels still sold well, especially *Citizen Tom Paine*, *Freedom Road* and *The Last Frontier*. Many of his novels had huge print runs in the Soviet Union, which awarded him the Stalin International Peace Prize. But Soviet royalties were not forthcoming until 1957, by which time he rejected them, having left the Communist Party in shock and disgust at Khrushchev's revelations about the atrocities and moral corruption of the Stalinist era.

This was a deeply painful decision for Fast, who might have been accused of wilful ignorance about these appalling events. He gives a heartfelt, if intemperate, account of what he considered to be his ideological betrayal in *The Naked God* (1957) and a more reflective, if still defensive one in *Being Red* (1990), which some critics see as a partial retraction. Though still devoted to leftist ideals (he remained a socialist for the rest of his life), he had always had an ambivalent relationship with the CPUSA and its leaders. Looking back on his time as a member, he writes: "In the party I

found ambition, rigidity, narrowness, and hatred; I also found love and dedication and high courage and integrity—and some of the noblest human beings I have ever known" (*Being Red*, p. 355).

As a result of this very public "defection," Fast's star crashed out of the Soviet literary firmament almost overnight. Thus, in less than a decade, he achieved the dubious—and possibly unique—distinction of seeing his novels condemned and his literary reputation savaged by both the Right and the Left.

After running for Congress in 1952 on the American Labor Party ticket without a hope of success, Fast took no more part in public politics, and although his writing remained committed to the struggle of the dispossessed against oppression by the powerful, this was now portrayed on a more intimate canvas. *April Morning*, his classic novel of a boy's brutal coming of age during the Battle of Lexington, was published in 1961, and eleven years later came *The Hessian*, based on a small but shocking fictional incident during the Revolutionary War. Both novels, which Fast regarded as among his finest, explored the dehumanizing savagery of war through an ordinary person caught up in large events, and both were written, as was all his subsequent fiction, in a sparer, more emotionally detached style than his pre-blacklist books, those novels of his ardent, idealistic—even romantic—youth.

In between *April Morning* and *The Hessian* appeared *Agrippa's Daughter*, in 1964. It told the story of Berenice, King Herod Agrippa's daughter, who wrestled with her Jewish identity while conducting a long affair with Titus, the conqueror of Jerusalem and future Roman emperor. Although Fast had always enjoyed the company of women (agreeing with George Bernard Shaw that they were more intelligent than men), this was the first of his novels to have a female protagonist. It wasn't the last. During the 1970s and 80s he wrote a series of best-selling novels, "The Immigrants" sequence, which chronicled the fortunes of several generations of Americans as seen through the eyes of a woman to whom Fast gave many of his own personal experiences and beliefs.

By the 1960s, his books once again taken up by mainstream publishers, Fast had reached middle age, leaving behind the passionate engagement of his earlier novels, as we have seen, for a more reflective and low-key type of fiction. Having disengaged himself from active politics and public life, he now sought personal fulfilment and liberation in Zen Buddhism and an increasingly pacifist outlook.

But the Revolutionary War continued to be a source of inspiration. Bracketing The Immigrants series, came *The Crossing* (1971) and *Seven Days in June* (1994). *The Crossing* takes up where *The Unvanquished* leaves off, bringing Washington's Continental Army out of a series of crushing defeats to the tactically and psychologically important realization that retreat followed swiftly by surprise attack is a stunningly effective form of warfare against the British. *Seven Days in June*, a retelling of the Battle of Bunker Hill from both British and American viewpoints, is a prequel to *The Hessian* in that it shares the same protagonist when younger, a disaffected British Catholic physician who has settled in America and finds himself struggling with his conscience over questions of loyalty, freedom and the morality of war.

Fast continued his astonishing output well into his eighties. His last novels were *An Independent Woman* (1997), the final part of The Immigrants series, and the contemporary *Greenwich* (2000). But before these came two more historical novels—*The Pledge* (1988), a fictional rendering of Fast's own experiences as a journalist in India and victim of the anti-Communist witch-hunts at home, and *The Bridge Builder's Story* (1995) in which an American WASP is shattered by his personal encounter with Nazism and the Holocaust.

Source: Sarah Cuthbertson, "Hope for the Heart, Food for the Soul: Historical Fiction in the Life of Howard Fast," in *Solander*, Vol. 13, Spring 2003.

Ken Donelson

In the following essay, Donelson identifies the theme of April Morning *as the search for truth.*

In his "Speaking of Books" column in the *New York Times Book Review* for May 14, 1961, editor and critic J. Donald Adams began,

> Three weeks ago I had what was for me an uncommon experience: I read through a book at a sitting. I have done this before, but rarely. True, the book numbered only 184 pages, which means that the reading took something less than three hours. Another kind of book of the same length might well have taken me longer, but this was one of compelling narrative power, of unflagging interest. It was Howard Fast's *April Morning*, a story of the battle of Lexington as seen through the eyes of a 15-year-old boy who took part in it. When I had finished it, I said to

> WHILE IT HAS LITTLE TO DO WITH CHARACTERIZATION, READERS MAY ENJOY PLAYING— AS I DID—WITH THE BIBLICAL PARALLELS TO FOUR CHARACTERS."

myself. "This is an even better book than Crane's *Red Badge of Courage*." I still think so. All prophecy is dangerous, and literary prophecy in particular. Yet I readily wager that *April Morning* will some day reach the standing of an American classic.

Any invidious comparisons with *Red Badge* aside, I wish Adams had been right. But *April Morning*, fine as it is, has only rarely received the kind of praise it deserved then and deserves now. Adams' praise seems particularly ironic since the novel has often been pigeon-holed as an adolescent or YA novel, and Adams repeatedly attacked such books in his column. And since too many critics and teachers label Fast's novel as adolescent or YA literature (as opposed to all other books by Fast) and since those people *know* that such books can never be anything more than enjoyable and ephemeral, that neatly disposes of *April Morning*.

Careful readers and critics know better because they aren't so eager to categorize books. And Fast's apparently simple little story has more in common with fine works like *The Catcher in the Rye* and *The Chocolate War* and *Huckleberry Finn* than a few obvious and superficial characteristics of the initiation novel.

The plot is briefly told. In eight sections covering slightly more than a day in the middle of April, 1775, when a boy and a town and a people lose their innocence, the reader meets Adam Cooper; learns about the relationships Adam has with his father (Moses), his brother (Levi), his mother (Sarah), Moses' mother (Granny), his girlfriend (Ruth Simmons), and an old soldier who befriends him (Solomon Chandler) and watches Adam leave childhood and uncertainly enter the adult world. The novel is developed in three parts. Part one runs from our first meeting with Adam until his father's death at the hands of British redcoats, part two runs from Moses' death until the close of the

Battle of Lexington with the British, and part three runs from the close of the battle to the end of the book. In about 200 pages and a bit more than a day, we watch a serene land turn to war. We watch peaceful farmers and artisans die on the village green. We watch a group of individuals becoming a united people with a cause. We watch what the first moments of our Revolutionary War were like, not with zeal of patriotism sometimes preached in history texts but in the fear and hysteria caused by blood and death. We watch an immature 15-year-old grow up, not as he might have in normal times but as he was required by the time and the place.

While there are several characters who seem little more than stick figures, notably Adam's mother and brother, several characters jump off the pages and into the reader's life.

Moses Cooper. Adam's father, is one of the strongest and most fascinating characters in literature. Though he is killed halfway through the novel, the power of his personality stays with the reader as certainly as it inhabits Adam's life. Incapable of showing the deep love he feels for his firstborn son, Moses rebukes Adam for all his childish actions. Moses is strong and stubborn, unwilling to bow his head to anyone, even God. Early in the book, the Cooper family sits down to supper.

> The five of us sat down and four of us bent our heads while Father said grace. He didn't hold with bending his head, at grace or any other time, and when Granny once raised this point with him, he replied that one of the many differences between ourselves and Papists and High Church people—who were a shade worse than Papists—was that whereas the latter two sects cringed and groveled before the clay and plaster images they worshipped, we stood face to face with our God, as befitting what He had created in His own image. Granny said that there was possibly some difference between cringing and groveling and a polite bending of the head from the neck, but Father wasn't moved. The difference was quantitative, and therefore only a matter of degree. To him it was a principle. In two minutes, my father could lead any argument or discussion around to being a principle. So he said grace glaring across the table at the imaginary point where he placed God, and I always felt that God had the worst of it. My father couldn't just begin a meal with something direct and ordinary, like "Thank Thee, O Lord, for Thy daily bread and the fruit of the harvest," Oh, no—no, he had to embellish it. If there was no guest at the meal. God was always present, and tonight my father said sternly:

> "We thank Thee, O Lord, for the bread we eat, but we are also conscious of seed we have planted, of the hands that guided the plow and the back bent in toil. The ground is dry as dust, and I will take the liberty of asking for a little rain. I know that Thou givest with one hand and Thou takest away with another, but sometimes it seems to me to go beyond the bounds of reason. Amen!"

Granny is shocked, though not surprised, by her son's words, but the reader senses Adam's grudging respect for a father who fears no one and asks only for treatment he would accord any other man.

Moses often seems to Adam arrogant and unfeeling and incredibly stubborn. When Moses announced to his wife, "I am a man of peace," Adam adds—to himself—that his father was "the most belligerent man of peace I ever encountered."

Shortly before his father dies, the first victim of British bullets, Adam learns that Moses genuinely loves his son, and his father's apparently unfeeling and harsh treatment was only Moses' concern that Adam become the man that Moses wanted. If that perplexes Adam, Fast's characterization of Moses makes the father's past actions believable, not sympathetic but wholly understandable given Moses' high standards, for himself and for anyone he loved. Unfortunately for father and son, the reconciliation comes to a close on Moses' death. And his death makes Adam even less willing to accept the inevitability and finality of their separation.

Near the close of the book and after Adam has taken giant steps toward manhood, his neighbor, Mr. Simmons, urges Adam to remember his father honestly and accurately.

> "Your father was a hard man to know, Adam, and sometimes a body just had to grind his teeth and say, Well, that's Moses Cooper, and that's the way he is, and there isn't one blessed thing you can do to change him. But the way he was, Adam, was a most remarkable way. He was an educated man, like most of the men in our family. He was a prudent man. He was a man of many strong convictions, and you had to suffer somewhat to be his friend—or his son."
> "I'm not complaining." I muttered.
> "I know you are not. Nevertheless, if you recollect him as a saint, you will lose him. Moses Cooper was no saint. He was just as stubborn as a Methodist preacher, but he was a brave man with fine convictions, and I don't think there was ever a day

went by that I didn't feel pride and satisfaction in knowing he was my friend."

What a magnificent tribute, and by this time Adam knows how true and right the words are.

While Moses served as Adam's guide before the father's death, Solomon Chandler serves as guide afterwards. When Adam and others gathered on the village green that crucial day and heard the bullets and saw the bayonets, they fled. Adam says,

> You might think that with my father dead, my own fear would have lessened, but it didn't work that way, and all I knew was that I was alone—and who would take care of me or see for me now unless it was myself?

And the answer comes only minutes later when Adam tumbles over a wall and finds himself held, until his hysteria disappears, by the steel-vise arms of 61-year-old Solomon Chandler. Solomon has seen war before, and he is ready for this war as few others are, and for a time he teaches Adam some necessary lessons. When Adam berates himself for being a coward and leaving his father's body where it lay, Solomon says,

> "Cowards, you were, Adam?" he asked at last.
> "Yes—cowards."
> "Oh? I think you have got something to learn, laddie, about the nature of cowardice and bravery. It takes no courage to fire a gun and to kill, merely a state of mind that makes killing possible. Such a state of mind does not come easily to decent folk."

Those words, so apt for the time and Adam's state of mind, later come to haunt Adam and change his relationship with the old man. But for the moment, Solomon is the right person to be Adam's protector and teacher.

After becoming the leader of the rag-tag group of Americans firing at the British from behind stone walls, Solomon's an-eye-for-an-eye and God's-on-our-side principles are challenged by the minister when Solomon says to Adam,

> "Prime your gun careful, and don't ever fire unless the man's upon you. Count his buttons. A gun like yours won't stop a man at more than thirty paces."
> "Yes, sir." I said. "I'll heed your words."
> "Take no pleasure in it. Let it hurt, but become hard in the sorrow."
> "Would you tell him that?" the Reverend asked.
> "And you, too, Reverend. I tell you that. We'll weep for them, but they brought the killing to us, not us to them."
> "God help all of us," the Reverend said.
> "I say amen to that. We fight in God's cause."

> "Nobody fights in God's cause," the Reverend replied harshly. "Isn't it enough to kill in freedom's name? No one kills in God's cause. He can only ask God's forgiveness."
> The old man heard this respectfully. "As you say, Reverend. I would like to dispute it somewhat, but there ain't time." (p. 128)

Adam is confused by the argument, but he begins to recognize that Solomon's words are religious justifications—or madness, as Twain recognized in his "War Prayer"—for carnage. Only a little bit later, Adam knows that his feeling of respect for the old man is gone.

> I no longer felt any warmth toward the old man. I would kill and he would kill, but he took pleasure in the killing.

And at the end of the book, Adam no longer needs his father to lead him, though Moses will always be there with him, and Adam has rejected Solomon in almost every way. By that time, Adam has become his own man. As the book opens the reader sees a young man who allows things to happen to him. He reacts but he is almost incapable of acting. That changes when he decides to join the local committee to fight the British, even though his mother and brother know that Moses will oppose Adam's wish. To Adam's surprise, Moses recognizes that Adam has been propelled by circumstance into manhood though Adam doubts it. Solomon looks at his watch and says,

> "Twelve minutes after nine," he said, "and you've lost your youth and come to manhood, all in a few hours, Adam Cooper. O, that's painful. That is indeed."
> "I wish it was true that I have come to manhood," I said bitterly.
> "Give it time, Adam. Give it time." (p. 107)

Time has little to do with manhood, as Adam learns but the times have much to do with manhood. The times force Adam into responsibilities he does not want but responsibilities he must accept. When he returns home after the first battle of the war, he finds that his mother is incapable of action—hardly surprising to Adam since Moses had never delegated real responsibility on serious matters to Sarah at any time—and, worse yet, Granny, who had always seemed so strong, is aging almost before Adam's eyes. Adam left his family as a child and returned a man, all in a little more than a day. If Adam might have preferred to go back to the childhood he left only a day before he cannot. His family and the times demand otherwise.

While it has little to do with characterization, readers may enjoy playing—as I did—with the biblical parallels to four characters. Ruth, though less developed as a character, exemplifies the earlier Ruth, "whither thou goest (Adam) I will go." Moses Cooper is much like the prophet. Adam's father is intelligent and a respecter of ideas and learning who knows what is right and stubbornly leads his people (both his immediate family and the townspeople) onward toward the promised land (for his family, security; for his sons, maturity; for the townspeople, a land again safe and tranquil) but who is never allowed to see the promised land himself. Solomon is a hard and harsh lawgiver, deeply committed to the rightness of Old Testament justice, sure of himself and unwilling to compromise, a leader never wholly trusting his followers. Adam is like the first man, unformed and incomplete, a bit too sure of himself, superstitious and ignorant yet eager to know the truth, but temporarily satisfied with the peace of family and home.

The theme of *April Morning*, or rather the ambiguous and multiple themes, fascinate me, partly because my first reading convinced me that here was an obviously superior initiation novel. Clearly the book is a *bildungsroman*. A young man is separated for a time from a loving family on a quest. During the quest, whether alone or with friends, he undergoes tests of courage, both physical and emotional, and he ultimately returns to his home in a new and changed role.

On second reading—and you'll need to remember this was back in the late, troubled '60s—Fast's novel seemed even clearer; but this time I saw the theme as generation gap, Adam and Moses, Moses and Granny. While I no longer find this compelling, I suppose others might.

During that second reading, or perhaps a third, I read *April Morning* concurrently with *Red Badge* and a good deal of Twain, particularly "The War Prayer" and *Huckleberry Finn*. That was when Vietnam was becoming troublesome, and less a holy war, for lots of us. I admired Fast's honest patriotism which was far removed from paranoid patriotism or chauvinism. I admired Moses and Mr. Simmons and others caught up in something beyond their comprehension. I admired their simple and genuine statements about why they were fighting, not for God's cause or for the good of humanity or to save the entire country from tyranny but because the British had violated their land and their people.

Simple, direct, honest and admirable. I'd read so many novels virtually sanctifying American Revolutionary War heroes that it was delightful to read an honest account of people forced into actions they deplore, actions that will have consequences none of them can possibly foresee. I wondered if a more obvious theme was war as a determiner of values, the kind of thing Hemingway had written so often, though Fast and Hemingway had little in common about their conclusions. For Hemingway, war was often good because it allowed man's greatness to emerge. Fast's attitude was more to my taste.

But all those interpretations/themes bothered me and left me unsatisfied. I noticed on a slightly later reading what Elizabeth Collamore discussed in her "False Starts and Distorted Vision" in the November, 1969, *English Journal*, that *April Morning* is a search for truth. When the reader meets Adam, he is drawing water from the family well and muttering incantations to take the evil spell off the water. His father, a worshiper of reason and learning, rebukes Adam for the display of superstitious ignorance, but Moses himself tends to talk in maxims and platitudes. Adam questions much about the world, but his questioning of God to Granny establishes his shallow thought, most of it announced to shock people. Later after his father has been killed, Adam temporarily takes refuge in a fantasy, pretending that Moses is still alive and there to lead Adam; but he soon realizes that pretense is a child's substitute for truth, bitter as it sometimes is. When he returns home, a man, he has learned to accept truth and to live with it. And he learns what we must all learn, that some people like superficial, easy truths. When he is approached by a reporter from the Boston *Advertiser*, Adam is asked what happened on the village common that began the battle.

> I was past being able to think clearly, and I begged him to put his questions to someone else.
> "Don't you have an interest in the truth, Mr. Cooper?" He called me master, anticipating that I wouldn't be able to resist the flattery.
> "I'm too tired to know what the truth is."
> "A patriot always knows what the truth is."
> I stared at him dumbly...I shook my head and pushed past him out of the church.

Truth is never something easily come by, and superstitions and platitudes and pretense and popular myths are no substitute for truth. Adam learns that ever so slowly just as we all must. The reporter is unhappy proof that not everyone wants the truth or cares to search for it.

In Anne Commire's *Something about the Author* (Vol. 7, Detroit, Gale Research Company, 1975), Howard Fast said, "*April Morning* is as good a book as I have ever written, as nearly perfect a book as I could hope to write." In his later, and more commercial work, he's never surpassed *April Morning*, nor would I expect him to. It's a high compliment to Fast that so many readers—but not enough—have found in Adam Cooper a boy out of the past who is as contemporary as Huck Finn, a boy worth knowing and learning from.

Source: Ken Donelson, "*April Morning*: Coming of Age, All in a Few Hours," in *Virginia English Bulletin*, Vol. 36, No. 2, Winter 1986, pp. 8–13.

Elizabeth Collamore

In the following essay, Collamore identifies the search for truth as Fast's focus in April Morning.

Road maps and novels have much in common. One shows the relationships of places, the other the relationships of people. Since both create patterns not actual, but bearing a discernible resemblance to reality, we come to have certain expectations of them. If, when we are following a road map, the anticipated intersections and towns appear at the right times and places, then we begin to trust the map. But what if such a map shows us mountains when in fact there are oceans? We feel angry, confused, even disoriented. Map makers do not do this to us, but novelists sometimes do.

Such was the experience my eighth-grade class and I had last year while reading Howard Fast's *April Morning* (Bantam Pathfinder, 1962). We had read several chapters, always following the signs, or so we thought. We had noted the many varieties of conflicts in the first chapter, the interplay of conflicts and anti-conflicts in the second chapter, the dreams and initiations in the third, and the slaughter in the fourth. We felt quite confident as we examined the fear and flight, and then the beginnings of recovery, in the fifth chapter. What we had been led to expect was happening: Adam's personal growth and our country's national growth were both being accomplished through pain and struggle. Life was winning over Death. We were sure that old Solomon's pronouncement that "life is potent" carried with it all the weight of the original Solomon's wisdom. It seemed not at all accident (nor merely historical authenticity) that our hero's name was Adam,

his father's name Moses, and this surrogate father's name Solomon.

But we were wrong. We soon discovered that Solomon is quite fallible, even vicious. What else could we make of Adam's statement: "I no longer felt any warmth toward the old man. I would kill and he would kill, but he took pleasure in the killing." As we watched the change in Solomon we realized that something was wrong. Either the signs were wrong or we were not reading them correctly.

And so we started over. We reread the first chapter to see what we might have missed. This time the overwhelming emphasis seemed to us to be not on conflict, but on truth. Our first evidence was the concern with superstition: Adam's spell over the water and his father's resultant fury. Are they not arguing over what is true? And why does Moses birch Adam exactly seven times? Is he not superstitious, too? We also noticed the father's constant reliance on folk sayings such as "slow to start and quick to finish" and "wasted steps are like wasted thoughts, just as empty and just as ignorant." Are not these a form of inherited truth?

Adam's mother's comment, in which she refers to him as a "silly dreamer," would seem to indicate a belief on her part that the truth is only that which is tangible, but later she is visibly upset when Adam uses the phrase "good heavens." Such irreverence seems to her to have real power.

We puzzled awhile over Granny's statement, "I see less and less," and Adam's reply, "I don't think your eyesight is going. It's just getting dark in here." We had previously noticed this passage for the warmth and kindness between these two, but now we wondered about the reference to sight and seeing. Were they really talking about knowledge and insight? Perhaps. Why else their long discussion about belief in God, and Adam's remark, "I think we keep saying things we don't really mean at all"?

Granny accuses Adam of asking too many questions, a typical reply to a child by an adult who is tired of the subject, but it seemed to us that a questioner is one who is looking for truth, and we began to believe that we were asking the right questions. Why else the emphasis on Isaiah Peterkin's hypocrisy when he never shows up in the story again? Why else Granny's insistence that "shaking a body loose from her faith is about the most sinful thing you could do"? Why else the man from Boston who said "the highest good was to doubt"? And why else Granny's fury when Adam offers to cross his heart as a sign of truth?

Viewed in this way, the conflicts in the first chapter seem to serve a greater cause: that of getting at the truth. The purpose of argument becomes the clarification of right thinking. And that of war becomes the preservation of true justice and rightful property. Although war is portrayed in all its confusion and ugliness, *April Morning* seems to maintain that it is sometimes necessary.

With the search for truth suggested as the controlling focus of *April Morning*, we readily found new reasons for many other episodes and statements. Now we saw a clear purpose to the dream/nightmare sequence in the third chapter, with its "fever" of signing the muster book and its "madness" of atmosphere. Now it mattered that Ruth says, "I get to feeling that we're all asleep still, and this is just a dream," or Mother, "I can only say that you and all the rest of them have taken leave of their senses entirely."

Now the references to illness and insanity had a clear connection with the dreams, all of which represent unreality, but all of which are very real. Thus we paid close attention to Adam saying,

> ...at fifteen, you can still manufacture a fantasy and believe it for at least a few moments; and I had need for such a fantasy, or I would lose my wits and senses completely; so I began to tell myself that none of this had happened, that it was all something I had invented and dreamed.... I didn't believe any of this fantasy, you must understand; I knew I was inventing it; but I had to invent it and use it to get hold of myself.

This deliberate escape into the untrue in order to be able to bear the true, and to know which is which, brings all of the heretofore loose threads together. Dreams and fantasies assume their proper function. In the remaining chapters we found a proliferation of references to excitement, to insanity, to drunkenness, to craziness, and to change: all unstable, or distorted, states of being. A man's character seems to change when he mounts a horse, and Adam himself changes from boy to man. Growing up becomes a search for the truth of self.

After the battle, at the beginning of the next-to-last chapter, comes a paragraph containing the words "warm," "sweet," and "good." This is the homecoming. And here is the only reference to sanity—not insanity, but sanity. From here on there are many comforts, in particular food and candles ("Mother wants them at the meeting-house, so Father won't lie in darkness.") Surely candles represent the light of truth. On the last page Granny says, "you may lie to others, Adam. But don't lie to me." Adam replies that he is not lying, he's just too tired to think. They both know what he will do, and so do we. In the language of doubt, there is certainty.

One question remains. Did Howard Fast make his road signs confusing on purpose, so that we readers might serve as a laboratory for truth? Did he want us to get lost so that we would have to start over? In any case, it is what I want for my students. It builds confidence in them, and a willingness to start over without feeling defeated.

Source: Elizabeth Collamore, "False Starts and Distorted Vision in *April Morning*," in *English Journal*, Vol. 58, November 1969, pp. 1186–88.

SOURCES

Adams, J. Donald, "Speaking of Books," in *New York Times*, May 14, 1961, p. BR2.

Fast, Howard, *April Morning*, Bantam Books, 1961.

Fearing, Kenneth, "A Meeting at Concord," in *New York Times*, April 23, 1961, p. 438.

Griffith, Samuel B., "An Affair That Happened on the Nineteenth Inst.," in *The War for American Independence: From 1760 to the Surrender at Yorktown in 1781*, University of Illinois Press, 2002, pp. 157–74.

Homberger, Eric, "Howard Fast: Prolific Radical Novelist Who Championed the Cause of America's Common People," in *Guardian* (London, England), March 14, 2003, p. 25.

Hooper, Brad, "A Tribute to Howard Fast," in *Booklist*, May 15, 2003, Vol. 99, No. 18, p. 1639.

McLellan, Dennis, "Howard Fast, 88; Novels Included *Spartacus*," in *Los Angeles Times*, March 14, 2003, p. B.13.

"Sowing the Seeds of Liberty: Lexington and the American Revolution," in *National Heritage Museum*, http://www.nationalheritagemuseum.org/Default.aspx?tabid=162 (accessed December 18, 2009).

"Today in History: April 19," in *Library of Congress: American Memory*, http://memory.loc.gov/ammem/today/apr19.html (accessed December 16, 2009).

FURTHER READING

Emerson, Ralph Waldo, *The Complete Works of Ralph Waldo Emerson*, General Books, 2009.

> Emerson, whose grandfather was involved in the first battles of the Revolutionary War, wrote a poem in honor of the men who lost their lives fighting the British in the 1700s. It is from Emerson's "Concord Hymn" that the famous line about the first shot fired in Lexington being heard around the world is taken.

Ferling, John, *Almost a Miracle: The American Victory in the War of Independence*, Oxford University Press, 2009.

> This concise history of the Revolutionary War, written by a distinguished historian whose research is notably extensive, is well worth the effort of reading. This book offers the story of the endurance of the colonists, which caught the British off guard and eventually helped the colonists to win their independence.

Fischer, David Hackett, *Paul Revere's Ride*, Oxford University Press, 1995.

> This young-adult book provides an extensive story about the young messenger who rode his horse ahead of the British forces to warn the colonists of their coming. Though Fast does not name the messenger in his novel, Paul Revere is the figure most often referred to as the one who rode through the night so the colonists would not be unprepared. Though he was a somewhat minor character in the war, Paul Revere's ride was a pivotal event that helped the colonists gain victory.

Galvin, John R., *The Minute Men: The First Fight: Myths and Realities of the American Revolution*, Potomac Books, 2006.

> The Minutemen were an intricate part of the Revolutionary War, and this book explains who they were. As the author sorts through the stories, disclaiming some of the myths and supporting the facts, readers learn about the lives of these ordinary farmers and shopkeepers who quickly transformed themselves into soldiers when they were needed.

Scheer, George, and Hugh F. Rankin, *Rebels and Redcoats: The American Revolution through the Eyes of Those That Fought and Lived It*, DaCapo Press, 1987.

> Written in a narrative style with comments from people who lived through it, this tale of the American Revolution is told through the experiences of both the colonists and the British soldiers who were on the battlefield. Research was done on the major players of this great battle for independence, such as George Washington and Benjamin Franklin, but the authors also capture how the foot soldiers endured this war.

Tourtellot, Arthur Bernon, *Lexington and Concord: The Beginning of the War of the American Revolution*, W. W. Norton, 2000.

> Here are the historical facts of the first days of the Revolutionary War as presented in Fast's novel. Tourtellot describes the roles that two Massachusetts towns, Lexington and Concord, played in starting the colonists' fight for freedom.

SUGGESTED SEARCH TERMS

Howard Fast bio

Howard Fast AND April Morning

Howard Fast novels

April Morning AND young adult novel

April Morning AND Revolutionary War

April Morning AND American Revolution

April Morning AND Lexington and Concord

April Morning AND minutemen

April Morning AND bildungsroman

The Contender

ROBERT LIPSYTE

1967

Robert Lipsyte's young-adult novel *The Contender*, published in 1967, tells the story of a seventeen-year-old high school dropout who turns to amateur boxing in an effort to make something of his life. The story takes place in Harlem, a New York City neighborhood with a rich African American history, during the 1960s, a time when the civil rights movement was just beginning to unfold in the African American community. Tensions run high throughout this story as the protagonist, Alfred Brooks, pushes against the more popular dropout mode in his neighborhood: turning to drugs and crime. Though taunted by the local bullies and worried over by his Aunt Pearl, Albert is out to prove to himself that he is a winner.

Lipsyte, an award-winning sports writer, transports readers to the training gym throughout this novel to witness Alfred's transformation as he works out each day, seeking to better himself. Readers travel along with the protagonist as he enters the ring for the first time as an amateur boxer. Sitting ringside, readers wait with the fictional spectators in the novel to see if Alfred has what it takes to move up the ranks and become a professional boxer. Prior to writing this novel, Lipsyte witnessed many boxing scenes firsthand, and his training as a journalist allowed him to authentically share those experiences with his readers.

The Contender, Lipsyte's first novel, was listed as one of the American Library Association Notable Children's books from 1940 through

Robert Lipsyte *(Duffy-Marie Arnoult / WireImage)*

1970. The novel also won the Child Study Association Wel-Met Children's Book Award the year it was published.

AUTHOR BIOGRAPHY

Lipsyte was born January 16, 1938, in New York City. His father, Sidney, was a school principal and later the director of all the New York City schools for emotionally disturbed children. His mother, Fanny, was a teacher and counselor. By the time Lipsyte was nineteen, he had already earned a bachelor's degree from Columbia University. Two years later, he earned a master's degree from the same school.

Over his long career, Lipsyte worked in various writing positions. He began working for the *New York Times* in 1957, first as a copyboy and later as a sports reporter and columnist. He covered the first New York Mets game in 1962 for the *New York Times*. In 1964, he reported on the now infamous boxing bout for the world heavyweight championship between Sonny Liston and Cassius Clay (who later changed his name to Muhammad

Ali). It was this fight that inspired Lipsyte's first novel, *The Contender*.

Lipsyte's second novel, *One Fat Summer* (1977), is based on the author's childhood experiences. At his personal Web site, Lipsyte describes himself as an overweight youth who never played sports and did not lose the excess weight until he was a teen. His young-adult novels *Summer Rules* (1981) and *The Summer Boy* (1982) are also based on the author's personal experiences of being overweight as a child.

Lipsyte held positions at the Columbia Broadcasting System (CBS-TV) as a sports essayist, and at the National Broadcasting Company (NBC-TV) as a correspondent. He also hosted the television series *Life* for the Public Broadcasting Service (PBS).

At his Web site, Lipsyte states that he has always been two kinds of writer: a journalist and a novelist. He has written both styles throughout his long, award-winning career. In 1992, Lipsyte was a runner-up for the Pulitzer Prize for his sports writing. In 2001, he won the Margaret A. Edwards Award from the American Library Association for lifetime contribution to Young Adult Literature. In 2010, two books were published: Lipsyte's memoir, *An Accidental Sportswriter: Lessons from a Lifetime in the Locker-Room*, and his novel *Center Field*.

Lipsyte is married to Lois B. Morris, who is also a writer. His son, Sam, is a novelist. He also has a daughter, Susanna.

PLOT SUMMARY

Chapters 1–4

The Contender is set in the 1960s in Harlem, a neighborhood in New York City. It begins on a Friday night, as protagonist Alfred Brooks is waiting outside his apartment for his best friend, James, to show up. Alfred is seventeen years old and has dropped out of school just one year short of graduating. He lives with his Aunt Pearl. His father has deserted the family, and his mother is dead.

Alfred and James have been best buddies since elementary school. They have consoled one another through many challenges, such as the death of Alfred's mother. They have also enjoyed expanding their imaginations together, going to the movies and later discussing how they would remake the film they just saw. They have a secret hiding place in a nearby park—a cave they discovered behind some bushes. They often meet there. But recently, their friendship appears to be falling apart. Alfred fears that James has become involved with a gang of boys who are using and selling drugs.

When James does not show up, Alfred wanders over to a neighborhood hangout, which he refers to as the clubroom. James is there, along with other teenage boys. Of this group, Major is the leader. Other boys in the gang include Hollis and Sonny. Alfred reminds James that they had planned to go to the movies. When James says he has no money, Alfred offers to pay for his ticket. This arouses the attention of the other boys. Alfred has money because he works as a stockboy at the Epsteins' grocery store. The boys make fun of Alfred for working a meaningless job for a white man. In the course of their teasing, Alfred inadvertently reveals that on Friday nights, the Epsteins, who are Jewish, leave a large amount of cash in the register because they do not handle cash on their Sabbath, or holy day.

The other boys develop a scheme to rob the store and want Alfred to become involved, but he refuses. After the boys leave, Alfred remembers the new silent alarm system that the Epsteins have recently installed and wants to warn them. As he runs toward the store, Alfred hears police cars approaching. He is too late. So he walks quickly in another direction, hoping James has not been caught. Alfred goes to their secret cave to wait for James. But James never comes. Later Alfred learns that James was the only person who was caught and is now in jail. Major, Hollis, and Sonny hunt down Alfred and beat him up. They believe Alfred set them up.

Henry Johnson, a school friend, and his father happen upon Alfred as he is staggering home, his face bloodied. Alfred does not remember all the details of that night, but his Aunt Pearl tells him how he made it home. Alfred does not want to tell his aunt about the burglary or the beating. So he tells her he fell off a wall. Aunt Pearl is suspicious, but she does not press Alfred for more details.

When Alfred finally feels strong enough to go outside, he ends up at the entrance to Donatelli's gym. Henry, who works at the gym, had told Alfred how much he enjoys working, there watching young men train for boxing. At the top of the stairs, Alfred sees a light and walks into the gym where he meets Mr. Donatelli, a man of few words. Donatelli has trained many boxers. He does not coddle the young men. He knows some might make it to professional status, but only a few. Most will quit, lacking the discipline and the commitment it takes. He tells Alfred this, neither encouraging nor discouraging him. Alfred takes in the information and before he leaves, he tells Donatelli that he wants to be a boxer.

On Sunday, Alfred travels with his aunt and her three daughters to Queens, a large neighborhood east of Harlem. They are visiting Aunt Pearl's sister, Dorothy, whose family is better off economically that Pearl's. Alfred's uncle, Wilson, has encouraged his son, Jeff, to succeed by studying hard and earning scholarships for college. However, when Uncle Wilson talks to Alfred, he implies that Alfred does not have what it takes to succeed as well as Jeff. As Uncle Wilson puts it, Alfred should merely make the best of his circumstances, trying to become a grocery store manager. Alfred prefers the message that Mr. Donatelli gave him, one that promises Alfred that he can become a contender if he works really hard.

Chapters 5–8

On Monday morning, Alfred is up with the sun, running at a local park. It is his first day of training. Two policemen yell at him, asking where he is going so fast. Alfred tells them he is training to be a boxer. The policemen's attitudes change from being suspicious to being supportive. They know of Mr. Donatelli's successes with young athletes.

When he later shows up for work, Mr. Epstein questions Alfred about the recent burglary. He knows that Alfred and James are friends. Though Mr. Epstein says he trusts Alfred, he no longer allows the boy to take the cash to the bank. In a moment of weakness and anger, Alfred thinks about robbing the store himself, but he quickly changes his mind. Before he leaves for the day, Henry comes in and tells Alfred how happy he is that Alfred has begun training at the gym.

Chapter Six takes place inside the gym while other boxers are training. Alfred is ready to begin the routine with the boxing equipment. But when he walks in, no one greets him. Mr. Donatelli is not there, and neither is Henry. Alfred looks around and does not know where to start. Everyone but him is very busy. There are boys in boxing trunks in the ring. Some others are punching the heavy bags along the sides of the gym. Others are jumping rope. Everyone seems to know what to do, except for Alfred.

The first person to introduce himself to Alfred is Dr. Corey. He is a dentist whose office is downstairs. Dr. Corey gives Alfred some tips on boxing, telling him he should aim for the stomach of his opponent, the weakest spot on a boxer's body. That is why Alfred should work on tightening his stomach muscles, Dr. Corey tells him. A boy called Red laughs at the way Alfred does sit-ups but does not want to waste his time demonstrating the right way. Another boy named Denny shows Alfred a better way to do them. Before Alfred leaves for the day, Bud Martin, Mr. Donatelli's assistant, gives Alfred and Henry tickets to attend a boxing match at Madison Square Garden.

That night's boxing bout is the first Alfred has ever seen in person. Willie Streeter, Mr. Donatelli's most promising boxer, is fighting. In the middle of the bout, Streeter takes a punch to his face, which causes a serious cut near his eye. Mr. Donatelli stops the fight because he sees that the cut has distracted Streeter, and Donatelli worries the boy might be more seriously harmed. After the match, Alfred meets Bill Witherspoon, who used to fight for Donatelli but is now a teacher. When Alfred gets home, Major, Hollis, and Sonny are waiting for him outside his apartment.

In Chapter 8, Alfred stands up to Major's bullying, even though Major pulls a knife on Alfred. Major needs Alfred's help in burglarizing the Epsteins' grocery store again. Though Alfred is fearful for his life, he refuses to buckle under Major's pressuring him. He walks away from Major, feeling as if he has won the confrontation.

Chapters 9–12

Alfred is getting stronger, mentally and physically. The policemen whom he sees while he is out running encourage him. When he comes home, Alfred confesses to his aunt that he is training to be a boxer. Aunt Pearl is relieved. She had thought he was up to no good with James. She would prefer that he not box, but she is also glad that Alfred is not in trouble.

Weeks pass, and though Alfred is getting into shape and learning how to use all the training equipment, he thinks no one is paying any attention to him. He needs feedback, but no one is offering it. At work at the grocery store, Mr. Epstein tells Alfred that he was once a boxer when he was young. He was known as Lightning Lou Epp. This information gives Alfred a different, more impressive image of Epstein. However, Epstein tells Alfred that the sport of boxing has

changed for the worse. He implies he is a bit concerned for Alfred.

Major shows up at the gym and tries to entice Alfred to attend a party at the club. Bud Martin makes Major leave. Henry tells Alfred that he is suspicious of Major's intentions. Alfred misses James and believes James may be at the party. It is a Friday night, and Alfred is tired of all the training and having no fun. So he heads for the club after he leaves the gym.

Major greets Alfred, calling him Champ. Alfred looks around but does not see James. Major assures Alfred that James will come. In the meantime, Major offers Alfred alcohol and drugs. Alfred resists at first but then caves in. He spends the night at the clubhouse and in the morning he feels very sick. James shows up finally. He looks miserable—thin and sickly. He wants little to do with Alfred, telling him that their friendship is a thing of the past. James has come to the club, looking for drugs.

Alfred feels very sick through most of Saturday. He finds himself home at the apartment alone, barely remembering how he got there. His aunt is away. Major calls to remind him of plans they had made to go to Coney Island on Sunday. The next morning, Major shows up with Hollis and Sonny in a stolen car. Major drives recklessly, and when he sees a cop coming, he abandons the car. Everyone gets out and runs. Alfred twists his ankle as he attempts to get away. He no longer cares about his body. He has decided to quit boxing.

A few days later, after twice missing training, Alfred goes to the gym to collect his things. Mr. Donatelli is there. Alfred, though he has decided to quit, asks Mr. Donatelli if he thinks he might have made it if he had stuck it out. Donatelli tells Alfred that there is only one way to find out. Alfred would have to face a fight. Alfred decides to continue training a little longer. He wants to know if he can make it to contender status.

Chapters 13–16

Alfred is back on track with his training and is constantly improving. He finally is strong enough to spar, or practice boxing, with some of the older boys who are training at the gym. He learns how to defeat Angel, Denny, and Jose. Mr. Epstein shows up at the gym. As he is leaving, Mr. Epstein informs Alfred that he would like to train him on the cash register, insinuating that he now trusts Alfred to take on more responsibilities. Then Mr. Donatelli tells Alfred to check in with

Dr. Corey, the dentist, for a custom mouthpiece. This is the sign that Alfred is ready for his first amateur match.

Alfred's aunt becomes suspicious when he does not get up early to run the next day. She questions if he is sick. Alfred does not want to tell his aunt that he will be fighting his first bout that night. He is concerned that his aunt will worry too much.

Mr. Donatelli treats Alfred to lunch. Afterward, Alfred and Henry go to Witherspoon's apartment, where Alfred will rest before his fight. When Betty, Spoon's wife, comes home, she fixes Alfred a steak dinner. Then she tells Alfred to take a nap. Later, Donatelli drives Alfred and Henry to Long Island where the match is to be held. Alfred fights a boy named Rivera. The bout lasts three rounds. Alfred wins, but he is hurt. He listened to the boos of the crowd instead of following Donatelli's advice to punch and then to evade the boxer. The crowd wanted Alfred to stand and face Rivera. Because Alfred ignores Donatelli's advice, Rivera lands several damaging blows on Alfred.

In November, Mr. Donatelli arranges Alfred's second amateur fight, which Alfred wins with a powerful punch in the third round. However, Alfred does not feel good about having hurt his opponent. He is afraid that he might have killed him. His opponent is all right, but Alfred still feels sick about punching the boy so hard.

Chapters 17–20

In Chapter 17, Aunt Pearl takes her family to her sister Dorothy's house again, this time for Thanksgiving dinner. Jeff, who is Alfred's cousin, is home from college for the holidays. Though Uncle Wilson constantly praises his son's achievements, which often irritates Alfred, Alfred is surprised that he and Jeff get along so well. Jeff is even interested in boxing and wants to hear Alfred's stories. Jeff demonstrates pride in Alfred for having already fought two boxing contests and winning. Jeff also says he is interested in working for the local black communities rather than going into the Peace Corps to work with families in Africa as his father hoped he would. Alfred is inspired by Jeff and tells his aunt that he is thinking of finishing his high school degree. Jeff has lit a fire inside of Alfred, giving him hope for the future. Jeff has told Alfred that with his boxing experiences and training, he could be an inspiration for children in his neighborhood.

In contrast to the positive image Jeff has provided, when Alfred gets back home, he sees what at first looks like an old, ragged man, slumped over some garbage cans. It turns out to be James, who begs Alfred for money. Alfred wants to take care of James, so he offers him his home and some good food. James refuses. All he wants is money. Alfred only has a few dollars, which James takes and runs off.

Alfred's third match ends in a draw, or tie. It is obvious to Donatelli that Alfred does not want to hurt his opponent. He is concerned that without this ability, Alfred will end up being seriously hurt himself. So Donatelli tells Alfred that it is time to quit. But Alfred has one more match scheduled. He is determined to fight it so that he will know for himself whether he has what it takes to be a contender. Though Donatelli is reluctant, he gives in to Alfred. When they show up at the amateur bout, they learn that Alfred's opponent is Elston Hubbard, an older boxer with more experience and much more strength. Donatelli complains to the officials that the bout is not fairly matched. He is concerned for Alfred's safety because Hubbard is so much bigger than Alfred. But again Alfred insists. He accepts that he may be hurt, but he wants to know if he can take it.

Once in the ring, Alfred is overwhelmed by the older boxer and is knocked down within seconds of the opening bell of the match. He is down again before the first round is completed, but he does not want to give up. In between the second and third rounds, even the referee is concerned about Alfred's welfare and asks Donatelli if he wants to continue the fight. Henry stands up for Alfred, telling Donatelli to give Alfred the chance to finish the fight. Donatelli allows the match to continue. In the third round, Alfred fights stronger, but he loses the match. However, everyone is proud of Alfred for the way he stood up to the more powerful fighter.

When Alfred arrives home, his aunt tells him some bad news. James has broken into the Epsteins' grocery story again. He is hurt, and the police are searching for him. James apparently cut himself on some glass as he tried to gain access to the store. There is blood on the scene. Alfred thinks he knows where to find James. He runs to their secret cave where he finds him. Alfred sees that James is badly hurt and tries to convince him to go to the hospital. James refuses. He has lost all hope for a better life. He believes he has nothing but trouble to look forward to. Alfred honors James's request to leave him there. But as Alfred starts to walk away, James calls out to his friend. The two young men leave the cave together.

CHARACTERS

Alfred Brooks

Alfred is the protagonist of this novel. He has decided to drop out of school because he does not see how graduating will help his future. He lives with his Aunt Pearl because he has been orphaned. However, Aunt Pearl has three children of her own that she must support, so Alfred feels the need to help earn his keep. For this, Alfred works at the Epsteins' grocery story, making a meager wage as a stock boy. He wants to become someone special, thus proving to his Aunt Pearl and his Uncle William, Aunt Pearl's sister's husband, that he can make a successful life for himself.

Though he is, at one point, tempted to take the easy road—stealing money and doing drugs—Alfred eventually sticks to his plan of pushing himself as far as he can in becoming a professional boxer. In the end, even though he does not have what it takes to fight and hurt another boxer, he does prove to himself that he has the discipline necessary to do whatever he puts his mind to.

Dr. Corey

Dr. Corey is a dentist who has an office in the same building as Donatelli's gym. Dr. Corey fits the boxers with personalized mouthpieces when they are ready to box in the amateur ranks of local matches. He sometimes offers encouragement to Alfred, giving Alfred the strength and determination to continue his training.

Mr. Donatelli

Mr. Donatelli owns the gym in Alfred's neighborhood. He challenges Alfred to get into good physical shape by telling him that many young boys try but few succeed in becoming a boxer. Donatelli is like a father figure for Alfred. He has a good reputation as a trainer. Even the local policemen respect him for how he handles the young boys in training. In a time when many other trainers are out for as much money as they can get from promoting up-and-coming contenders, Donatelli cares for his boys in and outside of the boxing ring. He wants them to fight hard, but he does not want them to permanently do damage to their bodies. Donatelli is also a straight-speaking man, telling Alfred exactly what he must do to win as well as how difficult the challenges are before him.

Aunt Dorothy

Dorothy is the sister of Alfred's Aunt Pearl. Dorothy lives in a more prosperous part of the city,

thanks to the financial success of her husband, William. Dorothy is the mother of Jeff, a boy Alfred's age. Dorothy is supportive of Alfred, at least on a psychological level, encouraging Alfred when he visits.

Mr. Epstein

Mr. Epstein owns the grocery store in which Alfred works as a stock boy. Epstein is pictured as a caring man who becomes suspicious after Alfred's friend James is caught stealing money from him. Though Epstein distances himself from Alfred after the burglary, he later regains his trust in Alfred. He even shows up at the gym to watch Alfred work out.

Hollis

Hollis is a friend of Major's and one of the boys from the clubroom. He often does whatever Major asks him to do. He represents a boy who is up to no good—someone whom Alfred should not try to emulate.

Elston Hubbard

Elston is the last fighter that Alfred confronts in the ring. He is an ex-Marine who is older and much bigger than Alfred. Elston is also very boastful and loud concerning how well prepared he is as a boxer. After the bout with Alfred, however, Elston compliments Alfred for not giving up, even though Alfred was badly beaten up during their fight.

James

James is a long-time childhood friend of Alfred's. When the story opens, there are signs that James is in trouble. Later, readers learn that James has become addicted to drugs. As the story continues, James's condition worsens. Twice, James is involved in burglaries. He begs Alfred for money so he can buy drugs. At first, James refuses Alfred's help. But in the end, after James is severely hurt after attempting to rob the Epsteins' store, James gives in and accepts Alfred's friendship. Though the story ends before readers witness James recovery, the author provides hints that James might have finally decided to follow a different path under Alfred's influence.

Jeff

Jeff is Alfred's cousin, the son of Alfred's Uncle William and Aunt Dorothy. For most of the novel, Jeff is away at college. Whenever Alfred visits his aunt and uncle, however, much of the conversation involves stories of Jeff's continued successes. In the last visit, during Thanksgiving holidays, Jeff and Alfred get together. Jeff is very interested in boxing. Jeff tells Alfred that he could easily be a positive influence on the young children in the community and encourages Alfred to become involved in a recreational program to help youths.

Jelly Belly

Jelly Belly is one of the older boxers in training at the gym. His love of food is stronger than his love of the sport. As a consequence, he maintains a physique that is not suitable for boxing. He is a warm-hearted person who encourages Alfred.

Henry Johnson

Henry is the person who gets Alfred to go to Donatelli's gym. Henry works there and hopes to become a trainer for boxers one day. Henry believes that James and Major are bad influences on Alfred and tries to steer Alfred in a more positive direction. Mr. Donatelli gives Henry a chance to prove that he is capable of becoming a trainer by assigning him to Alfred. Henry helps Alfred strengthen his body and to keep his mind focused on what he has learned in the midst of Alfred's boxing bouts.

Major

Major is the leader of a group of boys in Alfred's neighborhood. Major asks Alfred to help him steal money from the Epsteins' store. When the robbery is not successful and James ends up in jail, Major beats up Alfred. Later, Major tries to convince Alfred that they are friends and then influences Alfred into taking drugs and getting drunk at a party. Later, Alfred stands up to Major, marking a turning point in Alfred's development.

Bud Martin

Bud Martin is Mr. Donatelli's assistant. He offers encouragement to Alfred when Mr. Donatelli is not present.

Aunt Pearl

Aunt Pearl is the mother-figure in Alfred's life after he is orphaned. She is a single mother trying to make the best of a very difficult life, raising four children. It is apparent that Aunt Pearl loves Alfred. Though at times, she worries if Alfred is going to get into trouble like his friend James has, Pearl most often trusts Alfred to do what is right. She does not completely approve of his interest in boxing because she fears he will get hurt, but she is proud of Alfred's commitment to get in physical shape in order to achieve his goal.

Sonny

Sonny is a member of Major's gang. Though Sonny talks tough around Alfred, he does whatever Major tells him to do. At one point, Sonny beats up Alfred because he believes Alfred set him up to be caught stealing from the Epsteins.

Willie Streeter

Willie Streeter is Donatelli's best boxing prospect. However, Willie gets injured in a boxing bout, and Donatelli stops the fight. Donatelli can tell that Willie's injury is distracting him, making him susceptible to a more serious injury. The author uses Willie as an example of a fighter who will not last long in the ring. Alfred is determined not to be like Willie.

Uncle William

Uncle William is the husband of Aunt Pearl's sister, Dorothy. William is always bragging about his son, Jeff. Jeff is everything that Alfred is not, and William lets Alfred know this. William sees little worth in Alfred and does not take the time to get to know him. William believes he has done an excellent job of fathering his son and is proud of his own efforts. He is completely caught off guard, therefore, when his son finally stands up to him and develops ideas for his own future.

Betty Witherspoon

Betty is Bill Witherspoon's wife. Betty acts as a minor mother-figure for Alfred, preparing him for his boxing bouts, which Alfred's Aunt Pearl is unable to do because she worries so much about Alfred's getting hurt inside the ring.

Bill Witherspoon

Bill was once a boxer. However, he lost interest in the sport and decided to go back to school and earn a teaching degree. Bill supports Alfred psychologically. Bill represents another path that Alfred could take should he decide to continue on to college. Bill encourages Alfred to earn a high school diploma and shows Alfred how he can do this.

THEMES

Fear

Fear is one of the more significant themes in *The Contender*. Fear affects most of the characters in this story. In particular, Alfred's most important fear is that he will not be able to handle pain. As Mr. Donatelli tells Alfred in the beginning chapters,

TOPICS FOR FURTHER STUDY

- Write an alternative ending for this novel. Choose from a variety of possibilities in which Alfred might either succeed in boxing or might fail socially, following in Major's or James's paths. Could you see Alfred going to jail for stealing from Mr. Epstein? Could you imagine an ending in which Alfred discovers a mean streak and hurts someone in the ring in order to win a championship? How would the novel have ended if Alfred won his last bout? Or what if Alfred decided to attend college to become a teacher? Make your ending at least 1,500 words long and read the alternative chapter(s) to your class.

- Create a Web site for Alfred Brooks as if you were Henry and wanted to promote the young boxer. Imagine that this Web site was created at least ten years after the story ends, with Alfred not quitting boxing but rather continuing successfully. Create a statistics table of all Alfred's fights, making up bouts that he might have fought. List any titles he has gained and the names of his competitors. Also include a biography for Alfred, giving personal information. Is he married, with children? Where has he traveled to fight? Did he win by any knockouts? Was he ever injured? How much money has he earned with each fight over the years? Share your results with your class.

- Research the Black Nationalist movement, part of which involved Malcolm X and Elijah Muhammad, the leader of the Nation of Islam in the United States in the twentieth century. Lipsyte creates a scene in the opening of Chapter 4 in which people are handing out pamphlets at a black nationalist rally. Provide brief backgrounds of Elijah Muhammad and his relationship with Malcolm X. Also find out what the major tenets of the Black Nationalist movement were. Who is credited with bringing these concepts to the United States in the nineteenth century? Create a multimedia presentation of your research, including music background, photographs, and narration. Present it to your class as a documentary.

- Make a map of New York City, showing the various boroughs and neighborhoods mentioned in the novel. Include places such as Harlem, Jamaica, Queens, and Manhattan. Provide statistics for each community using U.S. Census Bureau figures or any other information you find to distinguish what are the median incomes, the socioeconomic backgrounds, and the breakdown of age groups and ethnicities for each section of the city. Be sure to find enough details about each community to give your fellow students an idea of the general makeup of the city. Make a chart of the statistics to accompany your map and present both to your class.

- Read the young-adult collection *Here in Harlem: Poems in Many Voices* (2008), edited by Walter Dean Myers. Choose five or six of your favorite poems and ask some of your fellow students to join you in reciting them in front of your class. Study the poems well before reading, practicing the voices you will use as well as the expressions. Pretend you are the narrator of the poem, telling your class what it was like growing up in Harlem. Perform these poems as if you were an actor on stage.

---

one of the first signs that a young man is not psychologically ready to become a contender is that he becomes afraid of pain. Donatelli expects boxers to get hurt when they are in the ring, but when all a boxer does is focus on that pain, then even greater physical damage can be inflicted on him by his opponent. This is exemplified when Donatelli stops Willie Streeter's boxing bout after Streeter receives a wound on his face. Willie cannot take his mind off the wound and thus loses his focus

Boxing is the means through which Alfred grows from child to man. *(Image copyright Marc Dietrich, 2010. Used under license from Shutterstock.com)*

on his boxing technique. Boxers' minds must be strong enough to brush away their fear of pain until the bout is completed. Alfred insists on fighting his third match because he wants to prove to himself that even though he might not win the last bout at least he has the mental strength to overcome his fear of pain.

Alfred's accomplishment in fighting his fear in the ring is foreshadowed when he overcomes his apprehension of Major. After having been beat up by Major after the failed burglary attempt, Alfred has good reason to fear Major. But instead of cowering under Major's threats to hurt him in a second fight, Alfred decides not to give in to the boy. In spite of the threat of the knife that Major pulls on him, Alfred stands his ground and refuses to let Major pressure him to take part in a second attempt to burglarize the Epsteins' grocery store.

Other characters who experience fear include Alfred's Aunt Pearl. She is at first fearful that Alfred is becoming influenced by James and getting into trouble. Later she is afraid of Alfred's boxing, concerned Alfred will get hurt. Another

character, James, is afraid of turning himself over to the police at the end of the novel, even though he is hurt and in danger of losing a critical amount of blood. It could be argued that Alfred's Uncle William experiences the fear of losing control of his son, Jeff. Uncle William has spent many years and a good deal of energy in planning Jeff's future. When Jeff announces at the Thanksgiving dinner that he does not plan on joining the Peace Corps and going to Africa, his father is taken aback. It is the first time, according to this novel, that Jeff has made a decision of his own. This startles his father, and readers can assume that this makes William fear he has lost his son.

Self-Knowledge

Knowing oneself is a process that young people go through that is exemplified in a coming-of-age novel such as *The Contender*. The character James is on one end of the spectrum of self-knowledge and Alfred is on the other.

James is easily swayed and eventually demoralized by his submissive stance in trying to figure out for himself who he is. Once a vibrant youth who loved to use his creativity playing imaginative games with Alfred, James has slipped under the detrimental influence of drugs. Readers are not told who got James started on drugs, but the story insinuates that Major might have been the source. Whereas Alfred also stumbles at the party at the club, losing himself to alcohol and drugs, he realizes that the sickness and loss of discipline that he momentarily experiences is not the path that he wants to follow. He does not want to give away his sense of self to any substance or to anyone other than himself.

At one point in the story, Alfred sees the difference between someone who has a strong sense of self-knowledge and one who does not. He compares himself to his friend James. When he comes home late one night, Alfred sees what he thinks is a derelict, a groveling old man with no self-worth looking through the trash. This person turns out to be James, who has come to beg for money so he can feed his drug habit. In contrast to James, when Alfred realizes his mistake in indulging in drugs and alcohol, Alfred pulls away from Major and returns to his training. He cares about his body. He wants to become someone special. He knows himself well enough to realize that drugs are like thieves that can steal his sense of self away from him.

STYLE

Black Dialect

There are numerous phrases of slang from the black community that Lipsyte uses in *The Contender*. Though Lipsyte is white, his knowledge of (or research into) the phrases used by black youths in inner-city environments during the 1960s adds interest and authenticity to this story.

Some of these terms include Hollis calling Alfred "Uncle Alfred." This is a reference to the character of Uncle Tom in Harriet Beecher Stowe's novel *Uncle Tom's Cabin*, a classic piece of literature about slavery written from an abolitionist's point of view. When Hollis refers to Alfred in this way, he is insinuating that Alfred figuratively bends over backwards to please white people. Sometimes the abbreviated term, "Tom," is used to mean the same thing. On the other side of the issue, the term "The Man," refers to a white man who holds a position of power over a black person. Knowing and using these terms in this novel helps to create realistic characters who speak as their

counterparts in real life would talk, making the characters more believable.

Confronting Real Issues

Lipsyte has been praised by many literary critics for his style of not sugar-coating the issues that his characters must face in his novels. Lipsyte was one of the first authors to tackle some of the real, often life-threatening issues that some teens confront. He did not simplify his character's experiences, making the transition from youth to adult appear to have no difficult challenges.

For example, in *The Contender*, Lipsyte uses the character Major, a young boy who appears to be bent on creating havoc in the lives of the boys who are drawn to him, to show the difficult choices and conflicts Alfred faces. Major encourages theft as a way to make money. He inspires the youths who hang out with him to do drugs and to get drunk. He steals cars and drives recklessly, threatening the lives of the boys who go along with him for the thrill. By the end of the story, Major has not changed. He has not transformed himself from being a bad influence on the boys to being sorry for what he has done to them. This does not mean that Lipsyte believes that an inner-city youth cannot be changed. Rather, Lipsyte, through his novel, points out that there are some teenagers who get trapped into believing that drugs and crime are sometimes the only path they know to follow. His style is to show life as it is, not what it should be.

Lipsyte also allows Alfred to fail in some ways. In doing so, Lipsyte emphasizes the effort Alfred must exert in becoming the best he can be. Lipsyte has Alfred temporarily slip into the culture that Major represents rather than being strong enough to completely resist Major. The author also has James collapse so badly into that world of drugs and crime that James almost loses his life. Lipsyte does not have Alfred rescue his friend until the very end of the novel.

HISTORICAL CONTEXT

Muhammad Ali

The most popular boxer in the 1960s and 1970s, Muhammad Ali, who was born Cassius Clay, shocked his growing audience when he became the youngest boxer (at age twenty-two) to defeat a reigning heavyweight champion. The bout took place in Miami, Florida, on February 25, 1964.

COMPARE
&
CONTRAST

- **1960s:** Cassius Clay (later known as Muhammad Ali) wins a gold medal in boxing at the 1960 summer Olympics and four years later becomes the youngest-ever U.S. heavyweight boxing champion.

   2000s: Muhammad Ali, suffering from Parkinson's Syndrome possibly induced by blows to his head during his boxing career, is sent to Afghanistan as a United Nations messenger of peace.

- **1960s:** Harlem, which is recognized nationally as one of the centers of black culture, suffers from poor schools, rundown housing, and racial tensions.

   2000s: Harlem is witnessing economic renewal as people with money, including former president Bill Clinton's offices, move into the neighborhood and gentrify, or renovate, the community.

- **1960s:** Malcolm X states that U.S. society is generally racist and that he therefore believes black people will never enjoy equal rights in this country.

   2000s: Barack Obama is elected U.S. president, exemplifying that African Americans can attain high-level elected offices in the United States.

Hardly anyone expected Ali to defeat Sonny Liston. But he did and afterward, Ali became a star.

Ali first gained national attention when he won the gold medal for his light heavyweight title at the 1960 Summer Olympics in Rome. Nine months later, Ali won his first professional fight in his hometown of Louisville, Kentucky. In the next three years, Ali won nineteen fights and lost none. But it was not just his wins that brought him all the attention. In part, people noticed him because of his mouth. Ali liked to boast a lot. He often would predict the round in which he would defeat his next opponent. He also appeared on television talk shows and recited poems he had written. Ali was proud of his accomplishments, and he let everyone know it.

The years that Ali reigned as champion are often referred to as the golden age of heavyweight boxing. The sport enjoyed an increased popularity, due, in large part, to Ali's grace inside, and his personality outside, of the ring. In 1993, the Associated Press listed Ali as the most recognizable U.S. athlete (tied with baseball legend Babe Ruth). In 2005, Ali received the Presidential Medal of Freedom, the highest civilian honor bestowed in recognition of an individual's contribution to the national interests of the United States.

Harlem in the 1960s

Harlem, located in the Manhattan borough of New York City, has in modern times often been referred to as an African American neighborhood and a center of black culture. The percentage of blacks living in Harlem peaked in the 1950s with over 98 percent of the population comprised of African Americans.

As people became more involved in the civil rights movement throughout the nation, the residents of Harlem followed suit. Rent strikes occurred, in which people demanded that landlords fix up apartment buildings that were notoriously infested with cockroaches and rats. Many buildings lacked heat, and the people of Harlem were tired of being cold in the winter. Citizens also organized and demanded better schools.

Though Martin Luther King, Jr.'s policy of non-violence was an inspiration for the people of Harlem, so too were more radical leaders and their movements. The Black Nationalists, for example, were active throughout the district, and one of the organization's leaders, Malcolm X, was well known. Other groups that had a strong presence in the black community included the Congress of Racial Equality (CORE), the Student Non-violent

Alfred loses his last fight. (*Image copyright Karen Struthers, 2010. Used under license from Shutterstock.com*)

The underlying concept was that there was no chance of African Americans ever gaining equal rights and therefore they had to have a place where they could create their own nation, where the black culture could thrive.

During the 1960s, the concept of Black Power swept through African American communities as the movement toward civil rights grew. Even as Martin Luther King, Jr., organized non-violent demonstrations to help integrate African Americans into the largely white U.S. society through the passage of civil rights laws, some African Americans preferred the tenets of Black Nationalism, which advocated separation. It was at this time that Malcolm X appeared as a leader for those who wanted nothing less than a black nation. Malcolm X and his followers believed that the white society in which they lived was hopelessly corrupted by racism, and that no matter what laws were put in place, African Americans would always suffer. Malcolm X later softened his views. Before his death in 1965 by assassination, he promoted the ideas of integration.

Coordinating Committee (SNCC), and the Black Panthers.

In 1964 Harlem suffered a race riot, stirred by the fatal shooting of a black youth by a white police officer. The riot led to one fatality and many injuries as well as property damage. In an attempt to prevent future riots, the federal government provided financial support for programs to better the lives of African American youths living in the area of Harlem. After news spread of the murder of Martin Luther King, Jr., in 1968, riots again raged through Harlem.

Black Nationalism

To counter the lack of civil rights prior to the 1960s, a movement called Black Nationalism became prominent. Based on the principles set forth by Marcus Garvey in the 1920s, the ideas expressed varied from a complete exodus of African Americans from the United States to Africa to the forming of a separate nation of African Americans within the boundaries of the United States.

CRITICAL OVERVIEW

The Contender has topped the list of recommended young-adult literature since its publication in the 1960s. The book was featured on the *New York Times* 1967 list of The Year's Best Juveniles. One of the reasons for the novel's high approval ratings, according to John S. Simmons in the journal *Elementary English*, is that it meets the criteria for successful young-adult literature. Lipsyte's novel handles "the matter of taboos with restraint and imagination," Simmons writes. The novel also centers on the theme of "young people searching for a place in a modern urban setting." Another important factor in successful young-adult literature, Simmons writes, is demonstrated by Lipsyte's "skillful mixing of extended descriptions with suspense and action."

Though Nat Hentoff, writing a review of *The Contender* for the *New York Times Book Review*, finds fault with Lipsyte for his need "to teach rather than to create textures of experience," in parts of the novel, he also praises the author for his exciting and realistic presentations of the sport of boxing and the training that the sport requires. Lipsyte is at his best, Hentoff writes, when he describes the "inner transformation" that Alfred must go through in order to become a contender.

In an introduction to an interview in *School Library Journal* with Lipsyte, Walter Dean Myers states that "anyone who cares about YA literature knows *The Contender*." Myers then continues by calling the book a "groundbreaking novel." The reason Myers classifies the novel in this way is that *The Contender* was one of the first novels in the young-adult category to take on the task of exploring "the scary, confusing terrain of teenage boys struggling to fit in, to make hard choices, to become men."

In an article for *Harper's* magazine, Frances Fitzgerald writes about the evolution of the young-adult novel. From the 1920s to the 1960s, Fitzgerald writes, novels for children tended to depict idealized story lines, in which childhood was "portrayed as a happy, protected stage of life." In the 1960s, however, this depiction changed. And, according to Fitzgerald, Lipsyte's novel would go on to prove to be one of the new models for this transformation. Lipsyte, along with a few of his contemporaries, "produced many of what are now considered the classics of YA literature," Fitzgerald writes.

CRITICISM

Joyce Hart

Hart is a published writer and creative writing teacher. In this essay, she explores the symbols that Lipsyte uses in The Contender.

For the most part, Lipsyte's novel *The Contender* offers a straightforward narrative, relating the details of a critical point in a young teenager's life. The story contains a rhythm of built up tension and then release as the protagonist, Alfred, faces challenges and eventually solves them. The story follows Alfred through a period of grueling training at the local gym, where he chisels his body and his mind into a more powerful form. However, not everything about this novel is a day-to-day account of how a young teen matures into a young man. Throughout the story, running like a quiet river through a forest, are clever images that Lipsyte implants, providing refreshing moments of reflection for the careful reader. Three of them stand out. There is the clubroom, where Major and his followers plan illegal escapades; the three sets of stairs that lead up to Donatelli's gym; and the cave, where Alfred and James go to hide away and to share secrets.

At the clubroom, Major is king. It is here that he collects his followers, distributes mind-numbing drugs, and, in as many ways as possible, distracts the young teens from bettering themselves. The clubroom, in this story, is the exact opposite of Donatelli's gym. At the gym, young teenage boys build their bodies to make them stronger. At the clubroom, boys could not care less about what they are doing to their bodies as they consume detrimental chemicals. At the gym, Mr. Donatelli works the young boys' minds, challenging them to dig deep within themselves to find the mental strength to face opponents who want to knock them out in the ring. At the club, Major entices the young boys, tempting them with grandiose schemes of how they can make easy money without working. There is no worth to slaving away as their ancestors once did, breaking their backs for the White Man, Major convinces them. Why not let the White Man do all the work and then steal the money from him? The image of the club could be likened to a black hole in space, one that sucks everything in and swallows it. If a teenage boy falls for Major's false promises at the club, as James does, he might as well hand over his mind and body to Major to do with whatever he wants. James, by listening to Major, gives him his thoughts, his dreams, and his future. James becomes more like a robot than a human being. The club thus becomes a symbol of negativity to the extreme—a dark room in the pit of despair.

The three flights of stairs leading to the gym also represent an interesting image. First of all, with the gym on the third floor, readers might note that the gym is elevated, obviously on higher ground than the clubroom. However, there is more going on with this image. The first time Alfred approaches the gym, he is nearly wiped out physically in trying to climb the stairs. He is winded and almost turns back from the effort of ascending all those steps. It takes a great effort to get up those stairs. That effort, in a less determined teenage mind, might have been enough to discourage a young boy from reaching the top floor. By not giving up, by pushing himself all the way to the third-floor landing, Alfred demonstrates that he has a will. He might not know at that moment whether he will actually become a boxer, but he at least has enough determination to reach the gym and find out.

Later, as Alfred rises early each morning to run and afterward comes to the gym to work out, readers can judge Alfred's progress by how he mounts

WHAT DO I READ NEXT?

- Like Lipsyte's tale of Alfred Brooks, many other fiction writers have created stories about boxing. Jeff Silverman collected some of these stories in *The Greatest Boxing Stories Ever Told: Thirty-six Incredible Tales from the Ring* (2004). Some of the authors in this collection include Joyce Carol Oates, George Plimpton, Jack London, and even Homer, the Greek writer from antiquity. Among the themes included in this collection are the greater meaning of how boxing affects society and the personal tragedy of death inside the ring.

- For a more realistic glimpse into the world of boxing, John Gattuso and Jim Lommasson have put together a collection of vivid photographs and a nonfiction narrative that takes readers into the gym to see what it takes to be a boxer. *Shadow Boxers: Sweat, Sacrifice and the Will to Survive in American Boxing Gyms* (2005) provides readers with an up-close view of real contenders.

- Lipsyte included his protagonist Alfred Brooks in a type of sequel to his first novel in his 1993 book *The Brave*. In this young-adult novel, Sonny Bear is a Native American teen who has grown tired of living on the reservation. He travels to New York City and meets up with Alfred Brooks, who is now a policeman helping troubled teens. Alfred eventually sends Sonny to Donatelli's gym, where Alfred once trained as a boxer. Sonny has a fire inside of him that is much hotter than Alfred ever experienced. But like Alfred, Sonny learns to mold himself through the grueling training.

- Lipsyte concludes his trilogy, which began with *The Contender*, with his 1995 novel *The Chief*. Sonny Bear, who had become disgruntled with several incidents of cheating in the boxing world, heads back home to the reservation. There he gains the opportunity to fight a legitimate boxing bout and takes on the challenge. Before he steps into the ring, though, Sonny must fight his own self-doubts.

- Anne Moody's autobiography about growing up in the South, *Coming of Age in Mississippi* (1968), offers a different take on the challenges of being a teen. The author, besides confronting family and school issues, including poverty and divorced parents, also must deal with the deeply entrenched segregation of the Jim Crow laws that were prevalent in the South during her youth.

- *Into the Widening World: International Coming-of-Age Stories* (1994), edited by John Loughery, is a collection of tales about teens facing dramatic situations that become pivotal in facing the adult world. Coming-of-age lessons are shared by teens all over the world, and this collection demonstrates just how common these lessons are no matter where one lives. From authors like Nadine Gordimer and Ben Okri from Africa, to South American Gabriel García Márquez, these writers tell stories of love, racial inequalities, and obesity, challenges that many teens will be familiar with.

---

those same stairs. While at first, Alfred trains to reach the top, later he uses the steps to increase his stamina. He runs up the steps, and that makes him feel good about himself. He, too, sees how much stronger he is becoming. The image of the stairs gives readers a vivid visual representation of how far Alfred has to go from where he once was to

where his dreams exist. Running up three flights is not an easy task. Running up in top form is even more difficult. But every time that Alfred accomplishes this task, he can see how much closer he is coming to his wish to be the best he can be.

Sitting on the steps in front of his apartment at street level is where Alfred had watched the turmoil

---

Alfred climbs the stairs to the gym and climbs his way out of a life of crime and drugs. *(Image copyright Viachaslau Kraskouski, 2010. Used under license from Shutterstock.com)*

of city living. At street level are the young boys who hang out on the corner looking for trouble. Here too is where Alfred runs into James, who is constantly in search of money to feed his drug habit. Major hangs out on the street, looking for weaker boys who will do as he tells them. But at the top of the three flights of stairs, young boys are reaching for something better. They want to be winners and are willing to work hard toward that goal.

Finally, there is the symbol of the cave. The cave is unusual. Who would think of New York City or any major metropolis having any caves? But there it is, hidden behind some bushes in a park in Harlem. When they were young boys, Alfred and James discovered the cave. They kept it a secret, a place just for them. They would go to the cave to loosen their imaginations, creating fantasies that were sparked by the movies they attended. They would also go there when they were grieving and needed to separate themselves

from all the other people in their lives. It was in the cave that James consoled Alfred after Alfred's mother died.

When Alfred is looking for James after the failed burglary attempt, he goes to the cave. Though Alfred's relationship with James was disintegrating, Alfred returns to the cave, the place where their friendship grew. It is as if in Alfred's mind, their friendship still exists in the cave, as if the cave has preserved it.

The cave thus becomes a vessel that holds and protects Alfred's memories, especially the pleasant ones he once shared with James. The cave is a sanctuary, too. It has become a place that soothes Alfred because of those memories. In the cave, all the pressures of his life are kept at bay. In the darkness of the cave, anything is possible. With the walls of the cave wrapped around him, Alfred feels safe and reassured.

It is therefore fitting that Lipsyte ends his novel at the cave. Alfred has learned that James is in trouble again. This time James is also seriously hurt. When Alfred hears that James has run away from the police, the first thing that comes to Alfred's mind is the cave. Where else would James feel safe? Where else would James go to figure out what to do next? So Alfred runs to the cave and finds James there. It is inside the cave, that secret room of their own, that James and Alfred's friendship is renewed.

James needs a lot of help, physically, mentally, and morally. Alfred is there to help him. Eventually the two of them have to emerge from the cave, or James will die. In this way, looking at it as a symbolic image, the cave could be likened to a mother's womb. The boys' emergence is like a re-birthing. When James and Alfred finally emerge from the cave, they come out not as boys but as newborn men. They have made the decision to face their life, their challenges, and their responsibilities.

Source: Joyce Hart, Critical Essay on *The Contender*, in *Novels for Students*, Gale, Cengage Learning, 2011.

Walter Dean Myers

In the following interview, award-winning YA writer Walter Dean Myers talks to Lipsyte about topics such as masculinity, encouraging young men to read more, and writing for young adults.

In the mid-1960s, a sportswriter for the *New York Times* decided to try his hand at fiction. His novel, about a young man who finds himself through boxing, was marketed as "young adult" fiction, a then-new category. Today, of course, anyone who cares about YA literature knows *The Contender* and its author, Robert Lipsyte. In this first, groundbreaking novel, and in several others that followed, Lipsyte maps the scary, confusing terrain of teenaged boys struggling to fit in, to make hard choices, to become men. For *The Contender*, as well as three other books of enduring appeal—*One Fat Summer*, *The Brave* and *The Chief* (all from HarperCollins)—Lipsyte was named this year's winner of the Margaret A. Edwards Award for lifetime contribution to young adult literature. (The award is sponsored by *School Library Journal* and administered by the Young Adult Library Services Association, a division of the American Library Association.)

To talk to Lipsyte about his life and work, who better, we thought, than Walter Dean Myers, another Edwards Award winner and another writer whose books explore ideas about manhood and morality. Lipsyte spoke to Myers by phone from his home in New York City, where, when

> **WHEN YOU WRITE FOR ADULTS—AND I THINK MUCH OF MY SPORTSWRITING AND HEALTH WRITING IS FOR ADULTS—YOU'RE EITHER A GENIUS OR A JERK, DEPENDING ON WHETHER YOU STROKE OR RUFFLE THEIR FEATHERS. BUT KIDS ARE SEEMINGLY READING WITH MORE OF AN OPEN MIND."**

not traveling the country to cover sports for the *Times*, he continues to write for adults and young adults. One of his latest projects is writing the libretto for an opera about Muhammad Ali.

Walter Dean Myers: When I was growing up, I lived in a rough Harlem neighborhood, where reading was synonymous with weakness. As a result, I became a secret reader and book lover. Did you have a similar experience?

Robert Lipsyte: Well, I didn't really have to be a secret book lover. I was fat . . . and hated my body and hated to go out in the world. So books were a real refuge. Also, I grew up in pretty much of a lower-middle-class striving Jewish ghetto in. . . . [Basically], in that society, I was the marginalized boy. I was a girl. You know, if you were fat or disabled or had very thick glasses or a stutter or whatever it was, that put you last to be chosen on the team and sent to play with the girls. So books and writing were a real refuge for me. When I lost my weight at the age of 14, it was like those operations where a kid's blind all his life and then suddenly, "I can see!" And from the age of 14 for the next I don't know how many years, I didn't read, I didn't do anything, except, you know, play ball and screw around.

WDM: Your books nearly always deal with masculine identity. By that I mean the idea of boys being aware of what it is to be a boy, of competition with other males. I think that's a vastly underrated concern of teenaged boys and that it's really important for them to realize it's not just them having those feelings. But you don't find this dealt with very often in young adult literature.

RL: Well, I think that maybe so many guys who are writing tend to take that for granted or haven't understood that, simply because they were not in some ways placed on the sidelines. I think that I'm very much aware of it because it was a long time before I was allowed to participate. I never took it for granted, being male. Probably in the same way that gay men, and others who've been told that they're not quite on the team, are marginal. I think that in those years of being fat and being an observer and being very much aware of watching guys—and then, you know, after 14, being allowed to participate, I don't think I ever really lost the idea that I don't quite belong.

WDM: One of the things that comes off very strongly in your books is that even the most physically aggressive guys—Alfred in The Contender, *for example, and Sonny Bear in* The Chief—*all have this marvelous awareness of "becoming" males. Of the way that, from boyhood to manhood, there's this idea of "How male are you?" You expect it in* One Fat Summer *[the story of an overweight teen] because here's a kid who's marginalized. But in your books, even the fighters, the toughest guys, are aware of this question of manhood, of another man imposing his will on you.*

RL: I think kids talk about it and respond to it because we have been taught not to show our inner life. Because we're not supposed to be vulnerable to each other. It's interesting: I never got into it, but that whole Iron John movement—remember Robert Bly? Guys hugging each other and playing drums in the woods? There were guys who really went for that, and others who obviously felt threatened by it and mocked it. The idea is that there is this tremendous need for guys to trust each other, to be friendly, to be vulnerable to each other. But we're constantly being taught, for very good reasons, not to. [Instead we're supposed] to keep up the game face—the constant facade of masculinity, of toughness, and never to let down.

You know, the whole thing about homophobia, I mean when you think about it, who should really give a s—?... But the threat, you know, that you would be cast out from this male society if they found out you were a fag, was really another way for parents and teachers and coaches to keep us under control.... And I think that it became then increasingly important to never show any kind of weakness or vulnerability or sensitivity, because then you're a faggot. And I think guys kind of closed into themselves. And I think they like to hear that other people have, you know, lives and feelings, and are scared. I mean, guys are scared.

WDM: Absolutely. And I think that in this country the boys read less than in, say, Europe. You know, we spend about six weeks a year in London and it's not uncommon to see young guys on the Underground reading. Here, I never see that. And yet if you go to comic book fairs, they're full of young sweaty boys buying comic books. But it seems that once they reach a certain age, they don't transfer it to books. I read comic books as a kid. I'm sure you did. And just reading other stuff, this came naturally to me. How did you get into reading?

RL: I didn't go to ball games with my father, I went to the library with my father. That was our thing. We went to cowboy movies and we went to the library at least once a week. And I could take out as many books as I could carry. That's how I built up upper body strength [laughs]. So reading was very much encouraged in the household. My father had a lot of books. And I moved from comic books to pulp magazines. I read a lot of mostly westerns, then later, science fiction and some detective. But I read a lot of pulp magazines, and then into "book-books."

WDM: How do you think we could encourage more boys to read now?

RL: Well, I see around the country, there are librarians who kind of feed boys books, one book at a time. I suspect that it's the same way how you find, you know, an alpha boy in high school, a kid that everybody looks up to, and you make sure that he's wearing, you know, "Air Myers" sneakers. And if you can get him a book and turn him on to a book, and if he's not afraid to walk around with a paperback in his baggy back pocket, you could do it that way. The [problem] is that the people who are involved in books, say, "Hey, this is kind of a wonderful thing. We're just going to wait until the light goes on over America." And that's never going to happen.

WDM: It's never going to happen.

RL: I mean [reading] really has to be sold and pushed.... But there's never been that kind of an effort. Although there are these pockets... [for instance] I was just in a library in Philadelphia. It was kind of a tough neighborhood—they had more guards than librarians [laughs]. And the place was packed with all these kind of real tough-looking kids. And man, they were great. They had a lot of questions—good questions—about the books, about me.

Two questions I hadn't been asked before: One, do I ever use drugs to help me write? And two, the killer—the one that I'm still stewing over—was, "Are you rich enough now to stop writing?" The answer to both was a resounding no. But they were really into it. They were into the books. They had read the books. And it was because librarians and teachers had fed these books to them slowly. And they talked to them and the kids got turned on by them, as I think they'd get turned on by any books that were sold to them in the right way. I mean that's not really happening in any kind of a mass way. For all the talk, I don't think the culture really wants young people to read. I think reading is ultimately dangerous and subversive to any kind of authority.

WDM: One thing in your books is interesting in light of the recent school shootings and people suggesting that when kids hear another student talking about this kind of thing, they should go to the authorities. I think that's such nonsense. I mean, I think kids should go to the authorities— that would be nice. But kids are not like that. Even when kids know there's something wrong going on, they have these divided loyalties. And one of the themes you treat so clearly in your books is the value young people place on peer loyalty. In The Contender*, Alfred doesn't approve of the guys planning to rob the grocery store. In* The Brave*, Sonny Bear doesn't want to betray Dolly and Stick. I don't think adults always understand these conflicts. And I think some kids just want to know that it's okay even to think about some of these things. But I don't find that in enough books.*

RL: Well, I guess one of the problems in the books we write is that it's very much of a genre. And as a genre, it has conventions and customs, one of which is the idea that these books, because they are for children, for this kind of vulnerable audience that has not yet reached the wisdom of the writer, has to be on the side of authority. You know what I mean? On the one side is the kids and on the other side is the teachers and the librarians and the cops and the parents.

I wrote a book called *The Chemo Kid*. After I had cancer and I went home, I was really sick from the chemo. And my kids were, like, 10 and 7. So I made up these stories for them about chemo giving you supernatural power. And at the end of the book, in the draft that I turned in, the hero is given the choice either to stop the chemo and be normal again, or to lose his supernatural powers. And he opts to keep taking the

chemo and to keep having supernatural powers. And the editor, whom I no longer will work with, went crazy on that. And not even from a literary aspect, but from the idea that the implicit message was that drugs were okay, you know?

WDM: Right, right.

RL: So we were at a real stalemate, because I wasn't going to change the ending. Then actually it was my son who helped me through it. He has subsequently written a book of short stories, and he has a novel coming up, but at that time he came up with the solution whereby—I forget now—there was a counterdrug and the character refuses the counterdrug that would cancel out the chemo—so it was worked out. But you know, I kept thinking about the idea that these books are so often placed on the side of the authorities that lie to the kids. And that in so many of the books, the endings are kind of clean and the adults tend to be either very good guys or a few evil ones. It's not really like life, where adults manipulate kids, where adults exploit kids. I mean there have been a lot of books now about sexual abuse of children. And I'm sure there's a lot of sexual abuse of children. But not everybody gets sexually abused, and that's not the only issue in which adults manipulate and exploit kids. It's often much more subtle than that.

WDM: It's emotional abuse.

RL: Yeah, it's emotional and it's on a day-to-day basis. So I think that the idea that we're a genre and that we're supposed to, you know, be saying, "Just say no," and be giving good, clearcut lessons, often gets in the way of—forget about storytelling—it gets in the way of telling kids the truth.

WDM: Another thing about your books, what's missing in them is the "ghetto to glory" concept.

RL: Actually there was a book called *From Ghetto to Glory* [about baseball great Bob Gibson].

WDM: Yeah, and it's really kind of absurd, because the guy is always a saint when he begins and the world just has to recognize it. That's missing in your books, and I'm very grateful about that being missing. The people and the gyms are so interesting in all of your boxing books. The people—they're real human beings. I read in one of your bios that you felt that putting sports in perspective was a real important thing to you.

RL: Well, yeah. I remember the first time I was sent to Yankee Stadium. This was kind of my turning point about those guys, about sports. I was on night rewrite—I was a reporter early, so I could have been like 22. And somebody had jumped out of the stands and hit Mickey Mantle. This could be like 1960. It was before [the idea of] recreational violence. I mean this was kind of off-the-wall stuff. And the *New York Times* "ambassador to baseball," whoever was covering the Yankees at the time, was not going to bother the great man by asking what happened. They go on a road trip and obviously Mantle had gotten hurt pretty badly. You know, his jaw was bruised. So now it's a week later and he's back, they're back in the stadium, and they send me up to interview Mantle about what happened that night. I'm sure I was wearing a suit and tie, as I did in those days. And Mantle and Berra were warming up in front of the dugout. And I'm sure I said, "Mr. Mantle," or something like that. And I asked him you know, really politely—I introduced myself—I asked him very politely about what had happened that night. And it was just in a kind of a casual way that he looked over his shoulder and said, 'Why don't you go f— yourself?' You know, I mean there wasn't even like, specific anger at [something], just 'Why don't you go f— yourself?' I remember thinking that I had either heard wrong or asked the question in an improper way, and I kind of rephrased it. And then he and Berra started throwing the ball through my hair.

WDM: Wow.

RL: At which point I knew that the interview was over. And so my first reaction was kind of shame and humiliation, and what had I done wrong that this, you know, American hero—butter wouldn't melt in his mouth—I read everything about Mickey Mantle before I went up there and I knew that he was a perfect human being. So I had misspoken, something I had done was wrong. And it took me a really long time to figure out that we had been lied to about Mickey Mantle. Many, many other sportswriters had been shamed and humiliated by him in all kinds of ways, and never reported it, never talked to each other about it, because we were all keeping up this invulnerability. And also we were protecting ourselves as much as we were protecting him. And here was this guy who, you know, kicked little kids and was sort of a stone prick. I went through a process of being very angry later and then to figure out that if I could be, you know, 22 and already half grown,

and could be lied to in this way and have bad feelings about it, what about kids? Why should kids be lied to? Why should kids have these guys as false role models?

WDM: Your bio says that when you were young, your role models were Steinbeck, Haliburton, and Salinger. But you know, when I read your work, I often think of Arthur Miller.

RL: Well, thank you. Wow.

WDM: Because he deals with some of the same issues. Have you ever done adult fiction?

RL: Yes. I've done two adult novels, *Liberty 2*, and *Something Going*. *Liberty 2* is a thriller about an astronaut who came back to lead America into the second revolution. And *Something Going* was a race-track novel. And both went in the toilet.

WDM: Oh yeah? Are you going to go back to that?

RL: I would, I have no reason not to. But I find writing YA so much more attractive in a lot of ways. I guess it's the messianic impulse. When you write for adults—and I think much of my sportswriting and health writing is for adults—you're either a genius or a jerk, depending on whether you stroke or ruffle their feathers. But kids are seemingly reading with more of an open mind. And you do have more of an opportunity to have an impact on somebody's life, and I like that.

Source: Walter Dean Myers, "Pulling No Punches: Edwards Award Winner Robert Lipsyte Talks to Walter Dean Myers about Tough Guys, Sissies, and the Struggle to Become a Man," in *School Library Journal*, Vol. 47, No. 6, January 2001, pp. 44–47.

Robert Lipsyte

In the following speech, Lipsyte reflects on writing The Contender *from initial idea to the sequels.*

As a sportswriter, I may be more sensitive than I should be to the meaning of a lifetime achievement award. In SportsWorld, you don't get such an award until after your knees are shot and your fast ball has lost its pop and fans start slapping you on your now considerable gut and saying, while trying not to laugh, "Lookin' goooood, Bobster."

Yeah. Great. So my first reaction to the award was, Uh-oh, it's over. The ALA is telling me to close the lid and hang up my laptop. Just when I thought I was finally figuring it out, the committee has declared, "It's been a lifetime, Bob, see ya around." I had this cold flash; it's a

> WRITING THE BOOK WAS A VERY HAPPY EXPERIENCE, TALKING ABOUT IT AT SCHOOLS WAS PURE FUN; THE LETTERS FROM GIRLS AS WELL AS BOYS WHO FOUND INSPIRATION IN IT WAS THRILLING TO ME."

few years from now, old timer's day at the big library stadium, and the Bobster totters in. There are kids reading the new young writers, Walter Dean Crutcher and Bruce Blume, and M. E. Zindel, and I creep up behind them and whine, "Read me, too, Sonny. We were tougher in my day, we actually had to touch our computers to make the words come out."

Well, it was this chilly Saturday in January when this all began. I'd just flown in from Charlotte, North Carolina. I'd given myself a new assignment for my sports column, stock car racing to get my blood boiling again. I got to ride 180 miles an hour—that wakes you up. I got back home to the East Village tired but renewed and I lowered myself into a hot bubble bath. Yeah, hot bubble bath, tell that to the boy readers. I got in with a glass of Jim Beam and a week's worth of newspapers. This is harder than it sounds, you have to keep the papers up high so they don't curl in the heat. You need superior upper body strength. It's the only reason I work out.

Well, the phone rang—I had the cordless by the tub—and there's a babble of excited voices, Judy and Jennifer were shouting, "You've won, you've won." I said, "Thanks, anyway I'll wait for Ed McMahon to ring my doorbell," but before I could hang up, the papers started to slip and as I grabbed them, Judy and Jennifer kept saying, "No, no it's Margaret Edwards"—and I said, "I swear, I never even dated a Margaret Edwards," and then my old friend Michael Cart got on and it gets serious. Michael is not often excited, and now I'm embarrassed—and I'm naked—so I ask everyone to wait and avert their eyes from the speakerphone until I can get out of the tub and put on a robe. And then I was very excited, too—and grateful and proud—and what I think must always happen, at least should always happen,

when you get a lifetime achievement award, my life flashed before my eyes. Actually in this case, my YA writing life.

I happen to know exactly when that life began. On November 20, 1965, about 9 P.M. Las Vegas time. I was sitting in the dark outside a casino hotel, by a deserted pool, with an old boxing manager I had taken to dinner. He was rheumy and garrulous and very old, I thought. In retrospect, I realize he was younger than I am now (as it turned out he hadn't had his second lifetime yet, the manager of former champions, he was on the skids and going through a depressed period—he would bounce back as Mike Tyson's mentor, adoptive father, and manager, but that's another story and Cus D'Amato's award).

So this ancient, washed-up boxing manager was telling me about his glory days when he owned a gym in a tough section of lower Manhattan, and late at night he would sit at the top of three dark, twisting flights of stairs, waiting for a kid to climb up—alone, at night, and fighting his fear of the unknown because he was so driven by the desperation of his life on the streets below.

A kid like that, he said, who used his fear as fuel, would have a chance to become somebody, maybe even a contender.

I was a boxing writer so I knew that a contender was a challenger for the championship, someone on the way up, someone with promise, someone who could fight. Being the champion is often luck, fate, the draw—but being a contender is about hard work and talent.

The picture of those stairs stayed with me all through the fight I had gone out to cover—Floyd Patterson versus Muhammad Ali—and all the way home. I became inflamed with the picture, and with the question: What kind of kid would dare to come up those steps—what would be going on in his life—what would he find at the top?

And I wondered what I needed to do to become a contender—what were my narrow twisting stairs?

I'd written a nonfiction book, Dick Gregory's autobiography, "*nigger,*" and sold some short stories, but I had never written a novel— would the chapters of a novel be my steps up to becoming a contender?

When I got back to the *New York Times'* office there was a letter from Harper & Row Publishers, from someone named Ferdinand Monjo. He wondered if I had ever thought of writing a book with boxing as its milieu—a common boxing term, milieu—I still can't pronounce or spell it, but I love that word. I called Ferdinand Monjo right up—Yes I would, and I babbled on, the book will have three flights of stairs, a kid hero, I'll call it *The Contender*, and Ferd said, "Go right ahead, dear boy," and I in my innocence thought that was a contract—Thank goodness—I never would have written the book if I was more sophisticated and less inflamed with becoming a contender myself.

Ferdinand Monjo was a terrific editor, and he was surrounded by terrific editors, Charlotte Zolotow, who became my editor when Ferd left Harper for a top job of his own, and of course, the queen—the Margaret A. Edwards of editors—Ursula Nordstrom, who just about invented YA.

Of course, I knew nothing about YA then—it was just my novel, with boxing as its milieu—and it was linear, it had a seventeen-year-old protagonist, and there was no sex that I can remember.

The Contender was a great success, less for my acknowledged genius—I guess I can't be too modest today thanks to this wonderful award—but the times were right for the book. Government money was available, there was a desperate need for books with minority protagonists, and perhaps most important there was a generation of librarians and teachers open to stories that were closer to the bone of real kids' real lives.

Writing the book was a very happy experience, talking about it at schools was pure fun; the letters from girls as well as boys who found inspiration in it was thrilling to me. But I thought it was a one-shot—the only YA I would ever write. Ursula gave me an advance for a second novel, which I tried to return for years. She wouldn't take it, but I was sure I'd never write it. After all, my plan was to rework King Lear not Kid Lear. So it was ten years—and three more books, including two Old Adult novels—before I returned to what has always been the most consistently rewarding and, I think, worthwhile part of my writing life.

The return was accidental. Well, my sister the Jungian analyst is here, so I have to say it was at least unconscious. I was writing an essay for *Mother Jones Magazine* on books that had influenced me as a kid and the phrase "in the prison of my fat" fell out of the typewriter. Just plopped out, I had never consciously thought of how trapped I had felt as a fat kid, hating my body and finding comfort in reading and in writing. As a writer I created a universe with words (in my

earliest fiction, skinny people died horribly). I'd wanted to write about being a fat kid for many years but never found the way in. I had written science fictions, metaphors about outsiders, lone rider cowboy tales, but never anything that directly confronted the emotions of feeling so different and alone. But the rawness of that image "In the prison of my fat" released all the repressed emotions. All I had to do was be honest, turn on the tap, get out of the way, and let my fingers tell the story. That night I started writing *One Fat Summer*, an emotionally true story of my fourteenth summer when I lost perhaps forty pounds—I don't really know exactly how much because I hated to weigh myself. In the writing, I fell so in love with the protagonist, Bobby Marks, who is an idealized version of myself, that I wrote two sequels just to keep him near me.

One Fat Summer was briefly banned in Levittown, New York, several years ago, a silly censorship, but it put me on lists with two people I admire enormously, Judy Blume, who is one of the most influential writers of my time—not YA writers, just writers period—and Francesca Lia Block, who I think is the most exciting new talent I've watched emerge. *One Fat Summer* was censored because a mother reading over her son's shoulder thought she saw a masturbation scene. She was probably right although I don't remember writing it. She complained and administrators took the book off the reading lists because they didn't want trouble—I didn't sense any morality on their part, just an unwillingness to attend more meetings, and have less time with their families—fair enough.

Teachers and librarians responded heroically, and the book eventually, after a fuss and a fight, was returned. But let me underline that this was not *Fahrenheit 451*, this was a mother taking an appropriate interest in her kid's schoolwork—there should be more such—and a lazy and unprincipled principal—there should be less like him.

I have no problem with a parent taking a book out of a child's hands—I have a lot of problems with their taking it out of the hands of other parents' children. Thank goodness for teachers and librarians who believe in the word and will stand up for it.

That helped lead me back to YA. I've always depended on happenings—I'm a journalist—and most of my books come from questions I can't answer just by interviewing someone.

Right now I'm in the middle of *The Warrior Angels*, the fourth in the Contender series. That came about because I'd been writing a lot about mental health among athletes—depression, rage, and eating disorders in particular—and I began to wonder how Sonny Bear, now that he was heavyweight champion, was dealing with his anger, a problem that's been plaguing him for two books now. And it would be a chance to check on Alfred Brooks, the hero of *The Contender*, the kid who put my kids through college, now in a wheelchair, his spine severed by a dope dealer's bullet.

The Contender was never supposed to be the first in a series. In fact, my kids always warned me against a sequel. They loved *The Contender* and were afraid a sequel would smudge the original. Thanks for the confidence, guys.

I went along with that until one day, as usual on a journalism assignment, I met a seventeen-year-old Indian kid on a reservation. He was afraid of ending up another alcoholic, jobless wreck like his dad and uncles; there were no opportunities on the res, but he was also afraid of the discrimination and lack of community out in the mainstream white world. He told me that he had run away once, come to New York City on a bus and spent a night on 42nd Street before the cops picked him up and put him on a bus home. That experience had given him hope—he had survived being off the res on his own, and now he was planning his great escape. I wondered, what would happen to a kid who fell in with drug dealers on The Deuce, as 42nd Street was called then. What if he was a boxer? What if Alfred was involved? Alfred twenty years later, a narcotics cop. I daydreamed about it a lot. In those days I had a city-based TV show and hung out with cops and social workers, went into prisons, and still kept up with boxing. In daydreams begin plot lines.

And sometimes in nightmares. Twenty-three years ago, when I got cancer for the first time, to keep my kids from feeling scared I would tell them a continuing story about a boy whose chemotherapy drugs gave him superhuman powers.

Writing that book, going back in time to think again as an adolescent, turned out to be very useful to me as a patient because I discovered how helpful it was to think of the cancer—and the chemo—as bullies I had to face. When I needed to suck it up, to really gather strength for a bad time, I could go back to a little room in the back of my head where I kept the memory of being that fat kid who for years was picked on by bullies, especially one in particular, until one day in junior high school, for reasons that have never been clear, the worm turned and I went berserk.

My bully was picking on me outside of school—nothing too serious that day, kind of a light off-day, no punching, no blood, no tearing off my shirt pockets, just pinching my elephant butt, kicking at my briefcase and calling it a fagbag. I snapped, maybe because girls were watching, and I dropped the briefcase and hurled myself at him. We both went down in a heap, me on top. I don't know who was more surprised. Because I was no fighter and didn't know the proper schoolyard rules of engagement, I probably would have killed him. I was beating his head bloody into the sidewalk when teachers rushed out to save him. They yelled at me! It was one of the greatest moments of my life. Even thinking of it now makes me smile. No one ever gave me a hard time again, in junior high or anywhere else. And it became a resource for me in dealing with illness.

Wow! Just thinking about it feels so good. Thanks to Margaret A. Edwards, and to you, I've been having this continuing lifetime flashback for the last six months, and I feel as though I'm setting out on another lifetime. I'm deep in the new book—probably not as deep as Alix Reid, my new editor, would like, and I've been talking in schools and libraries. And, of course, getting much more out of it than my audience.

I was recently at this tough branch library in Philadelphia—there were more guards than librarians—and the kids asked two questions that rocked my boat.

One kid asked, Do you use drugs to help you write? Another kid asked, Are you rich enough now to stop writing? I think the only thing I truly and unequivocally believe is that an adult should never lie to a kid. And so, I answered both questions truthfully. I just said, No. I've never used drugs to help me write and I don't have enough money to stop writing.

The kids seemed a little disappointed, and thinking about it, so am I. But about the same time, at my whining insistence, my old friend Michael Cart checked the bylaws of the Margaret A. Edwards award, and reported to me that in his librarian's opinion there was nothing to prevent winning the award again. Like Cus

D'Amato, the old fight manager, I could have a second lifetime.

And another chance to answer those questions:

Do you use drugs to help you write? Hey, who knows what I could write under the influence of steroids, marijuana, Propecia, Viagra. And maybe then I'd make enough money to stop. But not until then, and certainly not until I've had my second lifetime. So, look for me back here in another thirty-six years.

See ya around, and thanks again so very much.

Source: Robert Lipsyte, "The 2001 Margaret A. Edwards Award Acceptance Speech," in *Journal of Youth Services in Libraries*, Vol. 14, No. 4, Summer 2001, pp. 21–23.

Sari Feldman

In the following essay, Feldman asserts that while Lipsyte's 1967 novel The Contender *might seem sentimental, the book's themes and sports action continue to make it relevant.*

As a boy he read Hemingway and dreamed of writing in front of French windows like Gregory Peck's character in the film version of Hemingway's *Snows of Kilimanjaro*. In reality Robert Lipsyte descends the stairs around 8:30 a.m. to his basement office where he must wear hat and boots against winter cold spells.

Lipsyte, currently known for his popular young adult novels, is no newcomer to the daily grind of writing. From 1957 to 1971 he was a sports reporter and columnist at the *New York Times*. Lipsyte did not suffer from false hero worship or misconceptions about the role sports plays in the lives of Americans and, if anything, he was particularly attuned to the sociological significance of sports in our society. His career

spanned a time that saw the professional athlete change from a symbol of virtuous values to entertainment celebrity. He regrets that the genuine importance of athletics cannot filter through the commercial media hype that emphasizes the sports figure as superstar. "But I feel the whole sports thing has gotten away from what the real value of sports is which is: (1) to get people healthy and in good shape and (2) (this is where women have particularly suffered) to teach you how to work with people you don't necessarily like."

Another strong concern of Lipsyte's is that many youth, minority youth in particular, buy into this superstar image and hype that so few can attain, and turn away from education and other careers.

He left the *New York Times* in 1971 to pursue other kinds of writing, having felt stifled by sports journalism. "Covering sports is very cyclical and the faces change and the names change but its the same people, same event year after year. And I really was never that interested in sports, I was really more interested in the implication of sports. The way that sports are used."

The highlights of his sportswriting career are recounted in *Sportsworld: An American Dreamland*. Lipsyte's "Sportsworld" is concerned with the distorted influence of sports on everyday life. He is worried that the ethics of winning, in his view a perverted sports morality, permeate the workplace, relationships, and government. His anecdotes also create intimate portraits of Muhammad Ali, Connie Hawkins, Bill Bradley, and other personalities.

While Lipsyte was writing for the *New York Times* he had his first young adult novel published. *The Contender* is the story of Alfred Brooks, a young black growing up in Harlem who aspires to a better life than the ghetto can offer by training to be a boxer. The self-discipline and personal courage Alfred displays become the real rewards of the experience.

The Contender may seem quite sentimental, but in 1967 the realities of urban life were just beginning to be revealed, particularly to teenagers. The optimism of *The Contender* reflects the social vision of the "Great Society," a vision that remains unrealized. Today the well-meaning white adults of the novel are seen in a more sophisticated light and could be viewed as paternalistic or inadvertently exploiting impoverished neighborhoods and impressionable youth. It is the themes of *The Contender* and the vivid sports action that keep the book pertinent to a 1980 audience. "I think today *The Contender* is a girl gymnast in a well-to-do suburban high school," Lipsyte acknowledges.

The Contender owes its inspiration to a chance meeting with an aging boxing manager in Las Vegas. "He was old, he was going blind, kind of shuffling through the scene and he began to reminisce and he talked about this gym that he had once owned that was up three flights of stairs on the Lower East Side," Lipsyte recalled. "He used to sit at the top of those stairs listening to boys come up the steps and he could judge whether or not they would ever be contenders. He could tell because he was waiting for the boy who came up alone, one set of footsteps, a boy who came at night and a boy who came up scared, the footsteps kind of scurrying, or at least not confident. That boy was going to conquer his fear because he was so desperate to become somebody."

This image stayed in Lipsyte's mind and started him thinking about the word *contender* in a very symbolic way. What are the moments in life that are equivalent to "going up the stairs"? His ruminations led to the development of the Brooks character.

Today a white author might not risk creating a central black character. "In retrospect," Lipsyte revealed, "I'm appalled at my arrogance that I could have, I'm not so sure I should have." At that time Lipsyte had just come out of an intensive nine months with Dick Gregory, getting an exposure to black culture and gaining confidence to realistically relate to and write about the black experience. They coauthored *nigger*, Gregory's autobiography of his early years and personal struggles. "Just from working on *nigger*, talking to him (Gregory), meeting his friends, listening to reminiscences, talking about the sense of being black, I felt that maybe I could present a story in a reportorial way."

In a more recent novel, *Jock and Jill*, Lipsyte once again concerned himself with ghetto life. In this case Hector, a Hispanic gang leader from the South Bronx, dreams of revitalizing his community through the autonomous control of a housing project. Rather than tell this story through Hector, Lipsyte created from his sports knowledge Jack Ryder, a high school baseball star. Jack and Hector are brought together through Jillian, a teenage photographer concerned with conditions in the South Bronx. "I didn't really feel that I could take a Hispanic character and do a book from the Hispanic point of view. I just hadn't logged the time as I had with *The Contender*."

His second young adult novel, *One Fat Summer*, is about the summer Bobby Marks loses weight and gains self-esteem. The novel's humor and compassion make it easy for teenagers to identify with Bobby's personal problems. For Lipsyte the novel had deeper meaning because the story and character of Bobby Marks are autobiographical. "I always thought that I would write about the summer I had lost a lot of weight and had never been able to. Suddenly I was able to write some 24 years later," he disclosed.

The novel is set in 1952 but neither the historical time frame nor Bobby's naive character interfere with the sensitive portrayal of adolescent insecurities. "I really wanted to write about kids and their bodies. While the pressures and feelings might have been different in the 1950s, the internal thoughts on how one viewed his or her own body and how one viewed oneself in relation to friends and parents probably never changed."

In the intervening years between *The Contender* and *One Fat Summer*, Lipsyte had published two adult novels, *Something Going*, coauthored with Steve Cady, and *Liberty Two*. After *One Fat Summer*, however, he became more aware of young adult as a specialized genre of literature and the pleasure of writing for a teenage audience. "I began to realize that this was a very exciting field. Almost everything that I had done up until then, all the OA, old adult, was always either ruffling somebody's feathers or stroking them, almost never changing anyone's mind about something," Lipsyte explained. In contrast to a high-powered sports environment or the national recognition of a *New York Times* column, it was the more personal response from his readers that solidified Lipsyte's commitment to the field. "More and more young women were writing about *One Fat Summer* and how that had touched them. They were more relaxed talking about their bodies, or their feelings, certainly more than boys are, and I began to realize that I was getting a great deal more satisfaction out of writing young adult."

Summer Rules is a fast-paced sequel to *One Fat Summer* with a slimmed-down Bobby Marks. Bobby's hot on the trail of romance but suffering the tortures of being a summer camp counselor. The biggest change in his personality is that Bobby's ego expands in proportion to his weight loss. Although the novel stands alone, this book also serves as the transition from *One Fat Summer* to *The Summerboy*.

Body image and its effects on self-image play a significant part in Lipsyte's young adult novels. Although he claims not to be familiar with adolescent theory, he is completely in touch with the dynamics of body image. "During adolescence you don't have the mind and the soul you're going to have later so your body is really your manifestation of you, at least how people are going to judge you."

A second stage of adolescent development is the focus of his two most recent young adult novels, *Jock and Jill* and *The Summerboy*. In each book an older adolescent moves beyond personal needs, converting his narcissistic concerns for self into a concern for the outside world. In the hands of a less skilled writer these stories could have been doctrinaire, but Lipsyte's absorbing plots, strong characterizations, and insights into individuals' motivations create fine works of social realism.

In *The Summerboy* Bobby is forced to work with women laundry workers as his punishment for damaging a truck. Firsthand experience enlightens him to the women's unjust and inequitable working conditions, and Bobby makes a grand, heroic gesture on behalf of his coworkers. "Bobby Marks was sort of pre-ordained to do that because Bobby Marks is a person who lives as a hero in his own daydream. He's a continuing character in his own mind and he's a hero waiting for an event."

Jack Ryder in *Jock and Jill* takes up the cause of living conditions in the South Bronx with the same energy, commitment, and drive that had made him a great athlete. Jack Ryder is a hero, too, but for different reasons. "Jack suddenly understood that the system which for 17 years he had devoted his life to and that he had hung his star on was basically exploitive and corrupt. He felt betrayed and he took his narcissism, his sense of himself, and his image of his own power as a hero one step further. Jack Ryder is much less sophisticated than Bobby Marks and yet much more self-righteous and moral."

Fiction as social commentary has some of its roots in the works of John Steinbeck, a writer that drew Lipsyte as a boy. "For some reason his

(Steinbeck's) accessibility, his compassion for people, his outrage, somehow made it seem that there was a way to be a writer and still not be just a fantasist, just a storyteller, that there be kind of a social purpose."

Lipsyte defers to librarians and teachers as best equipped to turn teenagers on to reading, but suggests that getting them to write first may be the way to develop a reading habit. Knowing what books to suggest may be another part of the reading problem. Speaking on familiar ground, Lipsyte attacks sports biography as an example of the type of book arbitrarily pushed on different groups, in this case boys. "It (sports biography) has no relation to the guy's life, it is probably poorly written, probably written by some underpaid sports writer who pasted together some clippings from some second rate newspaper and it is presented to the kid and the kid reads it. So they give kids these bad sports biographies, junk food biographies and they are prepared for more junk food biographies. I don't think they're necessarily going to progress."

Free to Be Muhammad Ali is Lipsyte's own sports biography, an in-depth portrait of not only Ali's rise to fame but also the controversy and racism that surrounded Ali's career. This kind of biography was made possible by the intimate and mutually respectful relationship they enjoyed during Lipsyte's years with the *New York Times*. *Free to Be* . . . is not a secondhand account but personal observation that calls upon the reader to interpret the social and political climate surrounding the Ali mystique.

Young adult literature has certainly had positive impact on encouraging young people to read. Lipsyte reflects, "Maybe you should think of this kind of literature as a bridge between people who have just learned to read, reading children's books and reading textbooks, and to prepare them for the next step which is for a lifetime of reading, and give them books that pertain particularly to their own lives."

Young adult authors operate under certain constraints. They have less freedom in subject matter and presentation, and need to be less obscure stylistically and still not sacrifice quality. Above all, Lipsyte feels that young adult authors must be truthful not only in their facts but also in characterizations and life situations. "If you assume that your audience has substantially less experience than you do then you're under a kind of pressure to be truthful in ways

> MORE THAN ONE ALFRED BROOKS SITS IN OUR CLASSROOMS. ALFRED'S PROBLEMS ARE EVERYMAN'S IN THE GHETTO. JUST SEEING THAT IS THE FIRST STEP IN A YOUNG MAN'S COMING TO TERMS WITH HIMSELF. IT IS NICE TO KNOW THAT ONE IS NOT ALONE."

that you may or may not have to be truthful in books for an older audience."

For many years Robert Lipsyte was surrounded by great sports figures and other media personalities. He rejects the notion that teens need idols like these to emulate. "I don't think that we need heroes, I think that we need people who inspire us to be better ourselves." Today teenagers may be finding peer-heroes within young adult novels. Robert Lipsyte has created such characters with courage, determination, humor, and the ability to survive adolescence. Therein could be the major impact of his work.

Source: Sari Feldman, "Up the Stairs Alone: Robert Lipsyte on Writing for Young Adults," in *Top of the News*, Vol. 39, No. 2, 1983, pp. 198–202.

Saul Bachner

In the following essay, Bachner argues that Alfred's coming to terms with himself as an African American man is the most important lesson in The Contender.

In *The Fire Next Time*, James Baldwin, searching for his place in a threatening world, articulates the fearful problem of giving direction to his young life. He is Black; he lives in Harlem; his talents are few. His inventory is less than satisfactory.

> When I tried to assess my capabilities, I realized that I had almost none. In order to achieve like I wanted, I had been dealt, it seemed to me, the worst possible hand. I could not become a prize fighter—many of us tried but few succeeded. I could not sing. I could not dance.... The only other possibility seemed to involve my becoming one of the sordid people on the avenue, who were not really as sordid as I imagined but who frightened me terribly.

Baldwin's problem is given temporary answer in his move to the church. His career in the church turns out to be his "gimmick," his way of coming to peace with himself and his surroundings. It is a peace that had to be made. Survival demanded it.

Baldwin's fears and pressures to choose among questionable alternatives seem to be the adolescent heritage of too many of Harlem's young men. Alfred Brooks, central character of *The Contender*, finds himself in similar circumstances. He is a school dropout; the pressures of the avenue are mounting; he can't sing or dance. What will he do? He will see if he can box. His gimmick in the search for a place in the sun will be the ring. In his quest to become a contender Alfred will learn much about himself and those around him. He will also learn to make peace with himself as a man and with himself as a Black man. That is what Robert Lipsyte's award winning junior novel is all about.

If Alfred Brooks were not Black, he would be concerned only with the universal questions that trouble all adolescents: Am I worth something? What abilities do I have which make me feel that worth? What am I capable of that will earn the respect of my peers? These are the questions of self-esteem and belonging that all adolescents must work out. To young Alfred Brooks, however, is added the task of coming to peace with his Blackness as well. While being Black limits his choice of direction (to singing, dancing, boxing), it also conditions his relationship to his peers. Will he be part of the young protest movement? Should he work for a white store owner? Should he give his life to the church as a means of bearing the white man's burden? These are some of the questions he must work out as a Black adolescent.

In seeking answers to these questions Alfred Brooks turns to the ring. To the victors the rewards here are many: Status. Money. Self-esteem. And to those interested, a chance to do something for one's people. Alfred wants to be somebody. Responding to his friend Henry's urgings to try the gym, he approaches Mr. Donatelli and asks for a chance. Mr. Donatelli, gym owner and counselor-manager of young boxers, tells him that wanting to be a champion is not enough:

> Everybody wants to be a champion. That's not enough. You have to start by wanting to be a contender. The man coming up, the man who

knows there's a good chance he'll never go to
the top, the man who's willing to sweat and
bleed to go as far as his legs and his brains
and his heart will take him.

Alfred's seeking to be a contender is what
carries him to manhood. In the course of his
search the reader will get a good idea of what a
Black adolescent must contend with in his quest
for identity.

Alfred's family is his aunt and her three
daughters. His father deserted when Alfred was
ten. His mother died three years later. Helped
through this tragic time by James, his best friend,
Alfred determines to finish school and make
something of himself. Instead, he drops out eventually and goes to work for the Epsteins, Jewish
grocery store owners. His job, his family, and the
close friendship with James are pretty much his
uneventful life before he goes to the gym. James,
on the other hand, is drifting in a different direction. He moves with the neighborhood toughs.
Thus, while Alfred will find his challenges in the
ring, James will take his tests on the street.

Alfred's drive to succeed and desire to meet
and overcome the obstacles inherent in boxing are
what fashion him as a man. Regular hours,
restricted diet, roadwork, rigorous calisthenics
and sparring, in addition to clerking full time,
are bound to reveal one to one's self. But all of
that is prologue. The test in the ring is the ultimate
test of one's manhood. It is here that the contender is found out. It is here that one's worth
emerges. Success here is the positive answer to an
adolescent's crucial questions. Successful, he *is*
worth something, he *does* have talents, he *can*
command the respect of his peers. Lipsyte's portrayal of the four bouts in Alfred's short-lived
ring career is first rate. The author writes about
boxing like the man who spent years as sports
columnist for the *New York Times*. Each fight is
unique. Alfred wins on a bicycle, staying deftly
away from his first opponent. He wins again, with
a smashing knockout punch decking his second
opponent. This, however, proves his undoing.
After two fights, he can box and he can hit.
Unfortunately, he can't kill, nor does he want
to. Thoughts of that knockout haunt him and
inhibit him in his third fight. A dull draw is the
result and Donatelli wisely calls him off. Without
that killer instinct Alfred would never be more
than a journeyman fighter, he is told. Donatelli
advises him that his future lies elsewhere. Alfred
agrees but still hasn't learned what he must know.
Could he have been a contender? Could he stand

up and take it? His fourth bout, an overmatch
arranged over Donatelli's objections, brings that
answer. In some of the finest ring scenes one will
find anywhere, Lipsyte takes the reader through
three brutal rounds of one-sided fighting. Alfred
takes a fearful beating. But, in boxing parlance,
he is dead game. His defeat is also his victory. At
the fight's end, he is embraced by his opponent
and mobbed by his rooters. He has won the admiration and respect of the crowd. He is indeed a
contender.

Alfred's victory as a young man is only partial.
He is also Black. He must come to terms with his
Blackness as well. He must find his place in the
scheme of things as a Black man. The pressures
here are from without, but the soul searching is no
less troublesome. On Sunday evening just before
he begins at the gym, Alfred turns them all over in
his mind—the urgings of the nationalists, the pressure of the militants, the exhortations of the
church, and the counsel of his uncle (to go middle
class):

> Tomorrow was Monday, blue Monday, dirty
> Monday. The store would be filthy, there
> would be dozens of cartons and cans to stack.
> Opportunity for advancement? Sure, they might
> even let me deliver on the bicycle. He saw Major
> shuffle along the clubroom floor. Uncle Alfred.
> The Epsteins would be asking about the
> attempted robbery. About James. He would
> scratch his head and play dumb, like you always
> do when the white man asks those questions you
> better not answer. He's got his foot on your
> throat, you gonna lick his shoe? Come march
> with us Alfred. Maybe later. Happy little darky.
> World is opening up for colored people. Devil's
> got new uniforms. We'll get you. Everybody
> wants to be a champion. Alfred, slave, nothings
> promised you. Slave. Opportunity for advance-
> ment? You have to start by wanting to be a
> contender.

The pressures are unrelenting. While Alfred
trains and boxes, he must also contend with the
demands of the street. Major and his friends
want help in robbing the grocery store—help
from the inside. Alfred refuses. Help not forthcoming, James is caught after a botched attempt.
For his refusal, Alfred takes a beating from those
who got away. Later, after winning his first two
bouts, Alfred gains the respect of Major (and
Sonny and Hollis). The problem now is wine
and dope and good-timing it in a stolen car.
Alfred slips some but escapes that snare too.
James, however, does not. Hooked and driven
by need, he goes through a plate glass window in

a frantic attempt to feed his habit. Badly cut, he is eventually found by Alfred in a cave hiding place which the two shared in another time as young inseparables. After some impassioned pleading, Alfred leads James toward the lights of the avenue and help. Alfred has taken the first step on a journey which will carry him through much of the time ahead. He will help his people. He has made his place as a Black man.

Alfred is now eminently equipped and thoroughly motivated to remain where he is and help. Finished but respected as a boxer, he is ready to work with young people—his decision—and has all the qualifications. Young people will look up to him and listen. His desire to help and the encouragement he receives from Spoon (a former Donatelli boxer turned public school teacher) and the Epsteins lead him back to school where he will try to earn his diploma at night. Alfred has found himself as a man and as a Black man. He now knows who he is.

For the classroom teacher Lipsyte's book is invaluable. More than one Alfred Brooks sits in our classrooms. Alfred's problems are everyman's in the ghetto. Just seeing that is the first step in a young man's coming to terms with himself. It is nice to know that one is not alone. Alfred's solutions may not be everyman's, but they are articulated solutions. One can hold these up for his own individual viewing. That young reader may not be able to cut Baldwin, but he can handle *The Contender*. In his search for answers, he could do a lot worse.

Source: Saul Bachner, "The Junior Novel and Identity: Robert Lipsyte's *The Contender*," in *Negro American Literature Forum*, Vol. 9, No. 2, Summer 1975, pp. 62–63.

SOURCES

"Ali," in *ALI: the Official Site of Muhammad Ali Biography*, http://www.ali.com/ (accessed December 1, 2009).

Fitzgerald, Frances, "The Influence of Anxiety," in *Harper's*, Vol. 309, No. 1852, September 1, 2004, p. 62.

"Harlem: A History in Pictures," in *New York*, http://nymag.com/metrotv/02/blackhistory_photos/ (accessed December 1, 2009).

Hentoff, Nat, Review of *The Contender*, in *New York Times Book Review*, November 12, 1967, p. 42.

"History of Harlem," in *Harlem Heritage Tours*, http://www.harlemheritage.com/history-of-harlem/ (accessed December 1, 2009).

Lipsyte, Robert, *The Contender*, Harper Trophy, 1967.

Malcolm X, with Alex Haley, *The Autobiography of Malcolm X: As Told to Alex Haley*, Ballantine Books, 1987.

"Muhammad Ali Biography," in *Biography.com*, http://www.biography.com/articles/Muhammad-Ali-9181165 (accessed December 1, 2009).

Myers, Walter Dean, "Pulling No Punches," in *School Library Journal*, Vol. 47, No. 6, June 1, 2001, p. 44.

"Robert Lipsyte," in *Robert Lipsyte Home Page*, http://www.robertlipsyte.com/ (accessed December 8, 2009).

Schaefer, Richard T., *Racial and Ethnic Groups*, Little, Brown, 1979, pp. 177–201.

Simmons John S., "Lipsyte's Contender: Another Look at the Junior Novel," in *Elementary English*, Vol. 49, No. 1, January 1972, pp. 116–19.

"The Year's Best Juveniles," in *New York Times*, December 3, 1967, p. 431.

FURTHER READING

Boddy, Kasia, *Boxing: A Cultural History*, Reaktion Books, 2009.

This volume covers the sport of boxing as depicted in literature, film, and other media. Boddy examines the sport to see how it reflects concepts such as violence, politics, race, and national pride. Going as far back as ancient Greek culture, Boddy travels through time to examine the attraction for this sport, as well as the sport's influence on society.

Boyd, Herb, *The Harlem Reader: A Celebration of New York's Most Famous Neighborhood, from the Renaissance Years to the Twenty-first Century*, Three Rivers Press, 2007.

In the 1920s, a great resurgence of African American writers, painters, and musicians bloomed out of the part of New York City called Harlem. The outlay of creative work was referred to as the Harlem Renaissance. It marked a national awareness of art created by black people. Langston Hughes and Zora Neale Hurston were among the first noted figures. But Harlem was and continues to be much more than just a center for the Black Arts. The author provides a history of Harlem and speculates about its future.

Hardy, Sheila Jackson, *Extraordinary People of the Civil Rights Movement*, Children's Press, 2007.

Though most students have heard of some of the civil rights leaders who made the news, this book tells the story of some of the ordinary people who did extraordinary deeds during the fight for civil rights. Not only do readers have access to biographies of people like Fannie Lou Hamer and Robert Moses, they also learn who the Greensboro Four and the Freedom Riders were and how they helped the civil rights movement.

Kallen, Stuart, *History Makers—Political Activists of the 1960s*, Lucent Books, 2004.

Political activism was prominent in the 1960s. In this young-adult book, Kallen looks at some of the major players in the political movement of this decade. Brief biographies and statements of how these leaders affected the politics of the 1960s are provided to give readers an overview of the times. Information is included about Martin Luther King, Jr., Angela Davis, Cesar Chavez, and many others.

Marberry, Craig, *Spirit of Harlem: A Portrait of America's Most Exciting Neighborhood*, Doubleday, 2003.

Marberry has put together a collection of stories from long-time residents of Harlem to create a mosaic of history of this famous African American community. From the mouths of ministers, historians, gospel singers, dancers, and realtors comes an oral history of what Harlem means to the people who call this neighborhood home.

Tsoukalas, Steven, *The Nation of Islam*, P & R Publishing, 2001.

This book provides a basic understanding of the Nation of Islam and the creation of the Black Muslim movement in the United States. Tsoukalas tells the story of the important figures in this movement, including Elijah Muhammad, Malcolm X, and current leader, Louis Farrakhan.

Werner, Doug, *Boxer's Start-Up: A Beginner's Guide to Boxing*, Tracks Publishing, 1998.

Werner presents the basics of how to become involved in boxing. The book covers the equipment that is used, suggests safety tips, and explains offensive and defensive skills that need to be developed. A brief history of the sport is also provided.

SUGGESTED SEARCH TERMS

Robert Lipsyte bio

The Contender

Lipsyte AND coming of age

Lipsyte AND young-adult novel

The Contender AND novel

boxing novels

Lipsyte AND The Contender

Robert Lipsyte books

Lipsyte and boxing

Lipsyte and YA

Lipsyte and sports literature

Fever 1793

LAURIE HALSE ANDERSON

2000

Fever 1793 by Laurie Halse Anderson is a historical novel set during the yellow fever epidemic that decimated Philadelphia during the summer of 1793. The central character is Matilda "Mattie" Cook, a fourteen-year-old girl who lives in the coffee house that her mother and grandfather run. When the epidemic hits, she is forced to grow up very quickly as she faces not only her own illness, but those of her mother and grandfather. Mattie must rely on untested inner resources as she watches her familiar city become a place of danger and mayhem.

Mattie teams up with her most trusted friend, a free black woman named Eliza, to nurse the children in their care through the disease. Once her loved ones are out of danger, Mattie and Eliza become business partners and rebuild the coffee house. Over the course of the book, Mattie grows from a typical teen, interested mostly in avoiding chores and chasing excitement, to a fully grown young woman with a thriving business and a young child in her care. The novel, published in 2000, contains numerous actual historical characters, from General George Washington to Dr. Benjamin Rush, and provides a lively portrait of Philadelphia when it was still the capital of the United States.

AUTHOR BIOGRAPHY

Anderson was born on October 23, 1961, in Potsdam, New York, to Reverend Frank and

Laurie Halse Anderson *(Chris Whitney | Doylestown, P.A.*
Reproduced by permission.)

Joyce Halse. She grew up in Syracuse, New York, where her father served as chaplain for Syracuse University. After attending Onodaga Community College for two years, Anderson transferred to Georgetown University in Washington, D.C. She graduated with a bachelor's degree in languages and linguistics, and soon after married Greg Anderson, with whom she had two daughters, Stephanie and Meredith. The family moved back to Philadelphia and Anderson began writing as a freelancer while working on her own material.

Anderson's first publications were the picture books *Ndito Runs* and *Turkey Pox*. The idea for *Fever 1793* came to Anderson in 1993. In an article she wrote for *School Library Journal*, she said that she found an article in the paper about the yellow fever epidemic that had devastated the city two hundred years earlier and thought it was the perfect subject for a novel. Anderson researched the novel for nearly two years, delving into primary source documentation at the Historical Society of Pennsylvania, visiting historical re-enactors to find out how people of the period dressed, and reading up on the era's politics, architecture, religion,

class structure, and the role of coffee houses and taverns.

In 1998, Anderson took a break from *Fever 1793* to work on *Speak*. The story of a high school outcast who is hiding the dark secret that she was raped at a party, *Speak* was a surprise bestseller and won a number of awards. Anderson told *School Library Journal*:

> I never thought anybody would publish *Speak*. I had published a couple of children's books before *Speak* came out, and I was still slaving away at *Fever 1793*.... I had given myself a deadline by which I needed to have some books published. If I didn't meet the deadline, I was going to go to nursing school, because I needed to make some money so I could pay for my kids to go to college.

Fever 1793 came out a year after *Speak*. After two young-adult novels, Anderson returned to books for younger readers, writing the "Wild at Heart" series for the American Girl company (subsequently renamed *Vet Volunteers* by Penguin Books, who republished them after American Girl let the series go out of print). In 2002, Anderson published *Catalyst*, which is set in the same high school as *Speak* and contains some of the same characters. The same year she also published *Thank You Sarah! The Woman Who Saved Thanksgiving*.

In 2005, *Prom*, a comedy about a high school girl and her best friend Nate who must save the prom, was published. The book was a huge best seller and spent most of 2005 on the *New York Times* best-seller list. *Twisted*, which covered much of the same territory as *Speak* but from a teenage boy's point of view, came out in 2007. *Twisted* debuted on the *New York Times* best-seller list and was an American Library Association Best Book for Young Adults. In 2008, Anderson returned to historical writing, publishing *Independent Dames: What You Never Knew about the Women and Girls of the American Revolution* and *Chains*, a historical novel that follows a teenage slave girl through the American Revolution.

Anderson currently lives in Mexico, New York, with her second husband, Scott Larrabee. Anderson and Larrabee were childhood friends— she claims he taught her to whistle and tie her shoes—who reconnected after their first marriages ended. In addition to writing full time, Anderson also spends much of each year on the road, speaking to teachers, students, and librarians.

PLOT SUMMARY

Chapter One: August 16th, 1793

At the beginning of *Fever 1793*, a mosquito awakens Matilda "Mattie" Cook as her mother shouts at her to get up and get to work. Mattie is excited to see that Philadelphia is wide awake, and commerce has begun for another exciting day.

Chapter Two: August 16th, 1793

Mattie's mother and grandfather run a coffee house with the help of Eliza, a free black woman. Mattie's mother, Mrs. Cook, came from a wealthy family who disowned her when she married Mattie's father, a carpenter and tradesman who died when Mattie was a baby. Polly the servant girl is late, and Mrs. Cook is "in a lather." Mattie is sent out to water the vegetable garden, which has suffered greatly in the drought. While Mattie is in the garden, Mrs. Cook finds her and tells her that Polly has died from a sudden illness.

Chapter Three: August 16th, 1793

Mattie is distraught that Polly, her playmate since babyhood, has died. There are rumors of sickness in the city, but no real details are available. Eliza suggests sending a ham to the family, and Mrs. Cook objects. "The girl was our servant, not a friend," she explains. Mattie begs to be allowed to go pay her respects and to attend the funeral, but her mother, afraid of the sickness, refuses her.

Chapter Four: August 16th, 1793

Mattie is helping out in the coffee house in Polly's stead. Grandfather holds court in one corner with King George, his parrot, and several prominent Philadelphia business men. A doctor at a nearby table claims the sickness in the city is yellow fever, which causes everyone to pause. As the coffee house empties out, Mattie realizes how hard Polly had worked every day. Her mother sends her upstairs to bed, offering to do the dishes herself, telling Mattie to rest up because tomorrow is going to be another long day.

Chapter Five: August 24th, 1793

Sixty-four people are dead in the city and no one knows what is killing them. Mrs. Cook wants to send Mattie to the country to stay with the Luddingtons, a family of pig farmers. Mattie is given permission to go to the market, where she discusses the fever rumors with the Eplers, who sell chickens and eggs. Mattie runs into Nathaniel Benson, a painter's apprentice upon whom she has a crush.

MEDIA ADAPTATIONS

- An unabridged audiobook version of *Fever 1793* was published by Listening Library in September 2000.
- The Gifford Family Theater in the W. Carroll Coyne Performing Arts Center at LeMoyne College in Syracuse, New York, performed a stage adaptation of *Fever 1793* in May 2004.

Chapter Six: August 30th, 1793

Grandfather warns Mattie that she was seen talking to Nathaniel Benson, behavior that could be considered unseemly for a girl her age. At lunch, her mother and grandfather are discussing what to do with the coffee house profits. Mattie is full of ideas, and not hampered by her mother's class prejudice against being in trade. Meanwhile, an invitation to tea arrives from Pernilla Ogilvie, a wealthy member of their church. Before she knows it, Mattie is tied into a set of tight stays, and sewn into a dress that is nearly too small, but will do for a fancy occasion.

Chapter Seven: August 30th, 1793

Matilda and her mother arrive at the Ogilvies' large house where they are joined by the spoiled Ogilvie daughters, Colette and Jeanette. The daughters taunt Matilda and mock Mrs. Cook's inquiries about the Ogilvie sons' marriage prospects. As tempers flare, Colette complains of the heat and faints. She is burning up with fever.

Chapter Eight: September 2nd, 1793

The city fills with the sound of church bells and gunfire as the still-mysterious fever continues to spread. The heat does not break, and the wealthy flee the city. Mattie and Grandfather head out to do errands, and as they return home, they encounter a man dressed in rags, pushing a wheelbarrow with a limp person in it. To their horror, the man dumps a woman on their doorstep. It is Mrs. Cook.

Chapter Nine: September 2nd, 1793

Mrs. Cook is barely alive and Grandfather carries her inside. Mattie is terrified by her mother's condition. Grandfather brings home a doctor whom Mattie distrusts, since his hands are dirty and he smells of rum. The doctor declares that it is not yellow fever and prescribes regular cool baths to bring down the fever. Mattie finds it very strange to bathe her mother, and as Eliza leaves her for the night, she calms herself with the Psalms. Suddenly, she is awakened by her mother vomiting blood. As Mattie realizes she is alone and tries to think what to do, her mother yells at her and orders her out of the room, fearing that she will infect the girl.

Chapter Ten: September 6th, 1793

Mrs. Cook remains very ill. Eliza and Grandfather enlist the help of Dr. Kerr, who declares Mrs. Cook very ill with yellow fever. He declares that she must be bled because "pestilence boils within her blood." Dr. Kerr and Grandfather agree that Mattie must be sent to the country. As Grandfather sets out to hire a coach, Eliza packs them a hamper of food, and a package is delivered for Mattie. It is a painting sent by Nathaniel Benson. The next morning, Mattie and Grandfather head out of town in a rickety farm wagon. Grandfather is in his full regimental uniform and bears King George, the parrot, on one shoulder.

Chapter Eleven: September 7th, 1793

When Grandfather suffers a coughing fit, the farmer, alarmed, threatens to put him off the wagon if he has the fever. Mattie snaps that Grandfather is fine. Eventually, they both fall asleep, only to be awakened when the wagon is stopped by four armed men who demand that they prove they are healthy. When Grandfather does not wake right away, and seems confused, the farmer abandons them by the side of the road. Mattie and Grandfather are denied entry to the town, and told to walk back to Philadelphia, even though Grandfather is clearly ill.

Chapter Twelve: September 8th, 1793

Mattie and Grandfather begin walking but he is overtaken with chills, and so they find a tree, underneath which he falls asleep. Mattie is very frightened but tells herself she had better find them some food and water. She locates a stream, where she fills the canteen, and some raspberries, which she takes back to Grandfather. He seems a little better, but frightens her with his confusion.

Chapter Thirteen: September 10th, 1793

In the morning, Grandfather's heartbeat is strong, and Mattie goes off again in search of food and water. The farmer ran off with the food hamper and they are very hungry. Mattie makes a fish trap out of her petticoat and nearly catches a fish, but is foiled by King George. She returns to Grandfather with just a handful of berries and a canteen of fresh water. He sends her off to a nearby farm to buy food and blankets. They refuse to help her, accusing her of having the fever. Mattie continues on in the heat until she finds a pear tree. She loads up her apron, and heads back to where Grandfather waits under the tree. Suddenly, she is overcome with chills and weakness, and she passes out in the road.

Chapter Fourteen: September 12th–20th, 1793

Mattie wakes delirious in a strange place before falling back asleep. When she awakens again, Mattie recognizes that she is in hospital, and a Mrs. Flagg exclaims that she has come through the worst of it, feeding her a bowl of beef broth. Grandfather arrives. He is fine. He carried her to Bush Hill, a notorious fever hospital, where he has been flirting with Mrs. Flagg. Mrs. Flagg explains that Bush Hill has been restored to order by Mr. Stephen Girard, a wealthy Frenchman who has brought in French doctors with experience treating yellow fever. Mattie falls asleep as she is still quite ill.

Chapter Fifteen: September 22nd, 1793

As Mattie recuperates, she listens for news of her mother, or Eliza, or Nathaniel, but hears nothing. She has been in the hospital for ten days when Dr. Deveze examines her. He does not believe in bleeding patients and is pleased to see that she is hungry, a good sign. He orders her moved to the barn, an airy space for recovering patients. Grandfather keeps busy by organizing food deliveries and the burning of contaminated bedding. Because Mattie appears nearly well, a clerk threatens to send her to the orphan home. She is saved by an indignant Grandfather who works himself into a coughing fit.

Chapter Sixteen: September 24th, 1793

Mattie and Grandfather ride back into the city with Mrs. Bowles, a Quaker woman who offers her a position in the orphan home where she could work in exchange for room and board. Mrs. Bowles warns her about the lawlessness, food shortages, and thieves in the city. They see dead bodies in the street, and they pass the Potter's Field, where bodies are being buried without coffins.

Chapter Seventeen: September 24th, 1793

When Mattie and Grandfather enter the coffee house, they find that valuables have been stolen, their furniture is broken, and the kitchen is covered in broken pottery. Grandfather begins breathing heavily and goes red in the face. He tells her when he had visited the house days before, all was locked up. Mattie remembers the strongbox and is relieved to find it safe. She orders Grandfather upstairs to rest and checks the garden. It is nearly dead from the extended heat, but she waters what is left.

Chapter Eighteen: September 25th, 1793

Mattie realizes she is filthy, and despite the heat, hauls and boils enough water for a bath. After scrubbing herself she borrows clothes from her mother's trunk. She wakes Grandfather, who is still ill. Mattie makes a pot of soup from her few vegetables and begins cleaning the kitchen floor. Though they have little food, Grandfather discourages Mattie from leaving the house, as the city is dangerous. Mattie spends the afternoon watering the nearly-dead garden and making Grandfather rest. The garden begins to revive, and Mattie finds six potatoes for dinner. They go to bed early but Mattie cannot bear to sleep upstairs. She makes a pallet on the coffee house floor, but leaves the shutters open to catch a breeze.

Chapter Nineteen: September 26th, 1793

Mattie awakens as two men enter through the window in the middle of the night. She slips out of her pallet and holds her breath as the thieves put Grandfather's chess pieces into a bag. One of the thieves, playing with Grandfather's sword, nearly hits Mattie in the neck. She shrieks, and runs for the back gate, but one of the thieves catches her and hits her in the face, demanding to know where the silver is hidden. She tells him it has already been stolen. Grandfather appears in the doorway with a rifle. Grandfather shoots and misses, and the tall thief hits him. Mattie finds the sword on the floor and cuts the thief deeply on the shoulder, forcing him to flee through the window. Mattie chases him down the street and returns to find her Grandfather, dying. He apologizes for leaving her and dies as Mattie weeps and begs him to stay. She cannot

bear to cover his face, however, and sits beside the body until morning.

Chapter Twenty: September 27th, 1793

In the morning, Mattie is forced to put Grandfather on the dead cart. At the burial ground, Grandfather is sewn into a shroud by the men working there. When they go to throw him in the open grave, Mattie shouts to stop them. She insists they treat him with respect, and when the pushcart man pulls a copy of the Psalms out of his pocket, she reads the 23rd Psalm out loud as the gravediggers join her in prayer. On the way home, she finds the market empty, and later encounters Mr. Brown who he tells her that twenty thousand people have died. Wandering the empty streets, she finds an abandoned child with a broken doll, who tells her "Mama's broken too."

Chapter Twenty-one: September 27th, 1793

The girl's name is Nell, and Mattie cannot find anyone to take her. Carrying the heavy child through the streets, Mattie thinks she sees Eliza. Shrieking and running toward the apparition, she is waylaid by a drunken man who tries to take Nell from her. The child bites the man, and they escape. She is told that two black women from the Free African Society are in the neighborhood, and when Mattie cannot find them, she shouts Eliza's name. Finally, Eliza emerges from a doorway, and Mattie throws herself into her arms.

Chapter Twenty-two: September 27th, 1793

Mattie explains to Eliza that she never got to the Luddington's, and Eliza takes the two girls home to her brother's house. Eliza tells Mattie that Mrs. Cook is alive. At Eliza's house they are greeted by a very old woman, Mother Smith, who has been tending to Eliza's widowed brother Joseph and his twin boys. They stretch the soup to feed six instead of four, put the children to bed, and while Mattie helps Eliza mend clothes, Eliza explains that the Free African Society has been helping out, under the mistaken idea that black people cannot get yellow fever.

Chapter Twenty-three: September 28th, 1793

Mattie wakes early and realizes that all the small children need their bedding washed. Mother Smith arrives to help watch the children and tells Mattie she should take Nell to the orphan house, before she gets attached. Eliza arrives home after midnight, and the following morning Mattie lets her sleep in while she watches the children. Eliza says she will go to the orphan house with Mattie. The orphan house is overwhelmed with children, and they tell Mattie to keep the child. Eliza agrees that they are "all better off together." On the walk home, they pass the Ogilvie house, and Eliza tells her that the Ogilvie girls did not die, but Colette ran off with her tutor. As they pass the Peale house, daisies fall from the window, and Eliza points out that this is where Nathaniel Benson is apprenticed. At home, Joseph is much recovered, and he volunteers to look after the children while Mattie and Eliza go into the city to help others.

Chapter Twenty-four: October 1st, 1793

Mattie accompanies Eliza on her rounds, tending to the sick. They tend to rich and poor alike, coming home exhausted each evening. One night they find Joseph in tears. The twins have the fever. Mattie begs Eliza to take them to Bush Hill, but she refuses. Finally, Mattie suggests taking them to the coffee house, which has a big room with large windows.

Chapter Twenty-five: October 14th, 1793

Mother Smith finds a mule cart that very night, and Eliza and Mattie bundle the children and leave for the coffee house. They make beds for the children atop the tables and continue washing them, and their bedding, as they become sicker and sicker. As the fever reaches a crisis, Eliza wants to send for a doctor to bleed them, and Mattie argues with her, citing her experience with the French doctors at Bush Hill. The women tend to the sick children until they each fall asleep, Eliza on the table, and Mattie in the garden after pulling one last heavy bucket of water from the well.

Chapter Twenty-six: October 23rd, 1793

Mattie wakes in a garden sparkling with frost. The air is clean and pure. The women bring the sick children out into the frosted garden, where they seem to revive. When Joseph returns to the house, he finds the three children resting on a mattress under the cherry tree and gathers them all into his arms. He has brought toys, and news that the market is open once more. When Mattie goes down to see what news there is, she runs into the Eplers, who exclaim over how thin she is and press two fat hens and some eggs on her. As she is wondering what will happen if her mother is

dead, Mattie is surprised by Nathaniel. He walks her home and assures her that all will be well.

Chapter Twenty-seven: October 30th, 1793

Nathaniel becomes a regular visitor to the coffee house as people return to the city. Eliza, Joseph, and Mattie plan a small Thanksgiving feast and invite Nathaniel and Mother Smith. Mother Smith predicts that Mattie's mother will return safe, and talk turns to what Mattie should do with the coffee house. Mattie announces she is re-opening the coffee house the next day, with Eliza as her full partner. When Eliza hesitates, Mother Smith orders her to accept.

Chapter Twenty-eight: November 10th, 1793

The coffee house is open once more when Nathaniel runs in with news that President Washington has returned to town. As the President passes by, Mattie, in a moment of impulse, throws her arms around Nathaniel and kisses him on the cheek. As they return to the coffee house, they see a frail woman stepping out of a carriage. It is Mrs. Cook. She has returned.

Chapter Twenty-nine: November 10th, 1793

As Mattie and Mrs. Luddington help Mrs. Cook through the doorway, the men stand to honor her return. Eliza bursts into tears. Mrs. Cook is very frail; she has survived, but her heart is damaged. Mattie realizes, as she tells her mother an abridged version of recent events, how compromised she is, and what the future will hold.

Epilogue: December 11th, 1793

Mattie awakes with Nell tucked in beside her. Her mother is asleep after coughing late into the night. Mattie gets up, starts the fire, and sets out the breakfast dishes. They are all safe. Mattie sits on the front step and watches Philadelphia awaken, thinking of all they have been through. Then she gets up to begin work.

CHARACTERS

Nathaniel Benson

Nathaniel Benson is a painter's apprentice and the young man for whom Mattie has romantic feelings. At the beginning of the novel, he is considered unsuitable as a potential husband for Mattie because painters do not make enough money, but by the end he has proved himself loyal and caring, and he and Mattie have an understanding that they will marry when his apprenticeship has ended.

Mrs. Bowles

Mrs. Bowles is a Quaker lady who runs the orphans' house. She offers Mattie a position as a scullery maid and children's minder, but Mattie wants better for herself and determines to run the coffee house.

Andrew Brown

Andrew Brown is a local printer and a friend of Captain Cook. Mattie turns to him for news when she returns to the city because in the eighteenth century, printers' broadsides were a primary source of news.

Lucille Cook

Lucille Cook is Mattie's mother. Raised in a wealthy family, she was disowned for marrying Mattie's father, a carpenter. After he was killed in an accident, she opened the coffee house with her father-in-law, Captain Cook. While Mattie often feels she can never live up to her mother's expectations, Mrs. Cook's efforts to save Mattie from the epidemic make it clear how very much she loves her. Although Mrs. Cook survives the epidemic, her heart has been damaged by illness, and she returns to Philadelphia an invalid.

Mathilda "Mattie" Cook

Mathilda Cook, known as "Mattie," is the fourteen-year-old protagonist of the novel. When the book opens, she is very much a child, primarily concerned with getting out of chores, avoiding her mother's scolding, and escaping to the docks where she dreams of sailing off to Paris. As the epidemic spreads, she is forced to grow up, first by taking care of her grandfather when he falls ill, and later, after surviving yellow fever herself, by navigating the terrifying experience of being left alone in a city in chaos. Mattie refuses to let circumstances defeat her, even after her beloved grandfather dies. Mattie is determined to survive, and she does so by partnering with her old friend Eliza, re-opening the coffee house, and becoming the business woman she has always wanted to be.

Captain William Farnsworth Cook

Captain William Farnsworth Cook served in the Revolutionary War under General Washington and runs the coffee house with his daughter-in-law, Lucille. He is a flamboyant character, often

seen with his parrot, King George, on his shoulder. He is Mattie's champion, and although he dies of a heart attack after thieves break into the coffee house, it is not before he heroically rallies, despite his own ill health, to find help for Mattie when she falls ill with yellow fever.

Dr. Deveze

Dr. Deveze is one of the French doctors brought in from the West Indies by Mr. Girard to treat the citizens of Philadelphia. Unlike the local doctors, who have not seen yellow fever in over thirty years, Dr. Deveze does not believe in bleeding patients or in the use of strong emetics. He advocates rest, fresh air, and lots of fluids, the treatment still used today for yellow fever.

Eliza

Eliza is a free black woman who works for the Cooks in their coffee house. She is a great cook and is like a second mother to Mattie. A widow like Mrs. Cook, Eliza lives with her brother and his family, and after her sister-in-law dies of fever, she vows to protect her twin nephews. The boys also come down with the fever, and Mattie and Eliza work tirelessly to save them. When the epidemic passes, Mattie convinces Eliza to become her full partner in the coffee house.

Mr. and Mrs. Epler

The Eplers sell chickens and eggs at the Philadelphia market.

Mrs. Flagg

Mrs. Flagg is an Irish American nurse who works in the Bush Hill Fever Hospital. She nurses Mattie back to health, while flirting with Captain Cook.

Mr. Stephen Girard

Mr. Stephen Girard is an actual historical character. He was born in France, fought with the Americans in the Revolutionary War, and made a fortune in shipping. He survived the yellow fever himself, and at his own expense, took over and reformed the notorious Bush Hill Fever Hospital.

Grandfather

See Captain William Farnsworth Cook

Joseph

Joseph is Eliza's brother. He is also a free black person and works as a cooper, making barrels.

When his wife dies of yellow fever, Joseph is devastated, and Eliza, Mattie, and Mother Smith all come to help him. He is the father of the twins, Robert and William.

King George
King George is Captain Cook's pet parrot. He accompanies Mattie and Captain Cook on their journey to the country, but disappears after Mattie becomes ill and has to go to Bush Hill.

Polly Logan
Polly Logan was Mattie's childhood playmate who becomes the servant girl in the coffee house. She is the first character in the novel to succumb to the fever, although when Polly dies no one really knows what the mysterious illness is that is killing people across the city.

Mrs. Luddington
Mrs. Luddington and her family have a farm outside of the city where they raise pigs. Mattie and her grandfather are headed to the Luddingtons' farm when they fall ill. When she has recovered enough to travel, Mrs. Cook is sent to the Luddingtons' to recover. Mrs. Luddington nurses Mrs. Cook back to health and brings her back into the city when the epidemic has passed.

Nell
Nell is a toddler whom Mattie finds in a house that has been devastated by the epidemic. Her parents are dead, and so Mattie takes her in.

Colette Ogilvie
Colette Ogilvie is the spoiled eldest daughter of Pernilla Ogilvie. She accuses Mrs. Cook of shamelessly angling to marry Mattie to one of her brothers and rudely insults the coffee house by calling it a "grog shop." She collapses with fever while Mattie and Mrs. Cook are visiting, and later it turns out that she has secretly eloped with her French tutor.

Jeanette Ogilvie
Jeanette is the youngest of the Ogilvie daughters. She is as insulting and rude as her older sister during the Cooks' visit.

Pernilla Ogilvie
Pernilla Ogilvie is a wealthy woman who goes to the same church as Mattie and Mrs. Cook. When the wealthy residents flee Philadelphia, she invites Mattie and Mrs. Cook to tea.

Robert
Robert is one of Joseph's twin sons. He becomes ill with the fever, but is saved when the summer heat finally breaks and frost comes to the city.

Dr. Benjamin Rush
Dr. Benjamin Rush is also a historical character. He was the most famous doctor of his time in Philadelphia, was a signatory to the Declaration of Independence, and a founder of Dickinson College. While he was ahead of his time on many social issues including his opposition to slavery, his belief in purgatives and bleeding as treatments for yellow fever led to high rates of mortality among his patients.

Silas
Silas is the Cooks' pet cat. He has a penchant for catching mice first thing in the morning.

Mother Smith
Mother Smith is an elderly free black woman, and a member of the Free African Society. She comes to tend to Joseph and the twins after his wife dies so that Eliza can go out into the city to tend to the sick. She is a wise elderly woman with an almost magical ability to procure supplies.

William
William is one of Joseph's twin sons. He becomes ill with the fever, but is saved when the summer heat finally breaks and frost comes to the city.

THEMES

Black History
Fever 1793 has three free African American characters. Eliza's freedom was purchased for her by her late husband, while the origin of Joseph and Mother Smith's free status is not specified. In the 1790s, Philadelphia was a beacon of hope for African Americans, and there were over two thousand free blacks living there. As Eliza herself claims, "Philadelphia was the best city for freed slaves or freeborn Africans." It was possible in Philadelphia for free blacks to find work, to buy property, and to own businesses. In *Fever 1793* Joseph works as a cooper and owns his own business, while by the book's end, Eliza and Mattie have become full partners in the coffee house. Because Philadelphia was founded by Quakers, who in 1776 ordered all members of their denomination to free their

TOPICS FOR FURTHER STUDY

- The Free African Society plays a crucial role in the story of *Fever 1793*. Research the history of this organization. Who founded it? What is the role of the Free African Society in the history of civil rights for African Americans? Explore this topic in a three- to five-page research paper.

- The mechanism by which yellow fever was transmitted remains a mystery to the characters throughout the course of *Fever 1793*, in large part because the theory of germs had not yet been discovered. Do a research project to determine when germs were discovered and by whom. Make sure to cover how yellow fever in particular is transmitted. Create a Web page that traces the history of germ theory and the history of knowledge about yellow fever in particular. Be sure to write your own content and use links to outside sources to back up your assertions.

- In *Fever 1793* the capital of the United States is Philadelphia. When did the capital move to Washington, D.C.? How? Why? Research the history of the U.S. Congress and the move from Philadelphia to Washington, D.C. Prepare a visual presentation about the history of the capital.

- Anderson wrote another young-adult historical novel, *Chains*. In an interview with the *Post-Standard* newspaper in Syracuse, New York, Anderson said: "In the course of

writing [*Fever 1793*] I discovered a lot of things about slavery in the north that I never knew. That concept of so many people being held in bondage, often by the leaders of the American Revolution, when everybody around them is talking about freedom and liberty, but no one was talking about the slaves." Read *Chains* and create a chart comparing the lives of the black characters in *Chains* to the black characters in *Fever 1793*.

- Mattie and Eliza become business partners at the end of the novel. Was this legal in 1793? Were women and free blacks allowed to own businesses? Research the laws and customs that governed women's lives in the late eighteenth century. Build a PowerPoint presentation that illustrates with words, pictures, and sound what everyday life was like for the women of Philadelphia during that time.

- Many of Mattie's entrepreneurial ideas for the coffee house include adding more food items. Dig into the text of *Fever 1793* and identify what foods they are selling at the coffee house. Research coffee houses during that time. What did they sell? How typical are Mattie's ideas? Locate recipes from early Pennsylvania. Prepare a presentation on coffee house cuisine for your class, complete with a food item prepared from a historical recipe.

---

slaves and who enacted a gradual abolition laws in the 1790s, Philadelphia was one of the safest places in the new nation for African Americans to live. Although the city remained 90 percent white, by the 1790s, a black middle class, complete with a professional class, was becoming established in the city, just as we see happening to Eliza and Joseph over the course of the novel.

One of the virtues of historical fiction is the manner in which it can bring historical episodes

to life through the introduction of characters who lived during that time period. In 1787, Absalom Jones and Richard Allen, two free black elders, had founded the Free African Society also known as the FAS. The original goal of the FAS was to provide mutual aid to widows and the poor, although eventually they also took responsibility for marriage, burial, and birth records. In *Fever 1793* Eliza, Mother Smith, and eventually Mattie, all pitch in when the FAS calls for volunteers to nurse the sick. In part, this effort was inspired by the erroneous idea that African Americans were immune to yellow fever. As the death of Joseph's wife illustrates, and as science has subsequently discovered, all human beings are equally susceptible to diseases like yellow fever. A novel like *Fever 1793* that embeds realistic characters in the historical events of a specific time and place can give readers a means to imagine the lived experience of the people who volunteered for missions like the one the FAS carried out during the yellow fever epidemic.

Mother-Child Relationships

Mother and child relationships are complicated throughout *Fever 1793*. The book opens with Mattie chafing against her mother's reprimands and dreaming of running away to Paris, where she imagines everything will be different and wonderful. Like most teenagers, she resists doing her chores, and she resents her mother's attempts to make a "proper lady" out of her. Although Eliza is a sort of substitute mother, Mattie envies Eliza because she can move freely around the city, and because as an adult, she has control over her own life. These are the qualities Mattie most longs for at the beginning of the book: a life of freedom from responsibilities to anyone other than herself. This is a normal stage of mother-child relationships, when the child begins to move toward independence and define an identity for him- or herself.

Mattie's quest for independence becomes complicated when her mother is struck down by the epidemic. Although she does her best to nurse her mother through the night, Mattie admits to being very frightened, and when the crisis comes, her mother, although racked with sickness and vomiting blood, still has the power to order her from the room. Even deathly ill, Mrs. Cook remains the parent in this situation, while Mattie reacts as would any frightened child. The following morning, it is the adults, namely Eliza and Grandfather, who decide to send Mattie to the country despite her objections. Even though she is trying to rise to the occasion, Mattie at this point in the story remains a child.

When Grandfather becomes ill, Mattie faces a turning point where she is forced to begin growing up. Although her own bout with yellow fever and her stint in the fever hospital mean that Mattie has one more episode when she is treated like a child, from the moment she and Grandfather

return to the city, it is clear that Mattie must continue to rise to the challenges presented to her, and to become an adult in a rather abrupt manner. When she and Grandfather return to the city, he is not in good health, and rather than trying to evade work and responsibility as we saw her doing when the book opened, we see Mattie find food, clean up the coffee house, and eventually do her duty by Grandfather when he dies. She is forced during this time to become a sort of mother to Grandfather, and she finds the inner strength she needs to carry out this responsibility.

It is while searching for her substitute mother Eliza that Mattie actually becomes a sort of mother when she finds Nell, an abandoned toddler. Mattie does find Eliza, who gives her shelter, but the dynamic has shifted. Mattie is no longer a child; she must earn her keep being useful, keeping the children clean and fed, and helping Eliza as she tends to Philadelphia's sick. When Eliza's nephews become ill, it is Mattie who steps in to lead, insisting they move the children to the cooler and more airy coffee house. Together they nurse the children, and together they make all the decisions. There is no longer an adult-child hierarchy between Mattie and Eliza, and this new status of equality makes their eventual partnership possible. Even though Mattie's mother survives the epidemic, she returns so debilitated that Mattie must become the adult and make the decisions from now on. In addition, she has a child of her own, Nell. By the novel's end, Mattie has done the hard work of becoming an adult.

American Identity

One of the key motivating factors behind the American Revolution was a rejection of the hierarchical ideas that had ruled European society for centuries. The new American nation was going to be a place where there was no aristocracy and which set its foundation on the idea that all men were created equal. There were caveats to this notion. "Men" was not a metaphor for "all people"; it meant not only just men, but only white men. Women did not share the same property rights as men, and they were not allowed to vote. African Americans were, for the most part, enslaved, and even those like Eliza and Joseph who were free suffered from a curtailment of rights. There were also class distinctions to consider. One of the Founding Fathers' great fears was that democracy meant

A man helping a sick person during the yellow fever epidemic of 1793 *(© Bettman / Corbis)*

rule by the mob. While equality was the goal toward which the new nation strived, Philadelphia in 1793 was not a place where all people were necessarily considered equal.

Mrs. Lucille Cook is the character in *Fever 1793* who most demonstrates the class prejudices of her day. When Polly dies, she refuses to send a ham as Eliza suggests because even though Polly and Mattie were friends from babyhood, "The girl was our servant, not a friend." Class prejudice is also evident in the episode at the Ogilvies'. Mattie, who is truly a child of the American Revolution, having been born in 1779, is not at all interested in acquiring the sort of wealth and privilege the Ogilvies embody. She prefers the excitement of life in the market and at the docks, and the company of Nathanial Benson, a lowly painter's apprentice. Mattie is more color-blind than most of her historical period, seeing Eliza as an absolute equal, and in this she represents the ideals of equality that lie at the very foundation of the American identity. Like the new nation, Mattie is not impressed with inherited status, but rather seeks out energetic people like herself who want to make their own success.

STYLE

Historical Novel

A historical novel is one that seeks to bring to life a different time or place in order to re-create the time period imaginatively. The historical nature of this novel is signified first by the title *Fever 1793*, which clearly sets this book in a specific historical moment. Anderson noted in an article she wrote for *School Library Journal*, "Authors of historical fiction have two exciting challenges: to get the history right, and to tell a great story within the confines of the historical framework." Historical novels usually include both historical and fictional characters, and thus in *Fever 1793* the fictional character Mattie Cook intersects with actual historical figures like George Washington, Benjamin Rush, and Stephen Girard, while the fictional character Eliza is a member of the historical Free African Society.

This genre requires that the writer perform extensive research in order to create *verisimilitude*, the illusion of reality that causes a reader to feel that the world he or she is immersed in is real. Anderson states that she did nearly two years of research before writing this novel, and it shows in the details of the clothing Mattie wears and in the household technologies she uses, like pulling water from a backyard well, tending the chamber pots, and cooking over a kitchen fire. In addition, historical novels tend to encompass both public and private events as we see when Mattie, who is a fictional character, must negotiate the historical cataclysm that was the yellow fever epidemic.

Setting

The title of this novel, *Fever 1793*, denotes the sort of specific historical setting that is crucial to any historical novel. The setting here is Philadelphia, Pennsylvania, in a specific year and during an actual historical event. In order for the reader to believe the story being told, a historical novelist must do extensive research to get the details of the setting right. Anderson, in an article she wrote for *School Library Journal* states that she did background research on the time period, then created her own map of the city during that era upon which she superimposed the actions of the character. She then dove into eyewitness accounts of the epidemic housed in the Historical Society of Pennsylvania. All of this research allows a writer to create the illusion that their fictional character lives in a specific historical time and place.

First-Person Narration

Fever 1793 is written as though Mattie Cook is telling the story herself. The first-person narrator is characterized by the use of the first-person pronoun "I." A writer often uses the first person in order to create an illusion of intimacy, to bring the reader closer to the experience and inner life of the protagonist, the central character of the work. In the article she wrote for *School Library Journal*, Anderson recalls:

> Early drafts of *Fever 1793* were written in the third-person point of view. I thought it would be arrogant to assume that I could speak authentically in the voice of a character two centuries removed from my perspective.

One of the characteristic difficulties of writing historical fiction is this question of whether or not the author can really know the motives and feelings of people so removed by time and culture. The historical novel purports to transport a reader to a different time and place and to give some imaginative sense of what it might have been like to live there. Use of the first-person narrative point of view is a direct method for doing this, since it forces the reader to imagine him- or herself in the shoes of the central character.

Diction

Diction is another tricky problem that confronts the novelist writing in a time and place that is distant from the reader. Language changes over time; slang terms, idioms, and even grammar that evolve across decades may very well be unrecognizable to readers separated by centuries from the time period in which the story is set. Anderson admits in the *School Library Journal* article that she wrestled with exactly this problem. She writes: "Dialogue was a mucky compromise between my readers' ability and my need for authenticity. After much anguish, I chose in favor of readability. Kids were not going to enjoy the book if they had to fight through the language." Anderson chose a hybrid approach, using phrases that might seem archaic to modern ears but embedding them in a familiar grammar. For instance, early in the novel Eliza asks Mattie to go out back and pick some "asparagus grass," while Grandfather, who as an elderly character would use outdated language, uses exclamations like "Balderdash!" Anderson's challenge was to make sure that the archaisms she uses to denote period authenticity are nonetheless readily understandable by an audience of young readers who live in a world very distant from the action of the novel.

HISTORICAL CONTEXT

Capital and Hub of the New Nation

Although *Fever 1793* was published in the year 2000, it brings to life the cosmopolitan city that was Philadelphia in the latter decades of the eighteenth century. As Anderson herself noted in an article she wrote for *School Library Journal*, "Philadelphia was the capital of the United States in 1793, the cultural and political hub of the nation." While the Residence Act of 1790 established that the permanent capitol building of the United States would be located in the newly created District of Columbia on the banks of the

COMPARE
&
CONTRAST

- **1790s:** On January 9, 1793, Jean Pierre Blanchard launches the first hot-air balloon flight in North America. General George Washington is among the dignitaries gathered at the Washington Prison Yard in Philadelphia to witness the launch. Blanchard rises 5,800 feet into the air and carries the first airmail letter fifteen miles to his landing site in Gloucester County, New Jersey.

  2000s: On July 2, 2002, after five failed attempts to circumnavigate the globe solo in a hot-air balloon, adventurer-businessman Steve Fossett succeeds in his quest when he lands his balloon, "The Spirit of Freedom," in a dry lakebed in western Australia. The journey takes thirteen and a half days in the air in an unpressurized capsule seven feet long by five feet wide and five feet tall. Fossett is forced to wear an oxygen mask for almost the entire journey. In 2005, Fossett becomes the first person to solo an airplane around the world without refueling, and in 2007 he disappears into the high Sierra wilderness in his single-engine plane. The wreckage of his plane is found in October 2008.

- **1790s:** In 1793 the Second Congress, meeting in Philadelphia, passes a Fugitive Slave Law that authorizes the arrest or seizure of fugitives, and empowers "any magistrate of a county, city or town" to make an official ruling. By 1790, Philadelphia is home to some 2,000 free blacks and has enacted the first gradual abolition law. In addition, the establishment of organizations like the Free African Society and the African Methodist Church serve as a beacon of hope to enslaved blacks in other areas of the new nation.

  2000s: On January 22, 2009, Barack Hussein Obama is sworn in as the forty-fourth president of the United States. The son of a black Kenyan and a white mother, Obama is the first person of color to achieve this office. The inauguration is a joyous occasion, and crowds estimated to number up to two million people fill the length of the Mall, standing for hours in the freezing weather to witness the historic occasion. The new president notes the historic nature of the occasion, pointing out that "a man whose father less than 60 years ago might not have been served at a local restaurant can now stand before you to take a most sacred oath."

- **1790s:** Although New York City was the first capital of the United States, the Residence Act of 1790 establishes Philadelphia as the temporary capital of the new nation for a period of ten years, during which a permanent capitol building will be constructed in the newly created District of Columbia on the banks of the Potomac. While in Philadelphia, the Congress meets in Congress Hall across the street from Independence Hall. On September 18, 1793, General Washington lays the cornerstone for the new capitol building in Washington, D.C.

  2000s: On September 11, 2001, four airplanes are hijacked by Islamist terrorists. Two are flown into the World Trade Center's Twin Towers in New York City; one flies into the Pentagon in Arlington, Virginia; and a fourth plane crashes into a field near Shanksville, Pennsylvania. Investigations discover a high probability that the Capitol is the target of the fourth plane. This is the fifth time in U.S. history that the Capitol has come under attack, following attacks during the War of 1812, the Civil War, World War I, and isolated bombing incidents in 1971 and 1983.

Potomac river, Philadelphia was designated as the official temporary capital for the ten years during which that new city would be built.

Philadelphia was the busiest port in the United States during this period: more goods were shipped from Philadelphia to other parts

Disease-carrying mosquito *(Image copyright Vinicius Tupinamba, 2010. Used under license from Shutterstock.com)*

of the new nation and overseas than from any other port. Shipbuilding was a major industry, and shipping fortunes were used to establish Philadelphia as a major banking center while also funding libraries, museums, hospitals, and colleges. The city had been founded by William Penn in 1682 as a haven for Quakers, and while by the 1790s the Quaker population had become a minority, their ideas continued to exert a strong influence on the city, and values such as equality, modesty, and religious freedom contributed to the general openness the city enjoyed.

Abolitionist Center
It was in part due to this openness that Philadelphia became a magnet for free blacks in the new nation. In 1780, the State of Pennsylvania passed the Gradual Abolition Act, and by 1790, some two thousand free blacks were living in Philadelphia. Some had bought their own freedom from their owners; others had been freed by slaveholders moved by the ideals of the American Revolution. Philadelphia's population of free blacks founded organizations like the Free African Society (FAS), a mutual-aid organization that helped

newcomers find jobs. The Free African Society was also called on to help during the Yellow Fever epidemic by Dr. Benjamin Rush, who mistakenly believed that black people could not contract the disease. Richard Allen and Absalom Jones, who founded the FAS, also founded the African Methodist Episcopal Church (AMEC), which eventually became a major force in the civil rights movement and remains a mainstay of the African American community to the present day.

Legal Status of Women
In *Fever 1793* Mattie and Eliza form a partnership by which they plan to co-own and co-run the coffee house. While it was legal for both single women and free blacks to own property and run businesses, in the eighteenth century the law of coverture declared that any married woman must have her husband's permission to work, and any money she earned legally belonged to him. This means that should Mattie and Nathaniel marry, he would become the legal proprietor of the coffee house, a prospect that Mattie has not considered by the end of the novel.

Effects of Yellow Fever Epidemic

The yellow fever epidemic of 1793 was catastrophic for the city of Philadelphia, killing over 4,000 citizens, and yet as is true in most crises, the epidemic revealed both the best and the worst traits of the population. Many people fled, surrounding towns refused to allow those who were leaving the city to enter their towns, and some merchants raised prices to astronomical levels. On the other hand, prominent citizens like Benjamin Rush and Stephen Girard remained to tend to their fellow Philadelphians, and while they might have disagreed upon how to treat the disease, they both risked their lives and, in the case of Girard, considerable funds to tend to the sick. Members of the Free African Society also proved themselves, tending to the sick even when it became clear that they were not, after all, immune from the disease. It was only after the onset of the frost that killed the mosquitoes that carried the disease that Philadelphia returned to its position as the cultural, political, and commercial center of the new United States.

CRITICAL OVERVIEW

Before publishing *Fever 1793*, Anderson had a huge success with her award-winning first novel, *Speak*. In some ways, *Fever 1793* suffered by comparison. Where the first novel was set in a contemporary high school and delved deep into the interior life of a young girl carrying a terrible secret, *Fever 1793*, with its emphasis on exterior events, seemed somehow pale in comparison. For instance, while Constance Decker Thompson of the *New York Times* calls *Fever 1793* "a gripping story about living morally under the shadow of rampant death," a *Publishers Weekly* critic was disappointed that "Mattie's character development, as well as those of her grandfather and widowed mother, takes a back seat to the historical details of Philadelphia and environs." In general, reviewers who expected Anderson to repeat her first novel, missed the entirely different creative task that she had set for herself. Where *Speak* was driven by an intimate contemporary voice, *Fever 1793* is driven by external events. Eventually, critics and teachers came to see the accomplishment that this change in time period, voice, and literary ambition represents, and the book has become both a best seller and a favorite of teachers. Anderson's true accomplishment is the way in which she brings the

Federalist period to life, a period about which little has been written for readers of this age. That Anderson's project was a success with *Fever 1793* was confirmed when she won the American Library Association Best Book for Young Readers award, as well as the Teacher's Choice award from the International Reading Association.

CRITICISM

Charlotte M. Freeman

Freeman is a freelance writer and former academic. In this essay, she explores how marriage and property laws in Federalist Philadelphia might have impacted Mattie's ambitions and dreams in Fever 1793.

In the early chapters of *Fever 1793*, before the epidemic makes itself fully known, one could be forgiven for thinking that Mattie's marriage prospects are the pivot upon which the plot will hinge. While it might seem strange to modern readers that parents would be thinking about marriage prospects for a fourteen-year-old girl, in early Philadelphia, women married young. As Mattie notes, Mrs. Cook herself "ran off to marry a carpenter, a tradesman (the horror!), when she was but seventeen." A woman's marital status largely determined her social status, and entirely determined her legal status. A good match to a wealthy man meant a life of servants and fine furniture and French fashions, as we see when Mattie and her mother go to visit the Ogilvies. A poor match, like the one Mrs. Cook's parents thought she had made with her late husband, meant a life of hard work serving food and drink to strangers. Neither good nor poor have anything to do in this case with the emotional nature of the marriage, whether the husband and wife love one another, or get on, but rather, have everything to do with the economic nature of marriage and what it means to both parties. Before women achieved equal legal rights with men, marriage was necessarily considered primarily an economic decision, and only secondarily an emotional one. For instance, Mrs. Cook describes Mattie's prospects with the youngest Ogilvie son: "Edward Ogilvie has four older brothers. A bride with an established business, like the coffeehouse, is the best he can hope for."

In the early chapters of the book, Mattie's mother and grandfather are concerned to see her

WHAT DO I READ NEXT?

- *An American Plague: The True and Terrifying Story of the Yellow Fever Epidemic of 1793* by Jim Murphy is a nonfiction account of the epidemic at the center of *Fever 1793*. Written for readers in grades six through ten, it contains numerous firsthand accounts of the epidemic, as well as details about life in eighteenth-century Philadelphia.

- *Chains* (2008) is Laurie Halse Anderson's second historical novel. Set in New York City during the Revolutionary War, it is the story of Isabel, a teenage slave sold to a cruel Loyalist family. Although she risks her life to spy for the Revolutionary forces, Isabel discovers that the ideals of freedom and equality that fuel the American Revolution do not necessarily extend to slaves.

- *Washington Burning: How a Frenchman's Vision for Our Nation's Capital Survived Congress, the Founding Fathers, and the Invading British Army* (2008) by Les Sandiford is the story of the new nation's struggle to define and build a capital city out of a swampy wilderness. Sandiford brings a novelist's talent for narrative to this story of the larger-than-life personalities who forged a nation.

- In the novel *The Last Witchfinder* (2006), James Morrow creates an epic tale in which the scientific ideas of the Enlightenment are pitted against older superstitions. Jennet Stearne is caught between both worldviews when her father, a famous witch-hunter, has her beloved Aunt Isobel, an early proponent of scientific experimentation, burned at the stake as a witch. This begins Jennet's epic, including immigration to America, captivity with the Algonquin, and a romance with the young Benjamin Franklin. The book is a fast-paced epic that incorporates Newton's *Principia Mathematica* as a character in its own right.

- Jared Diamond's *Guns, Germs, and Steel* (1997) takes on the question of what led the Europeans to set out to explore and conquer the rest of the world instead of vice versa? A biologist by training, Diamond won the Pulitzer Prize in 1998 for this examination of how technology in combination with pathology shaped the history of European colonization of other nations.

- *Johnny Tremain*, Esther Forbes's 1969 classic young-adult novel of life in Boston during the Revolutionary War, follows a character who, like Mattie of *Fever 1793*, must grow up quickly as the world throws adult situations at him. Apprenticed to a silversmith, Johnny suffers a terrible accident that fuses his hand. Johnny is nonetheless determined to do his part for the Revolutionary cause.

- *Bone Rattler* (2008) is a historical mystery novel by the prize-winning Eliot Pattison that follows Duncan McCallum, a Scottish prisoner on a convict ship bound for America. When a series of murders breaks out shipboard, McCallum must follow the clues into the dark territory that is the estate of the man to whom he is indentured, Lord Ramsey. Thrust into the French and Indian war, this historical novel wraps the struggle for justice by the disenfranchised in a thrilling mystery narrative.

- In *Rise to Rebellion: A Novel of the American Revolution* (2001), Jeff Shaara brings the same talent he showed in his Civil War series to the American Revolution. Beginning in 1770 with the Boston Massacre, he brings to life historical figures like John and Samuel Adams, Thomas Jefferson, and the young Virginia planter George Washington. The first of a projected two-part series, the book follows the revolutionaries through the First Continental Congress and the drafting of the Declaration of Independence.

> MARRIAGE DOES NOT FACTOR INTO MATTIE'S DAYDREAM, WHICH IS PROBABLY FOR THE BEST SINCE IF SHE MARRIED, HER HUSBAND WOULD OWN THE COFFEEHOUSE. SUSANNAH'S FATE IS MUCH CLOSER TO THE HISTORICAL REALITY THAN EITHER MATTIE'S DAYDREAM, OR THE EVENTUAL STRATEGY SHE DEVISES TO SAVE BOTH HERSELF AND HER BUSINESS."

make a good match. While Mattie is not thinking of marriage yet herself, it is clear that she has feelings for her childhood playmate, Nathaniel Benson, although she is also quick to point out that the very idea of a husband is alien to her. "I don't need a husband to run the coffeehouse," she says to her mother, "You don't have one." Mattie has big dreams: she wants to visit Paris, France, a place she imagines "would smell like a lemon peel, far away and wonderful." She also has dreams for the coffeehouse. Unlike her mother who bears some residual shame at being in trade, Mattie relishes it. When Grandfather brings up the topic of what to do with the windfall they are earning, Mattie is full of ideas—from those that would improve immediate profits, like buying a second coffee urn—to bigger ideas, like expanding into the lot next door and opening a fancy goods store. One of the challenges of historical fiction is negotiating between the behaviors and morals of the time period one is writing about and the behaviors and morals of the time period in which the book will be read. While Mattie's entrepreneurial spirit and independence are admirable traits to readers of the present day, these qualities are more problematic for a young girl living during a period of time when, as Karin Wulf points out in *Not All Wives, Women of Colonial Philadelphia*, "The cultural construction of gender . . . emphasized the essential dependence of women."

Women of this time period were bound by a legal constraint known as coverture. Wulf explains that this legal status "placed married women under the legal wing of their husbands. Once married, women had no right, by law or custom, to act or speak as individuals. They were

literally in law and essentially by custom *covered* by their husbands." Because Mattie's mother is a widow, she is exempt from coverture, and despite the presence of her father-in-law as the head of household, Wulf notes that a widow like Mrs. Cook "can make contracts, own and devise property, and head a household. In short, she possessed the same legal capacity as any man."

While Eliza's status as a widow would seem to indicate that she has the same legal freedoms as Mrs. Cook, her case is somewhat more complicated. Although Eliza and her husband might have had a religious wedding, and might have considered themselves as married as Mattie's parents did, it was actually illegal for slaves to marry. Since marriage was a legal contract and since it was illegal for slaves to enter into a legal contract, Eliza's marriage would not have been considered real. However, her status as a single woman, whether never-married or widowed, does free her from coverture, and since she has free status in one of the most abolitionist and liberal cities in the new nation, she enjoys the ability to own property, and, most important, live in a place where there were significant legal protections to prevent her being kidnapped back into slavery.

Mattie's household is thus not a traditional household of the time. While Grandfather is the nominal head of household, it is Mrs. Cook, his daughter-in-law, who uses her status as a free white widow to act as head of household. Mrs. Cook makes all the critical decisions in the early part of the book. While she is deferential toward her father-in-law, in a time period in which legal, religious, and social relationships were based, as Wulf outlines in her summary of colonial marriage laws, on the assumption that women occupied a subordinate place in society and within the household, Mrs. Cook's position is nontraditional at best. Thus Mattie is being raised in a patriarchal society, one that treats women as inferior to men, but in a household in which it is women who hold all the power. Mattie also benefits by not having a brother. If she did, it would be her brother who would likely inherit the coffee house and upon whom all the educational and financial ambitions of the family would be placed. Mattie's position as the only daughter in a household headed by a woman enables her to dream big, even if her mother, whose ambitions are to secure a more traditional life for Mattie, disapproves of these traits.

The epidemic that threw Mattie's world into disarray could easily have had disastrous economic consequences for her. Colonial Philadelphia had civic organizations like the Overseers of the Poor whose job it was to maintain civil order by assuring that the needs of widows, orphans, and the poor were seen to. In many cases, the children of the poor were indentured to wealthier families as servants, often for time periods as long as ten or fifteen years. Mattie first comes into contact with this system when she is about to be discharged from Bush Hill, and the clerk wants to send her to the orphan house. Despite her grandfather's protestations, the clerk assures him that "the orphan house may be the safest place for her." Again, as Mattie and her grandfather ride back into town on the wagon, Mrs. Bowles, the Quaker woman who runs the orphan house offers Mattie work, and uses the fate of Susannah, a girl about Mattie's age, to explain what happens to girls who have been orphaned by the epidemic. Susannah, Mrs. Bowles explains, is:

> too old to be treated as a child but not old enough to be released on her own. Her parents owned a small house. The trustees will sell that and use the money for her dowry. We will hire her out to work as a servant or scullery maid. She's attractive enough. I'm sure she'll find a husband.

Mattie and Susannah are girls, and hence dependent; it is assumed that the best solution is to find them husbands. Mattie is horrified by Susannah's fate, and imagines herself instead running the coffeehouse, building her fancy goods store next door, and waiting at the door in a new French dress to greet her mother when she returns. Marriage does not factor into Mattie's daydream, which is probably for the best since if she married, her husband would own the coffeehouse. Susannah's fate is much closer to the historical reality than either Mattie's daydream, or the eventual strategy she devises to save both herself and her business.

Mattie faces the most danger from the authorities during that time period after her grandfather dies and before her mother returns from the country because during this time she is essentially an orphan. As an orphan, she would be considered a ward of the state and it is only because of the chaos in the streets, in conjunction with the overflowing state of the orphan house, that she escapes notice. It is Joseph who proposes what would have been considered the normal course of action for an orphaned girl of Mattie's station: "This business needs to be sold for Mattie's dowry," he says. As with Susannah, because Mattie is a girl, the society in which she lives assumes that she must marry, and that as in the beginning of the book, the normal end to her story must be finding her a good match. It is difficult to determine whether a young girl of her actual historical time period would be as dismissive of this prospect as Mattie is, and that Mattie's ambitions all lie in the direction of running her own independent business does mark her as unusually independent for her time period.

Mattie's proposed solution, that she takes on Eliza as a full partner, might have saved her from the Overseers of the Poor, but it might also have proved problematic. While Eliza, as a free black woman can legally own property, Mattie is a minor and would not have been allowed to enter into the kind of contract that would have legalized their relationship. As a minor, and a minor girl, if Mattie's mother had not survived the epidemic, she would probably have been forced to sell the coffeehouse for her dowry. However, since Mattie's mother does survive the epidemic, it is Mrs. Cook who still legally owns the coffeehouse. Whether or not the authorities would have tried to convince the enfeebled Mrs. Cook that Mattie would be better off indentured to someone who would support her until she reached majority is difficult to say. As with the clerk who tried to convince Grandfather to put Mattie in the orphan house, girl children were often seen as a burden, and placing Mattie in servitude would probably have been viewed by all as a practical solution to the problem. On the other hand, because both Mrs. Cook and Eliza are free single women, it is entirely possible that they could have entered into a legal partnership, and Mrs. Cook could designate Mattie as her sole heir, thereby solving the problem of Mattie's minority legal status. As for marriage, while Nathaniel and Mattie seem to have an understanding at the end of the novel, Mattie seems in no hurry to rush to the altar. Mattie notes that Mr. Peale, to whom Nathaniel is apprenticed, says that in "three years, maybe four, and he would be able to support himself. That wasn't long to wait."

The pleasure of historical fiction stems largely from the opportunity it provides a reader to imagine him- or herself in a different time and place.

While Mattie is probably more independent than most girls of her time, her ambitions and longings are something that most contemporary readers can recognize, even if she does manage to escape some of the actual legal and cultural restrictions that a girl of her time would have faced.

Source: Charlotte M. Freeman, Critical Essay on *Fever 1793*, in *Novels for Students*, Gale, Cengage Learning, 2011.

Kathleen T. Horning

In the following interview, Horning discusses with Anderson why she writes about the Revolutionary War and why she thinks today's teens are interested in it.

It's hard to believe that only 10 years have passed since *Speak* (Farrar) was published. Laurie Halse Anderson's edgy first novel for teens was immediately recognized as groundbreaking, and its little-known author was praised for her ability to write artfully about tough topics such as date rape. Since then, the Printz Honor Book has become required reading in many classrooms, and Anderson has written six more works for young adults, including two historical novels, *Fever 1793* (2000) and *Chains* (2008, both S & S), a National Book Award finalist, and most recently *Wintergirls* (Viking, 2009), a tough-minded account of an 18-year-old's struggle with anorexia. There's also a new, 10th-anniversary edition of *Speak*, which includes a haunting poem that Anderson created from snippets of messages she received from sexually assaulted teens who had found the courage to speak out. Given the impact of Anderson's works on kids' lives, it's not surprising that she's already received two awards for her contributions to young people's literature: the 2008 ALAN Award from the Assembly of Literature for Adolescents (a branch of the National Council of Teachers of English) and this year's Margaret A. Edwards Award, supervised by the Young Adult Library Services Association and sponsored by School Library Journal.

These days Anderson lives in Mexico, NY, a small town minutes away from Lake Ontario, with her husband, Scot Larrabee, her stepson, Christian, and a German shepherd named Kezzie, who, the author says, "excels at barking at chipmunks and laying on my feet." I talked to the 47-year-old Anderson just before she hit the road to promote her latest best seller.

Benjamin Rush, a Philadelphia doctor who attempted to treat those suffering from yellow fever in the 1793 epidemic (Public domain)

How has Speak *changed your life?*

Wow! I think it's easier to ask what hasn't changed in the past 10 years. That list would be shorter. Particularly with the ALAN Award last year and then being graced with the Margaret A. Edwards Award in January, I'm really taking this as a sign from the universe that it's time to stop and catch my breath and reflect. None of this is what I ever thought was going to happen. I never thought anybody would publish *Speak*. I had published a couple of picture books before *Speak* came out, and I was still slaving away at *Fever 1793*. My kids were young—they were in middle and elementary school. I was just kind of blundering my way through the world of children's literature, learning as I went. I had given myself a deadline by which I needed to have some books published. If I didn't make the deadline, I was going to go to nursing school, because I needed to make some money so I could pay for my kids to go to college. So I really, really never foresaw this day. I guess what has changed the most or that feels the most significant for me is that I finally feel like this is what I'm supposed to

"

A LOT OF PEOPLE—MY FRIENDS AND MY
BELOVED HUSBAND—WILL OFTEN SAY THAT I
STOPPED DEVELOPING EMOTIONALLY AT 15, WHICH IS
A REAL PLUS IN MY BUSINESS. I THINK I WRITE THESE
BOOKS FOR MYSELF AS MUCH AS ANYONE."

be doing. I have permission to do this, and it's something I can continue to do until my dying day. That's quite a comforting feeling.

Fever 1793 and Chains *both take place around the time of the Revolutionary War. What fascinates you about that era?*

It's when our nation was born. I adore this country. I adore being an American. And the revolution—it's a Revolution with a capital R. We lose sight of how extraordinary those series of decisions were, how they totally upended the status quo. We look from our perspective today, 200 years hence, and say, "Well, the white guys were still in control." Oh, absolutely! But they weren't the white guys who were supposed to be in control. And what the generation of the Revolution started was this incredible process of gradual democratization of a culture that we are still fulfilling today. It saddens me beyond belief that it's taken us this long to get to the point where pretty much all Americans are considered equal—and we still have a ways to go. But they started it back then. We learn about the leaders Washington and Jefferson and Franklin—but it was the working men and women who really bought into the concept that people were created with inalienable rights and they are guaranteed freedoms. Those people laid their lives and properties on the line and fought for seven years. That's an amazing story.

What do 18th-century kids have in common with today's teens?

They were struggling. It was a different kind of struggle. They weren't worried about peer pressure or being bullied in the classroom. They were worried about, am I going to be hungry when I go to bed tonight? Or in the case of *Isabel in Chains*, that woman just stole

my sister. Where is my sister? I think that kids are really drawn to those very life-and-death matters, stories set in history. If you wrote about them in today's world, it might feel a little overblown. But if you set a very serious topic in a historical setting, there's something about putting it at that remove that makes it more palatable to the reader. One of my favorite letters about *Fever 1793* came from a sixth-grade girl in New Jersey, who wrote about how much she enjoyed the book and the reason why was that her father had been in the Twin Towers on 9/11. He had survived, but she identified with those feelings of panic and disaster and being out of control and the world suddenly not being safe. It was comforting to her to identify with somebody else who had had these feelings, and she found that in a work of historical fiction.

When did you start reaching out to readers online?

My Web site was first put up in the year 2000. It was a very basic one with just my books on it. I almost feel it was drawn with a pencil, looking back on it now. I didn't do much with it for a long time. I started to get very proactive about outreach to readers right around the *Prom* tour—so that would have been about 2005. That was when I started blogging. It felt like the floodgates opened. I don't know if it was just me becoming aware of the potential of this, or if I was riding a wave that everybody was riding, including my readers. Now we've got all kinds of ways to keep in touch with readers and for readers to communicate back with me, and I love it.

Why do you think kids feel so comfortable writing to you?

A word that often comes up when they write me is they feel that my books are honest. I don't sugarcoat anything. When they're reading about an emotional experience in my books, it's something they identify with. It feels real to them. It doesn't feel fake. I would say that more than anything that's what motivates them to open up and email me. The older I get and the more I do this, the more I see how closely we are all connected by our experiences and by the human condition. And story is the traditional vehicle to relate with each other. I see the Internet as having brought me so much closer to my community of readers. It's an incredible blessing.

What do you hear from them?

There are two types of communication. I consistently get lots of requests for help with homework.

There's a very cranky note posted on my Web site right now that says, "Look, I already went to high school, so do your own homework. Read the book." It's a little frustrating to get an email from an 11th-grade reader at 11 on a Sunday night requesting that I explain to this kid who's got to turn in his essay the next morning all the symbolism in whatever book—fill in the blank. That's something I didn't think was going to happen. But I guess maybe it's a backhanded compliment if readers are feeling that they're so connected to me, or that it's OK to reach out and ask the question. The worst I can do is say no.

The other kind of emails I get are usually the kind that tug your heartstrings. Last week, I came back up to my office to shut the computer down before I went to bed and a boy had written to me. He had just spent the previous four hours reading *Twisted*. He was a high school senior, and it was the first book he could remember reading from cover to cover. There were a lot of elements about the relationship of the main character and his father that reminded him about his own dad. And he was struggling with his own dad. He said, "I don't even know why I'm writing this to you except that your book helped me make sense of a couple of things. So I guess I'm writing to say thank you." That's such an incredible honor that a kid would want to let me know that. Those are the emails that keep me going, keep me inspired to continue to write for these folks.

On your Web site, you've written, "The readers of Speak *have changed our world."*

Oh, I know they've changed our world. The classroom discussions about *Speak* have changed a generation. Not the book, but the way the kids have brought the story into their hearts and allowed it to inform their experiences and hopefully help them make some better decisions. Teachers are so smart about the opportunities *Speak* presents to them as educators, and they will often bring in someone from the community—like from the sexual assault crisis center—to talk about the laws regarding sexual assault and what this means. Our kids really need to understand what the laws are and the morality about this. I often hear from girls who write to me: "Now I know why my mom doesn't like me to go to those kinds of parties." Those girls just didn't get it before. They thought their moms were just being a pain in the neck. And now they realize, Oh, there are some things I need to be aware of and careful of.

Have boys bought into the story?

I know they have. So many boys have said to me over the years, "I didn't know that that would upset a girl so much. I had no idea." We can be horrified by that, or we can try to hold our judgment at bay and understand where it's coming from. It's because boys are inundated with very explicit sexuality in the media and they don't have enough trusted, loving adults in their lives to explain the emotional side of human sexuality and the consequences of some of these actions. I just have such respect for teenagers, especially the teenagers right now. It's so much harder than when we were growing up. But what I'm seeing is kids who are coming up with more tolerance, more respect for each other. I'm so in awe of this generation of kids.

For years Speak *was one of our nation's most challenged books, but lately it hasn't come under as much attack. What do you make of that?*

When *Speak* first came out, it was considered very cutting edge and daring. But since then, there have been books that have taken on equally important and raw topics and have done so in a way that's a little more explicit than *Speak* was. So by comparison, maybe what's happening is that *Speak* is looking mild to people who are upset by these things. And that's why I'm not seeing as many challenges. Or it could just be that the book is becoming a standard in curriculums. It's funny how the things that upset one generation become the standard of the next generation without a second thought.

Your latest novel, Wintergirls, *takes on anorexia—an issue that many teens face but rarely discuss. What inspired you to write it?*

I was beginning to hear from kids who had either been in the throes of an eating disorder or who wrote to me from clinics where they were. A lot of girls—and some boys—started to talk to me about cutting. They didn't know how else to deal with the pain that was overwhelming them. So that was the first piece. The second piece is I have a dear friend who is a doctor who had been bothering me for years in a very not subtle way to write about eating disorders, because she saw so much of it in her practice. She felt that there really hadn't been a good novel written about eating disorders, and she thought that might be helpful. I was really reluctant to do this because I have struggled since about 12 with my own body-image issues.

I never could be classified as anorexic, but disordered eating is definitely something that has been a piece of my life more than I probably care to admit. I realized that all of these threads were showing me a clear path, and it was time for me to take my own challenge and dive into something that was difficult and see what I could make of it. So that's what led to the writing of the book.

Where did you begin?

Before I really started to do the writing, I did a lot of research. I talked to my friend who's a pediatrician and she referred me to some psychiatrists. I did as much reading as I could in medical journals. I went to pro-ana Web sites [which promote anorexia as a lifestyle choice] to see what these girls—mostly girls—were talking about. Even though 10 percent of people in America with eating disorders are male, the public face of eating disorders continues to be female. So it was a process of gathering crumbs of information and stowing them all away and waiting for the voice to come. And then Lia [the main character] showed up in my head and started talking. It wound up being a much darker book than I thought it would be. It was hard to write this one. It really grabbed me by the throat. I was glad when it was done.

I love how you wove classical mythology into your story.

Last year at ALA, they had a presentation by the Printz reunion class. So I was on a panel with Ellen Wittlinger, David Almond, and Walter Dean Myers. David Almond talked about the need children have for myth. He talked about how sometimes, especially with really hard life issues, kids can see something more clearly in a myth than they can in their own experiences. His words totally triggered my reaching a little bit into magical realism with *Wintergirls* and leaning heavily on the myth of Persephone to try to tell the story. I love mythology, and I was starting to wonder, what is the larger story about eating disorders? And then I realized that it was Persephone's story. Persephone goes into hell and the world turns into winter—while her mother is scouring the earth, trying to figure

out how to help her daughter. Everything just fit into place for me at that point.

Why do you think you relate so well to kids?

A lot of people—my friends and my beloved husband—will often say that I stopped developing emotionally at 15, which is a real plus in my business. I think I write these books for myself as much as anyone. It's always so startling to look at myself in the mirror: that's not who I expect to see looking back.

Source: Kathleen T. Horning, "Fearless: Date Rape. Anorexia. Slavery. Is There a Topic That Laurie Halse Anderson Won't Tackle?," in *School Library Journal*, Vol. 55, No. 6, June 2009, pp. 30–33.

Laurie Halse Anderson

In the following essay, Anderson describes the steps she took to write the novel, including research, plotting, and characters.

A HISTORICAL DETECTIVE SEARCHES FOR THE TRUTH

The fever struck me in August of 1993. We were stuck in traffic on the Schuylkill Expressway on our way into Philadelphia. My husband groused about gridlock, but I didn't notice. I was sucked into the newspaper, reading about the yellow-fever epidemic that had devastated Philly 200 years earlier.

Zap! I was infected.

The story had strong elements of conflict: fear, ignorance, and death. The background was rich. Philadelphia was the capital of the United States in 1793, the cultural and political hub of the nation. The Federalist Period is an era rarely written about. And all this took place in my backyard.

The fever spread. I had to write this book.

Authors of historical fiction have two exciting challenges: to get the history right, and to tell a great story within the confines of the historical framework. In some ways, writing historical fiction is like writing outside of one's culture. The author must be scrupulous about detail and motivation, sensitive to cultural (and time) differences, wary of interpretation, and conscious of the reader's background and ability.

Erik Larson, author of *Isaac's Storm* (Crown, 1999), calls this kind of work "historical journalism." I take that notion one step further. Writing historical fiction for kids requires that the author become a historical detective.

"ALL TOLD, THE RESEARCH TOOK NEARLY TWO YEARS. IT COULD HAVE LASTED A DECADE. I LOVED IT, REVELED IN IT—ALL THOSE FACTS AND DETAILS— YUM! BUT THE RESEARCH WAS WORTH NOTHING UNLESS A STORY CAME OUT OF IT."

DIGGING FOR BONES

Researching *Fever 1793* was like digging at an archaeological site. I had written about women in the American Revolution, and thus had some knowledge of the world just before the epidemic. While the role of women shifted slightly from the Revolution to the Federalist Period, this background showed me where I had to dig. It also helped me understand the character of Mattie's mother, for whom the Revolution was a shaping experience.

I started with background research: reading up on the politics of the era, architecture, religion, food, class structure, the social roles of taverns and coffeehouses, education levels, and gardening. I visited museums, studied paintings and furniture, and pestered historical reenactors to explain how people got dressed and what held up their socks. I sharpened a goose quill and wrote with it. (This is when my family became nervous. The word "obsessive" was bandied about.)

Once I felt comfortable with the time period, I dug deeper. I needed to understand the impact of the epidemic on life in Philadelphia in the summer and fall of 1793. Using several period maps and annual city directories, I created my own map, which I tacked over my desk. Then I created a time line of the major events. Armed with these guides to my characters' universe, I dove into the juiciest research of all: primary-source documents.

(Note to readers: you know you're a serious history wonk when the phrase "primary-source documents" makes your eyes dilate, your mouth water, and your palms itch. Wipe that drool off your chin and continue.)

I wanted eyewitness accounts of the epidemic. I found them, thanks to the Historical Society of Pennsylvania. They house a treasure trove of primary-source documents. I expected to find transcripts of government documents from 1793. Instead, I found gold—letters, diaries, and account books, all in their original state. A young man named John Welsh wrote twice a day to his employer, a merchant who fled to Delaware after the outbreak of disease. The letters relayed news of the business and rumors about the spread of the epidemic until he fell ill. He survived, I'm happy to report. His letters were invaluable in helping me portray the course and impact of the epidemic.

I worked very hard to understand the medical aspects of yellow fever and the bitter debate that raged between two camps of doctors who supported vastly different "cures." I read medical textbooks from Scotland, worked my way through treatment details, and noted home remedies that were published in the newspapers. I waded through the bureaucratic minutes of relief committee meetings, and an astounding chart of daily weather conditions, mortality rates, and locations where people had died and were buried.

These were real people. I shook with goose bumps time and time again in the Society's reading room. Real people scrawled these letters, these prayers, these remedies. I had to do my best to honor them.

All told, the research took nearly two years. It could have lasted a decade. I loved it, reveled in it—all those facts and details—yum! But the research was worth nothing unless a story came out of it. It was time to crawl out of the pit and piece together my findings.

RECONSTRUCTING THE BODIES

My original vision of Mattie Cook, the main character in *Fever 1793*, was a 10-year-old orphan. Early drafts of the book opened months before the epidemic and dragged the waif through all sorts of interesting, but unnecessary, adventures in the city. I needed to speed up the pace. Time to cut and slash.

Mattie was a Daughter of Liberty, that first generation of American women who grew up in an independent nation. As befitted a young girl of her age and class, she had some education and knew how to work very hard. She was in conflict with her mother, at odds with her own body, and wondering about her future. The concept of a "teenager" may be a 20th-century construct, but the transition between childhood and adulthood was real for girls like Mattie. Diaries from the time period prove it. When I turned MaRie into an adolescent, the pieces of her struggle fell into place.

I also experimented with Lucinda, her mother. In several drafts, she was Mattie's aunt. But again, I realized that Mattie's journey was meant to be a hard one, and the stakes had to be high. In the course of the changes I made, Mattie's mother contracted yellow fever. I felt like an executioner.

Eliza walked into the story early on. Eliza and Lucinda had a peer relationship, one that both women valued.

As I learned more about the Free African Society's heroic volunteer work during the epidemic, it became clear that a woman of Eliza's integrity would have been in the thick of the action.

There is a point in writing a novel when the act of writing fades away and the author finds herself transported to that other world. For me that happened when Mattie's grandfather died. He was a Revolutionary War veteran, the raconteur of the coffeehouse, who spent his days playing cards and swapping stories with old friends. Like Mattie, I was quite fond of the old gentleman. I cried while I typed his last scene. For the first time, I slipped into Mattie's skin, felt her heart beat. When she closed Grandfather's eyes and looked up from his body, she was a different person, and I was a different writer.

UNCOVERING THE TRUTH

By now I had the elements of a novel—my plot and my characters. I knew the setting, I had a notebook of historical facts, and thematic elements were rising to the surface. But I continued to revise, cutting out extraneous historical details in search of historical truth. The last thing I wanted to do was to insert a 21st-century character into a book about the late 18th century.

I talked to social historians and read letters of women and girls from the time period (but not during the epidemic) to understand their dreams and how far they felt they could reach. I tried to create characters that were true to their world, not time travelers.

Early drafts of *Fever 1793* were written in the third-person point of view. I thought it would be arrogant to assume that I could speak authentically in the voice of a character two

centuries removed from my perspective. As I continued to read and write, however, my opinion changed. Unless I knew my characters and their world intimately enough to write in the first person, I had no business trying to tell their story. Time for another draft.

Dialogue was a mucky compromise between my readers' ability and my need for authenticity. After much anguish, I chose in favor of readability. Kids were not going to enjoy the book if they had to fight through the language: I tried to give a sense of 1793 with speech patterns and period slang.

I also decided not to include historical figures. Before the epidemic hits, Thomas Jefferson is the subject of arguments in the coffeehouse, but he never turns up in the book. Dr. Benjamin Rush, a central figure in the epidemic (who left voluminous correspondence) is referred to, but not seen. President George Washington rides by at the end of the book, but he is silent, just as he rode back into town in real life. I did not want to confuse readers by having historical and fictional characters interact. I was overjoyed when my editor suggested I write factual back matter where I could clear up questions I knew readers would have, and treat them to a few tidbits that wouldn't fit in the story.

People often ask whether I prefer writing historicals like *Fever 1793* or contemporary novels like *Speak* (Farrar, 1999). That's like asking which one of my daughters I prefer. Both types of writing frustrate me, but for different reasons. I enjoy each for its unique challenges and rewards. I consider myself very fortunate to try my hand at both.

It takes longer to find the truth in historical fiction. It requires meticulous observation, broad knowledge, and patience. Patience with the writing. Patience with layers of interpretation. Patience to listen for the quiet beat of a character's heart under the dust of time. You dig deeper, you dig slower, and the rewards are delightful. I can't wait to do it again.

Source: Laurie Halse Anderson, "The Writing of *Fever 1793*," in *School Library Journal*, Vol. 47, No. 5, May 2001, p. 44.

Anita L. Burkham

In the following review, Burkham praises Anderson's historical research but is less engaged by the plot of Fever 1793.

For fourteen-year-old Mattie Cook, the epidemic begins with the news of the sudden and unexpected death of her childhood friend Polly [in *Fever 1793*]. It is summer 1793, and yellow fever is sweeping through Philadelphia; the death toll will reach five thousand (ten percent of the city's population) before the frost. Mattie, her mother, and grandfather run a coffeehouse on High Street, and when others flee the city, they choose to stay—until Mattie's mother is stricken. Sent away by her mother to escape contagion, Mattie tries to leave, is turned back by quarantine officers, falls ill herself, and is taken to Bush Hill, a city hospital run by the celebrated French doctor Steven Girard. Without ever being didactic, Anderson smoothly incorporates extensive research into her story, using dialogue, narration, and Mattie's own witness to depict folk remedies, debates over treatment, market shortages, the aid work done by free blacks to care for and bury the victims, the breakdown of Philadelphia society, and countless tales of sufferers and survivors. With such a wealth of historical information (nicely set forth in a highly readable appendix), it's a shame that the plot itself is less involving than the situation. While Mattie is tenacious and likable, her adventures are a series of episodes only casually related to the slender narrative arc in which she wonders if her mother has survived the fever and whether they will be reunited. Sub-plots concerning Mattie's own entrepreneurial ambitions and her budding romance with a painter apprenticed to the famous Peale family wait offstage until the end of the book. Still, Anderson has gone far to immerse her readers in the world of the 1793 epidemic; most will appreciate this book for its portrayal of a fascinating and terrifying time in American history.

Source: Anita L. Burkham, "Review of *Fever 1793*," in *Horn Book*, Vol. 76, No. 5, September 2000, p. 562.

Christine M. Hill

In the following interview, Anderson discusses both her first novel, Speak, *and* Fever 1793.

Laurie Halse Anderson exploded onto the young adult literature scene when her first YA novel, *Speak*, became one of the inaugural Printz Honor Books last January. It was also a National Book Award finalist. Her second YA novel, *Fever 1793*, is reviewed in this issue of VOYA on page 344. Anderson grew up in upstate New York and now lives near Philadelphia, Pennsylvania, with

TO ME, WRITING IS LIKE BEING IN A VIRTUAL REALITY ENVIRONMENT, LIKE I'M THERE IN THE MIDDLE OF A MOVIE. MY JOB IS TO RECORD WHAT PEOPLE ARE SEEING AND DOING AND SAYING."

her husband and two teenage daughters. This interview was conducted by telephone on May 16, 2000, with e-mail additions on June 12 and October 4.

Hill: What did you like to read as a child and teenager?

Anderson: Everything that wasn't moving. Ketchup bottles. As I got a little bit older, I turned to science fiction and fantasy: J. R. R. Tolkien and *The Hobbit*, a dreadful thing called the Gormenghast Trilogy [by Mervyn Peake, 1950] that I just loved. It scared the daylights out of me. I read *The Outsiders* by S. E. Hinton. I read that diary by Anonymous, *Go Ask Alice*. Loved that. Was horrified by that.

Hill: What was your clan in high school?

Anderson: It changed. A lot of the emotions in *Speak* are true to my life because in eighth grade I was in a private school [on scholarship], which I really did love. Then we moved and I was put into a very wealthy public school, and we weren't wealthy. I had no clan. I didn't fit in. So the feelings of isolation in *Speak* came from my ninth grade year. If I had any friends, it was the waste case kids, who are in a lot of trouble with no place else to go. They used to call us "dirtbags." By tenth grade I had my act together a little bit more. My clan was this unusual mixture of jocks (because I was on the track and swim teams) and the kids who hung out in the foreign language wing—the exchange students. I really didn't like high school, so in twelfth grade I went to Denmark as a foreign exchange student and lived on a pig farm for thirteen months. I missed my senior year and I was very happy.

Hill: How did you begin writing for young people?

Anderson: I had two young kids at home. After my second daughter was born, I was being a full-time, at-home mom. I was taking some creative writing courses just to keep my head busy. [Then] I started working on some newspapers. I was simultaneously writing adult mysteries. The newspaper was wonderful. I really liked writing for the newspaper, but it was very depressing sometimes. At the beginning it seemed that writing for kids was sort of an antidote to that. But then I would get bored because I was only doing picture books in the early days and they didn't have enough sex and death.

Hill: Would you describe your writing process?

Anderson: I start to hear voices. I sit down with a pad of paper or at my computer and wait for the scenes in my head. And they do come and I write them down. To me, writing is like being in a virtual reality environment, like I'm there in the middle of a movie. My job is to record what people are seeing and doing and saying. One of the really important things in writing that *Speak* taught me is that I would be more successful if I was less deliberate about my writing. I wrote some very bad novels early on, where I plotted everything out in excruciating detail. I was in total control of the situation and I knew what was going to happen in the next scene. The difference in *Speak* was to focus on getting to know the character and just thinking about the character.

Hill: Have you read many of your reader reviews on Amazon? How about fan mail?

Anderson: I read Amazon slavishly. Fan mail has been a pleasant surprise. The letters are a lot different, more raw. I get a lot of notes from women who have been raped. That's pretty awful. There's a lot more—particularly date rape—than anybody is aware of. It's very gratifying because they find in my book something that helps. I also get these letters from kids: "Dear Mrs. Anderson, I was never raped and I get along with my parents, but I totally identified with your character." I'm coming to the conviction that all high school students feel as if they're outsiders at one time or another, even the kids who on the surface look as if they have everything. Inside, they go through these times when they feel pretty disconnected.

Hill: Has your life changed since becoming a National Book Award finalist and winning the Printz Honor?

Anderson: Yes, in different ways. The affirmation is the most important thing. It's kind of sad that it requires something of that magnitude

to make you believe in yourself. It makes it a lot easier to sit down and chase the demons off the keyboard and tell them I've got work to do now. Obviously I've made some money from *Speak*, which is very nice. They sold foreign rights. Paperback rights went for a tidy sum. They sold a movie option. I don't have as much time, though. My kids have a little more respect for what I do now. The real clincher, especially for my younger daughter, was when they included *Speak* in the Teen People Book of the Month Club. "Oh Mom, you do have a good job."

Hill: How did you feel when you first saw Speak*'s dust jacket?*

Anderson: I loved it. I loved it.

Hill: I think it's the best YA hardcover dust jacket I've ever seen.

Anderson: Not to sound self-serving, but I agree. I think this man is such an artist. He read the book. He read the book! Not all of them read the book. It's a respectful jacket. He's not talking down to these kids.

Hill: Please tell us the story of how the idea for Speak *came to you.*

Anderson: I woke up one night and I'm hearing a girl crying. Very, very upset, like on the verge of screaming—she was that upset—and I thought it was one of my kids. Both of my girls were fine. They were sound asleep. There were no tears, no sobs, nothing. I could still hear the crying girl. So I sat down at the computer right then to write about it. She started talking to me right then and there and she made it sound as if she was tapping on a microphone. She blew into it and asked, "Is this thing on?" And then she said, "I have a story to tell you." And that was it. It was eerie.

Hill: Is Melinda an unreliable narrator?

Anderson: Yes.

Hill: How much should we not believe her?

Anderson: I personally think that all narrators are unreliable. Anything told in the first person is unreliable. And what readers have to do for themselves is—given the circumstances, how the other characters respond to the narrator—they have to make up their minds about what is perspective and what is truth.

Hill: But if Melinda is telling us about their reactions. . . .

Anderson: Then you're stuck, aren't you? This is why I love young adult fiction. I actually find it harder to write for kids than I do for young adults. With YA fiction, because your readers are more sophisticated, you can leave a little bit more up to the reader. There's this whole question about do you believe everything she sees? Are people really treating her this way or is this how it feels people are treating her? Are they treating her because she's acting this way? These are the things that make for good discussion.

Hill: How do you know so much about high school?

Anderson: I lived it.

Hill: So it was more your experiences in the past than hanging out at high school?

Anderson: I didn't hang around any high school when I was writing *Speak*. My older daughter was in sixth grade. I didn't know anybody at our high school then, so I just went to where I knew they would hang out, in the food court at the mall and at Taco Bell. I eavesdropped on them shamelessly because I needed to hear the language. I figured if they were talking that loud that I could hear them, it was fair.

Hill: I'm glad that you mentioned writing mysteries because I thought that a lot of the plotting must come from mysteries. After all, Melinda has a secret. What has happened to her? The foreshadowing and the pacing and the way the secret is revealed is absolutely brilliant.

Anderson: Thank you. That's a very interesting observation. When I started the book, I didn't know what her secret was. I didn't know why she was crying. I didn't know what thing had happened. I knew she was an outcast from the get-go. I knew something had happened.

Hill: How about the art projects? I thought those were an important part of the foreshadowing.

Anderson: Yeah, just to set up the whole thing, the fact that she had this project that she had to work on—that was there from the beginning. It became very clear that the art teacher was the one teacher who was accessible to her and who she felt safe with—that she could, in her own limited way, speak to. I have an interesting comment to make on the foreshadowing. Women and girls [who read the book], for the most part, figure out what happened to her before she tells them. Men and boys do not do it as consistently. I think that for women, the possibility of attack and rape is always in the back of their minds. And for men—decent men

and boys—it's not there. They just don't think about it. It's a telling difference.

Hill: Over and over, something would happen to Melinda and I would think, "Okay, the healing is going to start now," but no. First, the boy who is in class with her—you think she's going to have a new relationship that will help her heal. No. Then the basketball scene. I thought, "Oh, sports are going to heal her." No.

Anderson: I thought they would heal her, too. I thought for sure David Petrakis was going to save her sorry butt, but no way. She wasn't ready for it. I actually tried really hard so that sports would do it for her and she just wasn't ready. I think sports are very important for girls, obviously. It was not accidental that it's the lacrosse team that rides to the rescue there in that last scene. But both the sports thing and David Petrakis showed up and I thought, "Here we go. You can relax now." But that's not the way it turned out to be. Not at all.

Hill: Michael Cart has described Speak *as "an arresting departure in form." How did the form develop?*

Anderson: I've been interested in pushing the edges of narrative structure for a few years. One of the beauties of YA fiction is that the audience is open-minded and willing to try new things. They are, after all, teenagers. Most of the structural quirks are the way I heard the book. I added some of them, like the division into marking periods and the report cards, during revision so that I had a better sense of the action.

Hill: Does Melinda still speak to you?

Anderson: I occasionally hear little bits of opinion from her. But I am leery of sequels.

Hill: How did the writing of Fever 1793 *intertwine with the writing of* Speak?

Anderson: Research for *Fever 1793* started the summer of 1993 when I read about the epidemic in the *Philadelphia Inquirer*. The writing started a year or so later and continued on and off for six years. I worked long and hard to get a sense of what the world was like back then so I could really see my characters operating in it. *Speak* was written during one of those periods when I had put the *Fever 1793* manuscript aside.

Hill: How did you develop the voice of Matilda, Fever 1793's *narrator?*

Anderson: *Fever 1793* was driven by plot; then character developed. *Speak* was driven by character; then the plot developed. I have an unsold nonfiction manuscript about women during the Revolutionary War. While researching that and *Fever 1793*, I learned a great deal about the dreams of women of that period, and how they thought and spoke.

Hill: How did your historical research affect your writing process?

Anderson: Because I was following the course of true events, the epidemic, that limited me a bit. I could not rely on my imagination to provide the details. I visited period houses and museums to learn what the furniture and clothing looked like. I read countless letters, diaries, newspapers, and books to understand the big issues of the epidemic and small details of daily life, like the sounds of the marketplace and the smells of a sickroom. Then I sat back and let my mind create the scenes and action of the book. It was actually a lot of fun.

Hill: What will your next book be?

Anderson: I don't really like to talk about what I'm working on. It's a new YA. I think it's about a girl's relationship with her father, and a world that wants her to follow the "traditional" path to success, instead of letting her find her own way. I really don't know what my books are about until I finish writing them.

Source: Christine M. Hill, "Laurie Halse Anderson Speaks: An Interview," in *Voice of Youth Advocates*, Vol. 23, No. 5, December 2000, pp. 325–27.

SOURCES

"Africans in America, Part Two, Resource Bank: Fugitive Slave Law," in *Africans in America*, http://www.pbs.org/wgbh/aia/part2/2h62.html (accessed December 4, 2009).

"Africans in America, Part Three, Narrative: Philadelphia," in *Africans in America*, http://www.pbs.org/wgbh/aia/part3/3narr1.html (accessed December 4, 2009).

Anderson, Laurie Halse, *Fever 1793*, Simon & Schuster, 2000.

———, "The Writing of *Fever 1793*," in *School Library Journal*, May 1, 2001, http://www.schoollibraryjournal.com/article/CA90345.html?q = Fever + 1793 (accessed December 5, 2009).

Anderson, Stephanie Holcomb, "Officially Long Biography of Laurie Halse Anderson," in *Laurie Halse Anderson Home Page*, http://www.writerlady.com/ (accessed November 5, 2009).

Baker, Peter, "Obama Takes Oath, and Nation in Crisis Embraces the Moment," in *New York Times*, January 20,

2009, http://www.nytimes.com/2009/01/21/us/politics/21 inaug.html?scp = 1&sq = inauguration%20dow %20jones &st = cse (accessed December 7, 2009).

Baldrick, Chris, *The Oxford Dictionary of Literary Terms*, Oxford University Press, 2009, p. 154.

Boyer, Paul S., ed., *Oxford Companion to American History*, Oxford University Press, 2001, p. 591.

Chang, Kenneth, "Balloonist No Quitter, Circles the World Solo on His Sixth Attempt," in *New York Times*, July 3, 2002, http://www.nytimes.com/2002/07/03/world/balloonist-no-quitter-circles-the-world-solo-on = his-sixth-attempt.html (accessed December 7, 2009).

Childs, Peter, and Roger Fowler, *Routledge Dictionary of Literary Terms*, Routledge, 2006, pp. 107–108, 182.

Cuddon, J. A., *Penguin Dictionary of Literary Terms and Literary Theory*, Penguin Books, 1999, p. 383.

Dickerson, Dennis C., "African Methodist Episcopal Church: About Us—Our History," in *African Methodist Episcopal Church*, http://www.ame-church.com/about-us/history.php (accessed December 7, 2009).

"The Great Fever," in *American Experience*, http://www.pbs.org/wgbh/amex/fever/peopleevents/e_philadelphia.html (accessed December 7, 2009).

"Historical Minutes: 1787–1800: The Senate Moves to Philadelphia," in *United States Senate*, http://www.senate.gov/artandhistory/history/minute/The_Senate_Moves_To_Philidelphia.htm (accessed December 7, 2009).

"Historical Minutes: 1964–Present: The Capitol Building as a Target," in *United States Senate*, http://www.senate.gov/artandhistory/history/minute/Attack.htm (accessed December 7, 2009).

Horning, Katheleen T., "Fearless: An Interview with Laurie Halse Anderson," in *School Library Journal*, June 1, 2009, http://www.schoollibraryjournal.com/article/CA6660876.html?q = Fever + 1793 (accessed December 5, 2009).

"Jean Pierre Blanchard (1753-1809)," in *U.S. Centennial of Flight Commission*, http://www.centennialofflight.gov/essay/Dictionary/blanchard/DI10.htm (accessed December 7, 2009).

"Residence Act," in *Library of Congress: Primary Documents in American History*, http://www.loc.gov/rr/program/bib/ourdocs/Residence.html (accessed December 7, 2009).

Review of *Fever 1793*, in *Publishers Weekly*, July 31, 2000, p. 96.

Ryan, Laura T., "Teen Spoken Here; Black-and-White World Resonates with Readers," in *Post-Standard* (Syracuse, NY), November 2, 2003, p. 4.

———, "Writer Up for National Award; Laurie Halse Anderson Says Nod Was Unexpected," in *Post-Standard* (Syracuse, NY), November 19, 2008, p. D5.

"Steve Fossett," in *Hot Air Balloon News*, http://hotairballoonnews.blogspot.com/2008/02/steve-fossett.html (accessed December 7, 2009).

Thompson, Constance Decker, "Children's Books in Brief," in *New York Times*, November 19, 2000, http://www.nytimes.com/2000/11/19/books/children-s-books-books-in-brief-130940.html (accessed December 3, 2009).

Vadboncoeur, Joan E., "*Fever 1793* Catches Feel of an Era," in *Post-Standard* (Syracuse, NY), May 24, 2004, p. D3.

Wulf, Karin, *Not All Wives: Women of Colonial Philadelphia*, University of Pennsylvania Press, 2000, pp. 3, 173.

FURTHER READING

Bernstein, R. B., *The Founding Fathers Reconsidered*, Oxford University Press, 2009.

> Noted historian Bernstein reconsiders the Founding Fathers not as the heroic figures of many history books, but as a flawed, intelligent, and quarrelsome group who nonetheless invented a new form of government. He pays particular attention to the ways that political necessity impacted their ideals about what the new republic should comprise and examines the ongoing political repercussions of Constitutional interpretation.

Ellis, Joseph, *American Creation: Triumphs and Tragedies at the Founding of the Republic*, Knopf, 2007.

> Ellis traces the ideas and actions of the key founders—Washington, Adams, Madison, Jefferson, and Hamilton—from the first gunshots fired at Lexington through the Louisiana Purchase.

Rinaldi, Ann, *Taking Liberty: The Story of Oney Judge, George Washington's Runaway Slave*, Simon & Schuster, 2002.

> As told in reminiscence by Oney Judge, this is the story of her childhood and young adulthood as one of Martha Washington's favorite slaves, as well as her escape to freedom in New Hampshire once she realizes that for all her favored status, she is only property to them.

Yates, Elizabeth, *Amos Fortune, Free Man*, Dutton, 1950.

> Winner of the 1951 Newbery Medal, this biographical novel follows Amos Fortune, who as At-mun, a prince of his tribe, is stolen into slavery and brought to Colonial America. Told chronologically, it follows Fortune's quest to obtain his freedom over the eighty long years that he lived.

SUGGESTED SEARCH TERMS

Laurie Halse Anderson

Laurie Halse Anderson AND interview

Fever AND 1793

Philadelphia AND Free Blacks

Free African Society AND 1793

women's rights AND colonial America

Jean Blanchard AND Philadelphia AND 1793

historical fiction award winners

Laurie Halse Anderson biography

Laurie Halse Anderson AND Fever 1793

Free African Society AND Philadelphia

Philadelphia AND 1793

Free African Society AND yellow fever

yellow fever AND Philadelphia AND 1793

yellow fever AND orphans AND Philadelphia

GraceLand

CHRIS ABANI

2004

GraceLand is a novel by Chris Abani, a Nigerian writer who has lived in the United States since 1999. It was published in 2004 and won many awards, including the 2005 PEN Hemingway Book Prize. *GraceLand* is set in Nigeria, a nation in west Africa, at various times and locations between 1972 and 1983. Most of the novel takes place in Lagos, Nigeria's largest city, in 1983. Sixteen-year-old Elvis Oke is trying, with little success, to make a living as a dancer and Elvis Presley impersonator. Chapters of the novel set in Lagos alternate with chapters that show significant events in Elvis's childhood, beginning at the age of five, when he lived in a small town eight hundred miles from Lagos. Coming from a dysfunctional family, Elvis has to struggle to find his way in Lagos, a city where violence and poverty abound. He gets caught up in illegal activities and runs afoul of the oppressive military government. Finally, he gets the chance to make a new start by immigrating to the United States.

A vivid coming-of-age novel, *GraceLand* presents a harrowing picture of life in the slums of Lagos and one young man's efforts to overcome the difficult circumstances in which he finds himself. Readers should be warned that some scenes in the novel graphically depict violence and sexual abuse.

AUTHOR BIOGRAPHY

Novelist, poet, and playwright Abani was born in Afikpo, Nigeria, on December 27, 1966. His father, a member of the Igbo (also spelled Ibo) ethnic group, had been educated at Oxford University in England, and his mother was white. Abani knew from a young age that he wanted to become a writer. He published his first short story when he was ten, and he wrote his first novel, *Masters of the Board*, when he was sixteen. This political thriller was published in 1985, with disastrous personal results for Abani. The Nigerian government noted that the plot had slight similarities to a recent coup attempt, and Abani was imprisoned for six months as a coconspirator. After his release, he attended Imo State University and was twice imprisoned for producing plays critical of the government. In 1987, he ran a theater group and was again imprisoned, this time for a year. In 1990, he was imprisoned yet again and held in solitary confinement for eighteen months. After his release he returned to Imo State University, graduating with a B.A. in 1991.

In 1991, he fled to London, where he continued to speak out about political injustice. In 1994, he enrolled at Birkbeck College, University of London and received an M.A. in 1995. In 1999, Abani immigrated to the United States. He received an M.A. from the University of Southern California in 2002 and a Ph.D. in 2004. During this time, he began to publish the fiction for which he is best known. *GraceLand* (2004) won several awards in 2005, including the Silver Medal of the California Book Awards for Fiction and the Hemingway Prize of PEN New England. It was also a finalist for the *Los Angeles Times* Book Prize. Abani's later work includes the novellas *Becoming Abigail* (2006) and *Song for Night* (2007), and the novel *The Virgin of Flames* (2007). He is also the author of four volumes of poetry: *Kalakuta Republic* (2000), *Daphne's Lot* (2002), *Dog Woman* (2004), and *Hands Washing Water* (2006).

In 2008, Abani received the Distinguished Humanist Award from the University of California, Riverside. As of 2010, he is a professor of creative writing at the University of California, Riverside.

PLOT SUMMARY

Book I

CHAPTER 1, LAGOS, 1983

GraceLand is set mostly in the slums of Lagos, Nigeria, in 1983, and in Afikpo, Nigeria, during the 1970s. The story centers on a teenage boy called Elvis Oke, who dreams of becoming a dancer. In Chapter 1, Elvis leaves his home, where he lives with his alcoholic father, and takes the bus to Bar Beach, where he tries without success to make money from tourists by doing impersonations of Elvis Presley. He returns home later, but his stepmother, Comfort, refuses to give him anything to eat. She is angry with him because he cannot find a job.

CHAPTER 2, AFIKPO, 1972

This chapter is set eight hundred miles from Lagos, in the small town of Afikpo. Elvis is five years old. His father insists on putting him through a gruesome initiation rite to make a man of him.

CHAPTER 3, LAGOS, 1983

Elvis decides to find a steady job. After seeking the help of Benji, a friend of his father, he is hired as a laborer at a construction site. One day on his way home he shares a meal with a beggar known as the King of the Beggars. That night it rains hard and his room at home is flooded and filled with rats.

CHAPTER 4, AFIKPO, 1974

Beatrice, Elvis's mother, is dying of breast cancer. Elvis has a playmate, Efua, his older cousin. One evening Beatrice is dancing with Elvis and Efua when Sunday, Elvis's father, returns and angrily tells them to stop.

CHAPTER 5, LAGOS, 1983

On his way to work, Elvis generously buys a meal for a hungry man named Okon. At home he does not get along with Comfort, who demands that he pay rent. Elvis visits his friend Redemption, who shows him his visa to visit the United States. Redemption urges Elvis to do something more constructive with his life rather than just waste his time.

CHAPTER 6, AFIKPO, 1976

Elvis is nine. His mother has been dead for a year, and the prescribed mourning period is over. Aunt Felicia is at Elvis's home with her young daughters, and they are preparing for parties.

MEDIA ADAPTATIONS

- *GraceLand* was adapted as an audiobook and released by Recorded Books in 2004. It is narrated by Abani.

Like the girls, Elvis has his hair done in cornrows; the girls put lipstick on him, and he wears a dress. His father returns and when he sees Elvis he is furious and beats him. On another day, Elvis sees some dancers performing in the market to music by Elvis Presley. He immediately knows what he wants to do with his life.

CHAPTER 7, LAGOS, 1983

Elvis is fired from his job because the company can no longer afford to keep him. On his way home he meets Okon, who is now earning good money by donating blood. Back at home, Elvis dresses up like Elvis Presley and dances to some Elvis music he puts on the record player.

CHAPTER 8, AFIKPO, 1976

Nine-year-old Elvis reads letters to his illiterate grandmother and also attends dance classes.

CHAPTER 9, LAGOS, 1983

In a nightclub, Redemption arranges for Elvis to receive payment as an escort for rich foreign women. Elvis dances with a young Indian woman named Rohini. Redemption takes a cut of his earnings.

CHAPTER 10, AFIKPO, 1977

Ten-year-old Elvis needs more money so he can go to the cinema with Efua. He decides not to mail the letters his grandmother entrusts to him, saving the stamp money. Realizing that Oye will no longer receive letters from her many pen pals, he writes the letters himself, inventing bizarre incidents. When he reads the letters to Oye, she does not seem to suspect that it is he who has written them.

CHAPTER 11, LAGOS, 1983

Elvis is recruited by Redemption to wrap cocaine in small packages that are then smuggled into the United States. Redemption pays him well for his work, and Elvis buys new clothes at the market. He also gives some money to the King of the Beggars. The King warns him about the company he is keeping. Elvis goes again to the nightclub. While dancing, he accidentally bumps into an army officer. The Colonel reacts aggressively, and Elvis is only saved by the intervention of Redemption, who knows the officer.

CHAPTER 12, AFIKPO, 1979

Elvis is twelve. He takes a bath and his Aunt Felicia rubs oil on him.

CHAPTER 13, LAGOS, 1983

Elvis tries to make it up with his father, with whom he has never gotten along, and buys him a drink. But Sunday is hostile and after a while tells him to go away. Elvis and the King go to see a European film, and later, Redemption tells Elvis that he has moved into Elvis's neighborhood. Redemption wants Elvis's help on another job—delivering something to Togo. The job will be well paid, but Elvis does not want to take the risk. He tells Redemption that the King has warned him against getting involved in crime.

CHAPTER 14, AFIKPO, 1980

Elvis is thirteen. He tells his father that Uncle Joseph has been abusing his daughter, Efua, but his father does not believe him. He threatens to kill Elvis if he ever mentions it again. Elvis goes to watch a western movie at a makeshift cinema in a motor park.

CHAPTER 15, LAGOS, 1983

Elvis goes to Freedom Square, where he listens to a speech by the King about how the country should return to indigenous culture rather than adopting Western ways. Later, the King tells Elvis about his past. During the Nigerian civil war, which took place from 1967 to 1970, he barely escaped death in a massacre perpetrated by the Nigerian Army.

Aunt Felicia comes to Lagos. Elvis has not seen her for two years. She is about to leave for the United States to take up a job as a nurse. She has recently gotten married to a Nigerian doctor who lives in Las Vegas. She tells Elvis he should go back to school. Elvis says no; he still wants to be a dancer. She also tells Elvis that his grandmother died the previous year.

CHAPTER 16, AFIKPO, 1980

Thirteen-year-old Elvis hears that the military government is to step down. Elections will be held for a new government. His father decides to run for the House of Assembly, and Elvis observes the hustle and bustle of the various election campaigns. Many of the candidates rely on bribery to win votes.

CHAPTER 17, LAGOS, 1983

Elvis asks his father about the disappearance of Elvis's cousin, Godfrey. Elvis says that Efua heard her father, Joseph, discuss killing Godfrey with Innocent, Elvis's older cousin and Godfrey's brother. Sunday denies all knowledge of the matter, but Elvis presses him, and eventually Sunday admits that he and Joseph had Godfrey killed because he was a criminal and was damaging the family name. Elvis visits Redemption, who gives him a ride home on his motorcycle.

CHAPTER 18, AFIKPO, 1980

Elvis and his friends Obed and Titus discuss sex in an empty chapel. Elvis's uncle, Joseph, enters the chapel and sexually assaults Elvis.

CHAPTER 19, LAGOS, 1983

Elvis returns home at three o'clock in the morning. His father warns him about hanging around with the King, whom he regards as dangerous. It also transpires that Sunday lost the election, and the military removed the new civilian government after only two months.

CHAPTER 20, AFIKPO, 1980

Innocent comes to Elvis's home in the middle of the night. He is hungry, and Elvis feeds him. Innocent tells him about his time as a soldier in the Biafran War in 1969. He witnessed a massacre of civilians by soldiers on his own side. They set fire to a church with many people inside. A year later, it becomes apparent that Sunday has lost his bid to win election. The winner is Chief Okonwo. Sunday has debts and must sell his home and move to Lagos to find a job.

Book II

CHAPTER 21, LAGOS, 1983

Redemption tells Elvis that they are working for the Colonel, the same soldier who confronted Elvis in the nightclub. Elvis is unhappy with this and believes they are involved in something illegal. He and Redemption watch a crowd kill a man accused of being a thief. Then a truck arrives to take them on the mission for the Colonel.

CHAPTER 22, LAGOS, 1983

With Anthony and Conrad, two of the Colonel's men, Elvis and Redemption set off on their trip. After a four-hour drive, they reach a hut, where the men load some coolers into the car. They also put six children with their hands tied in the back of the truck. It transpires that the coolers contain human body parts, and the children will be sold into slavery. Elvis is horrified. There is a commotion in the small town where they have stopped, and Anthony and Conrad are killed by angry villagers. Elvis and Redemption escape in a stolen car.

CHAPTER 23, ABEOKUTA, 1983

As they return to Lagos, Redemption explains that the body parts are to be sold to rich Westerners for organ transplants. Elvis thinks he sees his cousin Efua in the street as they pass by, but Redemption refuses to stop. They arrive home in Lagos.

CHAPTER 24, LAGOS, 1983

The government wants to bulldoze the slum where Elvis lives. People have gathered in Sunday's house to discuss what they can do to stop the demolition. Prompted by the King, they decide to barricade the main streets so the bulldozers cannot pass. Elvis learns from Redemption that the Colonel has ordered that both of them be killed.

CHAPTER 25, LAGOS, 1983

The barricades have gone up. The police arrive with a bulldozer. The protesters set light to some tires, and a fire truck douses the flames. Elvis's neighbor Jagua is injured by a jet of water. The bulldozer advances, but Freedom, a leader of the protest, has sabotaged it, and it breaks down. Frustrated, the police open fire and one man is injured. Two are arrested. Sunday offers to allow the demolition in a few days' time, if the police pull out, and so further trouble is averted.

CHAPTER 26, IJEBU, 1983

Needing to escape from the Colonel, Elvis joins the King and his performing troupe as they go on tour. They perform music, dancing, and a play. The King tells Elvis that the country is at the mercy of the army, the World Bank, and the United States.

CHAPTER 27, LAGOS, 1983

The police return and bulldoze Maroko as people run for their lives. Sunday runs at a bulldozer and is shot dead by a policeman. The army breaks up a performance of the King's troupe in Freedom Square. Elvis is arrested, taken to a police station, and tortured.

CHAPTER 28, LAGOS, 1983

Elvis has been missing for four days. The King enters the police station trying to find out where he is. He is told that Elvis has been taken to a military interrogation unit. At that unit, Elvis is tortured again. The Colonel wants Elvis to tell him where the King is. Elvis is finally released after he says the King lives under a bridge.

CHAPTER 29, LAGOS, 1983

The King leads a mob down Ribadu Road, where government headquarters are located. The army confronts them. The Colonel wants to kill the King but is told by his superiors to talk to him and end the demonstration with minimum violence. As the Colonel steps forward, the King recognizes him as the man who killed his family during the civil war. He draws a knife and kills the Colonel, and is then killed by army gunfire. In the riot that follows, about two hundred people are killed. In Maroko, Elvis finds his father's body, but a soldier will not allow him to take it for burial. Elvis wanders around and ends up in Bridge City. For a while he lives on the streets, sleeping for days at a time to recover from his injuries. He befriends a young girl called Blessed, then falls ill with a fever. Finally, he meets up again with Redemption, who gives him his passport, telling him to go to America to join Aunt Felicia. In the final scene, Elvis waits at the airport for his flight.

CHARACTERS

Mr. Aggrey

Mr. Aggrey is the dance instructor in Afikpo when Elvis is a child.

Caesar Augustus Anyanwu

See King of the Beggars

Joshua Bandele-Thomas

Joshua Bandele-Thomas is the Okes' next-door neighbor in Lagos. He is an eccentric man who wants people to think he is a surveyor.

Blessing

Blessing is a young street girl who is befriended by Elvis while he lives on the streets in Bridge City. Elvis promises never to leave her, but he soon does.

Madam Caro

Madam Caro owns a bar and restaurant down the street from where Elvis lives in Lagos. She survives the razing of the slum Maroko and opens a bar in Bridge City.

The Colonel

The Colonel is an army officer who is the chief of security to the head of state. He is a corrupt, arrogant man and is responsible for the deaths and disappearances of countless dissident Nigerians. He is also a sadistic crook. He traffics in cocaine and in human body parts, which are sold and used for organ transplants. He supervises and enjoys torture. After Elvis and Redemption escape from his organ-trafficking operation, he orders them to be killed. He is responsible for the torture of Elvis. The Colonel dies when he is stabbed by the King of the Beggars at a street demonstration.

Comfort

Comfort is Elvis's stepmother. She is divorced, with three children, and lives with Sunday Oke, although they are not married. Elvis does not get along well with Comfort. He thinks she only thinks of herself. Comfort survives the chaos around her by operating a small business.

Confusion

Confusion is three years older than Elvis. He is a sprinter who plays football for the local team. Elvis admires him.

Aunt Felicia

Elvis's Aunt Felicia is Beatrice's younger sister. She is only six years older than Elvis. When Elvis meets her again in Lagos, she tells him that she has trained as a nurse. She has also married a Nigerian doctor who lives in Las Vegas, and she is soon to join him in the United States.

Freedom

Freedom is a teacher who lives in the Maroko slum in Lagos. He is one of the leaders in the protest against the government's plan to demolish the slum. He sabotages the bulldozer and renders it useless.

George

George is a member of the King's performance troupe who befriends Elvis. He plays saxophone and clarinet.

Hezekiah

Hezekiah is an acquaintance of Elvis. Sometimes they chat together after watching a movie.

The King of the Beggars

The King of the Beggars, whose given name is Caesar Augustus Anyanwu, is in his late forties or early fifties. He chooses to be a beggar on the streets of Lagos, which is where Elvis first meets him. They become friends, and the King becomes a kind of mentor to Elvis. It turns out that the King is also a musician, a playwright, and a poet who can command attention for his performances in Freedom Square. He is also politically committed. He hates the army and wants a restoration of democracy in Nigeria. He tells Elvis that during the Biafran War, he witnessed his wife and children being killed by the Nigerian Army. He managed to escape and he has vowed to kill the man responsible for the deaths, the man who later turns out to be the Colonel. The King gets his chance when he leads a demonstration against the government. He comes face-to-face with the Colonel and stabs him to death before being cut down by army gunfire.

Beatrice Oke

Beatrice is Elvis's mother. She dies of cancer when he is a young boy. Before she became ill, she was a teacher in a primary school. She likes to sing and dance, and she is also a religious woman. She keeps a journal full of recipes for cooking and healing, and other jottings. Her husband, Sunday, is deeply attached to her and still thinks he can communicate with her after her death.

Efua Oke

Efua is Elvis's cousin. She is three years older than he, and they are playmates when Elvis is a young boy. Efua is repeatedly abused by her father, Joseph. After Elvis moves to Lagos, she leaves home, and no one knows where she went.

Elvis Oke

Elvis Oke is the main character in the novel. The story covers eleven years in his life, from the age of five to sixteen. He is the son of Sunday and Beatrice Oke and is named after Elvis Presley. His mother dies when he is young, and his brutal alcoholic father gives him little guidance in life. Elvis hates him. When Elvis is nine years, old he decides he wants to become a dancer, and this desire never leaves him. When he is fourteen, he and his father move from their village to Lagos.

Elvis is an intelligent, sensitive young man who likes to read and always carries a book in his backpack. He reads the German poet Rainer Maria Rilke, for example, as well as the British novelist Charles Dickens, and the African American authors Ralph Ellison and James Baldwin. However, he drops out of school and has few job prospects in Lagos. He gets work as a laborer for a while but is soon laid off. He develops an act as an Elvis impersonator but fails to make any money doing it. An older beggar named the King befriends him, and Elvis also makes friends with Redemption. Redemption leads him to become involved with illegal activities sponsored by the Colonel. Elvis makes some money from helping in a cocaine smuggling operation but rebels when he finds himself involved in trafficking in human body parts that are used for transplants. Despite the company he keeps, Elvis has a good sense of right and wrong. He only gets involved in bad things because he needs money and does not ask enough questions beforehand.

Elvis endures many painful ordeals. He is sexually abused, and he is imprisoned and tortured by the military government. But he comes through all these trials without feeling embittered. He eventually gets the chance to travel to the United States where a new phase of his life awaits him.

Godfrey Oke

Godfrey is Elvis's cousin, the son of Joseph. He is eight years older than Elvis. He is always getting into trouble, fighting and stealing and giving the family a bad name. Sunday and Joseph pay Innocent to murder him.

Innocent Oke

Innocent is Elvis's oldest cousin. The son of Joseph, he is ten years older than Elvis. He is paid by Joseph and Sunday to kill Godfrey, his brother. Innocent was a soldier on the Biafran side in the Nigerian civil war. He witnessed atrocities committed by both sides in the conflict and tells Elvis his story.

Joseph Oke

Joseph is Sunday's younger brother, Elvis's uncle. He is a violent man who beats his sons. He also sexually abuses his daughter, Efua. Joseph conspires with Sunday to pay his teenage son Innocent to kill his other son, Godfrey, whom he believes is tarnishing the family's good name.

Sunday Oke

Sunday Oke is Elvis's father. He is a roughly spoken man who shows little affection for Elvis and sometimes beats him. As a child Elvis is afraid of his father and also contemptuous of him. Sunday had a well-paid job in Afikpo in the 1970s as a district education inspector, and he supplemented his income by taking bribes. He took early retirement from that position and became a member of parliament before the military took over in a coup. In 1980, when a new civilian government is elected, Sunday runs again for office, but he does not have sufficient funds to succeed. He is left with heavy debts and has to sell his house and move to Lagos, where he is unable to find a job. He does, however, find a woman, Comfort, with whom he lives. But his life goes downhill nonetheless. He takes to drink and sits around the house aimlessly. He also develops a habit of talking with what he thinks is the ghost of his dead wife, Beatrice. He dies when in a fit of bravery, probably fueled by drink, he runs at the bulldozer that is about to raze his home and is shot dead by a policeman.

Okon

Okon is a beggar in Lagos whom Elvis feeds one day. Later, when Okon has started to make money as a blood donor, he repays the favor, giving Elvis food.

Chief Okonwo

Chief Okonwo is Sunday's rival in the elections. Okonwo wins because he has more money to bribe people.

Oye

Oye is Elvis's grandmother on his mother's side. She was married when she was eleven. After Elvis's mother dies, Oye gives him his mother's journal and does her best to look after him.

Redemption

Redemption is a friend of Elvis, whom Elvis meets in Lagos. Redemption is a few years older than Elvis. Elvis admires him and defers to him as he would an elder brother. Redemption is the kind of man who seems to know everyone and is always involved in some dubious enterprise. He is not held back by any ethical scruples about how he acquires his money. He says he wants to be a millionaire before he is thirty. Redemption finds work with the Colonel, first wrapping cocaine and then transporting human body parts that will be sold for organ transplants. He gets Elvis to help him. Redemption seems to live a charmed life. Even when he falls out with the Colonel, who sends someone to kill him, he manages to survive. Eventually he gives his passport to Elvis so Elvis can make the journey to the United States.

Jagua Rigogo

Jagua Rigogo is one of Elvis's neighbors in Lagos. He keeps a pet python and has strange spiritual beliefs. He is shot and killed by the army when the demonstration at government headquarters becomes violent.

Rohini

Rohini is a beautiful, wealthy, educated young Indian woman. When she goes to a nightclub, Elvis acts as her escort.

THEMES

Right and Wrong

As the young Elvis sets out to make his mark in the world he is somewhat confused and also rather innocent. He does not have a clear idea of how to make his living, since his desire to be a dancer and an Elvis impersonator is rather impractical. Lacking guidance at home, he must somehow survive and develop his own sense of values. He is easily influenced by the people around him, and he must make choices about how he is to live. The two main characters in his life, other than his family, are Redemption and the King of the Beggars. They represent two different moral choices. Redemption tempts Elvis into a life of crime, although Elvis is never comfortable with it. He seems to have an innate moral conscience that questions whether what he is doing is right. But lacking any other means of supporting himself, for a while he becomes a small cog in the Lagos underworld. The King, on the other hand, offers Elvis some cryptic warnings about the danger of associating with someone like Redemption: "Be careful. When a

TOPICS FOR FURTHER STUDY

- In *GraceLand*, Elvis's cousin Innocent was a boy soldier in the Biafran War. Research recent wars in Africa or elsewhere in which children have been forced to become soldiers. Give a class presentation in which you describe your findings. What can be done to stop children being used as combatants in wars? Use PowerPoint or a similar program to illustrate your talk and show its main points.

- With a small group of students, discuss the character Redemption. What sort of a man is he? Why does Elvis accept his friendship? How do he and Elvis differ in their attitudes to life? Is Redemption a likable character, or is he just a bad influence on Elvis? Use quotations from the novel to illustrate your points. Create a poster collage using Glogster or a similar program that illustrates the character traits of Redemption.

- Helon Habila is a Nigerian writer about Abani's age who also lived in Lagos. Read Habila's 2004 novel *Waiting for an Angel* and write an essay in which you compare his picture of Lagos in the 1990s with the picture presented in *GraceLand*.

- Read *Nigeria: 1880 to the Present: The Struggle, the Tragedy, the Promise* (2000) by Daniel E. Harmon, an historical account suitable for young-adult readers. Use information from this book to illuminate the setting of *GraceLand*, particularly the urban poverty and the corrupt military government. Is colonialism to blame for Nigeria's plight? Set up a Web-based tele-conference with a school in Nigeria and share information about the two cultures.

---

car hits a dog, its puppy is never far behind." His lowly status notwithstanding, the King represents integrity and moral strength. He has the courage, for example, to protest against the military government. Eventually, after Elvis has found out the hard way the consequences of his friendship with Redemption, the King rescues Elvis. He takes him on tour with his performing troupe and so allows Elvis to do what he loves most, which is dancing.

There are some ironies embedded in this theme. Elvis's father warns him against keeping company with the King, whom he regards as a bad influence, but says nothing about Redemption, who is the real problem. Another irony is that Sunday is in no position to lecture his son about good and bad influences, since he is himself a less than admirable role model for Elvis. Yet another irony occurs when Elvis throws in his lot with the King, joining his performance troupe. It is this decision that lands him in Freedom Square when the soldiers seize, imprison, and later torture him. Elvis made a good choice in going with the King, but it was also a dangerous one because it got him caught up in political protests, which is not his main interest or purpose in life.

Brutality

Elvis must find his way in a very brutal environment that adversely affects him at every level. His family is little help to him. His father is violent and abusive. Elvis makes friends with his cousin Efua, but she is forced to leave home because she is abused by her father. The conspiracy by Sunday and his brother to kill Elvis's cousin Godfrey is another example of the violence that surrounds Elvis from an early age.

At the societal level, there is also brutality and violence. The military government has no respect for people's rights. It is repressive and arrests and tortures those who oppose it. Soldiers strut around the streets and are a law unto themselves. They intimidate and shoot people without consequences. When in 1980, the military government steps down, the political process by which a civilian government is elected is hopelessly corrupt. The candidates who have the most money to bribe the voters win. But the civilian government lasts only a few months before the military takes over again, and the cycle of brutality returns.

Father-Child Relationship

Elvis's troubled relationship with his father is set at an early age. When Elvis is only five, his father insists that he participate in a cruel initiation rite. "Dis is about being a man," he says. Sunday may be well intentioned in his own way, but his tough

A Nigerian boy like the story's protagonist (*Joern Pollex - FIFA | FIFA via Getty Images*)

approach to parenting is not what a sensitive, artistic boy like Elvis needs. Elvis's relationship with his father is thus a broken one. Elvis despises his father, although there are times when he tries to reach out to him. Sunday also at times tries to repair the relationship, but the attempts on both sides always fail. Father and son do not know how to talk to each other in a way that conveys mutual respect. It is thus tragically appropriate, given the way the relationship has been, that when Elvis discovers his father's dead body, he is prevented by a soldier from giving it a proper burial. Even in death, the relationship between father and son cannot be healed.

STYLE

Postcolonialism

Postcolonial is the name given to literature by authors from nations that were formerly Western colonies. This type of literature is written from the perspective of the newly independent nation. It may assess the effects of colonization in terms of what kind of cultural identity the new nation should develop. Often there is a perceived need to develop indigenous cultural forms and to reject the legacy of colonialism. In *GraceLand*, the Nigerian boy Elvis grows up saturated in Western influences, primarily the popular culture of the United States. The influence of the colonizing power, Great Britain, is not so readily apparent, although Elvis Presley was as big a star in England in the 1950s and 1960s as he was in the United States. The novel presents several different views about the direction Nigeria, which became independent in 1960, should take. The King gives a speech in which he says Nigeria should return to indigenous ways rather than be corrupted by the West. However, Elvis thinks the matter is more complex than that. He knows that the country cannot go back to the way things were, because these were "new and confusing times." He seems

COMPARE
&
CONTRAST

- **1980s:** Although Lagos is the largest city in Nigeria and still the nation's capital, it is about to lose that status to Abuja, a city specially constructed to become the capital. Abuja will become the capital in 1991.

  Today: Lagos is the most populous city in Nigeria. It is Nigeria's chief port and a center of business and industry.

- **1980s:** Nigeria is ruled by a civilian government up to 1984, but after a military coup the country spends the remainder of the decade under military rule.

Today: Nigeria has a civilian government. The election in 2007 marks the first time in the country's history that one civilian government peacefully hands over power to another civilian government.

- **1980s:** During the period of military rule, the government relies heavily on the nation's oil industry, which supplies 80 percent of government revenues.

Today: In the first decade of the twenty-first century, the Nigerian government implements economic reforms at the request of the International Monetary Fund in order to qualify for debt relief.

---

to be thinking that Western influences must be accepted as a fact of life, but he also is aware of the indigenous culture. That culture has been overwhelmed in the swelling urban population of Lagos, many of whom live in slums. The old ways of Igbo culture are represented by his mother, Beatrice, who died in 1975. She kept a journal full of traditional recipes and Igbo tribal lore that is the link to the old indigenous culture. Elvis receives Beatrice's journal after she dies and carries it around with him everywhere he goes. It is the link that this Elvis impersonator maintains to his ancestral culture.

Symbolism

One of the themes of the novel is the choice the sixteen-year-old Elvis must make between right and wrong. This is symbolically foreshadowed in the scene in which the thirteen-year-old Elvis goes to the movies. Elvis is aware that the plots of the American movies he sees are "about the eternal struggle between the good of John Wayne and the evil of the villain." He is also reminded of what he learned from a Catholic priest about how evil and good, in the form of Lucifer and Christ, respectively, battle daily in an "eternal war." Shortly, that war is about to

break out within Elvis, as he is subject to the pull of good and evil and must decide on which side he stands.

HISTORICAL CONTEXT

The Biafran War

Nigeria became independent from Great Britain in 1960. For the next six years, the country had a democratic civilian government. This was the period in which, in the novel, Elvis's father, Sunday Oke, was a member of parliament. But in the mid-1960s tensions between the different ethnic groups in Nigeria increased. The civilian government was overthrown by a military coup in 1966. In 1967, Biafra, an eastern region of Nigeria, announced its intention to secede from Nigeria and become an independent nation. The war that followed lasted until 1970, when Biafra was defeated. The war resulted in approximately a million deaths. In *GraceLand*, Elvis and his family are originally from an area in the country that was part of Biafra. Innocent, Elvis's cousin, was a soldier in the Biafran Army; the King joined the Biafran Army after Nigerian forces led by the Colonel killed his family.

Nigeria (*Image copyright Olinchuk, 2010. Used under license from Shutterstock.com*)

Nigeria in the 1970s and 1980s

After the end of the Biafran War, national reconciliation in Nigeria was swift. However, military rule continued, in spite of the promises of the president, Major General Yakubu Gowon, of a return to civilian rule. In the mid-1970s, Nigeria prospered because of an increase in oil revenues, but Gowon was overthrown in a bloodless coup led by several army officers in 1975. The new military government accused Gowon of corruption and incompetence. Under the new president, General Murtala Mohammed, a timetable was set for the return of civilian rule. Mohammed's assassination in

1976 did not derail the process. In 1978, a new constitution for the country was written, and in 1979, the military government stepped down and a civilian election took place. Five political parties contested the election, which was won by Shehu Shagari of the National Party of Nigeria. Shagari's government won reelection in August 1983, but there were allegations of fraud in the election process. Just four months later, the military intervened, toppling the Shagari government and initiating a period of military rule that would last until 1999.

In the novel, Abani captures the flavor of the times without sticking to the actual facts. He has the military government step down in 1980 (rather than in 1979) and allow the election of a civilian government. That government is deposed after only two months (rather than the four months that the civilian government lasted in reality, in 1983). Abani's picture of human rights' abuses, including the detention and torture of political opponents, is an accurate representation of what happened in Nigeria under military rule, particularly in the 1980s and beyond. Journalists, political dissidents, and rival politicians were arrested and detained without trial. The repression during this period paved the way for the emergence of the human rights movement in Nigeria. Abani himself became part of this movement in the mid-1980s and was imprisoned without trial because of it.

CRITICAL OVERVIEW

GraceLand received generally positive reviews, although some reviewers had reservations about the quality of the novel as a whole. For example, in the *New York Times*, Sophie Harrison declares, "As a convincing and unpatronizing record of life in a poor Nigerian slum, and as a frighteningly honest insight into a world skewed by casual violence, it's wonderful." But Harrison adds that these elements are not integrated into the novel's "imaginative structure," and Abani's concern with explaining the exotic world of Nigeria to his Western readers leads the book "persistently in the direction of nonfiction." Dinaw Mengestu in the *New Leader* praises Abani's skill as a writer, commenting that the book, "often succeeds in its recording of violence. He [Abani] gathers together the details of a scene with a keen visual clarity and distills them into a haunting image." Mengestu faults the novel, however, for a lack of depth in its portrayal of the characters. But the reviewer concludes on a positive note: "Despite its serious flaws, *GraceLand* draws a searing picture of a country devouring its own children. What you learn about Nigeria will make you want to weep." A reviewer for *Publishers Weekly*, like a number of other reviewers, has doubts about the wisdom of including Nigerian recipes and other nonfiction material at the beginning of each chapter. The reviewer argues that the novel "is most powerful when it refrains from polemic and didacticism and simply follows its protagonist

on his daily journey through the violent, harsh Nigerian landscape."

CRITICISM

Bryan Aubrey

Aubrey holds a Ph.D. in English. In this essay, he analyzes the significance of the indigenous Igbo culture in GraceLand.

In *GraceLand*, Abani presents a desolate picture of Lagos in the early 1980s. This is Nigeria's biggest city twenty-three years after the nation won its independence from Great Britain. If Nigeria once had a strong indigenous culture, it is hard to see it in this Lagos. There is poverty, lawlessness, and violence everywhere. Homeless beggars wander the beaches, and people survive as best they can. Elvis Oke lives in a slum built on stilts over mud, where many people live in makeshift *bukas*, lean-tos made of corrugated iron and plastic. The place stinks from garbage and human excrement. In this city, vigilante justice takes care of thieves by means of a deadly burning tire around the neck. The bodies of pedestrians killed crossing the highway lie where they fall because their families cannot afford the fine levied by the government on those who cross the road illegally. Soldiers strut around the city like lords who can do whatever they please; the corrupt military government has no regard for human rights. It is clear that in the nation's rush to industrialize and modernize, Lagos has absorbed millions of people from small towns all over Nigeria—like Sunday Oke and Elvis—but it cannot cope with this vast influx of humanity. Like many Third World cities, it has huge gaps between rich and poor. There are wealthy neighborhoods, and Elvis estimates that they cover one-third of the city. However, Elvis thinks that the people who live there have made their money "with the help of crooked politicians, criminal soldiers, bent contractors, and greedy oil-company executives."

In presenting this panoramic vision of a restless city in which human happiness and dignity are rare qualities, Abani forces his point home with the ironic naming of his characters. In this culture, according to Elvis, names are "selected with care by your family and given to you as a talisman." But Elvis's cousin Innocent is anything but innocent. He was a boy soldier in the civil war and his nightmares still cause him to wake up

WHAT DO I READ NEXT?

- Abani is a poet as well as a novelist, and his fourth collection of poems, *Hands Washing Water* (2006), has been praised by critics. One section of poems is about two lovers who exchange letters with each other during the American Civil War. Other poems deal with topics such as exile, and Abani often brings a surprising humor to his serious work.

- *Things Fall Apart* (1958) is a novel by Africa's senior literary figure, Chinua Achebe, who, like Abani, is Nigerian. It was Achebe's first novel and has become a classic of African literature in English. It begins in the nineteenth century in an Igbo village before the British colonizers arrive. Then it shows how colonial rule and the Christianity brought by the colonizers undermines the traditional Igbo way of life. Finally, the protagonist, Okonkwo, tries to resist the destruction of his native culture.

- *A Long Way Gone: Memoirs of a Boy Soldier* (2007), by Ishmael Beah, is an account of how Beah became a child soldier during a civil war in the 1990s in the west African nation Sierra Leone. Beah was twelve years old at the time. Like Elvis in *GraceLand*, he loves American music and dance, but he is plunged into the horrors of war. He also resembles Innocent in *GraceLand*, who was only a boy when he fought in the Biafran War. Beah was a soldier until he was fifteen,

when he was rescued by a United Nations' organization. At seventeen, he fled to the United States, where he now lives.

- *Nervous Conditions* (1988) is a novel by Zimbabwean author Tsitsi Dangarembga. Set in the 1960s and 1970s, it shows how several young female characters deal in their different ways with the patriarchal structure of their society. In this coming-of-age story, the young narrator, Tambu, must show great determination if she is to realize her dreams in life. The novel gives much insight into the traditional life of the country's native Shona-speaking people and is an important contribution to postcolonial literature.

- *Nigeria in Pictures* (2003), by Janice Hamilton, is a book for young adults in the Visual Geography Series. The book contains information about the history, government, economy, people, and geography of Nigeria. It includes text, sidebars, statistics, an annotated bibliography, a glossary, and many color photographs.

- Like Achebe, the playwright Wole Soyinka is one of the most revered figures in Nigerian literature. His *Aké: The Years of Childhood* (1981) is a memoir of his childhood in the village of Aké up to the age of eleven. It gives a vivid and memorable portrait of life in Nigeria during the 1930s and 1940s.

---

screaming. Elvis's stepmother, Comfort, is no comfort to Elvis in her coldhearted attitude toward him—she never even gives him any food. Elvis's father, Sunday, has a name that suggests rest and ease, but this man is constantly tormented by his failures and lost opportunities. Elvis's friend Redemption leads Elvis not to redemption but to the Lagos underworld of crime (although he does, in the end, provide Elvis with the passport that enables Elvis to escape to the United States).

Elvis himself is named after Elvis Presley, since it appears that his mother, Beatrice, was a fan. His full name, Elvis Oke, gives a clue to one of the underlying themes of the novel: the overwhelming of the indigenous Igbo culture by Western influences. The Igbo are one of the largest ethnic groups in Nigeria; Elvis and his family are Igbos, although most people in Lagos belong to the Yoruba tribe. However, Elvis and the poorer folk of Lagos are saturated not with

IT IS EASY FOR THE READER, CAUGHT UP IN THE STORY, TO SKIP PAST THESE EPIGRAPHS THAT ARE PLACED AT THE BEGINNING OF EACH CHAPTER, BUT THEY ADD A DIMENSION TO THE NOVEL THAT DEEPENS ITS MEANING."

their own culture but with American popular culture. American music and American films are a constant part of the city's soundscape. Recorded music of stars of the 1980s such as Gloria Gaynor and the band Duran Duran are heard in bars and on the radio, and Elvis and his friends love to watch old American movies at the badly equipped theaters; they know all about *The Wild Bunch*, *The Good, the Bad, and the Ugly*, and a host of old John Wayne films. Nor is this a new experience for Elvis; it was when he was growing up in Afikpo, eight hundred miles east of the capital, that he first became familiar with movies such as *Casablanca* and *Breakfast at Tiffany's*. It was also at Afikpo that Elvis saw a group of dancers performing to Elvis Presley's song "Hound Dog" and decided there and then that he wanted to be a dancer.

Set against the pervasive trappings of American popular culture and the dysfunctional city of Lagos are the largely forgotten remnants of Igbo culture. References to this culture do appear and have an importance for the novel as a whole that is easy to miss. The indigenous culture first appears as part of the narrative in Chapter 2, after Chapter 1 has presented the unsavory reality of 1980s Lagos. In Afikpo in 1972, when Elvis is five years old, he is forced to take part in an initiation ritual supervised by the men of the family who watch and speak to one another in Igbo, not English. The scene is overlaid with irony and a certain macabre humor. Elvis is to kill his first eagle, his father tells him, except that it is not an eagle—eagles are too expensive—but a chicken. In fact, the sacrificial bird is a baby chick that has already been shot through with an arrow and is almost dead anyway. Elvis is frightened by the entire procedure and does not want even to look at the dying bird. After the "kill," the men anoint Elvis's head with

oil and give him a blessing. When the ceremony is over, Elvis feels like a man, but the reader is more aware of the ironies embedded in the scene; this is a culture that has seen more vibrant days, and in the background there is a hint of what it is that really animates so many of the Nigerian people: as the men and the boy set off for the ritual, a record of Elvis Presley singing one of his hits, "Return to Sender," can be heard coming from the house.

From this point on, the indigenous Igbo culture is virtually invisible in the narrative parts of the novel, but the author manages, for a very specific purpose, to slip it in, so to speak, between the cracks. Each chapter has an epigraph that purports to be an excerpt from the journal that Beatrice, Elvis's mother, kept before her early death. The epigraphs contain recipes for all kinds of traditional Igbo dishes and descriptions of herbs that can be used for the treatment of ailments. The epigraphs also describe an Igbo ceremony that utilizes the kola nut. The kola nut appears to have some kind of sacred significance for the Igbo ("He who brings kola, brings life") similar to that given by Roman Catholics to the bread and wine used in the Eucharist service. The epigraphs reveal some of the purposes of the kola nut ceremony, which is always offered when visitors arrive. The ceremony binds people together, helping everyone in the clan to remember their connections with one another, with the land, and with the history of all the clans that are present. The ceremony links the present to the past because the ritual has remained the same through countless generations. It ensures social stability on the basis of a shared understanding and acceptance of the way things are. Understanding the kola nut ritual is an essential rite of passage for the young Igbo male. There appears to be a philosophy of life embedded in the ritual that elevates and inspires those who take part: "We are all seeds, we are all stars," according to one epigraph.

What the epigraphs show is an entire way of understanding human life in society and in relationship to the natural world. Everything is bound together in a unity. Humans know their relationship to the earth, to plants, to the land, and to one another. It is clear that the epigraphs belong to a world that is quite different—more tranquil, more serene, more filled with real knowledge—from the one that is revealed in the desperate helter-skelter of life in Lagos in the 1980s.

This is a lost world to which young Elvis Oke has no key other than what he reads in his mother's journal. As a child he used to fetch the journal for her and was aware that, bound in leather, it "smelled of things old and secret." But he never learns in any practical way what those old secret things are. At one point, he grumbles that no one he knows uses recipes anyway—the significance of the Igbo traditions his mother recorded are completely lost on him. And with those epigraphs in mind, the reader can see that the initiation ceremony Elvis went through at the age of five was little more than a cruel parody of the ideals that nestle within the kola nut ritual. There is nothing available to him that would guide him smoothly through the complexities of his adolescence, and this applies to the other young men of his acquaintance also, such as Innocent and Redemption. They are cut adrift from any tradition and must make their own way in life. Not surprisingly, they all make a lot of mistakes and suffer because of them.

It is easy for the reader, caught up in the story, to skip past these epigraphs that are placed at the beginning of each chapter, but they add a dimension to the novel that deepens its meaning. The knowledge that would help to stabilize the lives of these uprooted people and give them peace of mind might be found, the author seems to suggest, in its indigenous culture that has been forgotten in the long process of colonization and the surrender to Western ways and Western culture.

Source: Bryan Aubrey, Critical Essay on *GraceLand*, in *Novels for Students*, Gale, Cengage Learning, 2011.

Stefan Sereda

In the following excerpt, Sereda notes three pop music references that are key to understanding the world of GraceLand.

...Chris Abani's *GraceLand* belongs to "the third-generation" of Nigerian authors, also termed "the children of the postcolony" (Waberi 8), (1) whose writing has recently exploded in the United States and United Kingdom publishing marketplace. (2) Novels such as Chimamanda Ngozi Adichie's *Purple Hibiscus*, Helen Oyeyemi's *The Icarus Girl*, Sefi Atta's *Everything Good Will Come*, Unoma Azuah's *Sky-High Flames*, Helon Habila's *Waiting for an Angel* or Uzodinma Iweala's *Beasts of No Nation*, as well as Abani's *GraceLand* and *Becoming Abigail*, all interpolate Western and Nigerian themes to convey their perspective on Nigerian culture in the context of neocolonialism, multiculturalism and globalization. All of these novels integrate intercultural themes in a form of ethno-cultural hybridity that "[incarnates] a complete fusion with the world" as Fanon suggests (*Black Skin* 45). In *GraceLand*, Abani offers a complex, multidimensional perspective on Nigeria, which is similarly reflected in other third-generation texts set in Nigeria (such as Adichie, Atta, Azuah or Habila). *GraceLand* juxtaposes Lagos of the early 1980s, a place "so ugly and violent yet beautiful at the same time" (7), with his quiet hometown of Afikpo. Yet, the traditional maternal culture represented by Afikpo, the mothers' cryptic recipes and Igbo proverbs, is fluidly fused with Lagos buka food, Nigerian juju and American pop culture by the teenage protagonist Elvis, an Elvis impersonator and avid Western movie fan. Just as Abani smoothly moves through English, Nigerian pidgin, Scottish dialect or cowboy lingo in his text, Elvis effortlessly navigates from the Moroko slums to highlife clubs, or reads Rilke, Ellison or the *Koran* just as readily as Onitsha Market pamphlets. Throughout the novel, however, Elvis must contend with global concerns, such as poverty, prostitution and human trafficking. The plot follows Elvis on his quest to escape Lagos as a dancer. His widowed, alcoholic father Sunday, a military colonel who dabbles in narcotics and organ harvesting, further complicates Elvis's flight. Encouraging Elvis to pursue his dream and escape neocolonial oppression are his friend, Redemption, and his mentor, the King of Beggars. As the novel's eponymous title implies, music is an overriding theme in *GraceLand*. (3)

Set in Lagos from 1972 to 1983, *GraceLand* demonstrates how music can be used as a cultural product to resist Euro-American neocolonial practices as well as the hegemonic discourses oppressing citizens in militarily governed nations, as Nigeria was in the early 1980s. The novel hybridizes Nigerian juju and asiko musical structures with the Western novel form as a defense against cultural violence and globalization. By appropriating Western pop music through intertextual references, Abani also critiques neocolonial Nigerian and American essentialism. In particular, the novel questions the West's economic exploitation of those living in Lagos and the government's reliance on military control when the West will not provide aid.

" SPECIFIC SONG REFERENCES OFTEN SPEAK

TO A PARTICULAR MOMENT IN THE NOVEL, BUT

THE RIFFS THAT ALLUDE TO FIGURES IN MUSIC

CRITIQUE WESTERN CAPITALISM'S CONNECTION TO

THE NIGERIAN GOVERNMENT'S OVER-RELIANCE ON

MILITARY COERCION."

Furthermore, in the novel music provides a space for women in the Igbo patriarchal society, as well as an escape from the violent definitions of masculinity. Allusions to Nigerian and American musicians also create a dialectic that exposes the oppression of the Nigerian people. In *GraceLand*, music proves to be a cultural element of resistance instead of a mere avenue of superficial escape from a neocolonial setting.

... Three specific pop music references shape the world presented in *GraceLand*, beginning with Bob Marley's "Natural Mystic." Elvis, who is 16 years old and music-obsessed, sings along with the first two lines: "There's a natural mystic blowing through the air / If you listen carefully now you will hear . . . . " before he realized "he did not know all the words" (4). Elvis is unfamiliar with existence's natural fluidity, which Marley's lyrics describe further:

> This could be the first trumpet
> Might as well be the last
> Many more will have to suffer
> Many more will have to die
> Don't ask me why
> Things are not the way they used to be
> I won't tell no lie
> One and all got to face reality now. (3–10)

This verse that Elvis cannot yet grasp foreshadows the rest of the novel, which reaches its climax in mass suffering and the deaths of his father, the King of Beggars (Elvis's friend and a resistance fighter), and the villainous Colonel. Furthermore, the line "things are not the way they used to be" highlights the present moment, while "one and all got to face reality now" insists on the importance of understanding one's situation rather than escaping it.

At the end of the novel, Elvis indeed flies away to America. However, before he can escape Nigeria to the United States, Elvis must gain an understanding of fluidity and neocolonial oppression. To do this, I suggest, Abani elaborates on the moment when Elvis is tortured by the Colonel's men. Elvis is flogged with a whip that, according to his torturer, the Fulanis use "to test who be man enough to marry." The moment that transforms Elvis's person is a moment of extreme suffering at the hands of the military regime; it seems that he must confront these horrors in order to learn that "nothing is ever resolved . . . it just changes." Although the Colonel calls Elvis "just a child" after the torture, Elvis's lyric moment brings him face to face with a violent masculinity that he manages to escape.

Two further references draw attention to recognizable political and social conditions in Lagos. Elvis whistles the theme song from *Casablanca*, a 1942 Hollywood film allegory that constructed America as a nation of refugees hoped to escape to and encouraged the country's involvement in World War II. The reference to "As Time Goes By" in Elvis's childhood questions American involvement in the country. In 1979 Elvis is seemingly waiting for his own escape from Africa or for America to step in and relieve the strife in Nigeria. The American government, whose economic interest in the country affected its politics, could have used its influence to improve the Nigerian situation. While 1979 was the year that Nigeria received a constitution, the rest of the novel clearly indicates that this year did not mark the end of military control in Lagos. Elvis has to continue searching for the lyric moment in this earlier period, as neither Americans nor Nigerians had resolved the nation's problems.

While the reference to the theme from *Casablanca* calls attention to the West's interest in Nigeria, an allusion to a 1966 James Brown hit questions Igbo patriarchy. When Elvis dances to "It's a Man's Man's Man's World" performed by a singer who "sounded nothing like James Brown with his high-pitched falsetto," the narrative undermines Brown's lyric. The singer's pitch feminizes his voice, mocking the notion of a "man's world" and riffing on the masculine ideals presented by Elvis' father throughout the novel. Indeed, music, which Sunday reveals he has lost touch with when he calls Elvis a "useless dancer," is often used to connect and sympathize with women and give them a space in the culture. In the late 1970s, the Lijadu Sisters predicted that the number of female artists who were given an opportunity to exit the domestic sphere through music would soon outnumber the men in the industry (Konkombe: *Nigerian Music*). Elvis's mother Beatrice reflects with her mother, Oye that "dirges" are sung by families when a daughter is born. The implication here stresses the family's disappointment and metaphorically suggests all girls are stillborn in this society. Since music is not regarded as masculine, women are able to contribute to society through song. For example, Sunday allows women to join in the protest against bulldozing Maroko by singing. When the bulldozer prepares to crush the barricade the Maroko inhabitants built, the women begin "humming gently, swelling the men's courage." As Brown wails, "this is a man's world / but it would mean nothing—nothing—without a woman or a girl." Although the women remain unequal, singing does allow them to display agency and engage in political protest.

If Nigeria is a patriarchal world that places undue importance on the name as passed down from father to son, Elvis's name and persona contradict definitions of masculinity. After Sunday tells Elvis he killed Elvis's cousin Godfrey to defend the family name he says, "all I have to give you is my name, your name, Elvis Oke. And when I die, it will continue to help you build something for your children. Dat's why I don't want you to be a dancer." Ironically, Elvis's name alludes to an American musician, given to him by his mother from whom he also inherits a record player and some records. Elvis's name and his interest in music distinguish his identity from the Igbo patriarchal tradition and thereby the essentialist expectations of responsibility and violence associated with it. If music is constructed as an escape from Lagos, it is a positive one that frees Elvis from being consumed by the cycle of hostility threatening the neocolonial experience.

Specific song references often speak to a particular moment in the novel, but the riffs that allude to figures in music critique Western capitalism's connection to the Nigerian government's over-reliance on military coercion. *Grace-Land*'s Colonel is a figure who embodies armed domination, the law's arbitrary and unequal application and globalization. The Colonel profits from the neocolonial situation through illegal organ harvesting. In the Redemption's words, "people like de Colonel use their position to get

human parts as you see and den freeze it." Through illegally exploiting fellow Nigerians, the Colonel profits in the global marketplace. The Colonel's rank and the abuse of power it allows connote an American historical figure: Colonel Tom Parker, Elvis Presley's manager. Upon meeting the Colonel in *GraceLand*, Elvis wonders how the Colonel "had earned so many medals, considering the military saw so little action." This suggestion of an undeserved rank also registers with Tom Parker, who received the honorary title of Colonel from his friend, Louisiana Governor Jimmie Davis (Nettles). Just as the Colonel exploited his people for profit, so Parker exploits Presley: in 1955, Parker signed Presley to an exclusive contract guaranteeing the Colonel 25 percent of the star's performance royalties as well as a percentage of Elvis's merchandising income (Szatmary 45). By the end of Presley's career, "three-quarters of Elvis's income went into Parker's pocket" (Nettles). The resemblance of the Colonel in *GraceLand* to Parker accentuates him as a figure of neocolonial economic exploitation, while also connecting him to the larger trend of Western misconduct in Nigeria evident in Mohammed's assassination, the oil boom and bust, as well as contemporary slave trafficking and organ harvesting. The association between the Colonel and a ruthless capitalist from the American music scene associates the West's arbitrary behaviour with the failure of Nigeria's economy and the country's subsequent reliance on military oppression. If Abani appropriates the figure of Parker through the Colonel, his suggestion of American mismanagement is furthered in the Colonel's attempt to manage the King of the Beggars. While Parker persisted in selling Elvis to the media (Szatmary 44), the Colonel does not have the same control over the King of the Beggars.

The novel's politically rebellious King of the Beggars opposes the Colonel. The King is another hybrid figure: his name riffs on Elvis Presley's status as the "King of Rock 'n' Roll," but he is also Nigerian, anti-capitalist and missing an eye, recalling the impoverished and blind konkombe musician, Benjamin Kokuru. Often considered the biggest influence on Lagos's contemporary musicians (Konkombe: *Nigerian Music*), Kokuru enjoys a status similar to Presley, but refuses the wealth. Both musical influences are brought together in the King of the Beggars, who represents the biggest threat to the Colonel. Much like juju, the King is a figure in which konkombe and rock 'n' roll converge, allowing him to break through boundaries of class, race, and culture just like Presley. When the King makes his final stand against the Colonel, his manipulation of the media allows him to spread anti-hegemonic ideas across cultures to white Westerners as well as his countrymen. The King leads the protest "singing in a deep Baritone." The protest takes a call-and-response form when the King insists "we want democracy!" and the mob echoes "Yes, democracy, no more army." The anti-militaristic dialogue only continues because the Colonel feels "it would not do to have an assassination taped, especially by the BBC. It would affect foreign investments, and his bosses wouldn't take kindly to that," although the Colonel would prefer to "blow the bastard's head right off." In calling the King a bastard and wanting to kill him, the Colonel recognizes the hybrid threat he presents: the King currently has the Nigerian people on his side and could easily attract foreign sympathy if the media were to film his slaying. The Colonel fears such coverage, especially by the internationally broadcast BBC, will result in additional financial withdrawals by foreign investors and in turn retribution from his superiors. The fear that the King instills in the Colonel is a reminder of the repression that occurs in Nigeria as a result of ruling-class inefficiency and Western economic abandonment. Abani's Beggar King, therefore, is able to desegregate Nigeria and the advantaged West through a multi-layering of cultural icons and voices to spread awareness regarding his people's oppression. In stabbing the Colonel in the throat, the King becomes an agent who silences this military figure's hegemonic voice.

GraceLand's assortment of musical references form an amalgamation of Western pop and konkombe into a hybrid soundscape that challenges the interaction between Nigeria and its people as well as Nigeria and the United States. Allusions to figures in the American and Lagos music scenes generate a dialogical protest against Western capitalism's encouragement of Nigeria's oppressive government, reminiscent of the antimonies found in afrobeat music (see Olaniyan). The Western music that pervades Nigeria is also reflected back on the United States to accuse Americans of imposing themselves economically on other cultures while refusing to come to their aid economically in times of crisis. Abani also utilizes the customary Igbo search for a lyric moment to shape his postfoundationalist novel and challenge the bastardization of his nation through Western influence with its own traditional beliefs. The book's fusion of the

Western novel's aesthetic with a Yoruban juju structure equalizes the two art forms and thereby African and American culture. The hybridity in *GraceLand* blends asiko song, Igbo tradition, and pieces from America, Nigeria, and Jamaica within a novel shaped by Yoruban juju to surpass binary dialectics and combat the oppression visited on neo-colonial subjects through globalization and abusive governments. By riffing on Nigeria's neo-colonial situation *GraceLand* constructs music as a weapon of the future for resisting globalization, political corruption, and cultural violence. Considering Abani's own desire to subvert aesthetic traditions, one of the novel's contributions to postcolonial literature is its incarnation of a bastardized form to contest the ills of a bastardized world.

Source: Stefan Sereda, "Riffing on Resistance: Music in Chris Abani's *GraceLand*," in *Ariel*, Vol. 39, No. 4, October 2008, pp. 31–47.

Colm Tóibín

In the following excerpted interview, Tóibín and Abani discuss Nigerian and Irish literature, commenting directly on GraceLand.

Chris Abani, a Nigerian novelist and poet living in political exile here in the US, is the author of the novels *Masters of the Board* and *GraceLand*, which won the 2005 PEN Hemingway Prize. He has also written several poetry collections and most recently, the novella *Becoming Abigail*, a poet's novella in its dreamlike juxtapositions and *Stepladder How*. His other prizes include a PEN Freedom-to-Write Award, a Prince Clans Award, a Hurston/Wright Legacy Award and a Lannan Foundation Literary Fellowship. He lives and teaches in California.

Colm Tóibín is an Irish novelist, journalist and playwright. His novels include *The South*, *The Heather Blazing*, *The Story of the Night* and *The Blackwater Lightship*, which was shortlisted for the 1999 Booker Prize. His latest book, *The Master*, aptly titled in reference to its protagonist, Henry James, and for the masterful writing deployed in conjuring him, was shortlisted for the 2004 Booker Prize and named the Los Angeles Times Novel of the Year. It won France's Prize for Best Foreign Novel in 2005.

In *Becoming Abigail* and in *The Master*, both authors, respectively, write about the nature of exile—in Henry James's case self-imposed—and its attendant loneliness. BOMB co-sponsored the

" IN MY BOOKS, THE DEAD RETURN AS TEXT, AS SKIN (DIARIES AND MAPS), AS INSCRIPTIONS THAT ACT AS THE MEDIUM, THE WAY TO VISIT THE GHOSTLY PLACES OF SELF AND YET RETURN SAFELY."

novelists' reading and conversation before a packed audience at KCB Bar in New York as part of the 2006 PEN World Voices Festival. Hear the audio at www.bombsite.com.

CT: . . . You've written recently about [Wole] Soyinka. How important has he been?

CA: You can't talk about Nigeria in any context without Soyinka. The country comes to birth in Soyinka's imagination. There's no political moment, no nationalistic moment that he doesn't have some involvement in. Purely as a voice of conscience, he's been the one constant. In Nigeria we have 250 ethnicities that are engaged in the often violent moments of self-determination. Soyinka is one of a few people able to occupy that duality that's required if Nigeria is to find itself. And you see that in his plays and novels as well. His work begins to achieve a universalism that has often led to criticisms over authenticity because he doesn't privilege folklore. For him myth and mythology exist only in terms of what they can do for the aesthetic moment, the way it did for the Greeks and the Romans. For me as a writer he is the most influential, both as a voice of conscience, but also in terms of aesthetic rigor and framework.

CT: Compared to Things Fall Apart, *I never liked* The Interpreters. *It seems to me very dull indeed. Is that just an outsider's view? Maybe his theater is his best work.*

CA: Theater is his best work, but I do think it is an outsider's view. In many ways *Things Fall Apart* performs a certain reassuring expectation of Africa. This means that most writers within my generation are resisting that performance. I am in fact lucky to get any kind of exposure because all my work is about resisting that performance. This new storytelling is a difficult balance.

CT: Yes, but it seems to me that you've taken both. In GraceLand *you're certainly alert to what*

Tutuola has done, in terms of your repetitions and style. But also there are pure pieces of nineteenth-century Russian realism, which both Achebe and Soyinka have worked with. So you're actually bringing the two forms together in order to dramatize what is quite a difficult public life for quite a fragile consciousness, your protagonist, Elvis. You're conscious of using both?

CA: Very, but more conscious of actually taking directly from the Russians. There are references in the book—the books that Elvis is reading—that talk about the way the book is made. I read Dostoyevsky very early—10, 12 years old—and became sucked into that ridiculous existential melancholy that 13-year-old boys feel, but haven't earned. Dickens, too. It's a colonial education, and so I had those references. Soyinka and Tutuola have been much more influential than Achebe in terms of my actual writing style. But in terms of how you build a worldview, Achebe has been more important, how you integrate what is essentially an Igbo cosmology into a very modern, contemporary, twenty-first-century novel. There are all of those things, but James Baldwin also plays into this.

CT: As does Ralph Ellison's Invisible Man. *I think that with every novel, there's this shadow novel: the novel that should have been and that was in my head at first, that was set in a much more public place. For example, I was in Spain when Franco died. I was at all the demonstrations. There was always a novel to be written. But when I went to write the novel, it was about those earlier years when there was nothing much happening. The Henry James book really should have been a novel about Oscar Wilde, which would have been much more exciting, funnier, more glamorous and sadder in the end. I was also conscious in* Grace-Land *that there are things you are leaving out; the war is mentioned only in passing. It must have been tempting to have done a very big war novel, written the novel of the Biafran war.*

CA: Do you get that?

CT: Of course, of course I do: "Where is the novel of Northern Ireland? Where is the novel of the civil rights movement? Where is the novel of the IRA?" Well, why don't you write it? (LAUGHTER)

CA: It's funny, because when I was reading *The Master*—the beautiful opening scene with James's play, when Wilde is mentioned—I can see that temptation. Yes, it is tempting, but *GraceLand* was doing the very reverse of that; it was trying to be both minute and epic, which is a contradiction in terms. Here's a book that's dealing with a whole generation—my generation—of Nigerians, and our coming of age and our notion of the country's coming of age. So it sprawls all over the place, but it had to follow this single consciousness if it was going to bear through with any degree of resonance. Otherwise it would veer too easily into the polemic. *GraceLand* is like a manifesto: I want to talk about gender, sexuality, the performance of masculinity, and how that is always associated with violence, the terrain of which is the female body within Nigeria; all of those spaces of silence that exist in Nigerian literature and are not privileged in the way that the easily political is privileged. *Abigail* comes out of that, as does a book I wrote about a boy soldier. They're both novellas. They're small and minute because I'm afraid of that easy political grandstanding. I'm looking for a more effective way of discussing both the political and human. I've returned more and more to Baldwin, because Baldwin is always about the quiet human moment. He never shied away from race, from the civil rights movement. He never shied away from dealing with issues of sexuality. Being 10 and reading *Another Country*, in a very homophobic culture, I realized that for James the only aberration in the world is the absence of love. And what's even more perverse is the giving up on the search for love, which is that melancholic voice that carries us in the quiet moments. That's what I want to return to. You too have this quietness at the heart of your work. Your writing is elegant, it's sparse—*Blackwater Lightship*, for example—and where the hell do you get these beautiful titles from? For you, is the more distilled voice—the better voice? Do you like it more in this sense?

CT: There's a lot of fear involved, that you're going to mess up the sentence, so you leave it short. It arises from having to struggle enormously just to get the thing down. I have no natural ability, I don't think. I have colleagues in Ireland who have a real natural ability—almost like having a natural singing voice—where you can write anything. I don't have that at all. So it always comes from fear, I think.

CA: It's funny you should say that. Do you know Dermot Healy's work?

CT: He has a natural ability to just do anything with words.

CA: But he says the same thing! He says that he's terrified. *A Goat's Song* took him 10 years and it's a beautiful book. Do you think that it's just that Irish writers are better writers precisely because they feel that they're not?

CT: I think that in societies like yours and mine, mothers realize: if my son can read and write, it'll be a way out of poverty. Reading and writing have a special sacred aura around them. You do not take them for granted. Because of the broken traditions and loose connections in our countries, what we write about also has its own rules and regulations. If you read your two books together, GraceLand *and* Abigail, *there's always dislocation, the dead father or the dead mother. You could say that* Ulysses *is about a man whose father committed suicide, whose son died, and whose wife is having an affair with somebody else, walking in a city to meet someone whose mother has died. And you'll say, "Ah, this must be an Irish novel!" I don't know how I would write a novel—this might sound like a joke but I mean it—with two parents who would be alive at the end of the book. Your two most recent novels are about someone whose mother has died and who's a ghostly presence in both of the books.*

CA: Yes. But everything in Nigeria is about haunting. It's about ghosts. The dead are everywhere, and just won't stay dead. In my Igbo culture, dead parents used to be buried in the middle of the living room and not in cemeteries. So in this way the dead are always there, to guide us, to teach us. I grew up around domestic graves and you couldn't have a drink without offering them libation. So the dead informed everything that the living did. They are in many ways our way of mediating self and history, partly because there's a real existential loss at the heart of what it means to be Nigerian, because three or four hundred years ago much of the culture was interrupted when the Portuguese arrived and began to deal in enslavement. What happens is that from that time on, Nigerian culture begins to cede itself to the invader, to this invasion of otherness. So even now in Nigeria, when we talk about "our culture," there's a certain Victorianness about what we think our culture is, which actually comes from Victorian England's colonial presence. It's that way in which all of our "selves" are built around ghosts, and sadly, mostly violent ghosts, malevolent ghosts. In *GraceLand* and *Becoming Abigail*, the mothers are dead and in a new book, *The Virgin of Flames*, the father's dead. So the body of becoming is often an absence made more present by its haunting, by the ectoplasmic residue. In my books, the dead return as text, as skin (diaries and maps), as inscriptions that act as the medium, the way to visit the ghostly places of self and yet return safely. So much of the ectoplasm of these ghosts is patriarchy and masculinity. My work asks if it is possible, if this absence, this malevolent place, can enfold and nurture and be reclaimed through prose and poetry, to turn into possibility. For me it's alchemy.

CT: Who is Percival Everett? He gets acknowledged in both of your books.

CA: He's an amazing African American writer who has been a huge presence for me. I started out as a genre writer, writing thrillers, and couldn't find a way to blend all that with the literary. He really brought things together for me. He has helped me solve one of the core challenges for contemporary African writers; how to occupy the spaces of imagination when the political moment is either inadequate or has exhausted itself. This is an interesting moment for Nigerian writers. We now have a more global moment, diasporas where even when you're in Nigeria you're on your Blackberry all the time. There are none of the usual places of engagement anymore. We have to find new topographies for our imagination.

CT: One of the ways that you have to solve this, by its very implication in GraceLand, *even by the title—and this is something that Ireland and Nigeria have in common, that both societies were ready to let America wash over them in every way. For example, there is no such thing as Irish capital. If Irish people have money, they put it in a bank or they buy more houses, but they wouldn't ever invest in something that might make or lose money. There's no tradition of that. Irish people adore American country music. If you're a writer, you love Hemingway, Scott Fitzgerald. We see ourselves in certain ways as an aspect of America, and we are happy for that to continue, despite the fact that there was very little support for the current American regime in Ireland. There are images throughout* GraceLand—*it isn't overplayed. There's the relationship between Nigeria and Portugal, Nigeria and Britain, Nigeria and its own internal disputes, and all that almost pales in comparison with this new one, which is Nigeria and America.*

CA: In many ways it's always been a concern of Nigerian literature, the engagement with the Western voice. But it has always been seen as the bogeyman coming in to erase the existing culture. But I was more interested in *GraceLand*

in the moments of possibility. Rather than its being a limitation, its being subversion too as well as possibility. Here's a Nigerian kid named Elvis, putting on whiteface to imitate a white guy who imitated black people, ridiculing the notions of race and ownership of art. I think my argument, or my belief, is that ultimately art in any form—literature, music, even cinema—offers dialogue. Once dialogue is introduced, the subversive element comes in. And so it can be transmuted into something else. America exports itself to Nigeria in this way, and Nigeria digests it and then exports itself back to America in a completely different way. A lot of things come from that conversation: possibility rather than limitation; something beautiful.

CT: GraceLand *is one of those books—I would love to have seen you writing it. To have known if it was day or night, the room, how many words per day. There are books like that, where you would love to see the thing being created. Could you give us some idea?*

CA: It was written in America, on a laptop, mostly in Starbucks, which seems appropriate. It was written very frenetically in nine months. I got obsessed with it. I was writing 16-hour days. The real difficulty was writing the fractured language. My tendency is to make everything beautiful. But I wanted to capture that cityscape. You were in the Lannan House, right?

CT: No I was never in Lannan. I was in Yaddo.

CA: I thought you were in Marfa, Texas?

CT: No, no. If you know them, do tell them I'd like to come.

CA: A train went by Marfa at three o'clock in the morning, and it had the most melancholic whistle. But this is a town where the cemetery is segregated, still. So, to be there working on my new novel, *The Virgin of Flames*, in a place where the sky blends with the landscape and it looks like you're caught in a glass bubble with all that contradiction was quite the gift. That's where I wrote *Becoming Abigail*—in three weeks. I wanted to ask you how you write, how you make the work you make. I'm very intrigued, because each of your books is very different. But at the core of everything—like this Henry James book, *The Master*, is this notion of exile: this separation, this displacement, this melancholy and loss. How do you infuse all of that into the sparsest sentences? How do you write?

CT: I wonder—and to ask you if this is true about you—if the first five or six books you read at a certain age matter to you more than any number of experiences? Or tend to merge with those experiences? And that they become your style, those books. Or a DNA in you, a magnet in you hits a magnet in them. Certainly, reading The Sun Also Rises *in Tramore on the beach, when I was 16 or 17, I was amazed. The hero being in Paris and going to Spain, having a whale of a time in Spain. But he was always separate from the others. I did all that, I did all that that happens in that book, after reading it. I didn't like the bullfighting thing; it wasn't my scene. Instead, I went to Catalonia. I was always there, watching the others, like the guy in book. And at the same age—I'm talking 1971 or '72—Penguin had published Sartre's trilogy, and it was being read by serious people. It's not read now. And Guernica was on the cover of the Penguin edition. It was everywhere you went. I didn't know anything about his philosophy—I still have no interest in his philosophy—but reading the first two books of his trilogy made an enormous difference to me. And then coming through those two books to Camus, to* The Outsider. *I ended up living like that. I didn't murder anybody, but nonetheless, those books didn't just affect the way I wrote, but they affected the way I lived. Notice that I'm not mentioning any Irish books, because in those years, the censors had been lifted and every book was coming in from the outside and the last thing you wanted to read was about Ireland. I read them later, but at that age those American and French books really hit me. Those books were what mattered, nothing else since of either reading or experience has mattered in any way like that.*

CA: I want to ask you about being Catholic or growing up in a Catholic household. I grew up very Catholic. I grew up going to a seminary and being kicked out, several times actually, for heresy. There's something about being Catholic that seems that you existentially displace all the time—it's almost like joy is a foreign country, and when you travel to it, you take all this flagellation. I'm talking about me here. I wanted to ask you if that informs any of the work you do?

CT: Catholicism didn't affect me very much, other than that the rituals were both interesting and boring. I was an altar boy. I find it very hard to create a Catholic character. Maybe if they banned it I would start wanting it. But I suppose there is an elephant in the room, which is the matter of being gay. That did make a very big difference. At the

moment I'm in the Castro in San Francisco, where every single person is gay. Which is most disconcerting because where I am in my head, there's no one gay guy for a hundred miles on all sides. Obviously, the business of holding a secret like that, which I did for years, affects you. It happens in Henry James. The best James books are where there's a secret and if told, it will be explosive. That is what interested me so much about James at the beginning, both personally and as a writer.

CA: To answer the question that I actually asked you about influence: for me it's a lot of Marvel and DC comics. *Silver Surfer:* all of my melancholy comes from the Silver Surfer. As a child, there were these books that they shouldn't have allowed children to read, these little comic books from England called the Commando series, about the Second World War. There was a particular one called *Darkie's Mob* that sort of stayed with me. It is all of the ways in which the English, completely unaware, celebrate their own racism. I play with sexuality in all my books. There's an ambiguity to all my characters. In *The Virgin of Flames*, the protagonist wants to be a woman. I write my characters from the inside out. There's no spectacle to it, so of course the first question is, Where is your body in relationship to this text? That always fascinates me. Before I wrote this book about this guy who wants to be a woman—I had always prided myself on, while being straight, being not homophobic at all. Until I wrote a scene where the character is finally about to make love to a transsexual stripper but realizes that that's not what he wants. In fact, he wants to occupy the stripper's position. And you have that whole *Crying Game* moment, but instead of the penis revelation being the thing, it's the penis disappearance. So this transsexual stripper is teaching this guy how to disappear his penis, so that he could wear a G-string were he to perform as a stripper. I researched it on the Internet. My girlfriend at the time read what I had written and said, "This reads like a manual." The rest of the book was beautiful but then it's, "Okay, over here we have the penis." I really had to go there, so I hired someone who performs as a woman. I said, "Okay, show me how to do this."

CT: Do you have his number? (LAUGHTER)

CA: I wanted to ask you, did coming out change your interaction with the text or with readership or with editorship or all of this?

Source: Colm Tóibín and Chris Abani, "Chris Abani and Colm Tóibín in Conversation," in *Bomb*, Vol. 96, Summer 2006, pp. 30–35.

Dinaw Mengestu

In the following review, Mengestu writes that while GraceLand *is "flawed," it is nonetheless a detailed and accurate picture of the tragedy that is Nigeria.*

With the largest population of any African nation and one of the world's major oil reserves, Nigeria once seemed set to become the economic and political pride of postcolonial Africa. Instead, since gaining independence in 1960, it has endured seven military coups, a civil war, and countless ethnic clashes that have left thousands of innocent civilians dead. Its history has been one of generals (Yakubu Gowon, Muhammadu Buhari, Sani Abache) and inevitably of violence—beginning with the mass murders during the war against secessionist Biafra in the late '60s and continuing with the wide-scale human rights abuses that until recently were a hallmark of every Nigerian government.

Born in 1966, author Chris Abani has had a painful and sadly emblematic relationship with his native country. His teenage writings—two novels and several plays—put him on the wrong side of the law. Arrested three times over the 24 years he lived in Nigeria, Abani was beaten, tortured and eventually given a death sentence he narrowly escaped. From those experiences have come two collections of poetry, and now Abani's first novel since his flight 14 years ago.

GraceLand's protagonist is Elvis [Oke], a young Presley impersonator. His name symbolizes the erosion of an indigenous culture. We see Nigeria through Elvis' eyes as the narrative oscillates back and forth between his early childhood in rural Afikpo and his life as a teenager in the slums of Lagos. The Afikpo passages take us from a farcical tribal initiation rite to a failed political campaign that forces him and his debt-ridden father to flee to the city. In the nine years that separate those events, Elvis' mother, Beatrice, dies of cancer; his father, Sunday, sinks into a permanent drunken despair; and Elvis' uncle rapes both his cousin and him.

The misfortunes of his boyhood occur in such quick succession that each tragedy comes to seem like just one more unhappy reality. Beatrice's death signifies grief without summoning the emotion in her son, or in us. Her presence clings to the rest of the book only because the pages of her journal—filled with recipes and descriptions of plants that she will need in the afterlife—are used to separate the chapters. Before her departure, Beatrice's character is hemmed in by the narrative's self-conscious anguish, and by Abani's insistence that we note the muted bravery of her passing away. Overwhelmed rather than stirred by the many horrors jammed into the Afikpo passages, we remain uncomfortably disengaged.

Elvis' escape to Lagos does not improve his lot. Sixteen and unemployed, he is a high school dropout who reads Rainer Maria Rilke and Ralph Ellison. His father has taken a new lover, named Comfort, who verbally abuses the boy and is short on motherly care. "The smell of garbage from refuse dumps, unflushed toilets and stale bodies" fills Maroko, the slum they live in. Lagos' streets are littered with corpses from hit-and-run accidents, men are publicly torched for stealing, and government soldiers exercise their vicious power at will. Against this chaotic background Elvis meets his friend Redemption, who drags him from a life of casual Elvis impersonations on the beach into an underworld of prostitution, drugs, and traffic in human body parts. Elvis meets the King of Beggars, too, a haggard, sagacious tramp and dance troupe leader who later dies a political martyr.

As an urban landscape Lagos strains the imagination: It is frenzied, poverty ridden, yet suffused with the throbbing pulse of a population struggling for its daily survival. A cruel indifference to human life breeds the collective resignation of a people who know all too well how capricious the difference between living and dying can be. Blessed with the lingering naiveté of his youth, Elvis stands heartbroken and frustrated, at once complicit in his own mistakes and outraged at the world around him. He comes most alive in the privacy of his own imagination, unencumbered by the troubling questions and condemnations that Abani has beset him with.

In one of *GraceLand*'s best realized scenes, Elvis goes into his bedroom and puts on "Heartbreak Hotel." He takes out the makeup kit that he uses to dress up as an Elvis impersonator and slowly transforms himself from black to white: "He walked back to the table and pulled the wig on, bending to look in the mirror. Elvis has entered the building, he thought, as he admired himself." This is one of the novel's few quiet moments, a self-indulgent act of love and desire that speaks perfectly to Elvis' hopeless plight. He will never become a famous dancer any more than he will become Elvis Presley, but his compulsion to imagine another life is an essential element of his survival.

Abani is a skillful descriptive writer, and *GraceLand* often succeeds in its recording of violence. He gathers together the details of a scene with a keen visual clarity and distills them into a haunting image, as when Elvis enters the ruins of a burned out church strewn with the remains of its slaughtered congregation during the Biafran War.

... Abani's fastidiously unsentimental eye notes the broken bodies and spirits of an entire community. For all the technical dexterity he demonstrates in observing the tedious yet essential details of life, though, he rarely provides more than a surface view of his characters. They stand out vividly for a moment, as Elvis does while donning his costume, then recede again behind a didactic voice determined to explicate and assign meaning where it is already obvious. Some, like the King of Beggars, narrowly trump their cartoonish introductions—"gnarled claws" "toothless grin" and sole eye "glittering insanely." Most, however, fail to register beyond the level of irony coded in their names. Sunday is only as sacred as the jugs of palm wine he swills, and Innocent, after his years in the Biafran War, is anything but. Redemption does fulfill the promise of his name, but first he drags Elvis through the seediest pits of Lagos. The irony, of course, is intended to point to what has been lost, but the device all too often renders that loss a cold abstraction.

The last chapters of *GraceLand* are spent in torture chambers drawn no doubt from Abani's own life. After being beaten to the verge of death, Elvis is dumped back into the world where what little he had is completely gone. Maroko has been demolished by the government, his father is dead, and Elvis' fate is left in the hands of a young girl, aptly named Blessing.

Despite its serious flaws, *GraceLand* draws a searing picture of a country devouring its own children. What you learn about Nigeria will make you want to weep.

Source: Dinaw Mengestu, "At the End of Lonely Street," in *New Leader*, Vol. 87, No. 1, January-February 2004, pp. 27–28.

John C. Hawley

In the following review, Hawley argues that the experiences of the young protagonist in Grace-Land *represent the hopelessness of Nigeria.*

If Chinua Achebe and Wole Soyinka are arguably the grandfathers of Nigerian literature, and Ben Okri and Buchi Emecheta are their successors, Chris Abani, Chimamanda Adichie and Helen Habila would appear to be coming into their own these days as the next wave. Adichie, author of *Purple Hibiscus* (Algonquin, 2003), tells the story of a fanatical Catholic father and his stranglehold on his family during Abacha's military regime in the 1990s and Helen Habila, author of *Waiting for an Angel* (Norton, 2004), offers a description of "Poverty Street" in Lagos in the 1990's. In *GraceLand*, Abani uses the experiences of a young adolescent, ironically named after Elvis Presley, to suggest the larger pattern of squalor and hopeless dreams that continues to define Nigeria.

Abani, a visiting assistant professor at the University of California at Riverside, is the recipient of the 2001 PEN USA Freedom to Write Award and a 2003 Lannan Literary Fellowship. He is best known for his poetry, including *Daphne's Lot* (Red Hen, 2003), about his English mother, and *Kalakuta Republic* (Saqi, 2001), about political incarceration. He knows something about the latter, since his first novel, *Masters of the Board* (Delta, 1985) earned him six months in solitary confinement. He wrote the novel when he was just 16—one wonders, how seditious could it have been?—but the government argued that his plot laid the groundwork for a political coup. He was soon picked up again, and this time held for a year in a maximum security prison. Friends finally bribed the authorities and effected his release.

For Abani, the tyranny of the state is reflected in the tyranny of the family. Thus, *GraceLand* is the story of an adolescent, Elvis Oke, who lives with his father and stepmother in Moroko, a notorious slum on stilts over a fetid swampland in Lagos. Throughout the story Abani plays on the traditional use of names as talismans, generally inverting their surface meaning. Thus, the stepmother's name is Comfort, but she is cold. His dead mother's name is Beatrice, but she is no longer present to guide him through this hell. His father is Sunday, but he has no access to rest or transcendence. Elvis himself cannot sing or dance, and his hopeless impersonation of his namesake for white tourists is painful to imagine. He is pulled in two directions: the revolutionary King of Beggars wishes him to stand up against the corrupt regime, with predictable results; the pragmatic and corrupt Redemption, on the other hand, is a character much like Dickens's Artful Dodger, who introduces Elvis to drugs and to the kidnapping of children for export to Saudi Arabia and the sale of their internal organs to rich Americans.

There are light moments in the book, but these are quickly submerged by the sadness, the rape of the boy by his uncle and the forced prostitution of his missing cousin. Most powerful of all are the scenes of the boy's torture near the novel's end. This is no surprise, since Abani himself was given daily beatings during his first incarceration and was tortured during his second.

Each chapter begins with a recipe and a fragment from the rubric for the kola nut ceremony (a rite of passage into male adulthood). This device is not particularly effective, but Abani remarks that his intention is to set the specifics of the plot against the broader sweep of Nigerian culture. Urban squalor is immediate, but Abani wants readers to imagine a possible future building on a rich cultural history. Yet his characters have little chance to do so. The climax of the novel comes with the government's Operation Clean the Nation, in which all slums are bulldozed. In another novel, the resistance offered by those who live in these slums might be the cause for some romanticized hope and reaffirmation of a common humanity. In Moroko, it is simply the final example of the intransigent inequity of conditions in many countries that have been used for years as convenient sources to fulfill the needs of wealthier nations. The final ironic talismanic name, of course, is the book itself. The only "GraceLand" is that of one's own making, cut off from God, nation or family, desperately scrabbled together from the garbage that can be guarded from one's neighbor.

Source: John C. Hawley, "Oke's Odyssey," in *America*, Vol. 191, No. 3, August, 2–9, 2009, pp. 25–27.

SOURCES

Abani, Chris, *GraceLand*, Farrar, Straus & Giroux, 2004.

"Background Note: Nigeria," in *U.S. Department of State*, September 2009, http://www.state.gov/r/pa/ei/bgn/2836.htm (accessed December 23, 2009).

Dunbar, Ernest, *Nigeria*, Franklin Watts, 1974, pp. 41–48.

Harrison, Sophie, "Jailhouse Rock," in *New York Times*, February 22, 2004, p. 78, http://www.nytimes.com/2004/02/22/books/jailhouse-rock.html?scp = 1&sq = Jailhouse %20Rock %20GraceLand&st = cse (accessed February 13, 2010).

Mengestu, Dinaw, "At the End of Lonely Street," in *New Leader*, Vol. 87, No. 1, January-February 2004, p. 27.

"Nigeria," in *CIA: The World Factbook*, https://www.cia.gov/library/publications/the-world-factbook/geos/ni.html (accessed December 21, 2009).

Review of *GraceLand*, in *Publishers Weekly*, Vol. 250, No. 46, November 17, 2003, p. 39.

FURTHER READING

Dowden, Richard, *Africa: Altered States, Ordinary Miracles*, Portobello Books, 2008.
> A journalist who has lived in Africa since 1971 gives a compelling account of the achievements of and the challenges faced by African nations.

Maier, Karl, *This House Has Fallen: Nigeria in Crisis*, Basic Books, 2003.
> Maier gives a portrait of the problems faced by Nigeria, from falling living standards to political corruption and ethnic tensions, suggesting that the nation may be close to collapse.

Meredith, Martin, *The Fate of Africa: A History of Fifty Years of Independence*, PublicAffairs, 2006.
> This is a history of Africa from the beginning of decolonization to the present. Meredith includes a chapter on Nigeria and the Biafran War.

Sherman, John, *War Stories: A Memoir of Nigeria and Biafra*, Mesa Verde Press, 2002.

Sherman is an American who served with the Red Cross during the Biafran War. Involved in relief operations, he saw firsthand the horrors of the conflict.

SUGGESTED SEARCH TERMS

Chris Abani

GraceLand

Abani AND postcolonial

Biafran War

Lagos

Nigerian literature

Abani AND coming-of-age

child soldier AND Abani

Third World literature AND Abani

Abani AND GraceLand

GraceLand AND Nigeria

The Joy Luck Club

1993 After Amy Tan's 1989 novel *The Joy Luck Club* became a best seller and was optioned for a film, there were questions about how its intertwined stories could be brought to the screen and whether it could be done with the sensitivity to Chinese culture that such a project needed. To address the first issue, executive producer Oliver Stone hired Tan herself to work on the screenplay, along with Ronald Bass, an Academy Award-winning writer (for his script for *Rain Man*) and one of the most respected screenwriters in Hollywood. To address the second problem, the project was turned over to director Wayne Wang, who, at the time, had not yet directed any major studio projects but who had built a solid reputation with the independent features *Chan Is Missing* and *Eat a Bowl of Tea*. The resulting 1993 film was a critical and popular success, earning award nominations for Tan and Bass from the British Academy of Film and Television Arts and the Writers Guild of America and grossing over thirty-two million dollars at the box office.

The film *The Joy Luck Club* brings together the stories of four Chinese women who met in San Francisco after immigrating to the United States in the 1940s. There, they form a social group, the Joy Luck Club. The movie tells the story of these women and their daughters, who have grown up as first-generation Americans of Asian heritage. Wang weaves their varied stories together with grace, drawing from a cast of little-known actors of Asian descent to bring the eight central characters, their families, their friends, and their enemies

to life. The different stories are merged through careful, lyrical storytelling. The modern world is connected to Chinese history in this film, but viewers of many backgrounds have found it easy to relate to universal familial relationships.

PLOT SUMMARY

The 1993 film *The Joy Luck Club* begins with the story that serves as a prelude to the novel's first section, "Feathers from a Thousand Li Away," about an anonymous old woman who tried to bring an expensive goose that was once a duck but had transformed itself, with her when she came from Shanghai to America. Customs officials refused to allow the swan into the country, so she kept just one feather from it, waiting for the right time to give the feather to her daughter.

While the credits run, the film follows a floating white feather. The story begins with people arriving at a party, which will later prove to be a party for June Woo, played by Ming-Na Wen. In the novel, Tan uses June's given name, Jing-Mei, though the film almost exclusively refers to her as June. As the camera moves around the apartment, introducing audiences to the characters they will come to know throughout the film, June, in a voice-over, explains that her mother has been dead for four months and that the members of the Joy Luck Club have asked June to take her mother's place for their regular mahjong game. She says that her mother met her three friends in church, skipping the novel's explanation that she had gotten the idea for the club when she was a refugee in Kweilin, China. Her mother's friends are Lindo Jong, played in the film by Tsai Chin; An-Mei Hsu, played by Lisa Lu; and Ying-Ying St. Clair, played by France Nuyen. Their daughters are Waverly Jong, played by Tamlyn Tomita; Rose Hsu Jordan, played by Rosalind Chao; and Lena St. Clair, played by Lauren Tom.

When June steps to the side of the room during the mahjong game to pour herself a cup of tea, she looks at the small piano in the corner. Looking at it triggers a flashback to when she was a young girl. She took piano lessons, she explains in a voice-over, from old Mr. Jong, a piano teacher who was mostly deaf. The voice-over fades away as the film shows her as a child, smirking at the old man's weak guidance. On the night that she is to play the piano in a recital, June feels confident that she will impress her audience to such a degree, her voice-over explains, that she even believes she

might become famous. She exchanges a sour, competitive look with Waverly Jong, whom she identifies as a chess prodigy. Her failure to take her studies seriously takes its toll, though. She soon hits a wrong note and becomes increasingly flustered, and the audience members become uncomfortable for her. The day after the concert, June explains, she did not want to play the piano anymore, but the film shows her mother, Suyuan, played by Kieu Chinh, physically forcing her to the piano bench. In the childish tantrum that follows, June shouts that she wishes that she was dead, "like them," which leads to a brief flashback of Suyuan leaving two infant children on the side of her road, underneath a tree.

Back in contemporary San Francisco, at the Joy Luck Club gathering in the apartment of June's father, the older women explain to June that they have located the two young daughters, whom Suyuan left on their own during China's Communist Revolution. June is amazed to find that they are alive. The women tell her that they will pay her way to China to meet her sisters. When June leaves, the older women discuss whether or not they should have lied in the letter that they sent to the sisters in China.

The scene dissolves into the memory of Lindo Jong, who remembers being four years old and flying a kite when she stumbles into a discussion her mother is having with two other women. One woman is a matchmaker, and in this meeting Lindo is being promised as the bride of the other woman's son; it is guaranteed that Lindo will produce many sons. A montage follows, showing ten years of Lindo's family eating together as she grows. Finally, she explains in narration, they moved away to the south, leaving her there. (In the novel, a flood forces them to leave.) Her mother says goodbye to her on a misty road, leaving her to her new family. On her wedding night, the camera shows her new husband's shoes as he approaches their bedroom while she sits on the bed, nervous with anticipation. The arrival of this husband, Tyan Yu, is anticlimactic: he turns out to be a chubby ten-year-old boy who immaturely waves a lizard in her face. Then he tells her to sleep on the floor. As time passes, Tyan Yu's mother berates Lindo for failing to become pregnant. She forces her to stay horizontal, to facilitate pregnancy, effectively making Lindo a prisoner in the house.

One day, Lindo overhears a servant girl talking with her boyfriend, distressed because she is

FILM TECHNIQUE

Flashback

This film is shaped by flashbacks, that is, portrayals of events that occurred prior to the main time frame of the story. Wang anchors the story in present-day San Francisco, at a meeting of the Joy Luck Club, where June Woo is invited to take her mother's place at the older women's regular mahjong game. The main action, though, is in the past. The film sometimes uses a mental trigger to transition into the flashback, such as when Ying-Ying hears someone mention how difficult it must have been for Suyuan to give up her twin daughters and it reminds her of the death of her infant son. Often a character's voice-over will be used to take readers back to her story, though sometimes Wang leaves the reason for the flashback uncertain, as when An Mei, discussing Suyuan's daughters with Rose, rubs her neck, taking the story back to a time that she was burned with soup.

Tracking Shot

A tracking shot is achieved when a camera moves on a wheeled platform, going through one continuous scene with fluidity. This is most apparent in the film in the first scene after the credits, when the camera moves from room to room during a meeting of the Joy Luck Club. It allows the filmmaker to show characters to the audience, establishing a first impression before viewers can get to know them individually. It also lets audiences see the scope and complexity of the club, with a variety of people—male and female, Asian and non-Asian, of at least three generations—spread out across the apartment.

Soundtrack

The music for this film is credited to Rachel Portman, a British composer who became the first female winner of the Best Original Score Academy Award in 1996 for her work on the film *Emma*. The score uses traditional Chinese instruments, particularly the flute and the guitar, to create a relaxed, haunting mood. Portman repeats variations on one main theme throughout the film.

A notable exception is when the soundtrack blares "One Fine Day," a 1963 hit for the Chiffons, during Waverly's story about her childhood. This song is conspicuous because it is so American and modern, drawing a contrast to the traditional Chinese music of the rest of the film and establishing the action on screen as occurring in the 1960s.

Close-Up

Wang uses a significant number of close-up shots on actors' faces in this film. One reason for this is that much of the film uses voice-overs, transferring Amy Tan's first-person narratives in her novel intact into the film's soundtrack. When the close-up is combined with the voice-over, the film indicates clearly that the words being heard are passing through the character's mind.

Wang also uses close-up shots to draw viewers' attention to significant objects, such as the vase that Ying-Ying breaks in her room at Lena's house and the swan feather in June's hand.

Montage

A montage is a series of quick scenes strung together to indicate a recurring pattern of behavior. An example of this occurs when Ying-Ying sits at her dining room table, waiting for her young husband to return: at first her hair is up and she is well made up, but over the course of several shots the lighting changes and she looks increasingly unkempt, indicating that she has waited in one spot for him without taking the time to refresh herself.

---

pregnant, and she devises a plan. She slashes her clothes, screams, and races out to tell the family that their ancestors have given her a warning,

telling her that the servant girl is pregnant with Tyan Yu's child, as she is his rightful wife. They look at the evidence, involving a mole on his back

that looks like the one on the ancestor's face in a painting and the fact that Lindo appears to be losing her teeth, and decide to send her away with money, so that Tyan Yu can marry the servant girl properly.

The story returns to the modern day, where Lindo is shaken out of her reverie by a phone call from her daughter, Waverly. She and Waverly argue and then meet at a beauty parlor, where Waverly's thoughts dissolve into memories of her childhood, when she was a famous chess prodigy. The soundtrack plays the Chiffons' 1963 hit song "One Fine Day" as young Waverly and Lindo walk through San Francisco. They have a copy of *Life* magazine featuring Waverly on the cover, comparing her to Bobby Fischer. Waverly is embarrassed by the way Lindo brags to people about her fame, and she tells her mother so. She runs off down the street. Returning home hours later, she sweeps her table clear of chess pieces, but her mother visibly ignores her. In a voice-over, Waverly explains that her mother never spoke about her decision to quit playing. When she decides to play again after ten months, her mother does not support her, saying that she always takes

the easy way out of things. She begins playing again but is no longer unbeatable.

Waverly explains in a voice-over that she married a Chinese man, who is not seen in the film. She has a daughter from that marriage. After that marriage failed, she dated and became engaged to Rich, a Caucasian man. In flashback, she recalls the disdain her mother showed for an expensive fur coat he gave Waverly. She recalls how he inadvertently insulted Lindo at a party by agreeing with her own humble assessment of her cooking. At the salon, Lindo reflects that Waverly is ashamed to be her daughter, while she herself wanted as a child to be like her mother. In a sepia-toned flashback, she recalls her mother combing her hair. Back in the present, she explains to Waverly that she actually does like Rich. They laugh. The scene returns to the Joy Luck Club, where Rich, now married to Waverly, is trying, unsuccessfully, to eat with chopsticks.

Ying-Ying St. Clair remembers being a sixteen-year-old girl in China and meeting a handsome man who courted her, had sex with her after a dance, and married her when she had a child. After they married, she watched him flirt with other women. One day he did not come home for supper; a montage shows her sitting at the table, waiting, for two days, until he finally comes in with the opera singer identified in a previous scene, explaining to her that Ying-Ying is a whore, "just like you." He lifts up his son with pride. When he tries to hand the infant to the other woman, Ying-Ying races forward protectively, and he throws her to the ground. She threatens to attack him with a shard of glass and finds that she cannot. Later, while bathing the baby, she reflects that the child is the only thing her husband cares about, and so she lets the baby slip into the water and drown. In Tan's novel, instead of this incident, she has an abortion performed before the baby's birth. By changing it to the killing of an infant, the film heightens the psychological trauma Ying-Ying is undergoing; this tactic also avoids the political controversy that would result from any mention of abortion in a commercial film.

Years later, Ying-Ying is remarried and living in America. She has a daughter, Lena, but she sits in a daze, having given up her spirit. In a voice-over, Lena explains that her mother gradually became better. The story shifts to Lena's life. She lives with her husband, Harold Livotny, in a tasteful but aesthetically sterile house. Harold insists on splitting bills down the middle, even though he makes seven-and-a-half times what Lena makes, working at his firm. They are in a dispute over who should pay to exterminate the cat's fleas when Ying-Ying comes to visit. Their dispute intensifies when Ying-Ying notes that there is an entry for ice cream on the list of expenses they are to share, even though Lena has not eaten ice cream since she was a child. (In the novel, Lena's aversion to ice cream is linked to eating massive quantities in guilt after wishing ill on a boy who died, but the film links it to a time she ate ice cream and liver.) When she hears a vase smash in her mother's room, Lena knows that it is on purpose, and she knows that she needs to demand that Harold give her the respect she deserves. A close-up of the vase is followed by a montage of Ying-Ying's disastrous first marriage.

At the Joy Luck Club, June tucks in Jennifer, the daughter of Rose Hsu Jordan, telling her the story of the swan feather that started the film, while Rose looks on. At the mahjong table, the camera closes in on Rose's mother, An-Mei, leading to a flashback of her childhood in China. The flashback begins with raised voices as her mother returns to the house where An-Mei was raised by relatives. She has been gone, living as a concubine, the fourth wife of a rich man, and has been shunned by her

family for abandoning her daughter. As they berate her, An-Mei's mother takes a knife to her own arm, while An-Mei's voice-over explains that the most dutiful daughter of the family would traditionally put a piece of her own flesh into soup to be served to a sick elder. After her mother's death, An-Mei's mother prepares to leave alone, but young An-Mei races forward, insisting that she will join her.

In the present, An-Mei sees Rose preparing a chocolate peanut butter pie for her meeting with Ted Jordan, the father of her daughter, during which they are to finalize their divorce agreement. Rose recalls her courtship with Ted. She met him in college, she says in a voice-over, and was surprised that someone from such a wealthy family would be interested in her. At a party, his mother insults Rose, feeling that an Asian wife would hinder Ted's business plans, and Ted stands up for her. They married soon after, she explains, and as the years passed he became a business success, but she lost her independence. She recalls that he tried to understand her distress, but eventually he entered into an affair, and so they split. Her mother warns her that the pie she is making for their divorce meeting is not the right way to assert her independence.

The story returns to An-Mei's past. Living with her mother in the house of the rich man, Wu Tsing, she sees that her mother did not leave her for a glamorous life. Her mother is treated badly as the fourth wife, worse than the first three, especially since the second one has the man's son. She explains how her mother came to be a concubine. She was a widow when the second wife invited her to the home to play mahjong. She stayed overnight, and the rich man came to her room and raped her. Her family would not believe she was raped, and, pregnant and homeless, she went back to the man's house. The second wife took the son she bore, and with it, An-Mei's reputation. Soon after telling her all this, An-Mei's mother killed herself with an opium overdose, and at her funeral service An-Mei stands up to the rich man and his remaining wives. After An-Mei tells this story to Rose, Rose stands up to Ted, waiting for him in the rain, shouting at him that he cannot take her house or her daughter from him.

At a dinner at the Woo apartment in the present day, an argument begins between June and Waverly, who does not want to publish some advertising copy June wrote. Their raised voices are cut off by Old Chong, the deaf piano teacher, who plays June's old piano in the next room. June remembers apologizing to her mother for being a disappointment, and her mother tells her that June gave her hope. She tells June the story of the abandoned twin sisters. Her mother was a refugee, fleeing the war, pushing her two daughters in a wheelbarrow, but she was sick and barely able to walk. Knowing that no one would take the girls if they were found beside a corpse, she left them at the side of the road, with all of her worldly possessions and a note that there would be more if the finder would get them to their father. Later, June's father, Canning Woo, gives her the white swan feather and tells June that she was indeed her mother's hope.

June arrives in China and is met at the dock by her two middle-aged sisters. She explains that their mother has died, though the "aunties," the women of the Joy Luck Club, wrote to them pretending to be their mother. They are all sad, but June is also thankful to have finally done something for her mother in being the one to reunite her family.

CHARACTERS

Old Chong

When June is a child, she takes piano lessons from Old Chong. She does not take her lessons seriously. He is mostly deaf, which gives her an opportunity to slack off if she feels like it, which leads to her disastrous recital performance. Later, when June is grown up, Old Chong is at a Chinese New Year's party and June and Waverly are on the verge of openly fighting, he starts playing the piano in the next room.

An-Mei Hsu

An-Mei is one of the founders of the Joy Luck Club. As a child, she was raised by her grandmother. When her grandmother was dying, her mother came to see her. The entire family rejected the mother because she had become a concubine for a rich man, and she had abandoned her daughter to live with him and his other wives. An-Mei witnessed her mother's devotion to the family that spurned her when she watched her mother use a knife to slice a piece of her own skin from her arm, to make a soup to help the dying grandmother.

After her grandmother's death, An-Mei insisted on going with her mother when she left. At the house of Wu Tsing, she sees that her mother is not living in luxury, as her family thinks she is. She is treated poorly by the other wives, especially Wu Tsing's second wife, who has a son. The second wife takes a string of pearls off her neck and gives them to An-Mei, over her mother's objections. Her mother smashes the pearls with a heavy cup, showing that they are just plaster.

Eventually, An-Mei finds out the real story: her mother became pregnant when she was raped by Wu Tsing, but her family turned her away because they did not believe that he had forced himself on her. She went to his house out of desperation, where the second wife took the newborn son from her. Having told An-Mei the truth, her mother commits suicide. As her mother lies in state, An-Mei, a previously quiet child, raised her voice, forcing Wu Tsing to vow to raise her brother and her as his honored children and to honor her mother's memory. She tells this story to her daughter, so that her daughter will not be subservient to her own rich husband and will stand up for what she wants.

Lindo Jong

Lindo is one of the women who founded the Joy Luck Club. When she was four years old, her mother entered into a bargain with a matchmaker, so that Lindo would marry the son of a rich family when she was older. Her family moved away when she was fourteen, and Lindo moved into the rich family's home. She did not see the man she was promised to until after they were married. He turned out to be a ten-year-old boy who was interested in tormenting her. He ordered her to sleep on the floor and turned his back on her in bed. When Lindo did not produce a male offspring, as the matchmaker had promised, Lindo is required to stay off her feet at all times, to help the fertilization process. Miserable and treated like a possession, she is able to leave that family only by making up a story about the anger of the family's ancestor, who intended the boy to marry one of the household servants. She is freed of that family and given money to go away to America.

In San Francisco, Lindo's daughter, Waverly, is a young chess prodigy, a fact that Lindo brags about to everyone she meets until, to spite her, Waverly quits playing chess. Lindo does not ask her to play again but waits for her to return to chess in her own time.

As an adult, Waverly sees Lindo as a cold, unforgiving person who is never satisfied. She fears her anger, and she desires her acceptance. She is surprised, therefore, to find out that Lindo, beneath her mask of dispassion, actually does approve of her engagement to Rich.

Waverly Jong

Waverly is the younger generation's most driven personality. She makes a name for herself early as a chess prodigy, feeling absolute confidence and constantly beating her opponents. Feeling the pressure of her mother's pride, though, she quits playing. Rather than pushing her, though, her mother, Lindo, leaves her to make her own mistake. When she decides to return to chess months later, the old confidence is gone, and she is not able to gain it back.

As an adult, Waverly still struggles for her mother's approval. She says in narration that she married her first husband, a man of Chinese descent, to please her mother. Her courtship with her second husband, Rich, is threatened by her fear of her mother's disapproval of him. Rather than stating outright that she is dating a Caucasian man, she drops hints, such as leaving his clothes around her apartment when her mother visits. Rather than saying that he is a good man, she tries to let the fur he gave to her show his generosity, but Lindo is unimpressed. Waverly takes him to her mother's birthday party, and he embarrasses her with his awkwardness about Chinese customs. It is not until Waverly and Lindo are at the hairdresser, preparing for her wedding, that they have an honest talk about Rich, and Waverly finds out that her mother really does like him after all.

Rose Hsu Jordan

Rose Hsu is the daughter of An-Mei. In the film, she recalls her relationship with Ted Jordan, beginning with their first meeting, in college, when he first asked her out: Ted was popular, handsome, and from a wealthy family, and Rose was amazed that he would be interested in her. At a party soon after, she finds herself thrilled to hear him refer to her as his girlfriend. At another party, Ted's mother takes her aside to warn her that his association with her could hurt his career, bizarrely citing the unpopularity of the Vietnam war, but Ted overhears and becomes even more supportive of Rose. They marry soon after.

Throughout their marriage and after the birth of their daughter, Rose becomes increasingly insignificant. Wang illustrates this in a scene at a party, when Ted spills his drink and Rose drops to her knees to wipe the floor, with just a vague glint in her eye of what is wrong with her behavior. Eventually, she finds out that Ted is having an affair, and they decide to divorce.

When An-Mei finds out that Rose is preparing Ted's favorite pie, the one she made for their first date, to take to the divorce meeting, she tells Rose about the man who raped her mother and then drove her to suicide, and how the experience of Rose's grandmother made An-Mei find her own voice and stand up for herself. Her story makes Rose defiant against Ted in the divorce proceedings.

Ted Jordan

Ted comes from a wealthy family, and, despite his mother's protestations, he falls in love with Rose Hsu and marries her. Throughout their marriage, though, he cannot get her to express herself. In one scene, he tells her that he wants her to make decisions for herself and not just repeat what she thinks he wants, but she finds herself unable to do that. Ted later enters into an affair, which destroys their marriage. When he arrives to discuss the divorce terms and finds Rose sitting in the rain, insistent that she will not give up her house or her daughter, he is perplexed by her behavior.

Harold Livotny

Harold is the husband of Lena St. Clair. Amy Tan's novel explains how Lena helped him further his career, encouraging him to leave a firm where they both worked to start his own firm; she went with him and helped him build a thriving business. Harold and Lena keep a list on the refrigerator of things that they have bought that are considered household expenses, though Lena's mother makes her see that Harold is unfair in listing ice cream, which Lena has not touched since childhood. This shows two things about Harold, his pettiness and his lack of attention to Lena.

Rich

Rich is the boyfriend of Waverly Jong. He is presented as one of the few positive male figures in the film. He serves as a form of comic relief. Rich is eager to impress Waverly's mother, Lindo, by embracing Chinese culture. He tries to eat with chopsticks and drops his food on his lap. He brings a bottle of wine to her birthday dinner but, in a breach of etiquette, drinks two glasses. He agrees with her assessment about her cooking, failing to realize that she was only being modest. Despite Waverly's fears, Lindo can see through this awkwardness to Rich's true good nature.

Lena St. Clair

Lena is the daughter of Ying-Ying, whose experience in China is mirrored in her own life in America. In China, her mother was involved in an abusive relationship with a brutal man who beat and neglected her. Lena's outward circumstances seem much better: Her husband, Harold, employs her at the advertising firm he owns and he has a stable home with her. The similarity with her mother's situation, which Lena does not see until late in the film, is that her husband is a controlling person. At Harold's suggestion, they split the bills, even though he makes more than seven times her salary. In voice-over narration, Lena makes it clear that this arrangement was fine with her for most of her life. When her mother comes to visit, though, she sees her marriage through Ying-Ying's eyes, which makes her realize that Harold does not love her the way she thinks he should.

Ying-Ying St. Clair

Ying-Ying is one of the founders of the Joy Luck Club. In China, she had been married to a cruel, abusive man. She had a child with him, but after his son was born he lost interest in her. He stayed away for days at a time, and one day he showed up at their home with a date, an opera singer. He referred to both the singer and Ying-Ying herself as prostitutes. (In the novel, Amy Tan explains that he left Ying-Ying for this singer.) When she realized that she did not have the will to attack him as he insulted her, she felt terrible, until a dreadful idea came into her mind as she gave their son a bath one day. Realizing that that boy was the only thing that her husband cared about, Ying-Ying let him slip down into the water and watched him drown.

When she is old, Ying-Ying goes to visit with her daughter Lena and Lena's husband, Harold. Harold is a successful businessman, but Ying-Ying recognizes traits in him that remind her of her own controlling husband. She disapproves of the way Lena is expected to share half of the living expenses. At first, her attitude is taken to just be a sign of her old-fashioned view of the world, but eventually Lena comes to view her life differently, through Ying-Ying's eyes. At that point, she stands up to Harold, telling him that she should not be taken for granted.

Wu Tsing

Wu Tsing is the rich man who rapes An-Mei Hsu's mother. When she is pregnant and her family rejects her, he takes her into his house as his fourth wife. After his abuse drives her to suicide, young An-Mei insists that he treat her and her young brother as his honored children, and, with the New Year's celebration days away, he agrees.

Canning Woo

Canning is June Woo's father. He is a widower of four months, trying to acclimate himself to his new life. He has trouble finding things around the house, imagining that his late wife, Suyuan, "hides" things. Canning is important in a scene near the end of the film, when he gives June the swan feather that her mother brought from China and explains to her how proud her mother was of her.

Jing-Mei "June" Woo

June Woo is the story's protagonist. At the party that begins the film, June explains that her mother has died recently and that the three surviving members of the original Joy Luck Club have invited her to join their regular mahjong game in her mother's place. It is during this game that she finds out that the twin sisters that her mother told her were abandoned in China are still alive. As the evening progresses, she finds that the women have arranged a trip to China for her to see her sisters, who do not know that their mother is dead. June's trip to China at the end of the film gives her the closure that she has been lacking since her mother's death.

June's relationship with her mother was a complicated one. The film shows one particularly powerful episode in her childhood, when she studied piano with little interest and took her ability to play for granted, only to perform poorly in a recital, embarrassing herself and her mother. For most of her life, she felt that her mother felt let down by her. She spends her life feeling that her mother's hope for her is a crippling burden. It is only at the end, when her father gives her the swan feather that her mother brought from China, that she realizes that her mother was sincere in her claim that June represented for her the hope that had died when she left the twin infants by the side of the road to die.

June has a competitive relationship with Waverly Jong. In the first scene, as the characters are being established, they exchange a look of mutual suspicion. As young June fails at her piano recital, Waverly, who is nationally famous as a chess master, beams. Later in the film, at a New Year celebration when her mother is still alive, Waverly brings up her truncated piano career, which June characterizes as "sneaky." An argument ensues about some ad copy she had done for Waverly's firm, which Waverly had rejected. They later mend their differences as June's self-esteem grows.

Suyuan Woo

This story takes place four months after the death of Suyuan, who was one of the founding members of the Joy Luck Club. The script is focused around the ambiguous feelings that her daughter, June, has about her relationship with her late mother. June knows that Suyuan had two children early in life and that she abandoned them in 1949 while fleeing from the Japanese army. June does not know, however, until the night of the party that is the focus of this film, that the daughters have been located in China. Suyuan's friends have written to them but have found themselves unable to admit that Suyuan is dead.

The infant daughters who were abandoned during the war are mentioned early, and viewers are left to feel that Suyuan left them to save her own life. Director Wayne Wang does not reveal the circumstances under which Suyuan left her own children on a roadside until late in the film. The film shows her along with the flow of refugees fleeing Kweilin; she is losing her ability to watch over them. Her hands bleed, and the wheelbarrow that she is using to transport the infants bounces in a pothole, falling over and spilling the girls into the road. In a voice-over, June's husband, Canning, is explaining that Suyuan was nearly dead when she left the girls and that she only did so because she thought that they would have a better chance of being picked up strangers if she did not die beside them.

As June comes to understand the abandonment of the twins, her father explains to her that her mother, who was not an emotional woman, had great hope for her.

Tyan Yu

Tyan Yu is the ten-year-old boy whom Lindo Jong was forced to marry when she was a teen, in a marriage that was arranged when she was just four years old and he was not yet born. Despite his mother's insistence that the couple produce a male heir, Tyan Yu has no interest in his bride. He teases her and becomes frightened of her when she presents herself to him naked, shifting to the far side of the bed that they sleep in together every night.

THEMES

Female Identity

All of the main characters in this film are female. In the stories of the older generation of women, men are seldom present, and those who are most conspicuous are there as antagonists. For instance, Suyuan Woo's husband is absent, as he is in Amy Tan's novel—he had gone to fight the Japanese army while Suyuan is left to cope with shuttling their infant daughters to safety. An-Mei Hsu's father is dead, and she is taken from the home of her grandmother, which is inhabited by shadowy, unidentified uncles, to the house of the man who raped her mother and who cares so little about the girl's existence that he does not care whether she is present in the bed while he requires her mother to have sex with him. Lindo Jong is bargained away by her mother to the mother of Tyan Yu, to be kept in a home where the emphasis is on the young boy and his prospect of producing a male child. Ying-Ying St. Clair's husband in China is unspeakably, unreasonably cruel, and as a result she commits the most heinous act possible in a patriarchal society, taking the life of a male infant.

In their daughters' generation, men are more relevant, if only because the United States of the late twentieth century has more gender integration than China in the early part of the century. They are still marginalized, though. Rich, though meaning well, is simply not culturally sensitive enough to understand the offense he gives Lindo by putting soy sauce on her cooking. Ted asks Rose to express her wants, but when she is unable to do so he takes it as license to have an affair. Harold is so blind to Lena that he never notices, in all their years together, that she never eats any of the ice cream he buys and makes her pay for.

There are positive male characters at the Joy Luck Club gatherings and at other parties, but they are given little screen time. This is a film about women's experiences, in which their interactions and rivalries with one another are the focus.

Mother-Child Relationships

A key theme running through this film is the way that the lives of the mothers who founded the Joy Luck Club affect their daughters' lives. Sometimes the connection is intentional, as when An-Mei Hsu demands that her daughter stand up to Ted Jordan in a way that she, as a child, learned to stand up to oppression, having symbolically drawn strength from her mother's suicide after she watched her

READ.
WATCH.
WRITE.

- Watch the film *Not One Less*, released in 1999 by Sony Pictures, about a thirteen-year-old girl who is conscripted to take over as a substitute teacher at a rural Chinese school and the lengths she goes to when one student leaves and she must get him back. Write a short story in which one of the characters from *The Joy Luck Club* accompanies the girl, Wei Minzhi, on her journey to the city, recording the character's observations about modern China.

- Technology has, in some ways, changed the nature of relationships, making it less likely that June Woo's life would be such a mystery to her half-sisters, and theirs to her, when she departed from the boat to meet them at the end of the film. Design a page for June like one that would appear on Facebook or some similar social networking page. Include as much information about her as you can find from the film.

- Some critics have taken exception with the ways that male characters are presented in *The Joy Luck Club*. Watch the film carefully, taking note of the male characters mentioned and whether you think they are portrayed fairly. Create a chart that lists the characterizations of the male characters and lead a class discussion about whether or not the positives outweigh the negatives.

- Research the life of children playing chess internationally now. Compile a list of videos of current grandmasters and view them beside the video of young Waverly playing chess in her two scenes in this film (both when she is winning and when she is losing). Write a persuasive essay that explains whether you think director Wayne Wang captured the look of the chess prodigy accurately.

- Academy Award-winning scriptwriter Ronald Bass wrote the screenplay for this film with the novel's author, Amy Tan. Bass also wrote the screenplay for *How Stella Got Her Groove Back* with Terry McMillan, the author of the novel from which that film was adapted. Watch both films and choose one scene from each that you think might display Bass's writing style. Show them together and explain why you think they are Bass's invention. Create a multimedia presentation that includes film clips along with analysis.

- In this film, Suyuan Woo's legacy to her daughter is the white swan feather that she kept from the time of her immigration to the United States and meant to give to her someday. Identify an object that each of the other original members of the Joy Luck Club— Ying-Ying St. Clair, Lindo Jong, and An-Mei Hsu—might save to give her daughter, and write an explanation about why these objects would be so important. They can be items mentioned in their stories, or, like the swan feather, things that do not become significant within the film's story.

- In Tan's novel, there is an extended segment about a trip to the beach with the Hsu family, during which Rose's youngest brother, Bing, is lost at sea. Read that segment and then storyboard it (create a series of drawings showing the important moments) so that it could be filmed in the style used in this movie.

- Oliver Stone produced this film. The same year it was released, Stone directed *Heaven and Earth*, much of which was filmed in Thailand. Watch that film and write a paper noting how this film would have been different if Stone had not hired Wayne Wang to direct *The Joy Luck Club* but had instead directed it himself.

---

mother's family, her husband, and her husband's other wives destroy the woman's life. Sometimes the relationship between the mother's life and the daughter's is unstated, though it is still clear. For instance, the son whom Ying-Ying allowed to drown is never mentioned, but the fact that she

© *United Archives | GmbH | Alamy*

committed such a terrible act shows the desperation of her life under the control of a domineering man, which motivates her to speak up when she sees Lena falling into the same sort of relationship. Viewers are also left to draw their own conclusions about the connection between Waverly Jong's success as a chess player and businesswoman and her mother's ability to cleverly uphold the marriage pact that her parents signed for her, and then to get out of it.

The film is shaped around June's struggle to regain her equilibrium after the death of her mother. Like the other younger women, she has trouble understanding her mother, and there is some hostility between them as she is growing up, but it is clear that she does miss her mother. The white swan feather, described in the prelude and shown during the credits, comes back later in the film, when June's father gives it to her and explains that her mother meant her to have it; this gives it the significance in her life that it has in the film. She goes to China in her mother's place, much as she sits at the mahjong table in her mother's place. Whereas the film ends with June reflecting that she has found her family, the novel ends with her

reflecting on how much she and her sisters look like their mother, Suyuan. Both endings indicate that completion is found, for June, through connecting with her mother.

Immigrant Life

The Joy Luck Club is about Chinese immigrants living in San Francisco, but many of the social interactions in the film apply equally to the immigrant experience anywhere. The lives of the film's main characters come together at meetings of the club in the film's title. The novel explains that the club was conceived by Suyuan Woo while she was fleeing the Japanese army, as a way of giving the refugee women she was with a sense of solidarity, regardless of their social class. In San Francisco, the club has the same effect. It is common and natural that immigrants would be likely to seek out those from their homelands, people who share cultural experiences, worldviews, and language.

In particular, the social gatherings in the film all center around food. The Joy Luck Club meetings include the backroom mahjong game that was their original purpose, but that is just a part of the event, along with eating. Several dinners are shown throughout the film. Food is a common element in the lives of many immigrants. For one thing, food is a comforting factor that is often associated with home and family. For another, immigrants often approach food preparation as a challenge: working with the ingredients that are available in their new homes, even the foods they prepare according to familiar recipes are not as they remember them.

The film has little to say about the difficulties that face immigrants. There is only one direct conflict from the mainstream culture, coming when Rose is confronted by Ted Jordan's mother. The mother is not overtly hostile, pretending that her dislike for Rose is not based on racial prejudice, but she gives herself away when she equates Rose, an American of Chinese descent, with the Vietnam War. When Rose points out that she has nothing to do with Vietnam, the mother nods and says that she understands, though she clearly does not understand at all. The one time the film openly addresses the difficulty of being in a minority group, it plays what could be a tense situation as a sad joke.

STYLE

Muted Visual Tone

The Joy Luck Club is filmed with muted, "cool" colors. Many scenes occur at night, or indoors, although even the scenes that occur outside during the day are softened to match the tone of the indoor scenes. The sets are designed primarily with pastel colors or with low-key browns and greens. Red appears frequently because it is often used in Chinese clothing and decorations, but even the fieriest red is photographed in ways that suppress its power. The visual tone matches the calm, even tone of the voices of the old women as they narrate the stories of their lives from long ago.

Language and Subtitles

Most of the dialogue in this film is spoken in English, even in the scenes that take place in China, among Chinese characters. This is altered at times, however, with dialogue spoken in Mandarin or Cantonese, with English subtitles. Wang's decision to use authentic language in some places, such as in Lindo Jong's and Ying-Ying St. Clair's childhood stories, gives these segments an air of authenticity. He could have used more Chinese, for the Chinese people living in San Francisco, for instance. Doing so would have been a risk for the filmmakers: this film was made primarily for audiences in the United States, and including too much foreign language would alienate large segments of the audience, who would be resistant to reading subtitles. Wang weaves samples of Chinese into the film to satisfy viewers of Chinese and Chinese American backgrounds, but he avoids making it a film that is predominately Chinese.

Narration

Films often use some voice-over narration to clarify points of the plot that are not clear from the action that is presented on screen. In *The Joy Luck Club*, the use of narration is frequent. One reason for this is that the stories that are told in Amy Tan's novel are all told from a first-person perspective—that is, using "I." Readers of the novel know what is going on inside the heads of eight different characters, which is difficult to show in a film without having characters make extended speeches about how they feel. By having the characters talk about events and then showing them in brief scenes, Tan and fellow screenwriter Ronald Bass are able to capture much of the internal thoughts of people who are not very expressive. Another reason so much narration works well in this film is that it enables the actresses to capture with their voices the personal tone that made the novel so popular.

CULTURAL CONTEXT

The Second Sino-Japanese War

Early in this film, Suyuan refers to fleeing Kweilin from the invading Japanese army. The incursion she is referring to is the Second Sino-Japanese War. After the brief first war, in 1894–1895, there had been an uneasy peace between the two countries. In 1931, this peace was broken when a Japanese captain was caught in Chinese territory on a mysterious undercover mission and then executed. Later that year, the Manchurian railway was attacked; though the railway was controlled by Japanese, historians often speculate that the attack was perpetrated by the Japanese army as an excuse to invade Chinese-controlled and mineral-rich Manchuria. Outright war was quickly halted, with the intervention of the League of Nations, but there were several events that brought both countries to the brink of war over the coming years. Wide-scale conflict was avoided until 1937, when the Japanese attacked the Marco

Polo Bridge outside of Peking. Fighting broke out throughout western China. Nearly twenty million Chinese civilians were killed in the ensuing war.

When the United States entered World War II after the bombing of Pearl Harbor in December of 1941, the outcome of the war was a foregone conclusion. There were slim odds that Japan could hold up against China, the United States, and the European Allies. After the nuclear bombs that destroyed Hiroshima and Nagasaki in August of 1945, Japan surrendered to the Allied Military Command, which ordered the country to withdraw all of its troops from China immediately.

Communist China

Before the war with Japan united the country against a common enemy, there had already been a struggle for control of China between the Chinese Nationalist Party (the Kuomintang) and the Communist Party of China, which received training and material support from the Soviet Union. Though fighting between the two forces was minimal while China was embroiled in the Japanese conflict, it broke out in full force at the end of World War II. After four years, the Communist Party of China,

led by Mao Zedong, declared victory, claiming the expansive mainland as the People's Republic of China and relegating the Kuomintang to leadership over the tiny island of Taiwan. Under the new government, land was taken away from those who owned it and redistributed to peasant farmers. The government tried various programs to bring the economy around to a functioning socialist program, including the Great Leap Forward (1958–1963), which established rural communes that proved incapable of coping with famines that ravaged the land, and the Cultural Revolution (1966–1976), in which the government tried to maintain control of the country by regulating all aspects of Chinese culture. Religious practices were outlawed, reproduction was limited, and free speech was curtailed. During these years, China closed itself off to the outside world: for instance, it is estimated that in 1964 there were only five hundred foreigners living in China, which came to one per one million Chinese people. President Richard Nixon's state visit to China in 1972 was considered a major breakthrough toward beginning tenuous relations, introducing opening the planet's most populous society to the rest of the world, but still the Chinese government worked to maintain strict control. After Mao's death in 1976, the government tried and executed four party functionaries, dubbed the Gang of Four, who attempted to take over in a government coup and were subsequently accused of causing the excesses of the Cultural Revolution, showing that things were moving in a new direction.

In 1989, the year that Amy Tan published *The Joy Luck Club*, the Chinese government's repressive nature came to the attention of the international community with the crackdown on protesters at Tiananmen Square. The protest at the square grew out of a gathering meant to mourn the recent death of a pro-reform politician, Hu Yaobang. As members of different political factions came to Beijing, a social cause developed. Eventually, more than a hundred thousand people had gathered at the square. Rather than allowing them to flaunt their opposition to the government, a decision was made to disperse the crowd. Tanks were sent in, and shots were fired, and hundreds of people were killed. The government went on to arrest thousands of dissidents across the country, but the actions against unarmed, peaceful protestors were seen across the world, raising awareness of the Chinese government's repressive techniques, defining Chinese society for a generation of the world's citizens.

CRITICAL OVERVIEW

Critics were surprised in 1993 when director Wayne Wang delivered an emotional, crowd-pleasing story with his adaptation of Amy Tan's novel. Wang had previously been the director of a few well-respected low-budget films, including the mystery *Chan Is Missing* and the immigrant comedy *Dim Sum: A Little Bit of Heart*. Most agree that the film *The Joy Luck Club* was heavy on sentimentality. An unsigned review in *Newsweek* uses the phrase "a four-hankie classic" in its title and warns viewers to "get ready to cry yourself a river." In *Time* magazine, Richard Corliss expands on the same theme, saying that "the typhoon of emotions makes this an eight-handkerchief movie. Bring four for the mothers, four for the daughters when they realize what brave resolve is hidden in an old woman's stern love." The *Newsweek* reviewer admits that the film is "melodramatic" and "manipulative" but notes that Wang and his screenwriters, Tan and Bass, "have come up with a shamelessly irresistible tale." Roger Ebert agreed, giving the movie a four-star review in the *Chicago*

Sun-Times and calling it "one of the most touching and moving of the year's films."

Some critics approved of elements of the film while disapproving of the film overall. John Simon, writing in the *National Review*, notes that "most of the performances are extremely appealing, and some of the humor provides welcome leavening," but Simon undercuts his praise with the next sentence: "Yet even the humor tends to leave a sudsy taste in your mouth." Overall, Simon's review focuses on what he calls the film's "intertwined miseries": "Tears of joy proliferate nevertheless, and the movie ends awash in liquid sentiment." He feels that the complex structure of Tan's book was doomed to fail in the adaptation, explaining that "however this might work in the wider scope and statelier pace of the novel, a movie—even a two-and-a-half-hour one—cannot bear this much freight."

Michael Sragow was even more blunt about the film's sentimental style when he wrote his review for the *New Yorker*. He faults the screenwriters for trying "to cram all of [the novel's] mininarratives into the script, diminishing instead of enlarging them." The contemporary scenes seemed to Sragow "pat or trite," while "the flashbacks to the mothers' woeful lives in China seem overblown or empty and portentous." "By the end," he says, "the filmmakers just about beg for tears."

Still, a majority of critics were inclined to focus on the film as a moving look at a particular subculture, as Deeson Howe does in a *Washington Post* review that notes that the film "gives refreshing—and bittersweet—dimension to the age-old clash between generations."

CRITICISM

David Kelly

Kelly is a writer and an instructor of creative writing and literature at two colleges. In the following essay, he examines the way director Wayne Wang weaves the many stories in The Joy Luck Club *together with the subtle use of camera work to frequently change the film's point of view.*

In adapting Amy Tan's *The Joy Luck Club* to film, Tan and writer Ronald Bass were faced with the uneasy prospect of weaving the various stories of a range of characters into one coherent narrative, or story. Their problem grew out of basic differences between film and text. For one thing,

WHAT DO I SEE NEXT?

- In 2007, the Public Broadcasting System released its acclaimed series *China from the Inside* in a three-disk DVD collection. This series examines modern China from a Western perspective. Episodes include a historical look at the Communist party's rule in "Power and the People" and an examination of the lives of women in rural areas in "Women and the Country."

- Director Justin Lin examines the stereotypes that face contemporary Asian high school students in his 2002 film *Better Luck Tomorrow*, about a high achiever (played by Parry Shen) who finds himself drawn into a life of crime. This highly acclaimed film is available on DVD from Paramount.

- In 1989, Wayne Wang directed *Eat a Bowl of Tea*, a comedy about mostly male Chinese immigrants in the 1940s, dealing with government restrictions that keep their loved ones back in the old country while they try to make a life for themselves in New York. The film is based on a novel by Louis Chu and written by Chu and Judith Rascoe. Sony Pictures released the DVD in 2003.

- The year before *The Joy Luck Club* was released, Steven Zaillian directed *Searching for Bobby Fischer*, about a seven-year-old boy who is compared, like Waverly Jong in this film, to the great chess prodigy who came to prominence in the 1950s. Starring Ben Kingsley and Joe Mantegna, it was released on DVD by Paramount in 2000.

- The same year *The Joy Luck Club* was released, acclaimed director Ang Lee released *The Wedding Banquet*, a comedy about a gay man living in New York who plans to marry a woman from mainland China to hide his sexual orientation, only to find his plans complicated when his parents arrive from Taiwan to take charge of his wedding. The film won Golden Globe and Academy Awards, both

for Best Foreign Language Film, and the Golden Bear Award at the Berlin International Film Festival. Metro-Goldwyn-Mayer (MGM) released it on DVD in 2004.

- The film *Like Water for Chocolate*, released in theaters in 1992 and on DVD in 2000 by Walt Disney Studios, is a comedy using magical realism, a type of storytelling in which fantastic elements are worked into a realistic setting. It follows the struggles of a Mexican woman, forbidden by her strict parents to marry the man she loves, who uses her culinary skills to express her passions.

- The film *Raise the Red Lantern* is a historical drama produced in China, concerning an educated woman in the 1920s who is forced to leave college to become the fourth wife of a brutal landowner. Directed by Yimou Zhang and starring international film star Li Gong, it was first released in 1991 and then released on DVD by MGM in 2007. The film is in Mandarin Chinese but is available with English subtitles.

- The film version of Whitney Otto's novel *How to Make an American Quilt* shows the same sorts of intergenerational relationships among women that are shown in Wang's movie. The plot concerns a graduate student and the members of her grandmother's quilting circle, who meddle in her love life. This popular American comedy stars Winona Ryder, Ellen Burstyn, Anne Bancroft, and the poet Maya Angelou. The DVD was released by Universal in 1999.

- The kind of extended family displayed in *The Joy Luck Club* is at the center of director Mira Nair's *Monsoon Wedding*, which offers the story of members of contemporary Indian society dealing with a traditional arranged marriage. The winner of numerous international awards, it was released on DVD by Universal in 2002.

> AUDIENCES UNDERSTAND FROM CINEMA
> TRADITION THAT THIS KIND OF CLOSE-UP, COMBINED
> WITH THE VOICE-OVER, TAKES THEM INTO
> LINDO'S MIND, AND THEY ARE READY TO TRAVEL
> WITH HER WHEREVER HER MIND GOES."

audiences have different expectations for films than they do for novels. In films, a certain degree of continuity is expected. A scene might just fade to black, the way a chapter in a novel ends, picking up immediately with another character in a different time frame, but the connection between the two has to become clear. Switching the narrative abruptly more than two or three times throughout a film will leave audiences confused and disoriented, which is not acceptable in a mass-market film aiming for broad distribution, like *The Joy Luck Club*. That problem results from a more basic difference between the two media: films are presented in linear time, playing out for their audiences minute-by-minute over the course of their two- or three-hour running times.

In recent decades, evolving technology has given viewers a chance to interact with films: pausing, rewinding, or even watching scenes in a different order than the way the film was originally presented. For some movies, several versions may be released at once, with different levels of sexual or violent content; it is not difficult to imagine that someday different versions will be available that reflect the different levels of cinema literacy of their audiences. Complex plot lines may be smoothed out for release to younger audiences, with the full version available for more sophisticated audiences. These options, though, do not change the basic nature of a film, which is that of a linear sequence of sights and sounds. Over the past century or so, moviegoers have learned to expect films to follow rules of continuity, showing a clear relationship between one scene and the one that follows it.

One way that scriptwriters meld scenes together is with the use of voice-over narration. Narration is the core of a novel writer's style, allowing a character in the story or a third-person narrator to comment on what is going on and to summarize what happened between scenes.

Narrative summary can use broad generalizations, defying a film's visual way of telling a story. Films generally ask their viewers to take their understanding of the story from what is presented before their eyes, not from abstract ideas presented in words.

In film, the use of narration is often considered cheating, a last-ditch effort to convey information that absolutely cannot be conveyed through dialog between the characters or through images. Great films can use narration, but good screenwriters know that narration is a diversion from the flow of their story, to be used as seldom as possible.

There is ample necessity for using narration in *The Joy Luck Club*. Tan's novel is not one person's continuous story, but rather the story of eight main characters and at least that many supporting characters. These stories take place in China and California across different times. Simply telling one story after another would make the film seem like an anthology that simply looks at the lives of certain people who fit into one cultural demographic. This problem is not one that can be solved by having each character narrate her own story: such a solution would still create the effect of a group of unrelated stories.

Voice-over can be a distracting interruption when used too much, but *The Joy Luck Club* manages to use it successfully. Director Wayne Wang's camera work uses just the right, light touch for taking viewers into the heads of his characters without drawing attention to itself. Once inside a character's head, Wang is able to travel through time and space to places that character has been to or heard about.

The first instance of this in the film is also the simplest, but it sets the pattern for what is to come. During the film's real time—that is, during the meeting of the Joy Luck Club of the title, filling the apartment of June's widowed father—June narrates the background information about the club and her mother's recent death. Wang introduces the flashback idea when June wanders over by the piano, and one of the older women asks her whether she is interested in taking the piano back to her own home. As June contemplates the question, the image of her as a young girl, practicing the piano, takes over the screen. Using an object, such as the piano here, to trigger a memory is a common cinematic and literary device, and viewers can be expected to understand the connection between June the adult and June the child, especially since the child is immediately called "June" in the flashback.

A few minutes later, though, Wang complicates the story. June's flashback progresses to a point where she and her mother are arguing, and June the child blurts out that she wishes she were dead, "like them." This leads to a scene of her mother, Suyuan, pushing her infant daughters in a wheelbarrow as they flee the war in China, back in the 1940s. The images are from June's mother's life, but the voice-over on the soundtrack is still June's, indicating that June is imagining a scene from her mother's life. June recalls hearing about her missing half-sisters at a church picnic a few months earlier, and that scene is shown, in a sort of stopover, before returning the film to the present time and the gathering at the Woo apartment.

The pattern continues and expands throughout the film. During one of the usual conversations that buzz around the background of a party, Lindo Jong hears someone speculate about what it must have been like for Suyuan's infant daughters to lose their mother at such a young age; that comment sends her on her own mental journey. As the thoughts in her head play on the soundtrack, the camera closes in on her eyes. Audiences understand from cinema tradition that this kind of close-up, combined with the voice-over, takes them into Lindo's mind, and they are ready to travel with her wherever her mind goes. In this case, it takes the viewer to the time when she was four and was promised in wedlock to a rich boy's family. The film follows Lindo's story for several years of her maturation. Like June's story, the flashback does not end with a return to the Joy Luck Club party: unlike June's story, however, it jumps forward to a full scene, with dialog, showing Lindo preparing for her daughter's second marriage.

During this scene, Lindo has a phone conversation with her daughter, Waverly, and the film's point of view is handed off. It stays with Waverly after the phone is hung up. She stares at herself in a mirror, and the camera closes in on what she is looking at: her eyes. Wang uses this portal again to now go into Waverly's flashback about her own childhood, when she was a chess prodigy. When that story is told, the film returns to the beauty parlor where it left the adult Waverly: she has one more flashback, about her mother's cool reaction to meeting her fiancé. Lindo joins her at the beauty parlor, and, when the two women reconcile their differences and end up laughing together, the

flashback is over. It is time to return the story to modern day, where the noise of the party rises and the visual image switches to Waverly, smiling at the memory. The flashback that left through Lindo's perspective returns to the party through Waverly's.

Wang's method of time travel is worth noting in one other trip. At the party, Ying-Ying St. Clair listens to the other two surviving women of the older generation as they talk about the tragedy of the babies who were abandoned in China. This time, the trigger is their speculation about the mother, Suyuan, and how difficult it must have been to lose her children. Following the now-familiar pattern, the camera moves toward Ying-Ying's eyes while her thoughts play on the soundtrack: their conversation makes Ying-Ying think that there is in fact something worse than what Suyuan went through, and as she tells the audience that she was young the story of her youth begins. The story continues through her courtship, her husband's brutal behavior, and her terrible decision to drown her own infant son. As before, the film does not return to the present, but to a time that is later than the flashback but preceding the party: Ying-Ying sitting by a window, staring catatonically, traumatized by the drowning, while Lena, a daughter born years later to a different husband, brings her a tray of food. The narration passes then to Lena, who, like Waverly, frets over her mother's seeming disapproval, failing to understand the traumatic past that the film just presented to the viewers. With Lena's voice-over, the story of her relationship with her husband, Harold, and how Ying-Ying helped her recover from it, plays on the screen. Again, the flashback ends when mother and daughter are emotionally united.

In less deft hands, *The Joy Luck Club* would appear to audiences as merely a sequence of loosely related events. In the novel, Tan is able to tie these events together thematically, as part of the female Chinese American experience. The medium of film, however, does not give artists much leeway with such abstract concepts. Adapting these diverse stories for the screen required Wang to make his viewers feel more than just that they are going *to* a character's story; they have to feel that they are going *into* it. Viewers travel within the minds of these characters to past times and places. Wang does this with voice-over, but also with a fluid understanding of how visual images can be used to imply thought.

© *United Archives | GmbH | Alamy*

Source: David Kelly, Critical Essay on *The Joy Luck Club*, in *Novels for Students*, Gale, Cengage Learning, 2011.

Mikel J. Koven

In the following excerpt, Koven examines women's narratives in films such as The Joy Luck Club *from the perspective of a folklorist.*

Marcia Landy, in referring to David Lean's film version of Noël Coward's *Brief Encounter*, notes: "the film does not appear to be talking to or about women. . . . it seems to be an example of a phenomenon described by Claire Johnston of making it appear that the subject is female when in fact the woman is the 'pseudocenter of the filmic discourse'" (228). Landy goes on to describe how this particular film constructs woman as pseudocenter: "she is another instance of the woman whose words never get public expression except through the male text" (228). For Landy, then, the significant factors of legitimacy for "woman's voice" in public is the gender of both the screenwriter and the director, and the latter is further privileged in film studies debates. Landy misreads Johnston, however: Johnston's "pseudocenter of the filmic discourse" refers to a denial of woman

as subject in favor of a "non-male"/other distinction (Johnston 211). Landy takes a radical stand even further than Johnston's: that the text, if controlled by a man, becomes a male text.

Conversely, perhaps Johnston is that radical: Hollywood narrative codes are inherently masculine, and for a woman's voice to be heard requires a radical shift of narrative coding and form.

> Romanticism will not provide us with the necessary tools to construct a women's cinema: our objectification cannot be overcome simply by examining it artistically. It can only be challenged by developing the means to interrogate the male, bourgeois cinema [i.e. Hollywood]. . . . The danger of developing a cinema of non-intervention is that it promotes a passive subjectivity at the expense of analysis. Any revolutionary strategy must challenge the depiction of reality; it is not enough to discuss the oppression of women within the text of the film; the language of the cinema/the depiction of reality must also be interrogated, so that a break between ideology and text is effected. (Johnston 215)

This premise for film studies has two implications: that should a film be directed (or screenplay written) by a man, then it can not be considered a

'WOMEN OFTEN CHOOSE TO TELL STORIES
IN WHICH THEY PLAY A MINOR, PROTOTYPICAL,
OR NO ROLE (VICARIOUS EXPERIENCE), THEREBY
DEFLECTING FOCUS FROM THEMSELVES'… AS SUCH,
THE NARRATIVES THESE WOMEN TELL, UNLIKE
THOSE IN *AMERICAN QUILT*, ARE NOT ABOUT
THEMSELVES; THEY ARE ABOUT THEIR MOTHER'S OR
THEIR OWN SITUATIONS."

female text and furthermore, the entire narrative form of Hollywood narrative cinema is inherently masculine.

Both Landy's and Johnston's position, cited above, could be identified, as E. Ann Kaplan suggests, as anti-essentialist. The processes utilized by theorists such as Johnston and Landy Kaplan describes as follows:

> …these authors contributed several elements central to later work from this perspective, namely (1) the notion…that, to be feminist, a cinema has to be a counter-cinema (the polarity Classical Hollywood Cinema versus the Avant-garde has been a dominant category in feminist film criticism…); (2) the idea, building on Althusser's work, that the realist strategy inevitably embodied oppressive dominant ideology, and thus was not useful as a feminist cinematic strategy; (3) the notion, relying on Freud's twin concepts of voyeurism and fetishism, that the dominant Classical Hollywood cinema is built on a series of three basic "looks," all of which satisfy desires in the male unconscious (161).

To some degree Kaplan disagrees with the anti-essentialist position: "feminist interventions… must prove their validity through their effects rather than through recourse to 'essence'" (169). It is through an essentialist position, then, that the "essence" can be identified.

I believe that the deciding factor of gendered cinema is not to be found in the biological sex of the director (or screenwriter), and that the only way a feminine voice can be heard is by a radical shift in the narrative codes, but in the understanding of the codes of gendered discourse, for example those codes and functions found by folklorists in

women's speech patterns and their communicative codes. A variety of theoretical models have been developed for such analysis, but they have yet to be applied to feature filming practices.

One such approach, and the one I am attempting to apply here, is the mnemonic SPEAKING model developed by Sociolinguist Dell Hymes (Hymes 65). Hymes breaks down a speech event into eight individual aspects: setting, participants, ends, act sequences, keys, instrumentalities, norms and genres. First, Hymes identifies a speech event as "activities, or aspects of activities, that are directly governed by rules or norms for the use of speech" (56). In any film, the speech events can be analyzed along the speaking model, and in this instance I shall be analyzing them as to their fidelity to the observations made regarding (profilmic) women's speech events. But more to the effect, Hymes's model also underlies the tension between the diegetic text (screenplay) and the performed text (movie). Hymes says,

> Many generalizations about rules of speaking will take the form of statements of relationship among components. It is not yet clear that there is any priority to be assigned to particular components in such statements. So far as one can tell at present, any component may be taken as starting point, and the others viewed in relation to it. When individual societies have been well analyzed, hierarchies of precedence among the components will very likely appear and be found to differ from case to case. Such differences in hierarchy of components will then be an important part of the taxonomy of sociolinguistic systems. For one group, rules of speaking will be heavily bound to the setting; for another primarily to participants; for a third, perhaps to topic (66).

In the application of Hymes's model to film, the different components of the speech act, rather than being culturally specific, although I do not doubt that may be a part of it, are predicated upon the different aspects of film authorship, the tension between screenwriter and director. Although the screenwriter controls, or rather presets, many of the diegetic components, and the director controls, or rather adapts these components, only two of the components (keys and instrumentalities), the two components the director has control over inform the performance of the text. "Keys" can be understood to be the tonal and textural qualities of the spoken act, while "instrumentalities" can be understood to be the figures of speech utilized, including, but not limited to, such things as dialect, accent, and idiomatic speech.

The question seems to be "who is the story-teller, the director or the screenwriter?" Film studies privileges the director as the author of a film, working from the auteur theory set up by André Bazin in the 1950s, but folkloristics leaves the question more open. For the folklorist, one must examine both the narrative (diegetic) means, as well as the performative means of the film.

. . . Many of the same dynamics of narration are in operation in the film, *The Joy Luck Club* (Wayne Wang, 1993). This is especially interesting in light of the anti-essentialist position. Should the anti-essentialist feminists be correct in their assertion that only women can tell women's narratives, otherwise women exist as "pseudocenter" of the filmic discourse, then Wang should not be successful at reproducing women's speech acts. But perhaps this is due to the film being based on the novel by Amy Tan, who also wrote the screenplay; and therefore a woman's voice controlled the structure and words used in the narrations, although Wang does bring these aspects to life. Here is the first instance that the issue of who is the story teller, the director or the screenwriter, becomes relevant. This is also the place to introduce the distinction between the diegesis of the narrative and the narrative's performance: the text of the film and the film's performance.

The Joy Luck Club tells the stories of eight women, four sets of mothers and daughters, and their marital relationships. Overall, these stories are dialogues between mother and daughter, about the expectations one has from the other, but taken together they share their narratives with each other, and at the end of each "chapter," the two voices merge into a single duet, a dynamic called "collaborative narration" (Langellier and Peterson 165). This can be seen as an alternative form of the type of mutual support which Kalcik identifies as indicative of woman's forms of talk (5).

Like *American Quilt*, *The Joy Luck Club*'s framing device for its story telling is an intimate setting, almost a familiar one: the respective matriarchs of the families, Lindo, Ying Ying, and An-Mei invite June, the daughter of their deceased best friend, Siu-Yun, to sit in on their Mah-Johng game, a great honor in Chinese-American culture. This comfortable setting is the catalyst for each woman's reverie about her own life and that of her daughter. The narratives follow a strict structure in that there are at least three time periods: the framing device (present), the recent past, and the far past. When the daughters take over their mothers' narratives, they never do so in the present tense, but in the recent past of their mother's story. Again as Baldwin notes, these narratives, although thought aloud, as opposed to spoken aloud, occur in private familiar settings (150). Also like *American Quilt*, these women are actively discouraged by each other to interrupt their play with "chit-chat." "Now is time for play, not talk," says the group's leader, Lindo.

A point that Kalcik makes is that two of the major themes in women's narratives are oppression experiences and self-discovery (4). While *American Quilt*'s narratives deal primarily with documenting women's external experiences, things done to them, *The Joy Luck Club*'s narratives are more thematically linked with Kalcik's schema: June's role as a "weapon of war" in her mother's status war with Lindo, Lindo's arranged marriage to a child, Waverly's constant fear of disappointing her mother Lindo, Yin-yin's abusive marriage, Lina's oppressive marriage, An-Mei's role in her mother's house as the "illegitimate" daughter of a third wife, Rose's disastrous lack of communication with her husband, and finally Siu-Yun's abandonment of her children in China. What Wang and Tan make absolutely clear, the second theme of Kalcik's schema, is that these tragedies are intended, not to evoke emotions of fear and pity in Aristotelian catharsis, but as a means to self-discovery and self-worth. These women narrate these tales, with their daughters, in an effort to share their experiences with each other as a means of support.

Kristin Langellier and Eric Peterson identify the following as a dynamic of women's storytelling, a dynamic which plays out in *The Joy Luck Club*: "Women often choose to tell stories in which they play a minor, prototypical, or no role (vicarious experience), thereby deflecting focus from themselves" (167). As such, the narratives these women tell, unlike those in *American Quilt*, are not about themselves; they are about their mother's or their own situations. The only exception to this rule is Yin-yin's story, but it falls under the "prototypical" categorization: Yin-yin's drowning of her infant son destroyed her own spirit, and therefore she "had none [i.e. no spirit] to give" to her daughter Lina, which is why Lina ended up married to someone as oppressive as Harold. Yin-yin's personal narrative about herself is more an explanation about why this situation evolved than about herself.

The diegesis and the performance of the film share many commonalties of Hymes's SPEAKING model, but the differences begin to highlight the various contributions of director and screenwriter as "author" of the film, specifically the keys and the instrumentalities which are controlled by the film's director. It is s/he who controls the tone which the diegesis is performed and, in the case of film, the cinematic codes utilized to tell the diegesis, or for Hymes, the "forms of speech" (63). It is the control of the cinematic codes which film studies has privileged as the "writing" of cinema, however in the case of *The Joy Luck Club*, Wang's achievement is in his fidelity to the keys and instrumentalities of Tan's novel; in effect, Wang has appropriated a feminine voice in order to perform this feminine narrative.

Even Tan's use of the act sequences and norms, the structural ordering of spoken acts (i.e. dialogical, monological, collaborative narration, etc.) and the culturally defined expectations of such acts, and Wang's appropriation of them, is less aligned to the Classical Hollywood structure of narrative. The closest thing to an enigma that the film has is whether or not June will ever understand her mother, and that is resolved, but it is resolved by June becoming a surrogate for Siu-Yun with her twin sisters left behind in China. "Resolution" in this narrative is the fusion between daughter and mother into a single unified "self," June. According to the studies published on women's speech acts, this discovery of the self is more indicative of "women's reality." Structurally speaking, *The Joy Luck Club* is less linear than Classical Hollywood cinema would dictate; the narratives within the larger narrative frame of the film circles back on itself, denying any specific singular enigma which needs to be resolved.

Source: Mikel J. Koven, "Feminist Folkloristics and Women's Cinema: Towards a Methodology," in *Literature/Film Quarterly*, Vol. 27, No. 4, 1999, pp. 293–300.

George K.Y. Tseo

In the following excerpt, Tseo argues that neither The Joy Luck Club *as a novel or as a film accurately conveys Chinese culture.*

Picture yourself in a Tokyo cinema. The film you are about see is based on a novel written by a young American woman who grew up in Japan, and her story is that of a foursome of expatriate American mothers and their ethnically American but culturally somewhat Japanese daughters. The lights go out, and the movie begins. The opening scenes depict life in the American-Japanese corporate community, and being an expatriate yourself the activities seem familiar. You are ready to go where the story will take you. The scene shifts, and a flashback brings you to of all places New York, your old home. It is an episode from the life of one of the mothers. She, her husband, and a corporate associate (judging from his suit) are seated around a living room coffee table. The woman, a young wife at the time, lowers her eyes, carefully pours out scotch into a pair of shot glasses and, with a smile and bows of her head, passes the glasses to the men. Without so much as a nod to his wife the husband says, "Mr. Anderson.... Terrible shame for you and your company the deal through to have fallen." He frowns and shakes his head gravely. The associate grimaces and draws air in through his clinched teeth with a loud sucking sound. "Mr. Taylor," he says shaking his head, "The contract with demands too great to be met was written." Hey, you suddenly hear a voice inside you say, wait a minute. Something in this picture doesn't fit, and I know what it is: These guys aren't speaking American English; they're talking Japanese! The two men on screen raise their glasses together, throw back their heads, and empty the liquid contents. They set their tumblers back down on the table with a single thump. These guys aren't American businessmen, continues the inner voice with a mounting sense of alarm, they're kereitsu "salarymen"! You look around nervously at the Japanese audience. Do they recognize this stuff for what it is? Or do they credit it as accurate by virtue of the ethnic background of the author? You have nothing against Japanese language and culture, but if only this movie could convey the tone of your language and the texture of your culture. The next thing you know the salaryman's young son buys a handgun and is killed in a high school shootout. The young wife in her grief runs off to join a religious cult. You sink deeper into your seat.

Several years ago I listened to the audiotape of *The Joy Luck Club* twice. Amy Tan had recorded it herself, and I liked listening to her read. Also, being a Chinese-American myself, the scenes of Chinese-American life rang familiar and true. Be that as it may, I needed to hear the parts set in China a second time. My Mandarin is fluent but precarious, my personal lexicon is abridged, and there is a definite limit to my eloquence. So I had to confirm my impressions. After second review, the dialogue did indeed seem wrong. In fact, it was worse than wrong; it was phony—stereotypically wooden and

> IT SEEMED TO ME THAT THESE SUBTITLES WERE NOT SO MUCH TRANSLATIONS OF THE ACTORS' LINES BUT RATHER PRECISE SPEECH PARAMETERS FOR THEM TO OBSERVE, AND THE ACTORS WERE TRYING TO WORK WITHIN THE CONSTRAINTS OF THESE PARAMETERS TO BREATH A LITTLE LIFE INTO THE DIALOGUE."

metaphorical. Chinese is highly metaphorical, but the full richness of the language derives from its mixture of metaphor, abstraction, and wit. Had Amy Tan written like James Fenimore Cooper and given her characters an acrobatic Oxbridge command and delight in the spoken word she would have come closer to the mark.

In the book's prologue the main character's mother contemplates her daughter's future in America through the statement "And over there she will always be too full to swallow any sorrow." There is the common Chinese expression "to eat bitterness," but this means to endure hardship as in "by taking twenty credits next semester you're really going to eat bitterness" or to put in hard work as in "you say you want to master the piano, but are you willing to eat bitterness?" No Chinese, whether in vernacular use, lyrical prose, or poetry, could conceivably make the awkward statement that the main character's mother does. Later in the story Auntie Lena tells her daughter, "You cannot put mirrors at the foot of the bed. All your marriage happiness will bounce back and turn the opposite way." In the film this comment is related by the daughter, and she and her friends share a laugh over its naivete. Again, there is the old Chinese custom of putting a mirror before the front door so that any evil spirits who enter may be confounded and frightened by the reflected light, but this practice is somewhat akin to the American one of avoiding walking beneath a ladder or cracking a mirror. Most Americans don't really believe that it's supernaturally hazardous to do either one, but just to be on the safe side. . . . So too in China with the very old or the peasants in the countryside. Most don't really subscribe to the belief, but some still refuse to take the chance.

As with Americans, superstition offers most Chinese only mild distraction if that. There are, of course, those Chinese who are superstitious to the point of obsession, but they are exceptional. In fact, the popular perception in China today is that it is Americans who tend to be simplistic in their outlook; witness religious cults and soothsaying con artists not to mention idiosyncratic baseball players. I take umbrage at Amy Tan's confused rendition of Mandarin not only because the true beauty of the language is obscured but because by doing so the Chinese culture is misrepresented. At one point early in the book the main character makes this remark with regards to her mother: "She said the two soups were almost the same, chabudwo. Or maybe she said butong, not the same thing at all. It was one of those Chinese expressions that means the better half of mixed intentions. I can never remember things I didn't understand in the first place." Chabudwo does indeed mean "about the same," but butong is not a veiled "expression" at all. It simply means "not the same." And so it is with *Joy Luck*'s fictional Chinese and the real thing.

When I learned that *The Joy Luck Club* was coming out as movie, I took heart in the fact that the Chinese portion of the story had been filmed in China. The tale of the main character's mother is set in Guilin, which is a spectacularly beautiful part of the world, and much more importantly, I assumed that Chinese actors had been engaged for the Chinese roles and hopefully also Chinese writers for the scripting. Surely together the native actors and writers would straighten out the twisted language. After the film debuted, I, my wife, and our friends went to see it on the first Friday night after its arrival in our town. As we sat there in the darkened theater and the scenes progressed, my wife—who was born, raised, and went to university in Beijing—noticed my squirming. I could not help but to notice her chuckling. "I kept rewriting the dialogue in my head," she confessed to me afterward. "It's so unnatural." At points in the film the words of the Chinese actors diverge from the subtitles. It seemed to me that these subtitles were not so much translations of the actors' lines but rather precise speech parameters for them to observe, and the actors were trying to work within the constraints of these parameters to breath a little life into the dialogue. In the final tale of the movie, Auntie An-mei's mother, who had been tricked into becoming the concubine of a rich man, encounters the second and dominant wife of the clan. Second Wife offers the then-little An-mei a string of pearls, insisting that the girl address her as the "Big Mother." In the subtitles the concubine replies with something like, "My daughter is not worthy of your gift," which is a typical bit of Western Oriental dialogue. What the actress really says is, "My daughter doesn't match your pearls," which superficially means that the child is too course for so fine a piece of jewelry but subtly implies that the trinket does not befit the girl. "If only a Chinese could have rewritten it," I lamented to my wife. "It might have been so much more expressive and novel." "Yes," she agreed. "It could have been rich."

My wife, Fu Hui, can see things in *Joy Luck* that I cannot precisely because she was born and raised in China. In the places where I can only sense flaws, she sees them as clearly as if they were cracks in a crystal. Where I see nothing wrong at all and am as fooled as any Westerner with zero knowledge of China, she can define the cultural distortions exactly. It was through Fu Hui that I gained a complete understanding of all the story's major problems in characterization and plot. Of the mothers' four tales, three are implausible to varying degrees.

To begin with, consider Auntie Lindo's tale. This woman's first marriage was brokered when she was a little girl. From that point forward her mother groomed her to be the daughter in the household of her eventual in-laws. This much is consistent with reality; under the circumstances almost any Chinese mother of the time would have done her duty by the marriage contract. "Don't eat so fast! Would you gorge yourself like a hungry wolf at your mother-in-law's table?" And so on. But to distance herself emotionally from her little girl is another matter entirely. Is it likely that an American mother, even of a bygone era, would emotionally sever herself from her daughter simply due to the awareness that her daughter would someday marry and leave home? Auntie Lindo's perception, if true, would be exceptional.

What occurs after she does become a bride is not merely exceptional, it verges on the impossible. Trapped in a barren marriage with a round pre-pubescent boy named Tyan Yu and constantly harassed by his mother, who is bent on the conception of a grandson, Lindo contrives a ruse. After staging a fit, she relates to her mother-in-law a terrible vision. The family ancestor had come to her and threatened unsavory physical afflictions unless she abandoned the marriage because "the servant girl is Tyan Yu's true spiritual wife. And the seed he has planted will grow into Tyan Yu's

child." The mother-in-law rises to this bait and actually compels the servant girl to confess her trace of imperial blood, which gratifies the old woman's conceit and makes this new match with her son palatable. Near immaculate conception does appear in the great mythological novel of Chinese antiquity The Western Pilgrimage (a woman becomes pregnant after drinking enchanted water), but that is not to say that rational Chinese would credit such a miracle. In the tales of King Arthur a boy is transformed into an owl, but how many Americans would believe it if somebody made that claim today or, for that matter, a hundred years ago? If accurate, Auntie Lindo's account describes a lunatic mother-in-law or one possessed of the most extreme gullibility. It is perhaps more likely that the ruse was interpreted by the mother-in-law as a somewhat melodramatic but nevertheless delicate and civil way of revealing the son's affair with a servant. Dissatisfied as she was with her daughter-in-law, she might very well have taken the cue.

In the film, Auntie Ying Ying St. Clair's first husband in China flaunted his numerous affairs, apparently out of a sadistic urge to torment her. While such loutish conduct is certainly believable (in fact, it seems to be making a comeback these days in China as the mores of the socialist past fade away), the husband's outward expression of his conduct is totally at odds with Chinese behavior. It is one thing for a man to cheat on his wife and to torture her with insinuation, subtle or bold-faced, but to barge into their own home with another woman and to announce to this woman that his wife is a whore "just like her" is grotesquely outlandish. Wouldn't such a scene set in a yuppie American apartment seem satirically, laughably exaggerated? In response to her husband's abuse, Ying Ying drowns their infant son in his bath water because this is the only way she can think of to hurt him. For both me and my wife this drastic measure lay just within the limits of plausibility since there are always those in any society who can be driven to desperate acts. However, for two of our female American friends such an act was simply unbelievable for a sane person.

. . . A clue as to how distortions may have been introduced into Tan's book and then deepened in the film may be found in Auntie An-mei's tale. As a young girl she experienced the suicide of her mother, whose motive was to transfer her life's strength to An-mei. In the film, the girl screams in pain and defiance during her mother's funeral, invoking the fallen woman's spirit against the crimes and outrages she has suffered at the hands of a brutish husband and the nefarious Second Wife. She takes back her little brother, who had in infancy been claimed by Second Wife (in the book as well as the film), and cows the evil woman as well as the lord of the estate into submission.

To begin with, the plot twist of the stolen baby boy so strongly resembles a certain historical event of the Tang Dynasty that it cannot help but raise suspicions. In that account, the empress, the infamous Wu Zetian, locks a hapless concubine in a cell, feigns pregnancy herself by padding her robes and thereby successfully effects the kidnaping of her rival's son upon his birth. Needless to say, in real life not even an empress, and a notorious one at that, possessed the audacity to steal another woman's child in plain view of the world. I would venture to guess that in the household of An-mei's mother, the boy was never really considered "Second Wife's son," although she may very well have monopolized his time and attention by acting as his de facto custodian. Moreover, after the death of An-mei's mother, An-mei was allowed to stay on in the household precisely because her acknowledged brother was the family's only son and heir apparent. That through a tirade a little girl might have gained an upper hand over the strong-willed and shamelessly manipulative adults of the clan is absurd on the face of it. Neither I nor my wife believed it for a minute. Perhaps Amy Tan didn't either since this is another gross inaccuracy that appears in the movie but not the book. Originally the husband vows to raise An-mei and her brother together as if they were both his own children by a First Wife out of his personal sense of guilt and fear of a vengeful ghost.

Whoever confided An-mei's story to Tan may have embellished upon the truth, perhaps in order to add heroic dimensions to characters that were more victims than anything else. And Amy Tan in spinning a novelistic episode might have altered the truth still further, either intentionally or through rough understanding of the details. The intricacies of another person's life are all too easy to confuse. What may lend indirect support to this conjecture is the fact that of the four mothers Suyuan tells the most believable account, and Suyuan, being the mother of Jing-mei (the main character), is presumably based to some extent on Amy Tan's own mother. It makes sense that with ready access to

her source, the author would have achieved greatest accuracy in this episode.

Finally, additional and rather large extrapolations were made by the filmmakers in their "jazzing up" of the plot, either out of commercial considerations or due to simple bad taste. In any case, the "abducted princeling" component may be a prime example of initial heroic embellishment. The suicide motive of An-mei's mother may be another. My wife tells me that any Chinese woman under similar circumstances and with the strength to endure would have done so since only by staying alive could she secure her daughter's place in the household. No rational Chinese woman could conceivably have entertained the notion that by killing her own spirit she might make her daughter's stronger. Rather she would have been sobered by the awareness that once she was gone her child would have as likely as not been turned out into the streets. If the real-life counterpart of An-mei's mother did indeed take her own life it would have been out of madness, desperation, or shame.

. . . Film can have such a strong impact on the public; this might have been what piqued me to write a review in the first place. I do not cherish the thought that America's impression of China might be unduly influenced by *The Joy Luck Club*. The prize-winning and truly Chinese art films of Zhang Yimou never reached a mass audience here, and in any case, their themes are mostly of peculiar and extraordinary nature. *A Small Town Called Hibiscus* and (or sometimes *Hibiscus Town*) and *Old Well* offer sophisticated, highly cinematic dramas that resonate with universal truth for the contemporary Chinese audience, but unfortunately, save for rare and isolated instances, these fine films have never found their way into American theaters. I regret that the critically acclaimed Chinese release *Farewell My Concubine*, which does give American audiences a taste of real Chinese cinema, language, and life, was not a better film and more deserving of its academy award and that *The Story of Qui Ji*, Zhang Yimou's best film with regards to its treatment of ordinary life in the Chinese countryside, went largely unnoticed by the American public. Would that America could be treated to the truly great Chinese features of older filmmakers, such as "second generation" master Xie Jin of *Hibiscus Town*, as opposed to only those of the new wave "fourth generation" directors, who have gained celebrity in the West but whose works nonetheless tend to lack the complexity in plot, depth of characterization, and sometimes sophistication of camera work (not to mention simple humor and warmth) to make them terribly popular inside of China. My only consolation is that *The Wedding Banquet* by Taiwanese filmmaker Ang Lee has enjoyed substantial commercial and critical success in the U.S. since this is both a vibrant story and an accurate depiction of Chinese society. His feature *Eat Drink Man Woman* about a father and daughters is the story about the cross-generational tensions in a Chinese family that *The Joy Luck Club* was taken to be.

The Joy Luck Club, as both film and book, is not about China. It is about a mythical conception of a country far away. It is about the Chinese-American experience, although even here possibly more successful works have been done by less well known authors such as Gish Jen. Ultimately, *The Joy Luck Club* is about mothers and daughters. It is in this realm that the story makes its greatest positive contribution; it is here that the book is so enjoyable and moving. The truth conveyed by Tan shone through even the movie's thin characterization, which may be why so many young women left the theaters in tears. To them the scenes must have triggered self-recognition.

Source: George K.Y. Tseo, "*Joy Luck*: The Perils of Transcultural 'Translation,'" in *Literature/Film Quarterly*, Vol. 24, No. 4, 1996, pp. 338–43.

John Simon

In the following review, Simon suggests that while the intertwining stories work well in the novel The Joy Luck Club, *the structure is too complicated for the film version.*

Hardly had I finished reviewing *M. Butterfly*, when already several other Chinese or Chinese-American movies were upon us. Take *The Joy Luck Club*, based on Amy Tan's bestseller about four women who regularly get together to play mahjong. They were all born in China but now live in San Francisco, and each trails behind her a dread past. Each also has a daughter for whom she harbors high hopes for a good American life. And all four women had, in their murky Chinese histories, mothers whose positions were inferior even to their daughters', yet who fought tenaciously for their girlchildren.

At once you will perceive a rather too fearful symmetry in those fearsome foursomes. It takes four to play mahjong, which is how Miss Tan must have gotten the idea to do everything foursquarely by fours. Yet however this may work in the wider scope and statelier pace of the novel, a movie—even a two-and-a-half-hour one—cannot bear this much freight. *The Joy Luck Club* must juggle the stories of four grandmothers, mothers, daughters, and, to make it a baker's dozen, a pair of sisters, whom their mother had to abandon in China, and whom, years later, their American half-sister, June, comes to fetch to America. To make this meeting more tearjerking, the elderly sisters expected to see their and June's mother, but learn now that Mother died recently, and that half-sister June is all they get. Tears of joy proliferate nevertheless, and the movie ends awash in liquid sentiment.

June conveys their bereavement in fluent Chinese, even though when she set out for China, she spoke not a word of the language. True, she made the trip by boat, but is there a slow boat to China quite so slow as to allow acquiring that difficult language during one passage? The movie not only piles thirteen heart-tugging stories on top of one another, it also dispenses with verisimilitude in sundry details. Mathematics clearly went by the board from the start. Thirteen dramas into two and a half hours means about ten minutes per sob story, and it must take a person very loose in his or her lachrymal glands to allow them to be jerked at such record speed, and with such frequency.

But things get even more complicated. Various characters are seen at as many as three stages of their lives, and it is no mean feat for a non-Chinese viewer to make the right connections between An Mei, age four, An Mei, age nine, and An Mei circa fifty or sixty, or whatever age she is at the mahjong table. So what we get here is pretty opaque, but sufficiently sentimental to qualify as an effective Sino-American soap opera, complete with exotic minority appeal.

Still there may be one positive aspect to this web of intertwined miseries. For miseries they are, despite some humor involving all these doting mothers and sometimes rebellious daughters. Matrimonial miseries, as we get three unhappy marriages: one in China, to a strikingly handsome but brutal philanderer; one in America, to a Caucasian socialite, who also cheats; and yet another in America, to a horribly Americanized Chinese capitalist, sexist, and miser. These three bad marriages serve to further idealize the mother-daughter relationship as something better and holier than that between spouses. Could this be reverse sexism?

Back to the positive aspect, however: NBC News assures us that this is the first Hollywood film in which Chinese people are presented as likable, normal human beings, even if one mother in desperate straits abandons two baby girls, and another, having no other way to get back at her brutish husband, drowns their baby in the bathtub. Yet I wonder whether, however sympathetically viewed, characters in a soap opera ever achieve enough genuine humanity to counteract all those Yellow Peril and Kung Fu stereotypes we have been plied with for so long. It will take a better screenplay than this, by Amy Tan and Ronald Bass, to do the trick.

On the other hand, most of the performances are extremely appealing, and some of the humor provides welcome leavening. Yet even the humor tends to leave a sudsy taste in your mouth. Wayne Wang has directed stylishly, and Amir Mokri's camera can wax duly poetic. And yes, it is nice to see Chinese-Americans achieve their embourgeoisement: what could be more middle-class than this movie?

Source: John Simon, Review of *The Joy Luck Club*, in *National Review*, Vol. 45, No. 22, November 15, 1993, p. 61.

SOURCES

Corliss, Richard, "All in the Families," in *Time*, Vol. 142, No. 11, September 13, 1993, http://www.time.com/time/magazine/article/0,9171,979182,00.html (accessed January 18, 2010).

Ebert, Roger, Review of *The Joy Luck Club*, in *Chicago Sun-Times*, September 17, 1993, http://rogerebert.suntimes.com/apps/pbcs.dll/article?AID = /19930917/REVIEWS/309170303/102 3 (accessed January 2, 2010).

"The Generation Gap in Chinatown: *The Joy Luck Club* Is a Four-Hankie Classic," in *Newsweek*, September 27, 1993, http://www.newsweek.com/id/115556 (accessed January 2, 2010).

Howe, Deeson, Review of *The Joy Luck Club*, in *Washington Post*, September 24, 1993, http://www.washingtonpost.com/wp-srv/style/longterm/movies/videos/thejoyluckclubrhowe_a0a ff7.htm (accessed January 2, 2010).

Hoyt, Edwin D., *The Rise of the Chinese Republic: From the Last Emperor to Deng Xiaoping*, McGraw-Hill, 1989.

Simon, John, Review of *The Joy Luck Club*, in *National Review*, November 15, 1993, p. 61.

Sragow, Michael, Review of *The Joy Luck Club*, in *New Yorker*, September 20, 1993, http://www.newyorker.com/arts/reviews/film/the_joy_luck_club_wang (accessed January 2, 2010).

Tan, Amy, *The Joy Luck Club*, Ballantine Books, 1989.

Terrill, Ross, *China in Our Time*, Simon & Schuster, 1992.

FURTHER READING

Chen, Victoria, "Chinese American Women, Language, and Moving Subjectivity," in *Amy Tan*, Chelsea House Publishers, 2000, pp. 83–92.

Although it is focused on the novel from which this film was derived, this essay gives readers useful background about the choices Tan made in her characters' speech patterns.

Feng, Peter, "Paying Lip Service: Narrators in *Surname Viet Given Name Nam* and *The Joy Luck Club*," in *Identities in Motion: Asian American Film and Video*, Duke University Press, 2002, pp. 191–208.

Feng, who has written extensively about film portrayals of Asia and Asians, examines the use of narration in this film, which many critics consider, for better or worse, to be its most conspicuous technique.

MacKinnon, Stephen, *Wuhan, 1938: War, Refugees, and the Making of Modern China*, University of California Press, 2008.

This book looks carefully at the events of the second Sino-Japanese War and how the displacement of the population changed the history of the country and therefore of the world. This displacement plays a role in *The Joy Luck Club* when Suyuan Woo is separated from her twin daughters.

Nga, Thi Thanh, "The Long March from Wong to Woo: Asians in Hollywood," in *Cineaste*, Fall 1995, pp. 38–41.

This article gives a brief overview of ways that images of Asians have changed over the history of American film.

Tibbets, John, "A Delicate Balance: An Interview with Wayne Wang about *The Joy Luck Club*," in *Literature-Film Quarterly*, Vol. 22, No. 1, January 1994, pp. 2–7.

This extensive interview, published soon after the film was released, covers Wang's feelings about his first major studio project and his aims in making this film.

Wong, Sau-Ling Cynthia, "'Sugar Sisterhood': Situating the Amy Tan Phenomenon," in *The Ethnic Canon: Histories, Institutions, and Interventions*, University of Minnesota Press, 1995, pp. 174-212.

Wong looks at the phenomenal success of *The Joy Luck Club* and the inability of Tan's next adapted novel, *The Kitchen God's Wife*, to replicate that success. She explores what these publishing trends mean to Asian American literature in general.

SUGGESTED SEARCH TERMS

Joy Luck Club

Joy Luck Club AND Wang

Wayne Wang

Wayne Wang AND Amy Tan

Amy Tan AND Ronald Bass

Ming-Na Wen AND Tamlyn Tomita

Asian American cinema

twentieth-century China

Joy Luck Club AND film

Joy Luck Club review

Joy Luck Club AND screenplay

Joy Luck Club AND Chinese culture

Make Lemonade

VIRGINIA EUWER WOLFF
1993

Virginia Euwer Wolff's award-winning 1993 novel *Make Lemonade* tells the story of Jolly, a seventeen-year-old unwed mother of two small children, and LaVaughn, the fourteen-year-old girl who takes it upon herself to help Jolly make a better life for herself and her children, though the odds are against them.

Written as a verse novel to reflect the scattered, somewhat free-association way teens often think and speak, the book is unique in other ways as well. Wolff never reveals the race of her characters, nor does she give them a last name or place them in a specific geographic location. By eliminating those elements, Wolff opened up her novel to individual interpretation, allowing readers to make the characters into whoever they need them to be.

Make Lemonade does not shy away from tough issues and themes. Wolff covers themes of choice and resulting consequences and hope while tackling controversial, realistic issues today's teens face: pregnancy, poverty, sexual harassment, and single parenthood. She encourages her readers to explore concepts such as the nature of family, the value of education, and the ethics of Welfare assistance.

Wolff supports this reality-based content with a format and style that, if not used judiciously, would fail. The entire novel is written in free verse from the perspective of LaVaughn. The language is not perfect, and the grammar is

at times incorrect. This is the language of the at-risk, inner-city, public-housing student, and it lends an air of realism to the plotline. The book reads almost like a diary, filled with a reporting of events, but also observations, thoughts, and memories.

Make Lemonade resonated with young-adult readers upon publication, and time has done nothing to decrease its popularity. The book has won numerous awards, including the *Booklist* Editor's Choice award and the magazine's Top of the List award.

AUTHOR BIOGRAPHY

Wolff was born on August 25, 1937, in Portland, Oregon. The second of two children, she lived with her brother and parents on a farm that included a log house that was without electricity until the author reached the age of eight. Hers was a loving home, filled with music and reading. Wolff's tranquil childhood was disrupted by her father's death. Five-year-old Wolff stayed on the farm with her brother and mother until she was sent to boarding school at age sixteen.

After graduation from Smith College in 1959, Wolff used her English degree to become a teacher at a junior high school in the Bronx in New York. Life in the city was an eye-opening experience. "I was hit with new sights, sounds and smells—crowds of people, all speaking different languages. The impact was tremendous," Wolff recalled in an interview with Lynda Brill Comerford of *Publishers Weekly*.

That same year, Wolff married Art Wolff. The couple had a son and daughter, but the marriage ended in 1976. After a year of teaching in the Bronx, Wolff stopped working to raise her children, and it was not until 1968 that she re-entered the work force as an elementary school teacher in Philadelphia, Pennsylvania (1968-72). That was followed by a two-year stint in Glen Cove, New York, again at the elementary school level.

In 1974, Wolff did her graduate studies at Long Island University and Warren Wilson College. She took various teaching jobs following graduate school, and in 1980, published her first novel, *Rated PG*. It is her only adult novel, and although it marked her debut as a writer, it did not sell well.

Wolff's first young-adult novel, the 1988 *Probably Still Nick Swansen*, brought the author to the attention of critics and won her a legion of readers.

The title won several awards, including the PEN-West Book Award (1989), and was an American Library Association Best Book for Young Adults selection. The story centers on Nick Swansen, a learning-disabled sixteen-year-old who still struggles with the death of his younger sister seven years prior while trying to fit in at school.

The Mozart Season was published in 1991. The protagonist of this novel is a talented twelve-year-old violinist who is preparing for an important music competition while wrestling with her self-identity, both in terms of how her parents see her and how she sees herself as a Jew.

Make Lemonade was Wolff's third young-adult book. Inspired by a television series about the poor, Wolff created characters teen readers can embrace and recognize. The book has won many awards and been recognized and honored by the American Library Association, the Canadian Library Association, *Booklist*, and the *School Library Journal*. Encouraged by reader response, Wolff penned two more books in the Jolly/LaVaughn series. *True Believer* was published in 2002, followed by *This Full House* in 2009. The books include Jolly but focus more closely on LaVaughn as she finishes high school. *True Believer* won the National Book Award.

In between the trilogy books, Wolff wrote another young-adult novel, *Bat 6* (1998). As of 2010, Wolff lives in Oregon and continues to write.

PLOT SUMMARY

Part One

Fourteen-year-old LaVaughn answers a baby-sitting ad and meets Jolly, a sixteen-year-old single mom of two young children. Jolly's apartment is run-down and filthy, with unwashed floors and cockroaches running around the place. LaVaughn notices that Jolly's home is even worse than her own, which lets the reader know both girls are poor, but Jolly more so.

Skinny LaVaughn looks too frail for the job of caring for two active, high-maintenance kids, but she wants the job anyway because she needs the money for college. Her dad died when she was young, so LaVaughn has only her mother, and college is an option only if she makes her own money and saves. LaVaughn's mom is proud of her daughter's ambition and encourages her to work toward her goals. Although not certain this is the job LaVaughn should have, she

MEDIA ADAPTATIONS

- *Make Lemonade* was recorded as an unabridged audio CD by Random House. Read by Heather Alicia Simms, the CD was released in February 2009.

gives her approval. She knows if LaVaughn can get out of the living situation they are in, she can have a good life. So she opens a bank account and begins putting away a little from each check. For LaVaughn, college is "why I babysit, it's why I do all the homework all the time, it's what will get me out of here."

When LaVaughn realizes what a handful two little kids are, how many messes they make, and the constant attention she must provide, she wonders why she goes back. Even her friends think the job is a bad idea, but she sees Jolly's reality and feels that now that she knows about it, she should do something about it. Doing something, in this case, means helping with the kids.

Knowing those little children see despair up close and in detail every day, LaVaughn brings over a pot with lemon seeds planted in it. She shows it to Jeremy and explains that the seeds will grow into something beautiful. Jeremy gets so attached to the idea that he literally sits by the pot, hoping to catch the seeds sprouting.

LaVaughn finds that she is falling behind on her homework because Jolly does not always come home when she says she will. She takes it upon herself to train Jeremy to use the toilet so that Jolly does not have to buy so many diapers. She is unknowingly taking on the role of mother for the two little children.

One night Jolly comes home all bloody and beat up. LaVaughn is forced to call her mom because she does not know what else to do. LaVaughn's mom rushes over and cleans up Jolly. While she does this, she advises Jolly to "take hold" and get herself together so she can be a proper mother.

In addition to teaching him skills like using the toilet, LaVaughn teaches Jeremy how to clean and scrub and make his bed. She knows that he will grow up knowing he is poor, but she tries to give him a sense of dignity and some sense of control over his situation. Jeremy is like a sponge, soaking up everything he learns from LaVaughn.

LaVaughn's mom wants her to quit, but LaVaughn knows that she is the only thing bringing joy to Jeremy and Jilly and relief to Jolly. She thinks of the time when the four of them ended up laughing like fools on the stained sofa in Jolly's living room. It was a small moment, but it had major impact. LaVaughn writes, "You ever laughed so hard nobody in the world could hurt you for a minute, no matter what they tried to do to you?" LaVaughn does not try to explain this to her mom; she just tells her she is working to save for college.

Jolly has no parents, and she is curious as to why LaVaughn has no dad. LaVaughn knows her dad was killed by a stray bullet one day while playing basketball with friends. She does not want to explain the details, so she says only that he died when she was little. Jolly tells LaVaughn she used to live in a refrigerator box under the overpass. She had a friend who overdosed, and she went to his funeral. Adding this to all the other sad and miserable details she knows of Jolly's life, LaVaughn realizes Jolly has too many burdens to count.

Jolly gets fired from her warehouse job because she would not have sex with her boss. LaVaughn describes how "Jolly comes in walking like somebody damaged, you couldn't see blood but it was worse: Fear." Jolly knows that without a job, she cannot care for her kids, and her boss warned her that she is powerless to do anything against him. There were no witnesses, and no one will believe her.

Jolly asks LaVaughn for a loan, knowing LaVaughn has been saving money. LaVaughn thinks of that hard-earned savings as her exit money, and though she wants to help Jolly, she resolves not to help her at the expense of giving up her dream. That money is "saved to help me not end up like her." This is a pivotal point for LaVaughn, who now understands that there are ways of helping that make a difference for someone else but do not require hurting oneself.

LaVaughn counters Jolly's question with the suggestion that she return to school to earn her GED (high school equivalency degree). She informs Jolly she could get Welfare for the children, a suggestion that sends Jolly into fits. She does not want to go on Welfare because she is afraid the System will take her children when they find out she has lost her job.

LaVaughn realizes at that point that there are a lot of unresolved issues between her and Jolly: Jolly resents the fact that LaVaughn is a better mother to her kids than she is; there is no money to pay LaVaughn, and so she will have no job; and the one direction Jolly could go, she rejects. LaVaughn's heart is heavy.

Part Two

LaVaughn decides to watch the kids while Jolly looks for work despite being warned by her mom that it is not a good idea. With the added stress at home, Jeremy is short-tempered. He becomes angry that the lemon seeds have not grown. After all, in a very short time, he has learned to use the toilet and developed other skills as well, yet still his mother yells a lot, and there is no lemon plant where he was told there would be one. LaVaughn takes Jeremy on the city bus to get shoes that she pays for. The adventure cheers Jeremy up.

Jeremy and LaVaughn save orange and peach seeds in hopes of growing a garden. Meanwhile, LaVaughn convinces Jolly to go with her to her self-esteem class, the name of which has been shortened by the students to Steam Class. A reluctant Jolly puts her kids in campus day care, where Jeremy is so excited he begins to dance. He does that a lot, LaVaughn notices. Even though his life holds so much sadness, he still finds joy enough to make him want to dance.

Afterward, when LaVaughn is home, she laughs at the image of what the four of them must have looked like on the bus, at school, and on the sidewalk: "We must have looked like some kind of family.... A family from the continent of I don't know what."

LaVaughn takes new lemon seeds to Jolly's, thinking that Jeremy can plant them himself. Jolly wants to secretly replace the old seeds and let Jeremy think they are the ones he planted earlier. LaVaughn disagrees. She thinks it would be wrong to let him be proud of something he did not really do. Jeremy comes into the room and makes the decision for the girls by taking the seeds into his own hands and planting them. LaVaughn takes this as a sign that despite

his life of struggle, Jeremy has not given up hope for something better.

LaVaughn asks Jolly about the fathers of her babies, why they are not in the picture. Jolly refuses to answer, instead turning on the TV and filing her nails. An exasperated LaVaughn approaches her Steam Class teacher the next day and asks for advice on Jolly's situation. The teacher implies that before Jolly lost her job, LaVaughn was taking advantage of Jolly by taking her money for babysitting so that she does not end up in the same desperate situation. LaVaughn had never thought of it that way, and she is confused and stunned. The teacher gives her the phone number for a woman named Barbara, who is a counselor with a program called Moms Up. If Jolly can get back into school, day care will be provided for free.

When Jolly refuses to call Barbara, LaVaughn does it for her and gets all the information about the program, but Jolly feels alone, like she will be the only girl in class with a sad story, the only one who has made bad choices. LaVaughn continues to try to persuade Jolly to return to school and has Barbara explain that the State will not take away her babies as long as she stays in school. Jolly relents and decides her shame is no reason not to try to improve things for her family.

Part Three

Jolly attends the Moms Up program in the same school LaVaughn attends, and they sometimes pass one another in the hall. LaVaughn's teacher makes a suggestion. The teacher wants LaVaughn to sign up for a leadership class, a college financial aid seminar, and a grammar improvement class when she is choosing her school schedule for the next fall. The teacher sees in LaVaughn a discontent with her situation, and she tells LaVaughn she is smart enough to go to college but just needs some help. This validation from someone she respects is another turning point for LaVaughn.

Now that Jolly is in school and the kids are in day care, LaVaughn's life returns to the way it was before she knew them. She spends time contemplating the nature of the help she gave Jolly and decides that babysitting for free was like giving Jolly Welfare right at home. On the other hand, doing a kind deed is the right thing to do. LaVaughn decides one has to be sure one is performing the right type of kind deed, which is not easy to judge. In the end, LaVaughn is confused about whether she did the right thing in helping Jolly's family.

Jolly does well in school, getting all As and Bs. Jeremy gets chicken pox, and Jolly misses class to stay home and care for him. When Jolly is absent, the program calls to investigate. She tells them about Jeremy being sick, and they explain that they can quarantine him so that the other kids will not get his chicken pox and Jolly can return to school. When Jolly tells this to LaVaughn, she explains that no one told her about this option, and LaVaughn experiences an epiphany (a sudden realization): "And when she says this it's like a flat tire got fixed in my head and I suddenly see the sign of her life: 'Nobody told me.'" Jolly has never had anyone in her life to guide her or tell her what to do. Children grow to be resourceful adults because more experienced, loving people help them. Without those people, where is a child left?

Jolly falls behind in her homework, and her grades suffer. A counselor calls in Jolly and LaVaughn for a conference. It is decided that Jolly needs some help at home, and LaVaughn fills that role for one hour a day. She is thrilled to spend time with the kids again, but she notices that Jolly has a hard time concentrating on her homework.

Jolly and LaVaughn get into a big fight when LaVaughn scolds Jolly for putting away Jeremy's shirts while they were still damp. Now the clothes smell. Jolly's solution is to pull a shirt out of the dirty laundry hamper and put it on Jeremy. Disgusted and frustrated, LaVaughn asks if that is how Jolly handled birth control—part way. Jolly accuses her of coming into her home just to make her feel like a cockroach. Crying, Jolly yells at LaVaughn for stealing away her role as a mother. LaVaughn starts to leave but instead hugs Jolly. Then the two girls sit on the floor crying until they laugh. That is the same day Jilly crawls across the floor for the first time.

Jeremy has to get eyeglasses, and he hates them. Jolly is furious when she finds out the glasses are paid for by Public Assistance because she feels she is not taking hold, as LaVaughn's mother said she must. LaVaughn thinks that accepting help should not be so confusing. Jeremy is upset that the lemon seeds have not yet sprouted.

Jolly sees a story in the newspaper about a billionaire who gives people money if they write him a letter and explain why they deserve the help. LaVaughn does not understand how this is any different from Welfare, and Jolly explains that the difference is in the deserving. She writes him a letter. She writes a rough draft and then carefully rewrites it, even though it takes her a long time. She does not get angry, even when she sees a mistake and has to start over.

Jolly tells LaVaughn that she used to have a Gram who took care of her and ten other foster kids, but that she died. She was the only woman who ever cared for Jolly.

Part Four

One of Jolly's required classes in the Moms Up program has her bring Jilly along to learn water safety and CPR. Without these skills, Jolly cannot graduate. The knowledge is proven to be practical one night when Jilly swallows a plastic spider and begins choking. Jolly saves her baby's life with her newfound knowledge. Paramedics had not yet reached the apartment, but as scared as she was, Jolly managed to keep her wits about her and administer CPR.

When an ambulance arrives and takes Jilly and Jolly away, LaVaughn is left standing in the street with Jeremy, who is confused. LaVaughn notices that many of the onlookers have nothing but pity for Jeremy and his sister, yet she wonders, "How many of these neighbors ... could go down on their knees and save their kid from choking to death ... while the world was going on outside in the sunshine?"

Even before this incident, LaVaughn notices how Jolly lashes out less often, how she has a quicker sense of humor and can look back on her life and make jokes about some things here and there. As the ambulance pulls away and LaVaughn hears the neighbors gossiping, she realizes she no longer pities Jolly, Jeremy, or Jilly. She loves them.

La Vaughn explains to Jeremy what has happened and what the doctors will do to make sure Jilly is safe. Then she calls her mom and tells her Jeremy will be spending the night with them. She and Jeremy take the bus to her home, and Jeremy enthralls fellow bus riders with the story of what just happened at his house.

Once home, LaVaughn and Jeremy tell her mom how Jolly saved Jilly, and LaVaughn's mom has just the reaction her daughter hoped she would. She tells Jeremy his mom is a hero, and when she learns that Jeremy punched the number 9 to start dialing 9-1-1, she picks Jeremy up and whirls him high in the air around her head, telling him how proud she is.

Months later, after Jolly has stopped calling LaVaughn and their relationship has shifted, LaVaughn understands that she is part of the saddest time in Jolly's life, and so Jolly has, in a necessary way, separated from her. Then one day in the hallway at school, Jolly pokes LaVaughn to get her attention. LaVaughn is startled by the gesture but is even more startled to learn that the lemon seeds have sprouted.

LaVaughn thinks back on her time with the little family and realizes that the image she most remembers is not the filthy floors or cockroaches or even bathing the kids. She most vividly remembers her mom whirling Jeremy through the air and praising him in his too-short pants and his mismatched socks. LaVaughn wonders "how it would be for Jeremy in another place, even in another time where he'd have new clothes that would go together in their colors and a dad." But she realizes that the here-and-now Jeremy, in spite of all the things wrong with his short life, forgot for a moment the sadness and the fear and the hardness. For that moment, flying through the air, he was happy. He was hopeful.

CHARACTERS

Annie

Annie is LaVaughn's friend, but she is against LaVaughn's working for Jolly and does not support her in any way. Annie and LaVaughn see each other mostly at school. She takes a cleaning job with LaVaughn and Myrtle at the end of the story.

Barbara

Barbara is a counselor with the Moms Up program who talks with LaVaughn and helps her get Jolly back into school. She arranges for Jeremy and Jilly to go to day care so LaVaughn does not feel obligated to keep babysitting for free. Barbara coordinates Jolly's life once she decides to return to school.

Fourth-Period Teacher

Although she appears in only one scene of the book, the fourth-period teacher plays a pivotal role in LaVaughn's life the day she acknowledges that LaVaughn is smart enough for college

and should make plans to attend. She helps LaVaughn by advising her to go to a financial aid seminar and to attend a grammar class so that she can talk properly.

Jeremy

Jeremy is Jolly's two-year-old son. He has had a hard life, one marked by poverty and a distracted, overwhelmed young mother who loves him but does not quite know how to care for him. Jeremy surprises LaVaughn the first time they meet by taking hold of her hand. LaVaughn immediately recognizes that Jeremy needs love and wants someone who can make him the center of attention.

As LaVaughn spends more and more time taking care of Jeremy and Jilly, she begins to slip into the role of mother. LaVaughn makes time to teach Jeremy how to make a bed and explains to him that doing so is a matter of self-respect. She toilet trains him and takes him shoe shopping, where she ends up using her own hard-earned money to pay for his new shoes.

LaVaughn sees in Jeremy an observant child who wants to do the right thing but needs to learn how. When she plants lemon seeds in a pot and assures Jeremy that they will grow into a tree that will bear wonderful fruit, he grabs onto that idea and literally sits by the pot, hoping to see the plant's growth. When the seeds fail to thrive, Jeremy is angry and disappointed. So LaVaughn gives him new seeds and lets him plant them. He is young enough that his hope is renewed, and the second time his plant does grow.

Jeremy becomes, by the end of the story, LaVaughn's symbol of hope. He is unkempt and living a difficult life that shows no signs of relief on the horizon, and yet he is happy, always ready to smile and forgive.

Jilly

Jilly is Jolly's young baby, not even moving around much at the beginning of the novel. By the story's end, Jilly is mobile and making all kinds of messes. As much as Jolly loves her, Jilly is a source of stress for her mom.

Jolly

A seventeen-year-old unwed mother of a two-year-old boy and an infant girl, the ironically named Jolly is one of the two main characters in the book. She is at once sympathetic, in that she is living a life of relentless struggle, and exasperating, in her tendency to give up too easily, without any real effort to improve her family's life.

As the story opens, Jolly realizes she cannot raise two children and hold down a job without outside help. She claims to be without parents or any other family, and from the look of her apartment and her children, it is immediately apparent that Jolly has never had anyone to teach her how to do much of anything. She has had to navigate through life on her own.

Jolly lives in squalor. She is trapped by the attitude that this is all there is to life and that all she can do is find a way to get by. She is lacking the thing so many people who live in absolute, constant poverty lack: hope. Jolly does not dream of escaping her circumstances; she is resigned to her situation. She does realize how necessary it is to have a job so that she can keep her children clothed and fed, but she lacks any marketable skills to land a decent-paying job. To make matters worse, she is a high-school dropout. From her point of view, there is no hope for a brighter tomorrow.

Jolly is not a very good mother. She has no energy to give her children the attention they need. At first it seems she is not aware of her shortcomings and passive neglect as a mother, but it becomes apparent that she does understand when she and LaVaughn fight. Jolly accuses LaVaughn of taking over as the children's mother. It is clear this hurts Jolly.

Jolly is the character in the book who experiences the most growth and change. The reader watches her go from a desperate, hopeless teen mother to a young woman determined to earn her GED and create a better life for herself and her family.

LaVaughn

Fourteen-year-old Verna LaVaughn is the narrator of the story. In an interview with *Publishers Weekly*, Wolff explains that initially, the narrator of *Make Lemonade* was both "nameless and faceless," nothing more than "an instrument to help Jolly." Wolff's editor insisted the author develop the narrator's character, so Wolff literally interviewed LaVaughn. Explaining the process, Wolff says, "I type a lot of questions and [LaVaughn] answers them: What do you like to do? What are your hobbies?"

The process the author used made LaVaughn a well-developed character. Fatherless since early childhood, LaVaughn is being raised by a feisty mother whose priority is to keep her daughter on the straight and narrow path to college. LaVaughn wants to go to college; it is the goal that keeps her focused and motivated to do well in school.

Although only fourteen, LaVaughn has a keen sense of awareness of everything around her. She observes not only what is said and done, but what is not said or done. As she learns to include Jolly in her life, LaVaughn's world expands, and she opens up her heart to a sadness bigger than the one she carries, born of the murder of her father. After learning that Jolly once lived in a cardboard box on the street and lost a friend to a drug overdose, LaVaughn thinks about Jolly's many hardships and says, "I see how Jolly's burdens is probably too many to count. Me, I got that big one, but at least I had a father." She is learning to empathize with those who might easily be harshly judged.

As LaVaughn's worldview broadens, she finds herself more at odds with her mom's way of thinking. While they do not fight, LaVaughn gets frustrated more easily, especially when it comes to her mom's responses to Jolly's behavior and circumstances. LaVaughn is too young to understand that her mom is concerned that Jolly will negatively influence LaVaughn, so she judges her mom's attitude to be one of condescension. LaVaughn and her mom have a solid relationship, however, and they manage to get through their disagreements with their love intact. LaVaughn realizes that she is lucky to have a mother to teach and guide her.

Because LaVaughn is a compassionate girl, she wants to help Jolly rise above her situation. So she goes beyond the role of babysitter and takes the responsibility of trying to find resources for Jolly. It is because LaVaughn took time to talk to a teacher who in turn sent her to Barbara, the counselor with the Moms Up program, that Jolly was able to find free childcare and return to school. Jolly would not have done so much without LaVaughn's patient encouragement to take those first steps. LaVaughn seems mature beyond her years in the way she takes the initiative to help Jolly be a better mother and improve herself.

Mom

LaVaughn's mom is a strong woman whose primary concern is keeping her daughter out of trouble and on the path to higher education.

Mom's husband died years ago, and she has been left to raise their daughter on her own. She works full time and is not around much of the time, but she trusts LaVaughn.

When LaVaughn describes her mom as big, she is not referring to her physical size. Mom's personality and strength of character shine through, almost to the point of filling up whatever room she is standing in. LaVaughn and her mom have built a solid, loving relationship, but as the novel progresses, it becomes clear that LaVaughn is beginning to disagree with her mom on certain topics. For example, she does not like the way her mom seems to talk disapprovingly about Jolly. LaVaughn feels almost defensive, as if she needs to protect Jolly.

Mom is proud of LaVaughn and tells her as much, but she is wary of LaVaughn spending so much time with Jolly and taking on her burdens. One minute Mom says Jolly made her choices and has to live with the consequences, and the next she praises LaVaughn for helping Jolly and reaching out in kindness. LaVaughn is not yet old enough to understand how both the condescension and the praise can coexist.

Myrtle

Myrtle is another friend of LaVaughn, and she is like Annie in that she does not agree with the idea of LaVaughn working for Jolly. Myrtle does not play a big role in LaVaughn's life. She accepts a cleaning job with Annie and LaVaughn at the end of the novel.

THEMES

Choice

Make Lemonade is all about choices and the resulting consequences. Wolff allows readers to decide for themselves whether her characters' choices should be perceived as good or bad; she explores the concept of choice without bias or judgment.

Jolly made the choice to have sex as a teen, although there is a hint that at least one encounter was not of her choosing. The result of her choices is that she got pregnant. Then she chose to have the babies and keep them. The consequence of that choice is that she had to drop out of high school, find an apartment in public housing, and take a full-time job.

Despite her desperate circumstances, Jolly makes another life-altering choice when she refuses to go on Welfare assistance. As a direct result, she can barely afford to feed her children, and she is so worn out from long work hours with minimal pay that she has time for little else, including paying attention to her children.

When Jolly chooses to hire LaVaughn, she unwittingly chooses hope over desperation, although that hope is slow to find its way into Jolly's outlook. She chooses to have LaVaughn help out even after it is impossible to pay her for her time, and when LaVaughn suggests that Jolly meet with a counselor so she can go back to school, Jolly is outwardly reluctant and doubtful, but she chooses to follow her friend's advice.

LaVaughn's choices throughout the story also have life-changing consequences. When she mentions one day to her mom that she might like to go to college, she forever changes the focus of every thought she will think and every action she will take from that point onward. To reach her goal, she chooses to look for a job and then chooses to take the babysitting position even though her initial reaction to Jolly's situation is one of doubt and distrust.

When Jolly loses her job and can no longer pay her, LaVaughn chooses to stay on and help. Around that same time, she chooses not to loan Jolly the money she has saved from babysitting because she knows that to do so would mean to lose sight of her ultimate goal: college. It was a choice to escape poverty. She has firmly decided: "It would be college for Verna LaVaughn and a good job and not any despair like I saw in these surroundings here."

Although LaVaughn was choosing self-preservation, she chose empathy and compassion as well. She was willing to help Jolly, but not at the cost of losing her own way. Instead, she chose to help by researching the possibility of Jolly's returning to high school to earn her GED. She shared what she found out and helped open that door to Jolly.

LaVaughn learns that even seemingly small choices can have far-reaching consequences. One night at Jolly's house, Jolly decides she only wants to watch TV, even though there are many other things she could and should be doing. She wants LaVaughn to join her, but LaVaughn has homework, and she needs to catch up on it because she has been babysitting Jeremy and Jilly even though Jolly cannot pay her. LaVaughn knows that "nobody on TV is

TOPICS FOR FURTHER STUDY

- Virginia Euwer Wolff never specifies the race of her characters. Did you make any assumptions regarding race as you read the book? If so, what were those assumptions? Make a list of the passages from the text that influenced your assumption.

- Rewrite one of the chapters in prose rather than verse. At the end of your rewrite, include a paragraph on how the change in format style changes the impact of the chapter and the book and indicate whether you like the verse or prose format better.

- Using a computer art program, create a scene from the story that could be used as a book cover design.

- Have you ever had an experience like Jolly or LaVaughn? For example, have you ever been harassed on the job? Or have you ever experienced an epiphany? Write an essay about your experience.

- At one point in the story, LaVaughn mentions that she, Jolly, and the children must have looked like a family. Think about what it means to be a family. Write an essay that includes your definition of "family." Think about these questions as you write: Does family include only those people you are related to by blood or marriage? Can a person have more than one family? What makes a family function well?

- Choose one character from the book and write a poem that reflects that person's life and attitude. The poem could also be set to accompanying music and performed as a song for your class.

- Compare and contrast the characters Jolly and LaVaughn and their situations. Create a Venn diagram or a PowerPoint slide presentation showing their similarities and differences.

- Welfare is an issue in the book. How do you feel about America's Welfare program as it is today? Do research on the Internet about the history of the Welfare system. Create a report that supports your opinion with research and/or real-life examples.

- Which character in the book did you like best or relate to most easily? Write a one-page response and give specific examples from the book that helped you form your opinion.

- Some readers think the ending of the book is up in the air. Write a final chapter or two in free verse that explains how life turns out for Jolly.

- Read Angela Johnson's young-adult novel *The First Part Last*. Together with a partner, compare Jolly's situation as a single mother to Bobby's situation as a single African American father. How are they similar? How do they differ? What character traits influence Bobby and Jolly's behavior and attitudes? Create a Web log (blog) about your comparison and invite your classmates to respond with their observations.

---

going to do my homework and I don't want to do it either . . . but [homework is] my ticket out of here."

That self-discipline—the knowledge that there is a choice and whichever one you choose makes all the difference in the world—is what makes fourteen-year-old LaVaughn more mature than seventeen-year-old Jolly.

Hope

Hope is arguably the most obvious theme in the novel. It underscores the title, which is taken from the saying "When life hands you lemons, make lemonade." Both of the book's main characters are somewhat marginalized from mainstream society, Jolly more so than LaVaughn. A seventeen-year-old unwed mother of two small children who has dropped out of school and holds no marketable skills, Jolly lives in public housing among the poorest of the poor. Mere survival seems to take every last ounce of energy and courage she has. She sees no way out of her situation, and then she hires LaVaughn.

LaVaughn does not have an easy life either. Her father died when she was young, leaving her and her mother to fend for themselves. Although they also live in poverty, it is to a lesser degree than that which molds Jolly's life. The difference is that LaVaughn is hopeful. She believes that if she tries hard enough, keeps her grades up, and saves her money, she will one day find her way out of poverty.

Hope is also illustrated in the way two-year-old Jeremy cares for the lemon seeds. When the first seeds fail to grow into a lemon tree, Jeremy is angry and disappointed. There is enough sadness and failure in his young life; those seeds gave him hope. When LaVaughn gives him new seeds, he carefully replaces the old ones with the new, and she observes, "he looks just like those picture books.... Where Mom wears an apron, Dad comes home from work ... and everybody has those NO PROBLEM looks on their faces." That "no problem" look is hope.

Charity

The theme of charity is woven throughout every story line in the novel. Wolff encourages the reader to ask himself not only the definition of charity, but also its purpose and effectiveness.

Jolly gets angry whenever LaVaughn suggests that she go on Welfare so she can focus on returning to school without having to worry about keeping food on the table and buying diapers. Jolly considers that sort of charity demeaning. She is too proud to admit she could use that sort of assistance, and yet the first time LaVaughn meets Jolly, at the very beginning of the novel, Jolly tells LaVaughn she cannot do it alone. She repeats that statement three times. She knows she needs help, but she is willing to accept only certain kinds of help.

After LaVaughn begins babysitting for free because Jolly no longer is employed, a realization hits her: "I been sitting the kids free and that's not right. But it is right. Me sitting the kids free is like Jolly gets Welfare right at home." LaVaughn's thoughts lead her to wonder how one knows when helping someone else is right and when it is wrong. LaVaughn has to

An overwhelmed single mother, like Jolly in the story (Image copyright Tomasz Trojanowski, 2010. Used under license from Shutterstock.com)

decide whether helping someone can be both right and wrong at the same time.

There are no easy answers to the question of the nature and influence of charity. There is sometimes an element of sacrifice involved in helping others, and LaVaughn comes to understand that her capacity for helping Jolly is limited. She will help her by taking care of Jeremy and Jilly for free, but only for a while, and will not give Jolly the money she is saving for college. Though she is just fourteen years old, LaVaughn understands that helping others is important, but not more so than helping oneself.

STYLE

Verse Novel

Make Lemonade is a verse novel, which means it is a narrative written in verses—similar to poetry—rather than the more traditional paragraph format. Wolff uses free verse, which gets its name from the fact that it is free from any constraints. There is no set rhyming scheme or metrical (rhythmic) pattern. Free verse has no structure.

Although verse novels are not common, the style works well for this story because it reflects the manner in which a teenager thinks and talks—in chunks of information, sometimes in a non-linear way. The story reads almost like a diary rather than a novel, especially because the chapters are noticeably brief; most of them are two or three pages long. This style, combined with the first-person narrative, gives the novel a more personal, intimate feeling. This in turn allows the reader to get a sense of being there, in the story, rather than standing at a distance, peering in.

In an interview with Roger Sutton for *Hornbook* magazine, Wolff explained, "The form just came to me.... I wanted young girls in Jolly's situation...to be able to say, 'I read two chapters!'"

First-Person Narration

The story is told in first-person narrative (using the word "I") from the perspective of LaVaughn, the protagonist (leading character). By using the first person, Wolff gives the reader a more intimate and immediate sense of drama because the unfolding of the story's events are being shared—as if between friends—rather than explained or reported. The reader has the privilege of going beyond her actions and into her thoughts and responses to what happens around her.

Simile

LaVaughn is a typical teenager in the sense that she relies on the familiar to explain those experiences or feelings that are new. For example, to make clear just how important going to college is in her life, LaVaughn explains, "This word COLLEGE is in my house, and you have to walk around it in the rooms like furniture." That simple simile (comparison of two unlike things) leaves no room for speculation: the idea of LaVaughn going to college is huge, and it is the basis for many of the story's discussions and the catalyst for LaVaughn's choices.

Simile is used throughout the book, and the entire first chapter is a simile. LaVaughn compares having a certain experience, but not being sure you understand or can explain it, to watching a bird pick up food. While watching it, one comprehends that it is a bird pecking at food. Then the bird is gone in traffic, and no one else can see it. One remembers how it looked and what it was

doing while it was there, but trying to describe the bird as it was is not always easy, in hindsight.

HISTORICAL CONTEXT

Economic Recession

From June 1990 through March 1991, America experienced an economic recession. From 1990 to 1993, median household income fell 6 percent as unemployment rose. In 1990, the unemployment rate was 5.6 percent; by 1993, that figure was 6.9 percent. Unemployed workers sometimes had to accept work that paid lower wages than they did only months before so that they could find jobs.

Times were hard for most people, but those already living in poverty—like Jolly—found mere survival a daily struggle. From the late 1960s through the 1980s, America's inner-city neighborhoods experienced an increase in the concentration of poverty. That is, the poor got poorer. *Make Lemonade* was published in 1993. The trend of increased poverty was well documented, and there appeared to be no hope for a turnaround, but throughout the decade, poverty gradually became less concentrated. At the time of writing, Wolff's topics—poverty, teen pregnancy, and single motherhood—were timely and of great interest.

Welfare Reform

Hand-in-hand with poverty goes discussion of Welfare, which was a hot topic in the 1990s. Wolff reflected the controversy regarding Welfare throughout the book. Jolly met all the requirements for Welfare assistance, yet she refused to accept it because she believed doing so would prove her irresponsibility. It would be evidence that she was not enough: enough of a mother, enough of a worker, enough of a person. LaVaughn holds a different view of public assistance. She believes assistance would allow Jolly more attention to "pay to her schoolwork and she has that much less she has to pay to getting some bad-wage job where she can't dignify."

These two views represent the early 1990s societal attitudes toward Welfare as well. One camp believed Welfare was nothing more than a handout that did little to encourage or empower individuals to stand on their own two feet. The other believed assistance should be made available for those who truly deserved it and who were trying to make the best of their situation

COMPARE
&
CONTRAST

- **1990s:** According to the Centers for Disease Control and Prevention and the National Center for Health Statistics, the birth rate for American teenage girls ages fifteen to seventeen is 37.5. This means that for every one thousand girls in that age range, 37.5 of them gave birth.

  Today: In 2006, the most recent statistics given, the birth rate for that same age group is 22.0.

- **1990s:** On average, 12 percent of all Americans aged sixteen to twenty-four are not enrolled in high school and have not earned a high school diploma or its equivalent. This is known as the status dropout rate.

  Today: In 2007, the status dropout rate is 8.7 percent.

- **1990s:** 33 percent of the nation's single-parent families live in poverty.

  Today: In 2005, the most recent year reported, the poverty rate for single-parent families is 23.4 percent.

---

but had various circumstances working against them. The issue became so controversial that in 1996, major Welfare reform legislation was passed. President Bill Clinton signed the Personal Responsibility and Work Opportunity Reconciliation Act of 1996, more commonly known as the Welfare Reform Bill. This law placed a cap on the dollar amount of assistance each recipient could receive as well as a time limit for receiving it. Most Welfare recipients were required to actively participate in activities such as community service, job training, and vocational education. In addition, the law enforced more rigid requirements for eligibility to receive food stamps. These new regulations made it more difficult for those taking advantage of the Welfare system to continue doing so. The revised requirements led to an immediate increase in median income as well. In 1997, the median income for a family on Welfare was $7,196; in 2002, it was $11,820. A provision that allowed for aggressive collection of unpaid parental child support particularly helped single mothers. In the final years of the decade, the poverty rates for single-mother families decreased from 42 percent to 33 percent.

Education

College is another major topic covered in Wolff's novel that was also of great interest in American society in the early 1990s. In 1983, the National Commission on Excellence in Education labeled America "a nation at risk" in terms of being able to compete with foreign countries in commerce, industry, science, and innovation. The commission's suggestion was to set higher goals and standards for students at all grade levels.

A study was conducted ten years after the commission's declaration, and the results were published in a report titled "High School Students Ten Years after 'A Nation At Risk.'" According to that report, by 1990, 90 percent of high school sophomores aspired to go to college. This was a 17 percent increase over 1980. Furthermore, the percentage of high school students making the immediate transition from high school to college continued to rise.

LaVaughn's desire to go to college and willingness to make sacrifices for that goal reflected what was going on in society during the time of the book's publication. LaVaughn was being raised by a widowed mom; resources were limited. If she hoped to make her dream of college come true, she would have to focus all her efforts and choices around that hope.

Although Wolff's book is marketed as fiction, most of its themes and topics serve as a mirror to the 1990s society.

CRITICAL OVERVIEW

Make Lemonade was published to great critical acclaim. Despite the fact that the book is written in free verse—an unusual style because it can seem forced if the content does not work with the format—and explores controversial issues like teen sex and pregnancy, it was praised almost unanimously as a realistic book to which teens everywhere could relate.

A reviewer for *Publishers Weekly* deemed the novel "radiant with hope... a stellar addition to YA literature," while calling its style "meltingly lyric blank verse." In an interview with Nell Colburn of *School Library Journal*, Wolff acknowledged that the novel's style has been called free verse and blank verse, but she quickly dismissed the idea of blank verse because it lacks the required iambic pentameter (a specific pattern of stressed syllables used in poetry). The author does not even agree that she wrote it in free verse, instead calling the text "prose and funny-shaped lines. I wanted white space around the words, to feel more friendly.... We think elliptically. We have a lot of pauses in our intake of breath." Wolff explains that LaVaughn is never quite sure of what she is saying, and so writing the book the way she did was a reflection of LaVaughn's figuring out her way through life.

A teacher by profession, Wolff had, according to Stephanie Zvirin of *Booklist*, "proven herself a skilled, innovative writer with a sharp eye for the joys and disappointments of young people outside the mainstream." In an interview with Zvirin, Wolff revealed that the idea for the story of Jolly and LaVaughn came from a television series about people who live in poverty and often fall between the cracks, becoming forgotten by the System. Jolly and LaVaughn were the first characters to form in Wolff's mind, and she calls their lot in life a "sloppy, drippy world, their world of hopelessness."

One of the most widely discussed issues surrounding the novel is one that is never even touched upon in the story: race. Wolff intentionally never reveals her characters' race. Wolff admitted to Zvirin that the idea of race did occur to her at the beginning of the story, but then it never came up again, so she left the interpretation of race to the reader. Then Wolff sat on a panel at a conference for librarians, where she "found 200 librarians all asking me whether the kids in the book were white or black. It's not a question I knew how to answer."

Make Lemonade won the *Booklist* 1993 Top of the List award for youth fiction. No one was more surprised by the onslaught of favorable reviews than Wolff herself, who admitted to Zvirin that she was "stunned" upon learning of the *Booklist* award. More important to Wolff, however, were the responses of her young readers.

In an interview with Linda Brill Comerford of *Publishers Weekly*, Wolff recounted the experience: "I got letters and letters from children who wanted to know: 'Does Jolly get her life together? Does LaVaughn ever make it to college?'" Those letters were the catalyst for Wolff to write the second and third books in the trilogy, an undertaking, she told Comerford, that required courage. Both books received high praise from critics and readers alike.

CRITICISM

Rebecca Valentine

Valentine is a writer with extensive background in literary theory and analysis. In this essay, she suggests that Jeremy, a secondary character, symbolizes hope more than either main character in Make Lemonade.

Virginia Euwer Wolff's 1993 verse novel *Make Lemonade* is all about hope. The idea of hope begins with the title, which is a short treatment of the old saying "When life hands you lemons, make lemonade," and is woven through events big and small up to the very last page of the story. Literary criticism and reviews focus on Jolly and LaVaughn, the two main characters, but it is two-year-old Jeremy who serves as the measuring stick of progress throughout the novel's plot. Though he is not the book's focus, Jeremy is the most developed symbol of hope in a story about two underprivileged teenage girls.

Jeremy gives LaVaughn her first surprise of the book. As she is standing in Jolly's startlingly filthy apartment, "Jeremy's hand is in my hand, he reached up for my fingers at the same time she says, 'I can't do it alone' for her third time." This simple sentence foreshadows two things: Jolly has finally recognized that she needs help and thus is taking that first step to bettering herself, and Jeremy will be the measuring stick of his mother's evolution.

WHAT DO I READ NEXT?

- *True Believer* is Wolff's second book in the "Make Lemonade" young-adult trilogy. Published in 2002, this title takes up where *Make Lemonade* left off. Protagonist LaVaughn reconnects with Jody, a childhood friend who suddenly opens the door to possible romance. This book follows LaVaughn through her sixteenth year of life.

- *This Full House* (2009) is the final book in the "Make Lemonade" trilogy. LaVaughn is in her senior year of high school and studying for a future in medicine when she discovers a secret that threatens to undermine everything for which she has worked so hard throughout her life. This book carries on with the themes of hope and choice.

- Matt de la Pena's 2008 novel *Mexican WhiteBoy* introduces readers to sixteen-year-old Danny Lopez, a Mexican American teen on the margins of his mostly white, elite school. Danny is a gifted baseball player. His story explores themes of self-identity, cultural identity, and divorce.

- Gabrielle Zevin's 2009 young-adult novel *Memoirs of a Teenage Amnesiac* features high-school junior Naomi, who is left without a memory after an accident. As she goes through her daily life, she is startled by its circumstances, and when her memory returns, Naomi struggles to decide which life is more authentic: the one she lived before her memory loss or the one she now leads.

- The 2009 novel *The Fortunes of Indigo Skye*, written by Deb Caletti, tells the story of Indigo Skye, a high-school senior who suddenly receives a gift of 2.5 million dollars from a stranger. Her search for answers leads her on a cross-country adventure.

- Steve Kluger's 2009 novel *My Most Excellent Year: A Novel of Love, Mary Poppins, and Fenway Park* tells the story of lifelong best friends T.C. and Augie as they meet Alejandra, a recent transplant from Washington, D.C. These three ninth graders survive an inspiring and revealing year as they each find out who they really are.

- *Broken As Things Are* is Martha Witt's 2005 novel that deals with family dysfunction as it relates to fourteen-year-old Morgan-Lee and her older brother, who speaks in poetry. Only Morgan-Lee understands him, and when she breaks out of the confines of her family with a teenage crush, her life and the lives of her family are forever changed.

- Readers of Laura Moriarty's 2003 literary debut *The Center of Everything* find themselves thrown into the middle of ten-year-old Evelyn Bucknow's off-kilter life. This coming-of-age novel explores themes of choices, self-preservation, and hope as Evelyn finds her way despite the odds being against her.

- *Lost Ground: Welfare Reform, Poverty, and Beyond* (2002) is a collection of essays about Welfare reform edited by Randy Albelda and Ann Withorn. The fourteen essays cover the breadth of the political and social aspects of the impact of the 1996 Welfare Reform Act.

As LaVaughn prepares for the conversation she knows she will have with her mom when she gets home from Jolly's apartment, she makes a list of reasons why taking this job is a good idea. Number seven on that list is Jeremy's gesture. Even in the earliest moments of the story, LaVaughn recognizes the importance of this child reaching out.

LaVaughn's mother agrees and tells LaVaughn, "That's a good start." LaVaughn realizes that this one brief moment clinched the deal for her. Before learning of Jeremy's gesture, LaVaughn's mom did

> LITERARY CRITICISM AND REVIEWS FOCUS
ON JOLLY AND LAVAUGHN, THE TWO MAIN
CHARACTERS, BUT IT IS TWO-YEAR-OLD JEREMY
WHO SERVES AS THE MEASURING STICK OF
PROGRESS THROUGHOUT THE NOVEL'S PLOT."

not seem supportive. Then, after they discuss how Jeremy took LaVaughn's hand, LaVaughn imagines herself walking up the steps to college and acquiring the skills she needs so that she will "never live where they have Watchdogs and self-defense ever again in my whole long life." LaVaughn is able to dream of all this because a tiny boy reached out for her hand.

Jeremy is the character most closely associated with the symbolic lemon seeds. Early in the story, LaVaughn brings a pot with lemon seeds over to Jolly's apartment and shows them to Jeremy. She explains, "If you want something to grow and be so beautiful you could have a nice day just from looking at it, you have to wait." This is the first time in his short life that Jeremy has ever been introduced to the concept of beauty for the sake of beauty, of being happy simply because something is pleasing to the eye. Again, Wolff subtly lets the reader know that Jeremy is the one to watch.

A major turning point for Jeremy occurs early in the story, in Chapter 14. LaVaughn takes it upon herself to train Jeremy to use the toilet. He is obstinate at first, not willing to do as he is told, but when LaVaughn is distracted with giving Jilly a bath, Jeremy successfully uses the toilet. As LaVaughn bends down to pull up his pants, she is eye level with him and praises him. She wants him to own his success, to realize that it is a big deal. LaVaughn describes how she and Jeremy "look at each other and there's some monster secret we both know and he's smart enough to take it all solemn like it should be." The secret they share is the knowledge that Jeremy is smart, and he is of value. It is all a part of the hope that Jeremy symbolizes.

Jeremy becomes a sort of sidekick for LaVaughn. She enlists his help in scrubbing the kitchen floor. She realizes this is the first time he has been taught how to help with the

housekeeping. Teaching a young child takes patience and a willingness to have things turn out less than perfect. Jolly does not have that capacity, but LaVaughn believes Jeremy is ripe for teaching, and her hunch proves correct. After six buckets of soapy water, the kitchen floor is cleaner than it has been in a long time. She praises Jeremy and tells him he is smart. When he says he knows, LaVaughn wonders how he knows—what makes him so sure. That certainty comes from a sense of hope, of understanding that what is true now may not necessarily be true of the future. Jeremy seems to have an internal wellspring of hope, despite the fact that his brief life has been one of struggle and fear.

By Part Two of the book, Jeremy is mad because his lemon seeds have failed to thrive. He needs those seeds to sprout. After all, he learns the skills LaVaughn teaches him, and he makes great efforts to stop hitting Jilly when she gets into his things or bothers him. Those seeds sprouting would have been his reward. He also needs them to grow because his Mom gets fired and is yelling a lot, and he needs proof that hope actually works. In his two-year-old mind, he has been good and done all that he should, so living with anger and sadness should not have been the result.

To take his mind off his anger, LaVaughn takes Jeremy shoe shopping. On his very first bus ride, Jeremy finds the world outside the windows rushing by more fascinating than anything he has previously witnessed. There, in that bus, Jeremy crowns himself King of the Shoe Bus. By the time they get to the shoe store, Jeremy is in good spirits, and he breaks into his Hacky Sack dance. Despite the suspicious glances of the store personnel, Jeremy is happy. He has found his fun again. He has rekindled his hope.

Nowhere is the purpose of Jeremy's character more obvious than in Chapter 34. Wolff describes him as follows: "Jeremy never walks, always dances, there's a band inside him giving him rhythm." He is poetry in motion, hope on the run. This passage is part of the scene in which Jolly is going with LaVaughn to her Steam Class. Jolly's body language clearly shows her mood: she does not want to be there. She is frightened and feels trapped. Her mind-set is very different from Jeremy's happy-go-lucky attitude, despite the fact that he is going to day care, a place he knows nothing about and has never been. He could share the same outlook as his mom, but instead he is excited.

When LaVaughn brings new lemon seeds over to Jolly's for Jeremy to plant, Jolly argues and says she wants Jeremy to believe those are the original seeds he planted, but LaVaughn wants him to know that sometimes, things do not work out the way you plan, and you have to be willing to start over. Jeremy plants those seeds in the pot on the windowsill, and LaVaughn notices that for one second, a "brief light comes around him from the window" and he looks like one of those kids in a picture book where everything is just perfect, everyone is smiling, and no one has any problems. The scene catches LaVaughn unaware, and she says, "I'm surprised and I take a picture of him in my mind for later." What LaVaughn saw in Jeremy in that moment was hope.

By Part Four, Jolly has made progress. She is attending school and has stopped relying on LaVaughn to help her get through daily life. LaVaughn still helps at the apartment one hour a day, but she admits she has returned to her old way of life, before she met Jolly, Jeremy, or Jilly.

Part Four is where all the hard work— Jolly's, Jeremy's, and LaVaughn's—pays off. Jolly tells LaVaughn the story of the old blind woman who is robbed of her oranges and given lemons back instead. She does not know they are lemons, and she is grateful to the boy who returns them. When LaVaughn points out that the woman should know they are not oranges because they are smaller, Jolly gets angry and explains that sometimes it is impossible to tell when someone gives you lemons. Most of the time, you thank the person for giving them to you, and only later do you realize you were given lemons. Then you have to make the best of them. In the story, the woman turns the lemons into lemonade and serves it to her starving children.

Because of this story, LaVaughn feels she understands how Jolly has come to live the life she has. She finally realizes that Jolly simply did not know any better, that she trusted and did the best she could with what she had been given. Almost simultaneously with LaVaughn's realization, Jilly takes her first steps. They are symbolic steps toward hope for a better future.

When the new lemon seeds fail to thrive, LaVaughn brings to Jeremy seven new ones, plus four orange seeds Jeremy collected at day care. Although Jeremy is rightfully suspicious,

he accepts those seeds, along with potting soil and fertilizer, and together they sow a tiny garden. Again, though he has been disappointed, Jeremy holds on to the hope that this time, things will be different, and the seeds do eventually sprout.

As the story draws to a close, Jilly swallows a plastic toy tarantula and is choking. Jolly instinctively takes the CPR knowledge she learned in class and treats Jilly, calmly and with intense focus. She yells for someone to dial 9-1-1, and it is Jeremy who pushes that first button on the phone before LaVaughn grabs it and dials the other numbers.

LaVaughn makes a big deal out of Jeremy's ability to keep calm and follow directions despite his fear and confusion. By the time the paramedics arrive, Jilly is breathing again. After the ambulance takes Jolly and Jilly to the hospital to make sure Jilly is completely out of danger, LaVaughn takes Jeremy home with her. There, LaVaughn's mom twirls the smiling little boy high into the air and tells him he is a hero and that she is proud of him.

In the last scene of the book, LaVaughn is reminiscing about her time with Jolly, Jeremy, and Jilly. She knows it was a transitional, temporary time, but one that left her changed, wiser somehow. LaVaughn thinks, "It's kind of strange that of all the pictures I might remember . . . sometimes it's only Jeremy up high in my mother's kitchen." Of all that transpired between LaVaughn and Jolly, it is Jeremy who lingers in LaVaughn's mind. When she wonders what life might be like for Jeremy in a place where everything is less of a struggle, she knows she cannot change that for him, but she feels that perhaps she does not have to. She writes, "Here he is now, this Jeremy, laughing in his voice I know so close, I think he's forgot the fear and all the hardness for a moment."

Jeremy is the character who both begins and ends the story of LaVaughn's time with Jolly. His impact on her is tremendous, and though his memorable moments in the story are comprised of the less dramatic events—planting lemon seeds and waiting for them to thrive, learning to use the toilet, pushing a button on a phone—is that not what hope really is? It is the persistence to forge on in the face of desperation or defeat—every day—the courage to dance when you have every reason to drag your feet. Jeremy is the epitome of hope in *Make Lemonade*. In his quiet, subtle way,

Jeremy teaches the most important lesson to be learned from the story.

Source: Rebecca Valentine, Critical Essay on *Make Lemonade*, in *Novels for Students*, Gale, Cengage Learning, 2011.

Nell Colburn

In the following interview, Wolff discusses her past and its influence on her writing.

It's a damp winter day, and Virginia Euwer Wolff is savoring the Hungarian mushroom soup at Old Wives' Tales, a popular Portland, OR, cafe. She's fond of this soup; it helped her quit smoking nearly 14 years ago. She had just turned 50. She had started taking violin lessons again, after a 30-year hiatus—and she had begun writing books for young people.

Wolff began receiving literary kudos with the 1988 publication of her first book for young readers, *Probably Still Nick Swansen* (Holt), a novel that the American Library Association's (ALA) Notable Children's Book Committee selected as one of the year's best. Four years ago, *Bat 6* (Scholastic, 1998), Wolff's story of softball and post-WWII bigotry, was also chosen as an ALA Notable Book. And last November, *True Believer* (S&S/Atheneum), the eagerly awaited second installment of the "Make Lemonade" Trilogy, received the 2001 National Book Award for Young People's Literature.

Wolff seems uncomfortable discussing her many honors. She says it's probably because she's wary of people who bask in their awards. "I'm a farm girl," Wolff explains. "I can't bask." Besides, she adds, "it's not winning that teaches you—not winning is what teaches you." Wolff, of course, explored that idea thoroughly through the eyes of Allegra Shapiro, the gifted young violinist of *The Mozart Season* (Scholastic, 1993). When Wolff is asked what's the most gratifying thing about being a successful writer, she answers without hesitation: "Finishing something that was impossible to complete. One of the things I like about getting older is continuing to find things I cannot do—and then doing them."

I know that you grew up on a pear and apple farm and now live in rural Oregon. Yet Make Lemonade *(Holt, 1993) and* True Believer *both take place in the inner city. Jolly, one of the main characters, is a single teenage mother who often does not know where her children's next meal is*

> " I WANTED WHITE SPACE AROUND THE WORDS, TO FEEL MORE FRIENDLY TO YOUNG MOMS WHO MIGHT NOT HAVE TIME AND CONCENTRATION TO READ A LOT OF WORDS ALL AT ONE TIME.... IT FELT RIGHT AND IT STILL FEELS RIGHT FOR LAVAUGHN TO SPEAK THAT WAY."

coming from. And LaVaughn, the heroine of both books, loses her father in a gang shooting. How are you able to write so convincingly about urban life?

I think that when I did live in the city, it had a stronger impact on me—maybe a heavier, more weighty impact on me—because I had come from so much fresh air. I lived in Queens, a borough of New York, when my babies were little. And the floor plan of Jolly's apartment, as well as the floor plan of LaVaughn's, is based on our apartment. Although ours wasn't as dirty, and we were not as downtrodden.

Still, I was a young married mom with two sloppy, drippy, adorable children in an apartment in Queens. The nightly news had an enormous impact on me.

LaVaughn reminds me of myself as a teenager. Do you see yourself in her?

LaVaughn seems to echo my kind of adolescence. Although I have to say, LaVaughn is not more contemplative than I was. But I think she's more substantial, more purposeful. Of course, she has somebody writing her, too, and she has only a certain number of pages in which she can work through whatever her problems are. But I think, in a way, what does bind LaVaughn and me together is the fact that she, too, lurches from mistake to mistake. Adolescence is not easy. Ursula K. Le Guin, in a book review, wrote this sentence: "Adolescence is exile."

Is that what your teenage years were like?

My mother got mad at me and sent me to boarding school when I was entering my junior year in high school—age 16. I suddenly had started reading; I suddenly needed glasses. My mom was mad at me and stuck me in boarding school. The boarding school that was available had a wonderful chaplain named Father Williams. He used to fly down the corridors of the school in his liturgical gowns, kind of humming, "You are old, Father Williams." It was wonderful.

He was 29, and he was so respectful of inquiry. I was angry, I was hurt, I was a mess as a teenager. We had church history and God stuff—we were required to take God courses and whatever I wrote in my papers, he was so delighted to have a student who was reaching for ideas, however cockeyed my reach was. I was reaching for huge ideas about existence and about God and about good and evil. Father Williams was one of my enormously important mentors. I was rebelling from religion, but just loving the man who was bringing religion to me. So, in a way, I wasn't rebelling from religion at all. I was just asking a whole lot of questions.

In True Believer, *LaVaughn and her friends Annie and Myrtle explore a number of religious and spiritual questions.*

I think teenage years are the years to explore religious questions. I don't remember Father Williams ever telling us we had to believe in anything. Just because it was an Episcopal school didn't mean that everyone had to be Episcopalian.

As I said, he was so fond of inquiry and he so wanted to nurture it in us girls. So he was a religious force. My mother was a religious force, she was a church organist and I went to Sunday school and church my whole childhood. I rebelled, of course, in my teenage years. I took one wonderful religion course in college, in Eastern religions, and later thought, "Oh gee, I could have majored in religion." It would have been fun. My son has a degree in religious studies.

But as for fundamentalist religion, where fundamentalists are different from others pursuing the religious quest is that fundamentalists are so sure they're right. Look at the Taliban. Fundamentalists of any stripe, in any part of the world, are absolutely convinced that they've got chapter and verse of how to live and why. That's what distinguishes fundamentalists of any kind. I'm not sure fundamentalists have much of a sense of humor. We who are less sure know it's okay to question. Whereas fundamentalists are absolutely sure they have the right answers. So Myrtle and Annie have one way of giving form to their religious questing, LaVaughn has another.

There's been a lot of speculation among librarians about the racial identities of the characters in Make Lemonade *and* True Believer. *I pictured LaVaughn as black and Jolly as white. Have you received questions from young readers about that? And why did you decide to omit the characters' ethnicities?*

Yes, I have had that question from young readers, but not as often as I've had it from grownups. I wanted the ethnicity of the characters to be the ethnicity that the readers needed. Kids seem to be a bit more accepting of that— understandably. I was much more accepting of stuff when I was a younger person. Why did I feel it wasn't necessary to identify the ethnicity? Dr. Martin Luther King said part of his dream was that there would be a time when his children would be judged not by the color of their skin, but by the content of their character. I was working with that idea. I wanted a raceless story; I wanted to see if I could do it. I kept wondering, is this one world that we envision possible? Is it possible to listen to a person's story and not know or care what race that person is?

Isn't it true that we all love and hope and are disappointed and fear and worry and hope again? Doesn't that link us all? The child born in the tundra, the child born in the savanna, the child born in the desert, the child born in the inner city—all those kids need some of the same things. Can I do this thing? And I thought maybe it was something that I couldn't do in the same way that I could not write it in funny-shaped lines. As long as I was writing it in funny-shaped lines, I wanted to try the non-ethnicity, too. Had I had a different editor, we might not have had the stories in funny-shaped lines. We might have had an ethnicity pasted onto the characters.

However, my editor, Brenda Bowen, said okay to both those things. I had to do some wrestling with my ego, because I was still caring about reviews. And I thought, reviewers will be very point-blank resentful of what I've done. I've written a story in funny-shape lines and I haven't identified the ethnicity of the characters or the city they live in. I haven't given any of them last names, which is less of an issue. But where is the city, what is the ethnicity, and why these funny-shaped lines? These are three offenses that I'm committing and reviewers are going to hate them.

Would you talk more about those "funny-shaped lines" that you use throughout Make Lemonade *and*

True Believer*? Some reviewers have described the narrative style as free verse.*

It has been called free verse; it's also been called blank verse. It's definitely not blank verse. There's not a bit of iambic pentameter in it. I'm a lifelong English major, I know that blank verse has to have iambic pentameter. So do you. But it's not free verse, either. I'm not trying to write poetry. That would be very arrogant of me. I'm not a poet. I am a prose writer and it's prose and funny-shaped lines. I wanted white space around the words, to feel more friendly to young moms who might not have time and concentration to read a lot of words all at one time.... It felt right and it still feels right for LaVaughn to speak that way.

It feels right for a teenager who's thinking about so many things so intensely.

We think elliptically. We have a lot of pauses in our intake of breath. I speak in a lot of dashes—dashes are my end punctuation a lot, before I embark on the next sentence, because the previous sentence didn't seem to be going anywhere. And LaVaughn doesn't speak in Emily Dickinson dashes. But she does speak in, I think, the length of a breath. And then she'll inhale and speak some more. LaVaughn, like her author, is never absolutely sure of what she's saying. And I don't think I've said that before anywhere to anybody but myself. But as I am feeling my way through a narrative, LaVaughn is feeling her way through life. I remember writing a section—I don't know what number it is in *True Believer*—she says, "I felt like a parenthesis."

I had had that in mind for months before it came to the place in the narrative to use it, because I have so often felt like a parenthesis. Everything else in the world seems sure and I'm not. And I know kids feel that way. I know adolescents very often feel, "I'm the only one in the class who doesn't get it. I'm the only girl who's not asked to go to the prom. I'm the only kid who wasn't chosen for the team. I'm the only one the college recruiters will not notice. I'm the only one who didn't hear the teacher say what page number." To feel like a parenthesis is a very common thing. The fact that I happen to feel it and I'm past 60 [means there] isn't much of a line of demarcation.

I was not surprised to learn that you play the violin. It seems to me that only a musician could

have written The Mozart Season. *Does music continue to influence your writing?*

Every day, all day. I started violin lessons when I was eight, after one year of piano, so I knew how to read music when I got the violin. I studied till just about the end of college. Then I put my violin down for about 15 years before picking it up again. Haltingly, as I've done most things in my life. Haltingly and with an enormous pause, characterizing every motion. But when I was 50, I began taking violin lessons again. Now that's a gap of 30 years. It was one of the most humbling, horrifying, and ultimately rewarding experiences I've had. I was just doing my early writing for kids. I started taking violin lessons again, and I play all the time now. I play far more than I ever did.

Was The Mozart Season *somewhat autobiographical?*

The Mozart Season is not the story of me at all. Allegra Shapiro is a much better violinist than I was at 12. She's a better violinist at 12 than I am now. She practices a lot. She has a wonderful kind of dedication. But I knew girls like Allegra. I knew girls who were that gifted and who had those wonderful, enviable families. Somebody called that an over-functional family. But my mom was a wonderful pianist and she always played with me—piano and violin. We did that stuff all the time, played a lot in church. She accompanied me to recitals. So I had music in my family, too.

But Allegra Shapiro in *The Mozart Season* certainly is not me, but she's a very privileged child, in that she gets to live a life with music. I seem to be bent on pointing out that privilege has nothing to do with fancy cars and cell phones and electronic gadgets and possessions. Although she does have a violin that's valuable and a valuable bow. But privilege has to do with enjoyment of beauty and the opportunity, the freedom, to enjoy beauty every single day. That's what I mean by a privileged life.

Source: Nell Colburn, "The Incomparable Wolff," in *School Library Journal*, Vol. 48, No. 2, February 2002, pp. 54–56.

Roger Sutton

In the following review and interview, Sutton and Wolff discuss how Wolff is a "master stylist," writing novels in free verse.

Virginia Euwer Wolff is the author of five novels for young adults, all of which are notable

❝ THAT'S A DANGEROUS THING, TO LOVE ONE OF

YOUR CHARACTERS, BUT I LOVE HER AT A DISTANCE

BECAUSE I HAVE NOWHERE NEAR THE STRENGTH

NOR THE ELOQUENCE SHE HAS."

for their emotional intensity, for their innovation, and for characters that "grab hold and won't let go," as the Horn Book review of her groundbreaking free-verse novel *Make Lemonade* said. In *True Believer*, the sequel to *Make Lemonade* published this spring by Atheneum, Wolff continues the story of vulnerable, resilient LaVaughn. In his January/February 2001 review, Roger Sutton noted how this "master stylist" makes "each line-break fall in exactly the right place, never relying on the bottom of a page to provide a punch line." Sutton started thinking more about novels in verse and decided to give Wolff a call.

ROGER SUTTON: When you were working on Make Lemonade, *did you know that you were going to be writing* True Believer?

VIRGINIA EUWER WOLFF: No, I didn't. But I became very interested in the questions that the first book raised, and I guess I just really got interested in LaVaughn. Thanks to my editor, Brenda Bowen, LaVaughn became a solid character in *Make Lemonade*, and I've been thinking about her ever since.

RS: And I see there's going to be a third book as well. Can you tell us what's going to happen in it?

VEW: No, because if I say it I will probably never get it written.

RS: Good for you. Sequels are tough. Booklist critic Hazel Rochman says that the best books make you want a sequel but refuse to give it to you.

VEW: Yes, and Anatole Broyard said "a good book is never finished; it goes on whispering to you from the wall." I knew the danger from the very beginning of *True Believer*. I knew that there was a likelihood that it would be pedestrian and mediocre, two of the sins in my church.

RS: One thing people have talked about with Make Lemonade, *as I'm sure they will with* True Believer, *is that we aren't told the race of the*

people in it. I assumed they were white; colleagues have assured me that they are black.

VEW: I was very careful of not having them be any race, any particular ethnicity. I had hoped that the readers of *Make Lemonade* would have the characters be whatever ethnicity they needed them to be. I have on my wall a drawing, made by an eighth-grader, in which Jolly and LaVaughn are clearly Asian. That was the sort of thing I had hoped for. It's true that their language is not the language of any ethnic group, and you could call that a virtue or a flaw, depending on how you look at it.

RS: But they don't come across as blanks. They're not generic characters; they're not archetypes.

VEW: My hope is that my characters are quirky and idiosyncratic enough to be real human beings.

RS: What brought about the form of that book, the free-verse narrative?

VEW: It's the way I heard the voice that was telling it. I had an index card on my desk for months that said, Sit here in the mornings like Ray Bradbury. Bradbury used to sit and improvise, just typing words to see what would happen. I finally sat down one morning and it got very scary. Just sit and improvise? I can't do that. So I gave myself a task, the creative writing exercise known as Be Something or Somebody. I said, Okay, I'll be a babysitter, and out came the first five lines of section seven of *Make Lemonade*:

Those kids, that Jeremy and that Jilly, were sloppy and drippy and they got their hands into things you'd refuse to touch. They acted their age so much they could make you crazy.

The kids had names from the start, and they were sloppy drippy messy kids, leaving the messes my own little kids had left around, leaking liquids everywhere. The form just came to me. It was less intimidating than trying to fill a whole paragraph. And so I kept it, hoping I wouldn't have to change it but being afraid I would. But Brenda Bowen said, No, this is fine, you don't have to change it into paragraphs. I did try changing part of a draft into paragraphs, and I just got all blocked and stifled and couldn't do it. It didn't want to get written. I also kept it that way because *Make Lemonade* is dedicated to young mothers. I wanted young girls in Jolly's situation, maybe pregnant or with babies, and maybe going back to school, to be able to say,

"I read two chapters!" In the amount of time they had, with the amount of concentration they could muster, I wanted them to be able to get through the book. I myself am intimidated by huge pages of gray without any white space. I wanted the white space to thread through the story and give it room to breathe. That sounds a little pretentious but it's kind of what I meant to do. I wanted the friendliness of white space on a page.

RS: What kind of thinking do you do about where to put a line break?

VEW: I talk it, all the time I write out loud. By now I have to work very hard to steer it away from pretentiousness, and that's a challenge. But in the beginning it wasn't so much of a challenge because I didn't know what I was doing!

RS: That's a problem I've had with some other books that have used this style, where the form is used either in an empty way, where you could put it in a regular paragraph and it would be fine, or melodramatically, where the last line provides a punch line. But yours have both natural speech patterns and the concentration of poetry. There's a reason for it to be in that form.

VEW: I hope so. I talk it, I say it aloud over and over again. I'm extremely aware of the danger of this different form preening. Is that a fair word to use? Showing off: look, I'm different or, God forbid, look, I am poetry.

RS: Even poetry that does that is horrible.

VEW: Writing my prose in funny-shaped lines does not render it poetry. And there's nobody more aware of that than I.

RS: I don't agree. I think it is poetry. Formally, it's poetry: once you've decided to use a line break for dramatic effect, whether for good or for ill, you are writing poetry. You're using the shape of the page and the length of the lines to help tell the story. At the same time you—you, Jinny—are writing good poetry in these two books because each line and each chapter has the concentration of language that one expects from good poetry.

VEW: That's the way I feel about it. I think meaning ought to radiate more fiercely in poetry than it does in prose; I'm certainly not alone in thinking that. I don't put those demands on my prose. Poetry should have more ergs per word.

RS: I think that yours does. I can think of some great novelists who write in entirely conventional forms whose power is achieved by mass.

VEW: Toni Morrison, for example.

RS: But a poem doesn't do that. It's compression that makes a poem work. If the lines in True Believer *didn't work from their compression it would seem just another way to paragraph, an easier way to read. With some of these "prose poem" novels we're increasingly seeing, it's possible to rearrange the line breaks into paragraphs without feeling as if anything has been lost. I can't do that with your books.*

VEW: If form is only an extension of content and we want to try to make our stories as convincing as they can be, we have to find the right form. I find the only form in which I can write the thing. I like to think of the young man in Chekhov's *The Seagull* who rants, "We must have new forms! . . . If we can't have new forms, we had better have nothing at all."

RS: I thought it was a pretty bold leap, in Bat 6, *to have those twenty-plus narrators.*

VEW: It was nothing but imitating Faulkner. I don't care how many children's and YA authors have done that before, we're all just imitating Faulkner. None of us made it up. With twenty-one narrators, I knew I was straining the reader's patience, but I wanted—you know, it takes a village to raise a child? I wanted a village to tell a story.

RS: You wanted every girl on the two softball teams to have a chance to speak.

VEW: Exactly. As in a traffic accident. Every eyewitness should be given a chance to speak. In the wake of last November's election, we are quite aware that not every vote was counted, and I'm furious. For better or worse we are in a democracy. Whitman wanted everybody to have a voice, and Twain felt the same way, and I wanted to let the girls in *Bat 6* each have her say, too.

RS: It must be dangerous when you're writing about characters like LaVaughn, or Nick Swansen, or Shazam in Bat 6, *all of them struggling and troubled, to resist the impulse to pontificate, to Make A Voice Heard.*

VEW: Actually, I don't have any trouble resisting that impulse because I don't have a clue what needs to be said. Marian Wright Edelman may know what needs to be said, or Howard Gardner, or Robert Coles—those people may have an idea of what needs to be said. I don't.

RS: But you do give your characters advice. That marvelous teacher, Dr. Rose. I wish she had been my teacher. She's clearly giving advice to the reader as much as she is to the characters, but she's so charismatic that you don't mind.

VEW: Well, I don't mind. I happen to love her. That's a dangerous thing, to love one of your characters, but I love her at a distance because I have nowhere near the strength nor the eloquence she has. But I did have a model for her, a person I never met in the flesh but saw a few times. I also didn't invent some of her dialogue. "Adjectives qualify the world" comes from poet Ellen Bryant Voigt in a lecture. I borrowed it and added my own stuff. It might offend some readers that there is this soapbox *True Believer* who says that we must do this and this and this, etc., but there she is.

RS: Didacticism is something we watch for in books for young adults. But the problem is not the teaching, it's when it's not convincingly worked into the world of the novel.

VEW: And if it's not, I start to barf.

RS: We recently ran an essay by Donna Jo Napoli about how her training as a mathematician helps her as a novelist ("What's Math Got to Do with It?" January/February 2001 Horn Book). You're a musician. What does that have to do with your writing? What has it taught you?

VEW: First of all, the fact that constructive criticism is necessary and inevitable! But I couldn't have written *Bat 6* if I hadn't been aware of the many voices in an orchestra. If the oboe's missing, we're in big trouble. And my sense of beginning, middle, and end. My sense that motifs can come back, be repeated (and I hope not ad nauseam).

I play a lot of chamber music. (Incidentally, I turned into a teacher and a writer because I wasn't enough of a violinist.) Chamber music consists of basically one person per part, and that's perhaps at the core of how I know every voice needs to get heard.

I'm always listening to classical music while I'm writing. When I think I'm in trouble, all I have to do is tune in more closely to Schumann, who went berserk; Brahms, who never found a woman to love him; Beethoven, who went deaf and didn't find love; Tchaikovsky and his tragic life; and I think, I can do this. All I've got is a paragraph problem. Big deal. Music touches the human heart with all its overwhelming sense of

tragedy all the time. Even the lightest of music always has that underside that we're going to die. Mahler wrote the most gorgeous, gorgeous of melodies when his daughter had just died. When I began writing *Probably Still Nick Swansen*, I saw in my mind a boy standing outside a building with all kinds of happiness, bright lights, and music going on within, and what was playing outside for him, his own private song, was "Eleanor Rigby."

RS: It's interesting to me that you can listen to music while you write. Don't you get distracted? Maurice Sendak, for example, has said that he listens to music constantly while he paints but has to wear earplugs when he writes.

VEW: If I don't have music, I'm half a brain. Because I don't think I have much to say, but when I'm combining some little impulses in my mind with the great ideas I'm hearing across the room from the great minds of the past, then I find I do have something to say.

RS: You began Make Lemonade *as an improvised writing exercise, but then you talk about loving classical music, which is a really ordered kind of performance. This is how it goes; this is where the oboe comes in...*

VEW: Improvisation is certainly at the beginning of how I write, but at the end it's carefully worked out. By the end I know exactly where the oboe has to come in instead of the six or seven other places where it might have come in.

RS: Other writers have told me that at the beginnings of their books they have to know where they're going to end, and depending upon the writer, will more or less have outlined how they're going to get there.

VEW: Katherine Anne Porter always wrote the last page first, evidently. I can't do that; I don't have any idea where it's going. Well, *Bat 6* came because I looked up in my brain and saw a whole crowd of people rushing toward first base, and I knew there was a crisis there. And so in a sense I wrote around that event, but that's not the end of the book. No, I never know how it's going to end.

RS: So how do you know when it's finished?

VEW: Do you mean after all the many drafts and the hundreds of changes within them? Oh, I probably don't recognize the end of the process at all. Brenda Bowen and I feel our way toward it together. I guess it's when I can no longer do any more pulling, stretching, twisting, yanking, carving, coaxing, rending, mending, splicing. I don't think there's a gleaming moment of discovery: "Oh, it's perfect now!" Nothing like that at all. More like a massive shrug of the shoulders, a huge exhalation. And in my case, it's always "I guess..." I'm never absolutely sure. Not of anything.

Source: Roger Sutton, "An Interview with Virginia Euwer Wolff," in *Horn Book*, Vol. 77, No. 3, May 2001, p. 280.

Publishers Weekly

In the following interview, Wolff discusses why she has revisited old characters in Make Lemonade.

PW: In 1993, your novel Make Lemonade *was published to great acclaim. What prompted you to return to the heroine, LaVaughn, after an eight-year-hiatus?*

VEW: Young readers, in letters, kept telling me that the ending [of *Make Lemonade*] was up in the air. It took me eight months to find a name for LaVaughn. Originally, in *Make Lemonade*, the narrator was nameless and faceless. She was an instrument to help Jolly. [My editor] Brenda Bowen forced me to make her much more than a messenger. Having found LaVaughn by my fingernails going up a cliff, I felt I knew her well. She felt like a person I wanted to revisit. I felt that LaVaughn was a friend, that she wouldn't assault me, saying, "How dare you write about me," which is what many of my new protagonists do.

PW: Even though Make Lemonade *is narrated by LaVaughn, in many ways it is the story of Jolly. How did you go about filling in LaVaughn's back story?*

VEW: You sit down with pen and paper—some people use a tape recorder—and interview her. I type a lot of questions and [LaVaughn] answers them: What do you like to do? What are your hobbies? At first [while writing *Make Lemonade*] she was stubborn: "Why should I talk to you now—you weren't interested in me in the first draft?" I work early in the morning, before my nasty critic gets up—he rises about noon. By then I've put in much of a day's work.

PW: The adults in LaVaughn's world, especially the teachers, are as fully formed as the teens. Have you had similar experiences, as a former teacher yourself, of those pivotal one-on-one connections between teacher and student?

VEW: I've probably had 100, but [none] that dramatic. I read about super-dedicated teachers who go above and beyond what's expected. I've taught with them. They're out there. Some people say it's not possible that a student would encounter several teachers like this in the same school. I disagree. I don't think it would be fair for me to write only about desolation for kids.

PW: Several of your characters pick up right where they left off in the previous novel. Did you spend much time revisiting Make Lemonade *before continuing these characters' stories?*

VEW: No, I didn't, really, because I knew it by heart. No one writes as slowly as I do, I'm convinced. It's so hard for me. I learn slowly; I make decisions at a snail's pace. I went back to check things, but I don't think I studied it.

PW: True Believer *handles the issues of faith and religion very respectfully. Even though LaVaughn feels excluded by Myrtle and Annie's narrow-minded take on God, she never dismisses her friends out of hand, but rather continues to explore her own sense of right and wrong. Why do you think so few novels take on the subject of faith?*

VEW: I haven't a clue. We're so mixed up about religion in this culture. We say the Pledge of Allegiance "under God indivisible" but there's no prayer in the schools. I would be so untethered without my personal faith. I wouldn't be able to go through a day—but that's my own experience. We're taught a respect for all religions; our founding fathers describe freedom for all faiths. Maybe authors are afraid of treading on toes.

I found it difficult to write about religion with lucidity; I wanted to be fair, strenuously fair. Readers have their own religious beliefs and questions. The teenage years are the years to examine faith—the need to be independent and the need to be anchored. Who made all this? And what do I have to do with it?

PW: This is the second book in a planned trilogy. Can you give us a preview of what's to come?

VEW: I can't talk about it because I don't want to jinx it. There will be a third book. I do have a plan. I measure my progress in millimeters, just as LaVaughn does.

Source: Publishers Weekly, "PW Talks with Virginia Euwer Wolff," in *Publishers Weekly*, Vol. 247, No. 51, December 18, 2000, p. 79.

Stephanie Zvirin

In the following interview, Zvirin and Wolff discuss the racial identities of Wolff's characters in Make Lemonade.

A relative newcomer to children's literature—her first YA novel was published in 1988—Virginia Euwer Wolff has nonetheless proven herself a skilled, innovative writer with a sharp eye for the joys and disappointments of young people outside the mainstream. A native Oregonian and a teacher by profession, she characterizes herself as a perennial English major "in love with the English sentence." This fascination with the power and beauty of words is evident in all her work, but no more so than in the poetically written *Make Lemonade*, her latest novel, which was *Booklist*'s 1993 Top of the List winner for youth fiction. Wolff graciously spoke with *Booklist* from Oregon, to which she'd recently returned following an appearance in Pittsburgh at an NCTE preconference sponsored by ALAN, the Assembly on Literature for Adolescents.

BKL: You're still a bit of an unknown author to many of as, even though you've published three very successful novels. When curious people ask you to describe yourself, what do you tell them?

WOLFF: Don Gallo edited a book about kids' authors, *Speaking for Ourselves, Too* (1993). In it, I said that three things seem to have determined a lot of what I am and what I do. I'm a woods kid—you know, the forest. I'm Pacific Northwestern. Two, I play the violin. And three, my dad died when I was a little kid. I'm also five foot three and very ordinary looking. My background is probably pretty average.

BKL: Are you a full-time writer?

WOLFF: No, I'm a teacher, and I have to go to work tomorrow. That's why we couldn't do this interview any other day this week.

BKL: Any particular subject?

WOLFF: Well, I've taught for many years. I teach high-school English now, but only during the ski season, three or four days a week from the beginning of November through the end of March. I teach at Mt. Hood Academy, a school for highly competitive skiers, kids who have gone beyond their school ski team and are aiming at the Olympics. I'm their English department. I also taught elementary school for 11 years in Philadelphia and on Long Island. That was before I thought I could write, when I thought of myself as a person without skills. Actually, I got into

> **THEN I WENT TO NEW YORK, TO THE PUBLIC LIBRARY WHERE I WAS TO APPEAR ON A PANEL, AND I FOUND 200 LIBRARIANS ALL ASKING ME WHETHER THE KIDS IN THE BOOK WERE WHITE OR BLACK. IT'S NOT A QUESTION I KNEW HOW TO ANSWER."**

teaching because I decided I wanted to go to school with my kids. Having taught for so many years now, I'm in a position to be profoundly respectful of teachers.

BKL: How did you make the jump from teaching to writing?

WOLFF: I just sat down and wrote one day. Actually, I was too foolish to know any different then.

BKL: You mean you wrote a book?

WOLFF: Yes, that's what I did. In the late 1970s. I had never taken a writing course, and I had never finished a short story. I just decided I would sit down and write a novel. You know "where angels fear to tread." I do everything "where angels fear to tread." I believe that's how our best writing gets done. I had a whole bunch of impulses and half-witted perceptions coming out of me, just coming out my ears, so I sat down and let stuff pour out onto the typewriter. That was my adult novel, *Rated PG*, which, happily, is now out of print.

BKL: It has an interesting title.

WOLFF: It's got a corny title, a terribly commercial title. I don't admire the book. I guess first novels are always embarrassing. I'd certainly never reread it. Writing it helped me find out how a book gets made, though—at least one of the ways—and by the time I sat down to write for kids, I had one humongous experience behind me.

BKL: What made you decide to write for young adults?

WOLFF: Actually, I just had a story. I really didn't know who I was going to tell it to, and I really didn't know if what I was writing would turn out to be a novel or a short story. I even thought it might turn out to be a poem. What it became was a book called *Probably Still Nick Swansen*, about a learning-disabled boy.

BKL: When I read that book, I wondered if you actually knew Nick or a boy like him. There aren't too many books about teenagers like Nick.

WOLFF: No. I had to do a lot of homework to write the book. I practiced being a boy.

BKL: You practiced being a boy?

WOLFF: Yes. I tried to understand how a boy would feel in the sort of situation in which Nick finds himself, and I wrote a short story and some poems. I never knew a boy like Nick, though. Lots of people ask that question, as if I were a nonfiction writer. I've never known a boy like Nick. I've never been a special-education teacher; my kids weren't in special ed, either. I write fiction. I do my research by wandering around. I watch and listen and look.

Also, I've been teaching in a public high school for a very long time. It just happened that one day I was in the cafeteria at a faculty table when I heard some teachers talking about a student who was looking forward to something. Four or five days later, I heard the same teachers talking about how the thing that the student was looking forward to hadn't occurred. I thought, boy, is that my kind of material. I major in disappointment. I guess Nick Swansen was basically me, having practiced being a boy and also having felt inept a whole lot of my life.

BKL: Was it difficult to find publishers for your first books?

WOLFF: Actually, I don't do any of that. My agent does. That's how I can live in Oregon, as far from the mainstream as I can possibly get. I also went to college with Jane Yolen, who's always been generous and kind to newcomers. After I'd written my adult novel, I asked her what to do with it. She told me to send it to her. So I got her agent. After that, the problem was writing, not selling, although *Nick Swansen* sat around in New York for 18 months before it found its right editor. It was turned down once before Mary Cash, who was then at Henry Holt, took it. She looked at this sow's ear and said, "I think there's a silk purse here." And she found it. She told me that the book went wrong about halfway through, and if I was going to work with her, I'd have to rewrite it. I said, "Okay," not having any idea what was involved. I found out that she meant I'd have to go back to square one and redo what I thought was perfectly fine

in the first place. I did, but I cried my way through it. I no longer think anything is perfect. I know enough now to know everything can be improved.

BKL: The Mozart Season is about a girl dedicated to the violin. You play the violin. Did that make this book easier to write than Nick *or* Make Lemonade?

WOLFF: In one way, it made the book easier. I've played the violin most of my life. I never was as good as Allegra is. I've never been an outstanding violinist, but I play in chamber orchestras a lot. I'm more comfortable in my skin when I have the violin going and have regular weekly lessons. Even so, the novel was still the most difficult of the books I've written.

BKL: Why is that?

WOLFF: Because there was so much in it. It was ambitious. I had many more characters in the world that surrounded Allegra and her violin than in my first YA book. I felt as if I were holding one of those great big bouquets of balloons and had lost all their strings. I thought the reviews were going to say "nice ambitious try that doesn't quite make it."

BKL: You've been quoted as saying that reading to children has a profound effect on who they will become. Were you made to as a child?

WOLFF: Oh yes. Winnie the Pooh and Christopher Robin left a great impression. And Eeyore and Piglet and Kanga and Roo. Winnie the Pooh keeps coming up in everything I write, either explicitly or implicitly. Those folks were in charge of my childhood. Mother read a lot of other things to us, but Milne's *Pooh* was the most comforting. I never got the joke about Eeyore until I was much older, though. I thought he really was unlucky, and all those terrible things were really happening to him. Mother never helped me see that he was just a self-pitying fool, and looking back, I'm glad she didn't.

BKL: In your essay for Don Gallo, you credited a number of teachers for steering you toward becoming a writer. Tell me, is that why education is such a prominent theme in your books?

WOLFF: Nobody has said that to me before, but you're absolutely right. I think so. Actually, I didn't know what education I was getting until years later. But that's the way we are. We all knew our fifth-grade teacher, Mrs. Fitzpatrick, was a strange and gifted person. I thought she was wonderfully quirky and great. We were in this little rural town on the side of a mountain, and she taught us about the structure of English—whether we wanted to learn it or not. As it turns out, I was a perfect candidate for learning it because I am in love with the English sentence. She taught us how to put the bricks in the wall to build one. Her husband was the principal and the band director of the high school, which had about 80 students in it. He embezzled the band funds and was caught, and Mrs. Fitzpatrick left in the middle of one night. They were just gone.

BKL: Let's go on to Make Lemonade *for a bit. Where did the idea for the book come from?*

WOLFF: I wish I could really pinpoint it. I watched a television series about the poor who fall into the cracks of the system and stay there generation after generation, and I was angry and sorrowful. And I watched several shows about tough, angry, loving women who take justice and safety into their own hands in inner-city projects because the city doesn't give a rip about keeping the children safe or is too snarled in bureaucracy to try. My admiration for those women was instant.

BKL: Women like LaVaughn's mother?

WOLFF: Yes, that's where she came from. But LaVaughn and jolly really came to me first ... their sloppy, drippy world, their world of hopelessness. I've never been hungry or gone without shelter unless I've wanted to, but I've felt hopeless and resourceless in my life. I could feel how those kids felt. I just didn't know if it would sound real to readers.

BKL: I never wondered about the reality of the situation, but I did wonder whether race was meant to be a factor in it. I kept wanting to pin labels and finding myself unable to do it.

WOLFF: Well, the idea of race went through my head at the beginning, but I settled into the writing of the book and the emotions of the characters and I honestly didn't think about it. Then I went to New York, to the public library where I was to appear on a panel, and I found 200 librarians all asking me whether the kids in the book were white or black. It's not a question I knew how to answer. I still don't, except to say that I didn't see faces so much as I heard voices when I was writing. I think that we do our best writing when we get out of the way and let our characters speak in whatever voices they have to speak in.

I also believe that it would have been very arrogant of me to try to write black talk. I am extremely white. It would be arrogant of me to write Irish talk if I'd never lived in Ireland. But I can write poor talk because I've been poor in spirit.

BKL: What about reviews for the book?

WOLFF: I was astonished and staggered by the good reviews it got. My editor, Brenda Bowen, still has a note hanging on her wall that I sent along with the last galleys. It says, "This is such a depressing story, I can't imagine reading clear through to the end. What if no one does?" we sent the book to press wondering if anyone would get the point. That was a gamble that my excellent editor took. She was willing to risk publishing a book without being sure whether or not anybody would get it. And they got it! Then, when such favorable reviews began to come in, I thought, "Now wait a minute, Wolff. One of the things you hate most is ego. Don't memorize these reviews. Put them in an envelope and file them away. Don't think about them." I've been around a lot of artistic ego in my life, and I don't want to get one.

BKL: You tried something very different with style in this book. It's written in very short, simple sentences, laid out on the page in what seem to be stanzas rather than traditional paragraphs. Why did you do the book that way?

WOLFF: Because that's the way I heard the voices. I love poetry; I read a lot of it and go to readings. Some of my favorite authors are Gerard Manley Hopkins, Dylan Thomas, Toni Morrison, and Shakespeare. Three or them are poets, and, of course, Toni Morrison is a poet in her prose. Also, I'm not unaware that kids often speak a funny kind of offbeat poetry. Nikki Giovanni put that kind of poetry on the page. People mostly talk in dashes; that's the way I speak, and I've taught school for so many eons and heard kids speak that way so long, it occurred to me that I ought to do the book that way. I hoped to do something with the rhythm of the voices that would sound real.

But I didn't ask anybody's permission. I didn't know to what extent precedent forbade me to write that way. Had I been keeping up in YA lit, as many of my author friends do, I probably would have been too intimidated to try something different. Another reason I wrote the book the way I did was that I know that mothers like Jolly have short attention spans.

They are often depressed, and when you're depressed you can't concentrate well enough to read very long. I wanted to create something they could read.

BKL: I wondered if that wasn't part of the reason you wrote it the way you did . . . short lines, simple vocabulary. It might be a good choice for reluctant readers.

WOLFF: Thank you. I hope so.

BKL: How did you feel about finding out that Make Lemonade *was* Booklist's *Top of the List winner for youth fiction?*

WOLFF: I was stunned, although I always put a damper on my exuberance. I don't want it to become a matter of ego, so I haven't told many people yet. I did tell one friend who said, "Welcome to the top of the charts." But I was truly delighted. I know I'm not giving you complete answers, if you were to call me two years from now, I would have thought this through much more. Were you to interview my editor, you'd get a very articulate answer. As a matter of fact, she was flabbergasted by the manuscript when she first got it. In fact, she was intimidated by it. Not by the problems it had, but by its potential. And it wasn't nearly the novel it is now. Brenda asked tough questions to help me make the book better. Good editors do that.

BKL: Have you heard from kids who have read the book?

WOLFF: The book is still so new that I haven't heard from many kids yet. I saw kids do a couple of scenes from it in a reader's theater performance in Pittsburgh recently. I hope they'll tell their friends.

BKL: Are you working on anything at the moment?

WOLFF: I am, but very slowly. My penchant for procrastination is amazing. I'm able to delay and delay and delay, and even sabotage a book. Still, I guess I'd rather write fewer books and have them be unusual, as all three of mine are, than write quantity. The book that I'm working on now is again on the sad side. It may be for younger kids, as young as nine. And it's probably more for girls than boys. I won't give the subject away, though. I'm afraid if I do, it might bring bad luck.

Source: Stephanie Zvirin, "The *Booklist* Interview: Virginia Euwer Wolff," in *Booklist*, Vol. 90, No. 13, March 1, 1994, pp. 1250–51.

SOURCES

"Annual Average Unemployment Rate, Civilian Labor Force 16 Years and Over (Percent)," in *Bureau of Labor Statistics*, http://www.bls.gov/cps/prev_yrs.htm (accessed January 13, 2010).

Colburn, Nell, "The Incomparable Wolff: Like Her Tough-Minded Characters, Novelist Virginia Euwer Wolff has Succeeded While Remaining True to Herself," in *School Library Journal*, Vol. 48, No. 2, February 2002, pp. 54–57.

Comerford, Lynda Brill, "Q & A with Virginia Euwer Wolff," in *Publishers Weekly*, February 5, 2009, http://www.publishersweekly.com/article/CA6634519.html?nid =2788 (accessed December 10, 2009).

"A Decade of Welfare Reform: Facts and Figures," in *Urban Institute*, June 2006, http://www.urban.org/UploadedPDF/900980_welfarereform.pdf (accessed January 13, 2010).

Grall, Timothy, "Custodial Mothers and Fathers and Their Child Support: 2005," in *U.S. Census Bureau*, August 2007, p. 4.

Holinger, Debra, "High School Dropout Rates," in *Consumer Guide*, U.S. Department of Education, No. 16, March 1996, http://www.ed.gov/pubs/OR/ConsumerGuides/dropout.html (accessed December 9, 2009).

"Income and Job Mobility in the Early 1990s," in *Bureau of the Census*, February 1995, p. 2.

Kaufman, Phillip, et al., "Dropout Rates in the United States: 2000," in *National Center for Education Statistics*, November 2001, p. 4.

"Make Lemonade," in *Publishers Weekly*, Vol. 240, No. 22, May 31, 1993, p. 56.

Martin, Joy A., and Brady E. Hamilton, et al., "National Vital Statistics Reports: Births: Final Data for 2006," in *National Center for Health Statistics*, Vol. 57, No. 7, January 7, 2009, p. 33.

Pettit, Kathryn L. S., and G. Thomas Kingsley, "Concentrated Poverty: A Change in Course," in *Neighborhood Change in Urban America*, May 19, 2003, http://www.urban.org/publications/310790.html (accessed December 7, 2009).

"PW Talks with Virginia Euwer Wolff," in *Publishers Weekly*, Vol. 247, No. 51, December 18, 2000, p. 79.

Smith, Thomas M., and Susan P. Choy, "High School Students Ten Years after 'A Nation at Risk,'" in *National Center for Education Statistics*, May 1995, pp. 3, 11.

"Status Dropout Rates of 16- through 24-Year Olds, by Race/Ethnicity: Selected Years, 1980–2007," in *The Condition of Education 2009*, U.S. Department of Education, http://nces.ed.gov/FastFacts/display.asp?id=16 (accessed January 13, 2010).

Sutton, Roger, "An Interview with Virginia Euwer Wolff," in *Horn Book*, May-June 2001, http://www.hbook.com/magazine/articles/2001/may01_wolff_sutton.asp (accessed December 10, 2009).

"Welfare Reform," in *Municipal Research and Services Center of Washington*, http://rainier.wa.us/Subjects/HumanServices/welfare/welfare.aspx (accessed January 13, 2010).

Wolff, Virginia Euwer, *Make Lemonade*, Henry Holt, 1993.

"Work, Poverty, and Single-Mother Families," in *Economic Policy Institute*, August 9, 2006, http://www.epi.org/economic_snapshots/entry/webfeatures_snapshots_2006 0809/ (accessed December 7, 2009).

Zvirin, Stephanie, "The Booklist Interview: Virginia Euwer Wolff," in *Booklist*, Vol. 90, No. 13, March 1, 1994, p. 1250–51.

FURTHER READING

Lindsay, Jeanne Warren, and Sharon Githens Enright, *Books, Babies, and School-Age Parents: How to Teach Pregnant and Parenting Teens to Succeed*, Morning Glory Press, 1997.

Written for educators, this handbook provides resources and advice for helping keep pregnant teens and teen parents in school.

Na, An, *A Step from Heaven*, Speak, 2003.

Winner of the American Library Association Printz Award for teen literature, this novel tells the story of Korean immigrant Young Ju and her family. Reluctant to leave her home, Young Ju moves to America with her family only to find life more of a struggle than it was before. When her alcoholic father's abuse goes too far, Young Ju summons the courage to force

change that will lead her mother and siblings down a new path.

Soto, Gary, *Buried Onions*, Harcourt Paperbacks, 2006. Teenage Eddie lives in poverty in Fresno, California. He tries to stay away from gangs in hopes he can lift himself up from his circumstances, but when his cousin is killed, his aunt encourages him to seek revenge. Life seems to work against Eddie as he faces his grim reality.

Woodson, Jacqueline, *The Dear One*, Speak, 2004. Rebecca is fifteen and pregnant, sleeping in twelve-year-old Feni's room. Though Feni wants to dislike her visitor, she realizes that Rebecca's tough exterior serves only to hide a vulnerable, scared girl who needs friends more now than ever.

SUGGESTED SEARCH TERMS

Make Lemonade

Virginia Euwer Wolff

Make Lemonade AND Euwer Wolff

teen pregnancy AND Euwer Wolff

trilogy AND Euwer Wolff

welfare AND Euwer Wolff

free verse AND Euwer Wolff

YA AND Euwer Wolff

troubled teens AND Euwer Wolff

poverty AND Euwer Wolff

Maus: A Survivor's Tale

ART SPIEGELMAN

1986–1991

Art Spiegelman's *Maus: A Survivor's Tale* is a two-volume graphic novel that documents the survival of the author's parents, both Polish Jews, during the Holocaust. Spiegelman depicts Jews as mice—hence the title—and Germans as cats as a metaphor for how Jews were hunted and killed in accordance with the Nazi Party's planned extermination of all European Jews during World War II. Spiegelman began work on the story as early as 1971, and he published portions of the story between 1980 and 1986 in the underground graphic journal *RAW*, which he edited with his wife, Françoise Mouly. The first volume of *Maus*, subtitled *My Father Bleeds History*, was published to critical acclaim in 1986; the second volume, *And Here My Troubles Began*, followed in 1991. *Maus* is as much a story about how the author's parents, Vladek and Anja Spiegelman, narrowly escaped death in Auschwitz as it is about their son's struggle to translate their personal history into a meaningful narrative and come to terms with the effect it has had on his own life.

Maus broke new ground in the graphic novel genre. Both volumes were nominated for the National Book Critics Circle Award, and in 1992 the work received a Pulitzer Prize in the Special Awards and Citations—Letters category. It also received the two highest honors in the field of graphic novels, the Eisner Award for Best Graphic Album and the Harvey Award for Best Graphic Album of Previously Published Work. *Maus* was

Art Spiegelman *(Sean Gallup / Getty Images)*

arguably the first graphic novel to reach a mass audience, and it paved the way for other serious works in the genre. As a work of Holocaust literature, it has garnered praise and critical analysis on par with landmark works of the genre, including Elie Wiesel's *Night* and Primo Levi's *Survival in Auschwitz*.

AUTHOR BIOGRAPHY

Spiegelman was born on February 15, 1948, in Stockholm, Sweden, to Vladek and Anja Spiegelman, Polish Jews and Holocaust survivors who immigrated to the country after World War II. When Art was three, the family moved to Rego Park, a neighborhood in Queens, New York. Spiegelman was captivated by *Mad* magazine and Golden Age comic books as a child and attended the High School of Art and Design in Manhattan. While at Harpur College, he began working for the Topps Chewing Gum Corporation, where he

created Wacky Packages and Garbage Pail Kids trading cards over the course of a twenty-year association with the company. When Spiegelman was twenty, he suffered a nervous breakdown and spent time in a mental hospital. Shortly afterward, his mother, who had suffered from depression for many years, committed suicide.

Spiegelman was a key figure in the alternative comics—or "comix" as they were affectionately known—movement of the late 1960s and early 1970s in San Francisco. During this time he published "Prisoner on the Hell Planet," an account of his mother's suicide that was later reprinted in *Maus* and that was also collected in 1977's *Breakdowns: From Maus to Now: An Anthology of Strips*. Spiegelman returned to New York in 1976 and married Françoise Mouly, a former architecture student from France. In 1980, they founded the alternative comics journal *RAW*, where portions of *Maus* first appeared. The publication of the first volume of *Maus* in 1986 thrust him into the spotlight as a major writer and leading graphic novelist. The second volume, published in 1991, garnered him a Pulitzer Prize and solidified his position as a major figure in Holocaust literature.

From 1991 to 2003, Spiegelman was a staff artist at *The New Yorker*. He contributed many covers to the magazine, the most famous of which is his September 24, 2001, black-on-black illustration featuring the barely visible silhouette of the World Trade Center twin towers. The image later became the cover of his book *In the Shadow of No Towers*, his graphic novel about the 9/11 attacks near his home in lower Manhattan. Though the anthologized panels that comprise the 2004 book were controversial because of Spiegelman's visceral reactions to terrorism and the wars that followed, critics praised the volume, and *Time* magazine listed Spiegelman as one of their Top 100 Most Influential People in 2005.

As an advocate for the graphic novel and comics in general, Spiegelman lectures frequently and has taught at the University of California at Santa Cruz and the School of Visual Arts in New York. Spiegelman and Mouly have worked together on a number of projects, including the "Little Lit" series, an anthology of comics for children by such authors as Lemony Snicket, Maurice Sendak, William Joyce, and Neil Gaiman.

PLOT SUMMARY

Volume I: My Father Bleeds History

The book opens in the mid-1970s with the adult Art, who is drawn as a mouse with a human body, visiting his father, Vladek, and his second wife, Mala, for dinner at their home in Rego Park, Queens. Art and his father are not close, and the tension between them is instantly apparent. Vladek and Mala have a tumultuous marriage—she complains that he is a miser, and he complains that she is a spendthrift. After dinner, Art asks his dad to recount his life before and during World War II in hopes of turning it into a graphic novel. Vladek reluctantly agrees.

Vladek's story is seen in flashbacks as he narrates it to Art. Vladek starts in the 1930s, when he was selling textiles in Czestochowa, Poland, near the German border. Through a cousin who lives in Sosnowiec, he meets Anja Zylberberg, a nice but nervous girl from a wealthy family. They are married in 1937, and Vladek begins working for his father-in-law.

On Art's next visit to Rego Park, his father throws out his long winter trench coat and replaces it with a short jacket. When Art discovers this, he is enraged. Vladek, who has one glass eye, cataracts in the other, and is diabetic, busies himself counting pills. Between these domestic events, Vladek continues his story. Early in his marriage, he catches Anja translating documents for the Communists. The police search their apartment, but Anja has left the documents with a neighbor who is arrested instead. Vladek orders Anja to cease all such sordid activity and she does.

Vladek becomes the supervisor of a textile factory in Bielsko, and Anja has a baby boy named Richieu. Anja suffers from postpartum depression, so she and Vladek travel to a luxurious sanitarium in Czechoslovakia. On the way they see their first Nazi swastika flag; it is 1938, and stories of violent pogroms against Jews are becoming increasingly common.

Vladek is drafted into the Polish army on the eve of World War II. In one of the war's first battles, Vladek kills a German soldier and is taken prisoner. One night he has a dream about Parshas Truma, an annual day on the Jewish calendar. An imprisoned rabbi tells him this is auspicious, and sure enough, three months later he is released from the prisoner of war (POW) camp on Parshas Truma. Instead of returning to Sosnowiec, he ends up at another POW camp in

MEDIA ADAPTATIONS

- The Voyager Company released *The Complete Maus* on CD-ROM in 1994. The multimedia disc includes the book, preliminary drawings, journal entries, home movies, and audio of some of the tape-recorded conversations between Art and Vladek Spiegelman.

- "Making Maus," an exhibition featuring Spiegelman's original artwork, ran at the Museum of Modern Art in New York City in 1991.

Lublin. He obtains his release by calling upon the assistance of some family friends in the town and sneaks back to Sosnowiec. A month after his return his mother dies of cancer.

When Art next visits Rego Park, he brings a tape recorder, and Vladek continues his story. Twelve family members, including Vladek, Anja, and Richieu, are living with Anja's father in their well-appointed Sosnowiec apartment, but life is not safe for the Jews. Many are carried off to work camps; food is rationed. Vladek forges useful alliances that enable him to keep working and to barter for food on the black market. Vladek's in-laws make a deal to sell their furniture to some German officers, but the officers take the furniture without paying for it. Vladek wants to send Richieu to live in safety with another family, but Anja refuses.

On January 1, 1942, all Jews in Sosnowiec are forcibly moved to the ghetto. Vladek, Anja, and eleven other family members now share two small rooms. Several of the men Vladek does business with are hanged. He stops selling cloth and starts dealing in gold and jewelry, which is easier to hide. Vladek mentions that Anja kept voluminous diaries about the war, and Art desperately wants them. Vladek says he has thrown them out.

Next, the Germans decree that Jews older than seventy will be taken to a special senior community.

They hide Anja's elderly grandparents behind a false wall in a shed. Officials threaten to take Anja's father in their place, and thus the grandparents are handed over. They are immediately sent to the gas chambers at Auschwitz.

Sosnowiec's remaining Jews are forced to have their documents inspected and stamped at the town's sports stadium. Healthy, able-bodied workers are separated from the elderly, the sick, and families with many young children. Only the healthy—about ten thousand people, Vladek and Anja among them—receive stamped papers and are allowed to return to the ghetto. Everyone else is taken away and never seen again. Mala says her mother was taken from the stadium that day and housed with thousands of other Jews in a nearby apartment building until they were discovered and sent to the gas chambers at Auschwitz. Art scours the house in vain looking for his mother's diaries. Mala complains that Vladek has saved everything—except for the diaries—and that he is more attached to things than people.

During Art's next visit to Rego Park, he discovers that his father has just read a comic Art wrote years ago about his mother's suicide. Titled "Prisoner on the Hell Planet," it is reprinted on the following pages. Drawn in a scratchboard style based on German Expressionist art, it depicts Art, recently discharged from a mental hospital, wearing a striped uniform much like the one worn by concentration camp prisoners. His mother slits her wrists and dies in the bathtub. Art blames his dead mother for his feelings of despair and his father for being needy and distraught. Vladek admits the story made him cry and brought back many memories of his beloved Anja.

On a walk to the bank, Vladek resumes his story. In 1943, the remaining Sosnowiec Jews are moved to the ghetto of Srodula, where they are under lock and key. Anja and Vladek decide to send Richieu to live with Anja's sister, where they believe he will be safer, but when the Gestapo liquidates that ghetto, Anja's sister poisons herself, her children, and Richieu in order to spare them from the gas chambers at Auschwitz.

The Germans begin to liquidate the Srodula ghetto, and Vladek builds a bunker in the cellar of their small cottage. When that becomes too dangerous, they hide in the attic of a different house. Eventually they are betrayed and taken to a prison to await transport to Auschwitz. Vladek tries to spare his in-laws by bribing officials.

They take his jewels but send Anja's parents to the gas chambers at Auschwitz anyway. Vladek survives by forming a friendship with a Jewish police officer who plays cards with the Gestapo. When Vladek and Anja are the only ones left in their family, Anja becomes hysterical and wants to die. Vladek tells her that to die is easy but to stay alive is hard. Together they will keep each other strong and survive.

Art and Vladek arrive at the bank, where Vladek gives Art a key to his safe deposit box. He complains that Mala wants to steal all his money. Art tells his father to enjoy his wealth, but Vladek insists on hiding it in the bank. He still has a few gold trinkets left from the war. On another visit to Rego Park, Mala complains to Art that Vladek treats her like a servant and does not give her enough money for essentials. Mala says his stinginess has nothing to do with surviving the prison camps, because she knows plenty of survivors, none of whom are as miserly as he is. Vladek complains that Mala is greedy and obsessed with money. However, both of them are impressed with Art's initial drawings for the book.

Vladek and Anja walk back to Sosnowiec after the Srodula ghetto is liquidated. For several months they alternate between hiding in a barn outside town and staying at a house in town owned by a woman named Motonowa. They arrange to escape to Hungary, which they believe is safer than Poland, but they are betrayed en route and delivered to the gates of Auschwitz. At Auschwitz they are separated, and neither believes they will survive.

Art asks again for his mother's notebooks. Vladek says he burned them after Anja's suicide because they held too many painful memories. Art yells at his father for saving useless junk and destroying priceless memories. He storms out in anger, calling his father a murderer.

Volume II: *And Here My Troubles Began*

In the summer of 1979, Vladek interrupts Art and Françoise's vacation with the news that Mala has left him and taken all his money. He urges them to spend the rest of the summer at his rented cabin in the Catskills. The thought fills them with dread, but they agree to visit for a few days. Art is finding his graphic novel difficult; how can he make sense of the Holocaust if he cannot make sense of his relationship with his parents? He feels guilty for having had an easier life than his parents and remarks that he had a childhood sibling rivalry with Richieu's portrait, which hung in his parents' bedroom.

In the Catskills, Vladek complains endlessly about Mala and asks Art and Françoise to come live with him in Rego Park. They do not want to live with him but recognize that he is in bad health and needs assistance. Vladek continues his story with his arrival at Auschwitz. Although he and Anja were quickly separated (she was sent to nearby Birkenau), he says they were always together during the war. Vladek and a wealthy former business associate, Mandelbaum, are processed and housed together. Their prisoner numbers are tattooed on their forearms. A rabbi tells Vladek that his prison number is auspicious, and this gives him hope. Mandelbaum is miserable. It is winter, and he has only one shoe, pants that are too big, no belt, and no spoon.

Vladek volunteers to teach English to the kapo (a Polish prisoner who serves as a supervisor). In return, the kapo saves him from the gas chamber and arranges for him to get a nice uniform and leather shoes. Vladek also obtains a belt, shoes, and spoon for Mandelbaum, who thanks him profusely and declares them gifts from God. Several days later Mandelbaum is taken away and never seen again.

In Chapter 2, "Auschwitz (Time Flies)," Art is at his desk working. He is wearing a mouse mask, and flies are buzzing around the room. Dead bodies are piled at his feet. He summarizes the story thus far: Vladek died in 1982, he is working on this page in 1987, and he and Françoise are expecting their first child. In 1986 the first volume of *Maus* was published, but he is uncomfortable with his success. He feels guilty; he wants everyone to feel guilty. In each succeeding frame he appears smaller until he is the size of a child, whereupon he screams for his mommy. He decides to visit his therapist, Pavel, who also survived the concentration camps. Both of them are wearing mouse masks. Art tells Pavel about his writer's block. Pavel talks about survivor's guilt and how maybe there should not be any more Holocaust stories. Art invokes a quotation from writer Samuel Beckett about silence. Walking home, Art returns to normal size and reports that he feels much better.

In Auschwitz, Vladek proves adept at forming associations with key people in order to get himself extra food and to prevent starving or being sent to the gas chamber. He is assigned to work in a tin shop after claiming he knows how to do the work. Vladek befriends Mancie, a beautiful Hungarian girl who is having a relationship with a German officer and who passes notes and food from Vladek to Anja. Mancie risks her life to foster communication between them, believing their love deserves it. In Birkenau, Anja, who has always been weak and now appears as little more than a skeleton, is forced to carry large pots of soup that are too heavy for her. She spills constantly, and the guards beat her for it.

Vladek volunteers for the work detail at Birkenau, risking his life in order to glimpse Anja. Once, Vladek is caught speaking to her and severely beaten. Back at Auschwitz, more and more prisoners are falling ill. The Germans kill all who are no longer capable of work. Vladek volunteers to become a shoemaker and quickly learns yet another new skill. He is very good at it and curries favor with some of the German officials. He receives extra food, which he barters for favors from the kapo. Anja is moved to a new barracks in Auschwitz that is closer to Vladek—it is the only time in the camp that he is happy.

Once when Vladek sneaks food to Anja, she is chased by a guard. The guard threatens to kill her, but she disappears into the barracks, and her identity is never discovered. The next day the guards urge others in the barracks to turn her in. No one does. Meanwhile, Vladek has become quite weak. He is in danger of being sent to the gas chamber, so he hides in the bathroom during one of the periodic "selection" examinations. By now the Russians are closing in. Vladek and a few others are sent to dismantle the gas chambers. He describes them in detail, and Art provides a drawing of them. A fellow prisoner tells Vladek that after each gassing, he was forced to pry apart piles of dead, mangled bodies and shovel them into the furnaces. He also describes throwing people into pits and burning them alive.

As the Russians get closer, the Germans abandon Auschwitz and force the prisoners on a hundred-mile death march to Breslau, Germany. Those who cannot keep up are shot. Breslau is in chaos; within a few days Vladek is herded onto a cattle car with roughly two hundred other people. The train departs from Breslau but does not go far before it comes to a halt. The prisoners are locked inside with nothing to eat for about a week. Vladek survives by forming a hammock out of his blanket, which suspends him above the crush of bodies and enables him to grab snow off the roof of the train. The Germans unlock the doors only long enough for them to throw out the dead bodies. Eventually, when only a few of them are still alive, the train begins moving. At a Red Cross station they each receive a care package of food. It is February 1945.

The train takes them to Dachau, where there is nothing to do but wait to die. Vladek survives by striking up a friendship with a Frenchman who shares food with him in return for the opportunity to practice his English. He trades some of this food for a shirt with no lice. He wears the shirt only at inspection time; only prisoners with no lice can receive food.

Vladek's situation becomes bleaker when he contracts typhus. He steps on dead bodies each night to get to the bathroom. He becomes so weak he cannot get out of bed or even eat. He trades his bread to two others in exchange for help in getting to the bathroom. Eventually his fever breaks. Again, the camp is evacuated, and all able-bodied prisoners are marched to a train to be exchanged for German POWs at the Swiss border. Vladek is carried to the train by the men he paid to take him to the bathroom.

Back in the Catskills, Vladek is still disgruntled over Mala's inconsiderate departure. He packs up her opened boxes of food and takes them back to the grocery store. He argues with the store manager, telling him he is a Holocaust survivor and receives six dollars' worth of food for only a dollar.

On the way back from the grocery store, Françoise stops to give a ride to an African American hitchhiker. Vladek becomes extremely irritated, calls the man a *shvartser*, and worries he will steal the groceries. They drop the man off without incident. Françoise and Art rebuke Vladek for his racism, but he is unrepentant. Françoise says he talks about the blacks like the Nazis talked about the Jews, but Vladek disagrees. There is no comparison between blacks and Jews, he says, and she should be smart enough to know better.

Back in Rego Park, Vladek laments that his money and his health are gone. Art asks more about Anja. She left Auschwitz earlier than Vladek and spent time in Ravensbruck, a women's concentration camp. Anja was liberated near the Russian front earlier than Vladek and returned to Sosnowiec.

Vladek's train from Dachau never reaches the Swiss border. Instead, it stops, and a rumor spreads that the war is over. German soldiers seem not to know what to do with them. They are rounded up several times, believing they will be shot but are then released again. Eventually, Vladek and a friend, Shivek, hide out in an abandoned house. The Americans arrive a few days later, and after a while Vladek and Shivek report to a displaced persons camp.

Vladek shares with Art old photos of those on Anja's side of the family, some of whom survived the war and some of whom did not. On Vladek's side of the family, only his younger brother survived. Vladek's heart starts bothering him, and he must rest. Art apologizes for making him talk so much, but Vladek says that it is always a pleasure.

Vladek goes to Florida, and Art and Françoise fret about what to do when he returns. He is too ill to live on his own, but they do not want to move to Rego Park. Mala calls from Florida; she and Vladek have reunited, but now Vladek is in the hospital. She wants them to come down and help bring him back to a hospital in New York. When they arrive, Vladek is bedridden. He continues his story: After the war he and Anja left for Sweden, where he reestablished himself in the garment industry and Art was born. Vladek wants to stay in Sweden, but Anja wants to move to New York where she has relatives.

Vladek and Mala return briefly to New York before deciding to permanently relocate to Florida. By now, Vladek is starting to have memory problems. In their final interview session, Vladek recalls how he and Shivek received new papers at the displaced persons camp and departed for Hannover to stay with Shivek's family. Vladek tries to learn Anja's whereabouts through the Jewish community center in Sosnowiec, but he fears the worst. He travels to Belsen, where many Jewish refugees are gathering, and runs into acquaintances from Sosnowiec who say Anja is alive. He makes the arduous journey home, which takes three or four weeks because of the destruction of the rail lines. Eventually they are reunited.

Vladek retreats to bed, mistaking Art for his dead son, Richieu. The final image in the book shows Vladek and Anja's headstone, adorned only with the years of their births and deaths. Art signs his name below with the dates 1971–1994—the years in which he wrote the book.

CHARACTERS

Mancie

Mancie is a prisoner in Birkenau, the death camp sometimes called Auschwitz II. She is a beautiful Hungarian girl who ferries messages and food between Vladek and Anja, which helps Anja survive. Mancie is brave—if her actions are discovered she will be killed immediately. She is also reputed to be having an affair with a Nazi officer, which accounts for her ability to move between the camps more freely than the other prisoners. She agrees to help Vladek and Anja because she believes their love deserves it. Vladek regrets that he never learned her last name and was thus unable to compensate her for helping to keep Anja alive.

Mandelbaum

Mandelbaum is one of Vladek's former business associates, a millionaire in prewar Poland who is transferred to Auschwitz in the same group as Vladek. Mandelbaum's miserable circumstances at Auschwitz provide a rare moment of comedy in the story. He has only one shoe, which keeps falling off, his pants are too big, and he has no belt. He dropped his spoon while he was trying to hold his pants up and now has no utensil to eat with. Vladek, through his association with the kapo, arranges to get Mandelbaum real leather shoes, a belt, and a spoon. For this, Mandelbaum thanks him profusely, saying they are gifts from God. Several days later Mandelbaum is taken away and never seen again.

Françoise Mouly

Level-headed and supportive, Françoise is Art's wife and artistic comrade. Art struggles with how to portray her. She wants to be a mouse because she converted to Judaism when they married. Art finally relents after considering making her a frog (because she is French) or a reindeer. Françoise helps sort out Vladek's finances after Mala abandons him in the Catskills but angers Vladek when she picks up an African American hitchhiker. She notes that his distrust of black people is reminiscent of how the Germans treated the Jews, but he rebukes her for her naiveté.

Pavel

Pavel is Art's psychotherapist, a Czechoslovakian Jew, and an Auschwitz survivor. He sees patients only at night and keeps framed pictures of his cats in his office. In his session with Art,

both of them are drawn as humans wearing mouse masks as they discuss survivor's guilt and whether or not Art should give the world yet another Holocaust story. Art says that Pavel always makes him feel better, which is illustrated by Art's growth from a child-sized representation to his normal size on his walk home from the session.

Anja Spiegelman

Anja Spiegelman is Vladek's first wife and Art's mother. She is the pivotal figure in both Vladek's and Art's stories, yet her suicide and the destruction of her diaries prevent her from telling her own story in the book. By all accounts, she is a nervous, frail woman who was on medication even before her marriage to Vladek. Following the birth of Richieu, her depression reaches clinical proportions, and Vladek takes her for a three-month stay at a ritzy sanitarium.

During the hardships of the war, Anja tells Vladek that she wants to die. Vladek makes her promise to stay alive, because dying is easy and survival is hard. She displays little of the ingenuity that Vladek so cleverly wields during their imprisonment, yet she manages to survive. After the war, they move to Stockholm, where Art is born. She persuades Vladek to move to New York so she can be closer to her surviving relatives. When her nephew Lolek is killed in a car accident, her depression spirals out of control. She never recovers and commits suicide four years later in 1968. Anja's suicide is the subject of Art's comic-within-a-comic, "Prisoner on the Hell Planet," in which he blames his dead mother for the perfect crime of psychologically murdering him. He depicts her as a needy woman, asking her son, who has just been discharged from a mental hospital, if he still loves her.

Art Spiegelman

Art Spiegelman is the autobiographer of *Maus*. He is Vladek and Anja's son, a comic book writer intent on publishing his father's Holocaust story as a graphic novel. At times he portrays himself in a negative light. In "Prisoner on the Hell Planet," he blames his mother for murdering him as a result of her suicide, and at the end of Volume I he calls his father a murderer for having burned his mother's diaries about the war.

Like his mother, Art has suffered from mental illness, having checked himself into a mental hospital at age twenty following a nervous breakdown. At the time of the story, he is happily married, and at the beginning of Volume II, he and Françoise are expecting a child.

Art struggles with survivor's guilt, even though he was born after the Holocaust. In the beginning of Volume II, this guilt manifests itself as writer's block. He is bothered by the fact that life has been much easier for him than for his parents. Even worse, he has had an ongoing sibling rivalry with the photograph of his dead brother, which hangs in his parents' bedroom.

Art presents himself as an honest autobiographer and biographer. He could easily have drawn himself in a flattering way, but he does not. He includes stories his father has told him to omit, such as his affair with a woman before he met Anja. Art is conflicted about his father; he admires Vladek for his perseverance during the war, but he loathes the miserly, racist old man he has become.

Art is overwhelmed by the success of the first volume of *Maus* and shrinks—literally—from the media attention he receives. He works through his conflicted feelings about survivor's guilt and writer's block with his therapist but presents himself as a person wearing a mouse mask rather than as having a real mouse head during their session. In fact, Art suggests that the true survivor of *Maus: A Survivor's Tale* is himself, not Vladek. The last frame of Volume II gives Vladek's death year as 1982, years before the first volume was published, and the last name on the page—underneath Vladek and Anja's tombstone—is Art's.

Mala Spiegelman

Mala Spiegelman is a Holocaust survivor and Vladek's second wife. She knew Vladek and Anja before the war in Poland. Her parents were killed when the Sosnowiec Jews gathered at the sports stadium and then were sent to the camps. She marries Vladek following Anja's suicide and wonders how Anja put up with him for so many years. She complains endlessly about Vladek's miserly ways, insisting that she does not have enough money to buy herself essential items. Other Holocaust survivors are not nearly as stingy, she believes. She frequently threatens to leave him and ultimately does, taking much of his money with her. She is high-strung and calls upon Art for assistance in dealing with Vladek, especially after they reunite in Florida and he has yet another heart attack. She thinks Vladek values things more than people.

Richieu Spiegelman

Richieu is Anja and Vladek's first son, born in 1937. After the war begins, his parents send him away, presumably to a safer place. Instead, his Aunt Tosha poisons him, along with herself and her own two children, because she fears they are about to be sent to a concentration camp. Volume II is dedicated to Richieu, whose photograph appears on the dedication page. Art states that he endured a sibling rivalry with Richieu's photograph for his entire childhood. Art got into all sorts of trouble, but Richieu's photograph never did. At the end of the second volume, Vladek, ill and confused, calls Art Richieu by mistake, a Freudian slip that may indicate that the dead son is never far from the father's thoughts.

Vladek Spiegelman

Vladek Spiegelman is the story's main character. He relates his experiences before and during World War II to his son, Art, during a series of conversations during the late 1970s and early 1980s. Vladek is a survivor of Auschwitz, a notorious Nazi concentration camp in Poland where millions of Jews were killed as part of Adolf Hitler's Final Solution. As a young man, Vladek is successful in business and marries Anja, the daughter of a wealthy man. When the war starts, Vladek's knack for making deals to ensure his survival becomes obvious. He finds his way back home after becoming a prisoner of war, and as food is rationed and Jews are restricted from many daily activities, Vladek finds ways to do business to feed his family.

When Jews are being rounded up and sent to Auschwitz, Vladek hides his family in a cellar and then in an attic. After the ghetto is liquidated, he keeps himself and Anja safe for quite a while by arranging to hide in a townhouse and a barn. He always finds food, pays others for protection, and never takes advantage of people unfairly. He is honest, faithful, cautious, and knows whom to trust. He has the will to survive when Anja does not, and he urges her to work hard to stay alive.

As an old man in failing health at the time he tells his story to Art, however, Vladek is manipulative, miserly, and racist. He throws his son's coat away because he does not like it, returns opened boxes of food to the grocery store, reuses tea bags, and calls an African American man a *shvartser*, a derogative Yiddish term. He complains that his second wife wants to steal his money, he sneaks into the swimming pool of a Catskills hotel, and he feigns a heart attack to get his son to visit him.

Other people's misery does not register with Vladek. Mala is infuriated by his attachment to things instead of people, but he thinks she is only after his money. He believes that when he and Anja were reunited after the war, they lived happily ever after, but twenty years later Anja commits suicide and his son has a nervous breakdown. Vladek is tormented over the suicide of his beloved Anja, but he never expresses regret over failing to do something about her misery. He burns her diaries of the war after her death because of the painful memories they harbor.

In Auschwitz, Vladek's bravery reaches new heights. He capitalizes on his English language skills to win favor from the kapo. He routinely risks his life to smuggle food to Anja and talk to her occasionally. He volunteers for work for which he is not qualified, knowing he can pick up valuable new skills quickly. He never passes up an opportunity to barter his skills for food. He is a faithful friend who arranges to get Mandelbaum a belt and shoes that fit.

After the prisoners are marched out of Auschwitz, Vladek's survival skills reach their zenith. He ties a blanket to the ceiling of a cattle car to suspend himself above the mass of dying prisoners and becomes one of a handful of survivors because he can reach the snow on the roof. Later, felled by typhus, he pays others to take him to the bathroom. Even with one foot in the grave, he finds a way to barter for what he needs to save his life. When he can no longer eat, he gives them his food, and in return they help him leave Dachau rather than let him die in the abandoned camp.

Despite his inconsiderateness, Vladek appreciates Art very much, supports his work on the book, and shares his story as a way to spend time with him. However, at the end of his story, Vladek, in a weakened state, mistakenly calls Art "Richieu," indicating that he has never forgotten the dead boy and may feel closer in spirit to him than to his living son.

THEMES

Survival

The theme of survival is evident from the book's subtitle: *A Survivor's Tale*. While Vladek is the most obvious survivor of *Maus*, he is not the only

TOPICS FOR FURTHER STUDY

- Marjane Satrapi's *Persepolis* is a graphic novel for young adults published in two volumes like *Maus*. It is the autobiography of a privileged young girl growing up in Tehran during the Islamic Revolution who eventually immigrates to Vienna to escape oppression. Though the circumstances are different, Satrapi experiences hardships similar to those suffered by Vladek and Anja in World War II Poland. Write an essay describing the similarities between the plights of the Satrapis and the Spiegelmans.

- Make a chart to document instances in which Spiegelman draws something in the frame yet does not comment on it in the text. For each example, explain what the unremarked visual item adds to the story.

- Spiegelman illustrated *Maus* in a much different style than "Prisoner on the Hell Planet." In an essay, explain why you think he did this and how both illustration styles impact their respective stories.

- Research post-traumatic stress disorder (PTSD) online and find out what its common symptoms are. Create a short class presentation about PTSD or invite a healthcare professional to discuss the topic. Then divide the class into three groups to debate whether Anja, Vladek, and Art suffer from PTSD and why. Have each group present their findings to the class.

- Visit a local Holocaust museum or read a nonfiction account of World War II (such as Primo Levi's *Survival in Auschwitz* or *The Diary of Anne Frank*, a favorite of teenage readers). Create a Wikispace about how Vladek's experiences compare to other accounts of life in the Jewish ghettos and the concentration camps. Invite others to post information on your space, including Holocaust survivors and their relatives who may be able to add information.

one. Anja, who also lived through the Holocaust, survived for a number of years before the psychological toll of events prompts her suicide. Art is a survivor too, as evidenced by his signature on the last page of the story beneath the drawing of his parents' gravestone. In fact, many critics have noted that it is Art, not Vladek, who is the survivor of the title. This is suggested by the frame story, in which Art autobiographically depicts himself as surviving Vladek's exasperating antics and prevailing in his decades-long quest to bring his father's story to light.

A corollary of survival—survivor's guilt—looms large in the story. Art's guilt over his mother's death is melded with his anxieties about the Holocaust most vividly in "Prisoner on the Hell Planet," which shows him wearing a prison inmate's outfit (indistinguishable from a concentration camp uniform) and incarcerated for his mother's perfect crime—injecting him with a lethal dose of guilt through her suicide. Art also discusses survivor's guilt with Françoise and his therapist, Pavel. He feels guilty for having survived while his brother died and for having a much easier life than his parents. Finally, Volume II of *Maus* is dedicated to Richieu, who did not survive, and Nadja Spiegelman, his recently born niece who will usher in a new generation of the surviving Spiegelman family.

Family Relationships

The frame story of *Maus* depicts the relationship between Art and Vladek Spiegelman in Vladek's later years. It starts with Art's first visit to his father's home in two years. Their strained relationship is put aside when Art persuades Vladek to tell his story of the Holocaust. These occasions become an opportunity for them to spend time together. Vladek enjoys having Art around, but Art is more interested in writing his book than enjoying Vladek's company. Art continually deflects Vladek's concerns about his troubled relationship with Mala, money, home improvement, and his failing health.

While Art and Vladek's relationship is central to the story, Anja's relationship to Art is also important. Art becomes interested in Anja's Holocaust story only when he begins his book, even though her diaries had been around until after her death. Just before her suicide, Anja asks Art if he loves her, and he begrudgingly says he does. He reacts violently to Anja's suicide and Vladek's grief, believing himself to be the

victim of the neediness of both parents. When he finds out his father has burned Anja's diaries, Art calls Vladek a murderer, echoing his words following his mother's suicide. The Spiegelman family seems dysfunctional for not being able to acknowledge one another's pain. Vladek, for his part, believes that he and Anja lived happily ever after following the war, oblivious to the fact that she was miserable enough to commit suicide. In his second marriage, Mala and Vladek argue continually, neither one obtaining any degree of compassion or insight into the feelings of the other. After Mala leaves him, Art and Françoise (who appear to have a very healthy relationship) reject the idea of taking care of Vladek themselves. During the Holocaust, Vladek went to great, if futile, lengths to keep Anja's family safe, and now Art tries desperately to avoid having to do the same for Vladek.

Suffering

Closely related to the theme of family relationships is the theme of suffering. There are two types of suffering depicted in *Maus*. The first is the suffering of Vladek, Anja, and their families during World War II, when they were imprisoned, forced to hide, suffer starvation and illness, or killed outright. The second type of suffering happens after the Holocaust and concerns not only Vladek and Anja, but also Art and Mala. Vladek screams in his sleep—a situation the youthful Art believes is normal, and Anja suffers depression that leads to suicide. These lingering effects of the Holocaust cause Art to suffer guilt over having a better life than his parents.

Art and Mala both suffer from Vladek's extreme stinginess and constant complaining. The story-within-the-story, "Prisoner on the Hell Planet," depicts Art's mental anguish in the wake of his nervous breakdown—more suffering, albeit without much explanation. In Volume II, Art explains his creative and existential suffering in the chapter "Auschwitz (Time Flies)," in which he wonders if the world needs to hear another Holocaust story and how he should tell such a story, and by illustrating his ambivalence over the success of the book's first volume by drawing himself rising above a pile of dead bodies.

Creative Process

The main theme of the frame story in *Maus* is the creative process. Art draws himself recording Vladek's story, laboring over the creation of

In 2005, a Hungarian publisher organized an exhibition of scenes from Maus in Budapest subway cars.
(Attila Kisbenedek | AFP | Getty Images)

Maus, and suffering from conflicting feelings about the work's success. The second volume opens with Art and Françoise discussing which animal she should be drawn as—her French nationality and conversion to Judaism presenting a predicament. The chapter "Auschwitz (Time Flies)" is key to the theme of the creative process. Art draws himself in his studio, suffering from depression and writer's block in the wake of the first volume's publication. Barbed wire is visible outside the window, along with a prison-like spotlight. Dead bodies pile up at his feet. He is trapped by history, imprisoned by his inability to render the rest of Vladek's story.

The second half of the sequence shows Art at his therapist's office. Their conversation about Art's writer's block touches on guilt and whether or not there should be more Holocaust stories. The scene ends comically with Art quoting Samuel Beckett on the meaninglessness of speech. Pavel, the therapist, comments that he should put

that quote in his book. The creative process theme is also evident in the dates Spiegelman ascribes to himself at the end next to his signature beneath his parents' grave: 1978–1991. These are not his birth and death years but rather the years in which he labored over writing the book.

STYLE

Frame Narrative

Maus is written in the form of a story-within-a-story. The story of Art and Vladek is the frame narrative that surrounds the Holocaust story of Vladek and Anja. The Holocaust narrative is told in flashback form, which allows Vladek to share his eyewitness account in Spiegelman's autobiography. Art plays the role of historian, coaxing details from Vladek and providing the central metaphor of Jews as mice and Germans as cats. Art is a witness to Vladek's story, rarely questioning his account (except for the part about the orchestra at Auschwitz), serves as a surrogate for the reader in reacting to the horrors Vladek describes, and provides visual details of Vladek's story through his drawings. By providing this frame story, Spiegelman gives additional context to the Holocaust, especially in terms of its lingering effects on survivors and the children of survivors.

The frame technique contrasts the difference between Vladek as a young man—smart, resourceful, willful, and deliberate—with his older self—miserly, manipulative, and racist. For example, in Auschwitz Vladek saves the paper wrapping from the kapo's cheese, on which he writes a note to Anja. While he relates his story to Art, he picks up a scrap of wire from the sidewalk, claiming it has many uses. The first action is resourceful, the second is obsessive (Vladek has plenty of money should he need to buy wire), but as the frame narrative makes clear, the only difference between the two instances is Vladek's circumstances. Spiegelman relates these events in his quest to uncover Vladek's true nature—maybe he was just as difficult during the war as he was afterward, but in one situation his resourcefulness saved his life and in another it represents an unhealthy attachment to things instead of people.

The story of Anja's suicide and its impact on Art is told within the frame narrative as well, through the inclusion of Spiegelman's "Prisoner on the Hell Planet: A Case History" comic, first published in *Short Order Comix* in 1972, an underground magazine that Spiegelman coedited. Its inclusion is jarring because of the stark woodcut-style artwork that renders Art and his mother as people instead of mice.

Autobiography

Maus was initially considered fiction—it even charted on the *New York Times* fiction bestseller list until Spiegelman persuaded them to move it to nonfiction. Despite the fact that the characters are rendered as animals, *Maus* is Art Spiegelman's autobiography of the period in his life where he seeks out his father's story and tries to make sense of it. Embedded in Art's autobiography is Vladek's autobiography; the frame narrative becomes a savvy way to provide a maximum amount of story in a minimum amount of space. Underscoring the autobiographical nature of both their stories is the inclusion of several photographs. The photograph of Richieu (on the dedication page for Volume II),

the 1958 vacation snapshot of Art and Anja at the beginning of "Prisoner on the Hell Planet," and the studio portrait of Vladek wearing a concentration camp uniform after the war reveal the human beings behind the text's generic mouse drawings.

Maus is a specific type of autobiography—a Kunstlerroman, literally an artist's novel (from the German word for artist, *kunstler*). A Kunstlerroman portrays the writer as he or she embarks on a journey to artistic maturity. Notable Kunstlerromans in literary history include Thomas Mann's *Death in Venice*, James Joyce's *Portrait of the Artist as a Young Man*, and Virginia Woolf's *To the Lighthouse*. The writer of a Kunstlerroman is often a sensitive youth who rejects the bourgeois (middle-class) notions of his or her upbringing. While Spiegelman was not necessarily young when he wrote *Maus*, he was sensitive. His precarious mental state is depicted in "Prisoner on the Hell Planet" and in the portions of the frame narrative that deal with his guilt, depression, and anger. The dates next to his signature at the book's end, 1978–1991, encapsulate the years of his artistic journey and signal that the journey has come to an end.

Metaphor

The metaphor of *Maus* is evident from the book's title, which was inspired by Adolf Hitler's assertion that Jews were an inferior race who bred like vermin, thus giving him the moral right to exterminate them. In drawing Polish Jews as mice, Spiegelman underscores how the Nazi Party dehumanized an entire race of people, and in showing Germans as cats he signals their power over the Jews. Spiegelman continues the metaphor with other nationalities: the Polish gentiles are pigs; the Americans are dogs; and the French are frogs. This visual symbolism underscores that fact that one cause of the Holocaust was the inability to see past people's nationality and ethnicity and evaluate them as individuals. Completing Spiegelman's mouse metaphor is the fact that the gas used by the Nazis to exterminate the Jews—the Zyklon B brand of hydrogen cyanide—had been previously used to kill cockroaches.

Using animals as stand-ins for people has an illustrious literary history. From Aesop's Fables to Franz Kafka's "Josephine the Singer, or the Mouse Folk" to George Orwell's *Animal Farm* and E. B. White's *Charlotte's Web*, generations of writers have anthropomorphized animals in the interest of storytelling. In comics the tradition is even stronger. George Herriman's *Krazy Kat*, originated in 1913, included a cat, a mouse, and a dog. Walt Disney debuted Mickey Mouse in 1928 and added numerous animal pals to the gang in subsequent years; Walt Kelley's *Pogo* and Charles Schulz's *Peanuts* are two more recent examples.

Graphic Novel

A graphic novel is a book-length story told through a combination of words and images arranged in panel format. As a literary form, it has a short history. Will Eisner's *A Contract with God*, published in 1978, is considered by many to be the birth of the genre. The mainstream success of the first volume of *Maus* just eight years later opened the door for many other graphic novelists.

The main unit of the graphic novel is the page. Within a page the artist draws panels that can be edited to a certain degree, similar to a scenes in a film, but once a page is designed it is difficult to rework it without impacting other pages as well. Whereas many novelists might think in terms of chapters, graphic novelists think in terms of the number of panels on a page and how to economize both words and images in order to capture only the details necessary to tell the story.

The advantage of *Maus* over other Holocaust memoirs is its visual narrative. Spiegelman illustrates Vladek's stories with drawings and diagrams of hiding places and the Auschwitz gas chambers and maps of Auschwitz and Birkenau. In Vladek's story of how he learned to be a shoemaker, Spiegelman draws a diagram of how his father sewed an officer's leather boots together, thereby securing himself extra food. In these instances, a picture really is worth a thousand words. Another advantage of graphic novels is the author's ability to draw one thing and say another or to have the image and the text subtly askew. This succinct dissonance adds richness to the story. For example, when Vladek, Art, and Françoise are driving to the grocery store, Vladek tells of four girls in Auschwitz who tried to revolt and were hanged. Rather than depict the girls in a flashback, Spiegelman draws himself, Vladek, and Françoise meandering through the Catskills on the way to the grocery store. The bare feet of the four hanged girls hover in the foreground of the frame.

Combining both stories into a single image exemplifies the narrative economy of a graphic novel. It also suggests that the ghosts of the Holocaust's six million victims live in the memories of the survivors, half a world away from where the horror took place.

HISTORICAL CONTEXT

The Jewish Ghetto

The details of Vladek's story are historically accurate. Beginning in 1939, the Germans quarantined Poland's Jews into small, tightly packed ghettos. They lacked sufficient food, clothing, and other amenities. As the war continued, the ghettos became de facto concentration camps. Of the Polish ghettos, Warsaw's was the largest, with three hundred eighty thousand residents— 30 percent of the city's population—living on 2.4 percent of its land. The ghetto was walled off, and those who attempted to escape were shot. Conditions were such that many died of disease and starvation. By 1944, many ghettos were liquidated, meaning everyone was killed or sent to concentration camps.

Sosnowiec, Poland, where Vladek and Anja lived, had roughly thirty thousand Jewish residents at the start of World War II. Because of its location on the German-Polish border, it was one of the first cities to be occupied by the Germans and one of the first to suffer wide-scale executions. During the early years of the war, the Jewish residents were used as slave laborers for the German war effort. In late 1942, just as Vladek describes, the remaining residents of the ghetto were moved to nearby Srodula or taken to Auschwitz. The ghetto was liquidated in the spring of 1944. Today, Sosnowiec is a thriving metropolis of two million people, but the number of Jewish citizens is unknown. Roughly twenty thousand Jews lived in all of Poland in 2006.

Auschwitz

The Final Solution was the Nazi Party's plan for carrying out systematic genocide against European Jews. The plan called for the construction of several extermination camps inside Poland to make the slaughter organized and efficient. Once the Jews were rounded up in the ghettos, they were transported to the camps via existing railroads. They were divided into two groups upon arrival, with one group sent immediately to the

COMPARE
&
CONTRAST

- **1940s:** Suffering from depression, Anja Spiegelman visits a sanitarium near the Czechoslovakian border—possibly in Gorbersdorf, a resort town that attracts wealthy visitors from all over Europe.

  1970s: Art Spiegelman suffers a nervous breakdown and is admitted to a state mental institution, a common treatment of the day, where he stays for several weeks. A nervous breakdown indicates a person is unable to function in everyday life because of anxiety and depression, although it is not a medical diagnosis.

  Today: In-patient treatment for mental illness is rare, as most state mental institutions have shut their doors. Treatment commonly consists of medication dispensed through out-patient clinics.

- **1940s:** The Nazis kill six million people during World War II. Jews, Polish gentiles, Soviet prisoners, homosexuals, Roma, and mentally and physically handicapped people are all targeted.

  1970s: Pol Pot, the leader of the Khmer Rouge and the de facto ruler of Cambodia, orders the deaths of two hundred thousand people, mostly Chinese, between 1975 and

1979. In total, 1.5 to 2.5 million people die from disease, starvation, oppression, and violence. Many historians consider it the worst genocide of the Cold War era.

  Today: Since 2003, the war in Darfur, Sudan, has displaced up to two million people and caused the deaths of three hundred thousand more people. Though some believe the conflict is a genocide, others disagree, stating that the intent to abolish an entire race is not present.

- **1940s:** Wealthy Jewish tourists visit European spa towns such as Czechoslovakia's Karolvy Vary, the site of a renowned mineral hot springs, resort hotels, and sanitariums, some of which allow Jewish guests.

  1970s: Jewish families living in New York frequent the many resorts run by and for Jewish people in the Catskill Mountains, but with many postwar immigrants nearing retirement, Florida gains in popularity as a vacation destination.

  Today: Jewish travelers can enjoy a variety of kosher tours worldwide, and young adults are encouraged to visit Israel through nonprofit organizations that sponsor free vacations as part of their birthright.

---

gas chambers and the other to barracks in order to provide slave labor until they were killed. Dead bodies were incinerated in crematoria or buried in pits. Auschwitz I opened in 1940 and was initially a work camp. As the Holocaust intensified, the camp was expanded. Birkenau (Auschwitz II) became operational in 1942, and a majority of the more than one million people who died in Auschwitz were killed in its gas chambers. As Spiegelman states in the chapter "Auschwitz (Time Flies)," the Hungarian Jews were killed at an unprecedented rate in the spring of 1944—over four hundred thousand in less than three months.

The Auschwitz death march Vladek endured began on January 17, 1945. Sixty thousand prisoners were evacuated to the Gross-Rosen concentration camp about one hundred miles away. Tens of thousands died along the way, either during the march itself or in overcrowded cattle cars as they were transported to their final destination. The seventy-five hundred remaining Auschwitz prisoners—those too weak to march—were liberated by the Soviet Army on January 27, 1945. In total about three hundred thousand former Auschwitz prisoners survived the war. In 1947, Auschwitz became a museum, and since then millions of visitors have walked beneath the infamous

Anti-Semitic sign (*Image copyright Timothy R. Nichols, 2010. Used under license from Shutterstock.com*)

Arbeit Macht Frei ("Work Brings Freedom") sign emblazoned over its gates, which Spiegelman reproduces in the first volume of *Maus*.

Holocaust Survivors in New York

From 1945 to 1952, between eighty thousand and one hundred forty thousand Holocaust survivors immigrated to the United States from the displaced persons camps in Europe. About half settled in the New York area, and many others moved to southern Florida. Rego Park, a neighborhood in Queens, a borough of New York City, welcomed a number of these immigrants with amenities that included existing synagogues, affordable housing, and plentiful business opportunities. Over the years, many of these Jews have moved away, and more recent Soviet Jewish immigrants have taken their place.

During the humid New York City summer, many Jews vacationed in the Catskill Mountains northwest of the city. Family-run resorts catered to a Jewish clientele and fostered an atmosphere

of community. Jewish comedians played in the resorts' lounges, a circuit that came to be known as the Borscht Belt. Children spent the summer in sleep-away camps, and during Jewish holidays the resorts were packed. By the 1970s as Jewish immigrants became more assimilated or retired to Florida, the resorts of the Catskills fell into decline. However, many older New Yorkers, such as Vladek Spiegelman, continued to vacation there.

The Rise of Independent Comix

In the late 1960s and early 1970s, Spiegelman was an influential figure in the rise of underground comics, or comix, as they were often called. Writers such as Spiegelman, Robert Crumb, and Bill Griffith self-published often graphic and profane autobiographical stories infused with large doses of self-loathing, violence, sex, and cultural criticism. The scene thrived in San Francisco, where Robert Crumb published *Zap* and Bill Griffith and Spiegelman edited *Short Order Comix*, an anthology devoted to stories of no more than four pages. Issue Number 1 in 1973 included "Prisoner on the Hell Planet." By the time Spiegelman returned to New York and launched *RAW* (in which *Maus* was initially serialized) with Mouly in 1980, the underground scene was morphing into an independent scene that paved the way for the alternative comics of the late 1980s and 1990s.

CRITICAL OVERVIEW

Maus was published to overwhelming critical acclaim. When the first volume appeared in 1986, graphic novels were unfamiliar to many readers. The success of the first volume fostered acceptance of the genre and paved the way for other graphic novelists, including Joe Sacco, Chris Ware, and Marjane Satrapi. As a Holocaust narrative, the book was lauded as well. In a *New York Times Book Review* assessment of *And Here My Troubles Began*, Lawrence L. Langer comments that "perhaps no Holocaust narrative will ever contain the whole experience. But Art Spiegelman has found an original and authentic form to draw us closer to its bleak heart." Writing in *VLS*, Laurie Muchnick applauds Spiegelman for creating "the perfect structure: *Maus*'s horror is intimate yet tolerable, its presentation gimmicky but expressive." In his review for *Newsweek*, David Gates admires "the comforting artificiality of an animal cartoon [that] worked both as savage irony and as a nearly transparent surface through which human horror could be imagined."

A few critics question Spiegelman's use of animals to represent ethnicity and nationality, claiming it perpetuates stereotypes. In an essay for *Commentary*, Hillel Halkin states that it is wrong to believe that Germans killed Jews and the Poles allowed it to happen because "cats kill mice, who do not attack cats, while pigs do not care about either." Instead, Halkin maintains, "the Holocaust was a crime committed by humans against humans, not—as Nazi theory held—by one biological species against another." Others think that Spiegelman did not take full advantage of the graphics portion of a graphic novel and that his drawings are mere illustrations rather than a vital component of the narrative. James Walton, who generally praises *And Here My Troubles Began*, writes in *Spectator* that by the time Vladek reaches Auschwitz, Spiegelman has run out of

sufficient tools with which to tell the story. "The most horrifying set pieces, the living and dead being burned together in mass graves...simply don't work as cartoons," Walton writes. "They seem both melodramatic and bathetic, inadequate images of his father's words."

In the years since the book's publication, many scholars have sought to assess *Maus*'s place within the body of Holocaust literature. Michael E. Staub, writing in *MELUS*, notes that *Maus* is "very much about...the tensions involved in understanding what it means to have a Jewish identity in a post-Auschwitz age."

Maus "has been embraced by both popular and academic readers," writes Joshua L. Charlson in *Arizona Quarterly*. Charlson admires how Spiegelman uses the "trivialized" art form of the comic strip, populated with anthropomorphic animals, as a "profound meditation on the historical event considered by many the gravest in its ethical implications for the twentieth century."

CRITICISM

Kathy Wilson Peacock

Wilson Peacock is a nonfiction writer who specializes in literature and history. In this essay, she analyzes Spiegelman's technique of breaking the fourth wall in Maus.

Spongebob Squarepants does it. *Malcolm in the Middle* does it too. Before that, it was evident in *Ferris Bueller's Day Off*, *Monty Python's Flying Circus*, Jane Austen's exhortations to her Dear Reader, and William Shakespeare's winking asides to the audience. It is the practice of addressing a reader or viewer directly, a metafictional technique known as breaking the fourth wall. In *Maus: A Survivor's Tale*, the wall between the reader and the story is already paper thin, given that key scenes depict Art Spiegelman himself writing the story, but in several instances the barrier falls away completely, allowing him to speak directly to his readers. While Spiegelman's breaking the fourth wall has an obvious comic effect, it also serves to involve the reader actively in the writing process.

The idea of the fourth wall dates back to the French Enlightenment philosopher Denis Diderot. He initially used the term for the theater, suggesting that the proscenium serves as a fourth wall of the stage separating the actors

WHAT DO I READ NEXT?

- Art Spiegelman's *In the Shadow of No Towers* (2004) is the author's account of 9/11, which he witnessed firsthand from his home in lower Manhattan. The collection of comics documents his struggle to come to terms with terrorism, Islamic fundamentalism, and the U.S. government's subsequent war on terror.

- Anne Frank began *The Diary of a Young Girl* on her twelfth birthday, and it chronicles the two years she and her family hid from the Nazis in occupied Amsterdam. Eventually discovered, Frank died in Bergen-Belsen concentration camp shortly before the end of the war. Her manuscript was first published in the United States in 1952 and has since been adapted for stage and film. The Frank family's experiences bear many similarities to those of Vladek and Anja as they sought to avoid being sent to the camps.

- As a teenager, Nobel Peace Prize laureate Elie Wiesel was imprisoned in Auschwitz and survived the death march to Buchenwald. His short memoir *Night* documents his plight, during which he ignores his father's dying words and explores his loss of faith in religion and humankind. Originally written in Yiddish and first published in 1955, the book met with indifference when published in the United States in 1960. It has since sold millions of copies and become the first volume of a trilogy that includes the novels *Dawn* (1961) and *Day* (also known as *The Accident*) (1962).

- Chris Ware's graphic novel *Jimmy Corrigan, the Smartest Kid on Earth* (2000) won an American Book Award in 2001. The story, first serialized in Ware's periodic *Acme Novelty Library*, is told partly in flashback form and concerns the relationship of an isolated, middle-aged man with his overbearing mother and his estranged father, whom he has met only once.

- Marjane Satrapi's *Persepolis: Story of a Childhood* (2003) and *Persepolis 2: Story of a Return* (2004) are autobiographical graphic novels about Satrapi's youth in Iran during the Islamic Revolution, a time of violence and social upheaval. Fearing for Marjane's safety, her parents send her to school in Vienna, where she finds life as an expatriate teenager difficult. Succumbing to homesickness, she returns to Iran and finds it a much different place than she remembers.

- Joe Sacco won the American Book Award in 1996 for his two-volume graphic novel *Palestine*, a journalistic account of his travels to the West Bank and Gaza Strip in 1991 to document everyday life in the occupied territories during the long-standing violent confrontation between the Palestinians and the Israelis.

- Scott McCloud's award-winning *Understanding Comics: The Invisible Art* (1993) is a comic book that introduces readers to the genre of comic books and graphic novels. McCloud traces the history of the medium and provides insight on specific advantages of the form.

- Gilbert Hernandez's *Palomar: The Heartbreak Soup Stories* (2003) is a graphic novel that collects thirteen years' worth of Hernandez's stories about the interconnected lives of residents in the small Central American town of Palomar. The stories embody the complex family histories and emotional lives of their characters in a concise, spare style that sometimes employs the kind of magic realism common in Latin American literature.

WHILE SPIEGELMAN'S BREAKING THE FOURTH WALL HAS AN OBVIOUS COMIC EFFECT, IT ALSO SERVES TO INVOLVE THE READER ACTIVELY IN THE WRITING PROCESS."

from the audience. An implicit divide between them would advance the realism of drama, he believed, allowing for more realistic exploration of the human condition than the previous theatrical conventions of comedy and tragedy. For close to two hundred years, the fourth wall stayed largely intact, until Thornton Wilder's Stage Manager character took the audience on a tour of Grover's Corners in his 1937 play *Our Town*.

Breaking the fourth wall is a technique of metafiction, a term that describes any work of literature that acknowledges its existence as a work of fiction. Frame narratives, the author-as-narrator, and parallel narratives are all forms of metafiction. The term was coined by the author William H. Gass in his 1970 essay "Philosophy and the Form of Fiction," but the practice has a long history. The ninth-century *A Thousand and One Nights* presents the wily Scheherazade prolonging her life by telling nightly stories to her punitive husband, and in the fourteenth century *The Canterbury Tales* was written by and stars the unreliable narrator Geoffrey Chaucer. Contemporary novelists who employ all manner of metafiction in their works include Kurt Vonnegut, John Barth, Thomas Pynchon, David Foster Wallace, and Jonathan Safran Foer. Breaking the fourth wall is a specialized metafictional device that accompanies several others in *Maus*, including the frame narrative and the author-as-character.

At its most basic, *Maus* is a self-reflexive story about storytelling: Art tells the story of his father telling his story about the Holocaust. Part of Art's story is his struggle to relate Vladek's story and his anguish over the loss of his mother's story. Thus, its metafictional status is apparent from the get-go. A good example occurs in the first chapter of Volume I. Vladek recounts an affair he had with a woman named Lucia before he met and married Anja. He makes Art promise

to leave it out of the book because it is disrespectful to Anja and has nothing to do with the Holocaust. Art briefly argues that it adds human dimension to the story but ultimately promises to leave it out. Obviously, he has broken his promise. In one fell swoop, Spiegelman tells the reader that he is a dishonest son but an honest historian. This self-reflexivity reflects poorly on Art—he is not as faithful to his father as he is in his pursuit of his story.

Although Spiegelman has serious aims in the book, he sometimes breaks the fourth wall for comic effect. For example, in Volume II, Art expresses to Françoise his childhood fantasies of Zyklon B and his guilt over having an easier life than his parents. He doubts his ability to render the Holocaust in comic book form and states that comics cannot encompass the complexity of reality. As proof of the distorted reality of comics, he offers up the fact that in real life Françoise would never let him talk so long. This sort of self-reflexiveness is typical of Jewish humor, according to Jeff Berkwits of the *San Diego Jewish Journal*, who wrote that quintessentially Jewish humor is "self-deprecatory and humorous without being hurtful."

Spiegelman's self-reflexive, self-disparaging humor was inspired at least partly by Harvey Kurtzman, the founding editor of *Mad* magazine. "[*Mad*] was *about* something—reality, for want of a better word," Spiegelman said in an interview with James E. Young for *Critical Inquiry*. "[It] was also highly self-reflexive, satirically questioning not only the world, but also the underlying premises of the comics medium through which it asked questions." Adam Gopnik, in an essay about *Maus* for the Museum of Modern Art, also noted and appreciated comics as the "metalanguage of modernism, a fixed point of reference outside modern painting to which artists could refer in order to make puns and ironic jokes."

Yet most of *Maus*'s fourth-wall breaking and self-reflexiveness has little to do with humor. As Spiegelman told Young, he prefers to call what he does "commix" instead of "comics" because the latter term

> brings to mind the notion that they have to be funny...humor is not an intrinsic component of the medium. Rather than comics...I prefer the word commix, to mix together, because to talk about comics is to talk about mixing together words and pictures to tell a story.

Certainly the totality of Spiegelman's words and pictures about the Holocaust are anything but funny. Such is the case with the book's most extended example of fourth-wall breaking, in the chapter "Auschwitz (Time Flies)" from Volume II.

Art interrupts his story to give readers a non-chronological list of events that weigh heavily on his mind, including the slaughter of Hungarian Jews at Auschwitz in May of 1944, the success of the first volume of *Maus* in 1986, the death of his father in 1982, and the impending birth of his first child as he writes the chapter in 1987. Art, wearing a mouse mask, is working at his desk with flies buzzing around his head. Dead bodies pile up at his feet, and the view outside his window resembles that of a prison. He is bombarded by interviewers and dealmakers as he shrinks into baby mouse size. He feebly defends the intent of his writing and cries out for his mommy.

He goes to see his therapist, Pavel, also an Auschwitz survivor. Art mentions that Pavel loves cats and keeps framed photographs of them in his office. Then he asks the reader whether or not that detail messes up the mouse metaphor—a humorous breaking-the-fourth-wall event perhaps designed to head off critics of the metaphor (or at least to keep them from taking it too seriously). A couple frames later Spiegelman draws the reader's attention to a framed cat portrait. Art and Pavel discuss survivor's guilt and whether or not people should continue to tell Holocaust stories. Art mentions Irish playwright Samuel Beckett's epigraph that "every word is like an unnecessary stain on silence and nothingness." Of course the fact that Beckett actually uttered such a phrase is ironic. Pavel suggests that Art include it in the book. His decision is self-evident and stands as an official rebuke of remaining silent on the Holocaust.

There are other examples of breaking the fourth wall in *Maus*, including the photograph of Vladek that appears near the end of Volume II. Although Richieu's portrait appears on the book's dedication page and a small photo of Anja and Art is reprinted in the comic-book-within-the-comic-book of "Prisoner on the Hell Planet," the sudden appearance of a young, handsome Vladek sporting a concentration camp uniform breaks through the layers of story in *Maus* and presents the reader with a bona fide, unfiltered primary document of history.

In the end, what do these fourth-wall examples add up to? According the Barry Laga of *Arizona Quarterly*:

> The point is that Spiegelman wants to make us aware of his intrusiveness.... The self-reflexive shaping and framing of the story has significant implications, particularly in terms of Spiegelman's coming to terms with the subtly oppressive Vladek. We almost get the sense that by being so self-reflexive, so "honest" as Françoise tells him, Spiegelman feels he can escape the "ghost of his father" which still haunts him.

Yet there is another reason Spiegelman breaks the fourth wall, and that is to obliterate the time-honored tradition of suspension of disbelief. The primary purpose behind erecting the fourth wall, Diderot believed, was to separate the audience from the action on stage in order to heighten the realism of the drama, but the Holocaust is already real, and by smashing the fourth wall, Spiegelman brings his readers closer to the events he is grappling with. Spiegelman gives us Vladek's words and heightens them with illustrations. Then he addresses readers directly, just to make sure they are paying attention. It is just one of the smorgasbord of literary devices Spiegelman employs in his quest to pack maximum impact in a book of minimal size.

Source: Kathy Wilson Peacock, Critical Essay on *Maus: A Survivor's Tale*, in *Novels for Students*, Gale, Cengage Learning, 2011.

Nina Siegal

In the following interview, Spiegelman discusses graphic novels and comic art as well as his experience on September 11, 2001.

Pulitzer Prize-winning author and illustrator Art Spiegelman, the man who made the comic book legit, has lived most of his life in New York. But he was born in Stockholm to parents who were both Holocaust survivors. He moved to Rego Park, New York, as a young boy. Although his parents wanted him to be a dentist, he was already drawing obsessively as a teenager and took his first art classes in high school. By sixteen, he was working as a professional artist.

He studied art and philosophy at Harpur College and later became a creative consultant for Topps Candy, designing Wacky Packages, Garbage Pail Kids, and other novelty items. In 1980, Spiegelman and his wife, Francoise Mouly, founded *RAW*, a large-format graphic magazine that featured strips by underground

A cremation oven at the Dachau concentration camp in Germany (Image copyright Phillip Holland, 2010. Used under license from Shutterstock.com)

> SO, I THOUGHT: WHAT STORY DO I HAVE THAT'S WORTH TELLING? AND AT THAT TIME IT SEEMED OBVIOUS TO ME THAT IT HAD TO BE THIS STORY I GOT FROM MY PARENTS—*MAUS.*"

comic artists such as Chris Ware, Mark Beyer, and Dan Clowes. In his contributions for *RAW* (subtitled "Open Wounds from the Cutting Edge of Commix"), Spiegelman experimented with drawing and narrative styles, producing strips that helped create an avantgarde of comic art.

During that time, he was also working on a graphic novel based on his parents' experiences during the Holocaust, and their later life in America. In this novel, *Maus*, published in two parts, he subverted the traditional use of comics—making funnies—to tell a tragic tale, portraying Jews as mice and Nazis as cats. Writing and drawing the book took thirteen years. It won Spiegelman the Pulitzer Prize in 1992—the first time a comic novel had won the prestigious award.

In 1993, Spiegelman became a staff artist and writer for *The New Yorker*, contributing some of the magazine's most memorable cover

art, including the black-on-black depiction of the Twin Towers that ran on the magazine's front cover just after September 11. He also collaborated with his wife, who is *The New Yorker*'s art director, on books for children, including *Little Lit: Folklore & Fairy Tale Funnies*, and *Strange Stories for Strange Kids*.

On September 11, 2001, he was in his home in Lower Manhattan, a few blocks away from the Twin Towers. He and Francoise ran to collect their son, Dashell, and their daughter, Nadja, who had just started the fall semester at Stuyvesant High School near Ground Zero. He saw the towers' unearthly glow just moments before they disintegrated.

He describes these experiences in his new book, *In the Shadow of No Towers*, which gathers together strips he drew mostly for European periodicals. It begins with the words, "I tend to be easily unhinged," and it explores Spiegelman's own frantic attempts to understand the events of that day and its aftermath. "Doomed, doomed to drag this damn albatross around my neck, and compulsively retell the calamities of September 11th to anyone who'll listen," he writes. Struggling to portray his own consciousness, he draws himself variously as a character from *Maus* and as classic cartoon figures from comics such as Happy Hooligan, Little Nemo in Slumberland, and Bringing Up Father.

A couple of weeks before the November election, Spiegelman was seated on a plush couch in the lobby of the Swissotel in downtown Chicago, chain-smoking and throwing back cups of coffee as if they were vitamins.

He talked to the *Progressive* about his new book, the politics of publishing, media censorship, his own drawing process, and the history of comic art. After the elections, I got back in touch with him.

Q: What was your reaction to Bush's victory?

Art Spiegelman: I'm still in too much of a depressed state to say anything about it.

Q: How did you come up with the image for The New Yorker *cover just after September 11, 2001, which is also the main image on the cover of your new book?*

Spiegelman: I think I channeled that image more than doing it. It wasn't what I was thinking of doing. On September 11, after we rounded up our kids and went home, one of the messages on our answering machine was from *The New Yorker* saying get down here right away for a special issue we'll be doing. That seemed so irrelevant to me, considering the cataclysm. I went to my studio for a while and I was processing the news. Because when we were in the thick of it, it just felt like Mars Attacks!, Is Paris Burning?, and I had no perspective. For a while, I thought I should go down and look for bodies. At the same time, since *The New Yorker* was looking for images, I thought, "Well, I'm more trained to look for images than for bodies."

The first image I came up with ended up being the cover of a book *110 Stories: New York Writes After September 11*, edited by Ulrich Baer, which was an image of the towers shrouded, floating above the city. It just wasn't working for *The New Yorker*. I was barking up the wrong tree—it had a blue sky and orange building; it was channeling [Rene] Magritte, with the thought bubble, "It's such a nice day, what a bummer." It was a reasonable cover for a book that came out a year later, but it just wasn't sufficient, because anything with a nice blue sky and pretty orange building was just too pretty. And pretty outweighed whatever meanings those shrouds had.

So I kept trying to gray down and dim down the image, so, OK, a less blue sky, less orange buildings. And I found out later that Francoise was under pressure to use a photograph instead of a drawing, which would have been a defeat of a hand-and-eye making an image, which was *The New Yorker*'s seventy-something-year-old tradition. I was looking at images and I was talking to friends and everyone had a consensus: Have no cover, have no image, maybe black. And that seemed like as much of a defeat as having a photograph. Then I finally said to Francoise that it should just be a black-on-black cover because every time I was walking to my studio from my house I kept finding myself turning

around to make sure the towers were not there, as though they were a kind of phantom limb.

Q: How would you describe the content of No Towers?

Spiegelman: This book is fragment of diary. In making the book, I'm trying to work my way out. By the end of the book I'm somewhere near the end of 2002. These are really over-articulated journal entries. We're still waiting to see the denouement, especially what it means to have reduced that event to a very jingoistic and belligerent set of responses. September 11 has been so co-opted, particularly by people who wanted to lead us into war. And that became a big part of the subject matter of the strips.

As pages, they were ephemeral. They were made for newspapers and magazines that were willing to have me, mostly in my own coalition of the willing, as I've described it. And they weren't really designed to be a book.

The idea of making a book implies for me a notion of posterity. At this point, yes it's true, most books have the shelf life of yogurt, but built into the notion of a book is something that has its own small monumental qualities. To find a book out of these fragments meant making something of these strips that actually had a reason to exist together. What I was able to find was a kind of art object appropriate to the occasion: a book that looked like a tower that was both incredibly fragile and was able to get scuffed but also has that monumental quality, and a book that had a thematic discourse.

Q: What was it?

Spiegelman: For me, it was, what's the nature of ephemera? Here's the best I can boil it down to: When the monumental—like two 110-story towers that were meant to last as long as the Pyramids—becomes ephemeral, the ephemeral, one's daily life, the passing moment, takes on a more monumental quality.

Q: Some of the criticism of the book has focused on the inclusion of archival broad sheets from classic comic strips. Michiko Kakutani of The New York Times *called the shift from your own narrative to the strips "jarring." How do you respond to those criticisms?*

Spiegelman: To me, the book requires that second part because otherwise it's just a fragmentary thing, a subjective part of a subjective meltdown. I was trying to scrape away the bullshit and piety that have come along with what we've seen so far. Some reviews have taken me to task for not being more temperate, for example. Some say it's impossible to say that we're equally threatened by Al Qaeda and our own government, even though to me that seems about as accurate a depiction I can find of where we actually are.

You then get to the second set of pages that finds the happy ending and the present in our history, in our past. You can look back to another moment when the world was ending, for example, September 11, 1901, when President McKinley had been shot. And the paper was full of bullshit lies of misdirection. Emma Goldman was immediately arrested for having killed the President. All of these pages have a kind of timeless quality—the quality that art's supposed to have—and they're also rooted in the present moment.

For example, I found a page with the help of friends that we called "Abdullah Hooligan the Arrogant Clown." Happy Hooligan pretends to be Abdullah, an Arab chief, riding a camel. Abdullah keeps turning around to wave to his nephews, and every time he turns around he whacks the camel. Finally, the camel gets understandably pissed off, and he tosses him into a tower of acrobats. That's a comic strip that could've been written by Susan Sontag if she had a sense of humor and was able to draw. It's essentially the same argument that got her so excoriated in *The New Yorker* when she said you have to look at how we've dealt with the Middle East to understand how we've created an environment that's gone so off the deep end.

Q: No Towers *employs a variety of different characters, drawing styles, and narrative threads to tell its story, creating a kind of frantic schizophrenia. Why did you decide to take that approach with this book, which is a dramatic departure from the style you used for* Maus?

Spiegelman: It actually just felt accurate to the inside of my head. Ultimately that was the pleasure of the work for me. The comics I made before *Maus* were dealing with structural aspects of comics. Doing that kind of work was finding me fewer and fewer readers every time I managed to get a page made.

At some point, I capitulated, and I decided that what people really want from comics is narrative. So, I thought: What story do I have that's worth telling? And at that time it seemed obvious to me that it had to be this story I got

from my parents—*Maus*. It involved using all the specific discoveries I'd made about how comics work formally and using those formal elements not to jump or undercut the narrative but to allow the narrative to happen more seamlessly. Eventually you were left with an IV that just delivered you narrative. After a few pages most people weren't even aware anymore that they were reading comics, and that was fine by me. I didn't want to get in the way of an already complex set of narrative events and themes that needed to be the focus of the book.

With the *No Towers* pages, I wasn't making them for anyone specifically. Unlike with *The New Yorker*, I was given a no-editor's clause and giant acreages of newsprint in which I could do anything I wanted. My goal was to be clear without overclarifying. Someone described the work as a work of "crystalline ambiguity," and that's what I was striving for. Because anything else is dumbing it down. The strategies that I used in *No Towers* return a much fuller voice to me, and I'm really thankful for that.

Q: You've talked a little bit about censorship at The New Yorker. *Can you tell us what it was like to try and get your work into* The New Yorker?

Spiegelman: I loved David Remnick's comment on this, which was, "Spiegelman confuses editing with censorship." And I have to confess that I think he's right because I have a very finite notion of what editing should consist of, and as soon as it transgresses, it becomes something else to me, and I call it censorship. It's not what the rest of the planet would call it. It's my own private vocabulary. The cover of *The New Yorker* is a very high soapbox, and so it's very tempting to want to climb on it and talk. But if what you want to say is limited and distorted by the time you get to the top of the soapbox, it's not quite worth speaking from. If I'd had a supportive editor, I probably would've found a way to make *No Towers* work within the context of the magazine. It was not necessarily Remnick's fault, because I was able to do things there as long as I could find the proper register or tone in which to speak. And it's very hard to scream "The sky is falling!" and keep your monocle in place.

Q: Did Remnick's overt support for the war have anything to do with your decision to leave The New Yorker *in 2003?*

Spiegelman: Remnick did something unusual in writing a "Talk of the Town" about being a reluctant hawk. And that was rather shocking, because it's not like the magazine is required to have an editorial. It's not like the *New York Times* in that way or *The Wall Street Journal*, where it's important to know exactly where the magazine is coming from.

The absolute cowardice of the mainstream American press at that time was overwhelming. The tendency is to find a consensual center, but because of a kind of hegemony that's set in, one side of the continuum has yanked the conversation way over to the right. So now the terms of the debate are shifted so far in that direction that there's virtually nothing taking place in news, except for places like the virtually unread *Progressive* and a handful of other publications in the so-called alternative press. And they're just not on the radar in terms of rallying the public to some radical shift in America's power and distribution of resources.

In that context, *The New Yorker* was one of the better places I know. It was reported often that I left *The New Yorker* in protest, but that's not true. I was ready to leave in 1993, 1995, 1997, and 1999. Being a staff artist was complicated because it drained much more energy than the output that could be arranged through *The New Yorker*'s pages.

Q: Do you think of going back to The New Yorker?

Spiegelman: Now that the zeitgeist has changed and Seymour Hersh's articles are in there and we're in a moment that's much more contested in terms of the war, it doesn't feel as oppressively censorious an environment as it did then. I just did a two-page strip for them, but I wouldn't want to go back as a full time culture worker at *The New Yorker*. To the degree that the magazine can accommodate me, that's great. What I don't want to have to do is to go back to even unconsciously try to figure out what *The New Yorker* might want. That's what to me felt like censorship.

Q: You often are quoted talking about how long it takes you to complete a page of graphic work. How many drafts of a single page will you do before you're satisfied with it?

Spiegelman: I can't even tell you. It's just like a mush on paper until it comes together. Sometimes I'm drawing onto a computer directly, sometimes I'm drawing on paper and redrawing on the computer from there, so I can't really talk

about drafts. It's just like having soft clay until it hardens. At least as much of the problem has to do with the decisions of what to represent, how to represent that, and how to reduce it down. The words in the balloons aren't particularly poetic necessarily, but it has the same problem as poetry, which is that one has to do great reduction. If I say things the way I say them in interviews, we'd have forty-page balloons. And if I tried to draw everything, you'd just have a tangled mess of a picture. The stripping down takes much longer than building up.

Q: Just one last question: You've been photographed a lot lately wearing that peace pin upside down. You're wearing it again today. Can you explain why you wear it upside down?

Spiegelman: I've been wearing it since September 12, or some version of it. And to me it's a little bit like a nautical convention. When a ship is at sea and it's sinking, it puts its flag upside down to indicate distress for a passing ship. So this is like a plea for peace as it sinks. It's a plea for peace against all odds.

Source: Nina Siegal, "The *Progressive* Interview: Art Spiegelman," in *Progressive*, Vol. 9, No. 1, January 2005, pp. 35–39.

Clifford J. Marks

In the following excerpt, Marks connects the publication of Maus *with President Ronald Reagan's decision to honor dead World War II German soldiers for political purposes.*

No two figures better represent the divergent range of remembering the Holocaust in the mid-1980s than the cartoonist Art Spiegelman and President Ronald Reagan. Spiegelman began drawing *Maus* in serial form in 1978. Reagan became President of the United States in 1981. Using family history and anecdotal political rhetoric respectively, Spiegelman and Reagan employed dramatic facades in order to articulate their versions of truth, memory, and history to the world. Spiegelman narrates the story of his father's survival of the Holocaust in comic strip form, using anthropomorphized animals as his facade to work through his complicated relationships with his past, parents, and status as the child of survivors. Reagan's facade involved the use of the anecdote. He skillfully reduced complex political and historical questions to exemplary stories that delivered the conservative "truth." Bypassing questions which would complicate political

TO SPIEGELMAN—AS WELL AS TO THE
CRITICAL WORLD—A NEW LANGUAGE WAS
NECESSARY THROUGH WHICH TO PORTRAY
AND EXPLAIN THE HOLOCAUST."

clarity, Reagan often seized upon a reductive theme to value, for example, "Democracy" over "Communism," or "free enterprise" over "big government."

These methods of arriving at truth metaphorically collided at Bitburg. Spiegelman's publishing of *Maus* in 1986 shortly followed Reagan's infamous decision in 1985 to honor German soldiers slain in World War II who were buried at a military cemetery in Bitburg, West Germany. Soon after Reagan accepted the invitation to visit the cemetery, the President, the American press, and the American public learned that Waffen SS members were also buried there. Volunteers who served in the SS executed orders that saw to the destruction of millions of Jews and other "undesirables." The Waffen SS was notorious for its death squads and ruthless tactics. The extremity of Reagan's blunder, and his patent refusal to acknowledge his actions as misguided, unethical, or disrespectful, signified a crucial pivot point in the history/development of Holocaust remembrance. This essay explores how the rhetoric of remembrance can be delivered in different dramatic forms, spurred on by a general cultural desire simultaneously to understand (as perceived by Spiegelman) *and* get beyond (as perceived by Reagan) the Holocaust.

Reagan used the language of conservative politics in an attempt to mend a perceived rupture that had affected West German-U.S. relations since the end of the war. Concentrating on language of healing and forgiveness, Reagan wished to form a stronger NATO to threaten the U.S.S.R. This rhetoric of comradery superceded his rhetoric of outrage to such a point that he still visited Bitburg cemetery and, by implication, honored those who willfully perpetrated the Holocaust. Spiegelman, on the other hand, rejected the anecdote in his rigorous search for truth. Repudiating the willed simplification of Reaganesque politics, *Maus*

celebrated the complexity of detail, hence creating a language that delivered a multi-faceted commentary on what it means to survive the Holocaust, grow up with an objectively mean-spirited Holocaust survivor father, and narrate a specific Holocaust story with conflicting implications. For Reagan, the Holocaust became an event where universal understanding could be agreed upon with former enemies and perpetrators. For Spiegelman, the Holocaust was the place where he could simultaneously examine the meaning of death-camp survival and growing up with a difficult parent. Reagan's anecdotal rhetoric—the attempt to simplify history in order to strengthen diplomatic relationships—manipulated the larger cultural understanding of the Holocaust in favor of a political understanding. Spiegelman's comic and detailed rhetoric—the attempt to deliver as many perspectives of the "truth" in order to seek a truth—emerged as a rhetoric that subverted the political. Surprisingly, perhaps, both Reagan and Spiegelman achieved more far-reaching goals than either conceived at the time.

... Despite Reagan's attempt to redefine genocide for political purposes, it was not completely coincidental that *Maus* was published as a book in 1986—a year after Reagan's visit to Bitburg. The specificity of Bitburg's politics helped inaugurate a new era in Holocaust testimony and survivor memoir. Bitburg pressured the world into taking a position on the Holocaust. In the years following Reagan's actions at Bitburg, *Maus I* and *II* were published (1986 and 1991), the construction of the United States Holocaust Memorial accelerated toward completion (1993), and Steven Spielberg began and completed production on *Schindler's List* (1993). The Library of Congress lists 538 books published about the Holocaust from 1975–1985, and in the ten years after Bitburg, 1986–1996, lists 1,219. Following Bitburg, the amount and diversity of Holocaust material virtually erupted. While the aging survivors and the transition of the Holocaust from memory to history prompted much of this societal need to memorialize, Reagan's powerful political will, in spite of its very different intentions, "forced a forgetful world through a most necessary grief" (214), as William Safire wrote the day after Reagan's fateful visit. Bitburg's rehearsed politics indirectly led to an unrehearsed recapitulation of many Holocaust narratives. Reagan's performance, although it achieved its political goals, led to the society needing works like Spiegelman's *Maus I* and *II* to grapple with the Holocaust.

I do not claim a causal connection between the publishing of *Maus* in 1986 and Reagan's visit to Bitburg a year earlier. Spiegelman had been drawing *Maus*, publishing it in installments in *RAW*, since early 1978. What mainly motivated Spiegelman to collect his story into one volume was fear that Spielberg would soon produce a movie, *An American Tail* (1985), featuring mice as characters enacting Jewish themes (Weschler, 67–68). Yes *Maus*'s emergence and the attending critical acclaim cannot be read completely outside of the milieu of Bitburg. To Spiegelman—as well as to the critical world—a new language was necessary through which to portray and explain the Holocaust. Bitburg, and its attempt to get beyond the Holocaust with the rhetoric of forgiven pasts and hopeful futures, provided the kind of background against which *Maus*, and other artistic representations of the Holocaust, flourished; as Reagan attempted to mollify the horrors of Auschwitz, the events at Bitburg reminded the world of the necessity to remember them. Artists, historians, philanthropists, and writers responded by accelerating Holocaust art, memorials, and memories at a brisk pace. Once Bitburg made the Holocaust the focus of a national debate, new histories and narratives were spawned.

It is precisely the novelty of comic rhetoric that strikes a reader when approaching *Maus* for the first time. By now, it is cliché to refer to *Maus*'s genre as bold or innovative; yet in 1986, for those who had survived, documented, studied, and analyzed the Holocaust, "bold and innovative" were words often used to define *Maus*. Spiegelman developed a complex history in a graphic novel whose non-fictional panels tell stories of survival, courage, and mixed emotions. The spare portrayal of the characters and the richness of the story combine to move readers from their comfortable position of Reagan-like forgetfulness or complacency. Opposing Bitburg's reductive historical moralizing, *Maus* tells one survivor's family story in elaborate detail. In fact, the story includes the author's struggle to obtain information from his father Vladek, a survivor, whom Spiegelman portrays, in his post-Holocaust life, as mean, penurious, and close-minded. Thus narrative and the narrative process merge in a way to produce an intimate version of the truth.

However, this truth has no facile definition. Each character—even the author's late mother (who committed suicide)—contains many contradictory aspects. As much as readers embrace Vladek for his heroic struggle to survive, they criticize the old man for throwing out his son's coat. As much as readers relate to Artie's attempts to understand his father's experience, they tremble at his ease in calling his father a murderer at the end of Book I. These counter-intuitive moves, designed to unveil the story's complex variety, disrupt any attempt at closure regarding the Holocaust. Even more, the opposite of closure occurs: readers question the author, the survivor, and the event in a way they had not yet done. These difficult questions, evoked by the multifarious narrative, reverse the Bitburg ploy of reducing the Holocaust to easy answers and political solutions. Because it is a cartoon, the audience reads *Maus* easily, yet struggles emotionally with the context. Likewise, the same historical event that would have Reagan urging us to move beyond horror and blame has the *Maus* reader making interpretive judgments about characters' somewhat elusive motives. Although Vladek occasionally appears heroic, his and his son's conflicted aspirations emerge more stridently because the narrative rejects simplistic heroic stereotypes. Likewise, as the artist depicts himself wrestling with issues of representation, history, and family dynamics, the reader cannot settle on a firm ethical description of him.

The cartoonist's lack of moral clarity contrasts with the President's reductive historicizing. As the creator of *Maus* confronts the demons that prevent the story of the Holocaust from being told, the leader of the Free World adapts the Holocaust's traumas to his version of freedom and truth. For Reagan, the Holocaust is too easy to "tell." The occasional ambiguity of Spiegelman's Holocaust can best be understood through the opening panels of *Maus*, where Vladek compares Artie's friends' offensive actions to how people behaved in a locked, abandoned railway car with no food, water, or place to eliminate. This child's perspective informs all of *Maus*. The child does not have the ability to draw together a narrative and then glean a moral from it. Art Spiegelman does not offer reductive morals in *Maus*; consequently, a reader does not emerge with a reductive understanding of the Holocaust. A compelling page from *Maus II* exhibits these characteristics.

Beginning with the specific date of his father's death (which pre-dates the publishing of *Maus* by three years) and ending with the off-page voice saying "Alright Mr. Spiegelman, we're ready to shoot," this scene captures the contradictions inherent in presenting a "factual" story of the Holocaust. These contradictions, however, do more to reveal the authenticity of the narrative then a straightforward reductive moral. On a single page, Spiegelman lists eleven facts, including (but not limited to): his successful publication of *Maus I*; his imminent parenthood; his father's death; his mother's suicide; and the gassing of 100,000 Hungarian Jews at Auschwitz. To draw connections among these events seems outrageous. The artist has chutzpah when he associates drawing a page in a comic book ("I started working on this page at the very end of February 1987" [41]), with his father's activities during the Holocaust ("Vladek started working as a tinman in Auschwitz in the Spring of 1944..." [41]). The general background of the page, loosely figured as a Swastika, the heap of rotting mice corpses in the bottom frame, and the guard tower looming over the corpses and the artist, reinforce the relationship between the Holocaust and drawing a comic book. The reader accepts the relationship because Spiegelman does not define his story through a moral or political perspective. By not reducing complex narrative moments to a single moralizing truth, Spiegelman fertilizes the ground for meaning to grow. Even with the weight of the Holocaust on his shoulders, he manages to emerge from the pressure to draw successfully. The drawing-board scene argues that individuals cannot control the horror or disappointment in their lives. Moreover, even success—surviving the Holocaust (Vladek) and publishing an immensely popular book about it (Artie)—cannot guarantee future happiness. Given the opportunity, Reagan would underscore the positive facts that Spiegelman recounts; alternatively, Spiegelman emphasizes his own inner turmoil. Although he depicts himself slumped over the drawing board, overwhelmed by pressure, he soon renders Artie visiting his psychiatrist who manages to alleviate the artist's depression.

I like to call this Spiegelman's trajectory of truth—not a moral truth, or a political truth, but the daily truth every human being lives with; this demotic truth exposes one's success at the risk of unveiling his darkest insecurities. In Spiegelman's truth, one day one suffers in the Holocaust, the next day reads about 100,000 people being

exterminated, and the next day draws history. By definition, the truth operates relative to its own historical and psychological position. Implicitly, the artist, the son of a survivor has the right to represent the rotting corpses of mass destruction. Explicitly, the claim throws the artist into a moral quandary because rationally he (and his audience) know that the historical fact of 100,000 exterminated Hungarian Jews is more significant than his ability to draw his father's story, or a picture of an Auschwitz tin shop depicted on the basis of his father's or psychiatrist's memory.

Reagan reduced conflicting discourses to a single theme of human redemption and unending fortitude. Spiegelman portrays the story's multiple perspectives, hence multiplying the themes. While Reagan appropriated a story of German-American cooperation during World War II to redefine the terms of Holocaust discussion, Spiegelman funnels all of the conflicts through himself. As the artist represents his own struggles as part of the finished artwork, the reader confronts the complexity of the artist's choices. Had Spiegelman left out his own involvement in the story, readers would have had a reproduction of a fascinating survivor's tale, but no way to understand the choices the child of the survivor must make so that he can tell his father's story. Audiences received no glimpse into how Reagan constructed his narrative. In fact, if the President's moral could be told without the story (for example, "It's morning in America," Reagan's 1984 re-election campaign theme), then he would gladly do so. That is a major reason he and his advisors did not initially want him to visit a concentration camp: it would have disrupted the narrative of forgiveness and hope. Nonetheless, Reagan still integrated his Bergen-Belsen speech with his German Military Cemetery visit to emphasize his vision of a future where the past is forgotten and the present means belief in a Soviet-free future. *Maus*, because it attempts an authentic portrayal of events using fictional devices, necessarily invokes, rather than settles, questions of synthesis. But part one ends with Art calling his father a murderer and part two ends with Vladek saying that he and Anja "lived happy, happy ever after" (136). It is to these two endings that I now turn.

In 1986, *Maus* ends with Vladek's revelation about burning Anja Spiegelman's diaries. Spiegelman deftly portrays Artie being upset (hand to forehead) in the upper right frame, infuriated in row two, right-hand frame, forgiving in row three, right-hand frame, and friendly in the bottom middle frame. The final panel has him walking away, head turned, uttering "murderer" (159). The implications of this scene are multi-faceted. Spiegelman portrays Artie having a full range of emotional responses to his father's revelation. Screaming murderer in one frame and dejectedly recalling the same word in another, Spiegelman illustrates his conflicted relationship with his work and his father. His father, meanwhile, characterizes his own difficult relationship with his past and his son. After many years of covering up his destruction of Anja's diaries, Vladek finally tells Artie what really happened. Vladek uses the same reason that Spiegelman has for drawing the story, more or less: "But I'm telling you, after the tragedy with mother, I was so depressed then, I didn't know if I'm coming or going" (159). Burning the diaries serves as a form of treatment for Vladek, literally destroying the recorded memories of the woman he loved. We can infer this as an action of anger, but it is also borne out of self-pity and frustration. How could Anja commit suicide after surviving the Holocaust?

Simultaneously, Vladek's past action damages Artie's pursuit of the truth. The diaries represent the only alternative to Vladek's version of events. *Maus* is dedicated to revealing as much of the convoluted past that can be revealed in a relatively short narrative frame. Anja's voice would have acted as a corrective to Vladek's. Destroying her history is like destroying his mother all over again, hence the ending appellation murderer. An older comic inserted in *Maus I*, "Prisoner on the Hell Planet," which recounts his mother's suicide, ends with Art saying "you murdered me, Mommy" (103). So in the stories most associated with his mother's independence—her suicide and her diaries—Art summarily calls both of his parents murderers. He had the artistic choice to recall these events and to represent them. Sadly, he associates murder with his mother and, by extension, his father. She kills herself, and this act leads Vladek to killing her diaries. Anger, forgiveness, frustration, and sadness intermix to complicate the story. Lacking a vital piece of information, Artie transforms this lack to an artistic space filled with serious accusations. As he tentatively forgives his father for his misdeeds, his father forgives him for his. Neither of the characters can be absolutely defined as a murderer or as a truth-saving artist. Specifying so many emotions in a compact narrative leaves the reader with a confusion similar to Artie's.

Although Artie calls his father a murderer, the reader cannot agree or disagree with this assessment.

Maus II ends with Vladek and Anja's reunion in frames three and four, Vladek saying good night to Artie in frames five and six, who he confuses with his Holocaust-victim son Richieu, and the tombstone bearing Vladek's and Anja's names, under which Art Spiegelman's signature dates the composition 1978–1991. Contrasting the tombstone, where Vladek and Anja's birth and death dates are recorded, with the beginning and end of Spiegelman's artistic composition, is a conscious effort on Spiegelman's part to portray physically how intermingled his art work is with his parents' lives and death. This is not a gratuitous appropriation of their lives; it is a statement about artistic reality. Anja's suicide and Vladek's riven existence drive Spiegelman to a thirteen-year project that critically tells a complex story. The text keeps memories of his parents alive, and serves as a source of personal salvation and revelation. While the story cannot be put to rest, Spiegelman's attempt to tell it can. And the final frames reveal that the truth is something comprised of many factors: Vladek and Anja do not live happily ever after, and Artie is Artie, not Richieu. These details matter because readers piece together their lives clinging to the best interpretations of difficult moments. Richieu, after all, was a victim of the Holocaust. While Artie cannot replace him, he can at least address the void that Richieu's death creates. And while Vladek and Anja do not live happily ever after, they live happily enough to produce Artie and generate their compelling narratives. There is no moral that can be drawn here; rather, the reader recognizes the power of the artist to tell a story. These figures point the reader to multiple meanings and the complexity of life.

Spiegelman does not make overt political statements with his art. Rather, he attempts a complicated rhetoric or revelation that would expose the contradictory nature of his father's survival and Spiegelman's relationship with his father. Reagan, on the other hand, eschewed personal details in conveying his sense of history while participating in conservative international politics. In his world, anecdotes served as guiding lights to political truth. Reagan often peppered his speeches with stories that demonstrated the value of his brand of conservatism and what embracing the conservatism might mean for an entire country. Thus Reagan, the consummate

Presidential politician, and Spiegelman, the underground comic artist, used dissimilar dramatic means to achieve vastly different cultural ends: Reagan sought Cold War geopolitical superiority for the United States at the expense of a complicated history; Spiegelman sought an audience to tell a personal story with complex historical significance.

Reagan reduced the Holocaust to a single meaning to give it closure. He appropriated trauma by taking advantage of people's desire to move beyond the traumatic event and, in the process, turned his newly created meaning to the conservative political purposes of the state. In a sense he tried to "fix" the Holocaust by giving people relief from memory and history. Spiegelman's work does the exact opposite. *Maus* recognizes the plurality of meanings associated with the history and memory of the Holocaust. Rather than taking his readers down a narrow path that would reveal a truth that is ideologically beneficial, Spiegelman exposes a truth whose meanings are multiple, contradictory, and rarely conform to an audience's narrative expectations. For Spiegelman, there is no escape from the contradictions inherent in memory and history. In the cultural milieu of 1985, Reagan attempted to narrow historical meaning at Bitburg and curb memory to reveal a Holocaust that, from the perspective of international politics, should be harnessed and controlled. *Maus*, as much as other attempts to recall the event, narrates a Holocaust that is full of contradictions, complex characters, and uneven understanding. In essence, *Maus* declares that audiences can try to understand the Holocaust by looking at anthropomorphized animals, but their understanding will always be tempered by the contradictions, misstatements, and wrongful actions that define the range of human behavior. In 1985, at a time when memorializing the Holocaust had become an official government function, President Reagan offered the public an easy political forgiveness to move beyond actions of racial hatred and prejudice. *Maus* reminds its readers that some actions are impossible to forgive and sometimes closure and understanding limit the ability to ask questions of a horrific event whose meaning we, as members of Western society, must still ascertain.

Source: Clifford J. Marks, "*Maus* and Bitburg," in *Midwest Quarterly*, Vol. 43, No. 4, Summer 2002, pp. 208–313.

> THE DECISION BY SPIEGELMAN TO REPRESENT THE HOLOCAUST IN A COMIC BOOK FORMAT IS A HIGHLY CONTENTIOUS ONE, CONSIDERING THE MOCKERIES OF THE HOLOCAUST THAT HAVE RESULTED FROM PREVIOUS ENDEAVORS TO REPRESENT THE HOLOCAUST IN POP CULTURE."

Sophia Lehman

In the following excerpt, Lehman discusses the difficulty American Jewish writers face in choosing to write about the Holocaust.

For American Jews, the memory of the Holocaust both contrasts with and implicitly threatens the vaunted freedom of America and the successful assimilation that defines American Jewish life in the latter part of the twentieth century. In Lore Segal's *Her First American*, a novel about the experiences of a young Holocaust survivor adapting to life in America, the protagonist tells her all-American lover that she must return home early that evening to care for her mother, who suffers from nightmares about the Holocaust; he responds, "open[ing] and drop[ping] his arms in an outsize gesture to demonstrate the breadth of her freedom, his powerlessness to hold her, 'Any time at all.'" The assumed freedom that characterizes his approach to life is diametrically opposed to the lack of freedom and the burden of memory connected with the Holocaust that characterize the approach of the protagonist.

The effect of the Holocaust on American Jewish understandings of the influence of history on the present has been interpreted in a variety of ways. Cynthia Ozick stresses the fear of a second Holocaust in America, based on the knowledge that the first one occurred in a place where Jews had become highly assimilated and successful. Robert Alter cautions against such fears, enumerating the ways in which our contemporary existence "is warped by being viewed in the dark glass of the Holocaust. We can never put out of our minds what happened to our people in Europe, but their reality is not ours." James Young suggests a compromise by exploring how memories and representations of the Holocaust shape the present, rather than simply relegating subsequent generations to living in the past. He envisions a dynamic interaction between past and present which encompasses the importance of memory while simultaneously allowing for future development and change.

The difficulty of writing about the Holocaust is compounded for American Jews by their distance from the event, both geographically and, increasingly, chronologically. Holocaust literature was not frequently written in the United States until the 1960s, when there was a sudden awakening of interest due to the Eichmann trial, the publicizing of which made the facts of the Holocaust newly accessible to Americans. This exposure was compounded by the occurrence of the Six-Day War and the Yom Kippur War, which together renewed anxiety about a repetition of the destruction of large segments of world Jewry. Since this initial burgeoning in the 1960s, the Holocaust has received an astounding amount of attention from American Jewish writers, in a manner which often eclipses all other facets of Jewish history and culture. It has taken on a problematic role as both a new center for Jewish commonality and a metaphor for all the injustices of the waning twentieth century. As the Holocaust itself becomes more removed, the range and number of representations of it seem to proliferate.

In writing about the Holocaust and the abundance of literary responses to it, it is important to distinguish between the Holocaust itself and the "rhetorical, cultural, political, and religious uses to which the disaster has been put since then." André Schwarz-Bart concludes his novel *The Last of the Just* with the tragic truth that "so it was for millions, who turned from Luftmenschen into Luft. I shall not translate. So this story will not finish with some tomb to be visited in memoriam." Just as translation renders the horror in a new and different form, so too do works of art and literature which serve as monuments. Nothing remains of the six million Jews and the European culture that died with them. In their places, we have the multitudes of responses from those who lived to bear witness and those who experienced the Holocaust only indirectly. Lawrence Langer delineates the difference between the event and the symbolism which has since accrued:

> For Dachau, like Auschwitz and in a related sense like Hiroshima, is no longer merely a place-name with grim historical associations

for those who care to pursue them. All three have been absorbed into the collective memory of the human community as independent symbols of a quality of experience more subtle, complex, and elusive than the names themselves can possibly convey.

Writing about the Holocaust thus produces new memories and associations.

These literary and artistic responses can be construed as both beneficial, in that they attest to continued commemoration of an event we must not forget, and also deleterious, in that they risk distorting the history which they strive to convey. Robert Alter refers to "the Holocaust phenomenon" in America, alluding to the way in which it has become tamed of its historical horror within academic, commercial, political, and religious spheres. Academically, it is used as a metaphor for twentieth-century existential and artistic crises and as a basis for propounding new literary theories, as in Dominick LaCapra's *Representing the Holocaust*. LaCapra justifies his use of the Holocaust by the contention that "there is in reality no history without theory." Such assertions remove the Holocaust from its historical mooring and transform it into a model on which to hone such concepts as "trauma." Commercially, the Holocaust has become a rich source of profit and entertainment, with disturbing implications about the ethics of making money from the Holocaust. Art Spiegelman, after the wild success of *Maus*, his comic book narrative about the Holocaust, recounts offers to make the book into a major motion picture, as well as other ventures for capitalizing on the success of his Holocaust narrative, including the packaging of *Maus* as Christmas/Chanukah gift sets. Politically, the Holocaust has become a standard against which is measured every other instance of oppression, murder, and racism, initiating a grotesque competition for the status of "most oppressed." Toni Morrison begins her novel *Beloved* (1987), about the atrocities of slavery, with a dedication to the "Sixty Million and more"; in a more communal spirit of shared historical horrors, the protagonist in Tillie Olsen's *Tell Me a Riddle* (1956) contextualizes her own suffering by comparing it with the suffering of those who endured trains to concentration camps, slave ships, and the bombing of Hiroshima.

It is in religious terms that the Holocaust assumes its most complicated role. The memory of the historical atrocity has in large part come to replace spirituality and traditional Judaic knowledge among assimilated American Jews, thereby providing a negative center for Jewish identification while at the same time secularizing an inherently religious tradition. As Jacob Neusner asserts, "What we have done is to make the murder of the Jews of Europe into one of the principal components of the civil religion of American Jews." Remembering the Holocaust—the "negative miracle," as it has been termed—becomes the only "tradition" that assimilated American Jews share. And as the Holocaust becomes more and more central to Jewish American identity, the fear of forgetting the Holocaust comes to represent and replace the loss of the rest of Jewish tradition and collective memory. Amos Funkenstein places the phenomenon within a larger trend: "The nation-state replaced the sacred liturgical memory with secular liturgical memory—days of remembrance, flags, and monuments." Memorializing the Holocaust thus becomes just one more instance of the secularization of Judaism.

Concomitant with the sanctification imposed on the Holocaust, there has been an insistence by many critics on the necessity of adhering to purely "factual" accounts. Ozick, for one, challenging her own literary practices, has stated, "I believe with all my soul that [the Holocaust] ought to remain exclusively attached to document and history.... If the Holocaust becomes commensurate with the literary imagination, then what of those recrudescent Nazis, the so-called revisionists, who claim the events themselves are nothing but imaginings?" Contemporary theory and literature have increasingly eroded the binary opposition between "factual" and "fictional" writing, thus questioning the very premise of Ozick's argument and rendering still more difficult the issue of "appropriate" Holocaust representation. Young asserts the necessity of metaphor even in the driest historical accounts and explores the ways in which metaphor shaped the events of the Holocaust themselves as well as their subsequent influence and representation: "How victims of the Holocaust grasped and responded to events as they unfolded around them depended on the available tropes and figures of their time." Moreover, fictional renderings of the Holocaust seem particularly wellsuited to eliciting imaginative responses from readers, an increasingly necessary component of Holocaust remembrance as the number of witnesses and survivors dwindles. In this capacity, fiction serves as a conduit between

the Holocaust and the present, an affirmation rather than an erasure of the Holocaust's historical import.

The writing of those who did not directly experience the Holocaust increasingly comprises the majority of Holocaust literature being produced. Accordingly, rather than addressing the Holocaust itself and survivor testimonies, I focus on contemporary works of literature which consider both the impact of the Holocaust on American Jews and also the ways in which the Holocaust is reimagined by those who were not yet born during the Second World War. Just as survivor literature gains a retrospective quality that can be contrasted with the immediacy of diaries, so does contemporary writing about the Holocaust gain a historical breadth that can be contrasted with the contemporaneousness of first-hand accounts. Because their memories and experiences of the Holocaust are already second-hand, writers lacking direct experience of the Holocaust are freer to experiment with new forms of representation, to rely more blatantly on the imagination, and to include multiple, conflicting accounts. Through the use of the imagination, such authors renew and transmit the memory of the Holocaust, portraying it in an interactive relationship with the present that accentuates its continued importance and influence.

Survivors and witnesses whose task it was to document the Holocaust struggled primarily with the issue of whether the Holocaust could be represented: in *Literature or Life*, Jorge Semprun remembers the shocked and suspicious expressions of the first people he encountered after leaving Buchenwald at the end of the war, expressions which gave rise to his own concern that "men from before, from the outside, emissaries from life" would never be able to comprehend what went on inside the camps. Contemporary writers, however, who inherit the bulk of literature and documentation that has been amassed, focus on "the consequences of interpretation"—namely, the responses to interpretation and its influence on later events. In *The Shawl*, for instance, Ozick explores the consequences of the survivor Rosa's memory in terms of her behavior in present-day Florida. Only a tenth of the novella occurs during the Holocaust; the rest concerns what follows. In *Maus*, Spiegelman is as anxious about his own dual role as son and author as about the transmission of his father's testimony. And in *The*

Ghost Writer, Philip Roth has Nathan Zuckerman create a fantasy about Anne Frank in response to challenges to his own, present-day Jewish loyalty.

... By filtering the survivor experience through comic book form and using the second generation, the children of survivors, as the dominant perspective in *Maus*, Spiegelman presents an antithetical supposition to Ozick's theoretical insistence on purely factual accounts and her concern with the interrelation of fantasy and idolatry. The two-volume work intersperses Spiegelman's interviews with his father, Vladek, about Vladek's experiences during the Holocaust with present-day conversations between Vladek and Art, thus providing an analogy to the two sections of *The Shawl* and again focusing predominantly on the legacy of the Holocaust.

The decision by Spiegelman to represent the Holocaust in a comic book format is a highly contentious one, considering the mockeries of the Holocaust that have resulted from previous endeavors to represent the Holocaust in pop culture. Lopate derides "the parade of shallow movie melodramas...that invoke the milieu of Nazi Germany as a sort of narrative frisson," thereby belittling its historical magnitude. In Hollywood, the Holocaust has become a rich source for entertainment productions, from Rabbi Marvin Hier's Academy Award for *Genocide* in 1982 to the more recent success of *Schindler's List* (1994). Popular representations such as these have contributed to the Holocaust's becoming a pervasive metaphor for questions of evil and of murder, no matter how inappropriate the analogy. A character in Norma Rosen's novel *Touching Evil* excitedly compares his report to the exterminator of insects found in his apartment to "telling the police where Anne Frank is hiding."

The casual and excessive representation of the Holocaust in pop culture is an inverse reflection of the long-standing debate about the impossibility of representing the Holocaust. The appeal of the Holocaust as a subject for pop culture stems in part from the drama inherent in the Nazi's Third Reich: the careful choreography behind all the marches and rallies, "all those red flags with swastikas, those jeeps and jackboots suddenly flashing in key-lit night scenes, the tinkle of broken glass." In *Maus*, Spiegelman both acknowledges the drama of the Holocaust and simultaneously questions the extent to which all representations, even the stories of survivors, threaten the integrity of the original experience. In a particularly relevant scene, Vladek recounts to Art how, after the end of the war, he "passed once a place what had a camp uniform—a new and clean one—to make souvenir photos" (Maus 2: 134). Vladek commemorates his real experience in the camps by having a staged photograph taken. Yet the photograph falsifies the original experience, not only in that it documents a later, freely-chosen performance, but also in that the uniform in the photograph is "new and clean," in contrast to the soiled, mismatching outfits of concentration camp inmates.

The issue of whether pop cultural dramatizations obscure the historical events of the Holocaust is compounded for Spiegelman by his own commercial success. An underlying concern is that he, like the tourist photo booth, is capitalizing on the Holocaust by simultaneously falsifying it and deriving profit from the fate of its victims. The back of *Maus II* depicts a mouse in a concentration camp uniform, over which is superimposed the bar code containing the book price. The stripes on the uniform are carefully made to meld into those of the bar code. Spiegelman discusses the issue further within the text, as he recounts being besieged by offers to film the book (which he rejects) and being approached by a profiteer holding a plaque which reads "*Maus*: You've read the book, now buy the vest!" The salesman tells him, "Artie, baby. Check out this licensing deal. You get 50% of the profits. We'll make a million. Your dad would be proud!" The vest, a replica of Art's own signature vest, is a perfect correlative of the photo booth uniform. The idea of "making a million" eerily echoes the statistic of the six million who were killed.

Spiegelman's choice of medium is not only a response to the increasing connection between the Holocaust and pop culture but also evidence of the way in which later generations use the imagination to envision history. The combination of testimony, comics (including the graphic style of most of *Maus* and the contrasting style of "Prisoner From the Hell Planet," a small section of the book which depicts dark, twisted humans, as opposed to endearing, humanoid mice), narrative, and photograph in *Maus* produces a multi-layered text which actively engages the reader and elicits new thoughts about the legacy of the Holocaust for later generations. Because of his distance, Spiegelman feels hesitant about ascribing a fixed meaning or trajectory to past occurrences.

The comic book format echoes the circuitous, conflicting, and multiple narratives of *Maus*, its layout increasing the sense of openness by means of the spaces between frames. In *Understanding Comics*, Scott McCloud writes, "In the limbo of the gutter [space between panels], [the] human imagination [of the reader] takes two separate images and transforms them into a single idea.... Comic panels fracture both time and space, offering a jagged, staccato rhythm of unconnected moments." The reader bridges the gutter and creates a sense of continuity by creating the missing connections. The necessity of imagination to complete the narrative parallels Art's own position as a generation removed.

The comic strip form is particularly well-suited to depicting the possibilities of sideshadowing, in that the words and pictures can suggest divergent rather than synonymous historical possibilities. When Art and Vladek disagree over the existence of an orchestra at the gates of Auschwitz, Art allows his father's words to take precedence, yet the picture offers a contrasting possibility. Verbally, the scene concludes with Vladek asserting, "No. I remember only marching, not any orchestras...." However, within the same frame we see the tops of the orchestra instruments sticking up from where the orchestra is situated behind the marchers. The scene questions the linearity and certainty of history both by revealing the struggle between Art and Vladek for narrative control and by examining the tension between collective and individual accounts of the past: whereas Vladek bases his assertion on his personal, "eyewitness" experience, Art derives his information from history books. The written text and the drawings provide simultaneous yet opposing narratives of Auschwitz.

In order to counter further the sense of a single fate which befell a generic victim, Spiegelman individualizes his parents' experiences of the Holocaust. Vladek's quirks and biases—for example, his niggardliness (he returns a half-empty box of cereal to the store) and his vanity about his ability to charm women (he compares himself to Rudolph Valentino)—indicate that his status as victim/survivor is not the sole factor determining his ideas and the shape of his testimony. People's experiences of the Holocaust differed widely and were informed not only by their particular fate during the war, but also by their individual lives and beliefs prior to the Holocaust. Vladek's parsimony and narcissism predate his time at Auschwitz, as Spiegelman repeatedly emphasizes. Vladek's own testimony contributes further to this process of individualization, recording the differentiation of his own experience from that of the collective. He recounts how he survives at one point because he teaches the block supervisor English in exchange for safety tips and extra food, and how his wife Anja survives at another point because the kapo cannot find the particular bed in which she is hiding. Individualizing the experiences of the survivors implicitly individualizes the unfulfilled lives of all the victims who were killed.

The process of individualizing the Holocaust finally leads to the creation of individual forms of commemoration. Vladek tells Art how as a prisoner of war, before the Holocaust, he had a dream in which his grandfather told him, "You will come out of this place—free!... on the day of parshas truma." Three months later, on the exact day predicted in the dream, he is indeed released. Vladek continues by explaining that it happened also to be the week of parshas truma when he married Anja and then again when Art was born. He concludes, "And so it came to be this parsha you sang on the Saturday of your bar mitzvah!" The repeated date of the chain of events shifts from being a divine prediction or coincidence to being an intentional commemoration of all the other events which have occurred on the same date. Each subsequent event thus stimulates remembrance and reflects the influence of history on present experience.

As an adult, Art internalizes the sense of interconnection between past and present. In the "Time Flies" section of *Maus 2*, he sets up a series of parallel occurrences: "Vladek started working as a tinman in Auschwitz in the spring of 1944... I started working on this page at the very end of February 1987. In May 1987 Francoise and I are expecting a baby... Between May 16, 1944, and May 24, 1944 over 100,000 Hungarian Jews were gassed in Auschwitz" (41). As a child of survivors, Art frames the events of his own life in America with corresponding events of the Holocaust. His pervasive awareness of the losses of the Holocaust leads to a continual sense of contrast with his own present successes, a contrast that cannot help but shape his response to the present.

The intermixing of imagination and memory, while inevitable for second-generation witnesses, leads to a dissolution of the boundary between imagination and historical experience. The collaborative creation of the book by Art and Vladek brings the Holocaust into the present of both Art's life and the reader's imagination, and, conversely, it relegates Art and Vladek to the past. Just as Art implicitly accuses Vladek of making him experience the Holocaust vicariously, so too he suffers from guilt at forcing his father to relive Auschwitz, as reflected in the subtitle of *Maus 1*, "My Father Bleeds History." Ironically, this blurring of temporal boundaries both generates and contrasts with the specificity of stories recounted and the unusual means of presentation.

Source: Sophia Lehman, "'And Here [Their] Troubles Began': The Legacy of the Holocaust in the Writing of Cynthia Ozick, Art Spiegelman, and Philip Roth," in *Clio*, Vol. 28, No. 1, Fall 1998, pp. 29–52.

SOURCES

Berkwits, Jeff, "What's with Jewish Comedy?," in *San Diego Jewish Journal*, August 2004.

Charlson, Joshua L., "Framing the Past: Postmodernism and the Making of Reflective Memory in Art Spiegelman's *Maus*," in *Arizona Quarterly*, Vol. 57, No. 3, Autumn 2001, pp. 91–120.

"The Extermination of the Jews of Sosnowiec, Bendzin, and Vicinity," in *Holocaust Education and Archive Research Team (H.E.A.R.T.)*, http://www.holocaustresearchproject.org/nazioccupation/sosbend.html (accessed December 9, 2009).

Gass, William H., "Philosophy and the Form of Fiction," in *Fiction and the Figures of Life: Essays*, Knopf, 1970, pp. 3–26.

Gates, David, "Stories Out of the Silence," in *Newsweek*, Vol. 119, No. 4, January 27, 1992, p. 59.

Gopnik, Adam, "High and Low: Modern Art and Popular Culture," in *New York Museum of Modern Art* exhibition catalog, 1991, pp. 153–229.

Groth, Gary, "An Interview with Art Spiegelman," in *Comics Journal*, No. 180, September 1995, pp. 52–114.

Halkin, Hillel, "Inhuman Comedy," in *Commentary*, Vol. 93, No. 2, February 1992, pp. 55–56.

Laga, Barry, "*Maus*, Holocaust, and History: Redrawing the Frame," in *Arizona Quarterly*, Vol. 57, No. 1, Spring 2001, pp. 61–90.

Langer, Lawrence L., "A Fable of the Holocaust," in *New York Times Book Review*, November 3, 1991, pp. 1, 35–36.

Muchnick, Laurie, Review of *Maus* in *VLS*, No. 101, December 1991, p. 16.

Spiegelman, Art, *Maus: A Survivor's Tale*, Volume I: *My Father Bleeds History*, Pantheon, 1986.

——, *Maus: A Survivor's Tale*, Volume II: *And Here My Troubles Began*, Pantheon, 1991.

Staub, Michael E., "The Shoah Goes On and On: Remembrance and Representation in Art Spiegelman's *Maus*," in *MELUS*, Vol. 20, No. 3, Fall 1995, pp. 33–46.

Walton, James, "Nothing Comic about the Holocaust," in *Spectator*, Vol. 268, No. 8543, April 4, 1992, p. 33.

Young, James E., "The Holocaust as Vicarious Past: Art Spiegelman's *Maus* and the Afterimages of History," in *Critical Inquiry*, Vol. 24, No. 3, Spring 1998, pp. 666–99.

FURTHER READING

Cohen, Beth B., *Case Closed: Holocaust Survivors in Postwar America*, Rutgers University Press, 2007.
    Cohen is a psychologist and social historian who examines primary documents in her quest to understand the difficulties that Jewish displaced persons—especially orphans and Orthodox Jews—had in adjusting to American life in New York and other locations.

Doherty, Thomas, "Art Spiegelman's *Maus*: Graphic Art and the Holocaust," in *American Literature*, Vol. 68, 1996, pp. 69–84.
    Doherty analyzes the power of Spiegelman's illustrations in terms of how they replicate cinematic conventions and compare with the Third Reich's predilection for idealized human forms in their own films.

Epstein, Helen, *Children of the Holocaust: Conversations with Sons and Daughters of Survivors*, Penguin, 1988.
    Epstein is the daughter of Holocaust survivors and examines the precarious mental balancing act it entailed, especially in childhood. She examines the history of Holocaust survivors as they made their way to South America and New York and discusses the idea of survivor syndrome at length.

Gass, William H., "Philosophy and the Form of Fiction," in *Fiction and the Figures of Life: Essays*, Knopf, 1970.
    Gass coins the term "breaking the fourth wall" in this essay, although he does not discuss the concept at length. The essay is deeply philosophical.

Geis, Deborah R., ed., *Considering Maus: Approaches to Art Spiegelman's "Survivor's Tale" of the Holocaust*, revised ed., University of Alabama Press, 2007.
    This collection of essays by prominent scholars offers numerous interpretations and insight into Spiegelman's opus, including its impact on popular culture, its graphic arts influences,

its relationship to psychoanalysis, and its success as a work of oral history.

Hatfield, Charles, "Irony and Self-Reflexivity in Autobiographical Comics: Two Case Studies," in *Alternative Comics: An Emerging Literature*, University Press of Mississippi, 2005, pp. 128–51.

Hatfield considers *Maus* at length (as well as Justin Green's *Binky Brown Meets the Holy Virgin Mary*) and praises it for its complexity and how it tackles a topic that the author himself considers unpresentable.

"Holocaust Encyclopedia," in *United States Holocaust Memorial Museum*, http://www.ushmm.org.

The United States Holocaust Museum's online encyclopedia presents photographs and data regarding many aspects of the Holocaust, including statistics regarding the Polish ghettos, the pogroms, and concentration camps.

Witek, Joseph, ed., *Art Spiegelman: Conversations*, University Press of Mississippi, 2007.

A volume in the "Conversations with Comic Artists" series, this volume collects interviews with Spiegelman from 1976 to 2006, including some never before published. Spiegelman discusses all aspects of his career, including *Maus* and *In the Shadow of No Towers*.

SUGGESTED SEARCH TERMS

Art Spiegelman

children of Holocaust survivors

Holocaust AND graphic novel

Maus AND survivor's guilt

graphic novel AND autobiography

Auschwitz AND Spiegelman

Maus AND Spiegelman

graphic novel AND Spiegelman

Complete Maus AND Spiegelman

themes AND Spiegelman

Never Let Me Go

KAZUO ISHIGURO
2005

Never Let Me Go is the sixth novel by renowned British writer Kazuo Ishiguro. Published in 2005, it was short-listed for the Booker Prize. Ostensibly set in England from the 1970s to the late 1990s, *Never Let Me Go* is a futuristic, dystopian (anti-utopian) tale about human cloning. At a secluded private school in the English countryside, young people who have been created through cloning are educated. Their lives will be short, since as soon as they become adults they will be required to donate their vital organs, one by one, to those who need them to recover from disease. The novel focuses on the lives of three of these clones: Kathy, who narrates the story; Ruth; and Tommy. The author examines how they grow up, the relationships they form, and the values by which they learn to live.

Ishiguro started writing *Never Let Me Go* in 1990. In its early stages, the novel was not about cloning. Instead, the characters were doomed because they had been contaminated by some kind of nuclear material. Not satisfied with his material, Ishiguro abandoned the story twice to write *The Unconsoled* and *When We Were Orphans* before finally finishing *Never Let Me Go*. Cloning was much in the news at the time, and this supplied him with his theme.

The novel has been acclaimed for Ishiguro's subtle handling of a nightmarish theme. It has also been praised as a moving meditation on how people create meaning in life in the face of loss and mortality.

Kazuo Ishiguro *(AP Images)*

AUTHOR BIOGRAPHY

Ishiguro was born in Nagasaki, Japan, on November 8, 1954. The family, including Ishiguro's two sisters, moved to Britain in 1960, when Ishiguro's father, Shigeo Ishiguro, an oceanographer, was employed as a researcher at the National Institute of Oceanography. Living in Guildford, Surrey, Ishiguro attended a grammar school in Woking, Surrey. In 1973, he worked as a grouse beater (flushing out birds for hunting) for the Queen Mother at Balmoral Castle, Aberdeen, Scotland. The following year he enrolled at the University of Kent at Canterbury, graduating with degrees in English and philosophy in 1978. From 1979 to 1980, he was a residential social worker in London, assisting homeless people. Ishiguro had been writing fiction since the mid-1970s, and he enrolled in a graduate creative writing program at the University of East Anglia, where he was taught by noted writers Malcolm Bradbury and Angela Carter. He completed his master of arts degree in 1980, and in 1981, three of his short stories were published in *Introductions 7: Stories by New Writers*.

Ishiguro moved to London, and his first novel, *A Pale View of the Hills*, was published in 1982. It received excellent reviews and was awarded the Winifred Holtby Memorial Prize. Encouraged by this success, Ishiguro decided in 1982 to pursue a full-time writing career. He also became a British citizen in the same year. His second novel, *An Artist of the Floating World* (1986), won the Whitbread Book of the Year Award and was short-listed for the Booker Prize. Both of Ishiguro's first two novels featured Japanese characters, but in his third novel, Ishiguro focused entirely on a plot and setting based in his adopted country. This was *The Remains of the Day* (1989), the novel that won the Booker Prize, became an international best seller, and made him famous. Set in the 1950s, it features an elderly English butler who looks back at his thirty-five years of service to an English aristocrat and tries to justify to himself why he chose this path in life. The novel was made into a 1993 film starring Anthony Hopkins and Emma Thompson that was nominated for eight Academy Awards.

Ishiguro's fourth novel was *The Unconsoled* (1995), which is about a concert pianist in Europe who suffers odd lapses of memory and seems to live in a dreamlike environment. The novel is unlike Ishiguro's previous work; it won the Cheltenham Prize but in general received a mixed critical reception. In the same year, Ishiguro received the Order of the British Empire for services to literature. In 1998, the French government named him a Chevalier de l'Ordre des Arts et des Lettres.

In 2000, Ishiguro published his fifth novel, *When We Were Orphans*, followed in 2005 by *Never Let Me Go*. Both novels were short-listed for the Booker Prize.

As of 2009, Ishiguro lived in London with his wife, Laura Anne MacDougal, and daughter, Naomi.

PLOT SUMMARY

Part One

CHAPTER ONE

Never Let Me Go is set in England in the late 1990s. It is narrated by a thirty-one-year-old woman named Kathy H. At the beginning of the novel, Kathy announces that she has been a "carer" for eleven years, working with "donors." She does not explain what she means by these terms, but she does say that through being a carer she has been able to reconnect with two of

MEDIA ADAPTATIONS

- A film adaptation (screenplay by Alex Garland) of *Never Let Me Go* will be released by DNA Films in 2010, directed by Mark Romanek and starring Keira Knightley, Sally Hawkins, Andrew Garfield, and Carey Mulligan.

---

her friends, Ruth and Tommy, with whom she went to school. The school was a private school in the English countryside called Hailsham. Kathy's reminiscences of the time she spent at Hailsham form a substantial part of the novel. In this chapter she recalls some incidents when she was about twelve or thirteen. Tommy was mercilessly teased by the other children. When he was not selected by the other boys to play soccer with them, he would lose his temper. The other students would make fun of him as he gave vent to his rage.

CHAPTER TWO

Kathy looks back at how she took an interest in Tommy over the few weeks following the temper tantrum. There were more temper tantrums and incidents involving pranks played upon him. The children think Tommy is lazy, noting that he fails to contribute anything to the Exchange, a quarterly exhibition and sale in which students trade little items they have made themselves. Kathy relates that she has spoken to Tommy recently about his troubles at the school, and he says it started when Miss Geraldine, one of the "guardians" (the term they use instead of teacher), praised some poor painting he had done, and this aroused the resentment of the other students. Kathy resumes her reminiscence, saying that after a while the teasing of Tommy stopped. He told her it was due to something that Miss Lucy, another guardian, had said to him.

CHAPTER THREE

Tommy explains to Kathy what Miss Lucy had said to him. She said it did not matter if he was not creative, and he was not to worry about

it or about what others were saying. Miss Lucy told him he was a good student. As she said this, she was shaking with rage, but Tommy did not know why she was angry. Tommy is helped by her comments, and his attitude changes, because he knows that what happens with the other students is not his fault. He also tells Kathy that Miss Lucy told him she believed the students should be told more about "donations," and Kathy seems to understand what is meant by this, but she does not explain it for the reader.

Kathy reminisces about a woman known as Madame, who comes to the school several times a year and takes the students' best artwork. The students think she puts the artwork in what they call the Gallery, but no one knows for sure what happens to it or why Madame takes it. Madame does not talk to the students, and Ruth thinks she is afraid of them. One day, a group of students surprises Madame after she has gotten out of her car, and Madame reacts with a suppressed shudder, and the students take this as confirmation that she is afraid of them. Looking back, Kathy says that even at a young age the children must have been aware at some level that they were not like other people, and that others might be afraid of them because of how they were created and what their purpose was.

CHAPTER FOUR

Kathy looks back to a time she calls the "tokens controversy," when the children were about ten. The students thought they should be compensated with tokens when Madame took something of theirs. A boy called Roy J. suggests it to Miss Emily, the head guardian, and eventually the idea is adopted. A girl called Polly T. asks Miss Lucy why Madame takes their work in the first place, but Miss Lucy does not explain.

Kathy then reminisces about the Sales, which were where the children bought with their tokens items such as toys and clothes. The items for sale were delivered in boxes by van every month. Kathy then thinks back to the early days of her friendship with Ruth, which started when they were seven or eight and they ride imaginary horses together.

CHAPTER FIVE

Kathy reports that as adults, when she was "caring" for Ruth in Dover, they discussed how Ruth had been the leader of the "secret guards" who protected their favorite guardian, Miss Geraldine. Kathy became one of them. She recalls how they protected Miss Geraldine from what they were convinced was a plot to kidnap her hatched by some of the other guardians. Kathy and Ruth have a falling out, and Kathy is excluded from the secret guard fantasy, but she still remains loyal to Ruth. About three years later, Ruth implies that a pencil case she has acquired was given to her by Miss Geraldine. Guardians are not allowed to show favoritism or give gifts. Kathy knows Ruth is lying and without confronting her directly finds a way of letting Ruth know that she knows.

CHAPTER SIX

Troubled by what she has done to damage her friendship with Ruth, Kathy finds a way of making it up to her. Ruth appreciates it and looks for some way of being nice to Kathy in return. The opportunity arises over a cassette tape of songs by a popular singer, Judy Bridgewater. Before Kathy explains what happens, she digresses, commenting on how smoking was forbidden at the school. Miss Lucy tells them that she once smoked herself, but it was far worse if the children were to smoke than it ever had been for her, although she does not explain why. Going back to the tape, Kathy says that her favorite song had a line, "Baby, never let me go." She imagines that it refers to a woman who has been told she could not have babies but really wants one and has one anyway. One day, she is dancing to the music in her dorm, holding a pillow to her chest as an imaginary baby. Madame comes by the half-open door and sees her. Madame says nothing but leaves sobbing. A couple of years later, Kathy discusses the incident with Tommy; they both know by then none of the students at Hailsham are able to have children. The tape was lost a short while after the incident with Madame. Ruth takes the trouble to replace it for her with a tape of ballroom dancing music. That kind of music means nothing to Kathy, but she appreciates the gesture.

CHAPTER SEVEN

When Kathy is thirteen, Miss Lucy decides to tell them all the truth. They will not be able to do what they want to do in life. Their futures are all determined. They have been created in order that, when they become adults, they will be required to donate their vital organs for others. The children do not react much; it seems that they already know this in a vague kind of way. They have sex education classes, in which they are told they must avoid disease, but sex will be different for them than for normal people because they are unable to have babies. The children discuss the future "donations" in a light-hearted way; in fact, it becomes a sort of running joke about what awaits them. This changes when they are fifteen; they talk more seriously about it.

CHAPTER EIGHT

At age sixteen, the topic of sex often comes up among the students. They receive contradictory messages from the guardians. The guardians tell them that sex is not something to be ashamed of, but at the same time they set rules that make it difficult for the students to engage in it. Kathy thinks there is less sexual activity among the students than many of the students like to think, although she knows Ruth and Tommy have done it. She herself has held back, but she decides she wants to experiment and chooses a boy named Harry C. She starts dropping hints to him that she is interested in him, but then Ruth and Tommy split up, and this puts her in a different position.

CHAPTER NINE

After Tommy and Ruth split up, a couple of girls mention to Kathy that they expect her to become a couple with Tommy. This surprises her, but she stops trying to start something with Harry. Then Ruth asks Kathy to help her get back together with Tommy. Kathy agrees. When Kathy talks to Tommy, he tells her about something Miss Lucy has told him. She said she had been wrong to tell him earlier that it did not matter that he was not creative. The art the students produced was important, she says, partly because it is "evidence." She does not explain what she means but encourages him to work again at his art. Kathy then mentions that Ruth wants them to get back together, but Tommy seems reluctant. The next day the students learn that Miss Lucy has left Hailsham, and Tommy and Ruth get back together.

Part Two

CHAPTER TEN

Kathy recalls that after she left Hailsham, she and seven others, including Ruth and Tommy, went to the Cottages, buildings on the site of a farm that had gone out of business. They live independently for two years in rather Spartan conditions, joining a group of students who already live there and are referred to as veterans. After about two months there, Kathy and Ruth quarrel. Kathy tells Ruth about an annoying mannerism she has copied from a veteran couple, Chrissie and Rodney. Ruth does not take this well and says that Kathy is upset because Ruth has managed to make new friends. Kathy then criticizes Ruth's behavior toward Tommy.

CHAPTER ELEVEN

Kathy feels betrayed by Ruth because in their argument Ruth made an unpleasant comment about Kathy having had sex with some of the boys at the Cottages, but now, in the present, Kathy reconsiders the situation from Ruth's point of view, deciding that perhaps Ruth had some cause to be unpleasant to her. She was trying to adapt to their new life in the Cottages, and Kathy realizes that she should not judge her friend. Recollecting once more their lives at the Cottages, Kathy says that when a student left the Cottages, people rarely spoke much of them again. She remembers someone named Steve whom she never met but who kept a collection of pornographic magazines. Some of those magazines keep turning up long after Steve had left. Kathy looks at them, and Tommy finds her doing so, but she does not tell him why she is looking, nor does she herself know.

CHAPTER TWELVE

Kathy, Tommy, Ruth, Chrissie, and Rodney decide to go on a trip to Norfolk. They go because on a previous trip, Chrissie and Rodney claim to have seen someone they regard as a "possible" for Ruth. A "possible" is a person who may be the model from whom a particular clone was made. The idea that circulates among the Hailsham students is that if they can find their model, they will have a deeper idea of who they are and what their lives might become. Ruth's possible is a woman who works in an office.

CHAPTER THIRTEEN

Rodney borrows a car, and they drive to a seaside town in Norfolk. At lunch in a café, they talk about a future for Ruth, working in an office, just like her possible. Ruth even thinks that Tommy will be with her. Chrissie mentions that she has heard that a couple, if they were Hailsham students, could get a "deferral." The couple must prove that they are in love, and then they would be allowed to have few years together before they are required to become donors. Kathy has heard this rumor before, circulating among the veterans at the Cottages.

CHAPTER FOURTEEN

They go shopping in the town. They pass an office with a big glass front, and Rodney points out Ruth's possible, a dark-haired woman of about fifty. Later, they see the same woman walking along the street, and they follow her into an art shop. They pretend to be interested in the pictures while observing the woman. After they leave, they decide that the woman is not a possible for Ruth after all. Chrissie and Rodney then take Ruth to visit a friend of theirs, but Kathy and Tommy decline to join them. There is tension between Ruth and Kathy.

CHAPTER FIFTEEN

Tommy and Kathy go to a shop where Kathy finds a copy of the Judy Bridgewater tape that she lost some time before. Tommy had suggested that they look for it. He had always wanted to find it for her. Later, they talk about deferrals, and Tommy wonders whether the rumor is true. He thinks it may have some connection to the Gallery, the collection of artwork that Madame took from them. The Gallery would help the authorities decide whether the couple who applied for the deferral were worthy of it. Tommy also tells Kathy he has recently been doing some art work of his own, drawing imaginary animals. Later, as they return home, Kathy feels that the tension between her and Ruth has been resolved.

CHAPTER SIXTEEN

One day Tommy shows Kathy his drawings of imaginary animals. He tells Kathy he sees no reason why he should keep his work secret, and she agrees with him. She tells him his work is good, but some time later, Kathy and Ruth talk about Tommy's animals, and they both laugh about them. When Kathy later meets Ruth and Tommy at a churchyard, Ruth is upset that Tommy told Kathy about his theory of the purpose of the Gallery but did not tell her. She then tells Tommy that Kathy thinks his drawings of animals are hilarious. Kathy is shocked that Ruth would say such a thing, and she turns and leaves.

CHAPTER SEVENTEEN

Over the next few days, Kathy realizes that Ruth and Tommy have grown apart; Kathy also finds it harder to talk to Tommy. Eventually she and Ruth try to patch up their quarrel. Ruth tells Kathy that she and Tommy probably will not be together forever, but even if they were to split up, Tommy would not be interested in taking up with Kathy. He regards her just as a friend, Ruth says. Kathy takes this without much comment, but the two girls come close to quarreling about something else and part on bad terms. Not long after that, Kathy decides to leave the Cottages and begin her training as a carer.

Part Three

CHAPTER EIGHTEEN

It is seven years since Kathy left the Cottages, and she reports on her life as a carer, saying she is suited to it. She drives around the country, taking care of the donors that are assigned to her. She has learned to live with the emotional difficulties of the work and the long hours. One day she meets Laura, one of her friends from Hailsham, by chance, and Laura says she has heard that Ruth had a bad first donation. Laura suggests that Kathy become Ruth's carer. They also discuss the fact that Hailsham has been closed. Three weeks later, Kathy does become Ruth's carer. Their relationship is still a little strained, and Kathy feels that Ruth does not trust her. They decide to go to see an old boat that is stranded in the marshes.

CHAPTER NINETEEN

On the way to see the boat, they stop at Kingsfield, which is a recovery center for donors. Tommy is staying there, and the three of them drive to see the boat. They talk about the news that Chrissie has "completed" (that is, died) during her second donation. On the way home Ruth asks Kathy to forgive her for trying, at Hailsham and the Cottages, to keep Kathy and Tommy apart. She wants Kathy to put it right by applying for a deferral, so she can spend some years with Tommy. She gives them Madame's address, which she discovered for herself. After this, Kathy's relationship with Ruth improves, and just before Ruth dies after her second donation, Kathy agrees to become Tommy's carer.

CHAPTER TWENTY

A year later, Kathy becomes Tommy's carer. He has just made his third donation. Their relationship deepens, but Kathy regrets that they left it so late. Tommy continues to do his drawings of imaginary animals. Some time later, Kathy tells Tommy that she has seen Madame after waiting outside her house in Littlehampton. They decide to visit her and ask for a deferral. Tommy says he will take his drawings.

CHAPTER TWENTY-ONE

Kathy and Tommy intercept Madame as she is about to go into her house. They say they must speak with her, and she invites them in. Kathy explains that she and Tommy are in love and want to apply for a deferral. Tommy explains his belief about the purpose of Madame's gallery, that the students' art will reveal who they are. Then someone in a wheelchair enters the room, and Tommy and Kathy realize it is Miss Emily, the former head guardian at Hailsham.

CHAPTER TWENTY-TWO

Miss Emily remembers both of them. She tells them the rumor about deferrals is untrue; there is no such thing. She also says that their artwork was taken to prove to doubters that these cloned people had souls, just like normal people. She explains that Hailsham was set up to improve the conditions under which clones lived, which had been deplorable. Those who set up Hailsham wanted to show that clones could become fully human if given a decent education but at some point there was a scandal involving a researcher who claimed to be able to help people produce superior children through genetic manipulation. People found this alarming, and funding for Hailsham began to dry up, even though Hailsham had nothing to do with the researcher's work. Miss Emily also explains that Miss Lucy was dismissed as a guardian because she thought the students should be told more of who they were and what their lives were for. Miss Emily believes Miss Lucy was wrong and that it was important to shelter the children from the full truth. When Kathy and Tommy drive home, Tommy says he agrees with Miss Lucy. He gets out of the car and gives vent to his feelings.

CHAPTER TWENTY-THREE

Tommy starts to identify more with the other donors at the center where he lives, and Kathy feels a bit left out. Tommy sometimes tells her she cannot understand certain things because she is not a donor. Tommy's fourth donation is coming up, and he tells Kathy he thinks he ought to have another carer because the job is too much for Kathy. She is angry at first but then agrees to his suggestion. In the last section of the book, Kathy looks back from the present. She is still a carer. Tommy is dead, but she thinks she will never forget her memories of him and Ruth.

CHARACTERS

Chrissie

Chrissie is one of the veterans at the Cottages. Chrissie is very welcoming to Kathy when she and the others first arrive from Hailsham, and everything about Hailsham fascinates her. She is always asking questions about it. Chrissie's boyfriend is Rodney, and they are always seen together. Chrissie is the dominant partner, and Rodney defers to her opinions. Chrissie becomes a donor and dies during her second donation.

Cynthia E.

Cynthia E. is a student at Hailsham and one of Kathy's friends. It is she who says she expects Kathy to take up with Tommy when Tommy and Ruth split up.

Miss Emily

Miss Emily is the head guardian at Hailsham. She is older than the other guardians, and the students are intimidated by her but they also regard her as fair-minded and do not argue with her decisions. At morning assemblies, she often tells the students they are special and should use the opportunities they are given. At the end of the novel, Kathy and Tommy meet Miss Emily again at Madame's house. She is in a wheelchair, and she explains to them how Hailsham was an attempt to give the students better lives than they would otherwise, as clones, have been able to lead. She believes that in her work at Hailsham she was able to give them their childhoods, even if that meant keeping them in the dark on some important matters.

Miss Geraldine

Miss Geraldine is one of the guardians at Hailsham. She is the favorite of the students, since she is always gentle and kind. She even finds something to praise in Tommy's bad drawing of an elephant.

Hannah

Hannah is a student at Hailsham. She and Kathy have been friends since they were five or six years old. She is also close friends with Ruth, but she does not play a large role in the story.

Harry C.

Harry C. is a student at Hailsham. He is respectable and quiet, and Kathy at one point wants to form a sexual relationship with him, but this never actually happens. Other than that, he and Kathy do not have much to do with each other, and Harry does not go to the Cottages. Many years later, Kathy sees him after he has made a donation.

Kathy H.

Kathy H. is the narrator of the novel. She is thirty-one years old and is looking back at her life and relationships. As a child, she is a student at Hailsham. Her best friend is Ruth, and she is also friends with Tommy. Later, she lives at the Cottages and then becomes a carer at the age of twenty.

Kathy gives the impression of being a calm, reflective, level-headed woman. She is not a leader, but she fits in well with others. Like the other characters, she does not protest against the course her life must take but accepts it. This does not mean, however, that she does not occasionally have a desire for some other kind of life. She is deeply moved by a popular song that contains the line "Baby, never let me go," and she imagines it being sung by a woman who has been told she cannot have children but who has a baby nonetheless. The fact that Kathy is so moved by this song suggests that deep down, she wants to have children of her own, which she will never be able to do. Also, when Kathy is in love with Tommy, she seeks a deferral so she will be able to enjoy their relationship for longer, although when she finds that is not possible she is not devastated by the news.

Kathy's job as a carer suits her. She travels from place to place, looking after those who are donating their organs. She becomes Ruth's carer and then Tommy's. Kathy values her relationships, especially those with Ruth and Tommy, and she spends much time cultivating them. She is a sensitive woman, able to appreciate the feelings of others and take them into account. She is continually reflecting on her experiences and what they mean to her. In particular, she cannot forget Hailsham, the private school where she and the others were educated. She knows that it was a special place, and she believes that she, Ruth, and Tommy were very fortunate to be able to go there. At the end of the novel, she has eight more months to serve as a carer, after which she will become a donor.

Keffers

Keffers is a gruff, uncommunicative man who oversees the maintenance of the Cottages.

Laura

Laura is a student at Hailsham and one of Kathy's friends. She is the joker in the group, always ready with an amusing remark. When they are all about thirteen she enthusiastically takes part in the mocking of Tommy. However, Laura does not fare well as a carer, frustrated by the demands of the job. When Kathy meets her after a gap of seven years, Laura has lost the lively spark she used to have.

Miss Lucy

Miss Lucy is one of the guardians at Hailsham. Her full name is Lucy Wainright. Miss Lucy excels at sports and is very strong and fit. Kathy realizes during her last years at Hailsham that Miss Lucy is different from the other guardians, although she does not really know why. Miss Lucy appears worried or frustrated by something. Then one day Miss Lucy addresses the students outside the sports pavilion. She has heard one of the students talking about possibly becoming an actor, and she tells them exactly what is in store for them. Their lives are predetermined. They should know who they are and what their lives are for. Not long after this, Miss Lucy leaves Hailsham, but the students do not know why. Many years later, Miss Emily explains to Kathy and Tommy that Miss Lucy was dismissed from her position. Miss Emily disagreed with her belief that the students should be told more about their lives. Miss Emily thinks Miss Lucy was too idealistic and did not have a good understanding of the practicalities of the situation.

Madame

Madame is presented at first as a mysterious woman who visits Hailsham several times a year and takes some of the students' artwork. The students think she must exhibit the art somewhere in what they call the Gallery. They call her Madame because she is French or Belgian. She is a tall woman who wears a gray suit, and the students think she is afraid of them—for some reason they do not understand. Many years later, Kathy and Tommy go to visit Madame at her house in Littlehampton. They learn that Madame, along with Miss Emily, was one of the main organizers of the Hailsham project. Miss Emily tells them that Madame, to whom she refers as Marie-Claude, worked hard to make the Hailsham project succeed but has been disillusioned about how things actually turned out.

Moira B.

Moira B. is one of Kathy's friends at Hailsham. Like Kathy, she is a member of the "secret guard" fantasy regarding Miss Geraldine, and also like Kathy, she is expelled from the group.

Patricia C.

Patricia C. is a student at Hailsham and is two years younger than Kathy. She has artistic talent, and Kathy acquires her beautiful calendar at one of the Exchanges.

Peter J.

Peter J. is a student at Hailsham. It is his comment about possibly becoming an actor that prompts Miss Lucy to explain to the students what their lives will really be like.

Polly T.

Polly T. is a student at Hailsham. It is Polly who asks Miss Lucy the question about why Madame takes their artwork.

Rodney

Rodney is living at the Cottages when Kathy first meets him. His girlfriend is Chrissie. Rodney wears his hair in a ponytail and is interested in religious concepts such as reincarnation. On a trip to Norfolk with Chrissie, Rodney spots Ruth's possible, and this prompts Ruth, Kathy, and Tommy to accompany them on another Norfolk expedition to find out if there is any truth in the sighting.

Roger C.

Roger C. is a former student at Hailsham. He was a year below Kathy. Kathy runs into him much later, at a clinic, and he tells her that Hailsham is about to close.

Roy J.

Roy J. is a year above Kathy at Hailsham. He goes to see Miss Emily to ask whether the students could receive tokens when their artwork is taken by Madame.

Ruth

Ruth is a student at Hailsham. She is close friends with Kathy from the age of seven or eight. Ruth is a leader of their small group of girls, and she can be outspoken, angry, and even vindictive sometimes. When she becomes a teenager, she and Tommy become a couple. Kathy and Ruth have a rather difficult relationship at

Hailsham. In one sense, Kathy feels she is able to trust Ruth and confide in her, but Ruth can be quarrelsome, and from time to time they fall out. However, Kathy still remains loyal to Ruth, and the two girls find ways of making up to each other. When they are together at the Cottages, the girls quarrel again when Ruth makes some unpleasant, catty remarks to Kathy. Kathy is also annoyed with Ruth because Ruth is always trying to impress the veterans—the other young people at the Cottages who did not attend Hailsham, and Ruth will sometimes ignore Kathy and Tommy. Acting out of jealousy, Ruth also tries her best to keep Tommy and Kathy apart. Much later, however, after Ruth has become a donor, she asks Kathy, who is her carer, to forgive her for her bad behavior. To make up for it, Ruth suggests that Kathy and Tommy seek a deferral, so they can spend some years together. This gesture of friendship and atonement results in an improvement in the relationship between Kathy and Ruth. Ruth, however, dies after her second donation. Kathy remembers her with affection.

Steve

Steve is a former resident of the Cottages. He does not actually appear in the narrative, but he is known for his collection of pornographic magazines, which keep turning up even though he is no longer there.

Tommy

Tommy is a student at Hailsham. When he is a young boy, Tommy is subject to temper tantrums at the school. As a result of this, he is teased relentlessly by the other children but this phase passes, and Tommy emerges as an intelligent, thoughtful boy. He is good at sports but appears to have little talent for art. Tommy forms a romantic relationship with Ruth, and he is also friends with Kathy. When Tommy and Ruth split up, it seems as if he and Kathy will get together, but Tommy and Ruth soon resume their relationship. After Hailsham, Tommy lives in the Cottages with the other students from Hailsham. His relationship with Kathy deepens, although for a long time they acknowledge each other only as friends rather than romantic partners. Tommy confides in Kathy more than he does in Ruth. He tells her, for example, that he has started doing some artwork, remembering that Miss Lucy at Hailsham had told him it was important (after she had initially told him it was not).

Tommy draws small imaginary animals. Even though Ruth acknowledges that she and Tommy are growing apart, she still does her best to ensure that Tommy and Kathy do not get close, either. Some years later, however, at Ruth's suggestion, Kathy becomes Tommy's carer. He has started his organ donations. Their relationship then flourishes as it had not been allowed to before. Tommy shows himself to be a mature, good-hearted individual, capable of loving Kathy. He and Kathy visit Madame so they can tell her they are in love and ask for a deferral of the time when they will have to donate their organs. They learn there is no such thing as a deferral. When Tommy's fourth donation looms, he tells Kathy he wants another carer, so that Kathy can be spared the strain of looking after him. Kathy reluctantly agrees to his request. After Tommy dies, Kathy, looking back on events, knows that she will never forget him.

THEMES

Cloning

Although this is in a sense a science fiction story in that the author presents a society in which the cloning of human beings is an accepted practice, he seems to have no interest in describing the kind of society that has permitted this practice to occur or how it developed. He does make it clear, though, that in this imagined society, life for most clones is not good. When the practice first began in the early 1950s, clones were raised in extremely inhumane conditions; people believed that the clones were not fully human and did not possess a soul. They existed solely for medical purposes and were required to donate their organs so that others might recover from previously fatal diseases, such as cancer. The private school Hailsham was established to counter that view, to allow the clones to have an education, and to show that they were capable of artistic endeavors that revealed their depth of character, if not their soul. In the 1990s, after the Hailsham experiment runs out of funds, the clones are raised in large government homes. These homes, according to Miss Emily, are slightly better than they were before Hailsham, but she also tells Kathy and Tommy "you'd not sleep for days if you saw what still goes on in some of those places." The novel might therefore be read as a warning against where the biomedical sciences may be heading and the moral issues

TOPICS FOR FURTHER STUDY

- In a small group of students, discuss the ethical issues associated with cloning, especially the cloning of humans. Should this be banned by law, or should scientists be allowed to explore the possibilities? If you argue for the cloning of humans to be banned, make sure you explain your reasoning. Is your objection moral or religious or practical (that is, cloning of humans could not be done safely)? When the group finishes the discussion, each member should write a position paper that summarizes their own views on the subject.

- Watch the movie *Blade Runner* (1982). One of the issues addressed in the film is cloning. How does the treatment of cloning in this film differ from how it is presented in *Never Let Me Go*? Write a short essay in which you present your findings.

- Read *Taylor Five* (2002), a novel for young adults by Ann Halam. Taylor is a fourteen-year-old clone living in Borneo, an island in Southeast Asia. She is one of the first human clones and resents it. During the course of this adventure story, she struggles to understand exactly who she is and what her life is all about. In an essay, discuss the similarities and differences between how Taylor learns to understands herself and how the clones in *Never Let Me Go* think of themselves and their own lives.

- Using your library and the Internet, create a time line for the history of cloning from the second half of the twentieth century to the present. What are the major landmarks in this developing science? What laws have been passed to deal with cloning in the United States and around the world? Create a presentation in PowerPoint or similar software and show it to your class.

it raises. In the society depicted in the novel, the desire for scientific progress and the curing of diseases is so great that a proper examination of

the moral implications of cloning has not been done, and the result is that thousands of clones are condemned to live short, circumscribed lives, regarded by most as sufficiently human in a physical sense to donate organs to the sick but not human enough to be given any basic human rights.

Relationships

The clones in the novel all have short lives, and they know it. It seems that they live only into their twenties or thirties. In these truncated lives, with a sure and known end, they do their best to create meaning. They come to know what is important in life, and it is not longevity. Far more important than a long life is a rich, satisfying one with warm and positive human relationships. Kathy and her friends Ruth and Tommy may be flawed as people, as all humans are, but they learn how to care for one another, how to overcome past slights or disappointments. They learn how to talk to one another, to communicate what is important to them. As they emerge from childhood into adulthood, they have plenty of time to reflect on their mortality, and they also accept their role in life. They do not protest about it or try to alter it. They are not angry about it. They accept their fates. On a few occasions they do entertain ideas about what they might do with their lives that turn out to be unrealistic—Ruth thinks she may work in an office one day, for example—but when the truth dawns it does so gently, without sparking great dismay. Even when Tommy and Kathy fall in love and seek a deferral so that they may have more time to enjoy their relationship, they are not seeking to escape altogether from their prescribed lives, only to postpone their donations for a little while. Through the lens of a highly imaginative story, the author has created in effect a universal meditation, through his doomed characters, on what makes life worth living in the face of the unalterable fact of human mortality.

Deception

At Hailsham, the children are not told much about what others have decided is their sole purpose in life. It is not that they are told nothing, but as Kathy remarks, looking back on the matter as an adult, it seems that they were given information that was always a little too advanced for them to understand. Either that or the truth was explained to them in a way that ensured they would not really be aware of its full import. An example of this is when they are told about sex at the age of about thirteen. Kathy thinks that when the guardians gave lectures about sex, they also explained about donations, but because the children were mostly curious about sex they forgot or did not notice the information about donations. This was probably, Kathy thinks, deliberate on the part of the guardians. The children were, as she puts it, "told and not told." They were also told about how important sex is because it can involve the emotions; therefore they should be careful and treat it as special, like everyone else did. This was in spite of the fact that they were not able to have babies. In other words, the information about not being able to have babies was slipped in along with a talk that still emphasized the importance of sex.

One day Miss Lucy does try to explain to the children what awaits them, but later Kathy is not sure how much Miss Lucy actually said. Kathy guesses that "once she'd seen the puzzled, uncomfortable faces in front of her, she realised the impossibility of completing what she'd started." Furthermore, Kathy recalls that after the talk, the students discussed Miss Lucy herself rather than what she said; some students thought she had gone crazy; others thought she had merely been scolding them for being too noisy.

When Tommy and Kathy later visit Madame and find Miss Emily there, Miss Emily explains the dispute she had with Miss Lucy. Miss Lucy was in favor of complete disclosure to the students about the real nature of their lives and their future, but Miss Emily wanted the children to be shielded from the full truth. She thought she was helping them by doing so; the deception, in her view, was necessary. Otherwise the children could not have been happy. She admits that "sometimes...we kept things from you, lied to you. Yes, in many ways we *fooled* you.... But we sheltered you...and we gave you your childhoods."

The theme of necessary deception suggests in a wider sense the fact that children are often shielded by their parents about truths they are too young to understand. How much to tell a child, and when, is a judgment every parent must make, but in the novel, as Kathy and Tommy leave after their conversation with Miss Emily, Tommy expresses his belief that Miss Lucy was right—the students should have been told more about the future that awaited them.

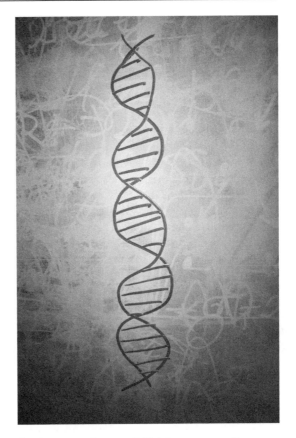

In the story, human DNA is a commodity.
(Image copyright Perov Stanislav, 2010. Used under license from Shutterstock.com)

STYLE

Dystopia

The novel can be described by the term dystopia. In dystopian fiction, the author takes a problematic aspect of contemporary society and projects it onto a larger scale, imagining a bleak and depressing future for humankind. Examples of dystopian novels include Aldous Huxley's *Brave New World* (1932), which features a society in which cloning takes place; George Orwell's *1984* (1949); and Margaret Atwood's *The Handmaid's Tale* (1985). Dystopian fiction is the opposite of utopian fiction, which describes an ideal way of life.

Euphemism

A euphemism is a term that softens the impact of something that is disturbing or offensive by making it sound vague or neutral. Dystopias often include the manipulation of language by those in power to blur the impact of oppressive policies.

In Atwood's *The Handmaid's Tale*, for example, a deformed baby is referred to as an "unbaby," which defines it in a way that makes it easier for the authorities to kill such babies. In *Never Let Me Go*, the clones refer to death as "completing." They never use the terms die, dying, or death. For example, Ruth says to Kathy, "I heard about Chrissie. I heard she completed during her second donation." "Completing" has none of the emotional impact of the word death. It does, however, express the idea that the clones have finished what they were created to do. They have completed their life purpose. The term therefore has for them a positive connotation, which may explain how they are able to face their inevitable fate with such tranquility.

Narrative Flashback

The story starts in the late 1990s, when Kathy is thirty-one years old. It is then told in the form of Kathy's memories of her life, starting when she was a young girl at Hailsham. This structure is maintained throughout the first two parts of the novel. Kathy reflects, from the standpoint of adulthood, on her childhood and adolescence. These reminiscences might be called flashbacks—a flashback is a scene that takes place before the main time frame of the novel—but since they form the bulk of the narrative they are rather too long for that term to be appropriate. The author's technique of telling the story is to provide long stretches of narrative in which Kathy recalls her childhood but occasionally (the beginning of chapter four, the second section of chapter six, the beginning of chapter ten, and elsewhere) return to Kathy's life in the present as she drives around the country fulfilling her duties as a carer. The structure changes in part three, in which Kathy tells of the more recent past, from her present perspective as a carer.

HISTORICAL CONTEXT

Cloning in the 1990s

Lee M. Silver, in *Remaking Eden: Cloning and Beyond in a Brave New World*, defines cloning as "the process by which a cell, or group of cells, from one individual organism is used to derive an entirely new organism." The new organism is genetically identical to that from which it is derived.

In 1996, there was a major breakthrough in reproductive technology when a British scientist, Ian Wilmut, working with colleagues at the Roslin Institute near Edinburgh, Scotland, successfully created a healthy lamb called Dolly from a single cell taken from an adult ewe. Dolly was in essence an identical twin of the ewe. This remarkable breakthrough was announced in the journal *Nature* on February 27, 1997.

According to Wilmut, one of the purposes of cloning sheep and eventually other animals was to transplant their organs into humans to cure disease. Quoted in Susan Squier's essay, "Negotiating Boundaries: From Assisted Reproduction to Assisted Replication," Wilmut said, "There are about 160,000 people a year who die before organs like hearts, livers, and kidneys become available to them." He added that cloning would be an effective way of providing organs that could be used to treat such conditions. At the time in Britain, however, there was a debate about the ethical issues that might be involved in transplanting the organs of animals into humans. Would humans be affected by this in some fundamental way? Would it blur the distinction between humans and animals?

The creation of Dolly in 1996 shows that in *Never Let Me Go*, which on the face of it seems a fantastic story, Ishiguro was merely drawing on current scientific research and controversy, merely substituting cloned humans for cloned sheep and other animals.

The announcement about the cloning of Dolly produced an avalanche of publicity and media speculation about cloning as it might be developed and applied to humans. Some scientists argued that the technology involved in cloning animals might not necessarily work to clone humans, that such a possibility was unlikely in the foreseeable future, and that there would be no reason to do it anyway. Other scientists believed that such technology could be applied safely to human cloning, without risk of birth defects.

Opposition to Human Cloning

Because of the serious ethical issues it raised, human cloning was already banned in Britain in the 1990s, and public opinion was firmly against it. In the United States, a Time/CNN poll appearing in *Time* magazine a few weeks after the announcement of the cloning of Dolly showed that 74 percent of respondents thought that it was against God's will to clone human beings. Another poll showed that two-thirds of Americans also thought that the cloning of animals was wrong.

Madame's tears suggest Kathy facing a new, emerging, and cruel world alone and asking for the old world to not let her go. *(Image copyright Pindyurin Vasily, 2010. Used under license from Shutterstock.com)*

Silver brought attention to the widespread fear of cloning that existed, and may still exist, among the general public. He argued that the fear was due to misperceptions among the public about what cloning is. It does not mean that a cloned human would be exactly the same as its original in terms of consciousness, personality, feelings, and other attributes. Silver explains as follows:

> Real biological cloning can only take place at the level of the cell—life *in the general sense*. It is only long after the cloning event is completed that a unique—and independent—life *in the special sense* could emerge in the developing fetus.

Ishiguro alludes to this question in the novel. The clones at Hailsham believe that if they could locate the person from whom they were created, they would have *"some* insight into who you were deep down, and maybe too you'd see something

of what your life held in store." In other words, they believe there will be some similarities between themselves and the person from whom they were "copied" (as they put it), but they will not be identical in every way to them.

The second misperception, according to Silver, was that clones would be an "imperfect imitation of the real thing. This causes some people to think that—far from having the same soul as someone else—a clone would have no soul at all." This idea finds its way directly into *Never Let Me Go.* The general population in the society depicted believes that the clones do not possess a soul. The school Hailsham was set up to counter this predominant view, and it is why the students there are encouraged to pursue art to reveal the depths of their inner life. Silver argues that such a debate about whether clones would have souls is based on a misunderstanding. He points out, "The newly created embryo can only develop inside the womb of a woman in the same way that all embryos and fetuses develop. Cloned children will be full-fledged human beings."

CRITICAL OVERVIEW

Never Let Me Go received universal praise from reviewers, many of whom regarded the novel as Ishiguro's best since *The Remains of the Day.* A reviewer for *Publishers Weekly* admires Ishiguro's style, commenting that the novel is "so exquisitely observed that even the most workaday objects and interactions are infused with a luminous, humming otherworldliness." The reviewer concludes that the novel is "a stinging cautionary tale of science outpacing ethics." For Joseph O'Neill in the *Atlantic,* the novel is "the saddest, most persuasive science fiction you'll read." O'Neill points out that Ishiguro brings attention to the fact that "modern desperation regarding death, combined with technological advances and the natural human capacity for self-serving fictions and evasions . . . could easily give rise to new varieties of socially approved atrocities." In *National Review,* Gina R. Dalfonzo calls the novel a "quietly devastating, beautifully written tale. . . . Ishiguro ensures that, having known Kathy's world, we will look at our own through changed eyes." Stephen Bernstein, in the *Review of Contemporary Fiction,* notes that Ishiguro's stylistic technique in *Never Let Me Go* is similar to that which he has employed in many of his previous novels. He describes it as "Ishiguro's penchant for the slow revelation of a first-person narrator's inner secrets." Bernstein concludes that the novel is a "powerful and sad narrative.... One whose lingering implications we will do well to take to heart." Finally, Sarah Howard, in *Kliatt*, recommends the novel for high school seniors. She writes: "Melancholy, suspenseful, and at times alarming, this novel is a compellingly dark page-turner."

CRITICISM

Bryan Aubrey

Aubrey holds a Ph.D. in English. In this essay, he suggests that what is most important about Never Let Me Go *is not cloning but the quality of the relationships that the central characters develop with one another over time.*

Never Let Me Go is a quiet novel that rarely raises its voice. Like many of Ishiguro's narrators, Kathy H. is a subdued character not given to emotional excess. She relates her story in an even, detached tone that conveys thoughtfulness and dignity, as well as insight into her personal relationships. Past dramas are viewed through the lens of understanding and even wisdom. Kathy is quite unlike her more volatile friend, Ruth, who is the only character in the entire novel who ever explodes in anger about her status as a clone. This comes on their trip to Norfolk, after Ruth has been disappointed that her "possible" (the person from whom she was cloned) turns out not to be a possible after all. Ruth declares that the whole expedition was futile.

> We're modelled from *trash*. Junkies, prostitutes, winos, trumps. Convicts, maybe, just so long as they aren't psychos. That's where we come from.... If you want to look for possibles...you look in the gutter. You look in rubbish bins. Look down the toilet, that's where you'll find where we all came from.

The others treat this outburst almost as a breach in decorum. Rodney tells her to forget about it and changes the subject, and Chrissie concurs. This shows that the clones accept the role in life that fate has dealt them. It is not really a big issue for them, and they indulge in no private rage or despair about it. Even when they consider possible futures for themselves outside of their allotted path, it is in a wistful, rather vague way that never results in a definite plan (with the one exception of Kathy and Tommy's attempt to seek

> ISHIGURO WANTS TO SHOW THESE YOUNG PEOPLE TRYING TO CREATE MEANINGFUL LIVES FOR THEMSELVES AND HOW ONE OF THEM, KATHY, LOOKS BACK AT THESE EFFORTS FROM THE BROADER PERSPECTIVE THAT THE PASSAGE OF TIME BRINGS."

a "deferral," but even that is envisioned only as a temporary postponement of the inevitable). As Ishiguro stated in an interview with Cynthia F. Wong and Grace Crummett, he focused in this novel on the degree to which "we accepted our fates, the kind of lives we were allowed to live as people, rather than focus on the rebellious spirit we gain and try to move out of our lives."

Ruth's outburst is interesting for what it reveals about the author's intentions. Other than Ruth's speculation in this one instance, Ishiguro never gives a clue about how the originals from whom the clones are made are selected. It is simply not his purpose. Although many reviewers of the book commented that Ishiguro's tale brings to the fore the moral implications of contemporary progress in reproductive technology, that was not Ishiguro's main intention. He does not spend any time creating a panoramic view of a society gone wrong or examine in detail how the society he depicts functions and how it got created. The focus is mainly on the lives and relationships of three of the clones in the context of the inevitable course of their short lives. Only briefly, near the end of the novel, does Ishiguro allow Miss Emily to explain something of the societal background that allowed the creation of clones and their relegation to a less than fully human status. In this sense it is not a fully fledged science fiction novel like Philip K. Dick's *Do Androids Dream of Electric Sheep* (1968) or a fully realized dystopian tale like Margaret Atwood's *The Handmaid's Tale* (1985) or *Oryx and Crake* (2003). Ishiguro wants to show these young people trying to create meaningful lives for themselves and how one of them, Kathy, looks back at these efforts from the broader perspective that the passage of time brings. His lack of interest in

WHAT DO I READ NEXT?

- *The Remains of the Day* (1989) is Ishiguro's third and most famous novel. Set in England in 1956, it features Stevens, an elderly butler who has served at Darlington Hall, a great mansion, for over thirty-five years. On a six-day motoring trip, he looks back at his life and profession, reflecting on what it takes to be an excellent butler. Stevens has so cultivated the personal dignity that he believes is essential that he has lived a life of great emotional restraint. Only at the end of the novel does he realize how much personal happiness he has sacrificed.

- *When We Were Orphans* (2000) is Ishiguro's fifth novel. In the early 1900s, when Christopher Banks is a young boy in Shanghai, China, his parents disappear. Christopher grows up in England, becomes a detective, and reflects on his memories of the past. Finally, in the 1930s, he returns to Shanghai to solve the mystery of his parents' fate. Within this framework, Ishiguro creates another haunting novel that revolves around the memories of the central character.

- *A Number* (2003) is a play by Caryl Churchill, one of Britain's leading dramatists, first produced in 2002. Set in the near future, it is about the conflict between a father and his three adult sons, two of whom are clones from the first son. The play explores not only cloning but the whole notion of identity. How does a person feel knowing that he is an identical copy of someone else? And does a person's identity derive from genetic inheritance or are environmental factors more important?

- Nancy Farmer, an award-winning author of young-adult novels, wrote *House of the Scorpion* (2004). This story takes place in the future, in Opium, a country that lies between the United States and what used to be Mexico, now called Aztlan. The ruler of Opium is one hundred and forty years old, thanks to organ donations from clones. The story focuses on one clone named Matt, who, as he grows up, gradually realizes what his fate will be if he does not escape.

- *The Parable of the Sower* (1993) by Octavia E. Butler, is a dystopian novel that begins in Robledo, twenty miles from Los Angeles in July 2024. The narrator is fifteen-year-old Lauren. California is presented as a violent and lawless society in which the rich hide behind walled estates and chaos reigns everywhere else. Over the next three years, Lauren seeks a better life by traveling north. By the end of the novel she has learned about freedom and self-reliance, and she has become a leader, founding a new community and a new religion, Earthseed.

- *Do Androids Dream of Electric Sheep* (1968) is a science fiction novel by Philip K. Dick. It is set in the near future following the devastation caused by a nuclear war. Androids are indistinguishable from humans except for one important fact: they lack empathy. The protagonist, a man named Deckard, is in pursuit of six escaped androids, while another main character, John Isidore, befriends some androids. Like *Never Let Me Go*, the novel explores what it means to be human. It was the basis for the well-known film *Blade Runner* (1982).

- Ian Wilmut and Roger Highfield present both sides of the cloning issue ten years after the creation of Dolly, the cloned sheep, in *After Dolly, the Promise and Perils of Cloning* (2006).

- *The Immortal Cell* (2003) is Michael D. West's own story of his role in the debates on human cloning. The use of diagrams and illustrations make navigation of the biology easier for readers.

the details of cloning is apparent also in the fact that the clones in the novel are unable to have children, which is odd given the fact that in all other respects they are fully human. There is no scientific reason why clones should not be able to reproduce—even Dolly the real-life cloned sheep was able to—but Ishiguro's purpose in introducing this detail is not difficult to determine. For Kathy, or Tommy, or Ruth to have children would complicate the story he wants to tell. As it stands, they and the other clones have no parents or any other kind of family connection. This makes them more alone in the world than most people, with a need to build from scratch the personal connections that will sustain them. Nothing in that respect is given to them; they must work it out for themselves. Allowing them to have children would make their predicament less stark; they might die young but find solace through the continued existence of their children, for example. In other words, for Ishiguro, the story in *Never Let Me Go* is more important than the science.

In his interview with Wong and Crummett, Ishiguro explained that his main purpose in the novel was indeed to present the concerns of his characters, despite their status as clones and their odd place in society, as very similar to the concerns that everyone has. "What are the things important to us while we are here?" he said. "How do we fit things like love, work, and friendship into what is a surprisingly short period of time?" He wanted the story of the clones to make its impact not so much because of its strangeness but because their story, with its typical human concerns, was a universal one.

Seen in this light, *Never Let Me Go* is a story about the cultivation of love, both in romance and simple friendship, and also about coming to terms with death. These universal themes are made more urgent and poignant by the brevity of the lives the three central characters, Kathy, Ruth, and Tommy, are to lead.

Kathy and Ruth become close friends in their early years at Hailsham. They have plenty of squabbles, but Kathy remains loyal to her more assertive and difficult friend. When they hurt each other's feelings, they tend not to talk openly about the breach, but each tries to make it up to the other in actions that she knows will be noticed. It is the sort of thing that must go on amongst girls—and no doubt boys, too—in middle schools and high schools everywhere. Things get more complicated between Ruth and Kathy in their mid-teen years, because Ruth, the pushier one, gets the boy she wants, Tommy. Kathy, less assertive and of course still very young, does not realize that although Ruth has Tommy, Kathy and Tommy are in fact able to talk and confide in each other much more easily than Tommy and Ruth can. Kathy and Tommy are therefore natural partners for each other, although it is not until they leave the Cottages and Tommy becomes a donor and Kathy a carer that they both find this out. In the meantime, Ruth and Tommy go through the usual teenage ups and downs as a couple: they break up, get back together, and then drift apart again. When they break up the first time, Ruth even enlists Kathy to help in getting them back together. She tells her friend, "You've always had this way with him. He'll listen to you." Then she tells Kathy all the admiring comments that Tommy has often said about her. Kathy, not making the obvious connection, that she is the one who should be with Tommy (as Cynthia and the other students in their circle are expecting), duly tries to talk Tommy back into his relationship with Ruth.

Later, at the Cottages, Ruth and Kathy share quarrels and closeness in roughly even doses, while the innocent intimacy between Kathy and Tommy continues to grow, still unacknowledged. Kathy observes on one occasion that she feels protected and comforted in his presence. Tommy unconsciously reveals his feelings for her when he is so concerned on their trip to Norfolk to replace Kathy's favorite music cassette tape that she has lost. It is easy to see where things are heading, and Ruth probably guesses it, too, but when Ruth knows that she and Tommy are drifting apart, her instincts toward Kathy are less than generous. Revealing a dog-in-the-manger attitude, she may not want Tommy any more, but she is determined that Kathy will not get him either. She tells Kathy, with a tone that suggests she is doing her friend a favor by imparting this particular piece of information, that Tommy would never consider her a "proper girlfriend" because she has had sex with some of the other boys. Kathy does not seem to grasp Ruth's manipulative intentions at this point, so it is not until years later that her relationship with Tommy reaches its natural fulfillment. The fact that Kathy and Tommy finally do

A cloned woman. In the story, humans are products used only for cloning donor organs. *(Image copyright Jose AS Reyes, 2010. Used under license from Shutterstock.com)*

get together is, ironically, largely due to Ruth, who, when she is a donor and Kathy her carer, decides that she wants to make amends for her past behavior in trying to keep Kathy and Tommy apart. She suggests that Kathy become Tommy's carer. Ruth, who does not fare well with her donations and will shortly die, exhibits some personal growth at this point, which is one of the central moments in the novel. Ruth knows how much Kathy's friendship has meant to them both, and she wants Kathy to find some happiness with Tommy in the time she has left. Ishiguro himself commented, in the interview with Wong and Crummett, about this aspect of Ruth's growth:

> I wanted to show that when her time is up, the things that had been important are not about material possessions or about being remembered in a particular way. Her instincts in the end are to do the decent thing.

That, in a nutshell, is really what *Never Let Me Go* is all about—people learning from their mistakes, trying to do "the decent thing" in the short time they have to live. The strange setting and the nightmarish vision of a society that creates and exploits human clones in a ruthless,

indeed murderous way, comes down in the end to this simple truth about human life: the desire, in the face of mortality, to make an imprint on life that is both good and kind.

Source: Bryan Aubrey, Critical Essay on *Never Let Me Go*, in *Novels for Students*, Gale, Cengage Learning, 2011.

Emily Mead

In the following interview, Mead talks to author Kazuo Ishiguro about Never Let Me Go, *science fiction, and fate.*

*PW: Why set this story [*Never Let Me Go, *reviewed on p. 46], with its sci-fi premise, in the late '90s instead of the future?*

Kazuo Ishiguro: I'm not much of a science fiction reader. I like James Cameron's type of science fiction in movies [*Blade Runner*], but I'm not really interested in reimagining the whole world and writing the details of everyday life—what cars will look like, what government will look like—80 years from now. In my fiction writing, I tend to start with a context, to ask a question: How does our childhood carry into our adult life? How do we slowly ruin our lives, become unhappy?

PW: There's a sense of inevitability surrounding the donors' fate, but no one is actually holding a gun to their heads. Why don't they rebel?

KI: We all face the inevitability of our lives coming to an end, of organs failing (if not being removed). People search for something that will carry on beyond death, through art or religion or love, but everyone has that same fate to accept. My interest, in this book, was in compressing that into 30-odd years of three individuals' lives. A lot of clone stories wind up being about slavery and a fight for freedom, but I was specifically interested in looking at how Tommy and Kathy, at least, try to love and be friends to each other in the time that they have.

PW: Is there another technology today that particularly concerns you, in terms of science outpacing ethics?

KI: All I did was imagine the world as it would be if our nuclear technology, our capacity to destroy ourselves many times over, was replaced with a kind of medical technology. The world could just as easily have developed the other way around.

PW: Do you ever find it alienating to be Japanese and living in England?

KI: I first came to the United Kingdom when I was only five years old, and I think that because of that, it wasn't as much of a cultural upheaval as it was even for my sister, who was nine years old and had already started school in Japan, It's only in looking back that I realize how kindly we were received, considering that we arrived only a few years after the end of the war. I think it indicates a real generosity of spirit in the English, who are capable of being very reserved.

PW: Your stories often have a "twilight" element to them, a sense of hope ebbing: Is there something in your own life that spawned that feeling?

KI: I think a lot of human hope does occur in the face of futility. And I think there's something very touching about that, about the strength and resilience of optimism. So I do try to leave my characters with some hope, even if it is an unlikely one.

PW: What's next?

KI: I have a sideline, which is writing original screenplays. Up until Christmas, I was working on one that was being shot in Shanghai, a Merchant Ivory production, directed by James Ivory. Now I'm working on a set of short stories, stories that relate to each other without being fully connected.

PW: Any recent books that didn't receive the attention you feel they deserve?

KI: Alex Garland's *The Coma* [which incorporates 40 woodblock illustrations by Garland's father]. It isn't a graphic novel, but it's more than an illustrated novel—it's an almost cinematic exploration of the unconscious. And I've been reading a lot of classics, trying to catch up after recently having the thought that I could quite possibly die without having read Proust.

Source: Emily Mead, "Future Present," in *Publishers Weekly*, Vol. 252, No. 5, January 31, 2005, p. 47.

Philip Hensher

In the following review, Hensher describes many of Ishiguro's novels as being, in some sense, sober parodies of familiar literary genres.

The time is the late 1990s; the setting a boarding school called Hailsham. This being a novel by Kazuo Ishiguro, the narrator, Kathy H., who attended the school, is looking back after some years and trying to make sense of her story. The school, it is quickly made clear, is not quite like other schools, the pupils not quite like people we know, and the 1990s slightly different from the decade we might remember. There is talk of 'carers', of the 'fourth donation', of 'completing', of someone called Madame. There don't seem to be any holidays, and, anyway, the kids don't have parents; nor are they orphans. In the outside world, they just have what are called 'possibles'; people who bear a strange resemblance to them.

Expensively and caringly educated, the poor mites are being groomed, not for careers, but for one particular use. You will have guessed quite early on that something gruesome is in store. Let's just say that none of them is going to be asked whether he wants to carry a kidney donor card in the future.

Basically, many of Ishiguro's novels have been, in some sense, sober parodies of familiar literary genres. *The Remains of the Day* is a version of those master/servant novels in which English fiction abounds; as it were, Thackeray's

> ON THE SURFACE, THIS ONE LOOKS LIKE
> A SINISTER VERSION OF THE TRADITIONAL
> SCHOOL STORY. BUT THE TRUTH IS THAT
> THE GREAT SCHOOL STORIES HAVE ALWAYS
> BEEN SINISTER."

The Yellowplush Papers with better spelling and no jokes, *The Code of the Woosters* as if it were about real people. *When We Were Orphans* similarly returns to an idea of 1930s stylish detective fiction, imagining Lord Peter Wimsey with a real history of hurt behind his chill. *Never Let Me Go*, I feel, is trying to fill the school story with nightmarish implications, to present an entire world run according to the principles of Angela Brazil.

Perhaps. The trouble with these ambitions is that, in each case, they stem not from any real engagement with the genres they aim to invert, but from a very loose idea of them. *When We Were Orphans* proved completely catastrophic in this regard. Purporting to be set in 1930s London society, its supposedly posh narrator sounded from beginning to end like Leonard Bast. It had some merits, but completely failed to engage with its subject, and did not even try to render the characteristic tone of its period. It was just a surreal, Daisy Ashford idea of poshness, in which the characters—as memory serves—were forever asking each other if the requisites were all in the toilet.

On the surface, this one looks like a sinister version of the traditional school story. But the truth is that the great school stories have always been sinister. Dickens's schools, Tom Brown's *Schooldays*, *Stalky & Co.*, Ivy Compton Burnett's *Two Worlds and their Ways*, Robert Liddell's *The Deep End*, Roy Fuller's *The Ruined Boys*, and, with particular relevance, Henry Green's book about a futuristic institution training children for bleak purposes, *Concluding*; the list is almost endless. Such books have always seen that real terror lies within the ordinary life of children at school; Ishiguro has to import a ludicrous cannibalistic farrago to create any kind of tension at all. *Young Torless* is a hundred times more terrifying, and infinitely more credible.

The good news about the style of this book is that Ishiguro has dropped the estate agent's prose which so deadens *When We Were Orphans*. In some respects, it's closer to natural spoken English than anything Ishiguro has written since *A Pale View of Hills*. But the style is very shakily done. Specifically northern locutions—'well, yes, if he's going to be that daft' or 'a right down'—mix with southern, rather bourgeois formulations, such as the 'really' intensifier or even public-school slang, like 'amazingly Dim.'

The narrator and the rest of the children have a most peculiar way with idioms: 'he could have done his smirk'; 'Miss Emily had an intellect you could slice logs with'; 'not very keen at all on letting me in on it, were you, Sweety Gums?'; 'I'd be able to talk the lot of them under the table' or (a sex scene) 'I slid a hand under his T-shirt. Pretty soon I was down around his stuff.' Often they are the wrong idiom for the speaker; a modern adolescent boy asks a girl if she looks at pornography 'just for kicks'; an adult professional woman says 'you stink of cow poo.' It's not a convincingly invented dialect: it simply sounds inconsistent and implausible.

The lack of plausibility in the style really begins to affect the interest of the novel. The narrator sounds so little like a woman that when she tells us she has been sexually promiscuous we don't believe it. The children seem unreal because, unlike all other adolescents, they almost never speak to each other ironically or sarcastically. Their concerns are barely imagined: at one point, Kathy says, 'I was sitting beside Cynthia E., and we'd just been chatting and complaining about the heat.' The conversation, in detail, has not been imagined, and is unimaginable. Like the novel's readers, the characters are constantly forgetting their names, it seems, and having to remind each other: 'Why are we stopping, Kath?' 'You remember, Ruth?' 'Okay, what I wanted to say, Kathy, is this. I was wondering, Kath, if I should go on keeping it secret.'

Nor is the plot really much more convincing than the novel's style. The ordinary, awkward objections rise up in battalions. For all this expensive education, the doctors only get at most four applications out of their subjects—a little arithmetic suggests that in this world every kidney transplant, bearing the cost of this education (at say, 25,000 [pounds sterling] a year per pupil), would cost an extra 100,000 [pounds sterling] or so. Why bother? When the products of these institutions become aware of their fate, why don't any of them ever run away? Why on earth should they be educated to a high point of liberal humanity, when human vegetables would serve the purpose just as well? What is the shortage of reckless motorcyclists that has required such unbelievably lavish state expenditure to create a new supply? If they are brought up all their lives in seclusion, why doesn't the outside world find them odder? (They certainly sound very odd.) Is it really believable that public opinion only moves against the programme when the children start being educated?

I can imagine why Ishiguro has avoided all these questions, hoping that we as readers will just accept a world where everyone, without obvious coercion, accepts their ghastly situation. Raising any of them would inevitably lead to the sort of breathless novelistic episode—a despairing escapee is dragged back, say, with Alsatian teethmarks in her bottom—which Ishiguro is reluctant to give us. The result, alas, is a novel quite without vulgarity, but one where the situation is totally implausible on every level. It is an awful thing to say, but I believed so little in any of the people, their situation, or the way they spoke that I didn't really care what happened to them. They could have been turned into tins of Pedigree Chum without raising much concern.

In the past, Ishiguro has been an exceedingly interesting novelist, but he looks increasingly like one at the mercy of his limited linguistic inventiveness. He has acquired a reputation for fastidiousness by writing, sometimes broadly and coarsely, about fastidious people. It worked very well in *The Remains of the Day*, which really sounded like a semi-literate butler's pompous locutions; *The Unconsoled*, set in a dreamworld, was utterly consistent in its strangeness, and wove a powerful spell. He has a fine capacity for pace and structure, even in *When We Were Orphans*. But a novel like this constantly brings you up against what he won't or can't do.

I kept thinking of what Henry Green said he wanted to do in *Concluding*, a book with quite a similar setting: 'something very beautiful thousands and thousands of girls, do you see—and a lot of moonlight, and a certain amount of sunlight.' That, concisely stated, is what Ishiguro never attempts, and the lack of it makes him a smaller novelist. A book with so little warmth has to rely, insecurely and with decreasing success, on the bare gestures of pathos.

Source: Philip Hensher, "School for Scandal," in *Spectator*, Vol. 297, No. 9212, February 26, 2005, pp. 32–33.

Valerie Sayers

In the following review, Sayers finds Never Let Me Go *a masterful contemplation of class and social responsibility.*

Kazuo Ishiguro's new novel [*Never Let Me Go*] opens in mysterious territory. We're in England in the late 1990s, not in some futuristic fantasy world, yet the way in which characters in this story use certain familiar words is disorienting. Our narrator, Kathy H. (a name that echoes both Kafka and the gradeschool classroom) tells us that her profession is "carer" and that she looks after "donors" who will ultimately "complete." When one of Kathy's donors, dying painfully, asks her to recount tales of her famous boarding school, Hailsham, she tells of a quite ordinary childhood—or a childhood that would seem ordinary were a reader not aware that Kathy's classmates, too, have gone on to become donors and carers, and that some of the childhood customs at Hailsham are distinctly puzzling.

Like all of Ishiguro's novels, *Never Let Me Go* is an introspective narrative concerned with troubling moral questions. His best-known work, *The Remains of the Day*, employs a hyper-dutiful, repressed English butler as witness to aristocratic sympathy for fascism. Ishiguro himself came to England at the age of six from postatomic Nagasaki (his first novel is set there, in the eerie aftermath of the bomb). His first-person narrators, in their emotional yearning, make muddled attempts to recall their own struggles as the world around them has gone through upheaval. They delude themselves and sometimes implicate readers, too, in delusion: Ishiguro uses irony to strong and subtle effect.

In order to reflect Kathy H.'s ordinariness, Ishiguro here employs a style more matter-of-fact than in his other novels, the language flatter and more workaday. The story of Kathy H.'s childhood, too, is a little slow and flat—but, because her seemingly pacific youth is set in opposition to the strange future awaiting her, narrative tension builds. Most readers will, from page one, have a rough idea of what is to become of Kathy and her classmates, but the novel unveils its mysteries gradually, and anyone who would prefer to solve the riddle of the book themselves should stop reading this review right here.

It would be coy to discuss this novel's concerns without revealing that Kathy H. and her classmates are human clones raised to be organ donors when their bodies mature; that they will serve brief terms caring for other donors before they become donors themselves; and that they will "complete" their donations in death. The clones assigned to Hailsham, a reader learns, are part of a benevolent social experiment designed to give these manufactured humans an education and make their childhood full (most clones are housed in Dickensian institutions they would prefer to forget). The students at Hailsham have a high status in the world of donors, but they are ordinary precisely because they are ordinary human children, perfecting the ordinary cruelties as they choose leaders and learn to conform. They shun each other, curry favor, hatch conspiracy theories.

Kathy, from the story's opening, is certainly capable of inflicting hurt, but she also distinguishes herself by her empathy. She has a special feeling for Tommy, humiliated by the other boys because they enjoy watching him throw tantrums. Those tantrums make him one of the few characters in the novel to protest mistreatment—not as a clone, but as the scapegoat of the other boys. The girls, too, join in deriding Tommy because he is no good at "creating" at Hailsham, where art is so highly prized. The social reformers who have created this experiment to improve the lives of the clones use the children's creations to demonstrate to the outside world that clones have interior lives—have, perhaps, souls—and are therefore worthy of decent treatment.

The effect on a reader piecing together the reason these children have been created is most unsettling. Kathy's friends lack curiosity (they answer references to their futures with silence and embarrassment) and defer to their guardians. They have, of course, been trained in obedience. As small children, they hear stories of a curious girl who climbs the fence encircling Hailsham—when she returns, the guardians will not let her back in. Such banishment is unthinkable. When they leave Hailsham as older adolescents, they are given nearly complete freedom before they begin their training, but it does not occur to them to flee or to question their fate. The most poignant scenes involve their fantasies about alternate futures: Kathy's friend Ruth imagines the "dynamic, go-ahead types" in offices. But when some friends go looking for a "possible"—the

human model from whom Ruth has been made—Ruth reminds them angrily that they all must have been modeled from trash.

Kathy, too, has fantasies: despite the physical impossibility, she dreams of being a mother, of singing a popular song, "Never Let Me Go," to her infant. When she and Tommy fall in love, they persuade themselves to believe the myth their friends believe, that Hailsham-raised couples who prove their love can win a deferral, an extended time together before they begin their donations. When they realize that this is not possible, their quiet responses may roil readers more than open rebellion.

On the most literal level Ishiguro is asking precisely the questions about cloning and other genetic experiments that we all should be asking—about what it means to be human and how far reproductive technology should proceed. But by setting the novel in the present rather than the future, he also suggests that acquiescence to one's class, duty, even fate, is a problem of not merely future technology but of our moral present. Early in the novel, Kathy asks Tommy why he's so much happier than he has been: "So what's happened?" she says. "Did you find God or something?" It is the novel's only mention of God— Hailsham is the product of a postreligious age that has taken social ranking and notions of human worth to a hitherto unimaginable level.

Ishiguro's interweaving of present and future moral catastrophe makes *Never Let Me Go* deeply disturbing, in the best sense. Though this narrative is not as taut as his earlier novels, the strange world it evokes is nonetheless compelling, the work's intelligence and concern for exploited souls a sad consolation.

Source: Valerie Sayers, "Spare Parts," in *Commonweal*, Vol. 32, No. 13, July 15, 2005, pp. 27–34.

Cynthia Grenier

In the following, review, Grenier assesses the social implications of Never Let Me Go, *declaring it a significant and substantial novel.*

Kazuo Ishiguro's latest novel [*Never Let Me Go*] is an important, serious, and deeply depressing work. Set in the 1990s—a kind of parallel '90s, not the one we all experienced—Ishiguro's story opens through the narrative voice of Kathy H. On page one, she tells us in a flat, matter-of-fact way that she is 31 and has been a carer now for over 11 years. By way of explanation, she says that she's been a carer for so long because "my donors have always tended to do much better than expected. Their recovery times have been impressive, and hardly any of them have been classified as 'agitated,' even before fourth donation." The monotone in which she delivers what amounts to the essence of the novel gives you a chill as you realize Ishiguro is telling us a story about what life would be like for the donors—clones—created by society to supply organs for those in need.

Kathy is thinking of the life she and her fellows led in what seemed like a fine private school, Hailsham, in the English countryside. Gradually, and without any explicit description of who these children were or the future planned for them, let alone defining "the fourth donation" or "completing," Ishiguro leads you through Kathy's memories as gradually the sheer horror of it all comes in upon you.

The children are told fairly early in life that they will never be able to bear children. At one point, as a young teenager, Kathy dances to her favorite cassette, whose theme is "Baby, never let me go." She is clutching a pillow to herself, swaying with her eyes shut, when, suddenly opening them, she sees one of the school's guardians watching her and sobbing. Kathy notes that the woman had the "same look in her eyes she always had when she looked at us, like she was seeing something that gave her the creeps. Except this time there was something else, something extra in that look I couldn't fathom."

The children are encouraged to be creative—painting, drawing, sculpting—and each month a woman would come to select the most promising work to take to a supposed gallery. You don't learn why until further in the story, when Kathy and her fellow student, Tommy, find one of their old guardians from Hailsham in the hope of obtaining a "deferral," as they are in love. Miss Emily, now in a wheelchair, tries to explain why art was being collected from the children: "We took away your art," she explains, "because we thought it would reveal your souls. Or to put it more finely, we did it to *prove you had souls at all.*" And they learn that there are no "deferrals" in their life.

Ishiguro does plant hints as to the nature of the children at Hailsham. Kathy recalls that the guardians were really strict about smoking—"If we were being shown a picture of a famous writer or world leader, and they happened to have a cigarette in their hand, then the whole lesson would grind to a halt." When one of the guardians is asked whether she ever smoked, "Mrs. Lucy weighing each word carefully says, 'It's not good that I smoked. It wasn't good for me so I stopped it. But what you must understand is that for you, all of you, it's much, much worse to smoke than it ever was for me.'"

In its way, *Never Let Me Go* reads like a mystery, Ishiguro dropping clues, details that join gradually until you know at last who done it. The story has a very real poignancy that goes considerably beyond its ambition. You come away caring about these "creatures," as one of the guardians refers to them.

And to lend a certain degree of horror to your reading, consider a recent story in the *Washington Times*: "Transplants from Living Rated Better than Deceased." In a study examining data from the Richmond-based United Network for Organ Sharing (UNOS) regarding pediatric liver transplants performed between 1987 and 2004, researchers discovered a failure rate of nearly 40 percent for transplants involving dead donors, compared with 27 percent in cases coming from living donors. Kazuo Ishiguro must have felt a genuine shudder seeing the potential for life resembling art—and looming, perhaps, on the not-too-distant horizon.

Source: Cynthia Grenier, "The Harvest Season," in *Weekly Standard*, Vol. 10, No. 40, July 4–11, 2005, p. 35.

Claire Messud

In the following review, Messud considers Never Let Me Go *a reworking of Ishiguro's narrative strategies and thematic preoccupations.*

Kazuo Ishiguro is a writer renowned for his capacity to create beautifully controlled surfaces and to beautifully evoke the roiling emotions beneath them. Most famously, of course, the voice of the butler Stevens in *The Remains of the Day* is a triumph of nuance and subtle unreliability: Here is a speaker whose apparently mundane obsessions with the qualities of a great butler and the importance of the proper polishing of silver mask his inner torments. Indeed, beneath his stiff upper lip, Stevens has come in later years to question not only his choices but the foundation upon which they were based.

. . . . The questions surrounding his latest, mesmerizing book, *Never Let Me Go*, would be

> " AS IN BECKETT, ISHIGURO'S CHARACTERS, IN THEIR DETACHED WORLD, SHOW US A VERSION OF OUR OWN MINUTE PREOCCUPATIONS AND PIDDLING DISTRACTIONS, AND RAISE LIFE'S LARGEST QUESTIONS FOR US ALL. IS THIS ALL THERE IS? MUST IT END SO SOON? WHY STRIVE? WHY PERSIST? WHAT IS IT ALL FOR?"

formulated rather differently. Here, through the narration of a 31-year-old named Kathy H., we are presented with a hermetic, fully imagined reality of the recent past—one whose details are as precise, as simultaneously petty and deeply significant, as Stevens's insufficiently polished fork or stray dustpan and brush—and yet it is a world almost wholly detached from the recent past as we know it. In other words, we are provided here with context, if only partially so, but it is context counter to fact. How, then, do we know our own reality? And what, indeed, might it be to see again and utterly askew what we thought we already knew?

. . . . We are told, a page before the story even begins, that we are in England in the late 1990s; but this could be a purely disarming strategy. (As a computer scientist recently pointed out to me, why should Internet users ever believe that we've entered a secure location just because a pop-up box assures us we have? To trust a few words on a screen, or page, smacks of a perilous credulity.) Before we begin reading, we have in hand, we feel, a comprehensive set of useful guidelines—the guidelines of our lived experience. Indeed, when Kathy informs us in the novel's second sentence that she has been "a carer now for over eleven years," we "naturally" assume she's at work in Britain's healthcare system, tending to the elderly or infirm. That this is an insufficient understanding is, within the paragraph, abundantly clear: The people for whom she cares are termed "donors," and a passing reference to their "fourth donation" suggests that this is not a one-off bout of purposeful generosity on their part (a kidney for a cousin, bone marrow for an ailing child) but a full-blown career. Still,

surrounded by so much that is familiar, by Kathy's calm conversational tone ("Anyway, I'm not making any big claims for myself. I know carers, working now, who are just as good and don't get half the credit. If you're one of them, I can understand how you might get resentful"), we assume that in spite of our slight disorientation, we will soon know where we stand.

What follows—Kathy's reminiscences of her years at a boarding school called Hailsham, and of her minute altercations and reconciliations with friends, in particular with two of them named Ruth and Tommy—is, in the context of our known world and the real past, of an indescribable banality. Ishiguro captures brilliantly the local rules and rituals of his imaginary institution, the cliques and spats and tiny treasured moments; but this involves Kathy relaying to us in prolonged detail the incident of Ruth's fancy pencil case, the disappearance of Kathy's favorite cassette tape and so forth. For a good third of the novel, we relive these events as if trapped at the dinner table with our suddenly voluble adolescent children—that is to say, with a mixture of mild interest, concern and deep exasperation. But over these childish dramas hangs an ever-growing sense of menace. Kathy observes:

> So you're waiting, even if you don't quite know it, waiting for the moment when you realize that you really are different to them; that there are people out there, like Madame, who don't hate you or wish you any harm, but who nevertheless shudder at the very thought of you—of how you were brought into this world and why—and who dread the idea of your hand brushing against theirs . . . It's like walking past a mirror you've walked past every day of your life, and suddenly it shows you something else, something troubling and strange

This is, indeed, the effect of Kathy's narrative itself, as we learn what lies behind her urgent prattling: that she and her fellow students are, like others in similar institutions around the country, clones, created and raised to adulthood in order to become multiple organ donors. As one of their most outspoken teachers, or "guardians," informs them, in response to their typical teenage fantasizing, "None of you will go to America, none of you will be film stars. And none of you will be working in supermarkets as I heard some of you planning the other day. Your lives are set out for you."

In this new context, of course, the mirror reflects a different reality, and the squabbles and triumphs of children become the high points of their lives, become life itself. Not far beyond the gates of school, they are destined for donation and ultimately death, or "completion," as it is delicately called. Just as Stevens has lived his adulthood entirely within the grounds of Darlington Hall (so much so that even a junket of a few days seems to flummox him), so too these people have lived entirely within Hailsham and The Cottages, a sort of halfway house where the older adolescents are sent to learn how to venture out into the world, engage with ordinary people and shop: "So we went to Woolworth's, and immediately I felt much more cheerful. Even now, I like places like that: a large store with lots of aisles displaying bright plastic toys, greeting cards, loads of cosmetics, maybe even a photo booth." They may be in England, but they are aliens in their country, a host of Frankenstein's children. They are fed upon literary classics, encouraged to make art and write poetry; they are civilized into an apparently meaningful humanity; and for what?

As in Beckett, Ishiguro's characters, in their detached world, show us a version of our own minute preoccupations and piddling distractions, and raise life's largest questions for us all. Is this all there is? Must it end so soon? Why strive? Why persist? What is it all for? At least the triumvirate of Kathy, Ruth and Tommy seem eventually to find an answer. Though not original—after all, these are not, by any definition, original people—it is nevertheless compelling: love. In time-honored tradition, they cling passionately to the belief that love will set them free; and needless to say, in time-honored tradition, love fails to oblige.

There is great dignity in Kathy H., and in her friends. There is also, ultimately, a pained and painful resignation. Like Stevens and Miss Kenton, the housekeeper who might have been his lover and wife, the Hailsham students seem, for all their musing, not to ask the essential question: Does it have to be this way? Rather as in Chekhov's *Three Sisters*, in which one might be forgiven for wondering just why the sisters cannot go to Moscow (as a friend of mine once insisted, they could surely get the train schedules, buy tickets and be off?), it is hard to understand fully why Kathy, Ruth and Tommy—or, for that matter, any of their cloned peers or acquaintances—don't contemplate escape, don't consider fleeing into the wider world—perhaps even to America.

This is a recurring element in Ishiguro's fiction; and surely an indispensable aspect of his vision. As he would have it, we are all trapped, whether in institutions or by mores or in a fantasy logic or in the past. His characters cannot jump out the window, because they do not believe there is anything outside the window to jump into. Even though we're told that Kathy lives in late-1990s England, in *Never Let Me Go* that place remains as flat as a stage set and as unreal, no possible Oz. This may be a radical and disturbing vision, of a world in which agency is so dramatically curtailed; but it is also an accurate rendition of the lives of so many, who are never granted the opportunity to imagine an alternative to the microcosm into which we have been born. Even when Kathy and Tommy seek out the powers that be to plead the case for their love, to beg a special dispensation, they do not dare to imagine any future to which a successful plea might entitle them; and that failure of imagination is perforce their *huis clos*.

If Ishiguro is a writer of uncommon restraint, he is also a writer who has increasingly made demands of his readers. Despite Kathy's easy and engaging narrative voice, this is true, too, of *Never Let Me Go*: A reader's patience and humility are required. Kathy H. is an ordinary young woman to whom circumstances have dealt an appalling fate; the ultimate emotional resonance of the book stems, at least in part, from that necessary ordinariness. And those who listen to her story will find themselves amply rewarded by this ambitious, peculiar and deeply affecting book.

Source: Claire Messud, "Love's Body," in *Nation*, Vol. 280, No. 19, May 16, 2005, pp. 28–31.

James Butcher

In the following review, Butcher questions the lack of a clear moral stance in Never Let Me Go *but contends that the novel is a superb achievement despite its flaws.*

On Dec. 23, 1954, Joseph E Murray did the first ever organ transplantation operation, a kidney transplant. 50 years on, kidney transplantations are now considered routine operations. However, according to the 2004 *Annual Report of the US Scientific Registry of Transplant Recipients and the Organ Procurement and Transplantation Network*, which was released on March 17, 2005,

60,000 people are currently waiting for a suitable donor kidney to become available in the USA. A further 30,000 are on the waiting list for other organs (http://www.optn. org/AR2004). A shortage of suitable organs is the main reason for these waiting lists. What can be done to help?

Some scientists think that xeno-transplantation might be a possibility. They envisage pig farms, stocked with animals bred especially for their organs. These organs would be genetically modified so that they do not produce alpha 1,3-galactosyl-transferase, the enzyme that is responsible for the production of Gal oligosaccharides that are expressed on cell walls and that contribute to transplant rejection (*Lancet* 2003; 362: 557–59). Other researchers speculate that stem cells might one day be extracted from ill patients and be used to grow new organs ex vivo, which can then be transplanted back into the patients without tissue rejection (*Lancet* 2000; 356:1500). But no sane researcher would publicly suggest that the two approaches be combined to produce clones of human beings who are farmed solely for their organs.

This distasteful and macabre proposition forms the backdrop for Kazuo Ishiguro's new novel *Never Let Me Go*. The book is set in England in the late 1990s, although it soon becomes obvious that this is not the same 1990s that we once lived in. The main protagonist and narrator is a 31-year-old called Kathy who is about to undergo a dramatic career change. For the past 11 years she has been a "carer," travelling to and from recovery centres, scattered across the country, looking after "donors" as they move to "completion." But the tables are about to turn as she herself will soon become a donor.

To help her face this reality Kathy describes her fond memories of her childhood, especially her time at Hailsham. It gradually becomes clear that Hailsham is a boarding school with a difference. None of the students has a surname, or indeed any family members to share a surname with; there are no school holidays; no one leaves the grounds; and the weekly medical check ups and emphasis on staying healthy become remarkably disturbing. Smoking is strictly forbidden by the Guardians—who are teachers of a sort—and all copies of Sherlock Holmes novels have been removed from the library because they contain too many images of pipe smoking.

The students' lives are sparse—mod cons are nowhere to be seen—but the atmosphere at Hailsham is fun and friendly. The Guardians encourage the students to create art, which the pupils then sell to each other at regular markets. These creations are the students' only real possessions and are highly treasured. However, the students have little idea of what life has in store for them when they leave Hailsham, as the Guardians remain evasive about the subject. Eventually, one of the Guardians cracks and tells them: "The problem, as I see it, is that you've been told, but none of you really understand, and I dare say, some people are quite happy to keep it that way. But I'm not. If you're going to have decent lives, then you've got to know and know properly. None of you will go to America, none of you will be film stars. And none of you will be working in supermarkets as I heard some of you planning the other day. Your lives are set out for you. You'll become adults, then, before you're old, before you're even middle aged, you'll start to donate your vital organs. That's what each of you was created to do. You're not like the actors that you watch in your videos, you're not even like me. You were brought into this world for a purpose, and your futures, all of them, have been decided."

Perhaps the most disturbing aspect of the book is the stoicism with which the clones face their fate. They fail to get to grips with the outside world that created them and are brainwashed into believing that donation is the only option for them. None of them seeks to escape to avoid their fate. But that is not to say that they are mindless automatons. On the contrary, these are people who are every bit as human as the members of the society who created them. They love and hate and want desperately to cling onto life, but do not know the rules that govern their existence. Kathy's calm and considered description of her upbringing and the way she resigns herself to her future is especially unsettling. There are many similarities between this work of fiction and Primo Levi's objective description of his time in Auschwitz in *If This is a Man*; both books are harrowing because of the matter-of-fact tone that the authors adopt.

Never Let Me Go is a dark and desolate novel, but it is not a direct indictment of science gone wrong. Unlike Margaret Atwood's *Oryx and Crake*, Ishiguro's latest book does not attempt to be science fiction. Indeed, *Never Let Me Go* sheds as much light on the cloning debate as *Remains of the Day*, Ishiguro's Man Booker Prize winning third novel, does on being a butler.

In many ways this is both the novel's outstanding strength, but also its most noticeable weakness: Ishiguro uses his disturbing backdrop to explore, in an unfamiliar setting, what it is that makes us human; but that same oblique approach means that the reader is left guessing as to how and why his dystopian vision came into being. Ishiguro is primarily interested in relationships and characters rather than exploring the morals of cloning, and the book is none the worse for that approach.

Ishiguro has lived in the UK for more than 45 years, but was born in Nagasaki, Japan, just after the war. He first heard about what the atom bomb did to his home city when he was 6 years' old. In a recent interview on BBC Radio 4, Ishiguro explained that *Never Let Me Go* is set in an alternative history in which the postwar scientific breakthroughs were in biotechnology rather than nuclear physics. He argues that since the human race managed to get itself into such a terrible situation in the 1950s and 1960s during the cold war, with nuclear obliteration a very real possibility, it would have been quite possible for rapid developments in biotechnology to create a similar, alternative, history. "In order to take medicine forward, in order to take cures forward, we often do have to take risks and some of them are very profound risks," he said.

Never Let Me Go is likely to challenge Ian McEwan's *Saturday* for this year's Man Booker prize, whose winner will be announced in October. Issues relating to medical ethics provide the backdrop for both novels and both books discuss aspects of human memory. But Ishiguro's novel is the most insightful and intelligent, and would get my vote if I was on the judging panel.

Source: James Butcher, "A Wonderful Donation," in *Lancet*, Vol. 365, No. 9467, April 2005, pp. 1299–1300.

Brooke Allen

In the following review, Allen deems Never Let Me Go *one of Ishiguro's finest works, and lauds the novel's quiet, mysterious tone.*

Kazuo Ishiguro, now 50 years old, is a much celebrated and decorated writer. He received the 1989 Booker Prize, he is an Officer of the Order of the British Empire, and he is a *Chevalier de l'Ordre des Arts et des Lettres*, among other honors. Yet it is only recently that he has come into his own, developing work that is truly personal both in style and subject. *The Unconsoled* (1985) was weird and marvelous, but it might have been written by Franz Kafka. *The Remains of the*

> THE REMAINS OF THE DAY SHOWED THAT ISHIGURO COULD BE MASTERLY IN HIS USE OF UNDERSTATEMENT; THIS NOVEL PROVES IT ONCE AGAIN. ITS TONE IS MUTED AND SUBTLE THROUGHOUT, PLAYING AGAINST THE SITUATION'S INTRINSIC DRAMA."

Day, his Booker winner, was an exquisitely written and delicately felt work, but it might have been written by E. M. Forster. Not until *When We Were Orphans* (2001) did Ishiguro begin to significantly distinguish himself from literary forebears and models.

His new novel, *Never Let Me Go*, deserves to become a classic, and if handled well it has the potential of being a great perennial seller in schools on the level of *Lord of the Flies*. Like William Golding's work it provides both an encompassing metaphor for the human condition and a cautionary tale about the nature of the human animal. *Never Let Me Go* might be the best novel, so far, to address our current brave new world of scientific possibility, in which each day brings some startling and unprecedented moral conundrum to our burgeoning flock of bioethicists. It posits a social order, "More scientific, efficient, yes," in the words of one of its characters. "More cures for the old sicknesses. Very good. But a harsh cruel world."

Most of the book takes place at Hailsham, a boarding school set in an idyllic corner of the English countryside. Kathy, Tommy, Ruth, and their friends enjoy more freedom than most schoolchildren, and they are encouraged to read, to write, to be "creative" in whatever way they can. They are given to understand that they are in some way special, and that Hailsham is an elite institution. It is, in many respects, a pleasant life.

From the beginning, however, the reader is aware that Hailsham is not an ordinary school. It is completely hermetic, for one thing: The children never leave the school grounds at all. And instead of teachers they have "guardians," though their function seems to differ little from that of teachers. Then there is the fact that Kathy, the narrator, never mentions anyone's parents. Just as the children have no last names, they have no families. Accordingly, they focus their often pathetic longing for affection on these guardians, the only adults and role models they know. "Didn't we all dream from time to time about one guardian or other bending the rules and doing something special for us? A spontaneous hug, a secret letter, a gift?"

Kathy also refers to the future beyond Hailsham, which for these children will be rather special. First they will become "carers"; later, "donors." They have merely the very vaguest ideas about this future and are diffident about inquiring into it too aggressively. "We certainly knew—though not in any deep sense—that we were different from our guardians, and from the normal people outside; we perhaps even knew that a long way down the road there were donations waiting for us. But we didn't really know what that meant. If we were keen to avoid certain topics, it was probably more because it embarrassed us. We hated the way the guardians, usually so on top of everything, became so awkward whenever we came near this territory." Not only are the guardians frequently awkward around the students: Some of them seem to fear the children, shying instinctively away if they come too close.

Never Let Me Go is neither a mystery tale nor a piece of science fiction, but a novel; the secret of Hailsham, and of these children, is central to the book's life and is therefore not kept from the reader for very long. The students are, it turns out, human clones brought into the world and raised to be organ donors. In effect, they are being farmed. As donors—by which time they will be in their mid-20s—they will enter a clinic and submit to operations to remove various organs. Eventually, usually after the fourth "donation" or so, they will "complete."

Ishiguro reveals their dreadful future at a poignant moment, after we have been drawn into the little circle of students and their doings through Kathy and her friends. They are for the most part typical children, with their petty rivalries, their foolish affections, their ridiculous fantasies about mundane people and events. They differ from ordinary children only in their vague awareness of what the future holds for them and in their resignation to it. There are in this group no rebels, no runaways. These children have

been created for a purpose, and they have no sense of their own independent being, or of any individual rights they might have. Indeed, they have none.

Kathy's simple narrative is mesmerizing as we discover the rules and limits of her world along with her. She puzzles over Hailsham's emphasis on being creative and wonders why all the students' best artwork is taken away: It is, we learn much later, so that interested pedagogues can examine it in an attempt to discover whether these clones have "souls." (That anyone might think they do not is as shocking to Kathy as it is to the reader.) At an age when most young people are preoccupied with sex—with where they came from, in other words—these children are more interested in their own genesis, that is, who their "possibles," their clone models, might be.

The three children at the center of the narrative are of contrasting types. The foil for the gentle, modest Kathy is her best friend Ruth, the kind of brashly confident girl who in normal circumstances would dominate friends and family. Tommy, who is loved by both girls, is a reasonable, empirical boy. When as teenagers the three move from Hailsham to a remote farm, "the Cottages," with other students, they have a bit more freedom to explore the world and begin to compare themselves with the "normals" they see on their travels. Having so little contact with "normals," or with adults of any sort, they live in a social vacuum. Kathy, for instance, realizes that many of her fellow students' mannerisms are copied from characters they saw on television, because they have no one else to emulate. "It's not what people really do out there, in normal life, if that's what you were thinking," she reprimands them.

Now that they are at the Cottages the students are fully aware of what lies in store for them, but they still fantasize about alternatives: Each of them has what they call a "dream future." "I'm not sure what was going on in our heads during those discussions," Kathy admits. "We probably knew they couldn't be serious, but then again, I'm sure we didn't regard them as fantasy either." What touches the reader, as it does throughout the book, is the *modesty* of their dreams. As Kathy says, "Mind you, none of us pushed it *too* far. I don't remember anyone saying they were going to be a movie star or anything like that. The talk was more likely to be about becoming a postman or working on a farm." Even Ruth, who in ordinary life would probably have aspired to become a supermodel or a captain of industry, settles for a dream future as an office worker in a provincial town.

The Remains of the Day showed that Ishiguro could be masterly in his use of understatement; this novel proves it once again. Its tone is muted and subtle throughout, playing against the situation's intrinsic drama. The students, like their preceptors, stick with the accepted euphemisms. The word "die" is only used once in the novel, and specific organs to be donated are never—or almost never—referred to by name. Kathy's narrative tone, for all her youth, can only be described as autumnal. If Ishiguro had insisted on accentuating the violent or disgusting details of his story, the result might have been a mere shocker. As it is, the details that stay with the reader are the tiniest and most painful. Above all, it is the students' quiet acceptance of their fate that breaks one's heart. A favorite topic in fiction is human durability, resistance, what people like to refer to as "the triumph of the human spirit"; less popular, because it so seldom makes for an uplifting story, is the flip side of human nature, its distressing tendency to be conditioned, brainwashed, even broken. Resignation is as human a characteristic as rebellion or rage. If a child is presented with a particular worldview as "normal," he or she generally accepts it.

Source: Brooke Allen, "The Damned and the Beautiful," in *New Leader*, Vol. 88, No. 2, March-April 2005, pp. 25–27.

Siddartha Deb

In the following review, Deb characterizes Never Let Me Go *as Ishiguro's most successful examination of childhood nostalgia.*

The past, filtered through memory, has always played odd tricks in Kazuo Ishiguro's fiction. It is a place full of arcane rules and uncertain events, the meaning of which can be decoded only gradually. This was the case from Ishiguro's first novel, *A Pale View of Hills* (1982), with its lonely Japanese protagonist recalling postwar Nagasaki from his house in the English suburbs. The very business of living, the novel suggested, can make us strangers to our former selves, a theme Ishiguro has sustained carefully in his subsequent fiction, through variations of form and subject matter.

Never Let Me Go, Ishiguro's strange new novel, approaches the same idea through a story set in England in the late 1990s. It is told from the point of view of 31-year-old Kathy H, who is about to change her vocation, having been a "carer" for more than a decade. It is not immediately clear what Kathy's job involves; we know that she looks after patients of some sort. Kathy herself is a pragmatic but slightly lonely figure who, as she drives from one medical centre to another, is preoccupied with memories of Hailsham, the boarding school she attended as a child. Hailsham occupies an idealised place in her imagination and is presented, in part, as a sanctuary from adulthood in which the young Kathy was able to develop close friendships— with, for example, the calculating Ruth and short-tempered Tommy. However, as one memory leads to the next, and as each event Kathy recounts is examined in the light of another, it becomes clear that there is something extraordinary about the students at Hailsham and their careful seclusion from the outside world.

The friends are clones, who have been nurtured at Hailsham only to serve adult roles as donors of organs to human beings. In that sense, they are bodies rather than individuals, and the relationships and ideas of selfhood that appear so crucial to them are secondary to their medical function. "Your lives are set out for you," one of their teachers tells them, unable to bear their chatter about possible professions. "You'll become adults, then before you're old, before you're even middle-aged, you'll start to donate your vital organs. That's what each of you was created to do. You're not like the actors you watch on your videos, you're not even like me."

This unusual premise, emerging through Kathy's memories, does not lead us into the realm of speculative science fiction. Unlike Margaret Atwood in *Oryx and Crake* (2003), Ishiguro is not interested in using the idea of cloning to conjure up a panoramic dystopia. His attention remains fixed on intimate things—on the small social groupings within a school, on the nuances of personal relationships. The larger world remains a distant, blurred backdrop, and is brought into focus only at the end. What holds our attention before then is the way Ishiguro uses the subject of cloning to focus on questions of human existence. Although the story of Kathy and her friends is especially poignant because of their status as clones, we can still identify with their predicament. Does not all childhood involve an interplay between knowledge and ignorance, hope and fear?

Ishiguro has always been good at presenting the past—and childhood—as a kind of universal affliction, but probably never so well as in this novel. There are moments when the pace of the narration seems slow, circling back endlessly on memories and desires, but, in a novel about transience, there is a point to this. The mythology of Hailsham involves the idea of a "lost corner" where all that has been mislaid will end up sooner or later:

> Someone—I can't remember who it was— claimed after the lesson that what Miss Emily had said was that Norfolk was England's "lost corner," where all the lost property found in the country ended up. Somehow this idea caught on and soon became the accepted fact virtually throughout our entire year.

The past may be a realm of loss, full of things that have to be let go of, but, in this wise novel, it is also a place where lost things may be recovered, and a form of redemption found.

Source: Siddartha Deb, "Lost Corner," in *New Statesman*, Vol. 18, No. 849, March 7, 2005, p. 55.

SOURCES

Bernstein, Stephen, Review of *Never Let Me Go*, in *Review of Contemporary Fiction*, Vol. 25, No. 1, Spring 2005, p. 139.

Dalfonzo, Gina R., "Lucky Pawns," in *National Review*, Vol. 57, No. 1, June 20, 2005, p. 53.

Howard, Sarah, Review of *Never Let Me Go*, in *Kliatt*, Vol. 40, No. 5, September 2006, p. 24.

Ishiguro, Kazuo, *Never Let Me Go*, Vintage Books, 2005.

Kluger, Jeffrey, "Will We Follow the Sheep?," in *Time*, Vol. 109, No. 10, March 10, 1997, p. 71.

O'Neill, Joseph, Review of *Never Let Me Go*, in *Atlantic*, Vol. 295, No. 4, May 2005, p. 123.

Review of *Never Let Me Go*, in *Publishers Weekly*, Vol. 252, No. 5, January 31, 2005, p. 46.

Silver, Lee M., *Remaking Eden: Cloning and Beyond in a Brave New World*, Avon Books, 1997, pp. 9–10, 93–94.

Squier, Susan, "Negotiating Boundaries: From Assisted Reproduction to Assisted Replication," in *Playing Dolly: Technocultural Formations, Fantasies, & Fictions*, edited by E. Ann Kaplan and Susan Squier, Rutgers University Press, 1999, p. 111.

Wong, Cynthia F., and Grace Crummett, "A Conversation about Life and Art with Kazuo Ishiguro," in *Conversations with Kazuo Ishiguro*, edited by Brian W. Schaffer and Cynthia F. Wong, University Press of Mississippi, 2008, pp. 214, 215, 219.

FURTHER READING

Levine, Aaron D., *Cloning: A Beginner's Guide*, Oneworld Publications, 2007.

> This is an explanation for beginners to the complex, developing science of cloning. Levine discusses, among many other topics, the ethical issues surrounding the idea of cloning humans.

Schaffer, Brian W., *Understanding Kazuo Ishiguro*, University of South Carolina Press, 2008.

> This is a guide to Ishiguro's work for students and general readers. Schaffer shows Ishiguro's debt to Japanese literature and writers such as Joseph Conrad, E. M. Forster, and James Joyce, as well as to Freudian psychoanalysis.

Sim, Wai-chew, *Kazuo Ishiguro: A Routledge Guide*, Routledge, 2009.

> This book contains a biographical survey and an introduction to all of Ishiguro's work, including an overview of different interpretations. There are also sections on issues connected to Ishiguro's work, such as postcolonial studies and narrative theory.

Wong, Cynthia F., *Kazuo Ishiguro*, Northcote House, 2000.

> This is a concise guide to Ishiguro's work and contains analyses of his first four novels, up to *The Unconsoled*. Wong emphasizes the role played by memory in these works.

SUGGESTED SEARCH TERMS

Kazuo Ishiguro

Never Let Me Go

Never Let Me Go AND cloning

Kazuo Ishiguro AND dystopia

Kazuo Ishiguro AND cloning

Dolly AND cloning AND sheep

Kazuo Ishiguro AND Never Let Me Go

Never Let Me Go AND song

Of Human Bondage

WILLIAM SOMERSET MAUGHAM

1915

W. Somerset Maugham's *Of Human Bondage*, published in 1915, is the coming-of-age story of the orphaned Philip Carey. Throughout the novel, Philip seeks freedom, above all else. He feels constrained by many things throughout the course of the story, including religion, morality, desire, love, and the need for money. Always looking ahead, eager for the next phase of his life to begin, Philip travels to Germany and to France before settling once again in England, studying literature, philosophy, art, and finally medicine. He prides himself on his ability to see things as they are, and his striving toward an objective, truthful view of life leads him to harshly judge those people in his life who seem to cling to a more idealistic view of the world and of human nature. This conflict between realism and idealism is one of the main themes of the work. His contact with various men and women during his travels and in his pursuits introduces Philip to a number of philosophical approaches to life, approaches that an always-fascinated Philip studies, appraises, and often discards. Despite the fact that Philip's experiences teach him about the ugliness that exists in the human heart, he nevertheless possesses the desire and capacity to find beauty almost everywhere; in this respect, he retains his own brand of idealism. The work is widely regarded as one of Maugham's masterpieces.

Published in 1915, by Heinemann in London and Doran in New York, *Of Human Bondage* is

W. Somerset Maugham (AP Images)

available in a more recent edition published by the Modern Library in 1999.

AUTHOR BIOGRAPHY

Maugham was born on January 25, 1874, in Paris, France, to Edith and Robert Ormond Maugham. He was their fourth son. Maugham's father was a lawyer for the British Embassy in Paris. In 1882, Maugham's mother died from complications related to tuberculosis and childbirth. Two years later, Maugham's father died of cancer. As there was little money to divide between five sons, the Maugham boys were separated after their father's death. Maugham went to live in Kent, England, with his father's brother Henry and Henry's wife, Sophie. Maugham's Uncle Henry was the vicar of a parish in Whistable. In 1885, Maugham entered the King's School in Canterbury, where he remained for four years. After suffering from pleurisy and recovering from the lung disease in France, Maugham, now sixteen, traveled to Germany in order to attend the University of Heidelberg. There, he met Ellingham Brooks, with whom

biographers believe Maugham had the first of numerous homosexual affairs. In 1892, Maugham returned to England and endeavored to become an accountant, a pursuit that he abandoned after a month. Maugham then turned to the study of medicine at St. Thomas's Hospital in London. His first novel, *Liza of Lambeth*, was published in 1897 and received favorable reviews. The same year, Maugham became fully qualified as a doctor. However, following the success of *Liza of Lambeth*, Maugham instead pursued a career in writing. For the next several years, Maugham continued to write, publishing a second novel and a play, and traveled to Spain, France, Greece, and Egypt. In 1906, Maugham returned to England. His play *Lady Frederick* was produced in 1907 and was regarded as a success. Soon, Maugham had other plays all running simultaneously. In 1910, Maugham visited the United States, where he met Syrie Barnardo Wellcome, a woman with whom he later had an affair and whom he eventually married. Maugham proposed marriage to another woman, Sue Jones, in 1913, but was rejected. Following the outbreak of the World War I in 1914, Maugham joined an ambulance unit in France. He met Gerald Haxton, a man who remained by Maugham's side many years, as a secretary, friend, and lover. The following year, Maugham published *Of Human Bondage* in both England and the United States. After initially weak reviews, the critical reception of the work was bolstered by lavish praise from American author Theodore Dreiser. Also in 1915, Syrie gave birth to a daughter, and Maugham joined the British Intelligence Service. Two years later, Maugham and Syrie were married. Maugham continued to write novels and plays over the next several years. In 1926, Maugham bought a home where he lived with Haxton; the next year, Syrie filed for divorce. Maugham, writing and traveling, spent time in India gathering material for his novel *The Razor's Edge*. He and Haxton were forced to leave their home in France in 1940 due to the Nazi invasion in the early phase of World War II (1939–1945). In 1944, *The Razor's Edge* was published; it is considered to be among Maugham's greatest works. That same year, Haxton died. In 1946, Maugham and his new secretary and companion, Alan Searle, returned to France. During the next several years, Maugham wrote his last novel, *Catalina*. His mental health began to decline in the mid-1950s. He died in Nice, France, on December 15, 1965.

PLOT SUMMARY

Chapter I

As *Of Human Bondage* opens, a young child, Philip Carey, is woken up and escorted to his mother's room by a servant. Philip's mother is lying in bed, and Philip cuddles up against her. He kisses her and drifts happily off to sleep. Philip's mother is not happy or well. A doctor watches over her. She sobs as she touches her son's deformed left foot. This deformity, Philip's club foot, will plague him throughout his life. (In this condition, the foot is turned inward and downward, so that the sole of the foot may not be completely placed on the ground.) Philip's mother has just given birth to a stillborn son, and she herself is in poor health.

Chapters II–VI

From the beginning of the second chapter onward, *Of Human Bondage* is told largely from Philip's point of view. The year is 1885. Philip is staying with Henrietta Watkin, his godmother. The servant from the first chapter, whom Philip now hails as Emma, tells Philip that his mother has died and that he is to live with his Uncle William and Aunt Louisa. Philip is introduced to his uncle, who has been handling funeral preparations. The middle-aged couple is childless, and William is not glad to have the child, but he sees it as his duty. William recalls how little money Philip's father, a surgeon who had died six months ago from blood poisoning, had left Philip's mother. Emma helps a tearful Philip prepare for his move to the vicarage in the village of Blackstable. (William is a vicar, or clergy member of the Church of England. His home is called a vicarage.) Philip feels alone and out of place.

Chapters VII–XI

As Philip accompanies his uncle on his Sunday errands, he grows accustomed to his new life. William's negative attitude toward Philip is easily aroused, and Philip is often scolded. Louisa attempts to keep Philip out of William's way and presents Philip with a variety of books filled with religious pictures, igniting Philip's lifelong love for books. Philip is soon enrolled at the King's School, which focuses on preparing boys for a life in the clergy. Intensely anxious, Philip is taunted by the other children about his foot. Already shy, he is now embarrassed as well. These initial experiences set the tone for the rest of Philip's academic career.

MEDIA ADAPTATIONS

- *Of Human Bondage*, adapted as a film by Lester Cohen and starring Leslie Howard as Philip and Bette Davis as Mildred, was produced and distributed in 1934 by RKO Radio Pictures.

- A 1946 film version of *Of Human Bondage* was adapted from Maugham's novel by Catherine Turney and starred Paul Henreid as Philip and Eleanor Parker as Mildred. It was produced and distributed by Warner Brothers Pictures.

- *Of Human Bondage*, adapted as a film by Bryan Forbes and starring Laurence Harvey as Philip and Kim Novak as Mildred, was produced and distributed in 1964 by Metro-Goldwyn-Mayer.

- An unabridged audio CD version of *Of Human Bondage*, read by Flo Gibson, was published by Audio Book Contractors in 2008.

Chapters XII–XVI

Philip's early days at school wear on, and he endures much bullying. Two years pass. Philip is now almost twelve years old, and he begins to feel a religious fervor growing in him. Over the Christmas holidays, Philip asks his uncle about the truth regarding a biblical passage, in which it is stated that faith can move mountains. William confirms that anything is possible with God. That night, Philip prays for a miracle, that his foot will be healed before he goes back to school. When Philip is not healed, he is angrily forced to conclude that the Bible meant something other than what it said, and that his uncle had tricked him. This marks the onset of Philip's mistrust of religion.

Chapters XVII–XXI

Tom Perkins, the new headmaster of King's School's upper grades, takes Philip under his wing and encourages Philip to consider becoming ordained. Philip's religious devoutness is renewed, but he is sometimes overwhelmed by his "desire for self-sacrifice." When Philip and a boy named Rose become close friends, Philip begins to feel fiercely possessive of Rose. However, after Philip suffers from a bout of scarlet fever that keeps him isolated for months, he returns to school to find that Rose has all but forgotten him. Philip loses interest in his schoolwork. Perkins reprimands him and asks him to think of his future. In response, Philip tells Perkins and his Uncle William that he will not pursue a life in the clergy. Seizing upon the idea that he would like to travel to Germany, Philip disappoints his uncle and Perkins, but he gets his way.

Chapters XXII–XXVI

A family friend of the Careys named Miss Wilkinson recommends a place for Philip to live in Heidelberg, Germany. Philip is welcomed into the home of Professor Erlin and his wife. At dinner, Philip is introduced to the Erlins' daughters and other boarders in the Erlin home. Philip finds himself, for the first time, a young man in the presence of young women. He feels awkward but happy. He learns Latin and German from Professor Erlin, and French and mathematics from other instructors. After about three months, an Englishman named Mr. Hayward boards with the Erlins. Hayward and Philip become good friends.

Chapters XXVII–XXXI

Philip is impressed with Hayward's worldliness and views on life, art, literature, religion, and philosophy. These topics are discussed among Philip, Hayward, and Weeks, an American student boarding with the Erlins. Philip is greatly influenced by both Hayward and Weeks, and he begins to reject some of the religious notions with which he was brought up. Philip eventually concludes that he no longer believes in God. During a winter spent attending plays and discussing philosophical matters, Philip grows restless and longs to travel. Hayward prepares to leave Germany.

Chapters XXXII–XXXVI

Philip returns to England and is introduced to Miss Wilkinson, who is visiting Philip's aunt and uncle. Miss Wilkinson, who is older than Philip, flirts with him, and he is attracted to her as well. She encourages Philip in his interest in art and Paris. Philip's uncle arranges for Philip to study accounting in London. Philip and Miss Wilkinson consummate their desire and exchange an awkward goodbye when Miss Wilkinson leaves

England. Philip then departs for London, where he begins work in the accounting office.

Chapters XXXVII–XLI

Philip makes a determined effort to learn what is expected of him at work. He is unhappy and friendless. As time passes, Philip realizes he has no aptitude for accounting. Mr. Goodfellow, an employee at the office, asks Philip to accompany him to Paris on business. Philip agrees, and when he returns he vows to finish the minimum term required of him at the firm and travel to Paris to study art. Philip appeals to his uncle for financial help. William refuses, but Louisa has money of her own that she secretly gives to Philip. Philip begins his studies at Amitrano's art school, where he meets an abrasive woman named Fanny Price, who, despite her demeanor, offers Philip advice on his artwork. He also meets Mr. Clutton, who invites Philip to lunch and introduces him to Mr. Flanagan and Mr. Lawson. These men form Philip's core group of friends during his time in Paris.

Chapters XLII–XLVI

Clutton, Flanagan, and Lawson take Philip to meet the poet Cronshaw. The men discuss Philip's favorite topics—art, literature, philosophy. At Amitrano's, Philip observes the master artists instructing experienced students, and he discovers that most of the students are quite poor. It is widely acknowledged that Fanny has little talent and less money. She takes Philip to various galleries to show him the work of famous artists. Philip's friends tell him that Fanny is in love with him, but he finds her repulsive. He spends his days painting and lounging in cafes with his friends. To save money, Philip and Lawson rent a studio together. Fanny grows jealous of Philip's closeness with Lawson.

Chapters XLVII–LI

Hayward visits Philip in Paris, and Philip is pleased to demonstrate his knowledge about art. When summer arrives, Philip's friends spend the season outside of Paris. Philip leaves as well, to Fanny's dismay, with Lawson and another student, Ruth Chalice. Philip discovers that Lawson and Ruth are having an affair. Once they have returned to Paris, Philip receives an ominous letter from Fanny. Arriving at her studio, he finds that she has hanged herself. Growing increasingly concerned about his financial situation and doubting his competence as an artist, Philip encounters one of the master painters, Foinet, from the school. He asks Foinet examine his work. When Foinet tells Philip he has no exceptional talent, Philip plans to return to England. He then receives a letter telling him Aunt Louisa has died.

Chapters LII–LVI

Philip returns to the vicarage for the funeral, after which Philip and his uncle bicker over Philip's future. Philip decides to become a doctor, and he begins his studies at St. Luke's Hospital in London. Philip becomes friends with a student named Dunsford, who takes Philip to tea. Dunsford is enamored of a woman, Mildred, who works in the tea shop. Philip finds her ugly and cold, yet he is drawn to her. Philip becomes obsessed with Mildred, and they begin dating.

Chapters LVII–LXI

Philip convinces himself he is in love with Mildred, although she is often cruel and is bored by him. She remains indifferent to him but continues to date him. Distracted by Mildred, Philip performs poorly in his medical exams. As time passes, Philip's feelings intensify, whereas Mildred is only occasionally affectionate. He professes his love; she responds coldly. In order to keep seeing her, Philip promises to keep his feelings in check and to not get jealous when she sees other men.

Chapters LXII–LXVI

Philip proposes marriage to Mildred, who considers Philip's income and rejects his offer. Continuing to struggle with his medical exams, Philip is crestfallen when Mildred reveals that she is marrying another man, Emil Miller. Philip attempts to forget her and enjoys a visit from Hayward. Hayward and Philip attend an art opening in which one of Lawson's paintings is to be featured. Philip's schoolwork begins to improve, and through Lawson, he meets the nearly divorced Mrs. Norah Nesbit, who earns her living writing romantic novellas. The two become friends and, eventually, lovers. Philip claims to not love her, although he is happy when he is with her.

Chapters LXVII–LXXI

Philip, Lawson, and Hayward begin spending time with a man named Macalister, a stockbroker, with whom Hayward went to school. They meet weekly. Philip's philosophical development continues, and he contemplates what he describes as

the illusion of free will. When Philip becomes ill, the medical student who lives upstairs from him, Harry Griffiths, befriends him and helps nurse him back to health. Mildred visits Philip, revealing that she never married Miller but had become his mistress. Now pregnant, Mildred has been abandoned by Miller. Despite his dwindling savings, Philip helps Mildred, his love for her reawakened. He breaks things off with Norah after lying to her about Mildred.

Chapters LXXII–LXXVI

For the next several months, Philip spends his free time with Mildred. Mildred has her baby and has decided to pay another woman to raise the child. With Philip's money, Mildred and the baby set off for Brighton, where she finds a surrogate mother. Afterward, Philip makes plans to take Mildred to Paris. After introducing Mildred to his friend Griffiths, Philip learns that they were instantly attracted to each other and have since met secretly. Mildred confesses to Philip that she hates him and wants only Griffiths.

Chapters LXXVII–LXXXI

When Mildred discovers that Griffiths has no money, she returns to Philip. He knows she still loves Griffiths, and he spitefully offers to pay for Mildred and Griffiths to go away together. He is shocked when they agree. Griffiths writes to Philip to apologize; he and Mildred are no longer together. Stunned, Philip seeks cheaper lodgings, as his savings are now depleted, and attempts to focus on his medical studies. He later learns that Norah is engaged and that Mildred is now alone and working in London.

Chapters LXXXII–LXXXVI

From Lawson, Philip discovers that Cronshaw has come to London and is very poor and very ill. Philip meets with him, and they discuss Cronshaw's life and impending death. He invites Cronshaw to move in with him. Cronshaw worsens quickly, and before long Philip finds him dead. As he did for Fanny, Philip takes responsibility for funeral arrangements. In the spring of that year, Philip treats a patient by the name of Thorpe Athelny, and the two become friends. Philip is drawn to Athelny's exuberant personality and philosophical nature.

Chapters LXXXVII–XCI

Philip visits Athelny's home and meets his family, which includes his wife, Betty, and his nine children, the eldest of whom is the fifteen-year-old Sally. In Athelny, Philip finds another man with whom he can share ideas about morality, religion, philosophy, and art. One evening, Philip sees Mildred and discovers she is working as a prostitute. As they talk, Philip learns that she was unable to find a job and could not get any money from Miller. She leaves the baby alone at night while she works. Philip, pitying her but no longer loving her, offers her friendship, a room to sleep in at his apartment, and work as his housekeeper. Mildred is surprised at his lack of desire but accepts his offer, and she and the baby move in.

Chapters XCII–XCVI

As time passes, Mildred continues to expect Philip to want a romantic relationship, and she is hurt that he does not. After making a small sum on the stock exchange, Philip decides to have his foot operated on, and he and Mildred and the baby go to Brighton afterward so he can recover. Mildred grows increasingly frustrated with his lack of interest in her. Back in London, Philip begins working in the surgical wards. He is once again concerned with money and encourages Mildred to find a job. Eventually she attempts to seduce Philip; he rebuffs her advances. Mildred is furious.

Chapters XCVII–CI

When Philip returns from work at the hospital, he finds that Mildred has destroyed his possessions and has left with the baby. Philip takes what few belongings he has left and finds cheaper rooms. He learns that Hayward is leaving for South Africa, where Great Britain is at war. (In South Africa, the British fought the Boers, descendents of Dutch colonists, from 1899 through 1902.) With Macalister, Philip makes an investment in the stock market that does not pay off. Philip is now practically penniless. He begins to pawn his clothes and eats almost nothing. Philip leaves school and abandons his apartment, as he cannot afford either. He sleeps outside and seeks employment during the day. After several days living in this manner, Philip seeks shelter with Athelny.

Chapters CII–CVI

Athelny helps Philip find a job. Philip is hired as a shop-walker, directing customers in a department store. Employees are given food and company lodging as part of their wages, and Philip moves into a dormitory. After months pass and Philip has been promoted to window dresser, he runs into Lawson and shamefacedly explains his situation. Lawson tells him that Hayward has died. Saddened, Philip contemplates the meaninglessness of life. By accepting that life has no meaning, Philip feels free from the responsibility of striving toward the success and happiness that always elude him. He chooses to view life as a creation, a work of art, in which happiness and pain matter only in that they contribute to the design of one's life. The thought comforts him.

Chapters CVII–CXI

Philip is now designing clothing for the store and is given a raise. Another winter passes, and in the spring, Philip is informed that his uncle is gravely ill. Secretly hoping for his uncle's death and the inheritance it will bring, Philip goes to Blackstable and finds William clinging stubbornly to life. The following winter, Philip receives a letter from Mildred. She has asked to see him because she fears she is ill, which Philip confirms upon visiting her. He tells her she must give up her current way of life (she has gone back to prostitution). Mildred informs Philip that her baby has died. Philip prescribes medicine, and gradually her health improves. When he follows her one night, he discovers that she is still working as a prostitute. She refuses to stop, and Philip walks away, never to see her again. Philip is called back to Blackstable later that winter; his Uncle William has died.

Chapters CXII–CXVI

With the money he has inherited from his uncle, Philip eagerly returns to school and begins studies in obstetrics. Philip completes his final year of study at the hospital. He receives his diploma seven years after he began; he is now nearly thirty years old. Seeking an appointment as a physician, Philip finds a temporary position assisting a Dr. South in a small coastal town. South is abrasive but gradually warms to Philip, and Philip enjoys his work.

Chapters CXVII–CXXI

Dr. South offers Philip a permanent position, which Philip declines. He wishes to travel and to work in Spain. After Philip is invited to vacation with the Athelnys, Philip and Sally acknowledge a mutual attraction. It is hinted that they become lovers. Upon returning to London, Philip accepts a position as an assistant house-physician at St. Luke's. Not long after, Sally confesses to Philip that she may be pregnant. While they wait to find out, Philip contemplates his future. He easily relinquishes his dream of traveling, drawn as he is to the notion of domestic life with Sally.

Chapter CXXII

Philip arranges to meet Sally. He has previously contacted Dr. South to confirm that the employment offer has remained open. Upon informing Philip that she is not pregnant, Sally wonders why Philip is not relieved. Philip has no wish to abandon his plan of marriage. He proposes on the spot, and Sally accepts.

CHARACTERS

Betty Athelny

Betty Athelny is the mother of Thorpe Athelny's children. She is referred to as Athelny's wife, but Thorpe Athelny explains that they are not actually married. When Philip becomes friends with the family, Betty dotes on him in a motherly fashion.

Sally Athelny

When Philip first meets Sally, she is a fifteen-year old girl, quiet and self-possessed. As time passes, Philip notices that Sally is growing into a young woman. Eventually, Philip and Sally become lovers. Philip finds himself content and happy when he is with her, and she is one of the few women he describes as beautiful. At the end of the novel, Philip and Sally decide to marry.

Thorpe Athelny

Thorpe Athelny works as a representative for a linen drapery. He has traveled widely; he was married, and when the relationship ended his wife refused to grant him a divorce. Athelny lives with Betty, the mother of his nine children. Philip finds Athelny to have a passion for life, literature, learning, art, and philosophy, and he is drawn to his new friend's enthusiasm. Philip is entranced with the domestic contentment the Athelnys enjoy. With so many children, the household is not a peaceful one, but everyone is happy, healthy, and infused with vitality. Athelny and his family demonstrate for the first time to Philip the best that family life has to offer, and it is at least in part due to this example that Philip embraces the idea of marriage to Sally.

Fraulein Cacilie

Fraulein Cacilie (*Fraulein* means *miss* in German) is a boarder in the Erlin home. Cacilie and Herr Sung, another boarder, have an affair and run off together.

Helen Carey

Helen Carey is Philip's mother. She dies after giving birth to a stillborn baby. Philip is a young boy at the time.

Louisa Carey

Louisa Carey is Philip's aunt and the wife of William Carey. When her young nephew Philip comes to live with her after his mother's death, Louisa is apprehensive. She has been unable to have children and desperately wants to mother Philip. Louisa strives to be a buffer between Philip and her husband William. Always supportive of Philip, she secretly uses her own money to help Philip pay for his trip to Paris. Louisa dies while Philip is there.

Philip Carey

Philip Carey is the novel's protagonist. Born with a deformed foot and orphaned at a young age, Philip is plagued by his shyness. He is ruthlessly teased in school and becomes very self-conscious. Philip is raised by his clergyman uncle and sent to a school designed to prepare young men for a religious life. Throughout the novel, the notion of self-sacrifice that seems to Philip to be integral to his Christianity is applied to various relationships after he rejects religion. Philip longs for romance, but when he believes he has found it, with Mildred, he resurrects the notion that pursuit of Mildred's love, like his former pursuit of God's love, must involve the humble abasement of himself. Philip destroys his life trying to win Mildred. Having freed himself from the constricting bonds of Christianity and the responsibility to behave according to a set of morals he comes to view as arbitrary, Philip becomes bound to his twisted notion of love, and soon he yearns to be free of love for Mildred. He briefly finds happiness with Norah, but he claims not to love her. Endlessly seeking a new purpose and more freedom, Philip travels, ponders life and its meaning, and changes careers. He demonstrates his kindheartedness and loyalty to his friends, but he also displays snobbery and callousness. Maugham's portrait of Philip is objective in this sense; the reader, like the other characters, sees both his commendable qualities and his flaws. In the end, he feels free of many of the bonds that he felt were hampering him. Having finally completed his medical studies and found a job, and having inherited money from his uncle, Philip is no longer constrained by the financial concerns that have plagued him. He has stopped judging the success of his life on the basis of happiness or suffering and sees the beauty of the pattern he has created. He reflects on what he has gained from all of his experiences and all of the viewpoints he has encountered. Finally free, Philip enters into a relationship with Sally with an open, happy heart.

William Carey

William Carey is Philip's uncle (he is the brother of Philip's deceased father). William is a gruff man who initially makes some effort to ease an anxious young Philip's heart after Philip's mother dies, yet William is irritated to have an unpredictable child in his life. William is a clergyman, a vicar in the town of Blackstable. Local church politics and routines dominate William's life, and he has difficulty in incorporating Philip into this world. William persists in trying to steer Philip toward a life in the clergy, and he is furious when Philip leaves school and expresses a lack of interest in becoming ordained. William is almost permanently disapproving of Philip, although he does make an effort to help Philip get a job in London with an accounting firm. When Philip has lost everything, his uncle refuses to give him any assistance. As William lies in bed, dying, near the end of the novel, Philip feels little emotion. In the end, it is William's death that saves Philip, for the money he inherits enables him to return to his medical studies and pursue his own goals once again.

Ruth Chalice

Ruth Chalice is an art student who studies at Amitrano's in Paris with Philip. She has an affair with another student, Lawson.

Mr. Clutton

Mr. Clutton is an art student at Amitrano's in Paris. The other students find him affable and accomplished. He is counted among Philip's circle of friends in Paris.

Mr. Cronshaw

Mr. Cronshaw is a poet living in Paris at the time when Philip is studying art there. Cronshaw is philosophical, intellectual, and an admitted alcoholic. Throughout his friendship with Philip,

Cronshaw offers a unique, often bleak, perspective on life. Philip considers everything Cronshaw says with great seriousness and is influenced by the poet's views. Of the many ideas Cronshaw presents to Philip to consider is the idea that the answer to life's mysteries may be found in a Persian carpet, and he sends Philip a scrap of one. Cronshaw returns to England, in the poorest of health. Philip offers him a room, where Cronshaw soon dies. Near the end of the novel, Philip contemplates the riddle of the Persian rug and feels he understands what Cronshaw had meant: that life, regardless of the happiness or pain it contained, could only be appreciated for its design, its patterns, like those in the rug.

Dunsford

Dunsford is a medical student in Philip's year. He attaches himself to Philip, as neither of them knows anyone else. It is Dunsford who introduces Philip to Mildred; Dunsford himself is fascinated by her.

Emma

Emma is Philip's nurse while his mother is still alive. She helps Philip prepare to move to his uncle's home.

Professor Erlin

Professor Erlin is a high school teacher with whom Philip lives during his time in Heidelberg, Germany. He teaches Philip Latin and German. He and his wife have two daughters.

Frau Professor Erlin

Frau Professor Erlin is Professor Erlin's wife. "Frau" means "Mrs." in German, and her title in the novel represents the respectful German convention of conferring the husband's title on his wife.

Mr. Flanagan

Mr. Flanagan is an American art student who is studying with Philip in Paris. Philip finds him to be easy-going and generally happy, and he observes that Flanagan seems to have more money than the rest of his peers.

Monsieur Foinet

Monsieur Foinet is one of the masters at the art school in Paris. When Philip begins to doubt his talent as an artist, he asks Foinet to review his work. Foinet tells Philip that he will never be a great artist. Based on this assessment and his own instincts, Philip decides to return to England.

Mr. Goodfellow

Mr. Goodfellow works in the accounting office with Philip. He takes Philip with him to Paris, where the accounting firm's services have been engaged by a hotel. It is after this trip with Goodfellow that Philip decides to give up accounting and move to Paris to study art.

Harry Griffiths

Harry Griffiths is a medical student who helps Philip recover when he becomes ill. Griffiths is gregarious and jovial, and he and Philip become friends. Griffiths is also something of a womanizer, and he has an affair with Mildred. As Philip has expected, Griffiths tires of Mildred quickly. He ignores her further pursuit and attempts repeatedly to make amends with Philip.

Mr. G. Etheridge Hayward

Mr. Hayward is an Englishman whom Philip meets in Germany. For a good portion of the novel, Hayward serves as an inspiration to Philip. Hayward considers himself a poet and is something of a philosopher as well, by Philip's estimation. Philip has a high regard for Hayward's worldly experiences and romantic point of view. After Hayward returns to England, he claims to feel like a failure. Hayward is disappointed in Philip. "You want to do things, you want to become things . . . It's so vulgar," Hayward says. Hayward is a symbol of idealism for Philip, who recognizes Hayward's overly sensitive and idle nature as well. Hayward's death, which has followed Cronshaw's, leads Philip to ponder the meaninglessness of life.

Fraulein Hedwig

Fraulein Hedwig is a boarder in the Erlin home. She is the daughter of a merchant in Berlin and corresponds with a lover of whom her parents do not approve.

Mr. Lawson

Mr. Lawson is an Englishman who is, like Philip, studying art in Paris. He and Philip become good friends. Years after Philip has left Paris, he and Lawson meet again in London, where the friendship is renewed. Lawson is sympathetic to Philip after he loses his savings on the stock market and lends him money, though as friends they drift apart.

Macalister

Macalister is the stockbroker Philip meets through Lawson. Philip loses all of his savings after taking some of Macalister's advice.

Mary Ann

Mary Ann is the servant in the home of William and Louisa Carey. As a child, Philip grows to love her.

Emil Miller

Emil Miller is a German man living in London who becomes involved with Mildred. Mildred tells Philip that Miller has proposed, when in fact he has only promised to keep Mildred as his mistress. He is already married to someone else. When Mildred becomes pregnant, Miller abandons her and has no future contact with her or her baby.

Norah Nesbit

Norah Nesbit is a woman, estranged from her husband, who writes romance novellas and whom Philip meets through his friend Lawson after Philip and Mildred part ways. Philip finds that he is extremely happy when he is with her, and he thinks of her as a truly good person. Their friendship becomes a romance, and Philip seems content until Mildred returns to his life. Norah handles Philip's callous treatment of her with grace and eventually marries another man.

Tom Perkins

Mr. Perkins becomes the headmaster at Philip's school. He takes an interest in Philip's education, and treats him kindly, unlike most of the other adults at the school. He encourages Philip to become ordained and is disappointed when Philip leaves school before completing his final year.

Fanny Price

Fanny Price is an art student at the school Philip attends. Philip finds that although Fanny offers helpful instruction, her work is unimpressive. Philip finds Fanny to be serious and abrupt. Her abrasive nature is noted by most of her peers, and Philip is surprised that despite this personality, she helps him in class and takes him to museums to show him the work of famous artists. Fanny grows increasingly jealous of Philip's other relationships. Her money runs out completely, and she hangs herself after not having eaten for days.

Mildred Rogers

Mildred Rogers is a woman who works in a tea shop; Philip meets her through his friend Dunsford. Philip finds her bony, unattractive, common, unintelligent, uninteresting, and extremely cold. Nevertheless he finds himself falling in love with her. The colder and crueler she is with him, the more obsessed Philip becomes with her. She repeatedly manipulates Philip. Mildred is depicted as almost inhuman in her conniving and heartless ways. It is largely because of her that Philip is reduced to poverty. When she appears one last time in the story, her baby has died and she is quite ill, possibly with a disease contracted through her work as a prostitute. Philip objects to the fact that she could transmit her disease to others if she continues in this line of work. Mildred responds that the men who hire her can take their chances. She feels that she owes men nothing. Philip's, and the reader's, last view of Mildred is significant in that it highlights Mildred's bitterness and her vindictiveness.

Rose

Rose is a boy who is a friend of Philip's at King's School. Philip adores Rose and feels jealous when Rose spends time with other friends. It is Philip's first close relationship with anyone near his own age, and it ends badly. After Philip is quarantined while he has scarlet fever, Rose moves on to other friends. He and Philip argue, and Rose calls him a cripple.

Dr. South

Dr. South is the doctor in a small coastal town who takes Philip on as a temporary assistant. Philip finds him to be gruff and old fashioned, but he is not perturbed by the doctor's demeanor. The people in the village adore Philip, and Dr. South offers Philip a permanent position. Philip initially declines this offer but later accepts it.

Herr Sung

Herr Sung (*Herr* means *mister* in German) is from China. He is a boarder in the Erlin home at the same time as Philip. He has an affair with Fraulein Cacilie and runs away with her.

Henrietta Watkin

Miss Watkin is Philip's godmother and was Philip's mother's close friend. She briefly cares for Philip in the transition period after his mother's death and before his move to his uncle's house.

Mr. Weeks

Mr. Weeks in an American living in the Erlin home in Heidelberg during Philip's stay there. Weeks is sarcastic regarding Hayward's romantic notions and lifestyle. Philip defends Hayward to Weeks. Weeks, Hayward, and Philip spend a considerable amount of time discussing literature and philosophy in Weeks's quarters in the Erlin home. It is at least in part due to Weeks's influence that Philip discards his religious faith.

Emily Wilkinson

Miss Emily Wilkinson is a family friend of the Careys who helps Philip find a place to stay in Germany. Philip meets Miss Wilkinson when he returns to England after leaving Germany; she is visiting his aunt and uncle. Philip knows that she is considerably older than he is. At times, he finds her attractive. Miss Wilkinson has been employed in Paris and in Berlin as a governess, and she tells Philip of the lovers she has had. She and Philip have a brief affair, in which Miss Wilkinson becomes much more emotionally involved than Philip. After she leaves England, Miss Wilkinson writes to Philip often, but he gradually tapers off his correspondence with her and the relationship dies. Near the end of the novel, Philip's uncle informs Philip that Miss Wilkinson has married.

THEMES

Idealism

Of Human Bondage may be viewed in one sense as Philip's journey from idealism to realism. As a child, Philip, like most children, has an idealized view of the world, despite the losses he has suffered at an early age. To view the world in an idealized way is to overlay the notion of perfection on one's world. Philip, for example, demonstrates his idealism regarding his faith in God when he prays for his foot to be cured, fully expecting that because he believes and because he has been told that with God anything is possible, his foot will be healed. When it is not healed, Philip's idealized notion of God is shaken. Similarly, Philip bases his initially idealized view of love on the books he reads and on the romantic experiences Hayward discusses with him after the two meet in Germany. Philip's notion of love is such that he expects to feel wild passion and the exquisite emotions he has read about and talked about with Hayward. Hayward is the epitome (the perfect example) of idealism. He views

TOPICS FOR FURTHER STUDY

- The early portion of *Of Human Bondage* focuses on Philip's formal education at a boarding school. Using sources such as Sally Mitchell's *Daily Life in Victorian England*, which was published in 2008 by Greenwood and which includes a chapter on education, research Victorian boarding schools. How did social class and the attendant issue of wealth affect where a person went to school? What was a typical school day like? What subjects were studied? How did the education boys received differ from the one that girls received? What other activities did students at boarding schools engage in, such as games or sports? Compile your findings into a written report; an electronic report, such as a PowerPoint presentation; or a Web page that your classmates can view. Cite all of your sources.

- In *Of Human Bondage*, Philip references Charles Darwin's 1859 scientific work *On the Origin of Species*. Seeming to accept Darwin's premises, he uses Darwin's ideas to support his own philosophy of individual versus societal self-interest. Using works such as Janet Brown's *Darwin's "Origin of Species": A Biography*, published by the Atlantic Monthly Press in 2007, research the public reception of Darwin's work in Victorian England. How controversial were Darwin's conclusions to conservative Victorian society? How did religious groups respond to the work at the time of its publication and in the years that immediately followed? Also consider how the work is regarded today. Do Darwin's conclusions remain controversial? Present your findings in a written, electronic format, or Web-based format.

- Philip's study of art, which he undertakes in Paris, becomes highly influential in his life even after he decides to no longer pursue artistic study, for it changes how he views the world and what he classifies as beautiful. Using Philip's own interests as a guide, study the artists whose work Philip sees when he is in Paris, including Claude Monet, Édouard Manet, and Edgar Degas. Create a Web-based report on these artists and the Impressionist movement of which they were a part. Describe the movement and its reception in the art community. Your Web page should include links to representative works by the artists you feature in your report.

- The young-adult coming-of-age novel *Esperanza Rising*, written by Pam Munoz Ryan and published in 2000 by Scholastic Press, features a wealthy teenage Mexican girl whose father is murdered when she is thirteen. She and her mother are forced to escape to California and take jobs as migrant workers. As the Great Depression strikes, Esperanza's mother becomes ill, and Esperanza must find a way to support both of them. Like *Of Human Bondage*, Ryan's novel deals with issues of social and economic class. Due to financial constraints, the young girl who was once treated as a princess must now do work she once considered beneath her. Read Ryan's novel with a book group of your classmates and consider the ways in which Esperanza's experiences are similar to those of Philip, who must also discard his notions of class status, at least temporarily. How do Philip's and Esperanza's experiences of poverty change them? Do they come to view class differences in a new way? Consider the fact that when Esperanza enters the United States, she is in a minority group. How does this contribute to her psychological development in the course of the novel? With your group, prepare an oral or written presentation for your class in which you discuss your comparison of the novels' main characters.

his world through a romantic, sentimental lens. As the narrator observes, Hayward's mind "saw everything a little larger than life size, with the outlines blurred, in a golden mist of sentimentality." When Philip begins to have his own experiences, he is disappointed, finding that they do not measure up to the idealized view. He experiences passionate moments with Miss Wilkinson, but he often finds she is more appealing in his thoughts than in reality. Philip possesses idealized notions of what life will be like in Paris, imagining adventures like those Hayward has reported. After a time, though, experience teaches him to be dissatisfied there as well. After the summer spent with Lawson and Ruth Chalice, Philip feels discontented: "Life was not giving him what he wanted, and he had an uneasy feeling that he was losing his time." It is Mildred who ultimately destroys any idealized notions Philip possesses about love. His obsession with her is self-destructive and brings him no joy. He thinks what he is feeling is love because the emotion, his passion, is so powerful, and when he feels it destroying him he learns to be fearful of such intense sentiment. In his subsequent relationships, Philip, who now has a more realistic view of what passionate love can do to a person, seeks out safe, comfortable women, such as Norah and Sally, who make him feel happy. Near the novel's end, Philip explicitly rejects the idealism that Hayward represents; "it was in reaction from what Hayward represented that Philip clamoured for life as it stood."

Realism

Just as Hayward serves as a representative of idealism, a notion that Philip ultimately rejects, Cronshaw represents realism, which Philip eventually embraces. (Realism in this sense refers to an outlook on life rather than approach to art and literature.) He may appear to have a bleak outlook, but Cronshaw takes life as it is, expecting little from it and accepting the consequences of his actions. Cronshaw discusses with Philip an understanding of human nature that to Cronshaw appears quite straightforward; he tells Philip, "Men seek but one thing in life—their pleasure." His world is one stripped of the ideals that Philip, at this point in his life (while he still lives in Paris), would still like to believe exist, ideals such as "duty and goodness and beauty." Philip gradually comes to agree, after he has lived a little more of life, that men and women are rarely, if ever, motivated by goodness for its

own sake. At one of his lowest points, when he is working in the shop with no end in sight, after he has been used and mistreated by Mildred and after his friends Cronshaw and Hayward have died, Philip realizes how few people appreciate the things he believes to be good. He thinks of Cronshaw and his notion of human motivation and comes to the same conclusion. People make choices in their lives or opt to view their lives in certain ways for no apparent need or use. "It was merely something [man] did for his own personal pleasure," Philip concludes. A view of life in which happiness bears no more significance than suffering, in which one tries for the sake of it, for the sake of living one's life, is the realistic approach that Philip arrives at near the end of the novel. Having accepted this brand of realism, Philip feels content.

Free Will

As Philip pursues various ambitions and relationships in *Of Human Bondage*, he begins to wonder how much his conscious choices matter within the large scheme of things. In a conversation with Cronshaw in Paris, when Philip is still pursuing romantic European adventures and before experience has disrupted his youthful idealism, Philip is shocked to learn that Cronshaw regrets nothing in life, for he believes his actions are inevitable. "But that's fatalism," Philip replies. Determinism is a school of thought in which it is believed that one's actions are determined by forces other than a person's own will, and fatalism is a closely related concept, focusing instead on the predetermined nature of events in the lives of individuals. Fatalism has the religious connotation that one's life is mapped out ahead of time by God. Cronshaw believes that free will is an illusion, but it is one he embraces. He acts as though he has free will but believes that he has no moral responsibility, because, in his view, he could not have chosen to act otherwise.

Eventually, although Philip still chooses to believe in his own free will, he nevertheless takes a view on morality similar to Cronshaw's when he concludes, for different reasons than Cronshaw does, that there is no good and evil. His notion is related to his growing belief in realism rather than idealism. Just before entering his medical studies, Philip has come to believe that society acts as an entity, toward its own preservation, whereas individuals act in a way advantageous to themselves. If individuals act in a way that benefits society, they are called virtuous, and if they act in a way that harms society, they are sinners. This, Philip

A waitress takes an order at a café. Philip meets Mildred at the café where she is a waitress. (Image copyright Brian A. Jackson, 2010. Used under license from Shutterstock.com)

concludes, is all that good and evil are. Philip feels that as an individual, "his power is the only measure of his morality." After Mildred has left Philip for Miller, however, Philip begins to subscribe to the notion that free will is just an illusion, as Cronshaw had stated. It is useless to regret, Philip says to Hayward: "It is no good crying over spilt milk, because all the forces of the universe were bent on spilling it." This is a repackaging of Cronshaw's determinism, and it emphasizes the lack of agency or control Philip experienced when he was with Mildred. Philip's understanding of this notion intensifies after he is further tormented by Mildred, he loses all his money, and Hayward and Cronshaw have died. He ruminates on the uselessness of trying, and on the way success or failure rest on "pure chance" alone. However, in this dark frame of mind, Philip finds a new way of making sense of his life. By embracing the idea that "life [is] insignificant and death without consequence," Philip suddenly understands

that "for the first time he was utterly free." All one can do is appreciate one's life for the beauty of its accidental creation and design. Still, Philip acts in a way that suggests that, like Cronshaw, he operates within the illusion of free will. When it seems that circumstances—Sally's possible pregnancy—will force him to abandon his plans of traveling to Spain, he nevertheless has the opportunity to chose his path when he finds out that she is not pregnant, and he chooses life with Sally.

STYLE

Bildungsroman

Of Human Bondage is a type of work known as a *bildungsroman*. This is a German word for a novel that focuses on the journey of its hero from youth to maturity, from innocence to experience. The word was originally used by German critics to describe a novel by a nineteenth-century German author and philosopher, Wolfgang von Goethe, but it later came into wider usage. In a bildungsroman, the protagonist (main character) undergoes a process of psychological and moral development. In *Of Human Bondage*, this is evidenced by Philip's philosophical explorations of morality, for example. He is transformed from a devout Christian, to a doubting Christian, to an atheist who accepts the moral teachings of the church but not the religious and spiritual beliefs, and finally to an atheist who believes in a subjective, individual morality rather than a universal one. This development parallels Philip's gradual rejection of idealism and embracing of a more realistic attitude toward life. Throughout the novel, Philip, always a thinker, absorbs and examines the philosophies and beliefs of his friends and peers. He examines everything that is said to him, attempting to determine its value and relevance in his life. In this manner, Philip actively pursues his intellectual, psychological, and moral development, from his days as a schoolboy at King's School throughout his travels in Germany and Paris, and finally through his life in London as a medical student.

Realism

Realism in literature is an approach that rejects the sentimentality of nineteenth-century romanticism. It gained momentum as a literary movement, particularly in France, England, and America, in the aftermath of the nineteenth-century romantic movement. Rather than portraying life and relationships in an idealized fashion, the author of realist fiction attempts to convey with real life accuracy the experiences of his or her characters. In *Of Human Bondage*, Maugham takes this approach, telling Philip's story in a straightforward, detailed manner that does not shy away from presenting the sordidness of life. The cruelty Philip endures and the suffering he causes are depicted as objectively as the happiness and pleasure he experiences. As is typical of the realist novel, *Of Human Bondage* is more focused on character development than on a fast-paced plot. Philip's psychological transformation and the psychology of the secondary characters are of primary interest to Maugham.

Third-Person Narration

Of Human Bondage is told using third-person narration. In this style of storytelling, an individual who exists outside the events of the story serves as the narrator. This person is sometimes associated with the author, an assumption that may or may not be accurate, as the author does not always make clear whether or not the narrator is a representation of himself or herself. In *Of Human Bondage*, the narrator tells the story largely from Philip's point of view. The majority of the storytelling is concerned with Philip's experiences, thoughts, feelings, and actions. The narrator's omniscience, or knowingness, is mostly limited to Philip. However, at times, the narrator strays from Philip's viewpoint and shares with the reader the thoughts of another character, as when Mildred ponders Philip's lack of romantic interest in her after he has rescued her from a life of prostitution. Third-person narration effectively supports the bildungsroman style of the novel, in that it allows Philip's experiences and progress along the journey of his development to be objectively conveyed by the narrator.

HISTORICAL CONTEXT

Late Victorian England Class Divisions

Of Human Bondage spans a period of approximately twenty years, from the time when Philip loses his mother when he is a boy of about eight until he is nearly thirty years old. In the opening chapters, the narrator specifies that it is 1885 when Philip's mother dies and he is sent to live with his uncle. The late 1880s and the 1890s (the time period during which most of the novel is set) marked the end of Queen Victoria's reign; she ruled from 1837 until her death in 1901, when she was succeeded by her son Edward VII. During this time, England was experiencing a period of prosperity that affected most of the classes in English society, according to H. C. G. Matthew, in *The Oxford Illustrated History of Britain*, published in 1984. As the working class (wage earners in factories and shops) and lower middle class (shopkeepers, bankers, and business people) earned better wages, the lines between the classes grew less distinct. As Matthew states, "Between 1860 and 1914 real wages doubled." The upper middle classes, those who drew their money from inheritances, investments, and property, and those who worked in professions for which a university education was necessary (doctors, lawyers, and clergymen) focused increasingly on their higher education and pedigreed family history as a means of distinguishing themselves from the rest of the middle class, as wealth alone was no longer a clear indicator of the difference that they worked to maintain. In *Of Human Bondage*, Philip struggles to make this distinction as well. His family sees only a few occupations as acceptable for a gentleman (an educated man of the upper class), and it pains Philip to have to accept a job for wages after the money he inherited from his father has run out. Philip refers throughout the novel to his notion that he is a gentleman, and he expresses disdain for shabbiness in appearance (as he does with Fanny Price) and condescension toward those whom he perceives are less intelligent than he is (as he does with Mildred). In addition to using Philip as a means of drawing attention to class issues, Maugham does so through the narrator, when, for example, extended discussion concerning Headmaster Tom Perkins's middle-class background is presented (in Chapter XV).

Second Anglo-Boer War and British Imperialism

One of the few direct historical references Maugham makes in *Of Human Bondage* is to a war being fought in the Cape region of South Africa. This region was inhabited by the Boers, descendents of Dutch colonists who settled the region in the late seventeenth century. In 1795, the British occupied the Cape in order to protect trade routes to India, which Britain had also colonized. (Colonizing territory in foreign countries and expanding control over that region is known as

COMPARE
&
CONTRAST

- **1890s:** In the late 1890s, Great Britain is embroiled in the Second Anglo-Boer War in South Africa, a conflict referenced by Maugham in *Of Human Bondage*. The British are fighting the Boers (descendents of Dutch colonists in the Cape region of South Africa) over territory rich in gold and diamonds. In 1902, a peace treaty is signed and the Boers surrender. Some British citizens protest the war.

  1910s: From 1914 through 1918, Great Britain, along with France and Russia and other allies, including the United States, fights the forces of Germany and Austria-Hungary in World War I. The war effort is a unifying force in Great Britain.

  Today: In response to the terrorist attacks on September 11, 2001, in New York City, Great Britain supports the United States' effort to combat terrorism by attacking the Afghanistan-based terrorist group. According to a 2009 British Broadcasting Corporation News report, more than seventy-one thousand British troops have been sent to fight in Afghanistan since 2001. The London *Guardian* reports in 2009 that although more British people oppose the war than support it, support has been increasing.

- **1890s:** During the late 1890s, impressionism characterizes much of the art being displayed in Paris. Masters of the form include Manet, Monet, Degas, Paul Cézanne, and Camille Pissarro. Impressionists seek to capture their intuitive perceptions about a subject rather than recreating fine details.

  1910s: While impressionists are still at work in Paris (Monet's famous water lily series is painted between 1914 and 1926), a new art movement, expressionism, is taking hold in Germany. Expressionists, including Ernst Ludwig Kirchner, Erich Heckel, and Karl Schmidt-Rottluff, originate a movement in which the artist seeks to capture emotion in a style that often distorts the subject's actual features.

  Today: New movements in contemporary art, such as stuckism, seek to revitalize an interest in figurative painting. Stuckists are critical of nonrepresentational postmodern art. Instead, representational painting (which depicts actual forms and figures) is embraced. Notable stuckists include Charles Thomson and Billy Childish. The New Leipzig school is another group of contemporary artists, who, like the stuckists, favor figurative painting and drawing. The New Leipzigs, such as Neo Rauch, focus on technical aspects of artistic rendering, such as perspective and color theory.

- **1890s:** Queen Victoria is nearing the end of her reign, ruling England until her death in 1901. Despite growing troubles abroad, Queen Victoria reigns over a vast empire with colonial holdings around the globe. Her popularity is bolstered by her subjects' approval of British imperialism.

  1910s: King George V ascends the throne in 1910 and rules over Britain's involvement in World War I. He is an avid supporter of his troops, and he visits military bases and hospitals hundreds of times during the war. While King George V is respected for this effort, his prime minister, Herbert Asquith, disappoints British citizens for his handling of the war. He resigns in 1916 and is replaced by David Lloyd George.

  Today: Queen Elizabeth II is the current monarch of the United Kingdom. She ascended to the throne after the death of her father, King George VI, in 1952. She has less power than her predecessors; governance of the United Kingdom is handled exclusively through Parliament and the prime minister, currently Gordon Brown.

imperialism.) As the British sought to maintain control over this area, two portions of it, the Transvaal and the Orange Free State, were allowed independent status, with some oversight by the British. In 1886, increased diamond mining in those areas, as well as the discovery of gold, resulted in the British increasing their exploitation of the region. The Boers struggled to retain control over the land they felt was theirs, land over which they had fought the native Africans of that region. An attack on the British settlement, the Cape Colony, by the Boers in 1899 led to a war that the British expected to end quickly. It is this war that Philip, in *Of Human Bondage*, sees friends such as Hayward leave to fight. The war grew increasingly violent, as the Boers refused to accept defeat. In response to the Boers' use of guerrilla warfare tactics, the British burned Boer farms and gathered Boers into camps, where many died. Protests were staged in Britain over the war by this point. In 1902, a peace treaty between the British and the Boers was negotiated, and the Boers surrendered.

The Onset of World War I

At the time that Maugham completed writing and published *Of Human Bondage* in 1915, World War I had begun just a year earlier. King Edward VII, Victoria's son, had ruled from her death in 1901 until his death in 1910. Edward's son, George V, now ruled England. During this early phase of the war, the British presence in the war was widely supported by the British people. The war effort in fact is thought to have united a nation divided by threatened strikes by an alliance of mine workers, railway workers, and other transportation workers. The British government was also faced with the prospect of civil war in Ireland, a nation at the time still under British rule. Britain entered the war on August 4, 1914, approximately a month after the assassination of the Austrian Archduke Ferdinand in Bosnia. This event is widely regarded as the spark that ignited the war in Europe; it caused a chain reaction of alliances being invoked and the defense of those alliances being put into action. Although the original conflict was between the Austria-Hungarian Empire and Serbia, backed by Russia, other nations quickly became involved. Austria-Hungary had ties to Germany, and France had an alliance with Russia. Great Britain was compelled to come to the aid of France, which was now being attacked by the Germans. Throughout the war, despite the death and suffering endured by British soldiers and the consequent

The Eiffel Tower in Paris, France. Philip goes to Paris and is inspired by the trip. (Image copyright Maugli, 2010. Used under license from Shutterstock.com)

hardships inflicted on British civilians, the British people maintained a steadfast support of their government during this prolonged crisis. According to Kenneth O. Morgan in the 1984 *The Oxford Illustrated History of Britain*, "Available evidence for the war years suggests that the broad mass of the population retained its faith that the war was just and necessary." The war lasted until the signing of the armistice, or peace treaty, in 1918. Maugham's own war experiences inevitably influenced his fiction. In 1914, he volunteered with an ambulance unit in France, and in 1915, he worked as a spy for the British Intelligence Service.

CRITICAL OVERVIEW

When Maugham first published *Of Human Bondage* in 1915, the work was, according to critic Richard A. Cordell, "quietly received." Cordell, in his 1937 review of Maugham's life and work, titled simply *W. Somerset Maugham*, explains that in 1915 (a year after World War I began), Maugham's "grimly realistic and uncompromising novel" did not inspire enthusiasm among English readers. In America, the critical response to the novel was boosted by author and critic Theodore Dreiser's exuberant praise for the work. Excerpts from Dreiser's December 1915 review in the *New Republic*, reprinted in the 1987 *W. Somerset Maugham: The Critical Heritage*, edited by Anthony Curtis and John Whitehead, reveal the high regard that Dreiser had for Maugham's novel. He describes it a work "of the utmost importance," and as "a gorgeous weave, as interesting and valuable at the beginning as at the end." Earlier that same year, however, Gerald Gould of the *New Statesman* took a less than favorable view of the work. In his review, also reprinted in *W. Somerset Maugham: The Critical Heritage*, Gould writes that the novel offers little in the way of technical skill in terms of the novel's construction. Gould faults the work as being devoid of the "sparkling verbal wit" that characterized some of Maugham's other works. It promises much, but delivers little, Gould suggests, stating that the work offered "minuteness without realism, passion without romance, variation without variety." Gould contends that the novel fails in its efforts at realism, capturing minute details without substance. An equally unfavorable 1915 review, reprinted in the same collection and originally published in the *Athenaeum* by an anonymous reviewer, describes the work as "a record of sordid realism."

As Cordell notes, Dreiser's effusive praise "saved the novel from oblivion." Since then, it has come to be regarded as Maugham's masterpiece. Archie K. Loss, in a 1987 study of Maugham's work, states that *Of Human Bondage* is viewed as the author's "finest achievement." Loss, commenting on the novel's autobiographical nature, goes on to explore its plot and characters. In addition, Loss addresses the issue of the novel's realism, which earlier critics had touched on, arguing that although *Of Human Bondage* is "strongly tinged by English realism of the Victorian and Edwardian periods," it is more accurately labeled a work of naturalist fiction. In this type of work, Loss explains, the naturalist writer stresses the lack of agency (power to make their own decisions) his characters have in their own lives. As a naturalist, Maugham emphasizes the hopelessness and

harshness of life, Loss contends. Taking another approach to assessing the novel, L. Brander, in a 1963 study of Maugham's works, *Somerset Maugham: A Guide*, examines the novel's structure. Brander observes that the novel's chapters are told "like a series of vivid and obviously true short stories, without the difficulty of beginning and ending each one." Brander goes on to emphasize the autobiographical nature of the work. Cordell, in his 1961 work *Somerset Maugham: A Writer for All Seasons*, also discusses the way Maugham drew on his own life experiences in the creation of the work. In prefacing his comparison of Maugham's life to the novel's plot, Cordell stresses that although Maugham's own life was an inspiration for the novel, "*Of Human Bondage* is not an autobiography but a novel. The reader must not take a word of it literally."

CRITICISM

Catherine Dominic

Dominic is a novelist and a freelance writer and editor. In the following essay, she explores Philip's perpetual examination of his past and current circumstances in Of Human Bondage, *arguing that the way in which Philip chooses to reframe his life is executed in a manner that enables Philip to avoid ever taking responsibility for his choices and his moral shortcomings. This habit, Dominic maintains, persists throughout the book and into its final pages, calling into question the idea that Philip has undergone significant psychological development.*

In Somerset Maugham's *Of Human Bondage*, Philip is perpetually seeking new experiences, as well as a way to reframe, or recontextualize, his past experiences. Reworking his personal history, Philip tries to find a way to make sense of his past experiences, almost desperate to prove to himself that nothing has been wasted. As the novel progresses, Philip's way of looking at his life seems to become more important to him than the actual events of his life. Eager to avoid acknowledging his own responsibility, Philip finds ways to absolve himself of blame. By the novel's end, despite Philip's persistent reworking of his personal philosophies, he has made little progress. Although he acknowledges that he has spent much of his life looking toward the future without

WHAT DO I READ NEXT?

- *Liza of Lambeth* was Maugham's first novel. Published in 1897, the work is focuses on the Victorian working class. Serenity Press published an edition of the novel in 2008.

- Although Maugham's modern literary reputation rests on novels such as *Of Human Bondage*, he is also an acclaimed author of short stories and plays. His *Collected Stories* was published in 2004 by Everyman's Library.

- While many of Maugham's plays are no longer in print, a few are available in recent editions, published by Metheun in a two-volume set. *Maugham Plays, Volume 1: "Sheppey," "The Sacred Flame," "The Circle," "The Constant Wife," and "Our Betters"* was published in 1997. *Maugham Plays, Volume 2: "For Services Rendered," "The Letter," "Home and Beauty," and "Lady Frederick"* was published in 1999. The plays in these volumes were originally published in the 1920s and 1930s.

- Maugham's novel *The Razor's Edge*, originally published in 1944, is counted with *Of Human Bondage* as a Maugham masterpiece. The work is concerned with an American who embarks upon a journey of self-discovery after the trauma of World War I has ended. A more recent (2003) edition is available from Vintage. The work was transformed into a film in 1946 and again in 1984, with the latter version starring Bill Murray.

- *Daniel Deronda*, published in 1876, was the last published novel by female Victorian author George Eliot. Although Eliot wrote in the earlier portion of the Victorian era, her works, like Maugham's, are realistic in tone and explore the psychological development of her various characters. Like *Of Human Bondage*, *Daniel Deronda* is concerned with Victorian society and its distinct ideas concerning class divisions. Eliot's novel also explores religious traditions, in particular Judaism. A 2000 edition is available through Everyman's Library.

- *Impressionism: Art, Leisure, and Parisian Society*, by Robert L. Herbert, published by Yale University Press in 1991, explores the relationship between the cultural atmosphere in Paris during the last decade of the nineteenth century and the artistic movement of impressionism. The leisurely lifestyle enjoyed by those in the middle and upper classes, such as the lifestyle Philip enjoys in Paris in *Of Human Bondage*, is examined in this work.

- *Four Views on Free Will*, by John Martin Fischer, Robert Kane, Derk Pereboom, and Manuel Vargas, is a collection of essays exploring the philosophical questions that plague Philip throughout *Of Human Bondage*. The essays discuss different views on morality and determinism versus free will philosophical debate. The work was published in 2007 by Wiley-Blackwell.

- *Passing Strange: The Complete Book and Lyrics of the Broadway Musical* is a musical play written by author and composer Stew, published in 2009 by Applause Books. The play, originally staged on Broadway in New York in 2008, takes place in the 1960s. It is the coming-of-age story of an African American musician, who, like Philip in *Of Human Bondage*, sets out for Europe (Amsterdam and Berlin) to study art.

- *A Little Princess*, by Frances Hodgson Burnett, was originally published in a serialized version in 1888 and later revised and published as a novel in 1904. Although it is a children's novel, it has a number of elements in common with *Of Human Bondage*, the early chapters in particular. Both works feature children living in the late Victorian era and deal with class issues, education, and the cruelty experienced by children in boarding school at the hands of other children, as well as British imperialism. An unabridged edition of *A Little Princess* was published in 2004 by Sterling.

> AS THE NOVEL PROGRESSES, PHILIP'S WAY
> OF LOOKING AT HIS LIFE SEEMS TO BECOME MORE
> IMPORTANT TO HIM THAN THE ACTUAL EVENTS OF
> HIS LIFE. EAGER TO AVOID ACKNOWLEDGING HIS
> OWN RESPONSIBILITY, PHILIP FINDS WAYS TO
> ABSOLVE HIMSELF OF BLAME."

focusing on the present, he nevertheless discovers a new way to view his past decisions and embraces a line of thinking that places the responsibility for his own choices on the shoulders of others. Philip's journey is a long one that takes him in circles rather than leading him to a more mature state of mind.

Philip first begins to seriously examine the notion of personal morality and responsibility in his conversations with the American student, Mr. Weeks, while the two young men are living in Heidelberg, Germany. In discussing religious faith, Weeks points out that there is no way of knowing that the truth about one's beliefs is any more accurate than the beliefs of our ancestors, which have since been proved false. Philip is shocked, as the conversation progresses, to hear himself say, "I don't see why one should believe in God at all." This realization regarding the futility of religious faith is a major turning point in Philip's life. From this point on, Philip will continue to question the nature of his beliefs concerning morality, personal choice, and individual responsibility. As he contemplates the matter further, he concludes "he had lost also that burden of responsibility which made every action of his life a matter of urgent consequence." No longer will he pause to wonder whether an act or a thought is an offense to God. He vows to be responsible only to himself.

After returning from Paris, Philip is forced by his uncle to account for his time in Paris. Uncle William asserts that, since Philip was unsuccessful in his pursuit of a career as an artist and must now find another way to support himself, surely Philip must agree that Paris had been a waste of time. Philip responds flippantly that he "had a very jolly two years," but privately he

considers the matter further. Thinking back to his rejection of Christianity, Philip realizes that at the time he clung to the moral teachings of the Church, even though he had embraced atheism. After his time in Paris, however, he has reached a new conclusion, that he will no longer content himself to accept society's view of morality. He rejects society's prejudices about what constitutes good and evil, "with the idea of finding out the rules of life for himself." Now, he feels "at last absolutely free."

While in Paris, Philip was exposed by Cronshaw to the idea of determinism, the notion that free will—the ability to make one's own choices—is an illusion. As Cronshaw tells Philip, "I act as though I were a free agent. But when an action is performed it is clear that all the forces of the universe from all eternity conspired to cause it, and nothing I could do could have prevented it." Philip does not embrace this philosophy at the time, and until he meets Mildred, Philip remains convinced that he is "absolutely free." However, Philip's obsession with Mildred causes him to feel as though "he had been seized by some strange force that moved him against his will." Up to this point, Philip has repeatedly reshaped his views regarding the parameters of morality, first rejecting the boundaries enforced by Christianity and then the moral codes of society. In doing so, he broadens his own notion of personal freedom and crafts a notion of individual morality by which he avoids judging himself too harshly. When he falls for Mildred, Philip gives up the idea that he has any choice at all, a notion, like Cronshaw's, that also absolves him of any responsibility or blame for his behavior. If he has not chosen to act, but been acted upon, he cannot be blamed for any of his actions. After Mildred has rejected Philip in order to be with Emil Miller, Philip looks back on the way he pursued her despite her decidedly cruel treatment of him. Rather than admit with shame that he behaved foolishly, Philip blames Mildred "because she had submitted him to so much humiliation." He continues to insert himself in her life when he knows she is seeing other men, and he knowingly allows himself to be used by Mildred. However, he accepts no responsibility for his own choices or the consequences of those choices, namely his misery and his drastically reduced wealth. In discussing the notion of free will with Macalister later, Philip recalls his so-called powerlessness where Mildred had been concerned. He repeats Cronshaw's lesson in determinism, voicing to Macalister Cronshaw's arguments about the forces of the universe conspiring to cause things to happen to him. Philip has now apparently accepted the belief that these "forces of the universe" craft his life and that his own decision-making plays no role in the events of his life.

Following the breakup of his relationship with Mildred, Philip becomes involved with Norah, with whom he seems happy, at least until Mildred appears once again. This time, Mildred needs him, and Philip is only too happy to spend his diminishing savings to help the pregnant and abandoned Mildred. He reshapes his feelings toward Norah, transforming his former affection to disgust in his own mind. Unwilling to endure the experience of telling Norah the truth about the change in his feelings, Philip avoids Norah and lies to her. He begins to feel angry with *her*, rather than himself, because he has had such an intimate relationship with her. Lying to avoid spending time with Norah so that he can be with Mildred, Philip is "angry with Norah, because she forced him to vulgar and degrading shifts." He actually blames Norah for his own act of deception. He is frustrated "that she should force him to tell lies." After Philip finally tells Norah the truth and has endured her grief, he begins to suspect he might bear some personal responsibility for her pain, but he immediately changes his mind and chooses to not blame himself. Philip "was inclined to reproach himself. But why? He did not know what else he could have done." Again Philip convinces himself he had no choice but to act in the way he has.

Once the intensity of all he has endured with Mildred subsides and Philip carries on with his life, he begins to struggle with the philosophy he has created for himself. He has become friendly with the Athelny family; thinking about why he is so drawn to them, Philip can only conclude that it is because of their goodness. However, he resists this notion because has long ago discarded the notion that anything can be described as good or evil. All that exists are the illusion of free will and the forces of the universe. In Philip's mind, he could not be praised for a good act, nor should he be punished for an evil one, for without choice, notions such as good and evil did not

exist. He thinks, "If morality were no more than a matter of convenience good and evil had no meaning." In the Athelnys, though, he sees "simple goodness, natural and without effort, and he [thinks] it beautiful." This crack in the shell of Philip's philosophy widens, when, as his fortune continues to change, he finds himself facing extreme poverty. He considers his life, shaping his memories in such a way as to find himself blameless, and wonders why he is experiencing suffering he does not deserve. He believes he "had helped people when he could" and that "it seemed horribly unjust" that he should be reduced to such circumstances. Philip, through this line of thought, has nearly returned to his Christian upbringing and notions of good people being rewarded and bad people being forced to suffer because of their sin. He feels that he has been good and does not deserve to suffer as if he were evil. At such a low point in his life, Philip finds it difficult to uphold the notion that good and evil do not exist, for he would like to think of himself as good, and worthy of more than what he currently is enduring. He wants to be praised, not punished, but he still does not acknowledge the suffering he has caused. He still views himself as blameless.

After the deaths of Cronshaw and Hayward, when Philip's own fortunes have changed only slightly (he is now at least employed), Philip once again reframes his past in order to view his life in a way that is acceptable to him. Just as he felt the need to convince his uncle, and himself, that Paris had not been wasted, Philip now begins to consider the notion that life itself has no meaning. Rather than shuddering under the weight of this bleak outlook, Philip feels a sense of peace. Again he feels free of "the last burden of responsibility." No longer does he have to feel as though he has failed for not achieving success and happiness; it is irrelevant. All sense of responsibility has evaporated, and Philip now chooses to view life only as a pattern that may be appreciated for the beauty created by the "accidents of his existence."

Later, after his uncle's death, Philip calls to mind this new philosophy he has embraced, that in which he viewed "the unhappiness he had suffered [as] no more than part of a decoration which was elaborate and beautiful." He reminds himself "strenuously" to accept everything with pleasure, for it enriches the design of his life.

However, as he watches children playing in the courtyard of his old school, he is able to see the beauty in front of him only "with his eyes." The phrase suggests that Philip does not feel the truth of what he longs to believe, that joy and sorrow weave the patterns of his life and that by appreciating the beauty of such elaboration, his life retains the only meaning possible. Philip struggles with the notion that this is enough, that this view of his life, his past, is sufficient to sustain him. During the final chapters of the novel, he continues to attempt to embrace this view, and he succeeds in appreciating the moments of beauty and happiness he feels. As always, though, he longs for the next part of his life. First Germany, then Paris, and then his study of medicine and life as a student in London were all objects of his desire. Now, Philip looks forward to traveling again, to Spain, and working as a doctor there. Sally's possible pregnancy forces Philip to consider a new future, one embracing domestic life in a medical practice in a coastal village. He finds he still wants to pursue this future, even upon finding out that Sally is not pregnant.

At this point, as Philip seeks to justify choosing one future over another, choosing Sally over Spain, a final reshaping of his past is set into motion. Philip continues, as he has done throughout the novel, to escape responsibility for his past. Now he feels that throughout his whole life he has embraced the ideals, the philosophies, of other people, "and never the desires of his own heart." He now claims that he was always moved to do "what he thought he should do" but that he was never influenced "by what he wanted with his whole soul to do." Philip somehow feels that in order to feel justified in marrying Sally and turning his back on Spain, he must put his past into a fresh context, a context in which he bears no responsibility for the choices he made. In this new version of the past, Philip never pursued his own desires. His ideas about what he wanted to do—travel to Germany, to France, his decision to become a doctor—he had arrived at as a result of the undue influence of other people.

Philip seems to be blaming other people for preventing him from chasing his own dreams, from pursuing "what he wanted with his whole soul to do." What Philip cannot seem to come to terms with is the fact that he has never even *known* a thing he has wanted with his whole soul. He seems ashamed to admit that after all his varied experiences, he has not yet figured out

In the story, Philip goes back to medical school.
(Image copyright barbaradudzinska, 2010. Used under license from Shutterstock.com)

what he has wanted. Rather than accepting that his experiences have actually been his journey toward finding out who he truly is and what he truly wants, Philip blames others for preventing him from getting what he wants. Philip is now certain that what he wants to do with his whole soul is marry Sally and have a family with her. In the final scene of the novel, Philip has looked back on his life and has failed to acknowledge that he has made errors in judgment, that he bears responsibility in the suffering he has endured and the suffering he has caused. He enters into a future with Sally with a clear conscience, not because he has made peace with the past but because he has placed any blame for the events in his life on others. As always, Philip hurries into the future, leaving the errors of his past resting on the shoulders of anyone but himself.

Source: Catherine Dominic, Critical Essay on *Of Human Bondage*, in *Novels for Students*, Gale, Cengage Learning, 2011.

Jack Matthews

In the following article, Matthews explains that movie remakes of Of Human Bondage *have failed because, like the hero of the movie, filmmakers would rather take their chances with the familiar than with something new.*

Hollywood's long tradition of remakes, brought to our attention by such recent efforts as "Red Dragon," "Swept Away," and "The Truth About Charlie," reminds me of the obsession at the center of Somerset Maugham's *Of Human Bondage*—a novel that was made into a movie several times itself.

Of Human Bondage is the story of an intelligent, genteel, well-educated man whose search for his place in society is derailed by his obsession with a low-born woman who takes from him and gives mostly pain in return. On occasion, she makes him happy; mostly, she rejects and humiliates him.

Filmmakers who attempt remakes face the same odds. They can hope, but the odds favor them having their hearts broken.

Brett Ratner has not had that experience with "*Red Dragon*," a remake of Michael Mann's 1986 "*Manhunter*." Ratner's film was a commercial slam-dunk. Mann's, though far better, did little business, and since 1986, its key figure—Hannibal Lecter—has become an international icon: the serial killer as rock star. Since Anthony Hopkins made him immortal in "*The Silence of the Lambs*," and did an appreciated encore in "*Hannibal*," it would have been foolish for the rights-holders to Thomas Harris' three Lecter books not to remake the first one with Sir Tony replacing the underappreciated Brian Cox.

Jonathan Demme's "*The Truth About Charlie*," a remake of Stanley Donen's 1963 "*Charade*," is a predictable failure. Whatever Demme's interest in that dated, period-specific international thriller, his pursuit of a remake seems foolhardy. *Charade's* appeal, in 1963 and today, is the made-in-heaven, one-time-only casting of Cary Grant, at the peak of his middle-age charm, opposite Audrey Hepburn at her most beguiling. It was the kind of matchup moviegoers virtually demanded in those declining days of the studio system, and swooned over when they got them.

Mark Wahlberg and Thandie Newton are in for Grant and Hepburn in the remake and all I can say is, it's a pairing that never would have occurred to me. I've heard that Demme originally wanted Will Smith in the Grant role of a mysterious U.S. businessman in Paris, and I can at least see the appeal of that. Smith does have an air of insouciance about him, and clearly has the looks and presence of a leading man. Wahlberg has neither. You might say he peaked in another remake, as the astronaut rebelling against primates in last year's "*Planet of the Apes.*"

Guy Ritchie's remake of *Swept Away* is a simple vanity production. It's almost admirable that Ritchie believed that by casting his wife, Madonna, he could make a good movie from a dated Italian cult film about a peasant sailor and a wealthy socialite stranded on an island. To anyone not in love with Madonna, it seemed futile from the start.

The reasoning behind so many remakes defies common sense. The 1967 comedy "*Bedazzled*," another Stanley Donen film, was made and succeeded because of the chemistry between Peter Cook, who played a con man Devil, and Dudley Moore, as a suicidal shlub who trades his soul for seven wishes, and bungles them. At the time, Cook and Moore were a fabulously popular comedy team whose shtick informed their screen characters.

Remaking the movie in 2000 with the amiable but limited Brendan Fraser in for Moore and the pretty but seriously limited Elizabeth Hurley in for Cook was a miscalculation that would have taken more than seven wishes to overcome.

Critics often complain about American remakes of foreign films, but I find most of them at least logically motivated. Most Americans won't watch a foreign film no matter how original or accessible its story, and the remake at least starts out with that story. Adrian Lyne's compelling "*Unfaithful*," starring Diane Lane and Richard Gere, is a remake of French director Claude Chabrol's 1969 *La Femme Infidele* and it works fine. So does Christopher Nolan's "*Insomnia*," a remake—with Al Pacino and Robin Williams—of a 1997 Norwegian thriller that featured only one actor, Stellan Skarsgard, who is known to American audiences.

Sometimes, remakes are justified because of advancing technology: David Cronenberg's 1986 *The Fly* was a brilliantly reimagined version of the 1958 horror classic about a scientist who accidentally trades body parts with a housefly. Sometimes, they're useful as a vehicle for a star:

Eddie Murphy has done well by remakes of and sequels to *Doctor Dolittle* and *The Nutty Professor*. And sometimes, they have marketing potential too good to pass up: Steven Soderbergh's all-star remake of the 1960 Rat Pack romp *Ocean's Eleven* was like stealing money.

But mostly, they are traps for lazy filmmakers who, like the hero in "*Of Human Bondage*," would rather take their chances with something familiar than with something new.

Source: Jack Matthews, "Most Movie Remakes Fail Because They Lack Brilliance of the Originals," in *Daily News* (New York), November 7, 2002.

Archie K. Loss

In the following excerpt, Loss illustrates the concept of bildungsroman, or character development, as a thematic pattern of Maugham's Of Human Bondage *and points out the maturity of Philip's character through the chronology of the bondage to Philip's "point of grace."*

Implicit in the concept of the bildungsroman is the idea of growth. It is not enough that the main character should simply experience a succession of adventures or suffer from the pangs of unrequited love; he must grow in understanding and sense of responsibility as a result of his adventures or loves. In the broadest sense, that is what the bildungsroman is about: following the main character to the point at which he is ready to assume responsibility for his life.

Of Human Bondage follows this pattern. It begins with the death of Philip's mother when he is a boy of ten and ends with Philip in his late twenties, his medical training complete, ready to assume adult responsibilities, his bride-to-be by his side. Thematically, it shows the growth of Philip's sense of reality, of his ability to distinguish what is true from what is false in the world around him and in his innermost being. It is only when Philip is able to reconcile to some extent the contradictions he perceives in himself and in the world that the novel achieves its end. To reach that goal, Maugham develops two major themes.

The first of these centers on the idea of bondage. Philip's relationship with Mildred is the primary vehicle for the development of this theme. Philip's bondage to Mildred is both physical and emotional—physical in the sense that he needs to have her by his side or be with her even if she doesn't want him around, emotional in the sense that whether he is with her or not she

> AS INTERESTING AS SUCH CONNECTIONS ARE, HOWEVER, *OF HUMAN BONDAGE* MUST ULTIMATELY BE JUDGED ON ITS OWN MERITS AS A NOVEL; WORKS OF ART ARE INDEPENDENT OF THE LIVES OF THEIR CREATORS, NO MATTER HOW CLOSELY THEY ARE ALLIED."

dominates his thoughts and actions as if she were actually there. From the beginning of their relationship, when Philip finds he cannot keep himself from going back to the tearoom where she works as a waitress, till the penultimate episode in their career, when Mildred, having had an affair with Griffiths, leaves Philip with the hated epithet "cripple," his feelings are the same.

Even after Philip realizes (fairly early in the relationship) that his attraction to Mildred is sick, he is still bound to her. Philip never has sexual relations with Mildred, yet he wants to assume the role of provider to her and father to her baby. In the terms of psychopathology, Philip is both a masochist and a voyeur. As a masochist, he needs to suffer to justify a love relationship. As a voyeur, he enjoys creating an opportunity for Mildred to have pleasure with another man. Even the love of a woman who genuinely cares for him—Norah Nesbitt—is not enough to change the pattern of his behavior. Before that can change, he has to hit bottom emotionally and economically.

The bondage theme also appears in relationship to other characters. Philip's Aunt Louisa lives in bondage to his Uncle William, the Vicar of [Blackstable]. Catering to his every whim, denying herself things she needs, Louisa is almost a parody of the wife as doormat so common to Victorian fiction. Hayward, Philip's friend from Heidelberg days, lives in bondage to a false ideal: an aesthetic view of life that prevents him from acting. He is the eternal dilettante, fluttering like a butterfly from flower to flower. Fanny Price, whose devotion to art is so misplaced and whose failure provides such a lesson to Philip in his Paris years, lives in bondage to an ideal she can never realize. Foinet's advice, savage as it is, is right: she is no artist, and chooses suicide over admitting the truth of his judgment. Cronshaw, another Paris friend who greatly influences Philip's view of the world, is in bondage to alcohol and a way of life that will ultimately destroy him. Cronshaw shows the dark side of the Bohemian life that appealed to Philip so much in his reading. These characters and others illustrate the pervasiveness of the bondage theme.

At the same time Philip puts himself into a state of bondage, however, he seeks independence. At King's School, he will not agree to try for an Oxford scholarship despite his admiration for the headmaster, Perkins, because he does not want to be ordained. Time and time again, in decisions about his studies and career, he asserts his independence from his uncle, who despairs of exerting any influence over him. Philip ultimately chooses medicine as his profession, much as he had tried art, because he believes it will give him the freedom he needs to survive. At the end of the novel, on the other hand, he almost decides against marriage because he is afraid it will limit his horizons and keep him from doing what he wants.

In describing Philip's ruminations on the subjects of marriage and personal freedom, Maugham makes use of the phrase "a more troubling grace." It occurs late in the novel, in chapter CVI, after Mildred has left Philip for the last time and he has come under the hedonistic influence of Thorpe Athelny. Running through the novel as a metaphor of Philip's frequent confusion of purpose is the image of a Persian carpet, first suggested to him in Paris by Cronshaw. In such a carpet, Cronshaw suggests, one might find the meaning of life. Philip, pondering his fate, thinks of that carpet again:

> In the vast warp of life..., with the background to his fancies that there was no meaning and that nothing was important, a man might get a personal satisfaction in selecting the various strands that worked out the pattern. There was one pattern, the most obvious, perfect, and beautiful, in which a man was born, grew to manhood, married, produced children, toiled for his bread, and died; but there were others, intricate and wonderful, in which happiness did not enter and in which success was not attempted; and in them might be discovered a more troubling grace. (524–25)

The "more troubling grace" of Philip's thoughts suggests at least a halfway point between the bondage of his relationship to Mildred and the ideal of a relationship, like the Athelnys', in which a lifetime is spent with a single partner. Like that ideal, Philip's more troubled grace is also an alternative of sorts to the absolute meaninglessness of life to which he has by now assented, after the death of Cronshaw and his friend Hayward ("There was no meaning in life, and man by living served no end. It was immaterial whether he was born or not born, whether he lived or ceased to live. Life was insignificant and death without consequence" [524].) Instead of the bleak prospect of a life totally without meaning, Philip can envision at least some figure in the carpet, "intricate and wonderful, in which happiness did not enter and success was not attempted."

Given these thoughts of Philip's, is it reasonable for him to choose the pattern that is "the most obvious, perfect, and beautiful, in which a man . . . married, produced children, toiled for his bread, and died," especially since he has made other plans and Sally is in fact not pregnant? In other words, is the ending of the novel honest? Or is Maugham pandering to his reading audience, giving it what he thinks it wants rather than what, logically, it should have? Every reader has to make his or her own decision on this matter.

Inevitably, in reaching that decision, the reader will be influenced by what he or she knows about Maugham's own attitudes toward marriage, love, and life. *Of Human Bondage* is an autobiographical novel: "fact and fiction are inextricably mingled," Maugham wrote in his foreword; "the emotions are my own, but not all of the incidents are related as they happened, and some of them are transferred to my hero not from my own life but from that of persons with whom I was intimate" (7). But to what extent does Philip Carey constitute Maugham's *alter ego*?

In terms of his physical characteristics and psychology, Philip is remarkably similar to his creator, though some details may have been altered. To cite only one example, Maugham suffered from a stammer that made ordinary spoken communication extremely difficult for him, especially when he was a child. In Philip's character, that difficulty is transformed into a clubfoot that makes him self-conscious and the butt of jokes at school.

Other matters can be addressed more readily now that a definitive biography of Maugham has appeared, with Ted Morgan's *Maugham* (1980). Morgan had access to materials that

Maugham did not wish his executors to make available to anyone, and he also had the advantage of researching and writing his biography at a time when many of Maugham's friends and colleagues were still alive. His book illuminates many characters and scenes from *Of Human Bondage* and helps to shed light on some of the novel's more ambiguous passages. It also helps the reader to establish the chronology of events in the novel as compared with those of Maugham's life.

. . . For many characters other than Philip, it is apparent that Maugham drew directly from his own experience. Uncle William and Aunt Louisa, for example, are precise portraits of Maugham's real-life uncle and aunt. Equally precise, apparently, is the portrait of Etheridge Hayward, based on Ellingham Brooks, whom Maugham actually met in Heidelberg. For other characters, however, there is no key. Most notable among these, the model for Mildred remains unknown. One can imagine that in creating characters as in describing events Maugham employed the freedom he suggests in his foreword, in some cases perhaps for reasons that had nothing to do with aesthetics.

In terms of chronology, the novel follows Maugham's early life fairly closely, though certain events are transposed or omitted, creating gaps of several years. In the novel, Philip's father is already dead by the time his mother dies. Philip becomes an orphan on his way to the vicarage at [Blackstable] within a few pages of the opening of the book. In real life, Maugham's father outlived his mother by several years. Maugham's mother died in 1882 (in Paris, not London), his father in 1884; in the novel, Philip's mother dies in 1885.

Another difference occurs later in the novel, when Philip decides to study art in Paris. Although artists were to occupy Maugham's attention in more than one story, he was never an art student and did not live in Paris during the corresponding period of his life. At the time Philip is in Paris, the young Maugham was already a medical student in London. Maugham did spend a year-and-a-half in Heidelberg, but, on the other hand, only one month studying accounting as compared with Philip's year.

As interesting as such connections are, however, *Of Human Bondage* must ultimately be judged on its own merits as a novel; works of art are independent of the lives of their creators, no matter how closely they are allied. In the

pages that follow, we will read the novel as a work of fiction with the major themes of bondage and troubled grace. If to some extent this reading repeats the events of the story, it should be kept in mind that any treatment of a novel so heavily chronological, built out of a series of incidents in the life of its main character, must itself be chronological and summary. Let us hope, however, that out of such a review will emerge the generalizations important to a critical judgment of the novel. Let us hope, too, that this reading will improve the enjoyment of the novel for a generation of readers now more than eight decades removed from the characters and events it describes.

Source: Archie K. Loss, "Major Themes: Bondage and Troubled Grace," in *"Of Human Bondage": Coming of Age in the Novel*, Twayne Publishers, 1990, pp. 15–20.

Forrest D. Burt

In the following excerpt, Burt contends that the persona of Maugham's writing reflects the personality and lifestyle of the man himself.

. . . At the age of sixty-four Maugham published the statement that although few writers achieve immortality through their works, any writer would consider it pleasant to think that "one may be read with interest by a few generations and find a place, however small, in the history of one's country's literature" (*SU*, 11). Of course, Maugham has been "read with interest" by several generations in not only his own country but in many countries and many languages, is still read with interest, and has a secure position in English literature. But of more importance is the fact that in this statement Maugham expresses "interest in the interest of others." Clearly Maugham here sees the meaning of life as contribution to others.

Since "interest" involves "value" (i.e., one places value upon that in which he or she is interested), social interest serves as a "guiding cognitive structure by which decisions are made." In other words, "the function of social interest is to direct the striving toward the useful side." By useful, Adler means "in the interest of mankind generally." And ultimately it is this criterion of usefulness versus uselessness (i.e., the consequence of what the individual does, more than what the individual says) that is the most dependable measure of his social interest: "Since the value of any activity is to be judged by its usefulness to all mankind, whatever may have been included under social interest, self-actualization and growth, are also subject to this stipulation." With this criterion, then, Adler allows even the highly unique individual his place in a creative, ideal society. By extending this concept of social interest into the future, one is able to see that the independent spirit not only has a place, but is the "ideally normal man." "The criterion of social usefulness, however, is applicable to nonconformity as it is to any other behavior. The question is whether the nonconformity is ultimately socially useful, in the interest of mankind, or valuable to mankind, or whether it is merely a rebelling for personal reasons."

After viewing the self-interested young Maugham in the early Philip, one must wonder how, in what way, and at what point he gained this interest in others. The theme of the novel concerns Philip's quest for a philosophy of life, a meaning to life, a freedom from human bondage, or bondage to passion. Maugham took the title from Spinoza's *Ethics*. He was attracted to Spinoza's statement that experience is only valuable when through our imagination and reason we are able to turn it into foresight, thereby shaping our future and freeing ourselves from the past; submitting to passion is human bondage, exercising reason is human liberty.

With this theme Maugham invents characters whom Philip observes to be in one way or another bound by passion. Philip's helpless bondage to Mildred is the epitome of human bondage for this protagonist. His friend Cronshaw gives him a Persian carpet which he says holds the meaning of life, but each individual must perceive it himself. The climax of the novel comes in a moving scene with Philip in the British Museum. Immediately before, he has been told of a friend's death. Seated before some Athenian tombstones in the museum, Philip feels the influence of the place descend upon him. All the figures on the tombstones seem to be saying "farewell"—"that, and nothing more." It is then that he begins to question again the meaning of life, for which he has searched so long. Thinking of Cronshaw, Philip remembers the Persian rug that he had given him and Cronshaw's claim that it offered the meaning of life. Sitting there, Philip is suddenly struck by the conclusion, the answer to the puzzle: life has no meaning.

Although Maugham the person reports no experience so specific as this, he did reach the same reconciliation early in his life. In this quite existential resolution he found a purpose and

meaning for life, a meaning in no meaning. His relations with others thereafter took on a special significance. No longer did he search aimlessly with the explicit purpose of expecting others to give him the meaning to life, but he now had an interest for the sake of giving meaning through his art, seeing now the meaning of life as contribution: "I have been attached, deeply attached, to few people; but I have been interested in men in general not for their own sakes, but for the sake of my work" (*SU*, 7–8).

This view is strikingly similar to that of Hans Vaihinger, a Kantian scholar at the University of Vienna, who influenced Adler: "It is senseless to question the meaning of the universe, and this is the idea expressed in Schiller's words: 'Know this, a mind sublime puts greatness into life, yet seeks it not therein.'"

Any consideration of Maugham's social interest must therefore center around the contribution he made through his works—what he put into life. Throughout his life he remained somewhat aloof, introverted, and more of an observer than a participant. The areas of friendship and marriage were clearly subordinated to that of work. It was here that he gave most valuably. Although he used his handicaps as excuses for withdrawing, he did extend his own sensitivity to include others. Combining this and skill in writing, probably compensatory for his stammering, with his zest for working—consciously or unconsciously a striving to concretize his own worth as an individual—he succeeded in making a significant contribution to his fellow human beings.

Maugham, like most writers, was not fully aware, of course, of the contribution he was making through his writings. That is, his attention was upon his work—creating emotions, characters, plots that are faithful, harmonious, and plausible—less than upon the audience and any contribution he may have been making. Often serving as a critic, rather than a supporter of present-day society, Maugham held the weaknesses and shortcomings of society and individuals up for exposure, even ridicule, often for laughter. Occasionally he was even cynical, but stopped short of being a reformer. But the important point here is that his contribution was often one of finding weaknesses and faults in today's world. Above all, though, Maugham gave pleasure and entertained his audience. This, he maintained, was the highest purpose of art.

The Maugham persona certainly varies from work to work. And the dramatized narrator-persona of the first-person narratives becomes a compensation for him, as Calder observes: "a representation of the kind of person he would like to be."

There is a striking similarity between the persona of the first published short story in 1898 and the persona of *The Razor's Edge*, published in 1944. And there is a striking similarity between the goals and values of the Maugham persona in all his works and the goals and values of Maugham, the writer—the man Somerset Maugham.

If the persona is only a literary mask, then it is such a mask, that, when removed, is found to be similar to the face. Essentially, the persona of *The Summing Up*, of the novels and short stories, as well as his letters—the guiding sympathy in the plays—are all rooted in the personality and life-style of Maugham. And the distinctive feature of this persona is its capacity for social interest.

Source: Forrest D. Burt, "Pattern of Life," in *W. Somerset Maugham*, Twayne Publishers, 1986, pp. 34–37.

William French

In the following article, French observes that despite his critics, Maugham's novels have not been forgotten.

Somerset Maugham's popularity has outlived his critics, and there's a lesson there somewhere. Here we are, 104 years after Maugham's birth (and 12 years after his death) and his novels and short stories are still being read while the books of many other writers of his generation, usually considered more important than Maugham, have all but been forgotten. A revival of his 1921 play, *The Circle*, recently spent a jaunty five weeks at the Royal Alexandra after a successful London run. The detractors who twitted him for lack of intellectual ballast, Edmund Wilson chief among them, are no longer around to scoff, not that it would have made any difference. The lesson that Maugham reaffirmed is that a good storyteller will never lack an audience.

While Maugham was a natural teller of tales who drew heavily on what he actually observed and on people he knew, he had a seemingly effortless knack of knowing how to please the public. As Anthony Curtis points out in this book, Maugham could find a good story anywhere, at any time.

He could sense a story in someone he sat opposite at dinner before he or she had hardly opened his mouth, writes Curtis, a London literary critic. Often the stories seemed to seek him out, to land ready-made in his lap in their finished form.

A case in point is Maugham's most famous short story, Miss Thompson, also known as Rain. The actual events occurred almost as Maugham described them, during a trip to the Far East in 1916, when he was tracking down the story of Gauguin for the novel that became *The Moon And Sixpence*. He didn't even bother to change the heroine's real name, which was Thompson.

There is more to writing fiction than mere reporting, of course, and Curtis gives Maugham credit for rigorous selection of details, scupulous editing, and arranging events into dramatic confrontation and resolution. And he managed to use the kind of precise and unaffected prose that he admired in de Maupassant but was not common in Victorian England.

Curtis' book is not conventional biography, although its main elements are biographical. What he attempts is to examine Maugham's life to find the sources of his fiction, so that we'll know where the fact ends and the fiction begins. It's an easier job with Maugham than with most writers, although not an entirely rewarding pursuit. And Curtis tries to find the sources of Maugham's talent, again an easier job with him than with more complex authors.

The first of the major motivations is transparent enough. As a 10-year-old orphan, Maugham was sent to live in rural England with an uncle who was a dour clergyman and his wife. Curtis argues that this trauma, after growing up amid the excitements of Paris, with the security of his parents, caused the stammer than afflicted Maugham the rest of his life. Its effect on the child was to prevent his speech from keeping up with the precocious rapidity of his mind, writes Curtis. There could hardly be a stronger stimulus to turn to writing as a source of self-expression than this.

Maugham of course transformed the stammer into a club foot in *Of Human Bondage*, and drew heavily on his uncle and his teachers. He borrowed other characters too, including the Canadian artist J. W. Mortice, on whom one of the minor characters was based. Maugham had met him socially in London.

Maugham himself said his five years in medical school was the best possible training for a writer for the insights it offered into human behavior. But a streak of malice was a strong motivation, too. In *Cakes And Ale*, for example, there was double revenge. The promiscuous Rosie was clearly based on the girl with whom Maugham had an affair for eight years before she rejected his marriage proposal. And he was revenging himself on the literary salons of London for spurning him for the likes of Hugh Walpole, who was ruthlessly satirized in the character of Alroy Kear.

This is a curious book, in some ways, a hybrid, all tarted up with glossy photos of Maugham at various stages of his long life and of everyone who crossed his path. Curtis is sympathetic, even defensive, in his treatment of Maugham, and supports him against the critics. He is most discreet in dealing with his homosexuality and his relationship with his longtime secretary and companion, Gerald Haxton. He agrees that Maugham was increasingly bitter and vindictive as he got older, but seems to suggest that he was mentally unbalanced when he vigorously attacked his ex-wife Syrie in his autobiography, which was serialized in *The Sunday Express* but has not been published in book form.

But in the end, Curtis' judgment seems sound. He admits that a good deal of what Maugham wrote, particularly the early plays, deserves the obscurity that has overtaken them. I think we would all agree that he was certainly not great in the sense that Henry James and Proust and Tolstoy are, he writes. Maugham does occupy the middle ground. He occupies it more brilliantly perhaps than it has ever been occupied before. And then he spoils his summation with this curious defensiveness: But then does one always wish to be living on the heights? The higher up you go the further away you get from the common universal concerns of men and women. Maugham understood how to dramatize those concerns in such a way as to be readily comprehended by many people not normally attracted by literature, as well as those who are.

And Maugham, he might have added, had the kind of life that would make a good subject for a novel.

Source: William French, "Maugham: A Good Storyteller Always Has an Audience," in *Globe and Mail* (Toronto, Ontario, Canada), January 19, 1978.

Robert Spence

In the following excerpt, Spence traces the novel's rise in popularity and notes the critics' role in the novel's emergence as a classic.

W. Somerset Maugham has been one of the most prolific writers of our time. However, of the

> 'MAUGHAM,' SAID MAIS, 'OUGHT TO BE ONE OF THE MOST FORMATIVE INFLUENCES OF THE PRESENT DAY. THERE IS CERTAINLY NO ONE WHO COULD EXERT SUCH A HEALTHY RESTRAINT ON THE YOUNG WRITER WHO FEARS TO FACE THE TRUTH.'"

more than fifty books which he has published—novels and volumes of plays, short stories, essays, and travel sketches—only *Of Human Bondage* has won the full admiration of serious, reputable critics. Although they tend to disregard Maugham's other work, they have been generally consistent in their praise of this autobiographical novel, comparing it with *David Copperfield* and *Tom Jones*. *Of Human Bondage* has been, in addition, enormously popular with the general reading public. It is, in the opinion of Theodore Spencer [in "Somerset Maugham," *College English* (October 1940)], "probably the most universally read and admired of modern English novels."

In view of the wide acclaim which has been accorded Maugham's masterpiece, it is of interest to notice that the book was not at first a success, either with the critics or the public. Indeed, success came tardily to *Of Human Bondage*, though it was not ephemeral. In this paper I shall endeavor to trace briefly the history of the reception of the novel, and to suggest what seem to have been some fundamental factors underlying its rise from temporary oblivion to a position in the first rank of modern English novels.

Maugham tells us [in *Of Human Bondage, with a Digression on the Art of Fiction*, 1946] that the book

> ... was published in England [and America] in 1915 and was well enough reviewed. But we were engaged in a war and people had more important things to occupy themselves with than the characters of a work of fiction. There had been besides a spate of semi-biographical novels and the public was a trifle tired of them. My book was not a failure, nor was it a success.

Evidence corroborates the suggestion that the book was not an immediate success. British reviewers in *The Tatler*, *The Westminster Gazette*, *The Nation*, and *Punch* all considered it perfunctorily, while others were generally critical. *The Satur-day Review* (September 4, 1915) objected to the evident relish of the author in depicting the sordid aspects of life. *The Athenaeum* (August 21, 1915) commented:

> The values accorded by the hero to love, realism, and religion are so distorted as to have no interest beyond that which belongs to an essentially morbid personality. In such a long novel reiteration is peculiarly tiresome and apt to reduce the gratitude which should be felt for the detailed portraiture and varied aspects of life the author presents to us.

... And *The Times* commented:

> The vivisection is at times a little too minute, the small incidents rather over elaborated, and there are certain episodes ... which seem both repulsive and superfluous. Nevertheless, Mr. Maugham has done a big piece of work.

The majority of the American reviews, however, reveal a reaction to the novel comparable to that of the British critics, and similarly proscribe the book. The critic for *The Dial* (September 16, 1915) wrote:

> When a novelist thus sets out to chronicle *everything* about his hero's life, he can hardly fail to leave us with the feeling of intimate acquaintance. But he can easily miss, as Mr. Maugham does, the broad effects and the larger issues of a human characterization. The only thing of this sort that we get from *Of Human Bondage* is a most depressing impression of the futility of life ...

... In view of this widespread denunciation by critics in 1915, and the novel's subsequent half-dozen years of dormancy, it is surprising to learn that in 1923 the George H. Doran Company classed it with works in continual demand, and that a commentator [Marcus Aurelius Goodrich] in *The New York Times Book Review* stated in 1925 that "*Of Human Bondage* has become a classic." There are probably several reasons for the new interest American readers showed in the novel during the twenties. Perhaps there was something in the story of Philip Carey which appealed to the psychology of what Franklin Roosevelt called "the apparently soulless decade which followed World War." Or possibly it was, as has been claimed by Richard Cordell and Stuart P. B. Mais, the publication in 1919 of *The Moon and Sixpence* which drew attention to the earlier "neglected" novel. Maugham has suggested, however, what appears to be a chief factor behind the success of his masterpiece. "It failed to do well," he says [in an interview in *The New York Times Book*

Review (21 April 1946)], "until, in the twenties, a number of your columnists picked it up and began to talk about it." [In an endnote, Spence adds: "I do not mean to intimate that the basic reason for the success of *Of Human Bondage* was the favorable comment of certain columnists and critics. Their function was to call attention to what previously had been considered a mediocre novel. Possibly the book's popularity with the public is due in part to Maugham's skeptical world view. Readers who experienced the feelings of despair, of frustration, and of the aridity of life subsequent to World War I perhaps found—with Philip Carey—a satisfactory solution to the problems of human existence in skepticism and iconoclasm."] He reiterated the statement when he presented the manuscript of the novel to the Library of Congress in April, 1946. *Of Human Bondage* was, after publication, apparently forgotten.

... Between 1917 and 1925, roughly, a number of columnists and critics did give much attention to Maugham and to *Of Human Bondage*. Early stirrings of interest, given impetus by what appears to have been a "Maugham cult," led ultimately to wide enthusiasm. Adams, who stated in a recent letter to this writer that he often alluded to *Of Human Bondage*, praised the novel in print as early as March 10, 1917. In his column in *The New York Tribune* under that date appeared this comment: "Home and finished reading Mr. Maugham's *Of Human Bondage*, which I think is a great book, and I am grateful to W. Hill the artist for having told me of it." The appearance in 1919 of *The Moon and Sixpence* seems further to have elevated Maugham in the esteem of the critics. Adams praised the novel, and Heywood Broun ranked it after *Of Human Bondage*. During the early twenties Adams helped to keep the spotlight on Maugham. He wrote in his column of November 5, 1921: "... I read Mr. W. S. Maugham's *Liza of Lambeth* on the train, and as good a book ever he wrote save *Of Human Bondage* ... So to bed and read Maugham's *The Circle*, a highly interesting and diverting play." The George H. Doran Company had, in that year, printed for the first time in America Maugham's earliest novel, *Liza of Lambeth*, which had appeared in London in 1897. During the previous year Doran had brought out his second novel, *Mrs. Craddock*, published in England in 1902.

Maugham's stature as a novelist was growing steadily in America—a fact due chiefly to the increasing popularity of *Of Human Bondage*. In

1922 Grant Overton stated confidently in *When Winter Comes to Main Street* that

> The day will come . . . when people will think of him as the man who wrote *Of Human Bondage*. This novel does not need praise. All it needs, like the grand work it is, is attention; and that it increasingly gets.

Adams, also, commented on May 5, 1922: "Thinking again on *Intrusion*, I mused that the girl [Mildred] in *Of Human Bondage*, which still to me is the best writing Mr. W. Somerset Maugham ever did, is as well drawn as Roberta in *Intrusion*." This conviction that *Of Human Bondage* was Maugham's best novel was echoed by Cornelius Weygrandt, who declared as early as 1925 (*A Century of the English Novel*) that the final judgment of Maugham would rest on the basis of that work. In 1923 Stuart P. B. Mais discussed the novel in *Some Modern Authors*, stressing its "realism" and the determination of the author to present all aspects of life, regardless of how unpleasant—those elements which Dreiser had lauded eight years earlier and which the devotees of the twenties generally pointed to. "Maugham," said Mais, "ought to be one of the most formative influences of the present day. There is certainly no one who could exert such a healthy restraint on the young writer who fears to face the truth."

. . . The new-found popularity of *Of Human Bondage* was not evanescent. As Maugham has said, since the critics began talking about and writing about his novel, "nothing has stopped it." Notice of it reached even the sports pages. Gene Tunney revealed, according to Maugham, that it was the only book he read while training for the famous fight with Jack Dempsey in Philadelphia in 1926. By 1930 Dorothy Brewster and Angus Burrell were expressing the opinion (*Adventure or Experience*) that "there are probably few characters in modern English fiction with whom readers more readily identify themselves than with Philip Carey."

. . . Suggestions that *Of Human Bondage* has been overrated appear (if anything may be inferred from the publication record) to have had little effect on the reading public once the columnists and critics had stimulated interest in the book. Goodrich, discussing at a ten-year distance the reception of the novel, reported that not until 1923—when the George H. Doran Company authorized a new edition—was there a serious demand for it. During the next two years it was reprinted three times, and by 1925, said Goodrich,

libraries and second-hand book stores were reporting increasing demands for it. The popularity of the novel appears to have mounted rapidly. In 1927 Doran issued a new edition, and in 1928 the book reached the cheap reprint stage. Odyssey Press brought out the first of these editions. Grosset and Dunlap published it in their reduced-rate Novels of Distinction series in 1929 and again in 1932, and the Modern Library added it to its list in 1930. By 1931 copies of the 1915 edition were to be found with difficulty. Frederick T. Bason, compiling a bibliography of the writings of Maugham in that year, reported that copies of the first edition of the masterpiece were among the most sought after books in the United States.

Public demand for *Of Human Bondage* continued undiminished through the thirties. The Modern Library advertised the novel in 1941 as one of its best-selling titles. The Garden City Publishing Company and the Dial Press each issued several reprints between 1933 and 1949. Even British readers, long reluctant to accept *Of Human Bondage*, apparently caught something of the American fever. William Heinemann, Limited, which published the novel in 1915, brought out in 1934 the first English edition in nineteen years. Reprints followed in 1935 and 1936. In 1936 Doubleday, Doran and Company published in New York the first of several limited deluxe editions. The following year the Literary Guild distributed the novel to its many thousands of members, and in 1938 Yale University Press printed it in two volumes, with an introduction by Theodore Dreiser, for members of the Limited Editions Club. The Clovernook Printing House for the Blind (Mount Healthy, Ohio) published a seven-volume edition in braille in 1941, and portions of the novel were recorded recently by Maugham. In addition to the many American and the two British editions, *Of Human Bondage* has been published in a number of foreign languages—in French (1937), German (1939), Italian (n. d.), Spanish (1944), and Hungarian (n. d.).

It would appear, on the basis of the foregoing data, that there is much justification for Spencer's assertion that *Of Human Bondage* is one of the most universally read and admired of modern English novels. His statement seems valid despite the generally unfavorable critical comment in 1915, and the subsequent half-dozen years of public apathy toward the book. Not until the early twenties did *Of Human Bondage* begin its climb toward a position in the highest level of English novels. As we have seen, the emergence of the work appears to have been due in large part to the critics and columnists who saw more in the novel than did the reviewers of 1915. Their interest stimulated public interest, and their unreserved praise was a fundamental factor in the making of a masterpiece. Maugham, when he presented the original manuscript of the novel to the Library of Congress [on April 21, 1946], acknowledged the debt he owed its champions:

> It is because the success *Of Human Bondage* is due to my fellow writers in America and to a whole generation of American readers that I thought the least I could do was to offer the manuscript to the Library of Congress.

That the novel has not slipped much in the esteem of American readers is suggested by the editorial comment of the Houston, Texas, *Post* (April 28, 1946), shortly after the presentation. The *Post* declared that *Of Human Bondage* is "one of the greatest novels in the English language." Maugham, in his novel *The Razor's Edge*, stated that "we the public in our heart of hearts all like a success story." Where could one find a better one than in the history of *Of Human Bondage*?

Source: Robert Spence, "Maugham's *Of Human Bondage*," in *Library Chronicle*, Vol. 17, No. 2, Spring-Summer 1951, pp. 104–14.

Woodburn O. Ross

In the following essay, Ross assesses Maugham's fiction, noting recurring themes of love, marriage, freedom, and adultery in his work, and he argues that despite some of its excellent qualities, Maugham's work is "restricted both in breadth and in depth."

Few contemporary authors have been praised as highly and condemned as completely as has W. Somerset Maugham. A recent critic enthusiastically says that today he is "perhaps the most creative talent in the field of the English novel." Another, while granting Maugham's talent, suggests that sinister influences have vitiated his abilities, a suggestion with which a great many competent readers, I think, would agree. "It is indisputable," he writes, "that Mr. Maugham, despite the authorship of one novel of almost universal appeal, ceased some time ago to be a force and was bought, as it were ... What metamorphosis took place? What happened? Were his desires worldly from the start; was he fired originally with no artist's longing to see and make, but with an earthling's lust to dine well and glitter? Or was a

> IT IS CHARACTERISTIC OF HIS WORK THAT THE RESPONSES OF HIS CHARACTERS ARE ALWAYS EXTREME, EVEN PERVERSE. PHILIP'S LOVE FOR MILDRED, BLANCHE'S LOVE FOR STRICKLAND, AND STRICKLAND'S DESIRE TO PAINT, ALL GO BEYOND ANY REASON."

man of genius, a virgin heart, seduced by the great world of riches and power?"

I

...Maugham's early fiction is little known; and this fact, I think, is responsible for a failure on the part of many of his readers to estimate properly his later artistic achievements.

...Nothing that Maugham had written up to 1912 gave him any substantial claim to fame. He had exploited the flashy possibilities of his conventional theme and at the same time had disported himself by attacking the conventions of others. He had not been blind to the deeper implications of his theme, but he had never dealt with them adequately. In short, he had gone through a fifteen-year apprenticeship, which prepared him to write a masterpiece on a single subject.

In 1912 he sat down to write that masterpiece, *Of Human Bondage*. He says that he had tried to write the book back in 1898; but it is fortunate that he failed and waited until he could bring long experience to bear upon its composition.

...The fact that *Of Human Bondage* is, to a considerable extent, autobiographical is frequently mentioned by critics of this work and is, of course, indisputable, regardless of whether the Mildred episode has any basis in fact. But to consider it as fictionalized autobiography is to make it appear a much more immediate and direct reflection of experience than it is. Theodore Dreiser, for instance, in his excellent review of the book which appeared in *The New Republic*, seems to regard it as a kind of spontaneous overflow of powerful feelings. It is, of course, nothing of the sort, as this discussion has shown. It is calculated and artificial; but the calculation which produced it was born of experience in writing and the artifice is the artifice which creates the illusion of reality.

III

...*Of Human Bondage* was not at all a work of great promise. It was a fulfilment of a promise made fifteen years before. From the beginning Maugham had seen human beings in a certain way, and he had now achieved, I think, the most perfect expression of his insight of which he was capable. But, though the play was over, the curtain refused to come down. Maugham was a professional writer, and a professional writer must keep on writing. His attitudes, however, did not change, except in one respect which I shall mention presently, and he did not develop new, significant ramifications of his ideas to which he must give expression. For the constancy of his opinions we have not only the evidence of his fictional works but also that of his autobiographical *The Summing Up*, published in 1938. Comparing his views then with those which he held when he was a student in St. Thomas' Hospital in the 1890's, he explicitly says: "The experience of all the years that have followed has only confirmed the observations on human nature that I made, not deliberately, for I was too young, but unconsciously...in the wards of St. Thomas's... I have seen men since as I saw them then, and thus I have shown them."

And the result? He has constantly repeated himself and has written nothing since which approaches the quality of his great work. But the answer to the charge that he sold himself out is that, on the contrary, he wrote himself out. Let us glance at some of his postwar efforts. *The Moon and Sixpence* (1919), his next novel, was apparently inspired by the life of Gauguin, but the result is pure Maugham. Strickland, the central character, is consumed by a passion to paint. He is a modification of Fanny Price and of another artist who appears in *Of Human Bondage*. Even the old formula of the unworthy beloved recognized as unworthy by the enslaved lover appears again in the Strickland-Blanche Stroeve situation. *The Painted Veil* (1925) describes the powerlessness of a woman to love a worthy man or to resist her desires for an unworthy one. *Cakes and Ale* (1930) conforms less to the pattern. Yet Rosie Driffield, the most striking character of the book, is interesting principally because of her surprising ability to be sexually promiscuous and at the same time remain a perfectly self-possessed, integrated character. The world expects one set of actions from her and gets another. In *The Narrow Corner*

(1932), Maugham remains preoccupied with the contradictions which can exist within characters. The book discusses, among other matters, the qualities of Captain Nichols, who is a thief, an all-round scoundrel, a more than competent sailor, and a potential hero; and of Louise Frith, a virtuous girl, a virgin, who gives herself almost instantly to a stranger. *Theatre* (1937) concerns the uncontrollable love of a great actress for an inconsequential young man many years her junior. *Christmas Holiday* (1939) presents a virtuous prostitute and describes her love for a kleptomaniac, homicidal husband. *Up at a Villa* (1940) and *The Hour before the Dawn* (1942) deal with the same old themes but, as books, are completely unimportant.

Maugham's latest book, *The Razor's Edge* (1944), however, though built around the usual themes, presents the first significant modification of them which he has effected since he created Fanny Price and Charles Strickland. The overwhelming desire of Larry Darrell, the central character, is not to win love or to paint but to find God. Though the book is not a masterpiece, it does seem to offer evidence that Maugham writes about what he considers important. For Larry's most striking quality is his goodness; and in *The Summing Up* Maugham says that, though he once regarded the creation of beauty as the most suitable end of human action, he now considers the good more important than the beautiful.

V

...As one attempts to formulate judgments concerning Maugham's work as a whole, one is struck above all by its limited range. It is restricted both in breadth and in depth.

It is restricted in breadth. The basic problem which he raises, when he raises problems, is that of the motivation of human choices. His solution, sometimes presented more or less tentatively, is that of the determinist; men choose what they do because they must. This kind of answer, though important—it denies free will—leaves altogether too much unsaid. When Maugham finds the ultimate causes of human choices to lie in the nature of things, he is thinking of the causative aspects of whole, vague, interacting psychological and environmental complexes. He is never specific. Concerning profound causes of particular psychological states in his characters he has nothing to say. And these vague complexes which in a sense are ultimate causes find expression in his works only in a very narrow range of actions. As we have seen, he uses countless modifications of a set formula; and, until lately, he has applied that formula principally to certain kinds of sexual frustrations or to needs for creative expression in the arts. How much of the broad human scene is omitted is evident.

A result of this narrow limitation of the area to which he restricts the activities of his characters is that the effect of his very considerable versatility in character drawing is seriously vitiated. Mr. Richard A. Cordell, the author of one of the two book-length studies of Maugham in English, emphasizes the fact that Maugham has created a wide variety of characters. He says, for instance, "The women of Somerset Maugham's novels are highly individualized. In the characterizations of Liza, Bertha Ley, Mildred, Blanche Stroeve, Kitty Fane, Rosie Driffield, Louise Frith, and Julia Lambert he does not repeat himself." But Mr. Cordell does not carry his discussion far enough. It is true that these women are separate individuals; they differ from one another in intelligence, in taste, in ability, in background, and in appearance. But such differences may have genuine literary significance only when they permit an author to illustrate various aspects of life; and Maugham uses all these characters to illustrate virtually the same aspect. The essential problem of these women is the same—to find some satisfactory solution to their sexual needs. Their solutions have this in common: each gives herself to a lover who, for one reason or another, is unsuitable for her. If Cordell wished to emphasize the diversity of character of Maugham's women, he would have done well to include Fanny Price in the group. She is different from all the rest; in her Maugham escapes in part from the constricting influence of his formula and is successful in illustrating a new aspect of life. But there are very few of his important feminine characters of whom this can be said. The same kind of criticism, of course, can be made concerning his men.

Just as Maugham's important comments upon life are limited in area, they are limited in depth. I have said that even in his most serious moments he is not concerned with profound causes of the psychological states of his characters. I do not mean that he does not provide adequate motivation for particular acts. He does. But he neglects what lies behind the immediate motive.

It is characteristic of his work that the responses of his characters are always extreme, even perverse. Philip's love for Mildred, Blanche's love for Strickland, and Strickland's desire to paint, all go beyond any reason. It is difficult to believe that the nineteenth century would have accepted these characters just as they are drawn. The twentieth century, I think, owes its willingness to believe in them to Sigmund Freud and his successors, who have directed attention to a wide variety of perverse responses and explained them by reference to the unconscious mind. Philip Carey, Charles Strickland, Rosie Driffield, and Robert Berger are all good Freudian characters, except that the Freudian explanation of their conduct is missing. Why does Philip Carey love Mildred? Critics frequently answer the question by vague references to an alleged feeling of inferiority caused by his club foot. I think, however, that M. Paul Dottin is much nearer the mark when he says that Philip hates himself and that his love for Mildred is an attempt at self-annihilation. But why should he hate himself? Or, for that matter, what is the specific evidence in *Of Human Bondage* that there is any relationship between his affection for Mildred and his club foot? The fact is that Philip's response to her is left unmotivated, as are the extreme reactions of all Maugham's characters.

In other words, when it comes to dealing with basic psychological states, Maugham does not interpret; he reports. He gives his readers no genuine insight into the fundamental—and consequently the most interesting and important—reasons for his characters' conduct. This is not to say that Maugham is merely a reporter. But the interpretation of life which he offers is abstracted from unaccountable, or unaccounted-for, patterns of behavior. His vision does not extend far beyond his formula.

Maugham has sometimes been spoken of as having been unusually successful in recording characteristic features of twentieth-century life—indeed, as having helped in some slight measure to create them. But, after one notices how repetitious he is and how restricted his serious interests have been, must not one conclude that he has failed to give himself sufficient scope to interpret much that is peculiar to our changing culture? Of the twentieth-century social or political manifestations of materialism he says nothing; the problems posed by the anti-intellectual neo-romantics apparently do not interest him. His basic philosophy is the conventional one of the brash, mechanistic nineteenth-century naturalists. It seems to me that one has but to mention the names of D. H. Lawrence, Aldous Huxley, Virginia Woolf, and John Dos Passos to realize how far Maugham is in spirit from authors who have given literary expression to crucial problems peculiar to the twentieth century.

He has been described as a revolutionist. Actually he is a sheep in wolf's clothing. It is almost fair to say that he has been revolutionary only in his opinions on the incidence and importance of adultery.

VI

Much of what I have written in the latter part of this paper is likely to appear disparaging. And certainly I have not dealt with some excellent qualities which Maugham displays—an unusual directness and simplicity of utterance and an extraordinary ability to articulate the parts of a plot and build them up to a dramatic climax. He pleases his readers. He interests them and, I feel sure, arouses a sense that what he is saying is important. But these are all matters which have been discussed repeatedly by critics of Maugham's work, and, further, they lie outside the area which I have been attempting to explore.

I have been principally concerned with isolating and describing the formula in terms of which Maugham has seen human life and with showing the influence which it has had upon his work. I think that to understand the development of his use of the formula is to understand a great deal about Maugham. His basic strength is shown by the remarkably persuasive and integrated expression of his formula which he achieved in *Of Human Bondage*. But his weakness was predicted by his long inability to bring it into satisfactory focus and is demonstrated by his subsequent incapacity to transcend it and enlarge his view of life. It is not primarily a facile willingness to meet the demands of the vulgar but rather an inability to expand the insights of his youth which is responsible for the dissatisfaction which many intelligent readers feel with his work. He has never escaped the young man who studied medicine at St. Thomas' Hospital in the late nineteenth century.

Source: Woodburn O. Ross, "W. Somerset Maugham: Theme and Variations," in *College English*, Vol. 8, No. 3, December 1946, pp. 113–22.

H. T. Webster

In the following essay, Webster points out the narrative parallels between Workers in the Dawn *and* Of Human Bondage.

Somerset Maugham has found material for two of his best novels in the lives of men as famous as himself—Paul Gauguin in *The Moon and Sixpence* and Thomas Hardy in *Cakes and Ale*. This raises the question: could Philip Carey's love for the appalling Mildred in *Of Human Bondage* have been suggested by George Gissing's first marriage, as it is recounted in that author's first novel, *Workers in the Dawn*. By its author's testimonial, *Of Human Bondage* is autobiographical, but Maugham makes it clear in the preface to the later American editions that he transfers some experiences of other people to his protagonist. This, of course, is implicit in the nature of fiction.

There are a number of marked similarities in Gissing's treatment of Arthur Golding's marriage to Carrie Mitchell, and Philip Carey's association with Mildred Rogers. In each book, a sensitive and refined man is drawn against his better judgment into an alliance with an uneducated and utterly worthless woman. Carrie and Mildred alike represent a mental and moral superficiality so great that it becomes the essence of evil. In each book, the woman reappears in the man's life after several betrayals and separations so that she remains a permanent blight on it. Carrie and Mildred similarly degenerate in character from tawdry respectability to prostitution and the extremes of degradation. There are a few circumstantial details common to each novel. Gissing's hero, Arthur Golding, is, like Philip Carey, a sometime art student. Carrie tears up his portrait of his real love, Helen Norman, in a scene that suggests Mildred's later destruction of Philip's pictures. Carrie, like Mildred, is in Gissing's words "suffering from a malady which was the consequence of her dissipated life," when we take leave of her.

But it is not so much the details as the general matters of shaping and narrative value which hint an affinity between *Workers in the Dawn* and *Of Human Bondage*. Of course, the stories are not without dissimilarities. Arthur Golding is held to Carrie by ties of sympathy tinged with Victorian moral earnestness, rather than by the poisoned fascination that Mildred exerts over Philip. As is often true of Gissing's characters, Carrie is reported to us rather than represented three dimensionally like Maugham's Mildred. On the whole, there is a close enough parallel between *Workers in the Dawn* and *Of Human Bondage* to suggest an influence without proving it. Only Mr. Maugham himself could establish this detail in literary history, if indeed he remembers the answer.

Source: H. T. Webster, "Possible Influence of George Gissing's *Workers in the Dawn* on Maugham's *Of Human Bondage*," in *Modern Language Quarterly*, Vol. 7, No. 3, September 1946, p. 315.

SOURCES

Brander, L., "*Of Human Bondage*," in *Somerset Maugham: A Guide*, Barnes and Noble, 1963, pp. 26–36.

Cordell, Richard A., "The Novelist," in *W. Somerset Maugham*, Thomas Nelson and Sons, 1937, pp. 65–142.

———, "Three Autobiographical Novels," in *Somerset Maugham: A Writer for All Seasons*, Indiana University Press, 1961, pp. 86–131.

DeForest, Julia B., "Impressionism in French Art," in *A Short History of Art*, Dodd, Mead, 1921, pp. 584–96.

Dreiser, Theodore, "As a Realist Sees It," in *W. Somerset Maugham: The Critical Heritage*, edited by Anthony Curtis and John Whitehead, Routledge & Kegan Paul, 1987, pp. 130–34; originally published in *New Republic*, December 25, 1915.

"Expressionism," in *History.com*, http://www.history.com/encyclopedia.do?articleId=208919 (accessed December 8, 2009).

Gould, Gerald, Review of *Of Human Bondage*, in *W. Somerset Maugham: The Critical Heritage*, edited by Anthony Curtis and John Whitehead, Routledge & Kegan Paul, 1987, pp. 126–29; originally published in *New Statesman*, September 1915.

"Historic Figures: David Lloyd George (1863–1945)," in *BBC History*, http://www.bbc.co.uk/history/historic_figures/george_david_lloyd.shtml (accessed December 8, 2009).

"Historic Figures: H. H. Asquith (1852–1928)," in *BBC History*, http://www.bbc.co.uk/history/historic_figures/asquith_herbert.shtml (accessed December 8, 2009).

Loss, Archie K., "Troubled Grace: *Of Human Bondage*," in *W. Somerset Maugham*, Ungar, 1987, pp. 14–36.

Matthew, H. C. G., "The Liberal Age (1851–1914)," in *The Oxford Illustrated History of Britain*, Oxford University Press, 1984, pp. 463–522.

Maugham, W. Somerset, *Of Human Bondage*, Modern Library, 1999.

Morgan, Kenneth, O., "The Twentieth Century (1914–1983)," in *The Oxford Illustrated History of Britain*, Oxford University Press, 1984, pp. 523–88.

Norton-Taylor, Richard, Julian Glover, and Nicholas Watt, "Public Support for War in Afghanistan Is Firm, despite Deaths," in *Guardian* (London, England), July 13, 2009, http://www.guardian.co.uk/uk/2009/jul/13/afghanistan-war-poll-public-support (accessed December 8, 2009).

"Operations in Afghanistan: Background Briefing," in *United Kingdom Ministry of Defense*, http://www.mod.uk/DefenceInternet/FactSheets/OperationsFactsheets/OperationsInAfghanistanBackgroundBriefing.htm (accessed December 8, 2009).

Review of *Of Human Bondage*, in *W. Somerset Maugham: The Critical Heritage*, edited by Anthony Curtis

and John Whitehead, Routledge & Kegan Paul, 1987, pp. 129–30; originally published in *Athenaeum*, August 21, 1915.

Simpkins, Scott, "W. Somerset Maugham," in *Dictionary of Literary Biography*, Vol. 36, *British Novelists, 1890–1929: Modernists*, edited by Thomas F. Staley, Gale Research, 1985, pp. 159–68.

"Stuckism," and "New Leipzig School," in *Contemporary Art Movements*, http://www.visual-arts-cork.com/contemporary-art-movements.htm (accessed December 8, 2009).

"UK has sent 71,560 to Afghanistan," in *BBC News*, September 17, 2009, http://news.bbc.co.uk/2/hi/uk_news/politics/8259818.stm (accessed December 8, 2009).

"United Kingdom Monarchs, 1603–Present: Victoria," "United Kingdom Monarchs, 1603–Present: George V," and "Her Majesty the Queen," in *The British Monarchy*, http://www.royal.gov.uk/HistoryoftheMonarchy/HistoryoftheMonarchy.aspx (accessed December 8, 2009).

FURTHER READING

Ledger, Sally, and Roger Luckhurst, eds., *The Fin de Siècle: A Reader in Cultural History, c. 1880–1900*, Oxford University Press, 2000.

> The period known as the fin de siècle (end of the century; pronounced "fan duh seeECKluh") spanned the years 1880 through 1900. Being the turn of the century, this period, according to the editors of this volume, was a time of conflicted attitudes in Europe, as nostalgia about the past and a yearning for the future coexisted. The editors have collected essays from this time period that represent various views from writers regarding art, literature, gender roles, politics, science, and psychology.

Mangan, J. A., ed., *A Sport Loving Society: Victorian and Edwardian Middle-Class England at Play*, Routledge, 2006.

> Mangan has collected a number of essays in which the relationship between sport as a leisure activity and various aspects of British culture, including class and education, in the late nineteenth and early twentieth century is examined.

Meyers, Jeffrey, *Somerset Maugham: A Life*, Vintage, 2005.

> Meyers offers a critical biography of Maugham's life and works, defending Maugham's work against detractors and demonstrating his influence on other writers.

Remington, Gwen, *The Way People Live: Life in Victorian England*, Lucent Books, 2005.

> In this young-adult nonfiction guide to Victorian England, Remington explores a variety of

aspects of life under the reign of Queen Victoria, discussing class issues, leisure activities, education, and religion, among other topics.

Roe, Sue, *The Private Lives of the Impressionists*, Harper Perennial, 2007.

Roe examines the lives of the Impressionist painters living and working in Paris in the mid- to late nineteenth century. Her analysis details the artists' financial struggles, personal relationships, and their professional efforts to build their reputations. In addition, Roe provides the cultural and political context that allows the artists' lives to be more fully understood.

SUGGESTED SEARCH TERMS

Of Human Bondage AND Maugham

W. Somerset Maugham

Maugham AND coming of age

Of Human Bondage AND realist novel

Of Human Bondage AND bildungsroman

Of Human Bondage AND free will

Maugham AND autobiography

Maugham AND novels

Maugham AND Victorian age

Oroonoko; or, The Royal Slave: A True History

APHRA BEHN

1688

Aphra Behn is credited with being the first female professional writer in England. In 1688, as a well-established dramatist, Behn published *Oroonoko; or, The Royal Slave: A True History* (also known by the shorter title *Oroonoko*), the story of an African prince who is forced into slavery in the South American country of Suriname, which in the late 1600s was an English colony. In her dedication to the work, Behn claims the story is true and establishes herself as the narrator in the novel. Scholars conjecture that Behn likely visited the English colony in the 1660s and based her work on her experiences there. The veracity of Behn's account is an area of modern critical debate.

In Behn's novel, the warrior prince, Oroonoko, falls in love with a young maiden, Imoinda, whom the king of their nation takes as his mistress. When the young lovers are discovered together, Imoinda is sold into slavery. Duped by an English slave trader with whom he has previously done business, Oroonoko is also captured and sold. Although he is purchased as a slave, Oroonoko impresses the plantation's overseer and is allowed to live separately from the other slaves and to do no work. After Oroonoko discovers Imoinda has been sold to the same plantation, the lovers conceive a child and attempt to bargain with their captors to return to Africa. Realizing that they will not be allowed to leave, Oroonoko leads a mass escape from the plantation. The group is quickly overtaken by the

Aphra Behn (*Public domain*)

English, and Oroonoko is punished. Fearing Imoinda will be tortured, Oroonoko kills her, and he is subsequently tortured and executed. Throughout the tale, the narrator stresses Oroonoko's nobility and expresses her deep sympathy for him. At the time the work was published, *Oroonoko* was treated as a romance, the love between Oroonoko and Imoinda being viewed as the work's main theme. Later critics have focused on the novel as an exploration of imperialism, slavery, and true nobility.

Originally published in 1688 by William Canning, along with two other works, in the volume *Three Histories: Oroonoko, The Fair Jilt, Agnes de Castro, Oroonoko* is available in a 2003 Penguin Classics edition.

AUTHOR BIOGRAPHY

Little is actually known about Behn's life, particularly her youth. It is believed that she was born around 1640, in Canterbury, in the county of Kent, in England, to parents thought to be named Bartholomew and Elizabeth Johnson. Scholars speculate that around 1663, perhaps

earlier, Behn visited the English colony established by Lord Willoughby in Suriname (now the Republic of Suriname). Although it has been theorized that Behn's father was a lieutenant-general in Suriname, based on the narrator's account in *Oroonoko*, most scholars believe Behn's parents to be of humbler birth. Once she returned to London, Behn likely married a German merchant, Johan Behn. The mysterious husband disappeared from her life shortly after; either he died, or the couple separated. In 1666, Behn was sent by the English government as a royalist agent to Antwerp, Belgium, to work as a spy. With England at war with the Dutch, Behn was assigned to gather information from a William Scot, who was providing information on the Dutch to England through Behn. Allegedly duped by Scot, Behn was cut from the English payroll and returned to London in great poverty.

At this point, Behn began to write plays for the English stage. Her first, *The Forc'd Marriage*, premiered in 1670. After the success of this play, Behn penned a number of subsequent plays. Some of her dramas were political in nature and supportive of the government of King Charles II. Behn also successfully published as a poet, and her work was known for its erotic nature, and she for her promiscuity. In 1688, following the success of her plays and poetry, Behn published *Three Histories: Oroonoko, The Fair Jilt, Agnes de Castro*. Two of these stories (*Oroonoko* and *The Fair Jilt*) are based on Behn's experiences in Suriname. In the last years of her life, Behn witnessed two royal transitions. After Charles's death and James II's ascension to the throne in 1685, James was ousted only a few years later. Just before Behn's death in 1689, James's daughter Mary and her husband William were crowned queen and king.

PLOT SUMMARY

The Epistle Dedicatory

Oroonoko, whose full title is *Oroonoko; or, The Royal Slave: A True History*, is prefaced by a letter of dedication, or "epistle dedicatory." In this dedication, Behn addresses the Lord Maitland, a Scottish minister under King James II, whose literary activities Behn admired. After praising Maitland's "wit and worth," Behn spends the better part of a long paragraph

MEDIA ADAPTATIONS

- *Oroonoko* is available on audio CD, published by Babblebooks in 2008.

explaining why a man with known faults may still be praised for his virtues, and she argues that such a man's true nobility reveals itself through his written works. Behn goes on to applaud Maitland's scholarly nature, his quest for knowledge, and his writings in which he defends the Catholic Church and explicates its teachings. Maitland's personal life and marriage are also the subject of Behn's effusive compliments. Behn then turns to her story, explaining to Maitland that what he is about to read is a true story. She defends the work against being labeled romantic (depicting an idealized world in the paradisiacal country of Suriname) by pointing out that the country she describes is extremely different from England and is full of wondrous things that may be hard to imagine, although Behn has truthfully written about them. Asking Maitland to forgive any faults in the book, Behn explains that she wrote it in a few hours.

The History of the Royal Slave

As Behn opens her story, she explains that while she was an eyewitness to what the royal slave endured after he came to Suriname, the earlier part of his story, which concerns Oroonoko's youth and how he came to be captured, is based on what Oroonoko told her. Behn narrates the story in the first person, referring to herself as "I." In the dedication and in the opening paragraphs, she identifies herself as the story's narrator. For the next several pages, Behn describes the native inhabitants of Suriname, the "Indians," as she states. At length she catalogues the various items the Indians trade with English colonists, which the English in turn take back to England to sell. Behn discusses some of the life and daily habits of the Indians. The English colonists lived "in perfect tranquility and good understanding" with these native people, for, as Behn points out,

it benefited the colonists to do so, as the Indians knew the land and where to hunt. The Indians also greatly outnumbered the colonists, Behn observes, so the English did not dare attempt to use them as slaves.

This statement allows Behn the opportunity to transition from a discussion of Suriname to the place where her story actually begins, in Africa, the country where the English acquired the slaves to work the Suriname sugar plantations. In the African nation of Coramantien, slaves are bought by the English and brought back to Suriname. (As Janet Todd explains in the footnotes to the 2003 Penguin edition of *Oroonoko*, Coramantien, or Koromantyn, was a trading post on Africa's west coast, an area that corresponds roughly with the coast of modern Ghana.)

Describing the structure of this nation, Behn characterizes it as a warrior society, ruled by an ancient king. On the battlefield, the young royal, Prince Oroonoko, who is the grandson of the old king, has earned a reputation as brave and daring. At the age of seventeen he becomes a general, when his commander is killed in battle. Behn paints a picture of the prince in which he is depicted as physically perfect and beautiful. Her description emphasizes the way his features are more European than African. Oroonoko falls in love with the daughter of his fallen commander, a girl named Imoinda, and to honor her he presents her with the slaves who have been captured in a recent battle. Imoinda returns Oroonoko's affections. The young couple make vows to one another.

The old king has, like Oroonoko, noticed Imoinda's exceptional beauty. Despite the fact that he has learned that Oroonoko and Imoinda are romantically involved, the king, who already has many wives and mistresses, desires her for himself. He sends Imoinda his royal veil, a symbol that designates Imoinda as the king's possession, his mistress. In keeping with the culture of their society, Imoinda cannot refuse the king's command. When Oroonoko learns that Imoinda has become the king's mistress, he is devastated. He knows that to rebel against the king would result in death for both himself and his beloved Imoinda.

With the help of a fellow warrior, Aboan, and one of the king's discarded mistresses, Onahal, who now tends to Imoinda, Oroonoko manages to spend a few stolen hours with Imoinda. When the king discovers that Oroonoko and Imoinda have been together, he sells Imoinda as a slave and has Oroonoko told that Imoinda has been executed. Gradually, the king begins to feel remorse for having wronged Oroonoko. Fearing that Oroonoko will plot revenge against him, he seeks Oroonoko's pardon. Oroonoko carries on, but he grieves for Imoinda.

When an English slave trader, with whom Oroonoko has previously conducted business, arrives, he invites Oroonoko and his companions aboard his ship, apparently as guests. Soon, however, Oroonoko and the others are overcome and bound, and they are destined to be sold as slaves. They are taken to Suriname, and Oroonoko is sold to a plantation owner. The overseer, named Trefry, who purchases Oroonoko is impressed by Oroonoko's regal bearing, his fine attire, his intelligence, and his ability to speak English. Trefry allows Oroonoko to live apart from the other slaves and to not work. Trefry promises that the situation is temporary and that he will endeavor to return Oroonoko to his own country. As is the custom with all the African slaves at the Suriname plantation to which Oroonoko has been taken, Oroonoko is renamed. Trefry calls him Caesar. When Oroonoko meets the other slaves at the plantation, he finds that they are people who he himself sold to the English. Knowing Oroonoko's royal status, they revere him and remain loyal to him.

Trefry tells Oroonoko about a female slave who has recently been brought to the plantation, a girl whom all the male slaves desire. The girl has been named Clemene, but when Oroonoko meets her he finds that she is none other than Imoinda. The lovers, who made their vows to one another in Africa, are allowed to live together as husband and wife, and they conceive a child. With Imoinda pregnant, Oroonoko continues to seek freedom for himself and his wife. He offers wealth and slaves in return for their passage home. As Behn points out, the slaveholders have no intention of letting Oroonoko go, but they pacify him by allowing him to hunt and to have more freedom than any of the other slaves at the plantation. Oroonoko even serves as an intermediary in disputes between the Suriname natives and the English colonists.

Oroonoko can only be appeased and distracted from thoughts of returning home for so long, and he begins to talk to the other slaves about escaping. They are loyal to him and follow him into the jungle. The deputy governor of the English colony in Suriname, named Byam, is brought in to help pursue Oroonoko and the slaves he has incited to escape. When they are surrounded by the English, the slaves initially fight by Oroonoko's side, but they are convinced by Byam to return with him to the plantation and to abandon Oroonoko. Forced to surrender, Oroonoko is brutally beaten.

As he begins to heal from his assault, Oroonoko realizes that he will probably still be executed, and if he is gone, Imoinda will be in grave danger. Both Oroonoko and Imoinda agree that she will suffer punishments worse than death at the hands of the English. The two escape into the jungle, and with Imoinda's blessing, Oroonoko kills the pregnant Imoinda. For two days he grieves by her body. When he realizes that he must go, as he has vowed to revenge himself and Imoinda on those who have captured them, Oroonoko finds that he is too weak to move. He languishes for another six days by Imoinda's body.

Another slave, named Tuscan, leads a search party to find Oroonoko and Imoinda. When Tuscan and another man from this party come upon Oroonoko, Oroonoko realizes he will not be able to carry out his revenge. Instead, he seeks to kill himself, and begins attacking his own body with his knife. Tuscan and the others are finally able to overcome him, and they return him to the plantation. There, he is operated on, his wounds closed, and he is revived, only so that his captors can execute him in their own manner. He is dismembered and finally killed.

CHARACTERS

Aboan

Aboan is a fellow soldier in the army of the Coramantien community. He fights alongside Oroonoko, under Oroonoko's leadership. Aboan is romantically involved with Onahal, the former mistress of the old king. Oroonoko establishes a chain of communication to Imoinda by passing messages to Aboan, who relates Oroonoko's feelings to Onahal, who finally delivers the messages to Imoinda.

Byam

Byam is the deputy governor of the English colony in Suriname. He is known for his brutal nature, according to Behn. It is Byam who leads the search for Oroonoko and the escaped slaves, and he who convinces the other slaves to abandon Oroonoko. At Byam's orders, Oroonoko is beaten and tortured, and later, after Oroonoko's murder of Imoinda and subsequent recapture, it is Byam who insists that Oroonoko, who has been almost fatally injured by his own hand, is healed and restored to health before he is tortured, dismembered, and executed. In Byam, Behn depicts the cruelest elements of the slave-holding system. All the evils of slavery rest almost exclusively on his shoulders, as the other whites Oroonoko encounters, save the English captain who tricks him, all treat him with a great deal of respect.

Caesar

See Oroonoko

Clemene

See Imoinda

Imoinda

Imoinda is the fifteen-year-old daughter of a fallen general, who was a man Oroonoko revered as a father. When Oroonoko presents Imoinda with slaves captured in battle as a means of honoring her and her dead father, Oroonoko is stunned by Imoinda's beauty. She becomes the object of Oroonoko's fierce passion and love. Imoinda soon confides to Oroonoko that she shares his feelings. Although Imoinda feels bound by duty and tradition—and fear of death—to accept the king's royal veil (his demand that she become his mistress), she, nevertheless, remains emotionally faithful to Oroonoko. When she allows him to visit her in her chambers and spends a romantic night with him, she is punished for disgracing the king; she is sold into slavery.

When the reader once again encounters Imoinda on the plantation to which she has been sold, she is again defined only by her beauty. Just as Oroonoko became entranced with her due to her beauty, and the king sought to possesses her because of her beauty, so do all the other slaves on the plantation desire her, according to the overseer, Trefry. Imoinda's beauty makes her an object of desire, and she is loyal to Oroonoko, gladly welcoming the fate he has decided for her—to be murdered at his hand rather than risk being tortured by the deputy governor Byam. Yet, Behn reveals little else

about Imoinda beyond her physical characteristics. A sense of duty commingled with fear are the driving forces behind her actions.

The King

The king, usually referred to as "the old king," is the leader of Oroonoko's people in Coramantien, and he is the grandfather of Oroonoko. Behn describes him as over one hundred years old. He has numerous wives and mistresses. His desire is rekindled by Imoinda, and he orders her to become his mistress even though she is already committed to Oroonoko. He cares not whether Imoinda feels any affection for him, knowing that she will see it as her duty to submit to him, which she does. Nevertheless, he jealously watches any interaction Imoinda has with Oroonoko, going into a rage, for example, when Imoinda accidentally trips and falls into Oroonoko's arms during a dance she is commanded to perform for the king and his generals. When the king discovers that Oroonoko has stolen into Imoinda's chambers and has been with her, he sells Imoinda into slavery out of spite and jealously, knowing it would be more honorable to have her killed. He lies, letting it be known to Oroonoko that Imoinda has been executed. The king seeks Oroonoko's forgiveness and realizes he has wronged him, but he does so out of fear of Oroonoko's rebellion rather than out of genuine remorse.

Narrator

In the dedicatory letter and in the opening paragraphs of the novel, Behn identifies herself as the narrator of the story. She remains a significant presence throughout the novel, commenting on events from her own perspective and describing her own interaction with the other characters. While Behn asserts that the story is true and although she appears in the novel as an eyewitness, it is believed that the work is a fictionalized account of Behn's experiences. As many facts about her life are unknown, critics have been unable to verify enough of the details she gives in the novel to label it as nonfiction, despite Behn's assertions to the contrary. Yet it has been observed that many of her descriptions of Suriname in the mid-seventeenth century are accurate enough to contend that Behn likely visited the English colony at some time.

Onahal

Onahal is an older woman, who is described as still beautiful. She was once one of the king's many mistresses. Like other mistresses of whom the king has tired, Onahal now tends to the newer, younger mistresses, and she is assigned to Imoinda after Imoinda arrives. Onahal and Aboan are romantically involved, and through this couple, Imoinda and Oroonoko communicate. Onahal helps arrange the fateful night that Oroonoko and Imoinda share, the event that results in Imoinda being sold into slavery.

Oroonoko

Oroonoko is a seventeen-year-old prince in the community of African people living in Coramantien. He becomes a general when his own general dies. Behn describes the nobility of Oroonoko in glowing terms. His physical perfection is admired as much as the integrity of his soul. In Behn's accounting of Oroonoko's physical traits, he is distinguished from other Africans and described in terms of his resemblance to Europeans. His love for Imoinda is also depicted in such a way as to highlight Oroonoko's purity of affection. Behn comments that in love, Oroonoko is even more honorable than Christians. His desire for Imoinda is described in physical terms; he longs to be with her, and he risks both of their lives in order to spend the night with her. After Imoinda has been sold into slavery, Oroonoko, who has been told that Imoinda has been executed, accepts the king's apologies and vows to never raise a weapon against him in revenge. Oroonoko languishes in his tent, despite the fact that his fellow soldiers beg him to lead them in battle. He finally collects himself and fights as though he seeks death. Oroonoko's anguish is intended by Behn to be regarded as a mark of his love for Imoinda and to indicate the depths of his grief for her.

Once Oroonoko himself has been sold as a slave in Suriname, having been tricked by the English captain, his nobility, according to Behn, is apparent to all. Although he is still bought as a slave, he is set apart from the other slaves and allowed freedoms the others do not possess. Promises are made that he will be allowed to return home, but they are never fulfilled. Oroonoko's reunion with Imoinda on the plantation is viewed with wonder by the white people on the plantation. Oroonoko and Imoinda are treated as curiosities, and they are allowed to live together. While Behn notes that she spends time visiting with Oroonoko and Imoinda, in general the whites' attitude toward the couple is one of amazement that slaves could demonstrate personal nobility, beauty, and affection for one another.

After Imoinda becomes pregnant, Oroonoko's captors begin to fear that he will rebel against them, as he is persistent in his attempts to bargain for his and Imoinda's freedom. He is given various tasks and duties in order to distract him from his goal and to make him feel purposeful. Behn demonstrates, through her recounting of Oroonoko's fate after he attempts to lead the slaves in escaping from the plantation, that it is Oroonoko's difference from the other slaves that results in his torture and ultimate death. He is clearly a leader and obviously a man who is certain that he, unlike his fellow slaves, does not deserve to be made subservient to others. Although he attempts to help free the other slaves, initially he only bargains for his own and Imoinda's freedom. It is also Oroonoko himself who, while still in Africa, sold many of the slaves to the English in the first place. Behn demonstrates Oroonoko's praiseworthy qualities—his ability to love Imoinda, his leadership qualities, his sense of honor. At the same time, these qualities lead to Oroonoko's death. His love for Imoinda leads him to murder her, to protect her from a fate worse than death. His abilities as a leader result in his punishment for tempting the slaves to escape. His sense of honor leads him to seek revenge against those who would hold him against his will, and this desire to violently attack Byam and his men, although he is unsuccessful in his efforts, results in Oroonoko's torture and execution.

Trefry

Trefry is the overseer of the slaves at the plantation where Oroonoko is destined. Trefry purchases Oroonoko but is so impressed with his nobility and intelligence that he does not treat him as a slave, and he even promises to obtain Oroonoko's freedom. While it is unlikely that Trefry ever intended to keep this promise, he does treat Oroonoko with respect, and he serves as an advocate for Oroonoko throughout much of Oroonoko's time at the plantation. After Oroonoko leads the slaves in an escape attempt, it is Trefry who prevents Oroonoko from being hanged on Byam's orders. In the end, Trefry is unable to protect Oroonoko.

Tuscan

Tuscan is another slave on the plantation to which Oroonoko has been sold. When Oroonoko tries to convince the slaves to follow him and escape their life of slavery, Tuscan confirms the slaves' loyalty to Oroonoko but also questions Oroonoko. Specifically, Tuscan points to the fact that the slaves all have families, and they do not wish to jeopardize the lives of their wives and children. Oroonoko still manages to convince Tuscan and the others. Tuscan stands beside Oroonoko and refuses to yield when the escaped slaves are captured by Byam. He is whipped alongside Oroonoko. When Oroonoko and Imoinda escape together so that Oroonoko can kill her, Tuscan is with the search party sent out to look for them. He attempts to help Oroonoko, but he is injured by Oroonoko in the process.

THEMES

Slavery

Behn's treatment of the issue of slavery in the seventeenth century is consistent with the commonly held opinions of the English population of that time period. Throughout *Oroonoko*, Behn depicts slavery as a practical economic necessity; there is little indication that she objected to slavery as an institution. However, Behn presents Oroonoko as an uncommonly noble African, and as such, a man who should not be a slave. In describing Oroonoko's own role in the slave trade with the English, Behn emphasizes her view of Oroonoko's superiority over his fellow Africans. This superiority, according to Behn, is acknowledged by the slaves Oroonoko has sold. When he encounters them on the plantation in Suriname, Oroonoko is still received as a prince by his former countrymen. He is honored and respected rather than attacked for his role in their current imprisonment.

In discussing the native people of Suriname, Behn describes them as innocent children. Her tone, which is condescending in the way she depicts their native habits, reflects the attitude of an imperialist nation. At the same time, the innocent and peaceful nature of the native people is not what keeps them from being enslaved by the English colonists, as Behn points out. Rather, the English are outnumbered by the native population, and they are also dependent on them for their knowledge of the land. While Behn illustrates the cruelty of the actions against Oroonoko taken by the deputy governor of the English colony in Suriname (Byam), she does

not do so as a means of protesting the slaveholding system. Other whites, herself and Trefry included, treat Oroonoko with respect, and few other transgressions against the slaves—save their being held as slaves—are described. Slavery, then in *Oroonoko*, may be viewed as a backdrop to the story of the tragic hero Oroonoko and his love Imoinda, providing the dramatic conflict required in such romantic tales.

Love

The love between Oroonoko and Imoinda in *Oroonoko* is lauded by Behn for its passion as well as its purity. Oroonoko and Imoinda desire only each other, despite the fact that Imoinda is forced to serve as the king's mistress. They epitomize tragic lovers not only in their devotion to one another and their nobility of spirit, but also in that they are forced apart. Even though the king knows that Oroonoko and Imoinda are romantically involved, he nonetheless indulges his desire for the beautiful young girl and demands that she become his mistress. Oroonoko cannot act to save her as her life, and his, would be in jeopardy. Imoinda also knows that death awaits those girls who refuse to accept the king's royal veil, the token of his desire for them. Still the pair risks their lives to be together.

Once they are reunited as slaves on the plantation, their love is admired and honored by their white captors; they are allowed to live together. The honorable Oroonoko, however, seeks to return to his homeland with his pregnant wife rather than remain at the plantation, even though he lives a unique life for a slave (he is not required to labor). After leading the slaves in an unsuccessful escape, Oroonoko is punished, and he knows that if he is executed, Imoinda will suffer at the hands of the cruel deputy governor, Byam, and that his unborn child will enter into the world as a slave. The lovers embrace the only fate that seems acceptable; the only escape from slavery and torture is death. Imoinda welcomes death at her lover's hand, and after she is gone, Oroonoko mourns her for so long he is unable to seek revenge on his captors. While he then attempts to kill himself, he is prevented from doing so, only to be tortured and executed.

In *Oroonoko*, Behn explores the details attendant to the notion of tragic love—her noble lovers are forced apart and meet a terrible fate. At the same time, Behn, who authored numerous erotic poems, incorporates into her story erotic elements of physical love. She makes it clear that

TOPICS FOR FURTHER STUDY

- *Oroonoko* has been compared to Harriet Beecher Stowe's *Uncle Tom's Cabin*, published in 1852, in that both authors depict brutalities endured by slaves in a plantation society. To explore this issue further, take one of two approaches. Either read Stowe's novel and compare Stowe's treatment of slavery to Behn's, or research the scholarly criticism on Stowe's treatment of slavery; use these critical responses as a means of comparing Stowe's attitudes with Behn's. In your opinion, can both works legitimately be called emancipation novels? How do the authors explore racial issues? Prepare a persuasive essay in which you present your view on whether Behn's novel is justifiably compared to Stowe's as an abolitionist novel.

- In the opening pages of *Oroonoko*, Behn offers a description of the land and people of seventeenth-century Suriname. Research the people and culture of modern Suriname. How does the nation's modern culture reflect its Dutch and English colonial history? What are the nation's culinary, literary, and musical traditions? Create a presentation for your class. Incorporate visual elements, such as copies of photographs of the people, landscape, and food of Suriname, for example. You may wish to instead create a Web page that incorporates these images, along with a sampling of local music or video clips related to the people or traditions of the nation.

- In 1739, playwright Thomas Southerne produced a drama based on Behn's *Oroonoko*. Read Southerne's adaptation of Behn's novel (available online through Google Books). How does Southerne's version of the material treat Behn's text? Does the playwright make drastic changes? Do his revisions alter Behn's themes? Are the characters as Southerne treats them substantially different from Behn's characterizations? Write a comparative essay in which you explore these topics.

- In *Oroonoko*, Behn explores the English colonization of Suriname in the mid- to late-seventeenth century. England had other colonies throughout the world at this time as well. Research English colonization during the mid- to late-seventeenth century. Where were the other English colonies located? Did the English use slave labor in other colonies, as it did in Suriname on the sugar plantations? What were the relationships like between the English and the native people of the colonies? Prepare a written report, a PowerPoint presentation, or a Web page in which you share your findings. Be sure to cite all of your sources.

- Behn explores the fate of Oroonoko after he has been sold into slavery, discussing his life in Africa, tracing his journey to Suriname, and following his experiences there. In the young-adult novel *The Glory Field* (1994), written by Walter Dean Myers, the author similarly follows the experiences of a young man, Muhammed Bilal, who is captured in Sierra Leone in Africa and sold as a slave in the American colonies in 1753. While Myers's work is set in a later time period than Behn's, the two novels feature young African men sold to British colonies in the Americas (Muhammed in North America, Oroonoko in South America). With a book group, read Myers's novel and compare it with Behn's. In what ways do Muhammed's and Oroonoko's experiences seem similar? How are the English portrayed in both works? Do the characters share a similar fate? How do the authors' different perspectives impact the tone they use in their novels? With your group, present your comparison to the class as an oral report.

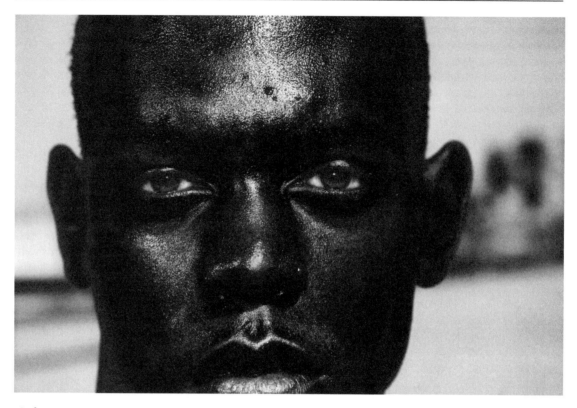

A slave (Image copyright CURAphotography, 2010. Used under license from Shutterstock.com)

one of the components of the attraction between Oroonoko and Imoinda is a powerful physical desire for one another, a desire that Oroonoko and Imoinda indulge to their detriment.

STYLE

First-Person Narration

Behn composes her novel *Oroonoko* in the first person. She incorporates a narrator who observes the events of the story and refers to herself as "I." In this type of story, the narrator is often associated with the author, although this assumption is sometimes erroneous, as the author of the story may be creating a narrator whose opinions and observations are meant to be taken ironically or as a satire of the prevailing opinions of the author's society. (Satire is the use of humor, irony, or exaggeration, for example, in order to expose faults or shortcomings.) Behn, however, in her dedication to *Oroonoko*, makes it clear that she is the narrator of the work, which she claims to be a true story. Modern critics

generally regard the work as a fictionalized account by Behn, and the narrator she depicts in the work as a fictionalized version of herself. Whether or not Behn's narrator is regarded as Behn herself or a fictionalized version of herself, the work is still regarded as a reflection of Behn's own views on such themes as slavery and her notion of love.

A Hybrid Genre: Tragic Romance and Travel Literature

Many critics have observed that in *Oroonoko*, Behn combines two popular genres, that of the tragic romance and the travelogue. Laura Anne Doyle, in the 2008 *Freedom's Empire: Race and the Rise of the Novel in Atlantic Modernity, 1640–1940*, states that Behn combines stories of "exotic adventure in Suriname" with "the high, tragic romance of noble lovers from Africa," along with "the brutal depiction of a colonial slave revolt." Similarly, Janet Todd in the 1998 *The Critical Fortunes of Aphra Behn*, observes that Behn "presents an old-fashioned romantic tale in the modern guise of a true travelogue, which allows her to assume authority." Behn, a successful dramatist, drew on the dramatic tradition available to her, incorporating elements of tragic romance plays into a story based on her travels to Suriname. Predecessors, including William Shakespeare (whom Behn was known to admire), and contemporary dramatists, including John Dryden, made frequent use of the tragic romance genre as well. In the tragic romance, lovers are prevented by circumstances from being together. The tragic hero is a brave and noble man with a fatal flaw that leads to his downfall, and the tragic heroine, like the hero, typically dies for the sake of love. Seventeenth-century travelogues often focused on the colonization of the New World. Like Captain John Smith's 1624 *Generall Historie of Virginia* and his 1630 *True Travels*, New World travelogues were nonfiction accounts of travelers or colonists to the Americas, and they often explored the relationship between Europeans and the native inhabitants of these lands. Behn's work combines these elements, an allegedly truthful account of her time in Suriname and the tragic romance, complete with tragic lovers, who, like their Shakespearean predecessors Romeo and Juliet, would rather die than live without the other.

HISTORICAL CONTEXT

Seventeenth-Century English Colonialism in Suriname

In the seventeenth century, the north coastal region of South America was the object of English, Dutch, and French colonial desires, as the region had not yet been settled by European colonists. The English Lord Willoughby, who had founded a colony in Barbados, an island in the Caribbean Sea, sent a party in 1650 to the Suriname region. Plantations were successfully established. Willoughby appointed William Byam as the colony's deputy governor. By the 1660s, the colony's plantations were producing sugar for the English market and incorporating slave labor in order to do so. From 1665 through 1667, the Second Anglo-Dutch War was fought, when the Dutch attempted to wrest from the English the land they colonized in Suriname. Suriname was ceded to the Dutch, while the English claimed New Amsterdam in Guyana. The Third Anglo-Dutch War was fought from 1672 to 1674. The Dutch reconquered New Amsterdam, while the English reclaimed Suriname. These possessions were reversed, however, by the Treaty of Westminster,

signed in 1674 by King Charles II of England. Scholars do not know for certain when Behn visited Suriname, but by the time her book was published in 1688, Suriname had been lost to the Dutch.

Seventeenth-Century Slave Trade in Africa

The English colonies in the Caribbean, including Willoughby's Barbados and Suriname colonies, were in need of laborers to be used in sugar production. Although some indentured laborers were sent from Ireland, Scotland, and Wales, the plantations needed more workers than could be serviced in this fashion. (Indentured servants worked in conditions similar to those endured by slaves, but were under contract to work for a specified amount of time, usually several years.) King Charles I, in 1630, granted the English slave-trafficking rights, and by 1672 the English had established the Royal African Company for the purposes of developing the slave trade in Africa. The Dutch competed with the English for the acquisition of slaves from Africa. As Janet Todd explains in her introduction to the 2003 edition of *Oroonoko*, the trade in African slaves in which the English and Dutch participated was "carried on by permission of the slave-selling African chiefs." Todd further observes that in the seventeenth century, the English did not enslave Africans exclusively, nor did they do so for racial reasons. Todd explains that the English in Barbados had white slaves, used European indentured servants as slaves, and on board ships and in English colonial settlements, Catholics and Protestants at various times enslaved the other group. Other scholars demonstrate the rapidity with which the slave trade developed to service the sugar industry in the English Caribbean settlements. In their introduction to the 2000 edition of Behn's novel, Catherine Gallagher and Simon Stern state: "Slavery became the dominant institution of the English Caribbean in less than a generation.... A few decades transformed the region into a ruthlessly efficient machine for supplying Europe with cheap sugar." At some point during this process, the critics suggest, slavery did become racialized. The Royal African Company was active in slave trading until the 1730s, at which point the British accomplished the task through other means. British slave trading was not abolished until 1807.

COMPARE
&
CONTRAST

- **1660s:** The English governor of the newly established colony of Suriname, Lord Willoughby, attempts to build the area of the West Indies, including Suriname and Barbados, into a sugar producing empire. He turns to acquiring slave labor from Africa to meet this goal.

  1680s: Suriname is lost to the Dutch in the Second Anglo-Dutch War, recaptured by the English in the Third Anglo-Dutch War, and eventually restored to the Dutch by the 1674 Treaty of Westminster.

  Today: Suriname is officially known as the Republic of Suriname, having won independence from the Netherlands in 1975. The lasting colonial influence of the English and the Dutch is revealed in that the nation's official language is Dutch, while English is also commonly spoken.

- **1660s:** King Charles II rules England. While the political parties of the Tories and Whigs battle over the balance of power in the English government (the Tories are advocates for the centralization of power with the monarch, while the Whigs maintain that Parliament should have more power), the bubonic plague sweeps over England in 1665, and in 1666, more devastation occurs with the Great Fire of London.

  1680s: King James II ascends the throne in 1685 after the death of his brother, Charles II. As a Roman Catholic, James is the target of heated criticism from his Protestant opposition. Largely due to the political conflicts aroused by these religious differences, James abdicates the throne in 1689. In his absence, King William and Queen Mary are crowned as the new monarchs of England.

  Today: The reigning monarch of the United Kingdom is Queen Elizabeth II. In 1707, with the signing of the Act of Union by Queen Anne, England and Scotland united to form the Kingdom of Great Britain. The United Kingdom, as of 1801, now also includes Northern Ireland. The role of the monarch of the United Kingdom of Great Britain and Northern Ireland is ceremonial, and the governance of the United Kingdom is handled by the prime minister and Parliament. Gordon Brown is prime minister in the second decade of the twenty-first century.

- **1660s:** There are few female writers in England at this time, and those that are known are largely prominent only within a small circle of admirers. Margaret Cavendish receives greater attention than most female writers for her poetry, the first volume of which was *Poems and Fancies* and was published in 1653, as well as for her plays and miscellaneous works on philosophy.

  1680s: The number of female writers in England remains relatively small. Some, like Behn, however, achieve prominence. Behn is a prolific writer of plays and becomes as well known as her male counterpart, John Dryden. Behn also becomes England's first female novelist with the publication of *Oroonoko* in 1688.

  Today: There is no shortage of female novelists in the United Kingdom. Authors of popular fiction, including J. K. Rowling, as well as authors of literary fiction, including Bernardine Evaristo, Gaynor Arnold, and Lissa Evans, abound. In 2009, Evaristo, Arnold, and Evans are all long-listed for the prestigious literary fiction award, the Orange Prize.

England in the Mid- to Late Seventeenth Century

The mid-seventeenth century was a time of great religious conflict, royal power struggles, and natural disaster in England. When Behn was a young girl, in 1649, King Charles I was executed in the aftermath of the Civil War, in which supporters of Charles battled the supporters of Parliament. The war was largely concerned with the balance of power between the king and the members of Parliament. The Puritan military leader Oliver Cromwell became the head of state and later, in 1653, was named Lord Protector. He refused the offer of the throne, and after his death in 1658, he was succeeded as Lord Protector by his son. Richard Cromwell, however, was unsuccessful in maintaining the Protectorate status of England, and in 1660, Charles II, who had been exiled to France, returned to England and claimed the throne.

Tensions regarding political power continued to divide the English government. The Tory Royalists served as advocates for the restoration of the powers of the king, while Whigs insisted on the use of Parliament as a means of balancing, or limiting, royal powers. During Charles II's reign, the bubonic plague devoured England in 1665, and this calamity was followed in 1666 by the Great Fire of London, which destroyed much of the city. The religious conflicts between Roman Catholics, the Church of England (also known as the Anglican Church, a Protestant church that incorporated some elements of Catholicism), and nonconforming Protestants (those Protestants, also known as Puritans, who fought for an English Protestant Church completely free from Catholic influence), continued to create political controversy. In 1662, the Act of Uniformity was passed, requiring the use of a common prayer book and demanding that clergy members conform to Anglican doctrines. In 1673, nonconforming Protestants and Roman Catholics were excluded from holding civil and military offices by the passage of the Test Act. Charles II died in 1685 and was succeeded by his brother James II. James was a Roman Catholic, and, not surprisingly, conflicts with Protestants ensued. James abdicated the throne in 1689 and the Protestant King William and Queen Mary were crowned.

Imoinda is given the sacred veil from the king.
(Image copyright Elko Dennis, 2010. Used under license from Shutterstock.com)

CRITICAL OVERVIEW

Published in 1688, shortly before Behn's death a year later, *Oroonoko* received the attention commensurate with the work of a popular author, and the work is commonly regarded as the most successful of her novels. As Frederick M. Link observes in the 1968 *Aphra Behn*, the novel additionally "had a topical interest derived from its setting in a colony recently lost to the Dutch." (The English colony in Suriname was attacked by the Dutch in 1667, and ceded to them by treaty in 1674.) Part of the lasting appeal of the work was due to its dramatization by playwright Thomas Southerne in the early eighteenth century, according to Janet Todd in the 1998 *The Critical Fortunes of Aphra Behn*. Abolitionist attitudes during the eighteenth century additionally contributed to the novel's continued popularity, Todd explains. By the early twentieth century, the abolitionist label was still being applied to Behn's novel due to her sympathies toward Oroonoko, and her depiction of the cruelties he endures. In a 1913 introduction to *The Novels of Mrs. Aphra Behn*, Ernest A. Baker regards *Oroonoko* as "the first emancipation novel," and compares Behn's dedication to the cause to "the same feeling of outraged humanity that in after days inflamed Mrs. Stowe" (the author of the antislavery novel *Uncle Tom's Cabin*, published in 1852). While Montague Summers, in the introduction to the reprint of *Oroonoko* in the 1916 *Oroonoko & Other Prose Narratives by Aphra Behn*, questions Baker's assertion, Summers does agree that Behn conveyed genuine "sympathy with the oppressed blacks." Summers goes on to examine the work's literary elements and to praise the lyric quality of Behn's prose as well as her ability to capture the details of her setting. Baker explores Behn's theme of man's savagery toward man, arguing that Behn paints Oroonoko as the "ideal man" and that she contrasts his noble actions with the "vicious manners of the colonists."

Later critics have focused on the work's structure and style, studying the way Behn combined elements of the tragic romance with the conventions of the novel and of the travelogue. As Lore Metzger asserts in the 1973 introduction to *Oroonoko, or the Royal Slave*, "Behn's fusion of romance motifs with novelistic verisimilitude does not consistently produce both wonder and delight." However, Metzger goes on, the attempt is an interesting one in the way it plays to the exploration of the "favorite Renaissance themes," such as the "antithesis of innocent natural and corrupt civilized man." Frederick Link similarly comments on this contrast in his literary biography *Aphra Behn*, but he points out that Behn takes pains to associate Oroonoko with European tradition. He is "not a true savage, nor is his nobility inherent." Rather, Link observes, the "true primitives in the story are the native Indians." Like Metzger, Catherine Gallagher and Simon Stern, in their introduction to the 2000 edition of Behn's *Oroonoko; or, The Royal Slave*, study Behn's attempt to employ different genres or styles in her work. Gallagher and Stern maintain that Behn did not seek to serve as a chronicler of slavery in the region of Suriname, but instead "to blend three popular forms of Restoration literature: the New World travel story, the courtly romance, and the heroic tragedy." Unlike their critical counterparts in the

early twentieth century, Gallagher and Stern find no traces of an emancipatory spirit in Behn's writing. They argue that Behn portrays slavery "as a practical economic matter; it neither needs nor gets transcendental authorization." Finally, Gallagher and Stern comment on the parallels between Behn as author/narrator and Oroonoko. The critics contend that Behn likens herself to Oroonoko by pointing out that they are both recognized as superior to the locals in Suriname, that "like him, she appears a shining marvel when she travels to the Indian village; and like his words, hers are always supposed to be truthful."

CRITICISM

Catherine Dominic

Dominic is a novelist and a freelance writer and editor. In the following essay, she explores Behn's views regarding the inherent superiority of a race or an individual as the author conveys them in the novel Oroonoko. *She finds that for Behn, an individual's superiority is related to his or her status as either a white Englishman/woman or as a member of royalty, regardless of race.*

The issue of slavery as Behn discusses it in *Oroonoko* and the attendant racial issues stand out for modern readers as the work's most dominant themes. Twentieth- and twenty-first-century scholars debate the extent to which Behn intended to explore the moral implications of the practice of slavery, with some earlier scholars insisting that Behn had abolitionist motives, and others contending she viewed slavery, like her contemporaries, as a matter of economic practicality. A close examination of Behn's characterization in *Oroonoko* reveals an ambiguity in Behn's racial attitudes. Behn's depiction of the native inhabitants of Suriname, as well as of many of the slaves, seems to indicate her sense of the white racial superiority of the English colonists. At the same time, Behn recognizes the royal superiority of the African character of Oroonoko. Behn's novel suggests that social hierarchies depend either on the innate superiority transmitted through one's race or through one's royal lineage, regardless of race; Behn recognizes as socially superior those born white and English, or those born royal.

The notion of innate superiority based on one's royal birth is one Behn was believed to

WHAT DO I READ NEXT?

- Behn achieved acclaim as a playwright before her novel *Oroonoko* was published in 1688. The Oxford World Classics edition of Behn's dramatic works *The Rover and Other Plays*, published in 2008, contains Behn's best-known play, *The Rover*, which was originally published in 1677, along with several of Behn's comedies and satires.

- In Angeline Goreau's *Reconstructing Aphra: A Social Biography of Aphra Behn*, published in 1980 by Dial Press, Goreau attempts to place what little is known about Behn's life into social, historical, and cultural contexts.

- John Dryden was Behn's contemporary and a fellow playwright. His drama *All for Love*, originally published in 1677, is counted among Dryden's most acclaimed. The work is a romantic tragedy concerned with the historical lovers Antony and Cleopatra. *All for Love* is available through Echo Library, and was published in 2007.

- *Caribbean Exchanges: Slavery and the Transformation of English Society, 1640–1700* by Susan Dwyer Amussen, published by the University of North Carolina Press in 2007, explores the history of the English colonies in the Caribbean in the mid- to late seventeenth century. Amussen studies the colonists' use of slaves in the production of sugar and additionally explores the ways in which colonial experiences shaped cultural and national identity in England.

- Editor Paula Burnett offers a collection of poetry by Caribbean writers in *The Penguin Book of Caribbean Verse in English*, published by Penguin Global in 2006. Burnett's collection features works from the Caribbean oral tradition, including centuries-old slave songs, as well as poetry from contemporary Caribbean poets.

- *Sold for Silver: An Autobiography of a Girl Sold into Slavery in Southeast Asia*, by Janet Lim, like *Oroonoko*, is the story of an individual who is forced into a life of slavery. Lim's work, however, is an autobiographical account by a Chinese woman of her life as a slave in Singapore in the 1930s and beyond. The work was originally published in 1958 and is available in a 2005 edition published by Monsoon Books.

- Sharon M. Draper's *Copper Sun*, published in 2006 by Athenaeum Books for Young Readers, is a young-adult novel that traces the experiences of a fifteen-year-old African girl who is sold into slavery in eighteenth-century America. While Draper's work is intended for teen audiences, it does, like *Oroonoko*, contain some graphic details concerning the brutalities suffered by slaves.

- Editors Elspeth Graham, Hilary Hinds, Elaine Hobby, and Helen Wilcox collect autobiographical essays by seventeenth-century English poets and essayists in *Her Own Life: Autobiographical Writings by Seventeenth Century Englishwomen*, published by Routledge in 1989. The collection offers a glimpse into the daily life of women during this time period.

---

have subscribed to, according to Catherine Gallagher and Simon Stern. In their introduction to the 2000 edition of *Oroonoko*, the critics maintain that Behn "was a well-known royalist," and that the novel indicates Behn's support for the rights of kingship. Behn's writing in *Oroonoko* clearly suggests her sense of racial and royal superiority. The work is in no way emancipatory, as early twentieth-century critics have suggested, nor does it indicate a detached view of racial dominance based on the economic necessity of having a slave labor force to work the Suriname sugar plantations, as later critics have argued. *Oroonoko* indicates that

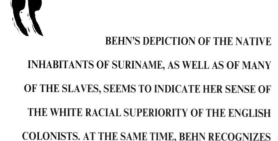

BEHN'S DEPICTION OF THE NATIVE INHABITANTS OF SURINAME, AS WELL AS OF MANY OF THE SLAVES, SEEMS TO INDICATE HER SENSE OF THE WHITE RACIAL SUPERIORITY OF THE ENGLISH COLONISTS. AT THE SAME TIME, BEHN RECOGNIZES THE ROYAL SUPERIORITY OF THE AFRICAN CHARACTER OF OROONOKO."

superiority—based on one's race or one's status as a royal—is an issue more deeply rooted than in economic concerns alone. Rather, Behn's story reveals that her sense of social order depends on her ideas of royal and racial superiority.

The first hint of Behn's sense of racial superiority is revealed early in her novel. In describing the native people of Suriname, Behn stresses the childlike innocence of the "Indians," as she calls them (as Suriname is included in the region known as the West Indies). She speaks of how the English "caress them with all the brotherly and friendly affection in the world." Near the end of her discourse on the idyllic lives lead by the Indians, Behn reveals the true reasons the English are friendly with the inhabitants of Suriname. She describes how useful the Indians are in their knowledge of the land and its treasures. They supply the English with items it is difficult or impossible for the English to acquire on their own. Behn compares them to the hounds the English usually use for hunting, as they can track and run down small prey. Behn states:

So that they being, on all occasions very useful to us, we find it absolutely necessary to caress them as friends, and not to treat them as slaves; nor dare we do other, their numbers so far surpassing ours.

In addition, then, to the economic usefulness of the Indians, they simply outnumber the English, and they are well armed, apparently, at least with bows and arrows, as Behn has previously discussed in her discourse on hunting. The English do not "dare" attempt to use the native people as slaves, out of fear they will be overtaken. The social order of the English colony, then, is at stake, and cooperation with the Suriname natives

is essential, despite the fact that Behn suggests that if it were not for the risks associated with being outnumbered by the natives, the English may well have used them as slaves. The natives, in their inferiority to the English colonists that Behn intimates would certainly make useful slaves to the English, but fearing for their safety, the English decide to take advantage of the native people of Suriname in other ways. Behn compares these native people to children and to animals, comparisons that place the English in the superior position in their relationship to the natives. They may not enslave the native people, but they clearly view them as inferior, even if they are potentially dangerous. Behn's analysis of the relationship between the English colonists and the native people of Suriname also suggests that the natives are simpleminded enough to be both used and kept in control by the English through the superficially friendly attitude the English employ.

After explaining why the English do not enslave the Indians, she turns immediately to the solution the English have identified for their labor issue. "Those then whom we make use of to work in our plantations of sugar are Negroes, black slaves altogether." An explanation of how the slaves are acquired from Africa ensues, and during the course of this discussion, Behn has the opportunity to introduce the Prince Oroonoko. In describing Oroonoko's qualities, Behn conveys her sense of amazement at Oroonoko's nobility. She wonders

where it was he learned so much humanity... where it was he got that real greatness of soul, those refined notions of true honour, that absolute generosity, and that softness that was capable of the highest passions of love and gallantry.

A portion of this noble nature Behn attributes to the Frenchman who tutored Oroonoko and taught him, among other things, "morals, language and science." Behn also observes that Oroonoko was motivated in his educational goals by the fact that "he loved, when he came from war, to see all the English gentleman that traded thither." At least a portion, then, of the admirable qualities Behn identifies as praiseworthy in Oroonoko are the result of the influence of (white) Europeans. She goes on to applaud Oroonoko's courage, wit, extensive knowledge of European history, and his lack of any traces of barbarity. He behaves as though he has been educated "in some European court."

Behn goes on to praise Oroonoko's physical appearance, delineating the many ways in which Oroonoko is unlike his fellow Africans. He is not "that brown, rusty black which most of that nation are, but a perfect ebony or polished jet." His nose is more Roman in shape than African, and his mouth is finely shaped and "far from those great turned lips which are so natural to the rest of the Negroes." In order to emphasize the prince's superior nature, Behn distinguishes Oroonoko from his countrymen, and in many cases, compares him favorably to Europeans. In particular, Behn appears to be impressed with the fact that Oroonoko is "as capable of love as it was possible for a brave and gallant man to be." His nobility, then, has been in part due to the Europeans who have instructed him. His physical beauty is compared with the features of Europeans. Anything that cannot be compared or attributed to European influence is treated with wonder by Behn.

The only means by which Behn can make sense of Oroonoko's uncharacteristically noble nature, then, is by studying Oroonoko through the filter of his royal birth. She reminds the reader of Oroonoko's lineage by referring to him as the prince and by observing that he is the grandson of the ancient king. On the plantation, Trefry finds "something so extraordinary in his face, his shape and mien, a greatness of look, and haughtiness in his air." Trefry sets Oroonoko apart from the other slaves at the plantation. Later, when Oroonoko is brought before the other slaves, the same people he himself sold to the English, Oroonoko is lauded as a king, and Trefry is pleased to see that his understanding of Oroonoko's royal bearing is supported by the way the other slaves treat him and honor him as a king.

Behn describes how Oroonoko and his lover, Imoinda, whom he has taken as his wife and whom he has discovered has been sold to the same plantation, spend many hours with her at her residence on the plantation. Oroonoko does not work as a slave but instead converses about literature, philosophy, and religion with Behn. She makes no mention of interacting with any of the other slaves in this fashion or of having any opinion at all on their well-being. But Oroonoko and Imoinda are of royal birth, and Behn, like Trefry, treats them as such. The brutality Oroonoko later suffers is lamented by Behn, but she does not seem to regard the torturing in terms of

its relation to slavery in general. It is an injustice to a man of royal breeding, to Oroonoko. When the slave Tuscan is beaten along with Oroonoko, Behn offers a report of it in a journalistic manner, but her tone is distanced; she appears unaffected by the savagery endured by Tuscan. Rather, Behn uses Tuscan, who remains loyal to Oroonoko, to highlight the honor and dedication Oroonoko inspires.

The only argument against slavery in the novel is made by Oroonoko. When he can no longer be "diverted" by the whites on the plantation from thoughts of freedom for his wife and unborn child, Oroonoko speaks to the slaves on the plantation about the evils they suffer as slaves, and how it is beneath them to be treated in such a manner. His argument, as Behn describes it, is not, however, based on an acknowledgment that slavery is inherently wrong. Oroonoko suggests that men have a right to treat people as slaves if they are won in battle. In his view, warfare ennobles the act of slave trading, and it also justifies his earlier actions as a man who won slaves in battle, presented them as gifts, like currency, and sold them to the English. Oroonoko states that if he and his fellow slaves had been "vanquished . . . nobly in a fight" or been won in "honourable battle" then they would not have cause, as noble soldiers, to be angry about their fate. Yet, they have not been so defeated in battle, he states, and therefore they do have cause to fight being treated as slaves. In this speech, Oroonoko attempts to identify the circumstances under which slavery would be justified. However, if, as Behn previously stated, the slaves at the plantation were the very people Oroonoko previously sold when he was a warrior prince in Africa, then Oroonoko's own argument makes little sense. He apparently felt justified in the selling of people he won in battle. Yet, now he tells those same individuals whom he has sold that their enslavement is not just, as it was not the result of an honorable battle. Oroonoko seems to have conveniently forgotten that his own conquering of these individuals is the reason they are now slaves.

One may draw the conclusion that if Oroonoko is as intelligent as he has been thus far depicted, he is well aware of his own complicity in the current predicament of his fellow slaves. One can only assume that Oroonoko is attempting to manipulate the slaves so that they will side with him and aid him in his own escape. It should be further noted that when Oroonoko had earlier been attempting to bargain for his and Imoinda's freedom, he was not so much concerned with the fate of his fellow slaves. As Behn reports, after it is discovered that Imoinda is pregnant, Oroonoko was

> more impatient of his liberty, and he was every day treating with Trefry for his and Clemene's [Imoinda's] liberty; and offered either gold, or a vast quantity of slaves, which should be paid before they let him go.

An astute reader will understand from Oroonoko's manipulation of the other slaves, and from Behn's continued sympathy for Oroonoko, that he and Behn feel that as a royal, Oroonoko should be exempt from a system that is perfectly acceptable for other, inferior individuals.

Although the rest of the novel details, with great and deserved sympathy for Oroonoko and Imoinda, the tragedies they suffer, Behn nevertheless has established quite starkly her views regarding the hierarchies that order her world. Both Behn and Oroonoko appear to share the view that the superiority of certain individuals is a necessity in order to preserve social order. Behn identifies circumstances under which toleration of an inferior race is necessitated in order to maintain social order, as well as circumstances under which the economic issues justify the slavery of individuals of a different race. Behn additionally uses Oroonoko as a means of demonstrating the natural superiority of those of royal birth; she repeatedly emphasizes Oroonoko's innate nobility, his potential as a wise ruler, and his status as a royal prince. As Behn describes, this status imbues Oroonoko with the right to sell his own people as slaves. The social order of his community is maintained by the "superior" members of the society exercising their rights over those deemed inferior by rank or by loss of status in battle. The inferior are utilized for the economic benefit of the community, or as a means of emphasizing the superiority of others, as when Oroonoko presents Imoinda with the slaves he has captured in battle. Imoinda, despite her own noble birth, is used in a similar manner when she is taken as the king's mistress. The world Behn describes is one in which those who are inferior in terms of rank and birth are viewed only in terms of the use to which they may be put by those who regard themselves as superior.

Source: Catherine Dominic, Critical Essay on *Oroonoko; or, The Royal Slave: A True History*, in *Novels for Students*, Gale, Cengage Learning, 2011.

Behn describes the beautiful blooming trees of Suriname, which take a separate meaning for the slaves. (*Image copyright Renate Micallef, 2010. Used under license from Shutterstock.com*)

Emily Hodgson Anderson

In the following excerpt, Anderson suggests that Behn experimented with different genres and styles of prose in Oroonoko *and such conscious experimentation characterizes the novel's form.*

SEEING BETWEEN THE LINES

...So, how does one teach *Oroonoko*, or Oroonoko for that matter? If novelty cannot be conveyed by either words or images, we seem to have ended at a paradox. And if Behn's spectacular war captains encourage the acts of independent interpretation that allow them to be evaluated repeatedly in novel ways, they also raise the traditional problem in the explication of spectacle or texts: how do we know a "right" interpretation from a "wrong" one? For all its emphasis on the independent evaluation of spectacle, this text remains peculiarly invested in explaining it. The war captains need to tell their visitors, through an interpreter, how they received their wounds (50), just as Oroonoko needs to justify Imoinda's murder verbally to the colonists (63). That Behn's text presents many of its "passive" spectacles as initially misread demonstrates both the flexibility of interpretation, and the instinct that some interpretations are better than others. Yet even as the narrator endorses a "right" reading, her very act of reinterpreting spectacles reminds us that we should not accept her final assessments too easily (see also Chibka 519).

But at the same time, we must acknowledge that our responses to this text, and these images, are not random or accidental; our resistance is encouraged by the narrator herself, from her deprecating "so they Slash on . . ." (50) to her insistence that Oroonoko (the man) transcends representation. By telling us this, she also tells us that *Oroonoko* (the text) transcends representation—that her evaluations cannot, as it were, be taken at face value. So when we question, when we resist, we are responding to a carefully placed challenge that encourages individual interpretation while it frames or guides it.

In *Oroonoko*, it is again the vision of the war captains that epitomizes both this challenge and this guidance. As with many prior images in the novel, the captains' mangled faces draw the gaze even as they transcend description: "so frightful a vision it was to see them no fancy can create; no such dreams can represent so dreadful a spectacle" (50). But this time, the narrator's description breaks down on several levels; at a loss for words, she challenges us to be at a loss for images—our fancy, dreams, or imagination cannot do justice to the spectacle the colonists see. Years after the publication of *Oroonoko*, Laurence Sterne would similarly challenge readers with his famous "blank page." As an ideal type, Sterne's Widow Wadman is more beautiful than words can say or eyes behold, but it is her uniqueness, more than her beauty, that would be lost were Sterne to use adjectives or even pictures to depict her. So he gives us an empty page, on which we are each supposed to impose our conception of the female ideal (331). The individual quality of each reader's "fancy" ensures Widow Wadman's perpetual uniqueness; she will forever and inevitably be without equal. Behn's insistence on imaginative insufficiency, apparently so opposite to Sterne's approach, has an identical effect: the result is not that we refuse to imagine her war captains, but that we refuse to imagine any conception of them as final or definitive. Thus her spectacle too remains beyond comparison, impossibly horrific and inevitably unique.

And so our imaginations run free—but not out of control. In both cases the guiding force of the narrator is present even as it is consciously effaced; the spectacle is conjured from within that kind of Kantian "frame" that "creates form while denying itself as a form" (Terada 154). Without the very unblank pages that surround it, Sterne's blank page would have neither meaning nor existence—just as a space without boundaries or demarcations cannot be perceived. And as Behn's readers recreate the garish faces that symbolize passivity, our own imaginative process discloses "the latent activity of the frame," of the narrative that produces our imagination (Terada 153).

Novelty is a transient, temporal state; it vanishes with the very curiosity it inspires. But the interpretative process, the process by which we come to know, is forever new, unique, and variable. To communicate novelty, then, is to guide interpretation, so that the professor devoted to teaching the novel can learn a lesson from Behn's mutilated captains—who are evaluated not on their acts of mutilation, but on their ability to live on and display the gaps and scars that mutilation leaves behind. While the Indian generals quite literally carve out a space in which their judges become conditioned to find valor, Behn and teachers of Behn use her narrative less literally to create room for the individual imagination. The repeated rituals within text and classroom frame, as opposed to fill, the space for personal epiphany, so that the new genre takes its name not for what it is but what it holds: Oroonoko, that prince whose novelty is repeatedly recreated in our mind's eye.

Oroonoko thus suggests two further and connected lines of inquiry for novel studies. As it shares with many eighteenth-century novels a concern for both didacticism and its own newness, it illustrates how the genre is particularly suited to highlight a synthesis between scholarship and pedagogy. Our criticism could benefit from attention to the theories of teaching and learning that these texts advance, and to how these theories gain complexity from their conscious situation in a generic framework that was at the time unfamiliar to their audiences. The epistemological problems developed and resolved within these texts resonate with the epistemological problem posed by the genre itself, and addressing these textual moments could lead to a richer and less limiting theory of this literary form.

For example, since Ian Watt, "the" novel, and the realism of the novel, have been linked to a description of the individual, and the investigation of interiority and psychological depth. Recently, Deidre Lynch has sought to debunk this claim, arguing that early- and mid-century narratives in particular exhibited types rather than individuals, and that over-particularization of a character was even frowned upon by eighteenth-century critics (9 and passim). What is at stake in this debate is how "character," or individuality, is effectively understood, communicated, and interpreted, and with her corrective reading Lynch identifies Watt's categorization as wanting. But, as illustrated by my reading of *Oroonoko*, this debate is not specific to twentieth- and twenty-first-century literary critics.

Oroonoko explores a related challenge, that of depicting and conveying novel characters and settings, and for Behn to convey Oroonoko and his environs realistically, the aspect of newness cannot be lost. The realism of Behn's narrative, then, resides in her ability both to represent and to preserve novelty, which it does not through visual description or probing psychological detail but through comparative references and a vocabulary of excess. Novelty exceeds visualization, though it depends upon the visualization or visual description of known objects (or types) as a conceptual starting point.

The challenge of communicating novelty is common to any realistic representation of the individual or individual experience, which is by definition unique and singular, that which we have not seen or known before (see Watt 13).

And when read within the contemporary desire to preserve novelty, a narrative's reliance on types or examples functions not to efface individuality but to promote it. For instance, in the passage from *Tom Jones* that probably inspired Sterne's blank page, Fielding invokes famous statues and paintings of great beauties, only to disclaim all these sights as representative of his beautiful Sophia: "Yet is it possible, my Friend, that thou mayest have seen all these without being able to form an exact Idea of SOPHIA: For she did not exactly resemble any of them . . . most of all, she resembled one whose Image never can depart from my Breast, and whom if thou does remember, thou hast then, my Friend, an adequate Idea of SOPHIA" (117). Fielding, like Behn, plays upon our imaginative limitations, for with the indirect reference to his dead wife (whom, of course, we do not remember), Fielding's narrator makes any "adequate idea" of Sophia quite impossible. But an "adequate idea" would not be quite accurate, either. The initial references to well-known images exist only to emphasize how a realistic portrayal of Sophia exceeds description or visualization; they ask readers to revise continually their conceptions of her, so that Sophia's uniqueness, her exemplarity—her individuality—are better attained and preserved in these attempts, than in any result.

So I suggest that, especially in those prose narratives that package themselves as new, if we situate our questions about narrative realism and character within the contemporaneous focus on novelty, then perhaps the goal of all these texts, both early and late, will appear to be more similar than has recently been proposed. While creative (and critical) approaches to characterization and realism have necessarily shifted over time, the resistance to particularized character that Lynch associates with the early examples of prose fiction might not illustrate a lack of interest in the individual, but be instead the signal for readers to extrapolate from these types—a historically specific narrative strategy designed to convey and preserve novelty and uniqueness. And then perhaps we may again productively consider the wide range of narrative texts from the 1680s to the 1780s as novels.

Source: Emily Hodgson Anderson, "Novelty in Novels: A Look at What's New in Aphra Behn's *Oroonoko*," in *Studies in the Novel*, Vol. 39, No. 1, Spring 2007, pp. 1–16.

> BEHN IS NOT INTERESTED IN ALWAYS REPRESENTING ABSOLUTE OR FACTUAL TRUTH. RATHER, AMIDST THE TRUTH CLAIMS AND HIGHLY DETAILED FACTUAL ACCOUNTS, SHE SHARES A MORAL CONCEPTION OF TRUTH."

Vernon Guy Dickson

In the following excerpt, Dickson advises that in the quest to ascertain the truth from fiction in Oroonoko, *the interpretation should not be separated from its context and moral focus.*

[T]he historian, wanting the precept, is so tied, not to what should

> be but to what is, to the particular truth of things and not to the general reason of things, that his example draweth no necessary consequence, and therefore a less fruitful doctrine. Now doth the peerless poet perform both.—Sir Philip Sidney (1)

For years, a central issue in the discussion of Aphra Behn's *Oroonoko; or, The Royal Slave. A True History* has been whether it is true or false, factual or fabricated. (2) While most now believe the tale's core to be authentic, based on Behn's real stay in Suriname, others question the need to ascertain the truthfulness of the work; after all, who would write pages on the factual fallacies of *Robinson Crusoe* or *Gulliver's Travels*? (3) There are reasons to question the incessant interrogation of truthfulness in Behn's text in comparison with more accepted canonical figures—her texts have received much unfair criticism, though this attention has also been productive of detailed and meaningful inquiries into her works. (4) While I believe the search for truth within Behn's work is still a meaningful one, there is a need to revisit the motives and aims of that search, to contextualize Behn's exploration of truth with respect to the period's changing notions of truth's relation to and representation of fact and fiction. (5)

Sir Philip Sidney, immediately following the epigraph I have given, argues that "whatsoever the [moral] philosopher saith should be done, [the poet] giveth a perfect picture of it in someone." (6) Behn, as I will develop further, enacts within Oroonoko's character this performance

of morality that Sidney locates at the juncture of poetry, history, and moral philosophy, displaying what she sees as appropriate truth—moral exemplarity and the truth of moral character that her finally bleak work suggests is missing within her own culture. Behn ostensibly argues against Sidney's praise of poetry, emphasizing in her opening lines the strict truth of *Oroonoko* without the embellishments of the "Poets Pleasure" as encouraged by her period's focus on empiricism and post-Baconian rhetorical practices. (7) However, Behn also performs the role of Sidney's poet, using *Oroonoko* as a representative of truth and wonders yet unknown (or misunderstood), a moral example of what "should be" in her own world. (8) In many ways, then, *Oroonoko* is a text about truth's place in Behn's world, fictional and actual. Accordingly, there is a need to refocus the text's analysis to a moral rather than biographical or historical reading for truth. Behn's frames for her work, before and within her tale, and her emphasis on authorizing her narrative through a variety of gestures suggest *Oroonoko* seeks to assert cultural models of moral truth and exemplarity.

Furthermore, the models that *Oroonoko* asserts are not new; rather, Behn uses wonder (especially in the character of Oroonoko) and the current vogue of travel narratives to reassert humanist traditions of moral exemplarity, tied up with noble and singular heroism—the "Great Man" to whom she refers repeatedly throughout her introductory epistle passing out of currency in her time (pp. 34–7). (9) This idea of singular exemplarity also reinforces Behn's royalist perspective. (10) As my epigraph from Sidney suggests, I believe that reading Behn as a participant in and conservator of an earlier humanist tradition of exemplarity instead of primarily, as is commonly done, the beginning point of the novel and new models of historicity helps to explain many of the seeming incongruities and ruptures of her text, especially in terms of her treatment of truth and fiction, history and morality. (11)

...According to Behn's account, then, veracity—including the Romantick (though true) "Wonders" of "the other World"—and the authorizing "Merit" of a royal and moral character create the core and the value of her work. (15) Behn is intent on using the honorable character of her royal and foreign subject to authorize the narration; she is merely a medium of the story.

This authorizing subject's place—a subject who, significantly, also acts as a primary agent in and of the narration—is reinforced by Behn's vehement avowal of the truthfulness of her tale, which is in turn strengthened by her frequent inclusions of verifiable facts mixed with detailed ethnographic observations that support her role as eyewitness to the narration's occurrences. (16) In addition, both truth and character also rely on the vogue for "Romantick" wonders that absorbed thinkers and audiences of the time. (17) Thus, within a frame of revealing "Truth," though "New and Strange," Behn's work rests its authority on an interlinking of observation and second-hand narration based upon the unimpeachable moral character of Oroonoko. Significantly, as I will develop further, Behn also hints at the fiction of her work, showing her piece to be interested in moral more than narrowly factual truth. (18)

Unconceivable wonders, for Behn, do not limit the delivery of truth. Rather, in her period truth is frequently tied to the wonderful and to the unknown. Katie Whitaker affirms the "broad interest in rarities and wonders of all sorts, natural and artificial" in the seventeenth century. (19) Whitaker's work also connects wonder to everything from feathers to the unusual human being (interestingly, each plays a role in *Oroonoko*) always emphasizing the place of reason and religion in the study and appreciation of wonder. (20) In his insightful examination of wonder and the marvelous in the early modern period, Peter G. Platt notes that even "late in the seventeenth century, wondrous beasts still make appearances in the Transactions of the Royal Society of London." (21) Aphra Behn plainly worked within very different understandings of science, nature, truth, and history than those to which we are accustomed, just as she worked within different conceptions of narration and literary form. As Nicholas Jardine and Emma C. Spary point out, "[T]he boundaries between the natural and conventional, artificial and social have been continually contested and relocated." (22) To Behn, and to many of her readers, wonder was closely related to truth as either a source of truth or an acknowledgment of truth unknown. Truth was not always about knowledge; in fact, many of the greatest truths were not known or thought to be knowable.

. . . Behn's primary interest in wonders is to authorize her work; to excuse (or to allow for) seemingly "Romantick," or fictitious, elements; and to prepare the reader to approach her work credulously, to accept things, including models, new and strange though real (true) in what she would consider the most significant sense of the term. As Mary Baine Campbell argues, wonder in Behn's work should be "taken on its own terms, not as or not only as a rhetorical masking or a deflection of 'reality.'" (26) Mary Baine Campbell also is aware of the blurring of fiction and fact that *Oroonoko* represents: "However much it may be simply true that Africans from the areas around 'Coramantien' had European features, it is surely not 'true' that they (or for that matter any European lovers or kings) spoke in a crisis in the precise accents of English heroic drama." (27) Behn is not interested in always representing absolute or factual truth. Rather, amidst the truth claims and highly detailed factual accounts, she shares a moral conception of truth. For Behn, wonders become the means both to introduce new truths as well as possibly to conceal untruth, allowing her fiction to transcend factual truth to establish moral and royal precedent—and to reify the function of texts in asserting proper moral practices. Wonders are Behn's method of enlarging the scope of understanding and perception to become aware of and to overcome contemporary social views and failings.

. . . By framing her work with factual details known to her audience as well as with a noble prince of impeachable character, Behn reinforces her work's worth, while diffusing her authority on to other sources and clouding a search for absolute historical and biographical truth within the tale. Behn frees her noble source from full accountability by relating the tale in such a way that shows her mediation and alludes to the mediation of others, as the narrator tells us of things that neither she nor Oroonoko could have known: events private to Imoinda and the old king, conversations between Aboan and Onahal, etc. (40) The narrator also describes Oroonoko in the third person at points that Behn (as a character) could never have seen, such as on the slave boat: "It may be easily guess'd, in what manner the Prince resented this Indignity, who may be best resembl'd to a Lion taken in a Toil; so he rag'd, so he struggl'd for Liberty, but all in vain" (p. 64). David Paxman has argued that much of the tale's "hyperbolic praise" of

Oroonoko must be self-referential. (41) While this assertion may be true, I believe the multi-vocality of the work's narration allows for a space of uncertainty, for Behn's supposition (as, possibly, evidenced in the relation of Oroonoko's actions on the slave boat) or hyperbole, and for other, and unknown, mediation. The tale derives from an unknown (and thus, again, unquestionable) shared source, centered in the royal character of Oroonoko but diffused by a multiplicity of sources and mediators of truth, allowing Behn to swear to the tale's truth as a sharer of received knowledge as well as firsthand experience, and leading us to trust in an inter-woven tale in which the boundaries of certain knowledge (especially factual knowledge) are always unclear and purposefully unimportant.

Behn, accordingly, creates in Oroonoko a self-referential source of truth and exemplarity tied into the moral and social aspects of her work. (42) As the history's value purportedly derives from the moral character at the story's center (and source), the work draws on his morality to overdetermine the truth of the work. Oroonoko becomes symbolic of moral truth and character to such a degree that nothing he does can be questioned, while the history constructed from amorphous and unknown sources becomes so interwoven with the factual and fictional aspects of the work that any attempt to separate historical truths from the narration's purported truth, without accepting the inner relations of truth and character within the work, would require a dismembering of the body of the text not dissimilar to the brutal dismembering of Oroonoko's body that takes place at the close of the work. Byam hacks up Oroonoko in order to impose upon the other slaves his own version of truth, indeed his own tale of absolute mastery over the land and peoples there—a tale equally based in fact and fiction, but lacking the moral core of character and truth that Oroonoko has come to represent. (43)

Truth then can be questioned and appropriated—which Byam violently exemplifies—but true meaning, signification, is located for Behn within the moral whole, within the authorizing agent of the work—the truth of character beyond discrete actions—with the burden of understanding and application upon the audience, as described by Erasmus. Again, we are reminded of Behn's insistence that the truth and value of her work (as well as others' works, as her preface

states) lie in the audience's ability to glean and to emulate the good from the necessarily (and unimportantly) fallible characters presented to them, in daily life, in fiction, in fact. Behn's truth is wonderful and thus not fully understood but certainly based in moral and royal character and observation. Another tale can be written about the factual truthfulness of *Oroonoko*, but such a work would betray and dismember the moral corpus of Behn's narration.

Source: Vernon Guy Dickson, "Truth, Wonder, and Exemplarity in Aphra Behn's *Oroonoko*," in *Studies in English Literature, 1500–1900*, Vol. 47, No. 3, Summer 2007, pp. 573–95.

Daniel Pigg

In the following essay, Behn's novel is described as a text that challenged the minds of Restoration English literature period but continues to appeal today.

Aphra Behn's *Oroonoko* (1688), an intensely stirring work, has captivated scholars of Restoration English literature in the last two decades with its obvious preoccupations with race, class, and gender. Behn, an underappreciated writer whose fortunes in the scholarly world are rising, is an experimenter in literary forms that attempt to characterize cultural and national identities. Among her works, *Oroonoko* is most keenly attentive to this issue. Studies of the "novel" have focused on issues such as the interplay among the writer, the constructed Behn of the narrative and the character Oroonoko, the notion of the noble savage or natural man, reliance on travel and romance narratives, fact versus fiction in the text, and political posturing within the scope of representing Oroonoko and Imoinda. What was seen in the Restoration and throughout the eighteenth century as an important abolitionist text has since the early '80s been investigated with methodologies—especially new historicism and feminist critique—that while not undermining obvious historicist assessments of the text, at least show socio-political ambivalence in Behn's posturing. In her 1981 article, Lucy K. Hayden observes that Behn's overall presentation supports slavery's continuation, and she asks "does she pity Oroonoko because he is a noble chief in captivity rather than because he is an enslaved human being?" (405). In an almost conscious way, William C. Spengemann in 1984, Laura Brown in 1987, Jacqueline Pearson in 1991, and

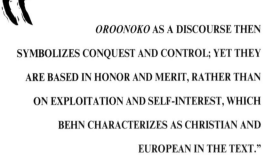

OROONOKO AS A DISCOURSE THEN

SYMBOLIZES CONQUEST AND CONTROL; YET THEY

ARE BASED IN HONOR AND MERIT, RATHER THAN

ON EXPLOITATION AND SELF-INTEREST, WHICH

BEHN CHARACTERIZES AS CHRISTIAN AND

EUROPEAN IN THE TEXT."

Moira Ferguson in 1992 attempted to answer her question. Ferguson, for example, contends that class may be Behn's greatest concern in representing Oroonoko and that she views him favorably as long as he upholds her clear royalist position. It is certainly true that on some level she is not present at some of the most critical junctures in Oroonoko's life (339–59).

While these studies have provided an important context for examining the work, none has attempted to explain those seemingly irresolvable issues in light of the text's own comments on the power of language and representation. Fissures or gaps in the text that we as late twentieth-century readers perceive as "Anglo-African"—a highlighting of the seeming superiority of European qualities—reflect more on Behn's own crisis in the creation of a discourse to represent a world which most of the time is the "Other" (Moira Ferguson 340). Oroonoko as a character is a construction of a variety of discourses—all of which he speaks or presents in gestures. He exists at the intersection of these voices, and thus as one of these shaping voices shifts and another gains dominance, his construction changes. He can be a talented speaker of European languages, be knowledgeable and sympathetic to some of the dire political events of seventeenth-century England, be a master of rhetoric, be a passionate lover, and even be a barbaric murderer.

This article asserts that Oroonoko as a character represents a different order of discursive model, unlike the typical European discourse, identified by verbal communication only. He represents a literary approximation of universal language theory. Throughout the text Oroonoko communicates by words but more importantly

through gestural signs by which Behn attempts to separate him from others, including other African slaves. Much of the nobility that Behn assigns to Oroonoko circulates around this model for characterizing him.

To understand Behn's development of *Oroonoko* as a discourse, we first need to define this "discourse" in terms of Restoration language theory. Then we can suggest a reading of the text in an historicist/semiotic mode that shows the process by which Behn creates *Oroonoko* as a discourse that ultimately cannot be contained within traditional frames. At the same time that this treatment forms a significant commentary on English colonialism and exploitation, it increases the worth of the African Oroonoko by allowing him to transcend the national limits of European discourse.

1

Behn wrote *Oroonoko* during a period of considerable discussion about the nature of language and the interconnectedness of languages throughout the world. Ideas of a universal language that might be discovered for and used by merchants to harness the economic potential of foreign trade by the application of both a Marxist-based vision of power as suppression and of the Foucaultian-based notion of power as creating a kind of network circuitry were the driving forces behind the activity. Linguists such as Cave Beck, John Wilkins, and George Dalgano attempted to develop a symbolic-based language much like that of Egyptian hieroglyphics or Chinese ideographs (Cohen 1–6). Among these linguists and among philosophers such as Descartes, there was a growing sense of the limitations of human speech and writing in representing thought. In a letter to Mersenne, Descartes contended there is a relationship between "natural language (as speech) and the natural language of emotions caused by sensations" (Reiss 280). Timothy J. Reiss notes that Descartes's notion relates to "'body language,' a language composed essentially (though not entirely) of gestures" (280).

Whether or not Behn knew these works directly is less significant than we might think at first. Many of these ideas are deeply rooted in texts contemplating colonialism as a discourse; she adopts and foregrounds this medium in her text as she attempts to use Oroonoko as a means for investigating a universal Adamic language underlying linguistic discourse. She elevates Oroonoko in her text above all other Africans, including Imoinda, as a bridge between European and African discourse—a term which can be defined as "the way in which the material embodying sign processes is organized. Discourse can thus be characterized as the visible and describable praxis of what is called 'thinking'" (Reiss 9). The position of radical instability allows her to "immortalize" him just as a Renaissance sonnet writer such as Spenser or Shakespeare would eternize the discursive representative of a person.

2

Part of the complexity in representing Oroonoko centers around the narrator's role in the text. Throughout the entire text there is a feeling of anxiety about representation if not, at times, an unrealized fear associated with it. On two occasions Behn articulates her position relative to her subject. Immediately after Trefry and Oroonoko meet in Suriname for the first time, Behn writes:

> But his Misfortune was, to fall in an obscure World, that afforded only a Female Pen to celebrate his Fame; tho' I doubt not but it had lived from others Endeavours, if the Dutch, who immediately after his Time took the Country, had not killed, banished and dispersed all those that were capable of giving the World this great Man's Life, much better than I have done. And Mr. Trefry, who design'd it, died before he began it, and bemoan'd himself for not having undertook it in Time.

As Laura Brown observes, the narrator's seeming "act of self-effacement" (50) allows her to pursue a topic that a male writer would have presented less graphically. The marginality topos for both writer/narrator and Oroonoko represents the text's announced problem. She is only able to capture her hero in several oral speeches, similar to those we would expect to hear from a hero in a Restoration heroic drama, his gestures, including the powerful gaze of desire, and his physical description. In her remarks she bows to male authority in writing and terms her own as a matter of expedience. On another level, however, presenting her own task as a matter of provisional discourse sets up an homology: she is to a male writer what Oroonoko is to a European prince. The frames are constructed to break from the beginning, freeing both Oroonoko in a discursive space of honor along with her own liberation from male authority.

At the conclusion of the text, reminiscent of an epilogue at the end of dramatic tragedy, the narrator again notes the difficulties of writing:

> Thus died this great Man, worthy of a better Fate, and a more sublime Wit than mine to write his Praise: Yet, I hope, the Reputation of my pen is considerable enough to make his glorious Name to survive to all Ages, with that of the brave, the beautiful and the constant Imoinda.

Margaret W. Ferguson observes that Behn may be playing a verbal game with the name of Imoinda as "I [moi] am Indian." Thus if she is even partially correct, Behn has inscribed her own identity into that of Imoinda on the discursive plane, and she becomes part of the discursive space that Oroonoko occupies. At the very least, she presents her abilities to arrange the discursive bundles that underlie her text in such a way that something of significance arises more than can be contained in a written text and thus more than words can frame. Both *Oroonoko* and Behn will occupy an existence in the gaps of literary production and Anglo-African discourse.

Another complexity in representing Oroonoko is a product of the discourse of fiction itself. The narrator notes that she first became acquainted with Oroonoko while he was a slave in Suriname and that he revealed his story to her of being an African prince. Thus on the fictive level, Oroonoko the character merges with the world view he narrates. He becomes synonymous with the action and thought processes which he embodies. Mixed with these discursive voices are various written texts representing African culture and Suriname, namely George Warren's *Impartial Description of Suriname*, that she consulted (Rogers 2–3). Critics who attempt to demythologize *Oroonoko's* Africa note Behn's "exaggerated sentimentality" (Rogers 3) and "material of fantasy" (Moira Ferguson 346). Such scholarly attempts, however, fail to realize that most of the mystique about Oroonoko is ethereal and cannot exist apart from the discourse which he voices. Without question, Behn has absorbed the English stage's material cultural presentation of heroic romance and has used it as one of the discursive strategies in the creation of Oroonoko as part of the process of feminizing her hero throughout the text. The love affair between Oroonoko and Imoinda, including the difficulties of Oroonoko's grandfather taking Imoinda for his wife and then subsequently selling her into slavery because of her sexual liasons with Oroonoko, could certainly have historical/cultural veracity in African culture as well as having parallels to events in heroic dramas such as Dryden's *Aureng-Zebe* (Moira Ferguson 346–47). Yet historicity has little to do with the creation of a discourse; language and thought processes are the roots of activity. The narrator's first description of the meeting between Oroonoko and Imoinda reveals much about the discourse that he comes to represent. Behn writes:

> So that having made his first Compliments, and presented her an hundred and fifty Slaves in Fetters, he told her with his eyes that he was not insensible of her Charms; While Imoinda, who wish'd for nothing more than so glorious a Conquest, was pleas'd to believe, she understood that silent Language of new-born Love.

These particular words reveal rich semiotic possibilities. Oroonoko presents slaves, a sign of his success in war, and at the same time, the narrator describes the love that Oroonoko bears for Imoinda as a refigured "conquest" with the suggestion that she too will be his captive. The gaze, while one of intense desire, although verbally undocumentable, has far stronger implications given class and gender attributed to Oroonoko. *Oroonoko* as a discourse then symbolizes conquest and control; yet they are based in honor and merit, rather than on exploitation and self-interest, which Behn characterizes as Christian and European in the text.

At a later meeting before the king, after he had given Imoinda the royal veil, Behn notes "Nor were his Eyes silent" and "'twas this powerful Language alone that in an Instant convey'd all the Thoughts of their Souls to each other." In this section of the narrative, Behn records very few words directly spoken between Oroonoko and Imoinda, choosing rather to focus on gesture and the power of the gaze—perhaps aspects that she learned from her experience as a writer of drama. On another level, however, she is setting the stage for a literary approximation of universal language theory in which communication is said to exist at the level of gesture. Yet it is this level of communication to which Behn is not privy—nor is anyone else—that seems to captivate her representation of Oroonoko.

Transferring Oroonoko into the world of colonial exploitation no longer as subject but as object further highlights his representation as a discourse of honor amidst double dealing. The major events leading to Oroonoko's brutal murder are his being reunited with Imoinda in Suriname and her becoming pregnant. The desire to return to his homeland, symbolically a return to the source which he figures, powers his actions. For Behn and likely for her readers in the Restoration and now, Oroonoko's initiating a slave escape on the estate, his later brutal killing of Imoinda to preserve her body from white European exploitation, and his own intentional mutilation of his own body are problematic. In these actions, part of the semi-European qualities that bridge the narrator's culture with Oroonoko's Africa disappear and are replaced by a darker vision of barbarity. In the final scene, however, Behn is able to shift these earlier scenes onto a barbaric, European-based society that oversees the bodily mutilation of her hero.

The actual description of the murder is significant to the reading of *Oroonoko* as a discourse. With ghastly realism, Behn writes:

> He had learn'd to take Tobacco; and when he was assur'd he should die, he desir'd they would give him a Pipe in his Mouth, ready lighted, which they did: And the Executioner came, and first cut off his Members, and threw them into the Fire; after that, with an ill-favour'd Knife, they cut his Ears and his Nose, and burn'd them; he still smoak'd on, as if nothing had touch'd him; then they hack'd off one of his Arms, and he still bore up, and held his Pipe; but at the cutting off the other Arm, his Head sunk, and his Pipe dropt, and he gave up the Ghost, without a Groan, or a Reproach.

Since the text has identified body with discourse, the author continues the image in the highly symbolic mutilation. The cutting of his genitals and his arms are specifically related to the image he created for himself in the first portion of the narrative. The erotic desire undefinable by language and crystallized in the gaze is terminated. The strength of his arms would symbolize his abilities in conquest and control. His continuing to smoke the pipe during the ordeal functions on two levels. First, it is a sign of honor which he represents through his silence. In fact, here we see the silencing of a discourse. On a second level, however, its presence is more ominous. It is a sign of colonial exploitation not only for the Africans who were known in the period to enjoy tobacco, but also as an image of European colonization which sought property on which to produce tobacco and to employ slaves to cultivate it. Thus in one painfully gruesome image, Behn crystallizes the discourse she has been endeavoring to frame throughout the text. Only for a brief moment does it last, and then it moves beyond the frame of the page.

Aphra Behn's *Oroonoko* was certainly a text that challenged the minds of Restoration and eighteenth-century readers, and it continues its appeal to our present. Conflicting cultures and discursive breaking are major concerns of the text. The presentation of Oroonoko is at the center of these issues, and it is Behn's attempt to frame the unframable Oroonoko as discourse that challenges our appraisals of the text. Oroonoko is more than a character; he is a pattern of spoken and unspoken thought.

Source: Daniel Pigg, "Trying to Frame the Unframable: Oroonoko as Discourse in Aphra Behn's *Oroonoko*," in *Studies in Short Fiction*, Vol. 34, No. 1, Winter 1997, pp. 105–12.

Martine Watson Brownley

In the following excerpt, Brownley discusses Behn's handling of the narrator in Oroonoko, *asserting that the narrative persona is used "to unify and to add realism to disparate elements" in the novel.*

In the past the narrator of *Oroonoko* has, with very few exceptions, been studied mainly in terms of the life and ideas of Aphra Behn. Since what little we know of Behn's life is just as exciting and romantic as any material in her writings, it is easy to see why the narrative *persona* of *Oroonoko* has taken second place to the woman who was traveler, spy, pioneer female author, and political intriguer. For the moment controversy over Behn's biography seems to have died down. Undoubtedly the lull is temporary, for many fascinating questions remain unanswered. Nevertheless, the pause offers a useful chance to consider the role of the narrator within the context of the novel itself. *Oroonoko's* importance in early English prose fiction has long been established, and, as George Guffey points out [in his *Two English Novelists*, 1975] the "particularly well-defined narrator" is one important element which distinguishes the work from other fiction of the time. Functioning as a strongly felt presence throughout *Oroonoko*, the narrator unifies the novel, enhances the tenuous realism of the basically heroic story, and offers a viable standard of judgment for the readers.

Since in general what the narrator says is more important than anything she actually does in the context of the story of *Oroonoko*

> *OROONOKO* IS AT LEAST PARTIALLY THE STORY OF THESE ORDINARY PEOPLE AND THEIR REACTION TO THE EXTRAORDINARY."

narrative control of language emerges as one of her most important functions. Other than the character of Oroonoko himself, the voice of the narrator is the major unifying element in the novel. Behn carefully develops a distinctive voice for her narrative *persona*; in *Oroonoko* the contrast of realism and romanticism in the narrator's expression gives the style its unique quality. This contrast in style, of course, reflects the uneasy alliance in *Oroonoko* of romantic elements from the heroic play and realistic elements later prominent in the novel. The synthesis is not entirely successful, but Behn's manipulation of the narrator's romantic and realistic styles to control point of view accounts for some of the success that she managed to achieve in *Oroonoko*.

The romantic element is apparent in the narrator's eloquent-style, found particularly in the elaborate rhetorical speeches which reflect Behn's dramatic background. The overstatement and hackneyed imagery typical of the heroic play also occur, as one would expect, whenever narrator or characters speak of love. When Oroonoko faces separation from Imoinda by military duty, "every Day seem'd a tedious Year till he saw his *Imoinda*"; after their reunion in Suriname, the lovers agree that "even Fetters and Slavery were soft and easy, and would be supported with Joy and Pleasure; while they cou'd be so happy to possess each other." The narrator pulls out all the stops in her heroic description of Oroonoko's appearance, which abounds in superlatives. His shape is "the most exact that can be fancy'd"; his mouth is "the finest shaped that could be seen"; he has "the best Grace in the World." She combines the best of nature and of art to depict him: "The most famous Statuary cou'd not form the Figure of a Man more admirably turn'd from head to foot," while "bating his Colour, there could be Nothing in Nature more beautiful, agreeable, and handsome" than his face. Having exhausted superlatives in describing Oroonoko, she can only do justice to Imoinda's charms by calling her a fit consort for Oroonoko, "the beautiful Black *Venus* to our young *Mars*." With one exception, the hyperbolic heroic style is always used in connection with Oroonoko and his activities. Only Oroonoko's execution, when he is finally destroyed by men who cannot tolerate what he represents, is described in realistic terms. In this passage the straight-forward language heightens Oroonoko's heroic actions by the narrator's grimly effective contrast of style and content. Through the rest of the novel, the heroic style sets him apart within the narrative just as his ideal love, truth, and honor separate him from the ordinary standards of those around him.

Oroonoko is at least partially the story of these ordinary people and their reaction to the extraordinary. Neither these people nor the narrator herself could be appropriately delineated in heroic terms, and so realistic colloquial elements are a part of the narrative style. This informal oral style suggests Behn's contemporary reputation as a witty and enjoyable conversationalist. The narrative is filled with conversational insertions: "I had forgot to tell you"; "as I said before"; "I must say thus much." Using this style, the narrator adds realism by infusing her own personality into the narrative, enhancing the story with her own experiences—"I have seen 'em [the Blacks] so frequently blush, and look pale"—and her personal opinions—"For my part, I took 'em for Hobgoblins, or Fiends, rather than Men." To modern tastes, this realistic element is the most familiar and pleasing aspect of the style in *Oroonoko*. Unfortunately, though the oral style adds realism and is most effective at times, the colloquial narrative is too often difficult to follow. Poorly structured sentences, the mixing of verb tenses, and especially pronouns with ambiguous references hinder the reader's understanding of the action. The clumsiness can be defended, just as Defoe's similar carelessness has been, by suggesting that the author intended the grammatical mistakes to characterize the narrator's mind and outlook. In both cases any gain in characterization would seem to be more than offset by the reader's confusion. The speed at which Behn and Defoe were known to produce also seems to indicate that authorial carelessness rather than deliberate artistry in characterization caused the stylistic problems. That Behn managed in any way to fuse the realistic and the romantic styles in *Oroonoko* is an achievement of sorts. The

effectiveness of the narrative voice unifies the disparate elements and appropriately focuses point of view. But style cannot finally account either for Behn's success in *Oroonoko*, or for her purposes in delineating the narrator.

. . . The characters of *Oroonoko* are in general no more realistic than the action and setting of the novel. Most of the characters in the story are described in exaggerated terms, emerging as excessively good or extraordinarily bad. Practically everyone in the novel is exceptional: Oroonoko and Imoinda are of course perfect; the Council "consisted of such notorious Villains as *Newgate* never transported"; Aboan is "not only one of the best Quality, but a man extremely well made and beautiful"; Banister is "a Fellow of Absolute Barbarity." Even the somewhat colorless Trefry is described as "a Man of Great Wit, and fine Learning," and "a Man of so excellent Wit and Parts." Only the narrator emerges as rather ordinary. Of her own characteristics, she heavily emphasizes only her credibility, obviously performing the standard obeisance to the antifictional bias of the age. She devotes the first two paragraphs of the story to establishing her reliability in the narrative role, assuring the reader of the literal truth of her tale and the trustworthiness of her sources. Astutely flattering her audience, she emphasizes her conscientiousness as a narrator; she is in complete control of her material and recognizes her obligations not to tell anything which "might prove tedious and heavy to my Reader, in a World where he finds Diversions for every Minute, new and strange." During the rest of the novel she establishes a pleasant enough narrative presence. Her most important trait is her fundamental decency and humanity, apparent in all of her actions and remarks. Critics note that she does try to emphasize her own importance whenever possible, but despite her insistence on her position, neither her remarks nor her actions establish her as an unusual person. No reader would characterize the narrator in the glowing terms she uses to describe the other characters in the story; she emerges as a character with whom the reader finds it easy enough to identify. Throughout the novel the narrator seems to be an ordinary woman in an extraordinary position, and she therefore adds a sense of realism lacking in the action, setting, and other characters in the story.

Thus in a strange and exotic world of romantic wonders, the narrator helps the reader to keep his bearings. She adds realism to the story, offering a standard of normalcy in an environment of extraordinary people and actions. As such, she can fulfill her other important narrative function, which is to provide an acceptable standard of judgment in ordinary terms for the events and characters in *Oroonoko*. Oroonoko himself of course provides the noblest example of human excellencies in the novel, but he is ideal rather than real. As Lore Metzger points out, Oroonoko's "heroic ideals cannot prevail in the real world" [introduction to *Oroonoko*, 1973 ed.]. The novel requires standards in ordinary as well as ideal terms, and the narrator, a decent, average woman, can focus the scale of values in the realistic terms required. As a participant in the story she several times serves as a link between Oroonoko and the European world, and in the novel she interprets him to this world. It is her standards which finally emerge as most interesting to the reader, because of their possible applicability to his own experience.

Source: Martine Watson Brownley, "The Narrator in *Oroonoko*," in *Essays in Literature*, Vol. 4, No. 2, Fall 1977, pp. 174–81.

Evangeline Wilbour Blashfield

In the following excerpt, Blashfield discusses the characterization in Behn's plays and novels.

Though [Mrs. Behn's] language is rich and sonorous, vigorous and racy, she cannot be counted among the group of comedy writers who clarified and disciplined our tongue. She has none of the filed and polished elegance of Congreve, none of the finish of the Augustans. She wrote hastily and carelessly, her style is often uncinctured, unmanicured, *en neglige*; its slipshod easiness is that of *billets du matin* dashed off on a toilet-table; indeed, Gildon noted that Aphra wrote while talking with her friends or receiving visits. . . .

[The] contention that Restoration comedy portrays the manners of the society of its time, is only half true. We could as well unquestioningly accept De Maupassant's French peasants as studies from nature, or D'Annunzio's novels as accurate pictures of modern Italian life. Aphra's flirts and bullies and rascals are "society" people; when not the conventional stock characters of Spanish comedy they are hangers-on at court, needy cavaliers with Worcester and Marston Moor behind them, and a sponging house before them,

> OROONOKO WAS THE FIRST CHARACTER IN ENGLISH FICTION POSSESSING A DEFINITE PERSONALITY, A PERSONALITY MARKED BY RACIAL CHARACTERISTICS AS WELL AS INDIVIDUAL TRAITS MODIFIED BY A FOREIGN EDUCATION."

swaggering fortune-hunters—Bassanios vulgarized, and thirsty Petruchios. The ladies are—when they are ladies—pert minxes, and highly born romps, all touched by the taint of Whitehall. Their manners and conversation are those of the court. The intrigues, disguises, practical jokes, heartless gallantry, indecent jests are those of the courtiers. . . .

Such a view of life was intensely artificial, it was parochial as well. Aphra may call her scenes Naples or Madrid, they are always Hampton Court, St. James's Park, Foxhall, or Bartholomew Fair, though in *The Widow Ranter*, where the scene is laid in America, and Bacon is hero, there is a dash of the local color so distinctive a feature in *Oroonoko*. Aphra's outlook in her drama is no narrower than that of her contemporaries and followers, but it is a small loophole from which to observe life. Certainly humanity is a sordid affair if we eliminate its finer elements, and nature is a sickening spectacle if we confine our observations to dung-hills. The choice is ours, the fertilizer and the flower lie close together, we can contemplate the flower or we can "concentrate" on the fertilizer if so inclined, but we must not insist that only the latter is real. . . .

Aphra and her kind dwelt contented in *Vanity Fair*. No shining visions floated before her as she drove her busy pen and took her plays to market. To write what would sell was her business, to please her public was her ambition, and after a false start and a couple of failures she fell into her stride and kept up the pace until the end of her busy life. No author of her time save Dryden was so prolific. Her material was ready to hand, her manner varied with her subject. Body of doctrine had she none, nor convictions, nor purpose, nor standard. She labored to amuse and surprise. She succeeded. Like those of all the playwrights of her time her characters were generally immoral, her situations often equivocal, her language frequently gross. Therefore, in spite of their undeniable qualities, their humor, sprightliness, and movement, her work has deserved oblivion, and no one, even to-day, would wish to revive her plays....

People were reading French novels when Aphra delivered *Oroonoko* "to the world" in 1688. Light literature was an *article de Paris*, like perfumed gloves, apricot paste, and other elegant trifles....

All through the eighteenth century the ponderous [French] tomes found English readers, even such readers as Dr. Johnson and Mrs. Chapone, and were still considered to furnish exemplars of gallantry and heroism, of noble deportment and fine language.

Into this realm of subdued half-tints, of discreet, reflected lights, of faintly defined forms, *Oroonoko* dashed like a tropical bird into a dovecote. It is easy to imagine the stir it caused, the surprise and interest it aroused after people had recovered from the first shock of its novelty. New indeed was a story told straightly, undeflected by digressions, its force undiluted by discussions; the abstract banished, and the concrete not only presented but visualized by all the means at the writer's disposal. The personal experiences, the autobiographical form, heightened interest, and the pictures painted from actual scenes and people added color to the narration. The action was not clogged by a multiplicity of minor episodes, attention was not disseminated by the abrupt intervention of new characters and their recital of adventures that had no immediate connection with the plot.... There were no delays in the development of the simple story, and none of the contemporary clogs on swift movement. The group of characters was a small one, and no elaboration of detail wearied the reader or diverted interest from the principal personages of the tale. The sentimental straw-splitting, the finikin refinements, the wire-drawn casuistry of the French novelists were forgotten; indeed in *Oroonoko* affairs of the heart are treated with a straightforwardness characteristic of the jovial gossips of the Queen of Navarre.

The form and pace of *Oroonoko* recalls the directness of attack of the Florentine *novella*, it has hurried away from the stately advance of the slow-paced seventeenth-century novel. In short, *Oroonoko* is composed; it focuses interest in one central figure. Its alertness is somewhat akin to that of Voltaire's tales. It could not, like its contemporaries, and many of Ibsen's plays, be continued indefinitely. Compared with the swift allure of this simple story the epistolary and picaresque romances of Aphra's distinguished successors are prolix and desultory. For the form of *Oroonoko*, for equal succinctness and concentration, we must hark back to the storytellers of the Renaissance.

It is naturally an aid to clear relation of facts to possess facts at first hand to relate, and for the expression and communication of emotion, the capacity for, and experience of, emotion is valuable. Aphra was deeply moved by the sufferings and tragic fate of her savage hero; admiration, pity, a horror of cruelty and injustice, are potent incentives to expression. The revolt of a high young heart against wrong finds eloquence ready to hand. Here *le style c'est la femme* ["style is the woman"]; Aphra recounted an actual emotional experience. Local color, studies from life, a narrative of personal adventure were as new in fiction as a plea for the oppressed, or an arraignment of ruling powers. Here was a frank departure from the Arcadia of aristocratic shepherds, and shepherdesses, exquisite and artificial as Dresden china rustics; into this fantastic throng, strode a bleeding slave, with manacled wrists and furrowed back to take his place among the paladins of romance and the princesses of fairy-land. Oroonoko was a prince also, it is true, but his court life was only an introduction to his adventures as a captive and a slave. The description of Coramantien reads like a concession to convention. In the seventeenth-century novel high rank was as necessary an attribute of a hero as personal beauty; Oroonoko was endowed with both as a matter of course, but it was as a man and not as a deposed prince that he was interesting....

Oroonoko was the first character in English fiction possessing a definite personality, a personality marked by racial characteristics as well as individual traits modified by a foreign education. In spite of his French breeding Oroonoko was depicted as a negro, and a savage, noble and kind by instinct, as the dog is faithful, and the blood-horse mettlesome. He was not a white man painted black with a white man's nature and innate ideas, he was not a negro St. Francis like Uncle Tom. There still was much that was fierce and untamed in Aphra's hero. He lacked, like most savages, sequence in action, constancy of purpose; his fortitude was physical only. He was not the gentle savage who illustrated the superiority of Nature over civilization, dear to the eighteenth-century philosophers. Though his instincts were those of the primitive man, no doubt his French training furnished him with a code of honor, and its language.... The words and acts of Oroonoko are consistent, they are never out of character, and consequently are convincing. With the exception of the adventures in Coramantien, which Aphra had at second hand, and which read like a twice-told story, the rest of the novel has an accent of truth, as well as an atmosphere of realism....

[Through] pity and admiration for this royal slave, a sentiment against slavery was awakened. Aphra's simple appeal to the emotions was more potent than a direct pleading or a protest. No ethical generalities, no preaching could have so touched the heart and quickened the imagination, and the readers of *Oroonoko* became the first Abolitionists. He was the Uncle Tom of the seventeenth century.

Oroonoko then was not only new in treatment and subject, but it was also the first novel with a purpose. Mrs. Behn was a pathfinder in fiction.

Source: Evangeline Wilbour Blashfield, "Aphra Behn," in *Portraits and Backgrounds*, Charles Schribner's Sons, 1917, pp. 113–284.

SOURCES

"Act of Union, 1707," in *United Kingdom Parliament*, http://www.parliament.uk/actofunion/index.html (accessed January 2, 2010).

Baker, Ernest A., Introduction to *The Novels of Mrs. Aphra Behn*, by Aphra Behn, George Routledge & Sons, 1913, pp. vii–xxvii.

Behn, Aphra, *Oroonoko*, Penguin Books, 2003.

"Charles I," "Interregnum," "Charles II," "James II," and "William III and Mary II," in *The Official Web site of the British Monarchy*, http://www.royal.gov.uk/Historyofthe Monarchy/HistoryoftheMonarchy.aspx (accessed December 27, 2009).

Cooley, Ron, et al., "Margaret (Lucas) Cavendish, Duchess of Newcastle (1623–1673)," in *Luminarium: Anthology of English Literature*, http://www.luminarium.org/ sevenlit/cavendish/cavendishbio.htm (accessed January 2, 2010).

Doyle, Laura Anne, "Entering Atlantic History: Oroonoko, Imoinda, and Behn," in *Freedom's Empire: Race and the Rise of the Novel in Atlantic Modernity, 1640– 1940*, Duke University Press, 2008, pp. 97–117.

Gallagher, Catherine, and Simon Stern, eds., "Introduction: Cultural and Historical Background," in *Oroonoko; or, The Royal Slave*, by Aphra Behn, Bedford/St. Martin's, 2000, pp. 3–25.

Hoefte, Rosemarijn, "A Concise History of Suriname and Marienburg," in *In Place of Slavery: A Social History of British Indian and Javanese Laborers in Suriname*, University Press of Florida, 1998, pp. 8–24.

Hooker, Richard, "The European Enlightenment: The Case of England," in *Washington State University's World Civilizations Internet Classroom and Anthology*, http://www.wsu.edu/~dee/ENLIGHT/ENGLAND.HTM (accessed January 2, 2010).

Link, Frederick M., "The Novelist," in *Aphra Behn*, Twayne Publishers, 1968, pp. 130–51.

Metzger, Lore, Introduction to *Oroonoko, or the Royal Slave*, by Aphra Behn, W. W. Norton, 1973, pp. ix–xv.

"Orange Prize for Fiction 2009 Longlist," in *Orange Prize for Fiction*, http://www.orangeprize.co.uk/show/feature/ orange-prize-2009-longlist (accessed January 2, 2010).

Porter, Andrew, "Britain's Empire in 1815," in *BBC's British History In-Depth*, http://www.bbc.co.uk/history/british/ empire_seapower/britain_empire_01.shtml (accessed January 2, 2010).

Summers, Montague, ed., Introduction to *Oroonoko; or, The Royal Slave*, in *Oroonoko & Other Prose Narratives by Aphra Behn*, Benjamin Blom, 1916, reprint, 1967, pp. 127–29.

"Suriname," in *CIA: World Factbook*, https://www.cia. gov/library/publications/the-world-factbook/geos/ns.html (accessed January 2, 2010).

Todd, Janet, Introduction to *Oroonoko*, by Aphra Behn, Penguin Books, 2003, pp. xv–xxxv.

———, Notes to *Oroonoko*, by Aphra Behn, Penguin Books, 2003, pp. 79–99.

———, "Oroonoko," in *The Critical Fortunes of Aphra Behn*, Camden House, 1998, pp. 114–30.

Walvin, James, "Ending It All: The Crusade Against Slavery," in *Black Ivory: Slavery in the British Empire*, 2nd ed., Blackwell, 2001, pp. 259–71.

FURTHER READING

Azim, Firdous, *The Colonial Rise of the Novel: From Aphra Behn to Charlotte Bronte*, Routledge, 1993.
    From a feminist perspective, Azim explores the work of female novelists writing during the years of English colonial expansion, examining the impact of England's imperialism on the writings of Behn and Bronte. In particular, Azim studies issues of gender and identity in the works of these women.

Morgan, Kenneth, *Slavery and the British Empire: From Africa to America*, Oxford University Press, 2007.

Morgan investigates the history of the British slave trade, studying the ways in which the British used slavery as a means of expanding their colonial empire.

Morris, Mervyn, *Making West Indian Literature*, Ian Randle Publishers, 2004.

Morris examines the development of modern West Indian literature and comments on the way the colonial history of the West Indies shaped the area's notions of identity, and subsequently influenced the literature of the region.

Scott, John A., *Settlers on the Eastern Shore: The British Colonies in North America, 1607–1750*, Facts on File, 1991.

Scott discusses the British colonization of North America in the seventeenth and eighteenth centuries. The work, which is targeted at a young adult audience, employs such primary sources as letters and diaries in order to covey what daily life was like for British settlers in American colonies. Scott additionally details the relationships between the colonists and the Native American people they encountered and discusses the colonists' use of slaves and indentured servants.

Todd, Janet, *The Secret Life of Aphra Behn*, Rutgers University Press, 1997.

Todd, who has edited Behn's writings, provides an examination of what is known about Behn's life and incorporates this scant biographical information with a detailed critical analysis of Behn's body of work.

SUGGESTED SEARCH TERMS

Oroonoko AND Behn

Aphra Behn

Behn AND slavery

Behn AND seventeenth-century novel

Oroonoko AND colonialism

Oroonoko AND tragic romance

Oroonoko AND travelogue

Oroonoko analysis

Oroonoko AND abolitionism

Oroonoko AND royalism

Oroonoko AND racism

The Outsiders

1983

Francis Ford Coppola's 1983 film *The Outsiders* is based on the 1967 novel *The Outsiders* by S. E. Hinton, and was adapted for the screen by Kathleen Rowell. The film is considered one of Coppola's weaker works. In the preceding decade, he had established himself as one of the most technically gifted young directors in Hollywood, scoring critical and popular successes with *The Godfather* in 1972, *The Conversation* in 1974, *The Godfather, Part II* in 1974, and *Apocalypse Now* in 1979. In 1982, Coppola tumbled from critical favor when he followed *Apocalypse Now*, a turbulent, soul-searching war film, with a light-hearted revisionist musical called *One from the Heart*. Critics found it a shallow exercise in technical filmmaking, a charge that was often repeated against *The Outsiders* the following year. However, the strong cast of young actors bound for fame, along with sixteen years of best-seller status for Hinton's novel, led the film to commercial stability.

The Outsiders did not win any major awards. C. Thomas Howell won a Young Artist Award for Best Young Motion Picture Actor in a Feature Film in 1984. The film was also nominated for Best Family Feature Motion Picture by the Young Artist Awards.

In 2005, Coppola's Zoetrope studios released *The Outsiders: The Complete Novel* on DVD. This revised version includes additional scenes at the beginning and end of the film and replaces some of the original soundtrack with pop music. Coppola also produced a short-lived television

series, *The Outsiders*, which ran on the Fox network in 1990, featuring further adventures of characters from the novel.

Hinton's novel tells the story of a gang of juvenile delinquents in Nebraska in the early 1960s and the social order that they form around the three Curtis brothers, whose parents are dead. Ponyboy Curtis, the novel's narrator, relates the growing tension between social groups that leads to a stabbing death, his flight from justice, and the final "rumble," or gang fight, to claim their territory. Hinton delves into the bonds that hold young men together when their families abandon them and society has no use for them.

PLOT SUMMARY

The plot for the 1983 movie of *The Outsiders* closely follows the events related in S. E. Hinton's novel. The film opens with Ponyboy Curtis, the narrator of the novel, opening a notebook and writing, under the title "The Outsiders," the first line of the novel. Though he narrates the novel, he does not reflect on the act of writing in it. His writing and the lined paper he is writing on are superimposed on the top of the screen, leading into the movie's opening credits.

After the credits, the scene opens on Ponyboy and Johnny Cale meeting Dallas Winston on a street corner and walking through town. They pass through a drive-in hamburger stand, where a fistfight breaks out, with both fighters eventually brandishing switchblades. The drive-in, along with the song on the soundtrack ("Gloria," released by the band Them in 1964), helps establish the time frame of the movie, while the knife fight establishes the animosity between the competing street gangs, the lower-class Greasers and the upper-class Socs. The three main characters continue to wander, stopping at the DX gas station where Ponyboy's brother Sodapop works. They come upon a small group of preteen boys playing cards for cigarettes in an empty lot, and they chase them away for fun.

At night, the three of them climb under a fence into a drive-in movie theater, which is showing a double bill of *Muscle Beach Party* and *Beach Blanket Bingo*, which were released in 1964 and 1965, respectively. Walking past the parked cars, the camera catches Cherry Valance and Marcia arguing with their boyfriends, although Ponyboy and the

others do not notice it. They sit in the small section of theater seats, and soon Cherry and Marcia arrive. Dallas makes crude insinuations, and he leaves when Johnny stands up to him. The girls leave the drive-in with Ponyboy, Johnny, and Two-Bit Matthews. While they are walking, a car, a blue Mustang, with their boyfriends screeches to a halt beside them. Two-Bit is prepared to fight, but Cherry agrees to go with her boyfriend, Bob, to maintain peace. Before leaving, she admits to Ponyboy that if she ever saw Dallas again, she might fall in love with him.

As they near Johnny's house they can hear the heated arguing of his parents inside. Stopping outside the house, Johnny says that he would rather sleep outside than go in. He and Ponyboy start a fire in the woods. The arguing parents can still be heard, and Johnny has tears on his face.

Ponyboy dreams about his parents. They are shown in long shots, so that their faces are indistinct. They are laughing at a picnic, and then the film shows a train barreling into their car. Ponyboy wakes to the sound of a train in the distance.

Ponyboy goes home. His oldest brother, Darrel, is reading the newspaper, furious that he is coming home at two in the morning. As they argue, Darrel pushes him; Ponyboy runs out the door and goes back to Johnny in the woods.

As Ponyboy and Johnny walk through the park, the film builds suspense with ominous music and crosscutting between their feet and the blue Mustang that followed them earlier. A gang of Socs comes from the car, led by Cherry's boyfriend, Bob, who drinks from the same distinctive round flask he carried in the previous scene. The tension builds, and then a fight breaks out. As the Socs hold Ponyboy's head in the fountain, the camera alternates between his underwater view and a close-up of Johnny taking a switchblade from his back pocket. The scene ends with deep red, with bubbles like blood, washing across the screen.

The next scene shows three bodies beside the fountain. Ponyboy has passed out, Bob is dead, and Johnny sits in shock at what he has done. When Ponyboy revives and sees what has happened they go to Buck Merrell's bar and ask to see Dallas, who comes to the door shirtless, having been asleep in a back room. He gives them money, shirts, a coat, and a gun and tells them to

FILM TECHNIQUE

Dutch Angle

The Dutch angle, also referred to as the canted angle, is the technique of filming from a slightly off-center angle, placing the camera at a stance that is not parallel to the ground. The effect, often seen in horror or crime movies, emphasizes a sense of strangeness and danger. *The Outsiders* uses the Dutch Angle twice: during the chase by the fountain, and then, later, when Ponyboy and Dallas arrive at the hospital after racing to talk to Johnny, who is about to die, about the rumble.

Foreshadowing

Foreshadowing involves the use of an element that is not immediately relevant to the plot but that later becomes significant. Unlike the novel, the film version of *The Outsiders* foreshadows the burning of the church by showing a smoldering cigarette falling into a dark space among spiders' webs. Because it is out of context, viewers might not realize that the scene shows the space under the church's floor until they ask themselves what caused the fire.

Crane Shot

A crane shot is a camera angle taken from above, used to show the layout of items in a scene. In the aftermath of the stabbing beside the fountain, Coppola fades in with a crane shot that allows the viewer to see three bodies scattered around the now-silent scene: Ponyboy is stretched out on his back, and Bob is curled up on his side with a pool of blood around him. Johnny is sitting up against the side of the fountain, sobbing. Capturing their postures like this allows viewers to instantly understand what has happened.

Flashbacks

Flashbacks are scenes showing audiences something that has already happened, taking them into the past. Several times in *The Outsiders*, Coppola presents flashbacks of the Curtis brothers' parents to show that Ponyboy is still thinking about them.

These flashbacks are photographed with a soft camera focus to indicate that the scenes are within a person's fading memory. One scene shows their car being hit by a train. It is unlikely that Ponyboy would have actually witnessed this, and he is probably just imagining it, so this is not a true flashback.

Wipe

A wipe is an optical effect that draws attention to the transition between two scenes. Coppola uses this technique only once in *The Outsiders*. At the close of the scene beside the fountain, when Ponyboy is passed out under water but viewers have been shown Johnny drawing his knife, a wipe crosses the screen that looks like spreading blood, complete with bubbles.

Pan

A pan is the camera technique of slowing moving across some area of ground, allowing audiences to gradually take in the situation. When the Greasers prepare for the rumble in this movie, the camera pans across them, moving left to right. (In cultures where reading also moves left to right, this is the standard, straightforward-seeming direction.) The film reacquaints audiences with all of the major and minor characters, and it shows viewers what each one looks like as he mentally prepares for battle.

Long Shot

A long shot is a camera shot taken from a distance so that it can capture entire figures within their setting. Coppola begins the morning that Ponyboy recites a Robert Frost poem with a long shot, in order to show Ponyboy and Johnny's figures dwarfed by the natural beauty of the sunrise. When their location is established, the scene uses medium shots, showing both boys from roughly the waist up, and then it closes in tighter onto Ponyboy's face, still retaining the colorful sunrise around the edges of the frame.

take the 3:15 freight train to Windrixville, where they can find an abandoned church to hide in. The film shows Johnny and Ponyboy sneaking into an empty boxcar at night and riding the train as it cuts through open prairie land at sunrise.

As they approach the church, the camera focuses on two frightened rabbits that are hiding under the steps. Ponyboy dozes off and thinks he sees his brother Darrel when he awakes, but the image disappears. Johnny returns with groceries, a copy of the novel *Gone with the Wind*, and peroxide to lighten the color of their hair. They cut each other's hair in the back yard. They watch a beautiful sunset, and Ponyboy recites a poem that it reminds him of: Robert Frost's "Nothing Gold Can Stay." He memorized it, he says, because he could not figure out what it meant.

The film shows Ponyboy's writing across a page of a lined notebook, superimposed across the multicolored sunset.

Dallas comes to visit, bringing them a letter from Ponyboy's brother Sodapop and news of the police search for them. He also announces a coming rumble, or fight, between the Greasers and the Socs. Cherry has been helpful in bringing the Greasers information about the Socs' plans. On the soundtrack, there is an indistinct voice, with one of them warning another to be careful about burning cigarettes. Dallas takes them out to a Dairy Queen drive-in. While they are sitting in an open convertible in the Dairy Queen parking lot, a little girl approaches the car with an even smaller girl. She asks for fifteen cents, and Dallas, worried that she will see the gun, chases her away abruptly. Johnny announces that he will surrender to the authorities for Bob's murder. He is tired of running and upset because his parents have not asked Dallas where he is, and he does not want Ponyboy and his brothers to suffer. Dallas says that he has been in jail and does not think surrendering is a good idea.

They return to the church to find it on fire, with some people standing around warning each other that some children are missing. Ponyboy leads the rescue, racing into the burning building, followed by Johnny. When Ponyboy comes out with some children, Dallas knocks him to the ground to put out his blazing jacket, and then he goes back in. The roof collapses, and the scene changes to the inside of an ambulance. Jerry, the adult who was at the church, tells Ponyboy that he and his friends are heroes, but Ponyboy responds that they are Greasers.

Ponyboy sits in the hall of the hospital with Jerry, smoking, when his two brothers enter. They hug and cry, and the music swells triumphantly. The next morning, while Ponyboy is making breakfast for his brothers, Two-Bit and Steve Randle arrive and eat the chocolate cake that is always in the refrigerator of the Curtis home. They all leave except Two-Bit.

Two-Bit and Ponyboy hitchhike downtown, and the same blue Mustang that followed them before pulls up. Randy, who is now the leader of the group, takes Ponyboy aside to talk. He is upset about losing his friend Bob and he is sick of fighting, he says. Before they part, Randy calls Ponyboy a Greaser, but then he catches himself and takes it back. Rejoining Two-Bit, Ponyboy refuses to label Randy as a Soc.

In the hospital, Johnny lies face down. He is burned and his spine is broken, and he probably will not be able to walk again. The boys visit Dallas, who asks Two-Bit for his switchblade (the novel explains that he uses this knife to force his way out of the hospital). Riding the bus home, Ponyboy dreams about his family on a picnic, filmed once again from a distance, so that faces are not distinguishable. He and Two-Bit meet with Cherry, who assures them that the Socs will not come armed to the rumble. She talks about good things she remembers about Bob. She is ready to admit that she and Ponyboy cannot be friends because their social conditions are just too different, but he points out that they see the same sunset from both sides of town.

Preparing for the rumble, the gang gathers at the Curtis house, drinking and talking bravely, and then bursting through the door, though with fewer acrobatic feats than in the book. They walk to the lot and meet with another group of Greasers, led by Tim Shepard. Shepard compliments Ponyboy on the killing of a Soc and his bravery at the church fire. He mentions that "Curley" is in reform school, though the film never establishes that Curley is Tim Shepard's brother.

When several cars full of Socs arrive, the camera pans dramatically across the faces of the assembled fighters. Darrel Curtis and a Soc named Paul say hello to each other, and Two-Bit explains to Ponyboy that they were on the football team in high school together. Dallas arrives running, a fist shoots out and punches Ponyboy in the face, and a heavy rain downpour begins abruptly. The rumble has begun.

During the rumble, there is no dialogue, but orchestral music plays. The fighters are back-lit (placed with a light source behind them) and outlined by the rain that falls on them. The action slows as the crowded field thins, and then the remaining Socs run away. The Greasers whoop in victory as the music swells triumphantly.

The action cuts to Dallas driving recklessly. His tires squeal, and the car skids on the wet streets. Beside him is Ponyboy, his face bloodied. A motorcycle policeman pulls the car over, and Dallas explains that his friend has been injured in a motorcycle accident. The policeman hesitates and then escorts them to the hospital.

They make it to Johnny's bedside in time to hear his last words; he tells Ponyboy to "stay golden," a reference to the Frost poem Ponyboy recited to him. As they leave the room, a doctor stops them to say they do not belong there. Dallas pulls his gun and points it at the doctor's head—but when he pulls the trigger, he shows that it is empty.

A test pattern on the television at the Curtis house shows that it is the middle of the night when Ponyboy comes home. He announces to his brothers and friends that Johnny has died.

The camera cuts to Dallas standing at the magazine rack of a convenience store, holding a magazine but looking distracted. The clerk asks whether he plans to buy any magazines, so he rips the one in his hand in half. He then points his gun at the clerk and demands all of the store's money. As he runs out the door, the clerk fires two shots at him.

Dallas stops at a pay phone and calls the Curtis house. Steve answers, and Dallas asks to speak to Darrel. Dallas asks him to meet him at the park and hide him. There is blood on the white bundles beside the phone. As the Greasers approach the park in a pack, they hear police sirens. Dallas approaches, followed by several police cars. The policemen leave their cars and shoot him down in a hail of gunfire.

Later, a sunlit room, Ponyboy picks up the copy of *Gone with the Wind* that he had given to Johnny in the hospital, and a paper falls out. It is a note from Johnny, who, in a voice-over, talks about the good things in life and his interpretation of the poem "Nothing Gold Can Stay." As Ponyboy reads the note, Johnny's and Dallas's faces are superimposed above his head.

Ponyboy puts Johnny's note aside and picks up the notebook. The film shows him writing the first line of the novel again, just as it did before the opening credits. The closing credits roll.

CHARACTERS

Randy Anderson

When he returns to town after Bob Sheldon's murder, Ponyboy is cornered by Randy, another Soc. He expects trouble, but Randy takes him aside and explains that the violent death of his friend has made him reconsider the pointlessness of being in a gang and fighting. As they part, he calls Ponyboy a greaser, but then he corrects himself, denying the significance of labels like "Greaser" and "Soc" and simply calling Ponyboy "kid."

Johnny Cade

Johnny is sixteen, the same age as Sodapop, but he is small and has delicate features, so he is often taken for younger. His diminutive size is why he often hangs around with Ponyboy, who is two years his junior. Life has made Johnny frightened and nervous, which is symbolized in the film by the two twitching rabbits that hide under the stairs of the church where Johnny and Ponyboy go to hide. One source of Johnny's nervousness is his parents, who are abusive alcoholics, so vicious in their arguing that their shouting can be heard from blocks away. Johnny often sleeps out in the woods to avoid facing them, but their opinion and attention are still important to him; he decides to turn himself in to the authorities when Dallas tells him that his parents have made no effort to find where he is hiding. Johnny is also nervous because he was beaten up by a gang of Socs fairly recently, an event described in the book. In the film, the scar on his cheek provides a constant reminder of the emotional pain that causes him to carry a knife. He recognizes Bob, the Soc who is trying to drown Ponyboy in the fountain, as the person who led his beating; killing Bob is at least in part a

response to the trauma that Johnny has carried since that night.

As played by Ralph Macchio, Johnny is unable to verbalize the worries that drive him. He is sensitive and curious, but his fears cause him to remain guarded. Still, when he realizes that there are children trapped in the burning church, he does not hesitate to race into the fire to save them.

Darrel Curtis

Darrel is the oldest member of the Curtis family, the father figure after their parents' death. He works long hours as a roofer and is often tired, making him seem stern to Ponyboy. In the novel, Darrel is almost always referred to as "Darry," though that name is not used in the film. Ponyboy explains in the novel that Darrel has a very close relationship with the middle Curtis brother, Sodapop, but the movie focuses too closely on Ponyboy's experiences to show the interactions of other characters.

Patrick Swayze plays Darrel. In addition to being the leader of his family, he is also, in effect, the leader of his gang of Greasers, which the film shows by having Dallas ask to speak to Darrel when he needs help running from the law. Just before the rumble with the Socs, Darrel greets a boy named Paul, who, Two-Bit explains, used to be on the school football team with him. This is the only glimpse the film gives of Darrel's life before his parents' death forced him into a parental role.

Ponyboy Curtis

Ponyboy is the protagonist of the movie version of *The Outsiders* and the narrator of S. E. Hinton's novel. He is fourteen years old, the younger brother of Sodapop and Darrel. Since his parents' death in an auto accident, he has lived with his older brothers. He idolizes Sodapop, who is sixteen, but his relationship with Darrel is more complex: He feels that Darrel, who is responsible for keeping the family together and is therefore prone toward harshness, does not like him.

Among the Greasers with whom his brothers associate, Ponyboy is the youngest, and he is accepted only because of his brothers' popularity. His closest friend is Johnny Cade, who looks as young as Ponyboy.

Although he tries to put on an antisocial exterior, Ponyboy is actually scholarly. He recites a Robert Frost poem from memory, though when he is done he sheepishly explains that he memorized it only because he did not know what it meant; he retreats back into his persona of an uneducated street hood. When Johnny brings a copy of *Gone with the Wind* to the church where they are hiding, he has Ponyboy read it aloud to him, indicating that Ponyboy is more literate.

Throughout the novel and the movie, Ponyboy is more of a reactor than a driving force. He forms a bond with a Soc girl, Cherry Valance, but their friendship is destined to be nothing more than platonic; she confides that she could imagine herself falling in love with his friend Dallas. He becomes a fugitive from justice because Johnny killed a man while Ponyboy was unconscious. He watches Dallas go off on the rampage that will end in his death, but Ponyboy is powerless to stop him.

The events of the movie do help Ponyboy realize the bond that he shares with his brother Darrel. When they are reunited in the hospital, after his flight from justice and his dangerous mission in the burning church, Darrel is moved to tears to see that he is all right. Ponyboy realizes that Darrel's concern for him is genuine. In the novel, he becomes anxious about the prospect that the recent attention might cause the state to put him in a foster home, though the film only mentions that fear once.

Ponyboy is played by C. Thomas Howell.

Sodapop Curtis

Although Ponyboy speaks of his sixteen-year-old brother often in the novel, describing him as a personal hero who is liked by all, his significance is greatly reduced in the film version. Played by Rob Lowe, Sodapop only appears in a few scenes, usually when other members of the Greaser gang are around, though the extended DVD version released in 2005 includes one scene of Ponyboy and Sodapop sharing a bed and talking.

Jerry

Jerry is adult leader of the school field trip near the abandoned church, during which several children are trapped in the burning building. He rides in the ambulance with Ponyboy after the fire, disturbed to hear the boy refer to himself as a Greaser, telling him that he is a true hero. In the hospital waiting room, while waiting for word about Johnny, Ponyboy smokes a cigarette. Jerry mentions his disapproval, but he is respectful toward Ponyboy.

Little Girl

When Dallas is unloading his pistol in the parking lot of the Dairy Queen, a young girl approaches the car. She is holding the hand of an even littler girl, who asks for fifteen cents. The girl who speaks is played by Sofia Coppola, the daughter of the director. She would become famous in her own right, acting in a featured role in *The Godfather, Part III* and directing such award-winning films as *Lost in Translation* and *Marie Antoinette*. She is billed in the credits as "Domino."

Marcia

Marcia is Cherry Valance's friend. She is with Cherry at the drive-in theater when they both leave their boyfriends and meet Ponyboy, Johnny, and Dallas.

Two-Bit Matthews

Two-Bit is the oldest member of the Greaser gang. He is good-natured and usually drunk. At the drive-in theater, when Johnny has stood up to Dallas and driven him away from Cherry, Two-Bit joins them, and he is ready to fight when a carload of Socs stops them on the street, delaying the confrontation that will later push Johnny to murder. After Ponyboy has returned home after the fire, Two-Bit stays with him while his brothers go off to work, and he accompanies Ponyboy downtown. When Randy takes Ponyboy aside to talk to him, Two-Bit taunts the other Socs. He is played by Emilio Estevez.

Buck Merrill

Buck Merrill is not mentioned by name in the film. He is a friend of Dallas, identified in the novel as his rodeo partner. After the fight that ends with Bob's death, Ponyboy and Johnny go to Buck's bar, which is just a house in the novel, to find Dallas staying in a room upstairs. Buck is played by singer Tom Waits.

Nurse

The stern nurse in Dallas's hospital room is played by S. E. Hinton, the author of the novel, in a cameo role.

Steve Randle

Steve Randle is a Greaser who is seldom mentioned in the novel or the movie, appearing in the background of the action. He is played by Tom Cruise, who later the same year shot to stardom with *Risky Business*.

Tim Shepard

Tim is the leader of a rival Greaser gang. He is Dallas's friend, though in his first scene in the film, at the drive-in theater, he is looking to beat Dallas up for slashing his tires. Two-Bit asserts that it will be okay for the friends to fight as long as neither of them is armed. Later, at the rumble, Tim talks approvingly to Ponyboy about his recent altercation with the law, mentioning that his own younger brother, Curly, is in reform school.

Bob Sheldon

Bob is a leader of the Socs. He does not appear often in either the novel or the film version of *The Outsiders*. In the few scenes he is in, he is drunk, drinking from a distinctive round silver flask.

The novel clearly identifies Bob as the leader of the gang that attacked Johnny a few weeks earlier, leaving him physically and psychologically damaged. The film alludes to this fact by having Bob's girlfriend, Cherry, shudder when she hears that Johnny's main attacker wore several rings, but the point is not emphasized in the film. Although Bob, played by teen singing star Leif Garrett, is only seen being violent in the film, Cherry later recalls his good points while talking to Ponyboy.

Cherry Valance

Cherry, played by Diane Lane, is a Soc girl. She meets Ponyboy, Johnny and Dallas at the drive-in theater when she walks away from her boyfriend, Bob Sheldon, who is drunk. She resists Dallas's attempts to pick her up and abruptly throws a soda in his face, but she later confides to Ponyboy that she could easily imagine falling in love with Dallas if she were ever to see him again.

Ponyboy and Cherry have a good talk together the night that they meet, but when Bob and the rest of the Socs come to take her away, Cherry acknowledges the social divisions between them, apologizing in advance for the times when she will not talk to him when she sees him at the high school they both attend. After Bob has been killed and Ponyboy and Johnny are out of town, Cherry meets secretly with the Greasers to tell them of the plans the Socs have for the upcoming rumble. She approaches Ponyboy after his return, angering him when she says that she cannot go to the hospital to visit Johnny, who killed her boyfriend. When he realizes how sad his anger has made her, Ponyboy brings up the sunrise, a subject that they talked about earlier and that connects all social classes.

Dallas Winston

Dallas is one of the Greasers and a friend of Ponyboy and Johnny. In the novel, he is usually referred to as "Dally," though that name is seldom used in the film. He is played by Matt Dillon. Hinton's novel explains the difficult life that led Dallas to be a street hood: he lived in New York for three years and was arrested when he was ten years old, spending time in reform school. He has had many run-ins with the police.

Ponyboy and Johnny look up to Dallas as an ideal street gang member. They run to him after Bob Sheldon's death, seeking him out at Buck Merrill's bar because they know that Dallas will be familiar with such violence. Their expectation proves correct: he has a gun and money to give them, and he already has a hideout in mind. He even knows the schedule of the freight trains that pass through in the middle of the night.

Dallas has a special fondness for Johnny. Johnny's death drives him out of his mind. He robs a store with an empty gun just to show his contempt for authority. When the police hunt him down, he is still brandishing the empty gun, which forces them to assume that he is armed and shoot him to death. While they are after him, though, Dallas phones the Curtis house, specifically asking to talk to Darrel, the only person he looks up to.

THEMES

Innocence

This film charts Ponyboy's loss of innocence. Even though he starts the film as a member of a street gang, he is still a sheltered youth. He is surrounded by friends who view the world as he does. His parents gave him the childlike name "Ponyboy" and named his brother "Sodapop." He sees the world as being nothing more than a struggle to keep competing street gangs away from his gang's territory. By the end of the film, however, Ponyboy has been driven into an early adulthood. He has seen two of his friends die. He has blurred the clear-cut definitions that society gives to "delinquents" and "heroes," and he has learned that the division between Greasers and Socs that defined the boundaries of his life is a meaningless distinction.

READ. WATCH. WRITE.

- In this film, Ponyboy gives a dramatic recitation of Robert Frost's poem "Nothing Gold Can Stay." Use a computer music-making program to set this poem to a two- to three-minute song that will make modern audiences focus on its words.

- *The Outsiders* and the 1994 film *Mi Vida Loca* (My Crazy Life) have many differences—one is an idealized picture of gang life in Tulsa, Oklahoma, in the 1960s and the other is a gritty, realistic look at Latina gang life in Los Angeles, California, in the 1990s—but there are similarities between them as well. Use examples from both movies as the basis for an essay that explains aspects of gang life that are likely to appear in every culture.

- The novel describes in detail Ponyboy's severe disappointment about having to cut his hair short and wash the grease out of it. In the film, he and Johnny do not change much after their haircuts. Discuss in an essay why the filmmakers did not make a more drastic change in the looks of two people who are supposed to be in hiding and how well you think this choice works. Research other films in which characters have to change their looks. Compare the extent of those changes and their effects on the plots in a Photoshop, Piclits, Flickr, or other visual representation program.

- The scene in which Ponyboy and Johnny discuss poetry at sunrise echoes a similar scene in the film version of *Gone with the Wind*, when the protagonist, Scarlett O'Hara, announces that she will never go hungry again. One scene is tender and the other is defiant. Take sides in an online debate using a blog site, discussing whether this type of scene is more effective in one movie than in the other.

- *The Outsiders* is told from the perspective of Ponyboy, a self-proclaimed hoodlum. Adults are usually seen as a threat to Ponyboy's world, particularly in the scene that shows a shadowy policeman shooting Dallas Winston. Using particular camera shots and dialogue from the film as evidence, discuss in an essay whether you think authority figures are or are not portrayed fairly in this film.

- The character of Dallas Winston used to live in New York. As you watch this movie, take note of Matt Dillon's performance as Dallas. Create a Venn diagram (a chart of overlapping circles) to track any acting choices he has made to set his character apart from the characters who were born and raised in Oklahoma.

- A rain storm begins when the movie's climactic rumble begins and ends when the rumble ends. Such a contrivance can help to establish the film's tone, but it could also hurt the story by making audiences too aware of the film's technique. Is the technique effective here? In small groups, take sides and debate the issue.

- This film shows a vision of the 1960s, presented from a 1980s perspective. Find a current film that shows what life was like for teens twenty years ago and compare it with *The Outsiders*. Point out the historical facts that seem accurate and those that seem inaccurate. In a small group, discuss the conclusions you can draw from these two films about how youths are treated in historical films, and why. Have a spokesperson from each group present the conclusions to the class.

- Many of the members of this film's cast soon went on to be major stars. Make a list of current actors that you feel should be in the film's major roles if it were to be remade today. Support your choices with details about acting styles, reputations, looks, or whatever else affected your decisions, and compare your list with those of other students.

The story uses Johnny Cade to represent innocence shattered. Johnny has a scar on his cheek, a reminder of the beating that he was given by a gang of Socs in the recent past. The emotional effect of that beating is clear, as Johnny is distracted and skittish, hesitant to speak up even when he is among friends. Whereas the other Greasers like Two-Bit and Dallas welcome any opportunity to fight, Johnny hangs back, intimidated by life. He carries a switchblade because he is frightened, but when he sees the Soc gang giving Ponyboy the same sort of beating they gave to him, he feels compelled to use it. In trying too late to fight against the beating that took his innocence, Johnny becomes a murderer, effectively destroying his life.

The film uses images to capture the sense of innocence still left in Johnny and Ponyboy when they are away from the social order, holed up in the abandoned church. As Ponyboy recites a poem he has memorized, the actors are brightly lit and filmed from an upward angle, with a pastel sunset in the wide, clear sky behind them, indicating the purity of their spirits. They both risk their lives to save small children who are even more innocent than they are. Later, the film shows the Greasers going off to the rumble filled with childlike enthusiasm; instead of being sullen and stoical, they jump around, do cartwheels, and scream for the sheer joy of screaming. Their enthusiasm is short-lived, however. Later that night, Johnny dies, and then Dallas, driven mad by Johnny's death, taunts the police into shooting him down. Trying to make sense of their deaths, Ponyboy is left in the same position Randy found himself when thinking about the death of his friend Bob. He faces the complex world with uncertainty.

Family

This movie shows several variations on the concept of family, reconsidering what the word means. The only traditional family structure presented in the film is the Cade family, which is presented as a nightmarish situation. Johnny's parents never appear on camera, but their violent argument can be heard as he walks up the block. When he reaches home, Johnny is visibly shaken and is unable to enter the house, choosing instead to sleep in the forest. Later, when Dallas comes to visit him and Ponyboy while they are hiding from a murder charge, he asks whether his parents have inquired about him. Dallas admits that they have

not, and he tries to console Johnny with the news that his own parents acted the same way.

The deaths of their parents have left Ponyboy and his brothers struggling to remain together as a family. Darrel, who has graduated from high school, works as a roofer. He is a parental figure to Ponyboy, even though his strictness makes Ponyboy believe that Darrel dislikes him. Sodapop was well liked at school, but he has been forced to drop out and work at a gas station to make ends meet. After Ponyboy has become involved with Bob's death, run away, helped save the children in the fire, and returned home, there is a palpable sense of fear in the Curtis house that the state will take him away from the custody of his brothers. This fear is mentioned in the film, but only in passing, and it is not given as much attention as in Hinton's novel.

The strongest element of family present in the film is the gang itself. Although each of the Curtis brothers has a distinct personality that helps make up the character of their household, the other Greasers provide an extended family for Ponyboy. When he is bullied by Socs, Two-Bit is there to help him, and Johnny eventually commits murder to protect him. The morning after his return home, when his brothers have to go to their jobs, Two-Bit volunteers to "babysit" him, so that he will not be left alone so soon after his traumatic experience. Overall, the Greasers fill in the gaps left by their own dysfunctional family situations, creating a replacement family of their own.

Identity

The search for personal identity is a driving force for all of the young men depicted in *The Outsiders*. Whether they belong to the Greasers or the Socs, the basic motivation is the same; they want to fit in with a group of other boys who look and act like them.

This is why the scene where Ponyboy and Johnny have their hair cut and colored is one of the most significant in the story. In the novel, which is narrated by Ponyboy, readers have direct access to his thoughts, and so can hear him talk at greater length about his deep disappointment. His hair is an important part of Ponyboy's identity as a Greaser. Changing it makes him safer while he is in hiding, but he deeply resents the idea of having to face the future without grease in his hair. In the film, Ponyboy mentions regret about having to change, but the film's pacing does not allow him to dwell on how much it hurts him to give up his greaser look.

© *Photos 12 / Alamy*

The young men's quest for identity is a menacing presence throughout this film, creating a dangerous situation whenever boys from different gangs are together. There is fighting among boys from the same social group, but it is considered playful, as Two-Bit points out when he hears that Tim Shepard is looking to fight Dallas: As long as they do not use weapons, he declares, there is nothing wrong. When Socs and Greasers find themselves in the same place, however, there is a chance for the kind of destructive violence that affected Johnny so deeply when he was beat up. The positive side of identifying with a gang is shown in the moments before the big rumble, when all the Greasers leave the Curtis house as one unit. For those moments, the film captures their feeling of youthful enthusiasm, of having a sense of purpose, as they all identify with something larger than themselves.

STYLE

Sound

Diegetic sound refers to sounds in the film that the characters themselves could possibly hear. A good example from this film is the way Coppola has the soundtrack of the film *Beach Blanket Bingo* playing in the background throughout the drive-in movie scenes. The characters carry on their conversations without reacting to it, generally, but even if they are not aware of it, they would be able to hear it. In contrast, the orchestral score that provides most of the soundtrack for this movie is used to emphasize the action and dialogue, but it is not supposed to be something that the characters themselves can hear.

Early in the movie, Coppola has the soundtrack playing the song "Gloria." It starts when the characters meet on the street corner and carries on for several scenes. The volume swells as they approach the drive-in restaurant, indicating that the music is present there, but the song continues even as the scene jumps to the DX gas station and then to the empty lot from which they chase the younger children. The fact that the scene has jumped but the song continues uninterrupted is the viewer's cue that the song is nondiagetic, that is, not existing within the world of the film. Later that night, the same song plays again, after the Socs drive up to take Cherry and Marcia away. It echoes in the background, almost imperceptibly, to evoke the wild feeling of youth and courtship. It fades away as Ponyboy, Two-Bit, and Johnny approach Johnny's house and hear his parents fighting: the powerful rock song is overcome with the sad reality of Johnny's life.

Voice-Over

This film begins and ends with Ponyboy's voice reading the words that he is writing on the notebook page before him. This establishes his point of view, similarly to the way that the first-person narration of the novel (that is, Ponyboy writes as "I") establishes his point of view. Moviegoers can tell that this is a story being told by Ponyboy, implying that the events presented are told from his perspective. Once this is established, viewers understand that they will not see things or find out information that Ponyboy would not know.

In addition to scenes at the beginning and the end of the film, Coppola uses Ponyboy's narration twice more in the film. Both instances occur when Ponyboy is at the abandoned church, a time in the film when there is not much dramatic interaction. One voice-over is used to establish that four or five days have passed, and the next establishes a scene at sunrise, with Ponyboy saying that he could not sleep. These brief instances of his narration, though infrequent, keep the film in the control of the voice and perspective that dominated the novel.

Ponyboy's voice is also heard in voice-over when he reads the letter Sodapop sent him while he is in hiding, and when he reads Johnny's letter at the end of the film. This is a fairly common way of using voice-over, saving the audience the trouble of having to read the words on the page.

Visual Effects

This film uses visual techniques to emphasize the youthful innocence of Ponyboy and Johnny. They are seldom photographed from a distance, which would make them look little or insignificant, like irrelevant parts of a big, mechanical world. Instead, the film offers frequent close-ups of them both, drawing attention to their open, questioning faces. This is particularly true in the scene when they watch the sunrise, when Ponyboy recites a Robert Frost poem. In that scene, they are photographed from a distance initially, but they do not look overpowered by their environment. Instead, they look like they are part of nature's beauty. The scene continues with medium shots, showing the actors from the waist up, and with close-ups. In all of these shots, the sunrise is apparent in the background, but it is used to frame the actors' faces in soft, natural light.

None of the gang members in this film is presented as being the sort of menacing threat that gang members would be in real life. They are played by photogenic movie stars, but Coppola uses camera techniques, makeup, and lighting to show their faces as clear and innocent, without the lines or bags that come with age. The film's aim is to make the Greasers and Socs look more like children than like criminals. This is most apparent in the climactic rumble: when a rainstorm begins at the very moment that the rumble begins, it is difficult for viewers to take the moment as realism. Blows are exchanged, but there is no real lasting damage done during the fight, and the choreographed moves of the actors show their physical prowess without focusing on the violent nature of this confrontation. Later, when Dallas is gunned down, the camera frames him to make him look surprised and distressed and, in particular, nonthreatening, like a victim. Coppola's visual style in this film is meant to show who they are inside.

CULTURAL CONTEXT

1960s Youth Culture

This film takes place in 1965, which Coppola establishes with the movies showing at the drive-in theater and the music that plays in the background. The film's focus on the lives of its young protagonists is no coincidence, as the 1960s saw a population explosion, as the first generation of the Baby Boom came of age.

The Baby Boom was the generation born just after World War II. Throughout the 1930s, before the United States entered the war, the country had suffered through the Great Depression, a difficult economic situation that caused massive unemployment and poverty. The depression thawed in the later years of the decade, and when war broke out across Europe in 1939, the United States became one of the world's great industrial superpowers, a position that it was to retain long after. Still, there was no time for the country to enjoy its wealth after the Japanese attack on Pearl Harbor in 1941 pulled the United States into the war. It was not until after the war was over that the country returned to the kind of peace and economic stability that it had known during the 1920s. Soldiers returning from the

© *Photos 12 / Alamy*

conflict felt more comfortable starting families in that stable environment than the previous generation had been. The resulting Baby Boom is measured by sociologists as spanning from 1946, the year after the war ended, to 1964, when the number of babies born finally receded. During that time, approximately 79 million babies were born to a population that began, after the war, with 132.5 million.

The growth of the Baby Boomer generation, coinciding with the postwar economic boom, created a shift in popular culture toward youth-oriented interests. In the 1950s, the ascent of rock-and-roll music tapped into the interests of young Americans, singing about the glories of being young and miseries of struggling to be appreciated in a world dominated by adults. Manufacturers and entertainment providers found during the 1950s that they could market products to adolescents, who had disposable income of their own, and so a culture rose up that catered to their interests and desires. Television, which had been created in the 1930s but did not become a widespread commercial product until the postwar economic boom, was part of daily life for young people by the 1960s.

The result of this new commercial power in the hands of youth, ironically, created in them a sense of alienation. The generation that grew up in the 1950s and 1960s felt themselves more cut off from their parents than previous generations had. For one thing, they did not face the hardships their parents had faced throughout the Great Depression and World War II; living in relative comfort in the shadow of their parents' struggles, they found it difficult to have their own concerns taken seriously. At the same time, the attention that advertisers paid to youth culture made them aware of their own significance. They were given a sense of importance at the same time that they were told that their troubles were less significant than those of their parents.

As the 1960s progressed, youth culture asserted itself. What had been a cultural force grew to be a political movement, as the Baby Boom generation went to college and found themselves in an intellectual environment of their peers. The young people who had set the fashions in music and clothing in the early 1960s turned their attention to social consciousness in the second half of the decade. Young white people who were raised watching the struggle for civil rights that African Americans went through expanded those ideas to rights for women, native Americans, and protesting the Vietnam War. The war that seemed necessary for the older generation was viewed with a new set of eyes by their children. A book like *The Outsiders*, about young men trying to establish their own social order in a world that rejects them, became a best seller in 1967 because it spoke to a generation.

Greaser Culture in Television and Film

At the time when this story takes place, the Greasers that are its focus were already going out of style. Greasers take their name from the way a certain subculture of young men wore their hair in the 1950s and early 1960s: long, with thick layers of grease. This hair was the chosen style of boys who took a tough, antisocial, combative stance. Usually, the name that they used to define themselves was "hoods," short for "hoodlums," a derogatory expression when used by authority figures. Because the Greaser identity was so closely identified with hair, it faded into obscurity in the late 1960s, when long uncombed hair came to define the hippie culture.

Interest in the Greaser as a cultural relic began in the 1970s. In 1972, the musical *Grease* was produced on Broadway, and it continued until 1980, one of the longest runs in theater history. In George Lucas's 1973 nostalgic film about the early 1960s, *American Graffiti*, most of the main characters dress like the Socs of *The Outsiders*, but one character, John Milner, wears grease in his hair, a tee-shirt with its sleeves rolled up, and blue jeans. The television series *Happy Days*, which was influenced by *American Graffiti*, (1974 to 1984) created a cultural icon in "the Fonz," a comic Greaser stereotype. By the time *The Outsiders* was made into a film in the 1980s, Greasers were long gone from the social scene, but they were familiar character types in movies and on television.

CRITICAL OVERVIEW

At the time of the film's initial release, *The Outsiders* met with mixed reviews. A review in *Variety* credits it for being faithful to the novel, noting that such diligence does not necessarily make for a good movie. "Dialog which reads naturally and evocatively on the page doesn't play as well on screen, and there's a decided difficulty of tone during the early sequences." "Although set in the mid-1960s, pic feels very much like a 1950s drama about problem kids." Roger Ebert finds the young actors convincing in their roles, but he objects to the film's conspicuous design. "The problem with seeing characters in a highly stylized visual way is that it's hard for them to breathe and move and get us involved in their stories," he writes in a 1983 review in the *Chicago Sun-Times*. "That's what happens here.... Nothing that happens in the movie seems necessary; it's all arbitrary." Ebert also identifies the specific cause of the problems he sees: "The problem, I'm afraid, is with Coppola's direction. He seems so hung up with his notions of a particular movie 'look,' with his perfectionistic lighting and framing and composition, that the characters wind up like pictures, framed and hanging on the screen." Gene Siskel, on the other hand, sings the film's praises in the *Chicago Tribune*. "I will always treasure this film for the way it photographs its subjects and for the poetic words they speak," he writes at the conclusion of his three-and-a-half star review. "The teenagers in *The Outsiders* are truly noble, and on that basis I can't think of a recent movie quite like it." Despite the differences of opinions among critics, the film gained a reputation of nearly cult proportions, in part because of Coppola's visual direction but even more so because so many of its stars had gone on to cinematic fame.

In 2005, Coppola released a revised "director's cut" version of the film, with new footage and new music on the soundtrack to offset the heavy orchestral score that his father, Carmine Coppola, wrote for the original. The revision showed briefly in a few theaters before its release on DVD. The changes made the film more appealing to some reviewers. Peter Travers, for instance, notes in *Rolling Stone* that "Coppola has given the film a fullness that makes it feel freshly minted," adding that the new version makes it clearer to viewers that the stylized visual technique is meant to be seen as Ponyboy's view of life, and not as the director's. "That clarity," he says, "results in a movie that will stay gold." Lewis Beale is a little more reserved in his praise of the new mix in *Film Journal International* when he comments: "Certainly Coppola has done his best to make *The Outsiders* an enduring work of art." Beale concludes, though, that "flawed though it may be, it's still an exciting piece of film made by an innovative director who was firing on all cylinders."

CRITICISM

David Kelly

Kelly is a writer and an instructor of creative writing and literature at two colleges. In the following essay, he discusses Francis Ford Coppola's distinct visual style in filming The Outsiders *and the way that it is used to emphasize points that are only implied in the novel.*

The film that Francis Ford Coppola made from S. E. Hinton's novel *The Outsiders* has a distinct visual style. Even the most casual viewer cannot help but notice the beauty of the world Coppola presents. The story takes place in lower-class areas of Omaha, Nebraska, and in a small town out in the country, but the film has no place for any downtrodden tawdriness that might naturally be a part of its characters' lives. Ordinary street scenes are made into carefully, conspicuously balanced compositions. The action scenes are choreographed, often in slow-motion, to emphasize the dreamy surrealism of the lives these characters lead; brawls play out with grace, not brutality. The film's leads are played by young actors (mostly male, except Diane Lane) who are photographed to make their faces look soft and fresh, framed in close-ups and two-shots (where two people are shown in the frame), and they are lit brightly, with hardly a shadow on any face. The beauty suggests goodness, and it is abundant here.

This emphasis on beauty seems an odd choice, given that the novel's story is about juvenile delinquents who live to fight. It is a story that hinges on bullying, abuse, and death. At first, Coppola's visual scheme might seem a contradiction to Hinton's coming-of-age story. In retrospect, though, the film's visual design provides viewers with the perfect complement for the characters' growing frustration with the cruel world they inhabit.

The Outsiders is a story about boys who discover the troubles of growing up. The novel was written when Hinton was a teenager herself; it was

> AUDIENCES ARE TOLD ABOUT THE HORRORS OF GROWING UP WITH PONYBOY'S STORY, BUT THEY ARE SHOWN, BY COPPOLA'S DIRECTION, THAT BEING YOUNG STILL HAS ITS WONDERS."

an immediate hit, and it has always had a strong following among people who are facing adulthood. The action concerns tensions between distinct social classes leading to a murder, but Hinton's real theme, about the darkness associated with adulthood, is not easy to miss. Without drawing undue attention to it, Hinton sets her story in the strange, uncertain void between youth and adulthood that is familiar to anyone who has made it into adolescence. Her characters have difficulties; for them, the social hostility that adolescents feel comes out in actual physical hostility, even combat. They also have a spirit of camaraderie, however, that is possibly found nowhere except among those who are young and threatened. On some level—though not a very advanced one—they are aware of being each other's only safety net. They dislike being young, and like many young people, they drink and smoke as if they are already grown up. In spite of what her characters think, Hinton makes it clear throughout the book that aging is a nightmare that her characters will eventually come to regret.

Maturity has been thrust too soon on Ponyboy Curtis, the book's narrator, and his two brothers. When the novel begins, they have been struggling to establish a life for themselves following the recent deaths of their parents. Darrel, the oldest, is so awkward at filling the role of authority that has fallen to him that his attempts to create security actually frighten Ponyboy, who sees any friction between them only in terms of sibling rivalry. Sodapop, the middle brother, has dropped out of high school to work in a gas station and is considering marrying his girlfriend, hoping for a definitive move toward adulthood.

The boys the Curtises associate with, their Greaser gang, all run free in the streets, fighting and smoking and drinking, living out a child's idea of what adulthood must be like. All, that is, except for Johnny Cale. Johnny is linked to

WHAT DO I SEE NEXT?

- While Francis Ford Coppola was working with S. E. Hinton on this film (she has a brief cameo as a nurse), he asked if she had any other works they could film. As a result, they began filming Hinton's *Rumble Fish* before this movie was completed. Like *The Outsiders*, it features up-and-coming stars (Matt Dillon and Diane Lane from this film, in addition to Mickey Rourke, Laurence Fishburne, and Nicholas Cage) and concerns an alienated but good-hearted juvenile delinquent. It was released by Warner Brothers in 1983.

- *The Outsiders* has often been compared to *Rebel without a Cause*, a 1955 film directed by Nicholas Ray that is considered the gold standard of films about disaffected youths. Starring film legend James Dean, the story concerns a teenager who is rejected by society in his new town. The Warner Brothers film also stars Natalie Wood and Sal Mineo.

- A decade before *The Outsiders* was released, George Lucas ascended to fame as the writer and director of *American Graffiti*, which is about recent graduates of a California high school and their uncertainty about the future. Set at the same time as *The Outsiders*, Lucas's film also introduced a generation of new actors, including Richard Dreyfuss, Harrison Ford, Ron Howard, and Cindy Williams. Lucas wrote this 1973 comedy about his own teen years at the suggestion of his friend Francis Ford Coppola, who produced it.

- Another S. E. Hinton novel to be adapted to film is *Tex*. Filmed by director Tim Hinter, this film is about two teenaged brothers who struggle to stay together after their mother dies and their father abandons them. It also stars Matt Dillon (as Tex) and Emilio Estevez. It was released by Disney in 1982.

- Before this film, Francis Ford Coppola had already broken with his reputation for working with serious thrillers like *Godfather* films and *The Conversation* when he directed *One from the Heart*, a 1982 romantic musical starring Teri Garr and Frederic Forrest. At the time of its release, it was almost universally panned by critics, but in the years since then it has developed a strong cult following for the director's heavily stylized visual scheme.

- Critics have compared Coppola's stylized and romanticized view of gang warfare to *West Side Story*, which is considered one of the great Broadway musicals of all time, winning ten Academy Awards. Filmed in 1961, with music by Leonard Bernstein and choreography by Jerome Robbins, it is loosely based on Shakespeare's plot about star-crossed lovers in *Romeo and Juliet*. Robert Wise directed the film, which was released by United Artists.

Ponyboy because they look the same age, though Ponyboy is fourteen and Johnny is actually the same age as Sodapop and his friends, sixteen. Ironically, though, Johnny is wizened beyond his actual age. His youth has been taken from him, first by his parents, who are abusive alcoholics, and later by a recent violent beating at the hands of the rival gang, the Socs, that was so terrible that Hinton can only have Ponyboy hint at what was done to him. As readers spend more time with Johnny, watching him kill to save Ponyboy's life and later sacrifice himself to save young children trapped in a fire, they see how pointless it is that the other boys are rushing toward adulthood. After Johnny's death and the subsequent suicide of gang member Dallas Winston, Ponyboy is thrust into the complex world of maturity that he and the other Greasers wanted.

Coppola's film of this story takes one element of the gang members, their youthful innocence, and expands its significance. All of the key roles in the film are cast with handsome young actors who are photographed in ways that emphasize their boyishness. It is a visual scheme that the film's marketers could love, a reason for the girls who had already been the core audience of *The Outsiders* for a generation, to buy tickets to a film about gang fights. It works as an artistic move in its own right, as well.

The opening sequence, a series of quick scenes added for the film, sets the tone, orienting viewers to the lives they are about to experience. After Ponyboy finishes the initial narration, taken from the book, the camera follows him from a movie theater. In the book, he goes home in the dark after the movie and is threatened by the Soc gang, facing a beating like the one that has psychologically damaged Johnny. In the film, though, he walks into a bright afternoon and meets up with Johnny and Dallas on a street corner. Their first dialogue couples the boys' aimlessness with their drive to view themselves as outlaws: "We're early," Ponyboy says, "What do you wanna do?" To which Dallas answers, "Nothing legal, man." If these words had been spoken by a character showing the wear of a difficult life, instead of by fresh-faced Dallas, these words would predict menace more than desperation.

The camera follows the boys to a drive-in restaurant, which helps the film establish its 1950s/1960s time period. While they talk to a friend in the background, the foreground shows a fight between two boys who can be identified by their clothes as a Greaser and a Soc. A knife is pulled, but a policeman shows up to impose order before any real sense of danger arises. The three Greasers then stop by a gas station where other members of their gang, including Ponyboy's brother, work, showing audiences that they are comfortable in certain secure zones within their turf. The final scene in this sequence has them coming across a trio of boys, younger than them by six to ten years, in an overgrown lot. They take a deck of cards away from the young boys and then chase them away, asserting their power over those who are weaker.

This opening sequence is important for two reasons. For one, it visually establishes the priorities of this movie: what follows is not an idealization of youth in an earlier, purer time, even when it shows bravery and sacrifice and bullying and death. It is a film about the joys of being young. This is established by the Greasers' carefree jaunt through town, chatting up friends and chasing away whoever they can, simply because they can. A visual symbol for the sordid lives of these lower-class hoods is the scraggly empty lot, which they dominate. These themes continue throughout the film, as the Greasers continue to rely on each other, and the façade of violence, to face their troubles. The purity of their bond continues right up to Dallas's cry for help, phoning the Curtis home before his suicide at the hands of the police.

More importantly, this opening sequence establishes the film's visual tone. Most of the shots are from a distance, so the actors are not shown with the clear, youthful faces the film will give them as their lives become more complicated. It is, however, filmed in full daylight on open streets. The world of *The Outsiders* is not the world of urban blight associated with dangerous gangs, it is a rural town, where young men do what they can to feel important. As the film goes on, the story becomes increasingly sad and angry, but the images become increasingly beautiful. Audiences are told about the horrors of growing up with Ponyboy's story, but they are shown, by Coppola's direction, that being young still has its wonders.

The Coppola film presents a world of unbelievable beauty. Clouds billow with rare colors, hoods look like movie stars, and a rainstorm begins just when it is needed, ending when its use is complete. Whether or not this is the Omaha that readers imagined in Hinton's book, it is, in fact, consistent with her vision of childhood as a wonderful place and adulthood as a world where natural goodness has been corrupted. Hinton does not show real adulthood, only an adolescent's idealized version, where heroes race into fires and misunderstood gangsters die in a hail of bullets because they are too good to be understood. Coppola puts that world on the screen. The film's opening sequence sets the tone, so that viewers cannot claim surprise that the onscreen world in *The Outsiders* does not resemble the one outside the theater.

Source: David Kelly, Critical Essay on *The Outsiders*, in *Novels for Students*, Gale, Cengage Learning, 2011.

Ed Grant

In the following review, Grant states that Coppola is empathetic to young-adult readers' requests for key missing scenes to be added to the film.

The most commonly known fact about Francis Ford Coppola's *The Outsiders* is that he

© *Photos 12 / Alamy*

made it because he received a letter from school-children asking him to. This retooled version of the film is the result of further requests from kids who loved S. E. Hinton's classic young-adult novel and were wondering where key scenes from the book "had gone." Several supplements in *The Outsiders*' two-disc set chronicle the film's original production, but the key bonus is Kim Aubry's featurette "Staying Gold," which contains reflections by Coppola as well as most of the cast members (missing are Tom Cruise and Emilio Estevez) whose careers were kick-started by the film back in 1983. The fact that the cast formed a tight-knit community and that Coppola shot an initial, practice version of the film on videotape are the initial focuses of Aubry's doc, but the whole thing soon gives way to a Coppola dinner party, as the director wines and dines four of the actors (Diane Lane, C. Thomas Howell, Patrick Swayze and Ralph Macchio) at his Napa Valley estate in preparation for their supplying audio commentary for the film's restored cut of the film. Matt Dillon and Rob Lowe also participate in the featurette and are seamlessly interwoven onto the cast commentary track. In his own director's commentary, Coppola is emphatic about how much better the film is

with 22 minutes of "lost" sequences and a new vintage rock 'n' roll soundtrack. He repeatedly mentions what he had eliminated in order to include his new soundtrack: an orchestral score by his father, Carmine, lamenting at one point, "may my father forgive me!"

Source: Ed Grant, "*The Outsiders*: The Complete Novel," in *Video Business*, Vol. 25, No. 36, September 5, 2005, p. 16.

Business Wire

In the following article, Coppola discusses adding a new beginning and ending to the DVD release of The Outsiders *because he wanted to correct the fact that so much of the novel was edited out of the film.*

The Outsiders: The Complete Novel —Francis Ford Coppola's 1983 film adaptation of the renowned S. E. Hinton best seller—arrives September 20 from Warner Home Video (WHV) as a restored Two-Disc DVD available in wide-screen for $26.99 SRP. It will be filled with pre-viously unavailable bonus content, including new commentaries by the director and several of the actors, three new documentaries, three featurettes, deleted scenes and more.

Coppola, a five-time Academy Award(R) winner, has added 22 minutes to *The Outsiders* including a new beginning and an ending which is more true to the book and enriches the characters' relationships.

Said Coppola, "*The Outsiders* is a teenage epic, beloved by so many young people—junior high school students especially—and it's often their first important experience with literature. It's always bothered me that, in the rush to distribution, so much of the novel was edited out. Once, after showing the original version to my granddaughter's high school class, where so many kids asked 'but what about the other parts of the story?'—I resolved I would restore it to be the complete novel. I just felt the film would be better if it played much longer. Warner Bros. agreed with this thought, and we both became excited to bring the entire story to the screen."

Coppola has also added a brand new rock 'n' roll soundtrack, with six songs from Elvis Presley and from Van Morrison, Jerry Lee Lewis, Carl Perkins, The Marketts, Sandy Nelson and others. "I had always hoped the film could have an all Elvis Presley score," noted Coppola, "which turned out not to be possible at the time. Now we have reconceived the score, based on what these characters would be listening to, while still retaining the movie's great original song, 'Stay Gold' by Carmine Coppola and Stevie Wonder."

The impressive array of young actors who starred in *The Outsiders* include C. Thomas Howell, Matt Dillon, Diane Lane, Ralph Macchio, Rob Lowe, Patrick Swayze, Emilio Estevez, Tom Cruise and Leif Garrett. "So many of the young and talented cast have gone on to great success that I think the new length will be that much more fascinating to audiences," Coppola added.

The idea for *The Outsiders* began with a letter to Francis Ford Coppola from a school librarian in Fresno, Calif., stating that the faculty and students had nominated the director to make a movie of their favorite novel; the letter was personally signed by 110 students. "What I am most proud of in this new release is that the film is now the truest expression of the novel. And of course, that I was able to be responsive to these kids' letter," said Coppola.

The movie version of *The Outsiders* —like the book—struck a powerful chord with audiences, capturing the intense feelings of being caught between childhood and adulthood, and not belonging anywhere. A classic coming-of-age story, *The Outsiders* is set in gritty Tulsa, Okla., during the early 1960s and centers on a teen rivalry between two opposing groups: the Greasers (poor kids) and the Socs (socials, the rich kids).

Source: Business Wire, "Francis Ford Coppola's Production of S. E. Hinton's *The Outsiders*: The Complete Novel: Two-Disc DVD, with 22 Minutes of Added Footage & Brand New Rock 'n' Roll Soundtrack, Arrives September 20," in *Business Wire*, June 13, 2005, p. 1.

Gary Arnold

In the following review, Arnold is not optimistic about the film version of The Outsiders.

The Outsiders, Francis Coppola's droopily faithful movie version of S. E. Hinton's best-selling juvenile novel (4 million copies in the United States since 1967), is dedicated to the librarian of a junior high school in Fresno, Calif.

It was her letter, accompanied by a student body petition, urging Coppola to consider *The Outsiders* as a movie project that first attracted the celebrated moviemaker to this curiously inappropriate subject.

Hinton's book, a short, awkward, exceedingly soulful romance of teenage gang culture, set in Tulsa in the middle 1960s, has achieved a peculiar eminence, especially with preadolescent readers. I suspect that this admiring public, which includes a 9-year-old in my own household, is also predominantly feminine.

Begun when Susan Hinton was still a high school girl herself, *The Outsiders* seems very much a nice girl's fancy of what gang members ought to be like—basically misunderstood, sensitive and dreamy beneath the facade of toughness and belligerence; in short, a legion of lost boys in need of comforting, understanding Wendy girls to console them.

If he were less enamored of the source, Coppola might have done *The Outsiders* an invaluable service by actually making belated dramatic repairs. Instead of starting with Hinton's characters and social setting and then filling in the missing links of motivation and causation, Coppola is content to treat the material like a holy text.

Opening today at area theaters, *The Outsiders* begins with the narrator, Ponyboy Curtis (C. Thomas Howell), a 14-year-old greaser with a literary spark, writing the novel's first sentence in his notebook. Among other drawbacks, this venerable cliché heralding the unfolding of a Prestige Literary Adaptation tends to eliminate any conceivable suspense about Ponyboy's fate, since whatever the story is, he's apparently come through it unscathed.

There are two antagonistic gangs in the high school culture evoked by *The Outsiders*—the working-class boys, known as Greasers, who live on the north side of town, and the privileged, upper-middle-class kids, known as Socs (short for "Socials"), who reside on the affluent south side.

Ponyboy is the youngest of three orphaned brothers; the parents were killed some time ago in a collision with a locomotive (this tragedy is visualized by Ponyboy in a dream), and the older brothers, Darrel (Patrick Swayze) and Sodapop (Rob Lowe) have curtailed their educations in order to work and keep the clan together.

An almost identical situation became the basis for dramatically interesting conflicts and misunderstandings in Hinton's later novel *Tex*. The sibling motif remains one of several undeveloped possibilities in *The Outsiders*.

In perhaps the best sustained sequence in the movie, an evening of preliminary romantic maneuvering at a drive-in showing the distraction-inspiring double-bill of *Beach Blanket Bingo* and *Muscle Beach Party*, it appears that the old *Romeo and Juliet* theme will give direction to the narrative.

Diane Lane, as a Soc princess named Cherry Valance (no, I'm not making up these names), spurns the drunken boyfriend who brought her and strikes up an acquaintance with Ponyboy and his sidekick Johnny (Ralph Macchio, a beautiful dark-eyed camera subject and a very skillful young actor). Although she also brushes off their hoody friend Dallas, it's also clear that she's attracted to him.

Since Dallas is played by Matt Dillon, adding more assurance and humor to a presence that is already slightly transfixing on the strength of a facial bone structure and set of eyes that mesmerize the camera, it's also reasonable to expect the initial contact between Cherry and Dallas to lead somewhere.

Unfortunately, this prickly opening encounter is also the end of the relationship.

Hinton veers off on an abrupt melodramatic detour—Cherry's boyfriend, looking for trouble in a greaser neighborhood later that night, ends up fatally stabbed by Johnny after he and his Soc pals jump Ponyboy. This twist turns Ponyboy and Johnny into fugitives, like the principals in

Rebel Without a Cause, but again the plot takes an arbitrary turn, so nothing decisive hinges on their fugitive status.

Between the aimlessness of the plot and the marshmallow sponginess of the sentimental content, Coppola is left with ingredients every bit as defective and softheaded as the ones he overrated in *One From the Heart*. This is another squishy one from the heart, I suppose, but the heart-of-darkness exertions of *Apocalypse Now* may have left Coppola in a suspended state of artistic convalescence.

The Outsiders works itself up into overstylized tizzies during things like the rumble sequence, but its overall energy level is alarmingly faint, and the failure to add new dimensions or new material to the Hinton original suggests an exhausted imagination.

Commercially, the film will no doubt sink or swim on the cutes of its young male leads. In that sweepstakes, Dillon would appear to have the inside track, with strong competition from Macchio on the outside.

As the jovial greaser called Two-Bit, Emilio Estevez, the exotically named son of Martin Sheen, makes a consistently funny, amiable impression. Considering the inertia of the vehicle itself, these personality kids really can't be too cute.

Source: Gary Arnold, "Greasy Kids' Stuff," in *Washington Post*, March 25, 1983, p. C2.

SOURCES

Beale, Lewis, Review of *The Outsiders—The Complete Novel*, in *Film Journal International*, http://www.filmjournal.com/filmjournal/esearch/article_display.jsp?vnu_content_id = 100109529 5 (accessed December 16, 2009).

Croker, Richard, *The Boomer Century, 1946–2046: How America's Most Influential Generation Changed Everything*, Springboard Press, 2007.

Ebert, Roger, Review of *The Outsiders*, in *Chicago Sun-Times*, March 25, 1983, http://rogerebert.suntimes.com/apps/pbcs.dll/article?AID = /19830325/REVIEWS/303250 302/102 3 (accessed December 9, 2009).

Hinton, S. E., *The Outsiders*, Viking Press, 1967.

Review of *The Outsiders*, in *Variety*, January 1, 1983, http://www.variety.com/review/VE1117793810.html?categoryid = 31&cs = 1&query = outsiders + coppola (accessed December 9, 2009).

"Rock and Roll Comes to Stay," in *Our Glorious Century*, Reader's Digest Books, 1994, pp. 284–85.

Siskel, Gene, Review of *The Outsiders*, in *Chicago Tribune*, March 25, 1983, p. C3.

Travers, Peter, Review of *The Outsiders*, in *Rolling Stone*, September 22, 2005, p. 116.

FURTHER READING

Bergan, Ronald, *Francis Ford Coppola Close Up: The Making of His Movies*, Thunder's Mouth Press, 1998.
As part of the publisher's "Close Up" series, this book gives a general overview of Coppola's career that makes it accessible to the student researcher. The chapter examining the period in which this film was made, "Teen Dreams," is particularly focused on the issues going on in the director's life as his career dimmed and his studio, Zoetrope, faltered.

Dargis, Manohla, "Coppola Pays a Return Visit to His 'Gone with the Wind' for Teenagers," in *New York Times*, September 9, 2005, sec. E, p. 3.
This article, regarding the video release of *The Outsiders: The Complete Novel*, discusses the new version and the changes that Coppola felt compelled to make after twenty years.

Farber, Stephen, "Directors Join the S. E. Hinton Fan Club," in *New York Times*, March 20, 1983, sec. 2, col. 2, p. 19.
Farber discusses how Hinton came to Coppola's attention. Reportedly, the director asked her in the middle of filming *The Outsiders* for another piece they could work on with the same crew. This collaboration resulted in the film *Rumble Fish*, which was released at approximately the same time.

Goodman, Paul, *Growing Up Absurd*, Random House, 1960.
This highly influential sociology classic helped steer the late-1950s debate about "juvenile delinquency" toward a sympathetic look at the frustration of being young at that time.

Hickenlooper, George, "Francis Coppola," in *Reel Conversations: Candid Interviews with Film's Foremost Directors and Critics*, Citadel Press, 1991, pp. 34–49.

Hickenlooper's interview with Coppola focuses on the director's struggles with the studios which produced his films. Though this interview offers a look at Coppola's transition from hot director of the seventies to shunned artist of the nineties, *The Outsiders* is not specifically discussed.

Phillips, Gene D., "Growing Pains: *The Outsiders* and *Rumble Fish*," in *Godfather: The Intimate Francis Ford Coppola*, University Press of Kentucky, 2004, pp. 203–25.
Phillips's telling of how Coppola came to make this movie and his struggles with the studio are similar to other versions of the tale, with some notable specific details.

Schumecher, Michael, "Paladin in Oklahoma," in *Francis Ford Coppola: A Filmmaker's Life*, Crown Publishers, 1999, pp. 315–35.
This chapter of Schumecher's exhaustive biography of the director concerns the time spent shooting this film and his follow-up, *Rumble Fish*, explaining much about his artistic approach and his dealings with the Warner Brothers studio.

SUGGESTED SEARCH TERMS

Coppola

Outsiders AND Coppola

Hinton AND Coppola

Hinton AND film

Ponyboy AND Howell

Macchio AND Dillon AND Swayze

1980s teen film

American Zoetrope Studio

Outsiders AND characters

Outsiders AND 1950s

Outsiders AND gangs

greasers AND films

The Sea-Wolf

JACK LONDON

1904

The title character of *The Sea-Wolf* is Wolf Larsen, the powerful and fierce captain of the *Ghost*, a seal-hunting schooner in the northern Pacific Ocean at the turn of the twentieth century. In the novel, the second published by Jack London, a young literary scholar named Humphrey Van Weyden is plucked from the ocean after a shipping accident and forced to serve in Larsen's crew. He survives storms, threats from fellow crew members, and Larsen's unpredictable temper, while falling in love and learning to be a competent sailor. Larsen, a self-taught philosopher and student of science, holds fast to his beliefs that life has no value and that there is no right and wrong, until he dies a lonely death.

The Sea-Wolf was originally published as a serial story in the January through November 1904 issues of the *Century* magazine. London, who as a teenager had acquired some experience as a sailor and a seal hunter, wrote much of the novel while aboard his own small boat, the *Spray*. It was published in book form in late 1904 and, on the strength of London's earlier success with *The Call of the Wild* (1903), quickly sold out of the initial printing of forty thousand copies. It has stayed in print ever since, and it has been the basis for at least nine feature films and television miniseries.

Jack London (The Library of Congress)

AUTHOR BIOGRAPHY

The writer known as Jack London was born John Griffith Chaney on January 12, 1876, in San Francisco, California. He never knew his father, and he eventually took the last name of the stepfather who raised him with his mother. As a teenager, London earned enough money doing odd jobs to buy a small sailboat, the *Razzle-Dazzle*, which he used for stealing oysters out of others' oyster beds. Soon, however, he found work with the California Fish Patrol. At the Oakland Public Library, he read widely in literature about the sea, and at seventeen he joined the crew of a sealing vessel bound for Asia. The adventures he had as sailor later provided the material for his writing. In 1893, he won a prize from a San Francisco newspaper for his "Story of a Typhoon off the Coast of Japan."

Life seemed dull after seven months at sea, so London set off for several months of tramping around the country before coming home in 1895 and finishing high school. In 1897, he tried to contact William Chaney, the man he believed was his biological father, but Chaney refused to acknowledge him. Disappointed, London headed for the Klondike River in Canada, where gold had been discovered, and spent the winter prospecting. Here again, he found adventure and danger, as well as inspiration and material for later fiction. Returning to California, he struggled to earn a living selling stories to magazines and newspapers. In 1900, he married Bessie Maddern. The couple had two daughters, but their marriage lasted only four years.

London's first novel, *A Daughter of the Snows* (1902), is about a privileged woman who finds adventure in the Yukon. In 1903, his second novel, *The Call of the Wild*, also set in the frozen North, made London an international literary star. Largely on the strength of the reputation of *The Call of the Wild*, London's first novel about the sea, *The Sea-Wolf*, became an instant success in 1904; the first printing of forty thousand copies was sold out before it even reached the stores. London was now wealthy and famous. In 1905, he married Charmian Kittredge, reported by some critics to have been the model for Maud Brewster, a character in *The Sea-Wolf*. Over the next decade, he traveled to Hawaii, Tahiti, and Australia, lectured at universities in the East, and built himself a sailboat he named the *Snark* and a mansion he called "Wolf House."

London continued to write and to live a fast-paced life. Over his short career he published almost fifty books, and he reported on the Russo-Japanese War, the San Francisco earthquake, and the Mexican revolution for national magazines. While he was in Mexico in 1914 he contracted dysentery, from which he never fully recovered. He died on November 22, 1916, on his ranch in Glen Ellen, California. The cause of death was unclear, but it is suspected to be a combination of dysentery, uremia, alcohol abuse, and an overdose of morphine.

PLOT SUMMARY

Chapters 1–3

The Sea-Wolf opens with the narrator, Humphrey Van Weyden, riding on a ferry boat across San Francisco Bay on a Monday in January. The fog is particularly heavy, and as he stands at the

MEDIA ADAPTATIONS

- *The Sea-Wolf* has been adapted for film at least nine times. The most well-known version is the 1941 film *The Sea Wolf*, directed by Michael Curtiz and starring Edward G. Robinson, John Garfield, and Ida Lupino. It is available on videotape but not, as of 2010, on DVD.

- The 1975 *Il Lupo dei Mari*, made in Italy and starring Chuck Connors, was released in the United States as a video with the title *The Legend of the Sea Wolf*. It is available on DVD.

- *The Sea-Wolf* has been recorded as an unabridged audiobook at least three times, in addition to abridged versions. Blackstone Audiobooks produced a full-length reading by Brian Emerson in 2000, available on CD or as a download.

- Frank Muller's unabridged audiobook, produced in 1988 by Recorded Books, is available on audiocassette and as a download.

rail of the ferry, a seasoned seafarer chats with him about how difficult it is even for the ferry's experienced pilot to steer in the fog. Suddenly, the ferry strikes a steamship crossing its path and begins to sink. The narrator puts on a life jacket and jumps over the side into the cold water. He spends several hours in the water, the current pulling him out of the bay into the sea. Finally, he sees a sailing vessel passing near him. He makes eye contact with a sailor aboard just before losing consciousness.

When he regains consciousness, he has been rescued and taken aboard the *Ghost*, a seal-hunting ship captained by Wolf Larsen. He is helped into dry but dirty clothes by the ship's cook, Thomas Mugridge. Larsen, a rough, angry man with tremendous physical strength, mocks him for being a weakling who has lived off inherited wealth rather than his own labor. In fact, Humphrey is a literary scholar, who has spent his days reading and writing.

On the deck of the ship is a dead man, wrapped in cloth. The crew unsentimentally drops the body overboard, and Larsen, refusing Humphrey's request to help him get back to San Francisco, instead presses him into service as a cabin boy to take the place of the dead sailor.

Chapters 4–5

Now that Humphrey is a cabin boy rather than a rescued gentleman, Mugridge treats him with cruelty, giving him the worst tasks and mocking him at every opportunity. Humphrey tries on his first day to get used to life aboard ship, learning to stand and move and learning to avoid being tossed about by waves that break over the ship. However, he injures his knee when a wave slams him against the galley. Nothing can be done but wrap a cloth around it and keep on working. Humphrey has never done any physical labor in his life, and he has never been around unwashed men who smoke and curse and drink. When he wakes up on his second morning aboard and retrieves his own clothes, he discovers that Mugridge has stolen the money that was in the pocket. He demands it back, but Mugridge challenges him to fight and he backs off.

That morning, while cleaning Captain Larsen's stateroom, Humphrey notices that the captain has a small library of poetry, scientific books, and philosophy. He decides that the captain might be more reasonable than he has given him credit for, and he reports to Larsen that his money has been stolen. This leads to the first of many philosophical discussions the two men will have throughout their time together; Larsen insists that "life is a mess" and that there is no immortal soul, while Humphrey disagrees. Humphrey cannot help admiring, however, the articulate way in which Larsen argues his case.

Chapters 6–8

Humphrey's education continues. He learns that the *Ghost* is one of the fastest schooners afloat and that the crew members hate the captain. Humphrey's conflict with Mugridge escalates, and he is exhausted from hard work. Humphrey sees just how brutal these men can be when they taunt an inexperienced young seaman who has to climb high in the rigging to free a stuck sail and refuse to help him even when he becomes scared and sick. This leads to another philosophical discussion with Larsen, this time about the value of human life. Larsen shows himself to be more complex than Humphrey originally guessed, sometimes quoting poetry, sometimes berating the sailors in a way that seems half crazy. Above all, Humphrey realizes, Larsen is lonely. After Larsen wins Humphrey's money away from the cook playing cards, he and the narrator settle down for a days-long discussion of the poetry of Robert Browning and then about science and religion. Larsen reveals himself to be a materialist, while Humphrey holds to his idealism.

Chapters 9–13

The long discussion ends suddenly when Humphrey says something too personal about Larsen, and Larsen snarls and grabs Humphrey's arm, leaving it sore for days. Humphrey decides to avoid Larsen from then on. Mugridge, meanwhile, has become jealous of Humphrey, and he has had to do Humphrey's work during his long debate with the captain. Sharpening his knife in a way that threatens Humphrey, he quarrels with another sailor, Leach, and slashes open his arm. Afraid, Humphrey gets a knife of his own and sharpens it, leading to a truce with the cook. Humphrey and Larsen resume their tentative association, though Humphrey knows now that he cannot trust the captain's mood to stay steady. He learns that Larsen had little formal education but has taught himself everything he knows about literature, science, and philosophy. He also learns that Larsen has a brother, called Death Larsen, who also captains a ship. Death has never learned to read, and he is a happier man than his brother Wolf.

The *Ghost* sails toward the Japan coast, where the seals will be hunted. There, the men anticipate finding the *Macedonia*, the steamship captained by Death Larsen. Wolf Larsen's brutality is again displayed when he and the first mate, Johansen, summon a sailor named Johnson and beat him viciously for complaining. Seeing what has happened, Johnson's companion Leach becomes angry and yells at Larsen; he then beats Mugridge just as viciously.

Chapters 14–16

One night soon after Johnson's beating, Humphrey sees Larsen climbing aboard the ship, soaking wet. There has been an attempted mutiny. When Larsen appears before the sailors, several of them fight him at once and attempt to kill him, but he escapes, using his seemingly superhuman strength to get away. Johansen is never seen again, though whether he went over the side with Larsen or was killed by the captain is not revealed. Larsen names Humphrey first mate in Johansen's place and regains control over the ship and the men, although he knows the men—especially Johnson and Leach—will kill him at their first chance. Larsen's temper becomes more violent, and the men become more full of hatred.

Chapters 17–22

At last, the *Ghost* reaches the coast of Japan, and the seal hunting begins. Humphrey observes that the slaughter is all in the name of women's fashion. The meat of the seals is not eaten; only the skins are brought back. To hunt for seals, small crews of three men go out in small boats, radiating out from the *Ghost* and being picked up at the end of the day. With most of the men gone during the day, Humphrey assumes more responsibility for maneuvering the sails and steering the ship; he is learning to be a sailor, as Larsen notes approvingly. In a bad storm, Humphrey successfully manages to find and recover most of the smaller boats, but four men are lost at sea. Johnson and Leach sneak off one night with one of the boats, intending to desert.

While Larsen attempts to track down the deserters, the *Ghost* crosses paths instead with a small lifeboat containing three hunters, an engineer, and a woman, Maud Brewster, who are apparently victims of a shipwreck. Humphrey establishes Maud in a small cabin with some privacy and a clean pillow. He is instantly attracted to her, with feelings he has never experienced before, and he stands up to Larsen, demanding that she be treated well. Johnson and Leach, meanwhile, are turned back by another storm, and they attempt to return to the *Ghost*. Larsen promises that he will not "lay [his] hands upon" them, but Humphrey learns to his horror that Larsen means that he will not allow them to come aboard. Instead, he leaves them to die at sea, and he tells Maud that he will not return her to Yokohama until the end of the sealing season.

Maud, it turns out, is a famous poet whose work is known to Humphrey, and she also knows his scholarly writing. They form a friendship, but Larsen feels excluded from their intimate talk of literature and art, and he sulks. In his bad mood, he dunks the cook over the side to punish him for wearing a filthy shirt, and Maud is horrified when a shark bites Mugridge's foot off before they can haul him back in. She blames Humphrey for not preventing the violence, but he tells her that she cannot understand what it is like to be among such men.

Chapters 23–26

The hunting continues, and the brutality continues. Comforting the frightened Maud, Humphrey discovers that he is in love with her. One day, the smoke from the steamship *Macedonia*, captained by Death Larsen, is spotted, and Wolf Larsen declares his intention to have revenge on his brother. In another philosophical discussion, he states that he wishes he were as innocent as Humphrey and Maud, who believe in right and wrong but who are ignorant of what the world is really like. When the *Macedonia* is close enough, Larsen kidnaps the crews of some of its seal-hunting boats. Later that night, Larsen tries to rape Maud, but Humphrey arrives just in time to keep him from harming her. When Humphrey strikes him, Larsen collapses, suffering from one of headaches that have tormented him occasionally during the voyage. While he is incapacitated, Humphrey and Maud steal a boat and some supplies and escape. They hope to make the coast of Japan in five days.

Chapters 27–31

It is cold and wet on the boat, and Humphrey has never steered this kind of vessel before. He and Maud both learn how to sail the boat, but a storm blows them off course and erases all their progress. Through it all, Maud is plucky and resourceful, and Humphrey's undeclared love for her grows. At last, they land on what they later name Endeavor Island, an unpopulated piece of land where the seals nest. The two castaways learn to make a fire, and they spend two weeks hauling rocks to make a small hut to protect them from the fierce winds. For the roof, Humphrey finds an oar and clubs some seals to death for their skins. While clubbing them, he realizes for the first time his true manhood—he is a mighty hunter and the protector of the woman he loves. They make a second hut for Humphrey, and they learn to use seal blubber for lamp oil and to make jerky from strips of flesh.

Chapters 32–33

Humphrey awakens one morning to find that the wind has died down and that the *Ghost* has shipwrecked just off the island. It seems deserted,

and its masts are gone. Raiding the ship for food and other supplies, he finds Larsen, alive but very weak from the brain tumor that has been the source of his headaches. He is still frightening, and Humphrey aims a rifle at him. Larsen taunts him, sneering that he is too impotent to shoot. He explains that his brother Death came aboard the *Ghost* and paid Wolf's men to join his crew; they left him alone aboard the *Ghost*, but before departing Mugridge cut the ropes holding the masts in place. Humphrey gathers up all of the weapons and knives on board and then goes back to Maud and the huts. Larsen remains on the ship, making no effort to come ashore. Maud cannot bear the thought of Larsen lying alone, dying and in pain, so she urges Humphrey to check on him. Humphrey finds him alive, but completely blind. Larsen tries to lock Humphrey in the hold, but he escapes.

Chapters 34–39

Humphrey and Maud decide to try to repair the masts, which are floating in the bay, and sail away on the *Ghost*. Humphrey rigs up an elaborate system of ropes and pulleys to get the masts out of the water and back in place. However, after days of hard work, Larsen sabotages the masts. He intends, he says, to die on the island, and he will not help them escape. Humphrey is forced to shackle Larsen out of the way and to begin the hard work again. Larsen's headaches continue, and a stroke paralyzes him on one side. Finally, the clumsy new masts are in place and the torn sails hoisted, and the ship gets underway. That night, Larsen dies, and Maud and Humphrey give him as proper a burial at sea as they can manage. As they bid farewell to Larsen, they see a steamship only a few miles away. The boat approaches to rescue them, and Maud and Humphrey share their first kiss.

CHARACTERS

Maud Brewster

Maud Brewster does not appear in the novel until Chapter 19, when she and four companions are shipwrecked in a storm on their way to Japan and rescued from their lifeboat by the crew of the *Ghost*. Maud is twenty-seven years old, a famous poet whose work, coincidentally, has been reviewed by Humphrey Van Weyden. She, like Humphrey, comes from the world of literature and ideas and has never had to perform manual labor. Also like Humphrey, she is horrified at the brutality of the men aboard ship. With her beauty, graceful manners, and sharp intelligence, she is admired and sought after by every man on the ship; Humphrey keeps his passion bottled up, but Larsen attempts to rape her. For her safety, Humphrey and Maud escape from the *Ghost* in one of the sealing boats. However, Maud does not stand back and rely on Humphrey to take care of her. She quickly learns to sail the boat and takes hours-long shifts steering while Humphrey sleeps; she carries rocks to build two huts after they are shipwrecked; she learns to cook over an open fire. In some ways, though, she is traditionally feminine, showing compassion and tenderheartedness. When it comes time to kill seals, she offers advice but does not swing the club, and it is she who cannot bear to leave Larsen alone on the *Ghost* at the end of his life. Maud and Humphrey declare their love for each other only in the last chapter of the novel, and they share their first kiss as the novel closes.

Cooky

See Thomas Mugridge

Hump

See Humphrey Van Weyden

Johansen

Johansen is the thirty-eight-year-old Swedish first mate on the *Ghost*. He seems loyal to Larsen and helps the captain beat Johnson savagely, to punish the sailor for complaining. During the attempted mutiny, when Larsen is forced over the side of the *Ghost* but manages to climb back aboard and retake control, Johansen disappears. No explanation is given for his disappearance, and critics disagree about whether he was thrown overboard with Larsen or was killed by Larsen while participating in the mutiny. In his absence, however, Humphrey becomes the ship's first mate.

Johnson

Johnson is strong and masculine, a highly skilled sailor who loves the sea, but he does not refrain from complaining when he sees unfair treatment. To goad him, Larsen calls him "Yonson," and Johnson protests every time, becoming angrier and angrier. When he is summoned to Larsen's cabin, accompanied by the first mate Johansen, he knows that they are going to beat him up, and he takes it bravely. However, soon afterwards,

he and his friend Leach steal a boat and try to desert. When a storm forces them back to the *Ghost*, Larsen refuses to let them come aboard, leaving them to die at sea.

Death Larsen

Death Larsen is the brother of Wolf Larsen and the captain of the steamship *Macedonia*. The two brothers, both seal-hunters, are rivals, and Wolf Larsen wants nothing more than to beat and shame his brother. Death, unlike Wolf, cannot read or write and does not live an intellectual life; Wolf tells Humphrey that Death "is all the happier for leaving life alone. He is too busy living life to think about it." When the two ships meet off the coast of Japan, Wolf kidnaps several members of Death's crew. Death gets his revenge later, while Humphrey and Maud are on Endeavor Island, by bribing all of Wolf's crew to join him, leaving Wolf alone on the disabled *Ghost*.

Wolf Larsen

Wolf Larsen, the captain of the seal-hunting vessel *Ghost*, is a complex character, a fascinating combination of brutishness and intellect. His real first name is not known; "Wolf" is only a nickname. Physically, he is impressive, described by Humphrey as "the man type, the masculine, and almost a god in his perfectness." He is strong enough to crush a raw potato in his hands and to fight off at least seven men at once. Unseen by others however, a tumor or disease is slowly destroying his brain, causing him debilitating headaches. Larsen, a Dane who grew up in Norway, has had no formal education, having gone to sea as a cabin boy at the age of ten. However, he taught himself to read, and from that beginning he educated himself in science, philosophy, literature, religion, and the arts. These interests lead him to hold long discussions and debates with Humphrey, who has more education but who is less skilled than Larsen at articulating his thoughts.

However, Larsen is not a happy man. He has developed a materialist philosophy, believing that there is no value to human life, no afterlife, no right and wrong. He controls his crew through cruelty and violence; they know that his temper is unpredictable, and that he is capable of coldly beating a man or leaving him to die at sea. He refuses to return Humphrey and then Maud to land, because it would interfere with his hunting, and he hates his own brother. Larsen is lonely. His self-education has brought him no comfort; noting that his brother cannot read and is the happier man, he says, "My mistake was in ever opening the books." In the end, Larsen is cheated by his brother, whom he has cheated before, and is left to die alone on the *Ghost*. When he shipwrecks off the island where Humphrey and Maud have also landed, he sabotages their efforts to repair the *Ghost* and get away, but he finally suffers a stroke and dies. He is buried at sea, with no one to mourn him.

George Leach

George Leach is one of the sailors. During an argument with Mugridge, the cook, his arm is slashed open with the cook's knife. He takes it calmly but promises revenge. When Johnson is beaten, however, he loses his temper, screams at Larsen, and beats Mugridge. He and Johnson steal a boat and try to escape Larsen and the *Ghost*, but in a terrible storm they decide to return to the ship and accept their punishment. Larsen. however, refuses to pick them up and leaves them to die.

Thomas Mugridge

Thomas Mugridge is cook on the *Ghost*. He is a cockney, or a working-class man from London, and for Humphrey Van Weyden he represents everything that is loathsome about the sailors: He is dirty, uneducated, unsophisticated, violent, and cruel, although he is said to be quite handsome. Mugridge fawns over Humphrey when he is first rescued, showing deference to Humphrey's superior social class, but as soon as Humphrey is made cabin boy, Mugridge begins to abuse him. When Humphrey establishes his peculiar friendship with Larsen, Mugridge becomes jealous and threatens Humphrey with a knife, but when Humphrey returns the threat, the two form an uneasy truce. Shortly after Maud Brewster is brought aboard the *Ghost*, Larsen orders that Mugridge be fastened to a rope and towed along in the water as punishment for the man's refusal to wash his shirt. Before he can be pulled up again, he is attacked by a shark, which bites off his foot.

Humphrey Van Weyden

Although he is not in some ways as interesting a character as Wolf Larsen, Humphrey Van Weyden is the character who undergoes the most change in the novel. Humphrey is a thirty-five-year-old literary scholar, recognized by Maud Brewster as "the Dean of American Letters, the Second," whose father left him enough money

that he has never had to earn a living. When he first comes aboard the *Ghost*, he is physically weak and finds peeling potatoes and scrubbing pots exhausting. Having lived with his mother and sisters all his life, he is unaccustomed to rough men who shout, curse, bathe infrequently, and settle their differences with fists and knives. Wolf Larsen, who is interested in philosophy, science, and literature, gives Humphrey the chance to demonstrate his superior mind during their long discussions, but Larsen is the more physically powerful, and Humphrey realizes quickly that at sea the physically stronger man can dominate the intellectually stronger one.

Humphrey becomes physically more adept through hard work, and after he becomes Larsen's first mate he learns to be a true sailor. Although he never adopts the other men's crude and violent ways, he learns to use his intellect to solve practical problems—a skill that proves useful when he is stranded with Maud on Endeavor Island. As he is developing his physical strength and mental range, Humphrey also finds for the first time his capacity to love a woman. By the end of the novel, Humphrey is a fully developed, mature man.

THEMES

Bildungsroman

As the story of Humphrey Van Weyden's maturation, *The Sea-Wolf* is an example of a *bildungsroman*, a German term that means "novel of education." This type of novel typically describes the progress of a young person from child to adult, including the difficult challenges and lessons along the way. Often, the road to maturity begins with a sudden event that forces the protagonist out of his or her comfortable life into a dangerous new setting. Novels of this type often conclude with their protagonists assuming their rightful places in the larger world. Examples of the bildungsroman include Charlotte Brontë's *Jane Eyre* (1847), Charles Dickens's *David Copperfield* (1850), and Harper Lee's *To Kill a Mockingbird* (1960).

Humphrey is somewhat unusual as the protagonist of a bildungsroman in that he is comparatively old—thirty-five—when he begins his education. He is an immature and innocent thirty-five, though, never having loved a woman, never having witnessed violence or crudity, never

TOPICS FOR FURTHER STUDY

- Watch one of the film versions of *The Sea-Wolf*—if possible, more than one. Write an essay in which you compare how one of the central characters (Wolf Larsen, Humphrey Van Weyden, or Maud Brewster) is presented in the novel and in film.

- Find illustrations, in books or online, of nineteenth-century schooners, and identify the different masts, sails, and riggings. Prepare a computerized illustrated presentation (using Flickr or another program) in which you explain the dimensions of the *Ghost* as described in Chapter 6 of *The Sea-Wolf*. Trace what happens to Harrison in the same chapter.

- Carefully read one of London's descriptions of storms at sea. You might consider the descriptions in Chapters 4, 17, 28, 39, or other chapters. How does London use word choice and imagery to show nature's power? What other literary devices does he use? Write a description of your own, in which you help your reader know what it was like to experience the worst weather you have ever faced.

- Read Theodore Taylor's young-adult novel *Ice Drift* (2005). Write a paper in which you compare the attitudes of the Inuit seal-hunters in Taylor's novel with those of London's characters.

- In Chapter 20 of *The Sea-Wolf*, Humphrey compares Maud's poetry to that written by the British poet Alice Meynell (1847–1922). Find and read a few of Meynell's poems to get a sense of what Maud's poems would be like, and then compose a poem that Maud might have written to commemorate her time on Endeavor Island.

- Using the Internet, research how seals were hunted at the end of the nineteenth century and the beginning of the twentieth. Prepare a PowerPoint presentation illustrating and explaining the ships, the weapons, and other equipment used.

- Using the Internet or books from your local library or theater, research the kinds of clothes that have been made from seal skins. You may also investigate fashions made from other rare animal materials, such as egret feathers. Prepare an illustrated presentation for your class.

---

having done physical labor. As the novel opens, he has much to learn. He does not seek out his education; one feels he could go on living his comfortable life without regret. Instead, he is forced to join the crew of the *Ghost* by forces larger than himself: the fog, the accident, and Wolf Larsen. Once aboard the ship, he learns to use his mind and body in new ways, and learns what it means to love a woman. Only then is he ready to be rescued and to return to San Francisco, a fully formed adult.

Seafaring

In using his experiences to write about life on the sea, London was following a long tradition. As a child, he read many of the most famous books about seafaring, including Richard Henry Dana's *Two Years before the Mast* (1840) and stories about the explorations of Captain James Cook (1728–1799), who sailed on the HMS *Endeavor*. He was well aware, therefore, of what readers of seafaring novels expected to find: exciting adventure in exotic locations, vivid descriptions of storms and waves, technical terminology for rigging and sails, and rough men uttering salty talk. A convention of these novels is the young crew member who learns to sail and to be a man, as Humphrey Van Weyden does. A shipwreck on a deserted island, a damsel in distress, and an inscrutable captain are all stock elements of the seafaring tale.

Edward G. Robinson as "Wolf" Larsen, John Garfield as George Leach, and Ida Lupino as Ruth Brewster in the 1941 film version of the novel (Warner Bros. | The Kobal Collection)

Materialism

Wolf Larsen subscribes to a philosophy known as materialism, and Humphrey refers to this philosophy several times as he relates the philosophical debates that he and the captain have on board the *Ghost*. At the core of materialism is the belief that only the physical world exists—there is no spiritual world or soul, and even emotions and the consciousness are simply the results of physical processes. As a materialist, Larsen's main concern is for material gain; he will not take time away from the seal hunt to take Humphrey or Maud to shore, and he says of the stolen money he has won away from Mugridge, "Being able to possess it, I wrong myself and the life that is in me if I give it to you and forego the pleasure of possessing it." He insists that human life has no value, that life is "a ferment, a yeasty something which devoured life that it might live," and continues, "the only value life has is what life puts upon itself." This philosophy

guides Larsen's actions—he is, as Humphrey notes, "at least consistent"—from his brutal treatment of his crew to his efforts to remain on Endeavor Island, but it does not bring him respect, success, or companionship.

Idealism

Humphrey Van Weyden's philosophy, diametrically opposed to Larsen's, is called idealism. Idealists hold that the material world is indivisible from, and less important than, the world of ideas and the mind. Another way of saying this is that the only way humans can perceive the material world is through the mind; the consciousness and the soul determine the value of material things. Humphrey believes in the soul, in the value of human life, in the importance of the arts and of beauty. He believes that good and evil exist and that, as he tells Larsen, "the highest, finest, right conduct . . . is that act which benefits at the same time the man, his children, and his race." Humphrey is idealistic in every sense of the term: he holds to high-minded virtues and an unwavering code of what is right, but he has never tested his ideals outside his sheltered world, in a setting where not everyone believes as he does. He soon learns—at least, the reader looking over his shoulder learns—that a man who holds to his idealism as a way of life among rough, savage sailors, letting trust, compassion, and generosity guide his actions, would soon lose his money, his dignity, and maybe his life. Humphrey's idealism does not help him in difficult situations among people who do not subscribe to his beliefs. When Mugridge refuses to return his stolen money, Humphrey has no recourse but to report the theft to the captain. When the crew goes after Larsen, Humphrey hides under the bed. Although Humphrey and Larsen derive some pleasure from trying to best the other in argument, neither man's philosophy can inform a full life.

STYLE

Antihero

In many ways, Wolf Larsen represents the figure of the antihero, a character from literature who demonstrates qualities opposite those we expect a hero to display. An antihero typically is friendless, socially awkward, unintelligent, uneducated, deceitful, and weak. Larsen is many of these things. He is, as Humphrey realizes, a lonely man, unable to maintain his unusual friendship with Humphrey or any sort of affection for his brother. He is a brute, controlling his men through force and intimidation and having no idea how, other than through force, to show his feelings for Maud. He has had no formal education, and he has no practical way to apply the things he has taught himself. Although he is straightforward in debate about his philosophical ideas and his ambitions, he is also conniving and deceitful when it suits him, as when he promises Humphrey that he will not lay his hands on Johnson and Leach, or pretends to be unconscious when Humphrey and Maud come to his aid on the shipwrecked *Ghost*. However, an antihero is not simply evil: the character must be compelling and attractive enough to capture readers' respect, if not their admiration. Larsen is quite intelligent and a nearly perfect physical specimen, handsome and strong. His philosophy has been formed

through careful and serious thought, and it has brought him a reasonable measure of success in the world of seal hunting.

Jargon

The setting of most of *The Sea-Wolf* is, of course, the Pacific Ocean, from San Francisco to Japan, aboard the seal-hunting schooner the *Ghost*. To help establish this setting and to constantly remind the reader that this is a different world, London frequently uses the terms that sailors use to describe parts of the ship and the actions the sailors must perform. The term for a specialized language like this that is used by members of a profession, or members of any group, is *jargon*. For example, when the young man Harrison climbs "out the peak-halyards to the end of the gaff itself," it is because "in the light baffling airs the schooner had been tacking about a great deal, at which times the sails pass from one side to the other and a man is sent aloft to shift over the fore-gaff-topsail." When Humphrey repairs the damage Larsen's sabotage causes to the shipwrecked *Ghost*, he notes, "In half a day I got the two topmasts aboard and the shears rigged and guyed as before." London was himself an experienced sailor, and he uses the sailors' jargon accurately and precisely, as his characters would, but he does not explain the terms. This creates in many of his readers the same slight disorientation that Humphrey feels at the beginning of the novel, when everything aboard ship is strange to him. The casual inclusion of this jargon, however, establishes London's and Humphrey's credibility as the readers' guides into this strange world.

HISTORICAL CONTEXT

Naturalism

In the late nineteenth century in Europe and the United States, writers began to move away from romanticism, a style of writing that was highly imaginative and highly emotional. Many writers began to depict realistic settings, rather than wind-swept moors and haunted castles, often researching locations and describing them in great detail. These writers, embracing the movement known as naturalism, created characters like Wolf Larsen, a man of lower-class background who cannot rise above his passions and his instincts, even through self-education. In a romantic novel, a handsome and physically

COMPARE
&
CONTRAST

- **1904:** According to modern scholar James A. Papa, Jr., the age of commercial sailing ships is nearly over. Steamships such as the *Macedonia*, because they are faster and more reliable, are rapidly replacing sailing schooners like the *Ghost*.

  Today: Most ships used for commercial hunting and fishing have diesel or electric engines, making them even faster, safer, and more efficient than steam-powered ships.

- **1904:** Because of rapidly diminishing seal populations, the age of extensive commercial hunting of the northern fur seal is coming to a close.

  Today: United States law bans the hunting of any marine mammal, including seals, except in limited numbers by some native peoples.

- **1904:** Because of the moral standards of the day and the fear of censorship, London's editor removes any hints of passion or impropriety between Humphrey and Maud, even to the extent of having them build two separate huts to protect them from the fierce winds.

  Today: Television shows and movies routinely depict men and women sharing living quarters without scandal or censorship.

---

strong man like Larsen could have used his intelligence to become a wealthy and influential hero, but in naturalism he cannot escape his heredity. Many characters in novels of naturalism are types, representatives of a group, more acted upon by environment and background than acting. There is no free will. Humphrey, for example, does not choose to have an adventure and change his life; a chance encounter between two boats sends him in a new direction, and he can only respond. As Christopher Gair explains in an essay titled "Gender and Nature," Humphrey is an inadequate specimen of a man at the beginning of the novel, but nature forces him against his will into situations where he learns what he needs to learn in order to survive. The natural world in a naturalist novel is indifferent to human desires, and characters are often seen battling storms or cold or hunger, as well as their own emotions. These novels depict physically strong characters who live violent lives and survive by dominating others. The novels are often gloomy and pessimistic, offering no hope that humans can transform their own lives or the larger world.

Naturalism arose partly in response to new ideas sparked by Charles Darwin and Herbert Spencer and intellectual debates about what Spencer called the "survival of the fittest." Naturalist novelists turned to science, looking for rational and logical reasons for characters' behavior. Most of the sailors on the *Ghost* are uneducated brutes, with no apparent capacity for deep thought or self-reflection. However, Larsen and Humphrey carry on a debate that puts the ideas of Darwin and Spencer, and the ideas behind naturalism, in the foreground. Larsen sums up his understanding of the meaning of life this way: "it's life eats life till the strongest and most piggish life is left," to which Humphrey replies, "You have read Darwin.... But you read him misunderstandingly." Larsen has also read Spencer but found him difficult to understand. As Gair points out, Humphrey describes Larsen and Maud as "the extreme ends of the human ladder of evolution." Even the cook, Mugridge, has absorbed this belief, responding to Humphrey's suggestion that "you can make anything you please of yourself" with, "It's a lie, and you know it. I'm already myde [made], an' myde out of leavin's an' scraps." In *The Sea-Wolf*, people cannot change their essential beings; they are who they are born to be, and the question of how heredity determines a person's life is a fascinating and important question.

Sailing ship *(Image copyright RCPPHOTO, 2010. Used under license from Shutterstock.com)*

Superman

In 1883, German philosopher Friedrich Nietzsche published the first part of his book *Also Sprach Zarathustra* (*Thus Spoke Zarathustra*). The book's main character, Zarathustra, proposes that humanity should try to overcome its weaknesses and produce a new kind of man, an *Übermensch*, usually translated as "Superman" or "Overman." This Superman would strive for satisfaction in this world, rather than looking toward an afterlife. He would not look to God to establish right from wrong, but would create new values that were sustainable and practical. He would be physically powerful, selfish, and ruthless, and he would know that his rightful place was above lesser men.

Nietzsche's idea of the Superman was a popular topic for debate in the later nineteenth and early twentieth centuries, as intellectuals wondered what Nietzsche meant by it and whether the Superman was an achievable or desirable goal for humanity. In *The Sea-Wolf*, in fact, Nietzsche

is mentioned in the second sentence, as one of the writers Humphrey's friend "loafed through the winter months" reading. London was also a reader of Nietzsche, but he found fault with the individualism and selfishness he saw in the Superman. His second wife, Charmian London, writes that as her husband was writing *The Sea-Wolf* he explained that the novel would demonstrate that "the superman is anti-social in his tendencies, and in these days of our complex society and sociology he cannot be successful in his hostile aloofness."

CRITICAL OVERVIEW

Although London was extremely successful commercially, and was by some reckonings the first American to earn his living completely from his writing, he was not taken seriously by scholars during his lifetime. Instead, he was dismissed as merely a popular writer, a creator of adventure novels for boys. In 1904, the *New York Times* reviewed *The Sea-Wolf*, calling it "a stirring and unhackneyed tale of life on the high seas, full of the seafaring spirit," but concluding, "We do not see our way to herald the book as an epoch-maker.... It is above the average alike in plan and execution." In the years since 1904, most critics seem to have agreed with a frequently quoted comment by the writer Ambrose Bierce, who in 1905 famously praises "that tremendous creation, Wolf Larsen" in *A Much Misunderstood Man: Selected Letters of Ambrose Bierce*. Bierce continues, "The hewing out and setting up of such a figure is enough for a man to do in one lifetime" but declares that "the 'love' element, with its absurd suppressions, and impossible proprieties, is awful."

London died in 1916; it was not until 1974 that the first full-length study of his work, Earle Labor's volume in Twayne's United States Authors Series, appeared. Labor has no hesitation in thinking of *The Sea-Wolf* as great literature, declaring, "It is structured upon the universal timeless motif of initiation; its setting is likewise archetypal: the ship as microcosm, the eternal sea as most fitting matrix, symbolic as well as literal, for death and rebirth." Since that time, several articles and volumes of criticism of London's work have been published.

The most frequently addressed issue in this criticism as it applies to *The Sea-Wolf* has been the matter of sexuality and what it means to be masculine in the world of the novel. Robert Forrey started the trend with a 1974 article in *Literature and Psychology*, titled "Male and Female in London's *The Sea-Wolf*," in which he examines the possibility that the conflict and attraction between Humphrey Van Weyden and Wolf Larsen is a representation of London's inner conflict over his own sexuality, a struggle of his "sensitive inner self against his public image of lone-wolf adventurer." In 1983, Charles N. Watson, Jr., agreed that the suggestion of homosexuality is an organic part of the gothic elements of the novel, as he explains in *The Novels of Jack London: A Reappraisal*. Jonathan Auerbach treats the matter in "Between Men of Letters: Homoerotic Agon in *The Sea-Wolf*," a chapter in his 1996 study of London's public persona, *Male Call*. *The Sea-Wolf* has drawn less critical attention than some of London's other novels, but the idea of gender and sexuality has informed nearly all of the criticism.

CRITICISM

Cynthia A. Bily

Bily is an instructor in English and literature. In this essay, she considers the role of books and "bookishness" in The Sea-Wolf.

Nearly one hundred years after its publication, Jack London's *The Sea-Wolf* (1904) remains one of the most well-known nautical adventure stories by an American author. It has been filmed at least nine times, starring well-known actors from every film era, from Noah Beery in a 1920 version, through Edward G. Robinson, Chuck Connors, Christopher Reeve, and Stacey Keach, and on to Tim Roth in 2009. It is easy to see why the novel should be so popular, and why filmmakers would be anxious to adapt the story: it features a handsome but evil-hearted captain, a weak and inexperienced man who finds his strength, and a beautiful woman who stirs both their hearts; there are dramatic storms at sea, fights with knives and fists, a shark attack, sails fluttering in the salt air, and at least three shipwrecks. Life aboard the *Ghost* is physically demanding, and many life-or-death decisions have to be made instantly, drawing on instinct and experience rather than slow, deliberate thought. Many of the lessons a new sailor like Humphrey Van Weyden must learn—how to

MAUD ATTEMPTS TO USE HER READING FOR PRACTICAL PURPOSES, BUT HUMPHREY, THE PROTECTOR, SHUTS HER DOWN."

manipulate the rigging and sails, or how to move about on a rolling ship—can only be learned by doing.

It is interesting, then, that the three main characters of the novel spend so much of their time reading and thinking about books. The three principal characters—Humphrey Van Weyden, "the Dean of American Letters, the Second"; Wolf Larsen, the self-taught philosopher; and Maud Brewster, author of poems, including "Kiss Endured,"—recite poems from memory, quote scientists and philosophers to support debate points, and spend their evenings analyzing books over supper, ignored by the sailors and seal-hunters whose lives are focused on their work. In the cases of both Humphrey and Larsen, books have blocked them from experiencing life. Humphrey has detached himself because he thinks the intellectual life is superior to the physical, and Larsen knows that his intellectual habits have stripped away much of the pleasure from his life. Of the three, however, only Maud achieves a proper balance between the practical and the intellectual. Maud is the character who seems to know when to read and when to act.

From the beginning, Humphrey Van Weyden is a man of books. He is a literary scholar, and he has just published an article about "Poe's place in American literature" when the novel opens. He is on his way home from a weekend visit with a friend who likes to "read Nietzsche and Schopenhauer to rest his brain." It is not just that Humphrey can read and write; his worldview has enabled him to develop these skills at the expense of others. Noticing a gentleman reading his Poe article in the current issue of the *Atlantic Monthly* magazine, he appreciates the division of labor that allows him to write articles and the gentleman to read them, without having to worry about how to operate a ferry. The first person Humphrey speaks to in the novel gives him his first lesson, if he would take it: that the world is not really that way.

WHAT DO I READ NEXT?

- Jack London's most popular work is his 1903 short novel *The Call of the Wild*, set in the Yukon Territory of Canada during the Klondike Gold Rush.

- *Master and Commander* (1969) is the first in a series of twenty novels by Patrick O'Brian. Set in the early nineteenth century, the novels feature Captain Jack Aubrey of the British Royal Navy and his friend, the naval surgeon Stephen Maturin. Elements of several of the books were blended to create the 2003 film *Master and Commander: The Far Side of the World.*

- The title character of Sheree-Lee Olson's *Sailor Girl* (2008) is Kate McLeod, a nineteen-year-old young woman who gets away from her family and boyfriend in Toronto, Ontario, Canada, by taking a summer job on a freight liner on the Great Lakes. This exciting novel vividly depicts the hard work, weather, and other dangers that help Kate find her strength.

- *Powder Monkey: Adventures of a Young Sailor* (2006), by Paul Dowswell, is a thrilling adventure yarn about Sam, a thirteen-year-old boy who is pressed into service as a "powder monkey," running gunpowder to the cannon crew.

- In the award-winning *The Cay* (1969) by Theodore Taylor, a young white boy, an elderly African American man, and a cat are shipwrecked together in the Caribbean after an explosion that also leads to the boy's blindness. This World War II story deals with racism, friendship, and trust, and it shows an inexperienced young man learning to survive in difficult conditions.

- A retired sea captain who is called back to the sea is the central character in Sammy Harkham's graphic novel *Poor Sailor* (2005). There are few words in this beautiful book, but Harkham's images tell a powerful story.

- One of the fables in Rudyard Kipling's collection *The Jungle Book* (1894) is "The White Seal." The tale is narrated by Kotick, a Northern fur seal, who looks for a safe haven for his herd.

- Seals, whales, dolphins and other sea creatures are the subject of Richard Ellis's illustrated natural history *The Empty Ocean: Plundering the World's Oceans* (2003). Commercial hunting, the book shows, has contributed to the near-extinction of several species.

The red-faced man, a fellow passenger on the ferry who had apparently once been a sailor, may or may not be able to read and write criticism, but he is able to translate "into articulate language the speech of the horns and sirens," and with that ability he is able to sense danger before Humphrey does.

London keeps the idea of reading in the foreground even as he tosses Humphrey into the sea. Humphrey twice takes note of the man with the magazine. He is still reading after he puts on a life jacket, and he asks Humphrey "with monotonous insistence if I thought there was any danger"; as the women scream, Humphrey sees the man "stuffing the magazine into his overcoat pocket and looking on curiously." This man, with whom Humphrey has already identified himself, and who is reading Humphrey's own words as the ship sinks, seems unaware that he is in danger. He is unable to help others, to calm the screaming women, or to take any action to help himself. His is the world of words, not of action. Humphrey believes, as all people who read books do, that he bridges both worlds, but books are more real to him than life is. He is surprised to realize, as he sees and hears other men trying to lower the life boats, "It was just as I had read descriptions of such scenes in books."

Much has been written already about what happens to this man of books on board the *Ghost*. There he meets the self-educated Wolf Larsen, a man who has taught himself to read and who has collected a small library of books by famous and well-respected authors—"Shakespeare, Tennyson, Poe, and De Quincey,"—as well as books of science, religion, grammar, and other fields. Larsen is attracted to the power of language and ideas, but he generally keeps that side of himself private and separate from his day-to-day life. For him, books are tools, conveyors of ideas that a man might use to amuse himself intellectually, but they cannot help him steer a ship or command a crew.

Humphrey learns on one of his first nights aboard the *Ghost* that he has landed in a world of words. On a particularly beautiful night, as he lies awake watching the waves from the ship, he hears Larsen reciting lines from Rudyard Kipling's poem "The Long Trail." Larsen's voice is "mellow with appreciation of the words he was quoting." When Humphrey expresses surprise at Larsen's enthusiasm, the captain responds, "Why, man, it's living! It's life!" As Larsen's recitation ends, one of the sailors begins to sing the "Song of the Trade Wind" in "a rich tenor voice" and Humphrey returns to his own thoughts.

Humphrey later learns that Larsen has read at least four books by Herbert Spencer, he appreciates the beauty of the language of Ecclesiastes, and he can quote from the poet Algernon Swinburne and from John Milton's *Paradise Lost*. Together Humphrey and Larsen read Robert Browning's poem "Caliban on Setebos," and Humphrey begins to see that there are more ways than one to be a reader. If Humphrey can be said to have led an empty but happy life, Larsen has led an exciting and unhappy one, and Larsen attributes his own unhappiness to reading. His brother Death, he tells Humphrey, "is too busy living [life] to think about it. My mistake was in ever opening the books." But Larsen cannot resist the pull of books. When the lovely poet Maud Brewster comes aboard the *Ghost*, he finds his knowledge both useful and enjoyable, trading recitations with her over the supper table. However, Larsen's attraction to books is twisted, perverted; he misunderstands its power. It is Maud's beautiful speaking voice, reciting a poem by Ernest Dowson one evening, that arouses Larsen's passion for her;

that night, Larsen attempts to rape Maud, and Humphrey and Maud leave the ship.

Maud, the youngest of the three main characters, is the only one who seems full-formed and mature from the beginning. She appreciates the beauty and inspiration of literature, but she also realizes its utility—unlike Humphrey, she earns her own living through her writing. Critics and reviewers have wondered in print what Maud is doing in the novel, since many of her scenes seem unnatural and, in Ambrose Bierce's word, "awful." Labor, author of the Twayne reference volume *Jack London*, argues that Maud appears in the novel "apparently to dramatize Van Weyden's newly-won manhood and fitness for survival." One of her roles in the novel may be to show Humphrey a way to balance the opposing forces in his life or how to remain "bookish" while facing the world head-on.

Once Humphrey and Maud land on Endeavor Island, their relationship to books and book learning changes abruptly. Although they have plenty of time on their hands, as they share meals and sit in the evenings, they never quote poetry or discuss the philosophers as they did with Larsen aboard the *Ghost*. Both have committed long passages of poetry and prose to memory, yet never once is either of them stirred to recite a few pertinent lines. Instead, their references to books all have to do with practical knowledge they might use to survive, and Humphrey again demonstrates his inadequacy. Immediately upon unloading the boat, for example, Humphrey realizes that he has forgotten to bring matches. Neither Humphrey nor Maud has ever had to build a fire on a beach, but Maud, remembering a novel by Daniel Defoe, makes a suggestion: "Wasn't it—er—Crusoe who rubbed sticks together?" Humphrey has read *Robinson Crusoe*, but it has not occurred to him that he could apply its lessons to the real world. He responds with his own memory of a journalist named Winter who concluded that "it's beyond the white man" to make a fire that way, and he does not even try. Maud attempts to use her reading for practical purposes, but Humphrey, the protector, shuts her down.

A bit later, when the two decide to kill seals to obtain skins for the roof of the hut, they again have no experience to guide them, and again they turn to books. "I think I have read something about them," Maud remembers. "Dr. Jordan's book, I believe." Maud is referring to the work of

The Captain puts Van Weyden through an initiation and controls him through much of the novel, until Van Weyden takes control of the ship at the climax. *(Image copyright Foto Factory, 2010. Used under license from Shutterstock.com)*

David Starr Jordan, a biologist who studied fish and mammals at the end of the nineteenth century. He published several scientific books about natural history, contributed to federal studies of seals and other northern species, and in 1898 published *Footnotes to Evolution: A Series of Popular Addresses on the Evolution of Life*, the source of Maud's motto, "Can we make it work? Can we trust our lives to it?" The fact that Maud, a poet from Cambridge, Massachusetts (home of Harvard University), has read and retained information from Jordan's work shows the breadth of her reading and the modernity of her thought. Her new hero, she tells Humphrey, is this modern man of science.

Humphrey begins as a weak and intellectual man, and his bookishness is something he struggles to overcome throughout the novel. In the beginning, he is clearly inadequate as a sailor. Even after he gains experience, physical strength, and confidence, however, he remains poorly equipped to live in the real world. At first he does not even recognize his own feelings for

Maud, as he notes that "long years of bookish silence had made me inattentive and unprepared" for love. He remembers his earlier decision not to pursue love, thinking of himself as "abnormal, an 'emotionless monster,' a strange bookish creature, capable of pleasuring in sensations only of the mind." Determined to protect Maud from Larsen's influence, he gathers strength, understanding that if he succeeds in saving her it will be "in spite of Wolf Larsen and of my own thirty-five bookish years." But even as Larsen is dying, and after Humphrey has used his brains and his brawn to make the first attempt to repair the sails of the *Ghost*, he still cannot declare his love, and sees himself as "not skilled in the speech of eyes. I was only Humphrey Van Weyden, a bookish fellow who loved." For Humphrey, bookishness is an impediment to his development. As a literary critic, he has dedicated his life to studying life through books instead of studying life directly.

Humphrey believes that his knowledge of books has practical use, but he is proven wrong when he needs to do practical things; Larsen believes that his knowledge of books has no practical use, but the only time we see him enjoying life is when he is reciting poetry or analyzing what he has read in books. Unlike Larsen and Humphrey, Maud has all the elements one needs to survive and thrive. Larsen notes this soon after he meets her, praising her for "books, and brains, and bravery. You are well rounded, a bluestocking fit to be the wife of a pirate chief." London seems to be saying that reciting love poetry is no substitute for declaring one's love, and reading about adventure is no substitute for getting up and having one. Of course, he is delivering this lesson to the readers of his novel, sitting comfortably in their armchairs reading about storms at sea. Although he does not expect his readers to put down the book and go find a ship, he encourages us to be more like Maud Brewster, to live life fully, to read and to act.

Source: Cynthia A. Bily, Critical Essay on *The Sea-Wolf*, in *Novels for Students*, Gale, Cengage Learning, 2011.

Edward W. Pitcher

In the following essay, Pitcher draws attention to the appropriateness of the title of Jack London's The Sea-Wolf *in relation to the characters and themes of his narrative.*

Some attention has been given to the several working titles Jack London entertained for the novel that was eventually published as *The Sea-Wolf*, but not much has been said of the appropriateness of his final choice to the characters and themes of his narrative. In the most recent edition of *The Sea-Wolf* (Oxford UP, 1992), John Sutherland has provided biographical, critical, and bibliographical information touching most aspects of the writing of the novel and has appended a glossary of nautical terminology; "sea-wolf" is not defined, however, and its several meanings are left undistinguished. Sutherland's appendix 1 obliquely links the use of "sea-wolf" to pirate or privateer; he reports London's statement (in his June 1905 letter to the editor of the *San Francisco Examiner*) that he had based his "*Sea-Wolf* character" on the piratical seal-poacher Alexander McLean. That Alexander McLean and his brother Dan McLean were models for the brothers Wolf and Death Larsen is also reflected in London's having once suggested for his novel the title "The Sea Wolves"; generally, this meaning of "sea-wolf"—a predatory, unscrupulous, piratical sea-captain—seems to have been accepted as London's primary or

sole intention. Certainly, by this association, Wolf Larsen can be conveniently distinguished from the "lesser" beings he calls "swine," but London, through Wolf, also insisted that all were swine, essentially. (1)

The pervasiveness of the swine/hog/pig motif is shown by reference to passages at 6 (women screamed like "the squealing of pigs under the knife of the butcher"); at 47 (Wolf: "It is piggishness, and it is life. Of what use or sense is an immorality of piggishness?"); at p. 88 (Wolf: "To get [my navigational invention] patented, to make money from it, to revel in piggishness ... while other men do the work"); at 96 (Wolf: "To crawl is piggish; but to not crawl, to be as the clod and rock, is loathsome to contemplate. [...] Life itself is unsatisfaction, but to look ahead to death is greater unsatisfaction"); at 106 (Leach: "May God damn your soul to hell, Wolf Larsen, only hell's too good for you, you coward, you murderer, you pig!"); at 107 (Leach: "Pig! Pig! Pig!"); at 205 (Wolf: "I'm going to give that brother of mine a taste of his own medicine [Death hogged the seal harvest]. In short, I'm going to play the hog myself. [...]"); at 220 ("Wolf Larsen it was, always Wolf Larsen, enslaver and tormentor of men, a male Circe and these his swine, suffering brutes that grovelled before him and revolted only in drunkenness and secrecy"); and at 266 ("It was a dark and evil-appearing thing, that hut [on Endeavor Island], not fit for aught better than swine in a civilized land, but for us [Humphrey and Maud], who had known the misery of the open boat, it was a snug little habitation"). In brief, from Wolf to those under him, and to Humphrey and Maud on Endeavor Island, everyone is associated with swinishness, but some wallow in the piggish side of their beings while others adapt to a swinish world, obliged to make a silk purse of a sow's ear, a "habitation" of a pigshed. Wolf, in particular, accepts his own essential piggishness ("I do no sin, for I am true to the promptings of the life that is in me" [136]), but he has determined to be the strongest among swine ("where there is room for one life, she [Nature] sows a thousand lives, and it's life eats life till the strongest and most piggish life is left" [62]).

Wolf clearly appreciated that his name did not distinguish him among his kind except by a superiority of power over others. He was master-pig over the peasant and slave pigs, the strongest yeastlife feeding on other yeast. That Jack London gave him the epithet "sea-wolf" to imply a distinction in kind between the wolf and the swine is contradicted by everything in the novel. Could London have punned on the meaning of seawolf as a name for wolffish and its synonym swine-fish? (2) This equation of "wolf" and "swine" would certainly remove any possible confusion between the novel's title and themes. It would, moreover, confirm that London had from the beginning a clear sense of the direction his novel would take: the steady stripping away of the outer mask of wolfish, Luciferian power to show the swinish, Satanic being beneath this Sea-Wolf.

Source: Edward W. Pitcher, "*The Sea-Wolf*: Jack London's Swinish Title," in *ANQ*, Vol. 16, No. 3, Summer 2003, pp. 42–45.

Pat MacAdam

In the following article, MacAdam shares a brief biography of the real-life Wolf Larsen, Captain MacLean.

He was portrayed in Jack London's novel *Sea-Wolf* as a Swede, Wolf Larsen. But in real life, Sea Wolf was a tough, brawling sea captain named Alexander MacLean from East Bay, Cape Breton.

When London's best seller appeared, Capt. MacLean jokingly threatened to throw the author into the sea for portraying him as Wolf Larsen, rather than as a Cape Breton Scot. We will never know how Capt. MacLean would have reacted to being played in the movies by, most famously, Edward G. Robinson, and later Charles Bronson.

Jack London's and Capt. MacLean's paths crossed several times—in the saloons of San Francisco, along the Oakland waterfront, probably on northwest Pacific sealing waters, and in the Klondike Gold Rush of 1897.

Capt. MacLean and his older brother, Dan, were sailing the Bras d'Or Lakes from the time they could walk. Wits joked the East Bay MacLeans had their own boat during the Flood and sailed alongside Noah's Ark.

A year after Alex was born in 1858, the MacLean clan christened the 23-ton schooner Alexander at a shipyard in Washabuck, Cape Breton. On her second voyage, bound for Newfoundland carrying livestock and produce, the Alexander went under in high seas and her master, Capt. Hector MacLean, and three young

> CAPT. MACLEAN PROBABLY WOULD NOT HAVE UNDERSTOOD THE SYMBOLISM BEHIND JACK LONDON'S STORY OF THE SEA WOLF—THE POWERFUL, RUTHLESS SKIPPER OF A SEALING SHIP, HIS GREAT PHYSICAL ENERGY—THE CULT OF "RED BLOOD" AND A BREED OF NIETZSCHEAN SUPERMEN ENGAGED IN VARIOUS AND VIOLENT INNER AND OUTER STRUGGLES."

MacLeans—James, Nicholas and Michael—were lost at sea.

The careers of the surviving MacLean brothers—Alex and Dan—and Jack London paralleled each other. They all left school at an early age to follow the sea. All three had larceny in their hearts. The MacLeans had a strict Scottish religious upbringing from God-fearing parents but Jack London, said to be the illegitimate son of itinerant astrologer William Henry Chaney, was raised by a family with neither a fixed address nor a fixed occupation.

London left school at the age of 14, bought a sloop and raided oyster beds along Oakland Bay. The MacLeans headed for the northern sealing grounds on board the schooner *City of San Diego* with older brother Dan as skipper and Alex as first mate.

The northwest Pacific sealing grounds were considered the private hunting preserves of Russia, the United States, Japan, Canada, and Britain. The Alaska Commercial Company owned a 20-year lease on the Aleutian sealing area and its monopoly was enforced by U.S. revenue cutters. But this was a minor inconvenience to the MacLeans and they ignored it, poaching at will.

In 1886, Capt. Dan MacLean returned to port with a record 4,250 skins and Alex took 3,300. Their combined harvest was worth more than $60,000.

In 1888, Alex dropped anchor in Victoria with the largest cargo of sealskins landed to date. When he learned a rival ship had off-loaded an even larger catch, he went back on a second hunt and came back with an even larger haul.

They normally sailed out of Victoria, flying the Red Ensign. Once, sailing the J. Hamilton Lewis, Captain Dan was challenged by a Russian gunboat which, by sheer coincidence, was named Alexander. Captain Dan had no qualms about running up the Stars and Stripes and ignoring the armed Russian patrol boat. His ruse worked.

On another occasion, Captain Alex wasn't as lucky. He was caught by the Russians raiding a seal rookery on Copper Island. Dan was wounded by Russian gunfire and a crew member drowned in the surf when swept overboard. The Russian gunship ordered Alex to heave to, but he ignored the warning. More shots were fired across his bow and still he ignored the Russians until the Russian vessel *Aleut* steamed down across his bow, carrying away the ship's forerigging.

An armed Russian party boarded the MacLean ship and escorted it to Vladivostok, where the crew was imprisoned briefly. The crew was permitted to roam the city freely by day but were locked up each night at 8 p.m.

Even while he was a prisoner of the Russians, Alex MacLean's brawling habits came to the fore. As he was negotiating duck boards over mud he was confronted by three decorated Russian officers from the area garrison walking abreast. Alex MacLean had no intention of being deferential to the three Russian militia, who soon found themselves up to their necks in mud. Soldiers rushed to their aid and Alex MacLean was manhandled back to his lockup.

An international tribunal later judged the MacLeans innocent of poaching or any wrongdoing, but their long incarceration meant they had missed the season's seal hunt.

Not to worry. Off they went to the Yukon to dig for gold. They found lodgings at a hotel in Bennett City owned by a MacNeil, a distant cousin from Washabuck.

Alex MacLean wasn't in Bennett City long before he was warned of a card cheat in the hotel's saloon. The crooked gambler played with two loaded pistols on the table in front of him. Alex called him a cheat and was challenged to a duel. MacLean said he had the right to choose the distance over which they would fire at one another and the card cheat agreed.

Alex said: "All right, you stand on one side of the card table and I'll stand on the other. Now."

The gambler would have no part of Alex's point-blank distance and begged for his life.

Alex took away his guns, administered a severe beating and threw the card cheat out in the snow.

Capt. MacLean's hunting was not restricted to seals or gold. He spent some time in the South Seas poaching French oyster beds for pearls. The French harvested the rich pearl beds every 10 years. Capt. MacLean plundered them in the ninth year. He was spotted anchored over the oyster beds by a French gunboat.

His ship, *Carmecita*, sailing under Mexican registry, was forced to heave to. Capt. MacLean's crew had hidden the pearls in tar pitch between the ship's planking. He told the French he was anchored in the lagoon to take on fresh water and fish. The French found no pearls on board but they were suspicious and the schooner was impounded.

Under cover of darkness and an approaching storm, the Sea Wolf and his crew overpowered the guards, rowed their ship out of the lagoon, set full sail and were never seen again by the French. A Maritime historian, W. A. Claymore, wrote that the French gunboat "couldn't have caught them had they tried. Most of these schooners being used by the sealers were Maritimers, direct forbears of the schooner *Bluenose*."

After the voyage, Capt. MacLean wore a pink pearl set in five golden claws as a tie pin.

Capt. MacLean and Jack London's Sea Wolf, Wolf Larsen, were both known for their great physical power and toughness, although MacLean did not possess the utterly ruthless nature of Larsen. Back home in East Bay, Capt. MacLean was known for his kindness and for his generosity with his money.

He was a fierce-looking sea captain. His trademark was his moustache—at almost 45 centimetres long, he could tie it in a knot at the back of his neck.

Capt. MacLean was five-foot-11 and weighed about 190 pounds and his feats of brawling on the deck are awesome.

He once took exception to the negligence of his 230-pound first mate. The mate had allowed several crew members to jump ship and join another sealing vessel—brother Dan's ship. Capt. MacLean announced he was "going to give him (the first mate) a licking." He ordered the crew below, locked the hatches, took off his shirt and for half an hour punched the first mate senseless. Capt. MacLean didn't have a scratch on him after the fisticuffs, but he bore no grudges.

He considered the first mate a good seaman so he gently dressed his cuts and abrasions, shook hands with him, and kept him on as his second in command.

Capt. MacLean probably would not have understood the symbolism behind Jack London's story of the Sea Wolf—the powerful, ruthless skipper of a sealing ship, his great physical energy—the cult of "red blood" and a breed of Nietzschean supermen engaged in various and violent inner and outer struggles.

Jack London's idols were Marx and Nietzsche, who were poles apart in their ideologies. London championed first one and then the other—both in his life and in his novels. Capt. MacLean probably never heard of either because he could not read.

There were stories Capt. MacLean had killed 50 men in his lifetime, but he denied them. He maintained he never killed a man in his life "though I've lost 59 men."

It has been recorded that he marooned men who fell afoul of his discipline and once he threw a man overboard, telling him: "If you want to go ashore, swim for it."

Capt. MacLean never left the sea. He was captain of *Favorite* when he drowned in Vancouver Harbour in 1914 at the age of 56.

Jack London put the sea behind him and tramped through Canada and the United States for two years before enrolling at the University of California for just one semester. The smell of gold lured him to the Klondike Gold Rush of 1897 but he failed at mining and panning.

He contracted scurvy and returned home to Oakland to write. By his death in 1916 at age 40, he had produced 19 novels and scores of short stories. His best-known works—*Call of the Wild, Sea-Wolf, White Fang* and *Jerry of the Islands*—made him as popular in the English-speaking world as Rudyard Kipling.

And Capt. MacLean, the real life Sea Wolf, never did get to carry out his threat to throw him into the Pacific.

Source: Pat MacAdam, "*Sea-Wolf* a Swede? Not on Your Life: Rough and Ready Cape Bretoner Was Real Inspiration in Jack London's Best-Seller," in *Ottawa Citizen,* January 15, 2000, p. A10.

Jeanne Campbell Reesman

In the following excerpt, Sandburg claims that Jack London's fame as a writer has been hard

WOLF LARSEN IS ONE IN WHOSE CHARACTER REVOLVE THE MOTIVES OF AMBITION AND DOMINATION IN THEIR MOST TERRIBLE FORM."

pushed by his notoriety as an agitator and London never neglected an occasion to boom his theories of "The System," a system on which his character Wolf Larsen from The Sea-Wolf *is based.*

... It is the common man for whom Jack London pleads and as he pleads he wants it understood that he too is a common man. Nor is it merely a plea he makes. It is also a threat, "the threat of socialism." It is the threat Mark Hanna had in mind when he said, "We've got to change the conditions that are breeding Social Democrats or the Republican Party will be lost in the shuffle." The masses are pitiful and pathetic in some respects, but there resides in them a huge, crude power that pushed too far spells blood and destruction. It is this that London points out to the men who think and control.

London's fame as a writer has of recent days been hard pushed by his notoriety as an agitator. Howells, "the dean of American literature," Bliss Carman, Richard Le Galliene, Edwin Markham, and other literary men are socialists, but they have made no noise about it. London, however, has neglected no occasion to boom his theories. He has gone up and down the land talking to thousands urging the need of a new "System." For the upper and middle classes he has tried to picture the hellishness of the social pit that forever yawns for the man and woman out of work. His book, *The War of the Classes* is a vivid presentation of the facts of the class struggle.

But towering above these transitory events are his works in the way of fiction. At twenty-three years of age his first stories were published and immediately sprang into popularity. They dealt with the Klondike regions, experiences of the hardy gold-hunters, so many of whom left their bones in the shadow of the Arctic circle. It has been his part to interpret the fear of "the white silence," that vast and awesome loneliness of the far north.

Among his various studies in the north, none shows a higher appreciation of the present

"System," none will set you thinking about how far the human race has progressed, the gulf between savagery and civilization, than the tale of Nam Bok the Unveracious. Nam Bok, after an absence of many years returns to an isolated fishing village on the shores of Alaska. They fear he has come from "the bourne whence no man returns," but he joins valiantly in a supper of fish and blubber and then asks triumphantly, "Can a shadow eat?" Late into the night they talk, and Nam Bok, who has been to California, tells them he has seen single houses in which lived more people than in all the village; he has been upon a boat larger than all the boats of the village in one; he describes the sails of the vessel and avers it made head against the wind as well as with it; he describes an iron monster that sped upon two streaks of iron faster than the wind, was fed upon black stones, coughed fire, and shrieked louder than the thunder. Early the next morning he is visited by his cousins and brothers, informed that his sense of truth is mournfully degenerate. Their message runs in this wise, "Thou art from the shadow-land, O Nam Bok. With us thou canst not stay. Thou must return whence thou camest, to the land of the shadows." So much for Nam Bok. I cannot name a piece of literature in which the contrasts of civilization and savagery are more livingly set forth. It should be a part of the reading-course of every school.

The Call of the Wild and *The Sea-Wolf* are his masterpieces. Of these not a great deal may be said that is not repetitive. *The Call of the Wild* is the greatest dog-story ever written and is at the same time a study of one of the most curious and profound motives that plays hide-and-seek in the human soul. The more civilized we become the deeper is the fear that back in barbarism is something of the beauty and joy of life we have not brought along with us. We all feel these artificialities that so easily cramp and fret our lives. But this sense of a too-extreme complexity of life, too many tailors, launderers and chefs, too many walls and ceilings that shut out the stars, too many carpets lacking the odor of green grass or the tang of crisp snow, it is this sense you can't educate or civilize out of man. It is in all of us. Not the rankest degenerate but vaguely feels this call back to "nature and his primal sanities," the call of the wild. That the race is soon ripe for new and saner modes of life is shown in the widespread reception of *The Call of the Wild*. The book appeals to people of red blood and clear eyes and the way I have seen boys and girls and old

men and hacked-up literary connoisseurs take to this book, makes my heart beat high for the final destiny of the human mob.

The Sea-Wolf bore down on me for all my brain-traffic would bear. I read it first as it appeared in [serial] form and found it wholesome and nutritious. Had I not held a policy in the Equitable and felt certain I was going to live, I would surely have written the publishers to tell me how it was all going to end. The reviews of *The Sea-Wolf* were fun. Almost every man-jack of the hired scribes missed the allegory of the book, the lesson. Wolf Larsen is one in whose character revolve the motives of ambition and domination in their most terrible form. He is a ship-captain and absolute master of the vessel's crew. What gets in his way goes overboard, be it scullion or first mate. Do you know of any Thing that relentlessly crushes whatever gets in its way, be it a frail child, a tender woman, or a strong man? Wolf Larsen is The System incarnate. London has him die of a slow, pathetic paralysis. No wonder the well-sleeked critics thought his end was not artistic!

It is the fashion nowadays in the cities when bridge, dancing, driving, or golf pall on the senses to go a-slumming. Tender-hearted, misguided people there are too, who want to "do good" and forthwith turn their steps to where poverty ferments. I have seen a woman carrying a basket of sandwiches into a ten-storey tenement and as she disappeared into the swirl of rags and dirt, it seemed to me the relief conveyed by the good woman into that abyss to want was about equal to that of a drop of water in the pits of hades.

When Jack London went a-slumming in London, England, he was original, as he always is. He dressed as a workingman. He looked for work. He applied for relief at the free-soup houses. He slept on the floors of police stations with the wretches that applied nightly. He knew what it was to be turned away, denied the balm of sleep on clammy stone floors. He "carried the banner"—walked the streets all night afraid to sit him down in fear that he would awake to the tattoo of a policeman's baton and be sentenced to the workhouse. Before you go a-slumming, read *The People of the Abyss*.

There, in "skeletesque" outline, you have Jack London. Not Gerald Thockmorton London, nor Francis Felix Quebec London. But just plain everyday Jack! I am not a prophet and I don't like to dabble in futurities, but I know

London to be a tremendous worker and of simple habits, so I put him down as X, a dynamo of unguessable power.

If he were not a Common Man I would call him a Great Man.

Source: Jeanne Campbell Reesman, "The Critics: Carl A. Sandburg," in *Jack London: A Study of the Short Fiction*, edited by Gary Scharnhorst and Eric Haralson, Twayne Publishers, 1999, pp. 228–31.

Lee Clark Mitchell

In the following excerpt, Mitchell states that Jack London was a novelist who most successfully celebrated the charm of social Darwinism, and nowhere as clearly as in The Sea-Wolf.

For a long cultural moment at the turn of the twentieth century, the Spencerian notion of social Darwinism held a special charm, and the novelist who most successfully celebrated that notion was Jack London. In widely read stories and novels, he fictionalized ideas about racial improvement, genetic selection, class warfare, and physical fitness, helping to popularize an ideal of vigorous Anglo-Saxonism that found support among figures as diverse as Henry Ford, G. Stanley Hall, Charlotte Perkins Gilman, and Teddy Roosevelt. But nowhere as clearly as in *The Sea-Wolf* (1904), his most accomplished novel, does London reveal at once the tenets of his evolutionary philosophy and their impossibility. Or rather, in the very dramatization of his rough-hewn Darwinian views, London exposes their incoherence—largely because he mistakenly assumes that the values he invests in gender and bodily change are effects of biology rather than culture.

Fiction regularly confers symbolic significance on forms of bodily movement, but few novels exceed a handful of turn-of-the-century American examples in equating certain distinct physical activities with a human ideal. And none more than London's *The Sea-Wolf* so unambiguously depicts bodily position itself as an ideological premise. Finding one's feet, standing erect, walking without assistance: all are highlighted not only as typical aspirations in a narrative where characters are repeatedly knocked down but also, more importantly, as confirmation of the Darwinian allegory of evolution through the body's physical ascent. Rising to an upright position is everywhere both test and sign of an ability to transcend one's animal past

> FOLLOWING NIETZSCHE, LONDON BELIEVES THAT CIVILIZED VALUES HAVE LED TO PHYSICAL AND EMOTIONAL DETERIORATION, PROMULGATING FEEBLE STANDARDS OF RESPONSE TO ADVERSITY AND INCULCATING A FALSE SENSE OF MORAL SECURITY."

and achieve human preeminence. More generally, London wants to explore the problem of the body itself—of what it means to have a body, and the relation that emerges between one's body and one's self. As several critics have observed, the plot traces the pallid idealist Humphrey Van Weyden's acquisition of figurative "sea legs"—indeed of an entire physical body—as counterpoint to the fiercely materialist Wolf Larsen's gradual loss of bodily functions. Throughout the course of their cross-exchange, the question left unanswered by London (and largely unaddressed by critics) is whether this transaction leads the two men to gain or lose their human "selves" as well.

That question is reproduced in the novel's unstable narrative voice—in the sudden, startling shifts between present and past tense that occur at various points in Van Weyden's account. This instability has the effect of inscribing the problem of split subjectivity onto the novel's rhetorical surface, reinforcing a larger thematic premise: that binding together one's various desires, perspectives, and energies into a coherent self is neither unproblematic nor at all natural. Quite the contrary, the process is always ideologically charged, with even apparently simple gestures inflected by social constraints. It should not be surprising, therefore, that the novel ends by dismantling the conception of a new self embraced so enthusiastically by both Larsen and Van Weyden. Larsen's odd self-demolition occurs, despite his vigorous efforts, as an effect of the gradual loss of a physical body that he can meaningfully call his own. Van Weyden's self-disintegration is less clearly defined but no less troubling, since it occurs through his reversion to the pattern of social interdependency with Maud Brewster that had characterized his earlier, highly specialized existence as an academic writer. Importantly, women are almost entirely excluded from the novel until its midpoint, as if to diminish the importance of sexual identity in the construction of an integrated self. But this exclusion only has the effect of highlighting the importance of gender as a *socially* constructed set of behaviors having little to do with sexual biology. Maud's appearance, then, is at once superfluous and indispensable, since the "feminine" has already been exposed as an arbitrary category that is nonetheless essential to social organization. She legitimates the fractured culture that Van Weyden says he wants to transform. And the novel's celebration of an integrated, multitalented self is revealed not only as an impossible achievement but as least achieved when most heartily celebrated.

STANDING UP, FALLING DOWN

It may come as no surprise that a novel about an inept landlubber's schooling at sea devotes so much energy to the acquisition of "sea legs," but the process of getting one's legs beneath one functions as a conceit more central to the meaning of *The Sea-Wolf* than simply adapting to turbulent seas. The phrase "finding one's legs" recurs insistently through the narrative and acquires multiple meanings; it refers not only to striving to rise above the horizontal but also to preserving one's life, discovering one's "soul," and defining one's status independent of culture. Indeed, through the pathetic fallacy the phrase is occasionally applied to all of creation, as when Wolf Larsen describes the onset of a storm by saying, "Old Mother Nature's going to get up on her hind legs." More generally, the topos is invoked to characterize human self-sufficiency, a freedom from the complacency-inducing support of class and social distinctions, expressed in Larsen's early retort to Van Weyden's announcement that he has an independent income: "Who earned it, eh? I thought so. Your father. You stand on dead man's legs. You've never had any of your own." That reference to an unearned legacy is reiterated throughout, as a goad to Van Weyden's learning to depend on himself.

Still earlier, aboard the *Martinez* (the ferry whose sinking initiates the plot), Van Weyden had met a retired seaman with artificial legs—as if London wanted to open his novel about the figurative importance of standing upright through an uncanny figure who has lost his physical legs, then regained them. "Stumping gallantly" on mechanical limbs just before the ferry

founders, the seaman helps women don life jackets, at the same time expressing disgust at their behaving hysterically, screaming wildly, and losing control as he undertakes to calm them down. At the novel's outset, the scene conjoins the ideal of principled restraint with physically strong legs, even if prosthetic. Following Nietzsche, London believes that civilized values have led to physical and emotional deterioration, promulgating feeble standards of response to adversity and inculcating a false sense of moral security. Confirming this vision (and contrasting with the unnamed seaman's strong stance) is Thomas Mugridge's loss of his foot. As ship's cook, his role is already stereotypically feminized, and his cowering, overly emotional demeanor and weak constitution establish him as someone who will be literally unable to keep his feet in this narrative. The transformation occurs during an enforced bath at sea, when a shark snaps off Mugridge's foot. The implications of this nearly predictable event are confirmed by the actions that frame the scene—Mugridge's breaking a steersman's leg in frantic resistance to being tossed overboard and his frantically "bur[ying] his teeth in Wolf Larsen's leg" after being hauled back.

The importance of keeping one's lower limbs is never far from the narrative surface, figured most prominently in the alignment of Van Weyden with Maud Brewster, who admits "we may be feeble land-creatures without legs." Maud's metaphor here acknowledges rather more than she means (that they lack only "sea legs"), registering a social Darwinist equation of weakness with earlier stages of development. By contrast, Wolf Larsen's most dramatic moment occurs when his first mate pitches him overboard. Dragging himself from the midnight sea, he quickly rises "to his feet" before descending to the dark forecastle to confront a mutinous crew. There, beaten and held by more than a half-dozen men, he slowly rises again: "Step by step, by the might of his arms, the whole pack of men striving to drag him back and down, he drew his body up from the floor till he stood erect. And then, step by step, hand and foot, he slowly struggled up the ladder." Few other scenes so clearly epitomize the novel's conflation of upright stance and evolutionary advance, as if an erect bodily posture represented the triumph of human development against all the forces opposing it.

Although particularly dramatic, this moment hardly stands alone in a narrative that persists in knocking characters down apparently just to see them rise again, whether it is the cabin boy Leach "staggering to his feet" after being decked by Larsen or Van Weyden, who "managed to struggle to [his] feet" after a mild wave upends him. Wolf discourses endlessly on being crippled yet "learning to walk," and in the process of gaining his sea legs, Van Weyden goes through a punctuated process of abject prostration and upright defiance. Repeatedly, he "sank down helplessly," or "[his] feet went out from under [him]" or he "tried to rise, but...was knocked back on hands and knees" before learning the secret to "standing erect." It is as if Van Weyden's emotional state could be graphed according to his changing physical position, with fear (for instance) measured in the degree to which he too is finally "knocked down." Nearly everyone else mirrors this pattern; the first mate Johnson, for example, is beaten mercilessly by Wolf and Johansen, then repeatedly picked up only to be brutally upended. Indeed, the moral implications of an upright position are conveyed by those, like Leach, who "stand" up against Wolf in "splendid invincibleness of immortality"—and even by Wolf himself, who vigorously resists his own crew and all of howling nature itself. By contrast, Mugridge's pusillanimous submission is everywhere signaled by his prone position, "knocked down" by others, left to "crawl weakly across the galley," no more craven when deprived of a foot than when he was physically whole.

Standing and falling are imaged in other ways as well, including the prominent framing of the narrative onboard the *Ghost* by scenes of ocean burial. Lifeless bodies are hoisted erect and dropped "feet first into the sea": at the opening, the dead first mate; at the closing, Wolf himself. In fact, death seems to result simply from lying down and giving up, with the plot echoing that pattern in displaced terms, as ships' masts are knocked down by Mugridge, raised by Van Weyden and Maud, lowered by Wolf, and finally resurrected in a sequence that resonates as much with evolutionary expectations as with nautical engineering. The entire novel traces a rough Darwinian allegory of *homo erectus*, reflecting London's rudimentary notion of the means by which the human body can be made to rise above an animal level. There is no need here to emphasize how much less London's ideas owe to Darwin's nuanced conception of natural selection than to Herbert Spencer's popularized views on social evolution

and survival of the fittest—except to help clarify the ways in which the novel tends to conflate behavioral progress with cultural and ethical standards. The evolutionary process of standing up and walking on two feet represents for London a series of less strictly physical qualities: independence, moral heroism, and virile manhood. By contrast, lying down denotes dependency, death, cowardice, and ultimately (or so the novel asserts) femininity. However little this weirdly skewed constellation owes to Darwin, it does exemplify the performative logic described by Judith Butler: "[T]here is no gender identity behind the expressions of gender.... [I]dentity is performatively constituted by the very 'expressions' that are said to be its results." This point has been made even more dramatically by Carol J. Clover in the context of horror films: "Sex, in this universe, proceeds from gender, not the other way around. A figure does not cry and cower because she is a woman; she is a woman because she cries and cowers. And a figure is not a psychokiller because he is a man; he is a man because he is a psychokiller."

Significantly, given London's crude set of binary oppositions, the entrance of the lone female (if by no means the initial entrance of femininity) occurs right at the novel's midpoint. The narrative's first half sets up clear expectations that any woman to appear will conform to a vertical-horizontal economy of manhood and womanhood. The importance of Maud Brewster, then, is that she is exaggeratedly supine—arriving on board the *Ghost* completely prostrate, lying down "in the stern sheets, on the bottom," at the "verge of physical collapse." Though various men counsel her to rest and do nothing at all, their advice is unneeded, since she remains asleep through much of the narrative. Even escaping the ship, she becomes quickly exhausted and "lies on her back on the hard deck, arms stretched out and whole body relaxed." As Van Weyden adds, "It was a trick I remembered of my sister, and I knew she would soon be herself again." The irony is that she is most herself here, when completely prone. Maud enters the narrative, in other words, to confirm that the "lying down" position has to be occupied by someone, since life requires death, heroism dictates cowardice, and masculinity necessarily defines femininity—at least within the novel's constricted logic of binary oppositions. What had seemed an evolutionary state (standing up) available to all becomes in the course of the novel a gendered prerogative, even if gendered by strictly performative considerations that have nothing to do with sexual difference. To ensure social equilibrium, some need to fall so that others may stand erect. But the question of what happens when women are absent from such a social economy requires further attention. Before exploring Maud's role in the plot, we need to clarify the performative implications of a "woman's place" among men alone, especially as it is defined in the charged relationship between Humphrey Van Weyden and Wolf Larsen.

Source: Lee Clark Mitchell, "'And Rescue Us from Ourselves': Becoming Someone in Jack London's *Sea-Wolf*," in *American Literature*, Vol. 70, No. 2, June 1998, pp. 317–22.

SOURCES

Auerbach, Jonathan, "Between Men of Letters: Homo-erotic Agon in *The Sea-Wolf*," in *Male Call: Becoming Jack London*, Duke University Press, 1996, pp. 178–226.

Bierce, Ambrose, "Letter to George Sterling, February 18, 1905," in *A Much Misunderstood Man: Selected Letters of Ambrose Bierce*, edited by S. T. Joshi, Tryambak Sunand Joshi, and David E. Schultz, Ohio State University Press, 2003, p. 131, http://books.google.com/books?id=Pz91n P8D7UEC&pg=PA131&dq=bierce+%22impossible+ proprieties%22#v=onepage&q=&f=false (accessed December 30, 2009).

Forrey, Robert, "Male and Female in London's *The Sea-Wolf*," in *Critical Essays on Jack London*, edited by Jacqueline Tavernier-Courbin, G. K. Hall, 1983, p. 131; originally published in *Literature and Psychology*, Vol. 24, No. 4, 1974.

Gair, Christopher, "Gender and Genre: Nature, Naturalism, and Authority in *The Sea-Wolf*," in *Studies in American Fiction*, Vol. 22, No. 2, Autumn 1994, pp. 131–47.

Hays, Alice N., *David Starr Jordan: A Bibliography of His Writings, 1871-1931*, Stanford University Press, 1952.

"Idealism," in *The Oxford Guide to Philosophy*, edited by Ted Honderich, Oxford University Press, 2005, pp. 412–15.

Jordan, David Starr, "The Evolution of the Mind," in *Footnotes to Evolution: A Series of Popular Addresses on the Evolution of Life*, Appleton, 1898, pp. 256–76.

Labor, Earle, "Chronology" and "Success," in *Jack London*, Twayne's United States Authors Series, No. 230, Twayne Publishers, 1974, pp. 15–16, 94, 98.

London, Charmian, *The Book of Jack London*, Vol. 2, Century, 1921, p. 57; quoted in Earle Labor, *Jack London*, Twayne's United States Authors Series, No. 230, Twayne Publishers, 1974, p. 96.

London, Jack, *"The Sea-Wolf" and Selected Stories*, Signet Classics, 2004, pp. 1–285.

"Materialism," in *The Oxford Guide to Philosophy*, edited by Ted Honderich, Oxford University Press, 2005, pp. 564–66.

Nietzsche, Friedrich, *Thus Spoke Zarathustra*, translated by Adrian Del Caro, edited by Robert Pippin, Cambridge University Press, 2006.

"NOAA Reports Northern Fur Seal Pup Estimate Decline," in *National Oceanic and Atmospheric Administration*, January 15, 2009, http://www.noaanews.noaa.gov/stories2009/ 20090115_sealpup.html (accessed December 11, 2009).

Papa, James A., Jr., "Canvas and Steam: Historical Conflict in Jack London's *Sea-Wolf*," in *Midwest Quarterly*, Vol. 40, No. 3, Spring 1999, pp. 274–84.

Review of *The Sea-Wolf*, in *New York Times*, November 12, 1904. pp. 768–69.

Spencer, Herbert, *Principles of Biology*, Vol. 1, 1864, p. 444; reprint, Cornell University Press, 2009.

Watson, Charles N., Jr., "Lucifer on the Quarter-Deck: *The Sea-Wolf*," in *The Novels of Jack London: A Reappraisal*, University of Wisconsin Press, 1983, pp. 53–78.

FURTHER READING

Hodson, Sara S., and Jeanne Campbell Reesman, eds., *Jack London: One Hundred Years a Writer*, Huntington Library, 2002.

> The Huntington Library in San Marino, California, holds the archive of London's letters, manuscripts, and other documents. The library prepared this volume of critical essays to commemorate the one hundredth anniversary of the start of London's career. The essays are wide-ranging, and supplemented by sixteen photographs from London's life and illustrations from the magazine publication of his novel *Martin Eden*.

Johnson, Donald S., and Juha Nurminen, *The History of Seafaring*, Conway, 2007.

> This illustrated volume explores the development of ships and navigation going back to the ancient world and the technological advancements that made it possible to travel across the oceans. This beautiful oversized book has many colorful illustrations, including historical maps and charts.

Kershaw, Alex, *Jack London: A Life*, Macmillan, 1999.

> One of the best-known celebrities of his time, London lived a life nearly as exciting as the lives of his characters. This lively biography covers his travels to sea and to the frozen North, his attempt to sail around the world, his drinking and his women, and his dedication to his craft.

MacGillivray, Don, *Captain Alex MacLean: Jack London's Sea-Wolf*, UBC Press, 2008.

> This biography is the story of a colorful character, the model for London's Wolf Larsen,

and a historical account of seal hunting in the Victorian period. MacLean sailed and hunted seals in the North Pacific for thirty-five years, had a long rivalry with his brother, and was known for his erratic temper.

Rosen, Robert, *Jack London's The Sea-Wolf: A Screenplay*, edited by Rocco Fumento and Tony Williams, SIU Press, 1998.

This book contains the screenplay used in making the 1941 movie version of the novel, which starred Edward G. Robinson as Wolf Larsen. In separate introductions, the editors analyze the difference between the novel and the screenplay, London's intentions as an author, and the reasons the novel has been filmed so many times.

SUGGESTED SEARCH TERMS

Sea-Wolf

Sea-Wolf AND London

Sea-Wolf AND novel

Sea-Wolf AND naturalism

Sea-Wolf NOT indie

Sea-Wolf AND Larsen

Sea-Wolf AND bildungsroman

Sea-Wolf AND quotes

Jack London AND seafaring

Shabanu: Daughter of the Wind

SUZANNE FISHER STAPLES

1989

Suzanne Fisher Staples's *Shabanu: Daughter of the Wind* (1989) is an important novel because it introduces its readers to a culture that is becoming increasingly relevant to modern America, a culture that would be recognizable throughout Southwest Asia from Iraq to Afghanistan. Staples, as a journalist and as a researcher for the U.S. State Department, learned the ways of Islamic tribal peoples in Pakistan firsthand and explains to her audience how that culture works from the inside. Staples sets her story entirely within the traditional culture of her characters and lets the inevitable conflicts in values with her Western audience subtly emerge from the interaction of reader and text.

In *Shabanu*, Staples is brutally honest in portraying the life of a girl passing from childhood to adulthood. She deals with many aspects of the adolescent experience that are the same the world over, and many others that are markedly different between Western and traditional societies. Although the book is aimed at an audience of young-adult readers, Staples never flinches from giving a realistic and authentic treatment of her characters and the events in their lives. This has naturally involved *Shabanu* in controversy, since it means that Staples treats sexuality as an ordinary part of life, integrated into the human experience. However, controversy has not prevented educators from seeing the value of a book that gives such a realistic picture of a particular age quite familiar to their students and a particular culture quite alien to them, nor

Suzanne Fisher Staples (Reproduced by permission of Suzanne Fisher Staples)

has it prevented Staples following the book's success with two sequels: *Haveli* (1993) and *The House of Djinn* (2008).

AUTHOR BIOGRAPHY

Staples was born Suzanne Fisher on August 27, 1947, into a professional family in Philadelphia, Pennsylvania. She married Wayne Staples while attending Cedar Crest College, where she majored in English literature and political science. From an early age, she intended to become a writer, but recognizing that it would be difficult to start a successful career as a novelist directly out of college, she went to work as a journalist for United Press International. Between 1975 and 1983, she was posted to various assignments, mostly in South Asia. By the end of that time she was Asia editor for United Press International, based in Hong Kong. Between 1983 and 1985, she was the foreign desk editor for the

Washington Post. After this, she left journalism and began to move in a more literary direction. She spent 1986 and 1987 working in Pakistan for the U.S. Agency for International Development. Her task was to record autobiographical narratives of women from the nomadic tribes that lived in the Cholistan desert in Pakistan. In 1989, she turned what she learned that year into the her first novel, *Shabanu: Daughter of the Wind*. Most of the characters and situations in the book were directly derived from the life stories of women she had collected in Cholistan. These she distilled into the story of the marriage of an adolescent girl, Shabanu, within the boundaries of her traditional culture. *Shabanu* was immediately praised for its authenticity and originality and was named a Newbery Honor Book in 1990.

Fisher followed *Shabanu* in 1993 with *Haveli*, which follows the adult life of her character Shabanu, and in 2008 wrote a third book, *The House of Djinn*, concerning Shabanu's children and the conflicts they face in a modern Pakistan. She has written novels dealing with other traditional cultures in south Asia, such as *Shiva's Fire* (2000) and *Under the Persimmon Tree* (2005). Another work, *Dangerous Skies* (1996), deals with Staples's own shock at discovering the persistence of racism in American culture once she returned to the United States following her decade in Asia. Staples's *The Green Dog* (2003) is a fictionalized memoir of her own adolescence. As of late 2009, she lived in rural Pennsylvania with her husband and children.

PLOT SUMMARY

Guluband

The first chapter quickly establishes the background and situation of the novel. The title character, Shabanu, is an eleven-year-old girl. She lives in an extended family (including her sister Phulan, parents, grandfather, aunt, and cousins) within a tribal framework. She and her family are nomadic cattle herders in the Cholistan desert in Pakistan. The family is preparing for Phulan's wedding. Although she is only thirteen years old, she will marry her cousin Hamir in the immediate future. In two years or so, Shabanu will marry Hamir's brother, Murad. Their father (usually called Dadi by Shabanu as the narrator) will have to pay a dowry at the time of each wedding of ten camels and provide cash or gifts equal to fifteen more camels, while her mother (Mama) is making dresses as part of the dowry. Their immediate problem is a search for water, but rain after a long drought eases their situation. Guluband is the best camel in the family's herd.

Birth

With water abundant after an unexpected rain, Shabanu is tending the camel herd by herself. One of the pregnant camels is bitten by a snake. As it is dying, Phulan must deliver its premature baby, fighting off hungry vultures. She succeeds and is eventually able to feed the new baby, which she names Mithoo.

Kalu

Kalu is a male camel that has been kept with the herd too long. He challenges the stud camel, Tipu, and the two of them have to be separated by Dadi, Shabanu, and Phulan. Tipu is extremely aggressive and has attacked his handlers. Shabanu disobeys Dadi and risks her life to protect Mithoo. Her father has to physically drag her away to safety. Shabanu's parents take this as a very bad sign, since her future husband (her cousin Murad) will expect unquestioning obedience of her.

Safari

Dadi and Shabanu set off to the market town of Sibi to sell camels for Phulan's dowry, taking fifteen animals with them. Now that Shabanu is twelve years old and is to be married in a year, her mother and aunt expect her to wear the chadr, or veil, but she refuses once she is out of their immediate control. On their trip through the desert, they pass the Derawar fort, a medieval ruin that is the most important architectural monument in Cholistan, and the Maujgarh fort, an eighteenth-century fort now also in ruins, that was the chief center of the Nawabs of Bahawalpur, where Shabanu's grandfather had served. When they camp for the night, Dadi is approached by Rangers, Pakistani soldiers who patrol the border with India, who want to buy Guluband the camel. Dadi replies that the Mujahadeen, the forces fighting the Soviet occupation of Afghanistan, will pay far more. The Ranger captain replies that their camels will quickly be killed by Soviet helicopters, and Guluband is too fine an animal to waste in that way. All of this is too much for Shabanu, who thinks of Guluband as a pet. She runs into the ruins and discovers the Nawab's harem, a structure more like a prison. She reflects that the condition of a daughter or wife is like that of a prisoner.

However, Dadi does not sell the camel, and he pacifies Shabanu by buying her a bracelet.

The Bugtis

Having joined a larger caravan, Dadi and Shabanu must cross the Indus River on the Gudu Barrage, a crowded road that crosses the top of an irrigation dam. In the tribal areas beyond, where the Pakistani government does not enforce its laws, they encounter a group of Bugti tribesmen who are searching for the niece of their leader, Sadar. She has eloped with a member of a different tribe, defying the authority of her family, and her uncle is hunting her down to kill her.

Sibi Fair

At the Fair, Dadi negotiates with various buyers for his camels, including Wardak, a Mujahadeen from Afghanistan. Because of the pressures of the war, the price of camels is much higher than Dadi had ever seen, and he thinks this one year's profits could give both Phulan and Shabanu higher dowries than he could have imagined. Shabanu visits the Fair's carnival grounds, which are reminiscent of an American county fair, with a merry-go-round, a Ferris wheel, a *hijra* (hermaphrodite), and side-show attractions.

The Bargain

Dadi negotiates to sell most of his camels to another herder whose stock was wiped out by disease. This pleases Shabanu, who is emotionally attached to the animals, especially Guluband, whom they would keep in that case. However, all of the camels are sold to Wardak for one hundred fifty thousand rupees, five times what Dadi would have gotten from the other buyer.

Shatoosh

Dadi and Wardak and their friends feast and dance to celebrate their transaction. As Dadi and Shabanu recross the desert, she still feels emotionally devastated by the loss of Guluband, but she gradually recovers from her emotional withdrawal: "I look up at the stars and am surprised at how brightly they pulse," she says. "I haven't noticed them in a while." At Rahimyar Khan, Dadi visits his brother to get pots and other gifts for his wife in the desert. He also buys clothes and jewelry for Phulan's dowry. One dealer, carrying out instructions that his dead mother (also named Shabanu) gave him in a dream, makes a present of one of her shawls to

Shabanu. It is shatoosh, a fabric made from collecting the beard hair of wild goats from plants the animals grazed upon. Although its manufacture is a traditional craft in Pakistan, because it is so labor intensive none have been made for a long time, and it is a priceless heirloom.

Dowry

Dadi and Shabanu return to the family and the herd to a general celebration of the unexpected success of their expedition. Phulan shows Shabanu the twenty or so baby camels that were born in her absence.

Nose Pegs

The family has to cooperate in the work of breaking several of the young male camels. Camels will not take a bit in their mouths as horses do, so their noses have to be pierced to hold the reins. This involves hog-tying them and wrestling them to the ground. After the nostrils are pierced, temporary wooden pegs are inserted.

Channan Pir

Pilgrimage, going to a holy place to seek a blessing, is an ancient Mediterranean practice that was taken up by both Christianity and Islam. The family goes on a pilgrimage to the Channan Pir Mosque, which contains the name of an Islamic saint associated with marriage, childbirth, and children. They are to pray for Phulan to bear sons and to be happy in her marriage (in that order). On the trip, Grandfather recounts stories from his military service, as well as snippets of the military history of Cholistan that he must have heard in the army; he is not quite able to distinguish one from the other. Once at the shrine, the women and men separate, and the women go to pray. The female group meets Sharma, Mama's cousin, and her daughter Fatima. Sharma became the second wife of an older wealthy husband who wanted a son, but when she bore Fatima instead, he began to beat both of them. She took a herd of goats and left, enduring the shame of being a woman living alone. Although Fatima is sixteen, she is unmarried and seems to have no intention of marrying. While Shabanu is off gathering firewood afterward, she strays near the encampment of the men from the families on pilgrimage and surreptitiously sees her father win a wrestling match.

Sharma

When the women are alone, they exchange stories about women being killed by the men of their own families for transgression of sexual codes, for dishonoring their families. Sharma, despite her own experience, reassures Shabanu that "the love of a good man is the most beautiful thing God can give us."

Desert Storm

The family's desert dwelling and waterhole are covered by a sandstorm, forcing them to move back to the settled area before the monsoon. Most of their camels survive the storm, but Grandfather, who was caught outside and in a very confused mental state, wandered out into the storm and seems near death when Dadi finally finds him in the desert.

The Thirsty Dead

In the aftermath of the sandstorm, the family sets out to Derawar. Grandfather, in what seems likely to be his last wish, has asked to see the nawab there, the former ruler of Cholistan in whose army he served. In Derawar, they will also be to find water.

Derawar

After they camp at Derawar, Grandfather dies during the night. Unable to gain permission to bury him in the cemetery attached to the fort, they bury him in the desert.

Ramadan

The family arrives at the farm of Hamir and Murad, the daughters' future husbands, at the village of Mehrabpur. It is desert land reclaimed by their father, who dug an irrigation canal. As they prepare for Phulan's wedding, they learn that Nazir Mohammed, the local landowner from whom the land had been purchased, is now jealous that the twenty-five acre- farm is so productive. He also is involved in litigation with the family because his son died by falling down a well on the property several years ago.

The Landlord

As they prepare for the wedding, the camels must still be tended. One day when Phulan and Shabanu take them out to graze, they encounter a hunting party led by Nazir. This is the very situation that their mother had warned them about: "Nazir Mohammed, the landowner, has hunting parties. He offers each of his guests a girl, usually a tenant from his land, for the time they are with him. When the man is finished with her, he gives her cash and sends her back to her family. Some people are grateful for the money and are willing to forget the indignity." The girls manage to ride away on their camel, but Dadi is convinced that the hunters intend to come after them, so he orders his family to flee into the desert while he takes his gun and goes to warn Hamir of what has happened.

Spin Gul

As the family flees into the desert, they become increasingly nervous that Dadi does not join them as he promised. They encounter a group of Rangers, whose officer, Spin Gul, offers them protection and feeds them. He relays a radio message claiming to be from Dadi that they are to return to Mehrabpur at once, but Mama does not believe it. Dadi soon does reach them, and it turns out the message was a trick by Nazir. In the meantime, Dadi and Hamir and Murad had had a confrontation with Nazir in which Hamir was killed. Phulan is overcome by grief. Auntie, stretched to the limit by their ride through the desert, miscarries her baby. The Rangers take the initiative to try to negotiate a truce between the two families, depending on Nazir's older brother Rahim, an important local politician who will not want his family involved in such trouble.

Yazman

The hoped-for monsoon rains, which have failed for two years, finally come, in ironic counterpart to the disaster suffered by the family. The Rangers escort them to a military base at Yazman for a conference with Rahim and Nazir. The meeting is moderated by Colonel Haq of the Rangers. While the meeting takes place, Hamir's sister Sakina tells Phulan and Shabanu the story of her brother's death. Dadi came to the farm to warn them that Nazir might come to threaten them also. Hamir wanted to immediately go and take revenge on Nazir for his insults to Phulan, and he nearly came to blows with his brother and Dadi over it since they wanted to restrain him. However, before that could be resolved, Nazir and the hunting party, all drunk, arrived in Jeeps. Hamir shot at them, but they returned fire and killed him. Later, while the men and women of the family are separately conferring about the future, Shabanu takes it on herself to rescue her young cousins, who have climbed a tree and cannot get down. A kindly old man who has just arrived by car helps her. She actually flirts with him.

Justice

Shabanu and Phulan are summoned by their mother to be told how the conflict has been resolved. Phulan will marry Hamir's younger brother Murad (who was to have been Shabanu's husband). Rahim will guarantee that his brother Nazir will cause the family no more trouble. Rahim, in turn, will marry Shabanu. She immediately objects but is told that Rahim is rich and an important religious and political leader, and she could never hope for a better match. Although he is fifty years old or more, she will be his youngest wife and therefore his favorite. More particularly, Rahim wants this match because he has already seen Shabanu and found her beautiful. It turns out that he is the man who helped her get her cousins out of the tree. She still refuses and says she will instead go to live with Sharma. Her mother slaps her for her insolence and tells her the matter has been decided.

The Choice

During the forty days of mourning for Hamir, Rahim floods Shabanu and her family with gifts. He builds several new houses for each of the various groups within the family, and he gives Shabanu jewelry worth more than Dadi's entire camel herd. Hamir's death comes to be regarded as something wonderful by local tribesmen and farmers who hear of the prosperity it has brought to his family, and his grave begins to become a site of pilgrimage. When Sharma arrives for the wedding, she questions the advisability of Shabanu's espousal to Rahim because his attention and eventually his inheritance will be divided among three other wives and their sons. Dadi replies that that is still more than she could hope for from any other possible match. Privately, Sharma suggests to Shabanu that she make herself indispensable to her new husband by pleasing him in order to counteract the influence of his other wives. Sharma offers, if Rahim is cruel to her, to take Shabanu in with her goat herd in the desert.

The Wedding

Phulan and Murad are married.

Cholistan

After the wedding, Shabanu returns to the desert with her family. When she reaches maturity (i.e., her first menstrual period), her parents decide to contact Rahim and set a date for the wedding. Overwhelmed by the prospect of her marriage, Shabanu decides to run away to Sharma. When she flees, though, the camel Mithoo follows her and breaks his leg before they get very far. She cannot abandon him, so Dadi quickly catches up with her. At a loss for what to do in the face of her disobedience, Dadi beats her, and then collapses in tears. Shabanu determines that she will go through with the marriage, but "Rahim-*sahib* will reach out to me for the rest of his life and never unlock the secrets of my heart."

CHARACTERS

Dalil Abassi

Dalil Abassi, usually called Dadi by Shabanu, is Shabanu's father. He leads his extended family in the traditional way of life of camel herders. He is indulgent of his youngest daughter, but he is completely immersed in his traditional culture. When she suggests the possibility of change, or even expresses simple willfulness, his answer is, "What Allah wills cannot be changed." He is not slow to punish his daughter, including beating her, when her behavior violates the standards of their culture. Dadi is extremely competent in his livelihood, and he breeds superior camels, valued by other dealers, as well as the soldiers of Pakistan and Afghanistan who must use them. He is also an excellent wrestler, a common pastime among men in his culture.

Auntie

Shabanu's aunt, who is not given a name in the novel, feels superior to the rest of the family because she comes from a comparatively wealthy family, has two sons, and is married to Dadi's brother, who works in a government office. She nevertheless lives with her brother-in-law's family because she can be comfortable only in her traditional way of life. At times, she is overbearing to her nieces Phulan and Shabanu. She is anxious to see them act in the correct way according to the traditions of their culture.

Sardar Nothani Bugti

Sardar is the leader of band of Bugti nomads, people richer and more aggressive than the Cholistanis, whose territory Dadi and Shabanu must drive their camels through to sell them at the

Sibi Fair. When they meet him, he is hunting for his niece to kill her for dishonoring her family.

Dadi

See Dalil Abassi

Fatima

Sharma's daughter and Shabanu's cousin, unmarried at age sixteen, is just as proud and independent as her mother. Shabanu looks to her as a model of independence: "How I long to be like her—never to marry, to say in the warm safe circle of women."

Grandfather

Shabanu's paternal grandfather lives with the family in the desert, even though he is too enfeebled by age to do much useful work; the family as a whole has a responsibility to care for him as he once cared for it. At one time, Shabanu was especially close to her grandfather, but lately he comes and goes, mentally, as Shabanu explains when she talks with him after the Sibi Fair: "This is the old Grandfather, back again after periods of frailty and seeming distant. Sometimes I worry that we'll never see the old Grandfather again before he dies." Shabanu's grandfather "tells stories about his days as a great warrior in the Army Camel Corps of the nawab of Bahawalpur." His death reveals the erosion of traditional social relations, such as those that tied him to the nawab.

Spin Gul

Spin Gul is a *subadar* in the Rangers, the Pakistani soldiers who patrol the Cholistan desert. He takes Shabanu's family under his protection when they flee from Nazir.

Hamir

Hamir is Phulan's fiancé. According to Shabanu, "He is wild. . . . He loves horses and rides them hard. But he's insensitive, coming back with his horse lathered and breathing heavily. He is handsome, and tall . . . and impatient, a dreamer. . . . But he is decent." His impulsiveness—valuing honor above status—is what caused him to confront Nazir, which resulted in his murder.

Colonel Haq

Haq is the commander of the Ranger Wing Command Base at Yazman. He acts as a mediator between Dadi's family and Nazir's.

Kulsum

Kulsum is the of widow of Lal Khan, the elder brother of Hamir and Murad.

Bibi Lal

Bibi Lal is the mother of Phulan and Shabanu's prospective husbands. Her own husband has been dead for two years.

Mama

Shabanu's mother. Like all the women of her culture, her life is filled with work necessary for the extended family to survive. Her main work is weaving, but after she sews Shabanu an adult dress for her twelfth birthday, her daughter notes that she also spends time "with gathering wood and helping Dadi and making Phulan's clothes and mending the mud walls and cooking and repairing the quilts." Like Dadi, she is a model of correct traditional behavior and is anxious to keep Shabanu's behavior within bounds, on one occasion slapping her daughter when she threatens to transgress those bounds.

Nazir Mohammad

Nazir Mohammed is a wealthy landowner who has a position of semiofficial overlordship with respect to Murad and Hamir (Shabanu's cousins), but rather than using his power to protect them, he abuses it in efforts to undermine and destroy them. He routinely allows his friends to dishonor the daughters of his tenants, offering cash to repay the insult. He eventually kills Hamir over the shame he felt at not being able to deliver Phulan and Shabanu to his friends to be raped. His elder brother Rahim eventually steps in to prevent him destroying the entire family; his behavior is so shameful it would disgrace their own family if it was not checked.

Murad

Murad is, at first, the fiancé of Shabanu (who does not seem to know him very well or think very highly of him), until his older brother Hamir's death. After this, he eventually marries Phulan.

Phulan

Phulan is Shabanu's sister, two years older than her. Her upcoming wedding dominates the action of the first part of the novel. She is at the same time happy to be entering the new world of womanhood and sad to leave behind the old world of childhood. Shabanu says, "As Muslim girls, we are brought up knowing our childhood homes are temporary. Our real homes are the ones we go to when we marry." Shabanu frequently thinks that Phulan is silly and impractical, but she envies what she considers Phulan's greater beauty.

Rahim

Rahim is Nazir's older brother, who eventually marries Shabanu. He is a wealthy and powerful landowner who holds political and religious office. When he first sees Shabanu, he is immediately taken by her and approaches her in a friendly way, to help her get her cousins out of a tree in which they were stuck. In deference to her as much as in shame over his brother's actions, he protects Shabanu's family and offers her a marriage very attractive by the standards of their traditional culture, including paying a bride-price.

Sakina

Sakina is the younger sister of Hamir and Murad, who tells Phulan and Shabanu the story of Hamir's death.

Shabanu

Shabanu is the main character and narrator of the novel. At the outset she is eleven years old and lives with her family, who are nomadic camel herders in the Cholistan desert of Pakistan. She can neither read nor write; she lives in an entirely traditional world based on tribal and cultural customs, hundreds or thousands of years old, a world that is highly resistant to change. She is fiercely independent. Although she has scope for independent action as a child, she realizes this is rapidly coming to an end as she approaches marriageable age.

Shabanu constantly recoils from the idea of a marriage arranged by her parents. She is also constantly horrified by the idea of her father selling her favorite camels, despite the fact that such sales are their means of livelihood. Within her culture, these desires seem childish. At the same time, though, she is possessed of very mature sensibilities. At the time of the sandstorm, although she shows an excessive concern for her favorite baby camel, Mithoo, she is not daunted by the scale of the disaster in the least. She confidently and rationally asserts that since their herd was largely intact, they could go on with their lives, despite the injuries to her grandfather. The more mature part of Shabanu's character is shown in her reaction to her sister's grief at the death of Hamir: "I pity her, but I can't help wanting to shake her, to tell her to wake up and prepare for what comes next." Ultimately, however, Shabanu is never (within the scope of the novel) able to come to grips with maturity. Although she realizes that Rahim wishes to marry her out of genuine love, she decides that if she cannot escape marrying him altogether, she will forever deny him the personal intimacy that comes with love, punishing him for her loss of freedom.

Shahzada

Shahzada is an older member of the nawab of Bahawalpur's military guard, who oversees the ruins of the fort at Derawar. Although he is sympathetic to Grandfather's wish to be buried there, he cannot give permission to do so. He does however, place the remnants of Grandfather's uniform and decorations in an empty tomb there.

Sharma

Sharma is Shabanu's mother's cousin. She is about thirty years old, but her "hair is streaked with gray, and her skin is dry and creased." This accelerated aging is due to the lack of proper nutrition, medical care, and even shelter that are part of the realities of life for the poor in Cholistan. Her parents arranged for her to marry an older man whose first wife had never given him sons. When Sharma also bore a daughter, he began to beat both of them. She left to live by herself as a goat-herder. This behavior is scandalous by the standards of Cholistan society, but it is barely tolerable because she has the respectability of marriage, even though she lives apart form her husband. Because of her isolation from the social norms of Cholistan, rumors circulate that she is a witch. Sharma's daughter Fatima is already sixteen and unmarried, a more problematic position. Shabanu looks to this unconventional family as a potential model for independence.

Sulaiman

Sulaiman is the keeper of the nawab of Bahawalpur's military cemetery, a petty official full of his own importance.

Wardak

Wardak is a one-eyed Pathan (Afghan tribesman) and Mujahadeen who is anxious to buy Dadi's camels at the Sibi Fair. He eventually buys them, including Shabanu's beloved Guluband.

THEMES

Orientalism

The literary theorist Edward Said (pronounced "Sah-EED") introduced the idea of Orientalism as a feature of Western art (such as literature or painting). The peoples and cultures of the non-Western world have long been of great interest to Western artists. However, Said's idea was that it is impossible for a Westerner to genuinely portray any element of a non-Western culture, such as that of Pakistan or China. Rather, the Oriental or the non-Western must become the Other, a screen onto which the Westerner can project anything considered non-Western: the primitive, the barbarous, the exotic. Even a non-Westerner could not, according to Said, create an authentic depiction of his own culture in a novel, for instance, written in Urdu or Mandarin, because the novel is an intrinsically Western form and writing a novel would presuppose a significant degree of Westernization on the part of the novelist, which would act as a screen between himself and his own culture. Said sees Orientalism in this sense as a result of the general colonialist framework by which the West approaches the non-Western.

Shabanu might seem an attempt to get beyond the Orientalist problem, since it was directly based on interviews with women from Cholistan, members of the culture in which it is set. However, while its main character, Shabanu, is largely integrated into her traditional culture, the main thrust of the novel is that she chafes against that tradition in one particular regard. Shabanu wishes to maintain the relative freedom she knows as a preadolescent girl largely in charge of her family's camel herd; this desire for freedom goes against the expectations of her family and her culture that she unconditionally submit herself to the authority of her father and eventually her husband. This kind of resistance does not find support in any institution within Cholistan society. Rather, it can more easily be explained as a conflict between Western ideas of individual liberty and feminism and the ideas of a traditional non-Western culture. In other words, the main tension of the novel is between Western ideas that are mysteriously present in a non-Western character and her traditional culture, which is viewed as the Other, something to be resisted and overcome. Rather than distancing herself from her own Western heritage, Staples creates a false presentation of the Oriental (that is, the

TOPICS FOR FURTHER STUDY

- Present to your class a PowerPoint presentation on the history and geography of Pakistan as it relates to *Shabanu*.

- Create a Web page that explains how Pakistan and Afghanistan have changed since *Shabanu* was published in 1989. For instance, the name of the Afghan character Wardak was completely unknown in America at that time. Why has it become better known since? Discuss American involvement in the region and America's relations with Pakistan. Explain the role of Pakistan in the war in the Middle East. Include on your Web page links to pertinent news articles and features to help inform your classmates.

- After reading *Shabanu*, write down some predictions about what may happen to Shabanu or what she may do during the next ten years of her life. Share these thoughts with your classmates. Then, read Staples's young-adult sequel, *Haveli*, published in 1993. Write an essay comparing your predictions for Shabanu and the new developments Staples invented for her character in the sequel. Were the plot twists a surprise? Do you think living nearly twenty years later influenced your predictions?

- Puppet theater is a traditional art in Pakistan. Perform a puppet show version for your class of a scene from *Shabanu*, perhaps the pilgrimage to Channan Pir or Phulan's wedding.

Cholistan society that she describes) by inserting Western thought at its heart, conforming, after all, to the Orientalist pattern.

Rebellion

Shabanu is a girl thoroughly immersed in the traditions of her nomadic culture. However, as her story progresses she finds herself more and more at odds with her position within that culture.

As a young girl below the age of marriage, she has considerable freedom and independence, and she has the responsibility, for much of the time without supervision, for her family's camel herd. As she approaches maturity and the age of marriage, her family begins to exert more and more of the rigid control that her culture imposes on adult women. Although it is ultimately her father and then her husband who have or will have authority over her, the pressure to conform comes from the adult female members of her family. It is her mother and aunt, for instance, who give her the *chadr*, or veil (the headscarf worn by adult women), but she refuses to cover her head with it. She wants to maintain the freedom of childhood even as she becomes an adult.

There is conflict between Shabanu's desire for her former freedom in rebellion against assuming the duties her family and culture expect of her. At one point, Shabanu comes across the ruins of the Derawar fort in the desert. She finds what she believes to be the remains of the harem quarters of the former ruler of Cholistan from centuries ago. She imagines that although his seventy wives might have lived in a pleasure garden, they nevertheless lived at the same time in locked cells: "Prisoners, willingly or unwillingly they lived their lives according to the wishes of their fathers and their prince." This mixture of history and fantasy presents a grim symbol of her own life, under the authority of her father and about to pass to that of her husband, a sixteen-year-old boy whom she did not choose herself and whom she could not find it in herself to respect. She rebels against accepting her adult identity as if it were a prison sentence.

Shabanu never fully comes to terms with what it means to grow up in her culture. Rather, she makes compromises with herself that move in the direction of adult responsibility but do not reach it, and she never goes one step further than she has to. When she is forced to accept something unpleasant, she rationalizes that the sale of Guluband, for example, "has taught me both the strength of my will and its limits. I know Dadi thinks my bent for freedom is dangerous, and I'm learning to save my spirit for when it can be useful." Although she seems to slowly start to accept marriage to Murad, when her circumstances alter in a way that her family and indeed her whole community view as an almost miraculous change for the better, she is only able to become sullen and resentful. Shabanu inwardly rejects

Bride and groom (Image copyright Cindy Huges, 2010. Used under license from Shutterstock.com)

jewelry given her as courting gifts by her new fiancé Rahim in this way: "I think vaguely of the blackness in my heart—I am wearing all of the light that was ever within me on nose and finger." Her basic attitude remains completely unchanged: "I am small and strong with too much spirit, and I think too much. I am lonely and fearful, and I long for the days when I was free in the desert." Shabanu remains in constant rebellion against what is expected of her by her family and the traditions of her culture. She rebels outwardly when she can and inwardly when she has to.

STYLE

First-Person Present Tense Narration

The novel is told as a first-person narrative by Shabanu; that is, she tells the story in her own voice, as "I." This limits the author to what

Shabanu can plausibly be expected to see or know, but it has the advantage of verisimilitude—seeming to be true—since everyone has had the experience of hearing someone tell a story about something that happened to the storyteller. Shabanu comments on this experience when Dadi tells her mother about their trip to Sibi, saying that she visits "where we've been through his remembering." For this reason, this voice is one commonly used by novelists (though not as common as an anonymous third-person narrator, which can be unlimited in the kinds of information incorporated into the narrative). More unusually, the narration is also set in the present tense, as if the reader were hearing Shabanu's internal monologue as events progress. This immediacy heightens the sense of verisimilitude, as though there were no time or place for any editing of the narrative. Staples uses the technique to sweep the reader along breathlessly, skipping ahead many days, sometimes, between chapters, as if to give snapshots of the relevant action, and providing a sense of rapid acceleration. "I talk quickly," Shabanu says, "with animation, the words tumbling out faster and faster, until I am breathless and have nothing left to tell."

Language

Pakistan is a multilingual country. Pakistanis speak not only a wide variety of languages but languages from different language families (although most are Indo-European). The principal language is Urdu, a form of Hindustani (the main language of India) that had been deeply affected by the Turkic language of the medieval Mogul conquerors of northern India. The second most common language is Pushto (or Pashtu), which is an Iranian language (that is to say, it is related to modern languages such as Farsi, Kurdish, and Ossetian, the same way that Romance languages such as Spanish or Italian are related to each other). English is commonly spoken by Pakistanis who receive a university education. Arabic, the language of the Koran, is widely known, especially among clergy. Staples does not deal in detail with linguistics since such subject matter would be far removed from Shabanu as her narrator. Shabanu and her family, and indeed all the other main characters from Cholistan, probably speak a dialect of Pushto.

Staples wishes to vividly emphasize the reality of the culture she describes as distinct from the lives of her American audience. One strategy that she uses to accomplish this is to present many terms from Shabanu's spoken language in transliteration (transcribing the sounds of the words into the Roman letters of the English alphabet) rather than translation. To make it easier for the reader to understand these foreign words, she provides a glossary in the back of the book. All of the words belong to the Pushto language, but most of the terms relating to Islam are "loan words" from Arabic, such as the common greeting, "Asalaam-o-Aleikum." Nevertheless, most of the foreign words are of Iranian origin. Two of the most important Iranian words (which are not in the glossary) are the names Shabanu uses for her parents: Dadi and Mama. These childish words for parents are among the most conservative words in the Indo-European family (that is, they are very basic words and do not easily change) and so are virtually the same among languages as distantly related as Pushto and English. The characters' names are also generally Iranian. Of Phulan, Shabanu says: "Her name means 'flower.'" This goes back to an Indo-European root meaning "to grow" that also turns up in English words such as *physics* (the study of nature). Shabanu suggests the meaning of her own name when she says: "I am Shabanu. Mama says it's the name of a princess." In fact, *shabanu* (more usually written *shahbanu*) is the Iranian word for queen, corresponding to *shah* for king. It could mean princess in the sense of an independent ruler, or the consort of an independent ruler. The Iranian word for a princess who is the daughter of a king is *shahdost*.

HISTORICAL CONTEXT

Nomadism

Nomadism, or pastoralism, is one of the oldest ways of life practiced by human beings. Nomads make their living by controlling herds of domestic stock (frequently cattle or horses, but in this case camels), moving them in seasonal patterns on land that is not too dry to support the herd, but not fertile enough for more profitable agricultural use. Unlike American Indians who depended on the buffalo, or Lapps who follow reindeer, nomads' herds are truly domesticated in the sense that the herders control where they go and which animals are allowed to breed. Four thousand years ago, Cholistan was the site of the lush valley of the Hakra River. It was part of the Harappan culture, one of the oldest civilizations in the world. The Bactrian, or two-humped, camel was a common domestic animal of the Harappan era. However, the Indus civilization eventually collapsed, in part because of the drying up of the Hakra by seismic activity, natural climate change following the last ice age, and agricultural degradation of the land. The dromedary, or one-humped camel, was fully domesticated only much later, not much more than two thousand years ago, by the Nabatean Arabs of modern Jordan, with the invention of the camel saddle. The animal quickly spread throughout Southwest Asia and came to India largely with Iranian nomads, for the most part after the expansion of Islam in the seventh century. The cultural world that Shabanu inhabits has hardly changed from that time. The camels are the source of most of what the herders need to live. They directly provide meat, milk, and leather, and excess camels can be sold or traded to obtain other necessities. As depicted in the novel, for much of the year, the camels can be tended by children, allowing adults to perform other necessary tasks. For example, as in almost any traditional society, the adult women in Shabanu's family spend most of their time manufacturing cloth and garments, supplying all of their own family's needs. The herd and the family move according to the season of the year. During the monsoon, they stay in the steppe (a plains region), which is watered by the rains, but during the driest part of the summer, paradoxically, they must go to the deep desert, where water is available in wells.

Pakistan and Its Role in South Asia

Geographically, Cholistan is a desert region, just north of the Thar desert in India, occupied by the dry valley of the Hakra river. It is the southernmost part of the Punjab. Cholistan took on a distinct political identity, as the state of Bahawalpur, in the eighteenth century when it was conquered by an aristocratic family descended from the Abbasid Caliphs, who had once ruled the entire Islamic world. In 1947, when India gained independence from the colonial power of Great Britain, the feudal state of Bahawalpur became part of Pakistan. In 1954, the nawab, or hereditary ruler, gave his rights to the Pakistan federal government. Pakistan (which originally included the geographically separate area of modern Bangladesh) was created as an Islamic-majority state, in contrast to the Hindu-majority state of modern India. This required the massive and frequently forced movements of populations, as well as a series of wars fought over control of the

COMPARE
&
CONTRAST

- **1980s:** Both Westernizers and traditionalists in Pakistan share a common enmity against the Soviet Union and support American efforts to supply and support the Mujahadeen, which is fighting against the Soviet occupation of Afghanistan.

  Today: Pakistani society is deeply divided over its government's support for American involvement in Afghanistan.

- **1980s:** Pakistan is one of the few countries in Asia with a parliamentary form of government.

  Today: Following nearly a decade of military dictatorship, Pakistan is again a functioning but fragile democracy.

- **1980s:** The Westernized elite in Pakistan are able to elect a woman, Benazir Bhutto, as prime minister (albeit a woman from a leading political family—her father and husband both served as prime minister).

  Today: The assassination of Bhutto in 2007, ending a campaign for reelection to the premiership, reflects growing tension in Pakistan between Westernizing and traditionalist factions.

- **1980s:** The number of girls receiving any level of formal education in Pakistan is less than half the number of boys.

  Today: Education is rapidly becoming more widespread, and the number of girls in at least primary education is approaching equality with the number of boys.

princely state of Kashmir. The violence of that time is sometimes recalled by Shabanu's grandfather, who fought in the army of Bahawalpur in that era. Staples suggests the artificiality of the partition of the subcontinent when Shabanu thinks: "Sometimes our animals wander across the border, and when I go to fetch them I look hard to see how it differs from our Pakistan. But the same dunes roll on into India, and I can't tell for certain exactly where Pakistan ends and India begins."

In the 1980s, when *Shabanu* is set, the Soviet Union had occupied Afghanistan on Pakistan's northern frontier, and there was some fear the Soviets intended to attack Pakistan itself to gain strategic access to the Indian Ocean and the Persian Gulf. Therefore, Pakistan cooperated with the United States to put pressure on Soviet forces in Afghanistan by supporting resistance groups fighting against the occupation there. Shabanu's father plays a small role in this by occasionally selling camels to the Afghan Mujahadeen fighters such as Wardak. They can pay more than anyone else for camels because of their international funding.

CRITICAL OVERVIEW

Since the novel's publication in 1989, criticism of Staples's *Shabanu: Daughter of the Wind* has focused on two issues. The book presents a detailed and forthright discussion of human reproduction and the paramount role it plays in human culture, especially in the life of a young girl of marriageable age, and it does so, moreover, in a culture that is alien to most of the book's readers, in which the social arrangements for sexuality, marriage, and birth are extraordinarily different. It also presents, for the most part, characters who live in an extraordinarily traditional world, where, as nomads, they practice a way of life that has remained virtually unchanged since prehistoric times and their culture has been almost untouched by contact with the modern Western world. In both cases, some authors have attacked *Shabanu* as unsuitable for use in middle- and high schools, while others have defended it as especially suited for such use on the very same grounds.

Helen R. Adams, in *Ensuring Intellectual Freedom and Access to Information in the School Library Media Program*, points out that reading

The family lives in mud huts at the border of India and Pakistan. *(Image copyright oksana.perkins, 2010. Used under license from Shutterstock.com)*

Shabanu in middle school or high school classes is often compared by parents to "teaching pornography." Staples's response to such criticisms is that she is merely depicting conditions as they exist and broadening the reader's perspective by making an alien culture familiar. Even sympathetic readers such as Joanne Brown and Nancy St. Clair, in *Declarations of Independence: Empowered Girls in Young Adult Literature, 1990–2001*, observe that *Shabanu* depicts "practices that for western readers constitute child abuse."

The elite class of Pakistan, and many Muslims in the West, wish to portray Pakistan and the Muslim world as modern and contemporary and as moving in the direction of many ideals of Western cultures (especially prosperity and the general sophistication of civilization). This tone is reflected in many works sponsored by the Pakistani government, such as A. B. Rajput's 1977 book *Social Customs and Practices in Pakistan*. In the chapter "Some Evil Customs and Practices," Rajput speaks about the very traditional ethos of tribal Pakistanis that Staples celebrates, in these terms: "There are many customs and practices prevalent in various regions of Pakistan, particularly in the rural areas, which though against healthy development of the society, are still carried on without any check or restraint due to want of education and lack of enlightened approach towards life." *Shabanu* is often criticized from this perspective, as Staples revealed to Adams: "One man (the director of an Islamic academy in Florida) said it wasn't inaccuracy that bothered him, but that 'if people read this book they'll think all Muslims are backward camel herders.'" Staples's response is that she is only interested in portraying life as it is lived in Pakistan, and that it is her critics who have a warped or distorted view.

CRITICISM

Bradley A. Skeen

Skeen is a classics professor. In this essay, he explains the basic concepts of honor that underlie the plot structure of Shabanu *in relation to its author's feminist ideas.*

WHAT DO I READ NEXT?

- The preparation of lessons plans and other teaching aids about *Shabanu* have been less controversial than the book itself. Although a great many resources of this kind have been posted online rather than presented in traditional media, a good example in book form by Mary Ellen Snodgrass is her 2003 *Literary Treks: Characters on the Move*. Snodgrass provides a geographical commentary on the novel and provides both a general and specific bibliography.

- *Haveli*, by Staples, is the 1993 sequel to *Shabanu*. This novel continues the story of Shabanu's life as a wife in competition with other wives in a polygamous marriage and the blood feuds in which her new family is involved.

- Margaret Mead's 1928 *Coming of Age in Samoa* is a classic of anthropological literature that describes the rites of passage of girls into adulthood in the traditional society of a village in the South Pacific island nation of Samoa.

- *In the Name of Honor: A Memoir*, by Muktar Mai, is the 2006 autobiographical account of a rural Pakistani woman who was sentenced by a local court to be raped by the brothers of a woman her brother had seduced. It is also the story of her triumph over this injustice; she saw her attackers executed by the Pakistani government and received compensatory payment, which she used to open a school for girls in her village.

- *Anahita's Woven Riddle*, a 2006 young-adult novel by Meghan Nuttall Sayres, set in the nineteenth century, tells the story of a young girl's marriage in a Turkic-speaking nomadic tribe in Iran. This story brings together themes of history, myth, and folklore.

- James Highwater's 1992 young-adult novel *Anpao: An American Indian Odyssey* tells the story of a young plains Indian's spiritual and physical journey across North America.

- *Desert Places* is a 1996 travel book by Robyn Davidson. He tours the Thar desert of Pakistan and India and writes a narrative of his journey, with an ecological and anthropological emphasis.

- The 1993 study *The Nomadic Alternative*, by Thomas Jefferson Barfield, gives a sociological survey by region of nomadic peoples throughout Africa and Asia.

- *People of the Wind* is a 1977 documentary film about the lives of nomadic tribes in Iran. It was directed by Anthony Howarth, and it was issued on DVD in 2000.

In *Shabanu: Daughter of the Wind*, Staples has a very direct way of simply describing social conditions and practices in Pakistan without giving away the significance of any given statement, but rather allowing the reader to build up a picture from the whole story. For example, in the very first paragraph of the novel, Shabanu and Phulan go by themselves to get water from a well. Although nothing happens at that time, it is a foreshadowing of the encounter with the hunters later in the book. In a traditional culture, going to a well to get water is almost the only time a girl might be out in public without an escort from her family. Thus, the well is often a place where women are courted, and equally where they are harassed. Perhaps the most famous instance is the Biblical Moses courting his wife Zipporah by protecting her and her sisters from aggressive shepherds at a well (Exodus 2:15–22). Knowing that Phulan and Shabanu are gathering water at a well by themselves, any observer from Cholistan would begin to think of them as young, marriageable women and begin to fear what might happen to them.

> IN TERMS OF STATUS, SHABANU'S FAMILY IS
> FROM THE LOWEST RANKS OF THEIR SOCIETY;
> HOWEVER, THEY HAVE AS MUCH HONOR AS ANYONE
> ELSE, SO THEY ARE ABLE TO INTERACT SOCIALLY
> WITH ARISTOCRATS SUCH AS RAHIM."

This foreshadows the main crisis of the plot and signals that the main theme of the novel will be the vulnerable role of unprotected women in a traditional culture.

Staples presents a traditional society in Cholistan that shares many of the social codes and norms that are common to traditional cultures all over the world, including the West before modern times, right up until the eve of the French Revolution in the late 1700s. In a traditional culture, one of the most important considerations is honor (*izzat* in the Urdu language). Honor is a difficult and much misunderstood concept. Perhaps the most useful way to think of it is as respectability, the quality that allows a person or a family to deal with others without those others turning away in disgust. Honor is different from status. In terms of status, Shabanu's family is from the lowest ranks of their society; however, they have as much honor as anyone else, so they are able to interact socially with aristocrats such as Rahim.

In an honor-based culture, a man may lose honor by some extraordinary transgression such as cowardice, but by and large, a family's honor is determined by the behavior of its female members, and a man's honor is judged by his ability to control the behavior of his female relatives. This is why Shabanu's mother and aunt are so anxious to have her act in the correct way, for instance by wearing the veil, a garment worn by women to signal that they live in an honorable way (a condition of *purdah*, in Urdu). They have internalized their society's honor code and want Shabanu to do the same. It is to maintain honor that marriages are arranged by the families rather than by young people themselves. The impulsiveness of youth might well lead to a match that would dishonor the whole family. One way that honor is regulated between families is through exchange or reciprocity. In terms of marriage, the groom receives a gift from the family—the bride—and repays with another gift—cash or valuable commodities such as jewelry, generally termed a bride price. A dowry, on the other hand, is property that, although it is to be controlled by the husband, is provided by the bride's family to support their daughter when she becomes a wife. Reciprocity from the groom, if all the parties are of low status, as in the proposed marriages between Shabanu and Phulan and Murad and Hamir, might be as little as his pledge to keep his wife in respectable circumstances. If a family's honor is attacked by an outsider, it can be restored only by exacting compensation from him. Compensation can be had in two ways: either by blood (killing the outsider) or by a cash payment. Most traditional cultures have detailed codes regulating exchanges of honor. If a member of the family transgresses the family's honor, that person too must give compensation. Familiar examples are found in the Hebrew Bible, a document equally foundational to Jewish, Christian, and Islamic cultures. Examples also exist in the Koran and its attendant literary tradition.

Another possible approach to marriage is for the young woman to choose her own husband, even or particularly if the groom is unacceptable to her family because his status or his honor is too little for him to engage in reciprocity with the family. In this case, the bride and groom go off together, an action the family would necessarily interpret as their daughter's abduction. Such an action is technically known as bride rape (in the original sense of the term as abduction, rather than sexual violation). The Hebrew Bible, for instance, permits the practice if the abductor is able to pay a fine to the girl's family (Deuteronomy 22:28-29). In *Shabanu*, this practice is illustrated through Shabanu's encounter with the Bugti tribesmen. Their leader, Sadar, is searching for his niece, who has "eloped with a Marri tribesman." Shabanu is intimidated by these men and for the first time is happy to hide behind her veil. Her father assures her that Sadar intends to kill his niece. She realizes that this is a warning that she too must obey the social controls placed on her. This incident lessened the Bugti family's honor. It could potentially be restored if the family accepted what to them amounted to blackmail from the groom and acted as though they had always approved of the marriage, essentially pretending the groom was capable of reciprocity. The other, more effective way of restoring their honor would be through blood, by the family killing the couple. Bride rape, despite its obvious dangers, is fairly common in traditional societies because of the strong impulse that many young people feel to pair off on their own initiative. It is well known in English literature as a motif of the Gothic novels of the eighteenth century, and especially in nineteenth-century satires of the Gothic, such as Jane Austen's novel *Sense and Sensibility* or John Keats's poem "The Eve of St. Agnes." Staples, however, uses the motif in a different way. In contemporary American society, couples routinely arrange marriages between themselves, with only a remnant of the need to seek the approval of the families involved. Being aware of this, Staples seeks to provoke a reaction from her readers, who will inevitably imagine that they, like Shabanu, would face death if they lived in her culture but acted according to the norms of their own society.

The crisis of *Shabanu* also hinges on the honor of Shabanu's family. In this case, Nazir Mohammed and his hunting party propose to rape Phulan, Shabanu, and eventually their cousin Kulsum. Nazir would then restore the family's honor with a cash payment. This is clearly nothing that the family would ever approve of, but something it might have to suffer because of the much higher status of Nazir. The practical difficulties of alternatives to seeking blood vengeance from someone of higher status is illustrated by the death of Hamir. However, this is a breakdown in the system of honor. Nazir sold their farm to Hamir and Murad's father and supplies them with water. They are therefore his dependents, and Nazir's honor requires him to protect them and their family. Instead, he exploits them, but he is largely able to escape the loss of his own honor because of his superiority in status. This illustrates a major theme of the book, when powerful men who ought to protect the weak no longer do so because of the changing conditions of modern life. Another example is the nawab of Bahawalpur, the hereditary ruler of Cholistan who has given up his rights and become a politician in Lahore (the Pakistani capital city), who has a duty to bury Shabanu's grandfather in his military cemetery, but whom the family cannot even contact to claim their rights. From the view point of members of a traditional society, the loss of social cohesion that modernity brings about entails a loss of honor.

In the conflict between Nazir and Shabanu's family, honor is restored to all parties by the intervention of Nazir's older brother Rahim, whose even higher status allows him to act as a judge in this matter. Rahim recognizes that his brother is abusing his status to act dishonorably without consequences. Rahim manages to convince Nazir to accept the death of Hamir as compensation for the insult to him, the insult being that mud was splashed on him and he was made to appear ridiculous by the girl he intended to rape, a disproportion that even his higher status cannot really excuse. Rahim also restores honor to Shabanu's family by personally engaging in reciprocity with them, showering them with gifts (houses, jewelry, etc.) as a bride price far larger than they could possibly repay, thus greatly increasing their honor and even their status. Everyone in their culture recognizes the family's good fortune—everyone except Shabanu. She does not seem to understand the honor that is being paid to her family to recompense them for the dishonor from Rahim's brother; instead, she thinks, "I do resent [Rahim's] trying to buy my heart."

Shabanu identifies entirely with her childhood freedom and refuses to accept the responsibilities of adulthood. This is symbolized by what she fears is the complete destruction of her identity at the sale of the camel Guluband: "But at the center of myself is an aching hole. With Guluband, my joy, my freedom, all of who I am has gone. I wonder if I will ever take pleasure in anything again." More precisely, she rejects the way of life of her people in favor of some other life that is never clearly defined. Again, Staples, expects her readers to know what Shabanu wants from their own American experience. Shabanu constantly reacts with horror to her impending arranged marriage. She is almost equally disturbed by the possibility of her father selling her favorite camels, although it is the family's only means of survival; she selfishly prefers to consider them pets. These are tropes (literary themes) common in American girls' coming-of-age stories, such as Louisa May Alcott's *Little Women* or E. B. White's *Charlotte's Web*, that Staples has imported into her novel. She uses the expectations of Shabanu's family and community, which are authentic to Pakistani culture, to contrast with Shabanu's reactions, which are modeled on those typical of American culture. Thus, Staples's novel is ultimately Orientalist, presenting an alien culture as

Shabanu's family breeds camels and heavily relies on the water from the local "toba" pond for their survival. (*Image copyright Agata Dorobek, 2010. Used under license from Shutterstock.com*)

an "other" that makes an exotic contrast to the reader's culture. She holds up Western feminism as an unspoken ideal that animates all of Shabanu's decisions. The ultimate purpose of *Shabanu* is to offer feminism and the ideal of women's freedom and equality of action as superior, reflecting the author and audience's beliefs, to the traditional system of honor.

Source: Bradley Skeen, Critical Essay on *Shabanu: Daughter of the Wind*, in *Novels for Students*, Gale, Cengage Learning, 2011.

Linda Brill Comerfield

In the following interview, Comerfield discusses Staples's personal background and writing career.

"She has no trouble finding her way around the Cholistan desert, but she can't figure out the streets of Harrisburg, Pa.," Suzanne Fisher Staples murmurs, poking fun at herself. There is

> DURING HER TRAVELS, STAPLES BEGAN TO SEE THE WORLD THROUGH THE EYES OF OTHERS AND, AT THE SAME TIME, CAME TO UNDERSTAND WHY AMERICAN PRACTICES ARE OFTEN JUDGED SO HARSHLY BY OUTSIDERS."

a twinkle in her eye and a hint of a smile on her face, so it's obvious that she is not too upset about spending most of the evening lost in Pennsylvania's capital city, where she agreed to be interviewed by *PW*.

The writer, who has traveled and lived all over the world, now resides in Chattanooga, Tenn., where her husband works for an architectural supply company. Once every six weeks, however, she returns to her home state of Pennsylvania to visit her 81-year-old parents at their retirement community in Elizabethtown, about 20 minutes southeast of the capital. Being temporarily disoriented in a new place (and later discovering that her parents' car, which she had driven into the city, was locked up inside a parking garage) does not ruffle the worldly writer. Tall, slender and good-natured, she meets opportunities to explore new territory with the same sense of adventure that she conveys in her YA novels, which range over more exotic ground than Harrisburg.

Three out of Staples's four books are set in southern Asia, where she was assigned to work as a UPI correspondent for 13 years in the 1970s and '80s. Her latest work, *Shiva's Fire* (FSG/Foster) due out in April, tells the story of a mystical Indian child, Parvati, whose birth coincides with the worst tornado her village has ever endured. Extremely talented as a dancer, and infinitely wise, Parvati follows her "dharma," or "true destiny," by leaving her beloved family to attend a famous dance school.

Staples's first two novels, the Newbery Honor book *Shabanu* (pronounced shah-BAH-noo; Knopf, 1989) and its sequel, *Haveli* (hah-VA-lee; Knopf, 1993), are set in nearby Pakistan and trace the struggles of a young woman reluctantly entering an arranged marriage. The first book focuses on the heroine's childhood as a nomad.

Free-spirited Shabanu loves tending her father's herd of camels while her older, more domestic sister, Phulan, would rather stay indoors learning the tasks that will make her a "good" wife. *Haveli* is set several years later and encapsulates Shabanu's feelings of entrapment after she weds a wealthy landowner with three other wives, all of whom are jealous of Shabanu's beauty and youth. *Dangerous Skies*, the author's only book with an American setting, was published by FSG/Foster in 1996.

Possessing a reporter's eye for detail, Staples gives an "insider's" view of Asian culture without imposing judgment or injecting American values. "*Shiva's Fire* required a tremendous amount of research and two trips back to southern Asia," she says. Not only did she go to a renowned dance school in India to observe the practices of young dancers both inside and outside the studio, but she also visited a religious leader, who shared religious stories, ancient legends and principles of Hinduism. While the connective tissue of her novels is purely fiction, most of the images and characters come from true experiences. "My books are made up of real stories about real people," the author emphasizes, citing the inspiration for a tiger attack scene in *Shiva's Fire*.

"I was in northern India riding through the jungle on an elephant with two friends and their two daughters as we came across a beautiful tigress sitting atop a rock," the author says. "We didn't realize that we were walking between her and her babies. The tigress leapt on to the elephant's trunk and climbed all the way up to his forehead, so that she was face to face with the driver." Staples was "terrified," but seizing the opportunity to capture the dramatic moment, she had the presence of mind to grab her camera.

PW had the chance to see a photo of the lunging beast the day after the Harrisburg interview, when Staples gave a slide presentation about her books and travels at her parents' retirement community. Most of the slides could be illustrations for her books, depicting other memorable characters and scenes. Pictures of India relate to *Shiva's Fire*; pictures of America's southeastern shoreline bring to life settings from *Dangerous Skies*; slides of Pakistan evoke aspects of *Shabanu* and *Haveli*. One of the most haunting portraits is of a strikingly beautiful girl with an impish grin and dark, mysterious eyes. She is the 13-year-old after whom Staples modeled her first protagonist.

"Although she was of age, this girl had no desire to get married," says Staples, explaining that this girl's independent-minded grandmother (like Shabanu's beloved Aunt Sharma) was forced to live a hermit's existence for leaving a husband who "beat her regularly."

Although the marriages of Asian women are not always happy matches in her books, Staples is not necessarily critical of parents choosing partners for their children. Like her perspective on many other traditional customs, her view on this issue is broad-minded. During her travels, Staples began to see the world through the eyes of others and, at the same time, came to understand why American practices are often judged so harshly by outsiders. She could, for instance, see how bizarre the American concept of dating seemed to Asians when a woman asked her "if it was true that American children were sent out to do the most important job of their life—finding someone to live with—alone, without the benefit of experience, age and people who love them." While living overseas, Staples found herself spending a lot of time explaining and "sort of apologizing for" American behaviors.

Staples's openness and adaptability led her to be readily accepted by Pakistanis and Indians, who, Staples points out, are "very hospitable" people. While working as a reporter, she traveled with Indira Gandhi ("bumping along the road with her as she campaigned for her second term as prime minister"), met Chinese refugees who were persecuted during the Cultural Revolution and watched boys "as young as 10, 11 and 12" going off to war alongside their fathers.

A few years later, when she was invited to take part in a women's literacy project in Pakistan, Staples lived with a family in a small village. One of her favorite parts of the experience was sharing their evening ritual of telling stories around a fire. She recorded many of the tales in notebooks and, in fact, had gathered most of her material for *Shabanu* before returning to America to work at the *Washington Post*.

Staples experienced less culture shock in Asia than she did upon her reentry into the States in the mid-'80s. "I felt like I'd been away a long, long time," she recalls. "There were a lot of changes. The cars looked really weird, and everyone had gone to using computers on a regular basis. I was amazed by how frivolous Americans seemed. There seemed to be a lot of gossiping and backbiting going on. People would ask me about Asia, but they did not seem to comprehend what I told them. Their eyes would start glazing over when I tried to explain things that had happened to me."

THE FRUITS OF TRAVEL

It was when she was in Washington, D.C., that Staples began "making up scenes" from the stories in her notebooks. She attended a writers' workshop at the Washington Writers' Center, but found the class to be more "confusing" than helpful. "I finally decided that the only way to write a novel was to dive right in," says Staples, who revised her writing as she went along. As would be the case with all her works, *Shabanu* took three years to complete. When it was finished, a writer friend, David Finkelstein, encouraged her to send it to his agent, Jeanne Drewsen, who in turn sent it to Frances Foster at Knopf. Although Staples had to "wait a while" for Foster to read her manuscript, she was rewarded for her patience and she has worked exclusively with Foster ever since the editor accepted Shabanu. "I hope Frances lives forever! We have a wonderful relationship," says Staples, who feels flattered that people sometimes mistake her for Foster's sister.

Shabanu won a Newbery Honor award in 1990. Staples was thrilled by the prize, but also somewhat intimidated, for she felt pressured to produce other novels of the same caliber. "Sometimes I believed that my success was just a fluke," she confides. "But now I feel more confident that if I run into a problem—and sometimes I do get a block—that I'll be able to solve it."

Reassuringly, Staples's second novel, *Haveli*, was also well received, although one Asian-American reviewer criticized her for taking her characters' problems "too seriously." According to Staples, his view has been mirrored by a few other Asians anxious to promote their countries' modernization, who express some bitterness over her books' graphic depiction of poverty and primitive lifestyles. Once, Staples was even harassed by a Pakistani woman angered by Staples's novels. After passing out protest pamphlets and accosting Staples at lectures, the woman finally tearfully exclaimed, "I should have written that book!"

Staples's third novel, *Dangerous Skies*, marked a dramatic transition in the author's personal life as well as in her subject matter. Having just moved to the Chesapeake Bay area, Staples wanted to "make sense" out of all her "feelings of dislocation." The culture shock she had experienced upon her return

to America was now magnified, as she felt very much an outsider among people "who were shore born and bred." She did, however, develop a friendship with two neighboring boys (one white and one African-American) who eventually became models for her characters Tunes and Buck, two children whose lives are deeply affected by their elders' prejudices. Before the publication of *Dangerous Skies*, Staples went through several more upheavals, including divorce from her first husband (whom she had met in Pakistan), yet another move (this time to New York City) and the news that her editor was leaving Knopf. The author, now working full time as a novelist, also had financial worries. Life in New York City was not entirely grim for Staples, however. She enjoyed reuniting with old friends, rekindled her romance with a college sweetheart (Wayne Harley, to whom she is now married) and changed publishing houses with Foster when the editor started her own imprint at Farrar, Straus & Giroux.

For someone who has endured so much upheaval in her life, Staples is remarkably evenkeeled. Whether she is thanking a helpful stranger (like the one who opened the locked Harrisburg parking garage, releasing her parents' car), responding to questions from elderly people at the retirement community or giggling over life's little absurdities with an interviewer she has only known a few hours, she radiates a sincere interest in and respect for other people. A "terrible daydreamer" as a child, Staples shows her quieter, more poetic side most eloquently in *Shiva's Fire*. The book smoothly links Hindu mythology with protagonist Parvati's spiritual journey, and Staples expresses cycles of destruction and rebirth in allegorical terms.

Now in her 50s, Staples continues to strike out in fresh directions as a writer. She speaks enthusiastically about her current project: a novel about a girl soccer player from a "highly dysfunctional" family. (The idea came from her husband's experiences as a volunteer soccer coach.) Though it unfolds worlds away from southern Asia, the new novel has at least one thing in common with the writer's previous books. "I thought that this would be a fairly simple project," says Staples. "But," she adds, smiling sheepishly, "it's turning into something quite complex."

Source: Linda Brill Comerfield, "Under Eastern Skies," in *Publishers Weekly*, Vol. 247, No. 7, February 14, 2000, pp. 168–69.

Suzanne Fisher Staples

In the following article, Staples argues that the question of authenticity seems to arise when a group of people feels that someone who has no right to do so speaks for them.

I first went to work in an Islamic nation as a news reporter in 1979 in Pakistan, where my novels *Shabanu* and *Haveli* are set. The news in the subcontinent that laid heaviest claim to the attention of Western reporters later that year was about the events that led to the Soviet invasion of Afghanistan on Christmas Eve. We spent weeks at a time in the Kabul Intercontinental Hotel. It was a scary time. Khad, the Soviet-led secret police, was everywhere, and threats to news people and those who associated with us were made openly and violently, if not directly.

A Swiss hotelier in Kabul told me his Afghan driver had not shown up for work in a week. He was worried about his employee, whom he described as a decent and educated man. When the driver finally returned to work one morning he wore a glove on his right hand. The hotelier learned Khad interrogators had torn off the driver's fingernails because they did not believe he had informed completely enough about his boss's contacts and activities. My own contact, a UPI stringer, disappeared completely. His family asked me not to contact them again.

It was in this atmosphere, where I once told my editors "the fear is as thick as the dust on the donkeys," that we reported on events in Afghanistan. Often our dispatches were reduced to a paragraph in "World News in Brief" columns in American newspapers. It was demoralizing. We were risking the welfare of Afghans who helped us to report news of vital significance to Western interests that was getting little attention. A new Afghan Soviet Republic would have given Moscow a good vantage point on the Arabian Gulf, which remains the world's most important petroleum shipping lane. In February of 1980 we were forced to move our base for Afghanistan news coverage to Pakistan.

The reason so many editors seemed not to care what happened in Afghanistan had to do with that nation's remoteness, illiteracy, and poverty, but more significantly, with ignorance on the part of Americans. At around the same time, terrorist acts supported by Iran and the Palestine Liberation Organization appeared on American TV with mind-numbing regularity. The news fostered a perception among Americans that

> THE QUESTION OF AUTHENTICITY SEEMS TO ARISE WHEN A GROUP OF PEOPLE FEELS THAT SOMEONE WHO HAS NO RIGHT TO DO SO 'SPEAKS' FOR THEM."

Islam was a brutal religion, and that those who practiced it were dedicated to killing Jews and Christians in general, and Israelis and Americans in particular.

I began to believe the news was not necessarily a good medium for fostering cultural understanding in America—at least news from parts of the world where the way of life is very different from the American one. I also grew increasingly interested in writing fiction. Whenever I had the chance I reported "color" features about people's lives. My notebooks were filled with textural details—the color of the sky, the smell of the earth, the feel of the bark of trees. I began to think in terms of story. But I still had to earn a living, and so I accepted a transfer to Washington, D.C., where I worked first on UPI's national news desk and later at the *Washington Post* as a part-time editor on the foreign news desk. By then I was tired and wanted out of journalism.

My opportunity came in 1985, when I moved back to Pakistan and was hired by the US Agency for International Development to investigate the lives of poor rural women. I studied Urdu, the national language, intensively for six months and began to travel and study women's lives in rural areas of Punjab, on Pakistan's border with India. It was in the course of gathering information for this project that I first visited the Cholistan Desert. There was something about the blue-tiled mosques, the honor and dignity of the people, and the ancient tales they told that made me know I wanted to write a story about this place and these people.

The story of *Shabanu: Daughter of the Wind* took shape slowly. It grew out of real incidents related to me by women around the cooking fires at the end of the day when our work was done, and during long walks to the wells during the dry season. These were stories about their own lives and about the lives of their sisters and cousins. Every scene and chapter in the book was based on a story told to me by a real person.

Over a three-year period I was in the desert or elsewhere in Punjab gathering information for my USAID work, or at the University of the Punjab in Lahore, or the Folk Heritage Institute in Rawalpindi, or interviewing scholars about traditions and culture in Cholistan. Before I submitted the manuscript for *Shabanu* to my publisher I had thirteen scholars and others who knew the area read it for accuracy. Each of them remarked that I had captured the place, the people, and their lives with a remarkable sense of realism. However, the fact remains that I am not a Muslim. I am not from the Cholistan Desert. I am not a camel herder. Should I have written about these people?

I have come to this subject that has become known as "authenticity" with the advantage of having seen it from more than one angle. When I lived in Asia I was aware of how the news media there portrayed life in the United States. Some Asian reporters based in American cities focused on crime, poverty, and disease in the world's richest nation. Their articles portrayed America as a nation where young people kill each other, where men and women are sexually promiscuous, a place of moral crisis that tries to tell the rest of the world how it should behave. While I did not think these reports were untrue, together they gave an unrealistic, incomplete, and negative impression of what life in the United States is like.

When *Shabanu* and its sequel, *Haveli* came under fire by some Muslims in the United States, I took it very seriously. I tried without success to find out exactly what it was that people found offensive. In February on a Children's Literature listserve, Jerry Diakiw, a teacher at York University in Ontario (Canada), posted a query in which he said a Pakistani student felt *Shabanu* "selected a very exotic aspect [of] . . . and did not portray her culture fairly." The student went on to say the book is "a subtle example of prevailing anti-Moslem feeling in North America." Diakiw asked if anyone had similar experiences. While a number of respondents said they had heard objections to the book, they did not offer a single concrete example of what was offensive or incorrect or misleading about it.

Last year I was invited to speak to students at the Islamic Academy in Orlando, Florida,

where I was living at the time. Before I went into the classroom the principal told me he had found *Shabanu* offensive. When I pressed him to tell me what it was that bothered him he grew agitated. "It is not the story, *per se*, that offends," he said. "What is so hard to swallow is that the rest of the world, if they read such things, will think that all Muslims are backward camel herders." Suddenly I saw a common thread in what other Muslims were saying about *Shabanu* and *Haveli*. The question of authenticity seems to arise when a group of people feels that someone who has no right to do so "speaks" for them.

I did not have in mind a portrayal or defense of Islam when I wrote *Shabanu* and *Haveli*. That is not what story is all about. My intent was to write a story about the people of Cholistan, a very specific subtribe of seminomadic camel herders in the small part of the vast Thar Desert that lies within Pakistan's Punjab province. Their history and culture are unique. That they are Muslim is a fact about them, but that fact is no more central to the stories in these books than the fact that Buck and Tunes in my most recent book, *Dangerous Skies*, are Christian. I tried to write all three books with all the particularity of detail about the lives of individuals that a story must have.

Representation is not what story is meant to do. Story is very particular. It speaks only for the author and the characters the author creates. Its power lies in its focus on the human heart, illumination, and connection. Story is not meant to represent or instruct about or speak for any group of people—and it should not be interpreted in that light.

So when we talk about "authenticity" what are we really talking about? Is it really about how true the author's vision is of made-up events that take place in a culture that is not the author's culture? Or is it a feeling of defensiveness on the part of readers when we cannot control images of our own culture as it comes under scrutiny by people from "outside"? Is the former question an intellectual rationalization of the latter? This is an emotionally charged and complex issue—one that I believe often reflects a mistaken notion of what a story really is.

Source: Suzanne Fisher Staples, "Writing about the Islamic World: An American Author's Thoughts on Authenticity," in *Bookbird*, Vol. 35, No. 3, Fall 1997, pp. 17–20.

Allen Raymond

In the following review, Raymond applauds Staples's ability to tell a powerful story while evoking a unique culture.

One would hope that someday you and I will be given the opportunity to curl up on a sofa with the autobiography—if she ever can be persuaded to write it—of Suzanne Fisher Staples.

It will be a gripping page-turner, not only because Suzanne's life has been, and is, the stuff of which page-turners are made, but because she knows how to write a book you'll find hard to put down.

That skill has been strikingly demonstrated in the first two books she has ever written, *Shabanu: Daughter of the Wind* (Knopf, 1989) and its sequel, *Haveli* (Knopf, 1993), which picks up *Shabanu*'s story five years later.

While it has been suggested that the audience for both books is young adults, experience tells us younger children become spellbound by the stories. And adults? Well, pick one up; you won't put it down.

Filled with vivid, mesmerizing descriptions of a young girl's life on Pakistan's Cholistan Desert, they're convincing evidence the *New York Times* knew what it was talking about when, in its review of *Shabanu*, it called the book "a small miracle."

Others recognized the miracle, too. *Shabanu* was selected as a Newbery Honor Book; a "Notable Children's Book" by the American Library Association; an "ALA Best Book for Young Adults"; and the International Reading Association selected it as both a "Teacher's Choice" and a "Young Adult's Choice."

But, in a distinction perhaps even more significant, as far as elementary and middle school teachers are concerned, in 1990 the National Council for the Social Studies honored *Shabanu* as a "Notable Children's Trade Book."

And little wonder. It's a social studies teacher's dream come true. When reading *Shabanu* and *Haveli* it is impossible to curb one's appetite to learn more. That appetite begins, of course, with geography.

Where is Pakistan? Where is the Cholistan Desert? What is the history of this country? How does one get to Pakistan? How big is it?

And how does one travel around Pakistan? Is it on camels, which Shabanu (and, one suspects, Suzanne Staples herself) love so much? Are camels everywhere, as it seems, or are they only to be found in the desert?

And is it true, as the author indicates in these graphic, often heart-rending books, that a woman's role in Pakistan is oppressively subservient to men?

Seeking answers, we find ourselves, in true teacher fashion, immersed in reference books, an atlas, an encyclopedia. The process of discovery brings back memories of our own childhood, and the excitement we felt—even now it's hard to explain, but it was palpable when an explorer/ adventurer (they seem to go hand-in-hand, don't they?) would pay our school an annual visit, showing movies of adventures, and of worlds and peoples we were sure we would never see.

Reading a book by Suzanne Staples conveys this same feeling. Her ability to recall stories told to her by nomads in the desert, and then re-telling those stories with a skill that transports us halfway around the world, makes us feel we're Pakistanis—that Shabanu's life is our life.

Suddenly, headlines in the local newspaper take on new meaning. Wars in Pakistan, or the rise and fall of its leaders, are not events occurring "somewhere else." This is our country, this Pakistan, and, such is the power of Staples' writing; when it bleeds, we bleed also.

Robert Cormier, who saw an advance copy of Staples' second novel, *Haveli*, published last fall, commented, "In language that both soars and sings, Suzanne Fisher Staples makes vibrant an exotic world, but be warned: she may just pierce your heart at the same time.

Ilene Cooper, in her review of *Haveli* which appeared in the June 1993 issue of *Booklist* added, "Staples brews a potent mix here: the issue of a woman's role in a traditional society, page-turning intrigue, tough women characters and a fluidity of writing that blends it all together."

The novels, with the courageous 13-year-old Shabanu as narrator, tell of her life in the Cholistan Desert of eastern Pakistan, on its border with India.

Following tradition (in which fathers pick a husband when a girl turns 13) Shabanu was married at 13 to a 60-year-old Pakistani landowner. In the sequel, *Haveli*, we discover how Shabanu, now with a four-year-old daughter, survives with courage in a culture where a woman's life is often harsh.

Describing her nomadic life on the desert, Shabanu says they are "People of the wind.

"When hot summer winds parch the land, we must move to desert settlements where the wells hold sweet water.

"When the monsoon winds bring rain, we return to the dunes. But this year and last the monsoons failed, and we must go now to Dingarh, an ancient village where the wells are deep."

The magical, almost poetic force of the author's writing carries us to this desert in Pakistan. Vicariously, we find ourselves sitting by the fire as Shabanu's extended family— grandfather, aunt, cousins, father, mother, sister—mesmerize us, in true oral tradition, with their nail-biting tales of life in the desert.

No history book could more effectively convey Shabanu's startling, often heartbreaking, almost unbelievable, but always courageous story. The author's ability to capture the matter-of-fact way in which the nomads of the Cholistan Desert live, cope and survive holds us glued to the page.

Torn between your own personal need for sleep and a passionate desire to know what happens next, you will become totally absorbed in a world that unquestionably proves truth is, indeed, stranger than fiction.

We inwardly cheer when the monsoons come and it rains and rains. We chuckle with delight as Shabanu, her father, mother, sister, aunt and cousins—to say nothing of the thirsty camels—romp in the precious water that has suddenly formed into giant lakes.

Suddenly, when we're least expecting it, the mood changes. A young man is cut down in a fusillade of bullets, as if he were nothing more than a target on a shooting range.

The men, many of them, are cruel, even to women. We know it's true, but we don't understand as, step-by-step and page-by-page, we are brought face-to-face with a culture in which women seem destined to lead what Staples describes as "a life of servitude and emotional bondage."

One wonders how an American woman, Suzanne Staples, could with such authenticity put all of us inside the head and mind of a 13-year-old Pakistani girl.

Not easily. It probably began while she was in school, where she developed a deepseated interest in South Asia.

Through a series of fortuitous career opportunities, she eventually became a foreign correspondent for United Press International, managing its bureau in New Delhi, India.

After three years reporting on the Afghanistan war, the comeback of Indira Gandhi and the upheavals in Bangladesh, she returned to the United States for three years.

Then it was back to South Asia, and Islamabad, Pakistan, working for the Agency for International Development.

Her work took her to the Cholistan Desert, her research took her everywhere in Pakistan, and her inquiring mind took her to campfires in the desert where stories are told.

And finally, her remarkable writing skills brought her to us.

Source: Allen Raymond, "Suzanne Fisher Staples: Magical Storyteller," in *Teaching Pre K-8*, Vol. 24, No. 6, March 1994.

Walter E. Sawyer and Jean C. Sawyer

In the following excerpted interview, the Sawyers and Staples discuss the influences on Shabanu.

[Jean C. Sawyer:] In reading about Shabanu it is clear that you could not have written the story without being Shabanu in a sense, or developing a kinship with her. The reader experiences and can relate to Shabanu's feelings as she goes through her life and as things change for her. What in your background or experience helped you accomplish this?

[Suzanne Fisher Staples:] Some of that is how I felt about where I grew up. I grew up in the countryside of northeastern Pennsylvania, and I loved it. I loved the mountains, the hills, and the forest. I never wanted to leave it.

I was able to relate to the feelings young girls go through when they're reaching puberty. It becomes much more poignant when the girl is about to be married against her will, and must give up the things she loves. Shabanu is frightened. She is at an age where she is not interested in sex, in moving away from her family, or in losing her freedom. Those are all things from my experience that were transposed to her culture.

[Walter E. Sawyer:] The setting has a profound influence on the story. The depiction of the

**IN A WAY, THAT IS HOW OUR MINDS WORK.
THINGS THAT ARE IMPORTANT TO US ARE THE
THINGS WE TELL OTHER PEOPLE ABOUT."**

*setting is more subtle than journalistic. There is a
distinct view of Shabanu's world even though it is
never discussed in great detail. Does a journalism
background help you to create such settings?*

SS: No. I had to unlearn everything that
I had learned as a journalist in order to write
fiction. Meticulous attention to detail should be
in your notebook as a journalist so that you will
know it in case you need to use it later. I remember covering the story of Breshnev (former head
of state of the Soviet Union) visiting India. He
had been out of the public view for quite awhile.
When he landed at the airport all of the ambassadors came. They made several speeches. This
happened right after Afghanistan was invaded
and everybody was focused on that story. When
I had finished writing my story, I received a
telephone call from a newspaper in Kansas
wanting a physical description of Breshnev.
They wanted an article on what Breshnev looked
like. I went back to my notebook and constructed it; it was all there. That's the training
of a journalist. You notice everything. You
record things and filter all of the human emotion
out. Fiction, to me, is just the opposite of this. As
a journalist I did consciously filter out the
emotion.

As a journalist in Asia, it was easy to gauge
whether your story would get into the newspaper. It often had to do with whether the World
Series was being played or whether the Pope was
in the United States. What was happening in the
United States was seen as much more important.
I realized that I was going out and risking my life
for something that often never saw the light of
day. I really lost faith in the news media as a
vehicle for understanding between people. On
the other hand, journalists have a lot of respect
for the people living in the places where they
themselves are assigned.

When I found out I was going to live in
Pakistan, I loved the idea. I love that country.

I had been all over it as a political reporter. The
idea of going back there and writing about the
people was so intriguing to me. I was working for
the *Washington Post* at the time, but you are not
allowed to report from the country where a
member of your immediate family is in the
diplomatic corps. Since my husband was in the
diplomatic corps, we made the decision to go
there based on my decision to leave journalism.
I thought it would be interesting to try to reach
the people by talking and listening to them. In a
sense, journalism influenced what I was trying to
do. Paying attention to detail was something I
did. Now, I had to learn a new subjective way of
expressing thought.

*WS: Deciding what details to include or
delete is a challenge for any writer. How did you
develop the ability to be discriminating about what
to include or not include?*

SS: I think it's a matter of experience. You
learn as you write or even as you grow to appreciate art. The telling detail, a distillation, is what
you are after. A telling detail might be when
Shabanu's mother is sitting and talking to her
as the sun is going down. The sunlight catching
in her nosepin tells you more about what the
light looks like than if you describe the sky.
That's what painters try to do. Instead of telling
every little detail, they present one very important detail that tells it all.

I remember discovering this when I was in
school. I had gone on a field trip to the Metro-
politan Museum in New York and was looking
at impressionist paintings. It dawned on me how
important it was to capture a tiny bit of the
whole thing and have that tiny bit tell the
whole story. When I write, I present vignettes
that tell more than I am actually putting into
words.

*JS: In one scene, Shabanu and her father
come back from the fair. Her mother wants to
hear all about the fair. As they tell her, she is
looking off in the distance, reliving her memories
through them. It told much about the society. Her
mother cannot go to fairs anymore; now she, can
only try to relive the experience. The reader can
picture much from just a line of conversation or
from a person's look.*

SS: In a way, that is how our minds work.
Things that are important to us are the things we
tell other people about. When the writer makes
the connection with the reader and something
rings true, it is very rewarding. Even if we are just

talking to friends, we often find that we can strike a common chord so that each knows what the other means. Creativity is related to this. We should demythologize the notion of creativity. It is something that everybody has, but it takes a lot of work to perfect. It takes technique to take a good idea and to execute it well. Some of us can do it in some ways but not in others.

WS: When you used the example of the light shining on the nosepin, your purpose wasn't to describe things literally. Rather, your purpose was to paint a picture with a telling detail. How can beginning writers or those working with developing writers encourage this ability to perceive significant details?

SS: One way might be to look at a slide for just a split second. Ask yourself what sticks in your mind about the picture, and then put that into words.

WS: In schools today there is an increased emphasis on establishing a more realistic balance between the meaningful content and the mechanics of writing.

SS: That's important. I was pleased by the fact that it didn't matter to my publishers how, why, or for whom I had written my book. They were interested in quality literature for young people. I have been reading young people's literature since writing this book. I didn't know anything about this type of literature before. Writing for young people is like having faith that you can talk about another culture because people are fundamentally the same. Children are fundamentally the same as adults. Their thought processes are very similar though perhaps a little bit less developed.

WS: There are many themes in the book ... duty, parental love, disillusionment, and making one's way in life. How do you establish themes in your writing?

SS: I don't think of *Shabanu* as being filled with themes. I was trying to tell a story in which everything made sense at some level. The finished manuscript, was about 25 percent fuller than it is now. I had to pull some things out, but I was afraid that in the process some things wouldn't make sense. For example, Shabanu's not having brothers makes her more independent. This opens up the question of the place of women in society.

WS: Do you let the themes emerge and then go back to clarify them?

SS: Yes. There were some things that I did have to go back and connect later. There were also some things that I had over-connected; I had to go back and untangle them.

The concepts of creativity, craftsmanship, and thematic writing make writing sound scary. I recall being at Breadloaf with people who talked about these things as though they were real things. I couldn't understand what they were talking about. Even now, when I go into a writer's group I don't understand or even care about those things.

JS: This sometimes happens to the reader as well as the writer. For example, take the notion of the word "choice." The reader learns that Shabanu has no choice about the sale of the camel. Later her aunt uses the word "choice." It came to be related to the inner self. Shabanu has a choice about her inner self and her own thoughts. It wasn't necessarily a theme, but the word came up twice and caused the reader to think about it. Do you consciously keep all of these things in mind as you write?

SS: I don't think I could write that way. One time I came home from Pakistan and attended a birthday party for a friend of mine who had introduced me to my agent. People were talking about things that were being published. These people were all successful writers, publishers, and agents. I became confused and upset by their terms even though I had read most of the things they were talking about. It made me think that I was never going to make it as a fiction writer.

One of the best pieces of advice I ever got about writing was from a writer friend. She said that when something bothers you as a writer, track it down and follow it until it disappears. That really made sense to me. If you can't nail it down, then take it out. You have to learn to trust your own judgment about it. I think you need to trust yourself to know that what makes sense to you is likely to make sense to others. This comes with a certain amount of maturity. You develop the confidence that it is worth writing a book, even if it is just because your family and friends will read about this culture that you have lived in, or because you loved doing it, or because it has helped you express yourself. You have to develop a faith in yourself that it is worthwhile.

JS: Do you read a lot of novels?

SS: I used to, but I don't anymore. It has too great an effect on me. If I'm reading at the same time I am writing, I find myself talking in other people's voices. So, I don't read fiction when I'm writing. It's just too hard for me to do. That disappoints me because I love reading fiction.

Writing is such a personal thing. Why do we tell stories that mean something to us? Everybody does it for a different reason. We need to help young writers get to a stage beyond where they are writing only as an assignment. We need to get them to the point where they hope that someone will identify with their writing.

In writing, you see how much your will can influence events. In my writing, I find distance very helpful. For example, I am writing a sequel to *Shabanu* that deals with her in an urban situation. She is eighteen-years-old, married, and has her own daughter when the book opens. Dealing with adult emotions, things which I might now be experiencing myself, are more difficult for me to write about than things like how she related to her father when she was younger. I can look back and remember my relationship with my father, and associate how I felt emotionally at the time.

I'm having a harder time with this book. For example, Shabanu learns very early on to use her body to please her husband. This is difficult for Western readers to accept and to still see Shabanu as a sympathetic character. Yet, it is so common. It is the way women insure their safety and survival in that part of the world. Everybody is not liberated. We don't realize how different our Western relationships are between women and men. I'm having to work at this book a little bit, go away, and then come back to it. It is very hard to get it right the first time.

Source: Walter E. Sawyer and Jean C. Sawyer, "A Discussion with Suzanne Fisher Staples: The Author as Writer and Cultural Observer," in *New Advocate*, Vol. 6, No. 3, Summer 1993, pp. 159–69.

SOURCES

Adams, Helen R., *Ensuring Intellectual Freedom and Access to Information in the School Library Media Program*, Libraries Unlimited, 2008, pp. 9–10, 233–34.

Ahmad, Kazi S., *A Geography of Pakistan*, Oxford University Press, 1964.

Alcott, Louisa May, *Little Women*, 2 vols., Roberts Bros., 1868–1869.

Austen, Jane, *Sense and Sensibility*, 3 vols., T. Egerton, 1811, http://books.google.com/books?id = eqdbAAAAQAAJ& source = gbs_navlinks_s (accessed December 16, 2009).

Brown, Joanne, and Nancy St. Clair, *Declarations of Independence: Empowered Girls in Young Adult Literature, 1990–2001*, Scarecrow, 2002, pp. 87–91.

Dar, Shujaat Zamir, ed., *Sights in the Sands of Cholistan: Bahawalpur's History and Architecture*, Oxford University Press, 2007.

Hedblad, Alan, ed., "Staples, Suzanne Fisher," in *Something about the Author*, Vol. 105, The Gale Group, 1999, pp. 208–10.

Keats, John, "The Eve of St. Agnes," in *Complete Poems*, edited by Jack Stillinger, Belknap, 1978, pp. 229–39.

Khan, Tahira S., *Beyond Honour: Historical Materialist Explanation of Honour-Related Violence*, Oxford University Press, 2006.

Khazanov, Anatoly M., *Nomads and the Outside World*, 2nd ed., University of Wisconsin Press, 1994.

Mandelbaum, David G., *Women's Seclusion and Men's Honor: Sex Roles in India, Bangladesh, and Pakistan*, University of Arizona Press, 1988.

McIntosh, Jane R., *The Ancient Indus Valley: New Perspectives*, ABC Clio, 2008.

Nanda, Serena, *Neither Man nor Woman: The Hijras of India*, Wadsworth, 1998.

Rajput, A. B., "Some Evil Customs and Practices," in *Social Customs and Practices in Pakistan*, Pakistan Branch R.C.D. Cultural Institute, 1977.

Said, Edward, *Orientalism*, Penguin, 2003.

Snodgrass, Mary Ellen, *Literary Treks: Characters on the Move*, Libraries Unlimited, 2003, pp. 153–59.

Staples, Suzanne Fisher, *Dangerous Skies*, Farrar, Straus & Giroux, 1996.

———, *The Green Dog: A Mostly True Story*, Farrar, Straus & Giroux, 2003.

———, *Shabanu: Daughter of the Wind*, Knopf, 1989.

———, *Shiva's Fire*, Farrar, Straus & Giroux, 2000.

———, *Under the Persimmon Tree*, Farrar, Straus & Giroux, 2005.

White, E. B., *Charlotte's Web*, Harper, 1952.

Wilber, Donald N., *Pakistan: Its People, Its Society, Its Culture*, Hraf, 1964.

Zarins, Juris, "Pastoralism in Southwest Asia: The Second Millennium BC," in *The Walking Larder: Patterns of Domestication, Pastoralism, and Predation*, edited by J. Clutton-Brock, Unwin Hyman, 1989, pp. 127–55.

FURTHER READING

Ahmad, Farooq, "Agro-Pastoral Systems in Cholistan," in *Pakistan Geographical Review*, Vol. 60, No. 2, 2005, pp. 65–69.

> Ahmad provides a technical description of the way of life followed by Shabanu's family in this book.

Chu, Man-Hua, "The 'Well-Behaved' Woman in Modern Pakistani Society in *Shabanu* and *Haveli* by Suzanne Fisher Staples," M.A. thesis, Providence University, 2007, http://ethesys.lib.pu.edu.tw/ETD-db/ETD-search/view_etd?URN = etd-0717107-103135 (accessed December 16, 2009).

> Chu examines Staples's novels as offering a pattern for the creation of a modern identity in traditional Islamic societies.

Hopkirk, Peter, *The Great Game: The Struggle for Empire in Central Asia*, Kondansha International, 1992.

> Hopkirk puts the recent political history of Central Asia in the larger context of the conflict for control of the continent between Russia and Great Britain going back to the eighteenth century, a conflict that has conditioned the modern history of Pakistan and that spills over into the story in *Shabanu*.

Staples, Suzanne Fisher, *The House of Djinn*, Farrar, Straus & Giroux, 2008.

> This is a second sequel to *Shabanu*. It largely concerns the lives of Shabanu's children while they are teenagers.

SUGGESTED SEARCH TERMS

Suzanne Fisher Staples

Shabanu

Islam AND West

Cholistan

Pastoralism AND camel

Shabanu AND Islam

Shabanu AND women's roles

Shabanu AND violence

Staples AND Shabanu

Shabanu AND empowerment

Shabanu AND Pakistan

Wicked: The Life and Times of the Wicked Witch of the West

Wicked: The Life and Times of the Wicked Witch of the West is the first adult novel that Gregory Maguire published after a distinguished early career writing fiction for children. It should be stressed that this novel covers adult themes and includes descriptions of adult sexual experiences, as well as significant violence, and is not recommended for younger readers.

In *Wicked*, Maguire explores the back story of two characters from L. Frank Baum's fictional land of Oz: the Wicked Witch of the East and the Wicked Witch of the West. Were they really wicked? And if so, what made them that way? He tells the story of Elphaba, the Wicked Witch of the West, who is born mysteriously green, very smart, somewhat prickly, and with a deep devotion to equal justice for all creatures in a world ruled by despots. He also tells the story of Galinda, who later changes her name to Glinda, who begins life as a spoiled and vain socialite and becomes a powerful sorceress. Whether Glinda is a "good" witch or not is ambiguous, although she is clearly not as tormented as either Elphaba, the Wicked Witch of the West, or her sister Nessarose, the Wicked Witch of the East. Neither sister sets out to become wicked, in fact, both sisters consider themselves to be working for the good, Elphaba by resisting the oppression of the Animals, and Nessarose by enforcing her vision of the virtuous Unionist religion on Munchkinland. One of Maguire's central themes in the book is the ways in which a quest for virtue and justice

GREGORY MAGUIRE

1995

Gregory Maguire *(Bruce Glikas / FilmMagic)*

can itself warp the seeker, leading him or her down paths that are as destructive as those against which they rebel.

AUTHOR BIOGRAPHY

Maguire was born on June 9, 1954, in Albany, New York. His mother, Helen, died giving birth to him. He and his three older siblings were split up among relatives, and for a short time, the baby was placed in an orphanage. His father, John, a newspaper reporter, eventually married Marie McAuliff, a poet, and reunited the family, adding a couple more siblings along the way. Maguire's history with the *Wizard of Oz* has its roots in his childhood. After seeing the movie on television, Maguire led a group of siblings and neighborhood children in a performance but expanded the cast to include Tinker Bell, Captain Hook, and Peter Pan. In an interview with Bev Goldberg on the American Library Association's Web log

AL Inside Scoop, he recalled that he told the other children "we need to have more than one bad guy so we can see who is worse." That particular game was interrupted when his stepmother discovered in the nick of time that Maguire's thirteen-month-old brother was suffocating in a hiding place under the porch. The baby was fine, but an imagination was fired. Maguire produced several hundred manuscripts between the ages of eight and eighteen, but as he told *Bookselling This Week*, he "was hopelessly fecund but not talented enough to be considered a wunderkind."

He completed his bachelor's degree at the State University of New York at Albany and his doctorate in English and American studies at Tufts University. While he was a student, he wrote a children's book titled *The Lightning Time*, which was published when he was twenty-three. He taught and codirected the Simmons College Center for the Study of Children's Literature and founded Children's Literature New England in 1985. Although he had been publishing children's books all along, it was while living in England in the 1990s that he suffered a bout of what he called, in the *Bookselling This Week* article, "financial embarrassment." Maguire wrote: "I began to be worried about being able to pay my bills.... I could see the time was growing ripe and that if I didn't do it, somebody else was going to have that very good idea and do it." *Wicked* was Maguire's first novel for adults, and its success freed him from teaching and allowed him to write full time. He has continued to write books for children and for adults ever since. In 2003, the Broadway musical *Wicked* debuted; it is based on an adaptation of Maguire's best-selling novel, and it has broken box-office records around the world.

In 2004, after same-sex marriage was legalized in Massachusetts, Maguire married Andy Newman, a painter. Together, they have adopted three children, Luke and Alex from Cambodia and Helen from Guatemala. In 2005, when asked by Bob Minzesheimer of *USA Today* about the intersection of the popular and the subversive in his life, Maguire said,

> I'm a father of three young kids, a practicing Catholic, a registered voter who does vote, a taxpayer, a volunteer on the boards of local charities.... Yet I am also an openly gay married man, a critic of the current administration, an occasional public dissenter about Vatican policy and practices.... so 'subversive' is perhaps more flattering than accurate.

PLOT SUMMARY

Prologue: On the Yellow Brick Road

The Witch descends out of the sky above Oz, where she eavesdrops on four travelers, a Lion, a Scarecrow, a Tin Woodman and a little girl, who gossip about the witch's true nature. As the group runs for shelter from the gathering storm, the Witch recognizes Dorothy's shoes and vows to retrieve them. When the rain begins, the Witch hides herself in the roots of a large tree, since water of any kind burns her like fire.

Part I: Munchkinlanders

THE ROOT OF EVIL

Frex, a Unionist minister, prepares for a crucial sermon as his wife, Melena, prepares to give birth to their first child. They spar affectionately over whose task is more momentous before Frex leaves for Rush Margins, the nearby town.

THE CLOCK OF THE TIME DRAGON

Frex stops in a neighbor's house to find a woman to help Melena with childbirth. Melena is unpopular because she was born wealthy, but the neighbor promises to send someone. Frex prepares to preach against the faith which is in opposition to his Unionist beliefs.

THE BIRTH OF A WITCH

Frex arrives in Rush Margins just before the Clock of the Time Dragon, an enormous mechanical dragon whose side opens to reveal a puppet show. As Frex preaches, the Dragon's puppets show a story of a preacher like Frex, with an unfaithful wife like Melena. As the puppet preacher is run through with a pike and roasted, one of Frex's parishioners attacks him. An old woman hides him in her storeroom. The crones who help Melena through childbirth hide her in the Dragon itself. When the baby is born, she is bright green, and they cannot determine her sex. The crones debate killing the green baby, and she bites the finger off one with her razor sharp teeth. They leave the baby and her unconscious mother inside the dragon and run away.

MALADIES AND REMEDIES

Melena's nanny arrives to help with the green baby, who is named Elphaba. Nanny quizzes both parents about what could have caused Elphaba's color, but she cannot find an

MEDIA ADAPTATIONS

- An unabridged audiobook of *Wicked* was recorded in 2005 and is available from HarperAudio.

- In May 2003, the Broadway musical version of *Wicked* opened at the Gershwin Theater in New York City. The music and lyrics were written by Stephen Schwartz, and Winnie Holtzman wrote the "book," or text, of the musical. It starred Idina Menzel as Elphaba, Kristin Chenoweth as Glinda, and Joel Gray as the Wizard. Menzel won the 2004 Tony Award for Best Actress, and the show has gone on to break box-office records in New York, Los Angeles, Chicago, and many cities around the world. Although there is no video of the production, the original cast recording is available from Decca Broadway on CD or as a download.

- Although it is not an adaptation of *Wicked* but rather the other way around, the 1939 movie musical *The Wizard of Oz* is a predecessor to *Wicked*. A holiday staple on television, the movie, starring Judy Garland, Billie Burke, Ray Bolger, and Jack Haley, with Margaret Hamilton as the Wicked Witch of the West, is available on DVD from Warner Home Video.

answer. Frex believes it is an evil spirit, but Melena confesses that she might have slept with passing strangers while Frex was away. Nanny tries several unsuccessful folk remedies, and when she is convinced she cannot fix the situation, she returns home.

THE QUADLING GLASSBLOWER

Melena and Elphaba are in the yard when they are surprised by a stranger, a Quadling glassblower named Turtle Heart. Melena feeds him, and he plays with baby Elphaba before blowing her a glass disk in which the future can be seen. He sees Frex and Nanny approaching, but he says they will not arrive until evening, so Melena takes the stranger to bed for the afternoon while Elphaba plays with the glass disk.

GEOGRAPHIES OF THE SEEN AND UNSEEN

Frex returns home with Nanny and is charmed by their new visitor. He explains the geography of Oz to Turtle Heart, who has never left Quadling country, and attempts to explain how the religious views of the Unionists are endangered by the pleasure religion. At dinner, Nanny adds the history of those who believe in Lurline, the Fairy Queen whose daughters, the Ozmas, have ruled for centuries. Frex objects to this talk of Lurline, while Melena reminisces about meeting the current Ozma as a young debutante.

CHILD'S PLAY

Nanny declares that Elphaba must have other children to play with. Melena objects, but Nanny threatens to tell Frex that Melena and Turtle Heart have been having a secret affair. They take the girl to Gawnette's home, where Elphaba joins a pack of grubby neighborhood children.

DARKNESS ABROAD

When Frex says that his mission is to the downtrodden, Turtle Heart says that the Quadlings are downtrodden, and he tells them of the ruby miners who have disrupted the delicate ecosystem of his country. Elphaba speaks her first word, "horrors," and Melena, trying to dissuade Frex from dragging her into the Quadling swamps, confesses that she is pregnant. Later, Elphaba disappears, and after a frantic search, during which Turtle Heart collapses, they find her in the arms of a terrible beast, repeating her first word.

Part II: Gillikin

GALINDA

Galinda, a vain and beautiful Gillikinese girl, meets Dr. Dillamond, a Goat who is a lecturer at her college, on the train into Shiz. Madame Morrible, the headmistress of the college, pairs her with Elphaba as a roommate. Galinda and Elphaba are very different, and they do not really like one another. The Wizard proclaims a ban on all Animal mobility, both in transportation and in the professions. Dr. Dillamond is deeply

upset, and Elphaba takes on his cause. Madame Morrible suggests that Galinda take up sorcery as her academic specialty and hints that if she does so, perhaps Galinda can be freed from her roommate.

BOQ

Boq, a childhood friend of Elphaba's and now a fellow student, climbs a tree to get a better look at the girls' dormitory windows and is caught by Elphaba. Boq admits to having a crush on Galinda, and Elphaba says she will arrange a meeting. When Galinda explains that she cannot return his feelings because he is from a different ethnic group and social class, Boq proposes that they all become friends. Galinda cannot see the point in that. Boq has a chance encounter with Elphaba, who is working for Dr. Dillamond, whom Boq admires, and they become friends over a shared interest in his research. When Elphaba explains that Dr. Dillamond's research is hampered by the inadequate library, Boq offers to use his library to help. Crope and Tibbett join the research efforts, and once a week they all meet at the café. When Elphaba receives an invitation from Galinda to join her and the other rich girls at a lake cottage, Boq insists she accept. When they arrive, they learn it is a cruel joke. Back in Shiz, Dr. Dillamond is murdered.

THE CHARMED CIRCLE

Dr. Dillamond's murder is covered up, and Ama Clutch succumbs to the very disorder that Galinda lied to Madam Morrible about earlier, and she now speaks only to inanimate objects. Galinda changes her name to Glinda, the name Dr. Dillamond called her on the train. Elphaba sends for Nanny and Nessarose. Boq meets Nessarose and Nanny at the coach and is amazed by Nessarose's beauty, despite her handicap of having no arms. Glinda is both awed by Nessarose's strange beauty and annoyed by her demanding neediness and overbearing religious fervor. In a lecture, Dr. Dillamond's successor, Dr. Nikidik, uncorks a bottle of "Extract of Biologic Intention" which accidentally animates a set of stag's horns, nearly killing a new student, the prince Fiyero from Vinkus, who enters the room late. The Thropp sisters are summoned, with Nanny, to Madame Morrible's chambers, where she delivers a pair of miraculous shoes, covered in glass beads that shimmer and pulse, that their father has made for Nessarose. There is no gift for Elphaba.

When Ama Clutch is about to die, Glinda uses all her skills to cast a spell that brings the old woman back to sanity. She tells them that it was the Grommetik that killed Dr. Dillamond. After a stingy funeral, Madame Morrible calls the girls into her office, casts a binding spell on them, and tells them that in return for great power, she can make them Adepts and give them each a section of Oz to rule over. In return, they will have to feed her information that will help keep the Wizard in power. When Glinda and Nessarose try to discuss it afterwards, both girls faint. Later, Avaric proposes they visit the Philosophy Club, a notorious sex club. Elphaba prevents Glinda from going along, while Nanny escorts Nessarose home. Boq, Avaric, Tibbett, Fiyero, Shenshen, and Pfannee all go to the Philosophy Club, which is run by the crone Yackle and the dwarf from the Clock of the Time Dragon. There is a disturbing incident involving a Tiger, from which Tibbett never quite recovers. Elphaba tells Glinda that they need to go to the Emerald City and meet with the Wizard. It takes them nearly a week to get there. After waiting five days, the girls get an audience with the Wizard, who appears as a dancing, luminescent skeleton. When Elphaba presents Dr. Dillamond's evidence—in full faith that if the Wizard only knew the situation, he would reverse his restrictions on Animals—he mocks her and tells her that morality has nothing to do with his decisions. Elphaba replies that if she believed that, she would be obligated to try to kill him. The Wizard accuses them of being pawns in a game they do not understand, and he vanishes. Elphaba tells Glinda she is not going back to Shiz and melts into the crowd.

Part III: City of Emeralds

Five years later, Fiyero encounters Elphaba, but she denies her identity. He tracks her to an abandoned building, forces his way in, and demands that she tell him why she disappeared. She finally admits that she has gone underground and is working to overthrow the Wizard. She tells him he must leave and never come back, that it is too dangerous to be seen with her. Fiyero is surprised by the strength of his attraction to her and vows to come back. She allows him to return, and they begin a deep and passionate love affair. They argue about Elphaba's political work. One day, Fiyero witnesses an act of unspeakable brutality against a family of Bears. Elphaba tells him she needs two weeks of solitude to prepare for what is to come. He objects, fearing she is using it as an

excuse to disappear. During this break, Fiyero encounters Glinda and Crope. Glinda is glamorous and married to a rich man. She tells Fiyero that Nessarose is in town with the Eminent Thropp and that she hates Elphaba for abandoning her. When the two-week break is over, Fiyero is relieved to find Elphaba in her apartment. She warns him not to be in any crowded places on Lurlinemas Eve, and they argue once more about the effectiveness of violence. On Lurlinemas Eve, Fiyero stalks her through the town, watching as she waits in the square outside a theater. Her target is Madame Morrible. Just as Elphaba is about to spring, Madame Morrible is engulfed in a crowd of small children. Fiyero watches Elphaba struggle, then fail in her quest to kill Madame Morrible. He goes back to her apartment, where he is beaten into unconsciousness. Elphaba seeks refuge in the mauntery, or convent, of Saint Glinda. There is blood on her wrists, but she seems unharmed.

Part IV: In the Vinkus

THE VOYAGE OUT

Seven years later, Sister Saint Aelphaba is released from the mauntery into the care of Oatsie Manglehand, a woman drover who is leading a caravan into the Vinkus country. The Mother Superior pays her to take Elphaba and a small boy. Elphaba is silent. She reflects on her life in the mauntery and how it was Tibbett, brought into her infirmary for the dying, who teased her back into herself again. Elphaba and a boy, Liir, befriend the cook's dog, Killyjoy. Elphaba invites a swarm of bees to come along, much to the alarm of the other travelers. As they climb the Kumbrica pass, the cook disappears one night. The caravan emerges from the pass, and a Yunamata messenger arrives to say that the body of the cook has been found at the bottom of a cliff, covered in lesions. The other travelers begin to call Elphaba a witch, and they claim that it was her bees that killed the cook. The group encounters the Scow tribe, led by the massive and elderly Princess Nastoya. Elphaba is summoned to the Scow temple, where the princess reveals herself to be an enchanted Elephant. She tells Elphaba that she must be careful and gives Elphaba three crows. As they approach Kiamo Ko, Elphaba rescues an infant monkey from the jaws of Killyjoy. At Kiamo Ko, Liir says he is staying with her, and although Elphaba still seems not to recognize him, the narrator states that Liir was coming into the house of his father.

THE JASPER GATES OF KIAMO KO

Elphaba arrives at Kiamo Ko determined to confess to Fiyero's widow Sarima that she had had an affair with Fiyero. Elphaba intends to head into the wilderness after that and become a hermit, but her plans are foiled when Sarima refuses to hear her confession. "This is my house and I choose to hear what I want," she tells Elphaba. She puts Elphaba and Liir up in the southeast tower. Fiyero's children take to tormenting Liir, who is slow and fat. Elphaba asks the sisters what happened to Fiyero, and they tell her that Sarima believes he was having an affair with Glinda and that Sir Chuffery had him killed, but they think it was for political reasons, as his body has never been found. Elphaba finds an enchanted Grimmerie, or encyclopedia of magic. Sarima tells her it was left at Kiamo Ko by an old wizard, who said it was from another world and needed a safe hiding place. Manek plays a prank on Liir, hiding him in the fishwell, and then forgets about him in the excitement of Nanny's arrival. She had tracked Elphaba down via Crope, who told her that Elphaba nursed Tibbett. Two days later, they find Liir in the fishwell, and Elphaba must give the boy mouth-to-mouth resuscitation. Sarima explains to Elphaba the Arjiki theory that men require hot anger to survive, while women must cultivate the cold anger of grudges and unforgiveness. While contemplating this, Elphaba gazes on a thick icicle, which then falls from the parapet and kills Manek in the courtyard below.

UPRISINGS

Nanny tells Elphaba that Nessarose has become the Eminent Thropp and Glinda, on a visit, has enchanted Nessarose's shoes to allow her to stand on her own two feet. Shell has become a secret agent in the Munchkinland independence movement. Liir, upon being saved from the fishwell, says that the golden carp told him he is Fiyero's son, an assertion that Sarima rejects. Nanny asks Elphaba whether Liir is her son, and she says she cannot know, since she spent the first year at the maunt in a deep sleep and the second year recovering. She does not remember giving birth, nor does she have any maternal feelings toward the boy, but when she left they insisted she take him along. Manek's death is a terrible blow to the family, as he was the only one who showed promise for recovering the position they lost when Fiyero died. Nor encounters a group of soldiers from the Emerald

City and invites them into the castle to stay. When Nor borrows Elphaba's broom to clean the soldier's quarters, she discovers that it can fly. Elphaba learns how to fly the broom, and after receiving a letter from her father announcing that Munchkinland has seceded from Oz and that Nessarose has declared herself the leader, she decides to travel home to see them. She has a tender reunion with her father and finds Nessarose as self-centered as always. Elphaba refuses both her father's and Nessarose's entreaties to stay and help rule Munchkinland. She returns to Kiamo Ko, only to find that Sarima and her family have been captured and Nanny is alone in the empty castle. Liir was spared, but he seems to have followed the soldiers.

Part V: The Murder and Its Afterlife

A tornado rips through Munchkinland, killing many before dropping Dorothy and her house on Nessarose. Elphaba flies home when she gets the news and finds her father brokenhearted. Glinda tells Elphaba the details, including that she gave Dorothy Nessarose's shoes and sent her to the Emerald City. Elphaba is furious, because Nessarose had promised the shoes to her. After Nessa's funeral, the Wizard summons Elphaba to an audience, where he demands to know whether she will be the next Eminent Thropp. He wants the Grimmerie; he claims that he came to Oz in search of it many years ago. Elphaba demands news of Fiyero's family and is horrified to discover that they have been murdered, except for Nor, whom the Wizard displays to her, mad and in chains. She attempts to trade the book for Nor, but the Wizard refuses. While looking for Dorothy, Elphaba encounters Boq, who is alarmed by her fury and tells her that Dorothy is just a child, not an agent of the Wizard. Elphaba is beside herself with anger at the brutality of the Wizard's regime and at her old friends' collusion. She flies to Shiz to kill Madame Morrible but arrives five minutes too late. Late at night in the park, she encounters the dwarf with the Clock of the Time Dragon. The dwarf shows her a puppet show that indicates the Wizard is her biological father, but Elphaba laughs it off. Agitated, she flies home to Kiamo Ko, where she ceases sleeping. When Dorothy and her friends approach, she becomes convinced that the Scarecrow is Fiyero in disguise. She sends the dogs to greet them and bring them to the castle, but the Tin Woodman kills them all. She sends the crows to pull the mask off the Scarecrow, but he frightens them away. She sends the bees to sting Dorothy to death, but the Scarecrow unstuffs himself to save the others. Finally, she sends the winged monkeys to bring Dorothy and the Lion to the castle. She locks Dorothy into the tower to interrogate her. Dorothy confesses that all she wants is forgiveness. Elphaba accidentally catches her dress on fire. Dorothy, seeking to save her, throws a bucket of water on her. In death, Elphaba discovers that she does indeed have a soul. Dorothy returns to the Emerald City bearing the old bottle of magical elixir. When the Wizard sees it, he flees in his balloon. No one ever sees Dorothy or the magic shoes again.

CHARACTERS

Avaric

Avaric is a handsome and wealthy Gillikinese schoolmate of Elphaba and Galinda, who is responsible for taking everyone to the Philosophy Club. After the death of Madame Morrible, Elphaba has a chance encounter with Avaric, who invites her to dinner. When his jaded friends take the news of Madame Morrible's death as a joke, Elphaba's agitation and despair is multiplied.

Bfee

Bfee is Boq's father and the mayor of Rush Margins.

Boq

Boq is a childhood playmate of Elphaba's whom she befriends while at university in Shiz. He falls in love with Galinda, who does not return his feelings. Boq and Elphaba become friends over a shared interest in Dr. Dillamond's work. After the death of Nessarose, Elphaba encounters Boq while trailing Dorothy. He tells her that Dorothy is just a child and tries to talk Elphaba out of her increasing paranoia, but his efforts only enrage her. She takes his defense as further evidence that Boq, like everyone else, has sold out and accepted the despotism of Oz.

Brr, the Lion

First introduced as a terrified cub upon whom Dr. Nikidik intends to experiment, Brr grows up to become the Cowardly Lion, Dorothy's companion.

Chistery

Chistery is a snow monkey that Elphaba rescues as an infant. Trying to prove Dr. Dillamond's theories, Elphaba teaches him to speak several words, although he never progresses beyond mere mimicry. Later, she surgically implants wings on him, making him her chief flying monkey.

Nick Chopper, Tin Woodman

Nick Chopper is an actual woodman upon whom Nessarose places a spell in return for the freedom of three Animals. The enchanted axe eventually chops off all his limbs and his head, but an enterprising tinsmith makes him replacement parts. He becomes one of Dorothy's companions.

Sir Chuffery

Sir Chuffery is Glinda's stupendously wealthy husband.

Ama Clutch

Ama Clutch is Galinda's chaperone. Her absence the first day of school leads to Galinda being paired with Elphaba as a roommate. After witnessing the murder of Dr. Dillamond, Ama is enchanted by Madame Morrible and then dies.

Crope

Crope is one half of a pair of "inverts," or gay students, who are part of Elphaba's circle at university. Crope eventually informs Nanny that it was Elphaba who nursed Tibbett at the end, thereby leading to Elphaba being discovered after many years' absence.

Dr. Dillamond

Dr. Dillamond is a professor at Shiz. He is a Goat and an advocate for Animal rights. Elphaba becomes his laboratory assistant, and it is through this work that she becomes determined to prove that there is no fundamental difference between humans and Animals. He is murdered by Madame Morrible's Grommetik, after which Elphaba disappears into the radical Animal rights underground.

Dwarf of the Clock of the Time Dragon

An immortal sent to Oz to keep watch over the Grimmerie, the Dwarf originally appears with the Clock of the Time Dragon the night Elphaba is born. Later, he seems to be running the Philosophy Club, and he orchestrates events the night of Tibbett's trauma. The dwarf reappears with the Clock of the Time Dragon after Madame Morrible's death, when he tells Elphaba about Yackle and that the Wizard is probably her biological father.

Fiyero

Heir to the Arjiki throne, Fiyero first appears in Dr. Nikidik's lecture, where he is nearly killed by a pair of enchanted stag's horns. He is a Vinkus prince, has blue diamonds tattooed down his face and chest, has been betrothed since childhood, and seems quite exotic to the students at Shiz. Five years after Elphaba disappears, it is Fiyero who finds her, and they fall deeply in love before he is killed by the Gale Forces. Fiyero is probably Liir's father.

Frex

Frex is a Unionist minister married to Melena, Elphaba's mother. A religious fundamentalist, Frex is determined to win the Munchkinlanders over to Unionism from the dangers of the pleasure faith that the Clock of the Time Dragon represents. He makes the beautiful shoes for Nessarose, shoes that Elphaba sees as proof that her father loves Nessa more than he has ever loved her. Frex knows that Turtle Heart is probably the biological father of Nessarose, but because he too loved Turtle Heart deeply, he sees it as an eternal bond between them all. A kind if ineffectual man, he is loved deeply by all his children, despite his failings.

Frexspar

See Frex

Dorothy Gale

Dorothy, the heroine of *The Wizard of Oz*, is blown into Oz on the tornado that kills Nessarose. She is only a child, and she becomes a pawn of Glinda and the Wizard. Although she has been sent to kill Elphaba, she does so only by accident.

Galinda

Galinda is a vain Gillikinese girl who becomes Elphaba's roommate at Shiz. Although Galinda is intelligent and shows a real talent for sorcery, her true ambitions are for social and financial security. Elphaba keeps trying to get Glinda (as Galinda comes to be known) to think about the political and social realities of Oz, but Glinda is content merely to flit across the surface, relying on her looks and charm to see her through. As

Elphaba and Nessarose become known as the Wicked Witches, Glinda becomes known as the Good Witch. She marries Sir Chuffery. They have no children, and she is stupendously wealthy.

Gawnette

Gawnette is an impoverished resident of Rush Margins who runs a grubby nursery for children. Boq and Elphaba meet in this nursery as children.

Glinda

See Galinda

Grommetik

Madame Morrible's tiktok machine, who serves as her servant, spy, and, in the case of Dr. Dillamond, assassin.

Irji

The eldest son of Fiyero and Sarima, Irji is a soft and dreamy boy who shows a religious bent. He is brutally murdered when the Wizard's forces use the "Paraffin Necklace" on him.

Killyjoy

Killyjoy is Elphaba's beloved dog whom she befriends on the caravan to the Vinkus territory. He becomes the father to a whole pack of wolf-like dogs, and he is killed by the Tin Woodman, who mistakes his mission of welcome for an attack.

Liir

Liir is an urchin boy who accompanies Elphaba to Kiamo Ko. Elphaba cannot be sure whether he is the son of her union with Fiyero or not, since she does not remember much of her first two years in the mauntery. Nearly killed by Manek, who locks him in a fishwell, Liir is both fat and slow, and he is a target of teasing by the other children.

Manek

Manek, the second son of Fiyero and Sarima, is bold and cruel. He tells Liir to hide in the fishwell, nearly killing him. He is in turn killed by a falling icicle, which may or may not be Elphaba's doing.

Oatsie Manglehand

Oatsie leads the caravan across the Kumbrica pass to the Vinkus territory and safely delivers Elphaba and Liir to Kiamo Ko.

Milla

Milla is a classmate of Elphaba's from Shiz; she eventually marries Boq.

Madame Morrible

Headmistress of the girls' college at Shiz where Elphaba, Nessarose, and Glinda all attend university, she is an evil woman, who seeks to enchant the three girls in order to bind them to the Wizard's tyrannical purposes. Elphaba tries to kill her the night Fiyero dies, but she fails. After the death of Nessarose, Elphaba sets out to finish the task, but she arrives too late and must settle for bashing in the head of a dead old woman.

Nanny

Originally Melena's nanny, Nanny arrives after Elphaba is born to help with the frightening green child. She is bawdy and honest, and she is the one person to whom everyone speaks the truth. When Melena dies, she raises Elphaba and Nessarose, and she accompanies Nessarose to Shiz. She finds Elphaba at Kiamo Ko and remains with her in old age.

Princess Nastoya

Nastoya is an enchanted Elephant masquerading as the princess of the Scrow people. She reveals herself to Elphaba and advises her on how to survive in difficult times.

Dr. Nikidik

Dr. Nikidik takes over as professor of life sciences after the death of Dr. Dillamond, but he betrays Dr. Dillamond's cause when he shows a willingness to experiment on the Lion cub, Brr.

Nor

Nor, the daughter of Fiyero and Sarima, is a dreamy child. It is Nor who invites the Wizard's forces into the castle. The lone survivor of the Arjiki royalty, she is kept in chains by the Wizard, and she appears to have lost her mind under his brutal treatment.

Pfannee

Pfannee is a wealthy girl at Shiz who plays a cruel prank on Elphaba and Galinda when she writes a false letter as Galinda, inviting Elphaba to come join them during summer vacation.

Sarima, Dowager Princess of the Arjikis

Sarima is Fiyero's wife, to whom he was betrothed as a child. They have three children together. After leaving the mauntery, Elphaba journeys to Kiamo Ko, the princesses' castle, in order to confess her affair with Fiyero and beg her forgiveness. Sarima, however, refuses to hear Elphaba's confession and refuses to bestow her forgiveness. She is captured and killed by the Wizard's troops while Elphaba is on a visit to Colwen Grounds.

Scarecrow

The Scarecrow is one of Dorothy's companions, whom Elphaba mistakes for Fiyero in disguise. He is also a source of folk superstition among the Munchkinlanders, who make little scarecrow pins and believe in the return of a mythical scarecrow figure.

Shell

Shell is Elphaba's youngest sibling, born during their years in the Quadling country. His birth was the cause of Melena's death, and he grows up to be a secret agent for Munchkinland independence.

Shenshen

Shenshen is one of the cruel wealthy girls at university at Shiz.

Eminent Thropp

Eminent Thropp, Elphaba's great-grandfather, is the head of the Unionist faith in Munchkinland and resides in Colwen Grounds. When he dies, his position is supposed to go to Elphaba, but in her absence Nessarose ascends to the Eminence. After Nessarose dies, Elphaba again refuses to ascend to the Eminence, preferring to leave the Munchkinlanders to rule themselves.

Elphaba Thropp

Also known as the Third Thropp Descending, though she disowns the title, and named Wicked Witch of the West by those who fear her, Elphaba is the protagonist of the novel. Born green, with a mouth full of razor sharp baby teeth, she is an outcast her entire life. She is loved by Fiyero and is probably Liir's mother; she is also, it seems, the biological daughter of the Wizard. Elphaba seeks justice for all creatures. Her lifelong struggle against self-loathing gets the better of her as she sees her hopes and dreams dashed one by one and after she loses her love, Fiyero. She is killed by accident when Dorothy throws a bucket of water on her to douse her skirts, which have caught fire.

Melena Thropp

Elphaba's mother, Melena, is a charismatic, sensual, alcoholic, beautiful woman who marries Frex in order to escape Colwen Grounds. She falls in love with Turtle Heart, and after his death she goes to the Quadling country with Frex as a missionary. She dies giving birth to her third child, Shell. She is loved and mourned by her family.

Nessarose Thropp

Elphaba's younger sister, Nessarose, is born spectacularly beautiful despite not having any arms. An invalid and a religious fanatic, she is needy and self-centered. Frex makes her a pair of exceptionally beautiful shoes, and Glinda enchants them to give Nessarose the balance she has previously lacked so she can finally stand unaided on her own two feet. When Elphaba disappears, Nessarose ascends to the role of Eminent Thropp, and when Munchkinland secedes from Oz, she names herself political leader. Her despotic rule leads her subjects to name her Wicked Witch of the East, and they do not mourn her when Dorothy's house crushes her to death.

Tibbett

Tibbett, with Crope, is one half of a pair of "inverted"—that is, gay—students at the university in Shiz. Tibbett has a traumatic experience in the Philosophy Club from which he really never recovers. Brought into Elphaba's ward of dying patients, he insists on her individuality, and he teases and gossips her back into the world before he dies.

Tin Woodman

See Nick Chopper

Turtle Heart

Turtle Heart is a Quadling glassblower who wanders into Melena's yard one day; the entire family falls in love with him. He stays with them until Nessarose is born. The night of her birth, he is brutally murdered by Munchkinlanders at the behest of the Clock of the Time Dragon. He is probably Nessarose's biological father.

Two, Three, Four, Five, and Six

Sarima's sisters who come to live in Kiamo Ko are named with numbers reflecting their birth order. They are a gossipy bunch who resent their sister for failing to provide them with husbands. They are brutally murdered by the Wizard's forces.

The Wizard

A human from Earth, the Wizard came to Oz in a hot-air balloon seeking the Grimmerie, a book of magic he had seen in Madame Blavatsky's crystal ball. Once in Oz, he becomes a despot and tyrant, dividing the nation along ethnic lines in order to consolidate power. He escapes Oz in his balloon mere hours before the revolutionaries who seek to kill him. He is probably Elphaba's biological father.

Yackle

By turns an old gypsy woman and an ancient maunt, Yackle is a constant and mysterious presence on the edges of Elphaba's story. The Dwarf tells her that Yackle is the opposite of a guardian angel, that while she has been sent to watch over Elphaba, it may not be for the best. It is Yackle who provides the herbs that might have caused Nessarose's disability, Yackle who comforts Elphaba in the mauntery after Fiyero's death, and Yackle who gives her the broom that she eventually discovers is enchanted.

THEMES

Evil

Maguire has stated in a number of interviews that he began writing *Wicked* because he wanted to explore the question of whether a person is born evil or becomes evil over time. Elphaba is certainly born with the fairy-tale indications of evil. She has skin "as green as sin" and a mouth full of razor-sharp teeth—with which her first act after birth is to bite off the finger of one of the crones. Her first word is "horror," and after disappearing she is found in the arms of a demonic animal whose presence is never explained. She certainly seems slated for evil, and yet, as Frex tells her after Nessarose dies, although during those first years she was "a little beast," it was by caring for Nessarose that she became a "normal child." For all her early signs of being "born evil," Elphaba grows up to be a studious, intense, and deeply

TOPICS FOR FURTHER STUDY

- *The Wizard of Oz* was a children's story published by L. Frank Baum in 1900, as a movie released in 1939, and as *Wicked* in 1995. Starting with the original, write a paper comparing and contrasting these three versions of the story. Pay special attention to issues of audience, historical context, and medium (film versus written word).

- Split the class into groups. Using the *Wicked* soundtrack and information available on Stephen Schwartz's Web site (http://www.musicalschwartz.com/wicked.htm), have each group choose an element of the novel that was *not* incorporated into the musical. Write a song, including both lyrics and music, that incorporates that element of the story into the musical. Stage the song, complete with costumes, and make a video of each performance. Have the groups discuss each other's choices of topic, music, lyrics, and performance.

- Maguire used the framework of Baum's novel as a starting point for his own reimagining of the Oz story in three novels. Do the same on a smaller scale. Pick a character and write a first-person monologue (that is, a speech by only one person, who refers to himself or herself as "I") in which your character explains why and how he or she is misunderstood or misrepresented in the novel. Follow your monologue with a short paper analyzing how the story might have turned out differently if this character had only been correctly understood or interpreted by others.

- Elphaba lives in a world in which physiognomy (facial features and appearance) are seen as markers of tribe, ethnicity, and social class. Although her greenness does not mark her as a member of an outcast ethnic or tribal group, the singularity of her skin color does affect both her self-image and her relationships with the people around her. Research the history of physiognomy as it relates to race, class, gender, and theories of human intelligence and character. Prepare a PowerPoint presentation, complete with illustrations, that traces how scientists have interpreted these features in the past and compare them to current views on the subject.

- The geography of Oz is central to many elements of the plot. Workings in teams and using the map in the front of the novel as a starting point, develop a computer game or board game that demonstrates what dangers lie in the various regions of the country and what obstacles must be overcome in order to free the Emerald City from the despotic Wizard. Use as many characters and plot elements from the novel as possible.

- Elphaba is obsessed with the oppression of Animals and is determined to prove Dr. Dillamond's theory that a common thread unites human beings, sentient Animals, and other animals. Although we do not have sentient Animals of the sort that Maguire imagines in the novel, there are many who argue that animals have inherent rights just like human beings do. Research animal rights activist organizations and their arguments. Analyze the premises from which they proceed—what legal rights and moral rights are they claiming for animals? What precedent exists for these claims? Make a multimedia presentation to your class that explains not only the controversy over animal rights but the legal and philosophical underpinnings for those arguments.

caring person. Although she rejects the faith in which she was raised, and indeed rejects even the idea that she possesses a soul, Elphaba spends much of her adult life resisting those who perpetrate injustice against others, whether those others be Animals or the poor or the dying she tends in the mauntery wards. She and Fiyero argue over her tactics when she is part of the terrorist underground, for if to do evil is to cause intentional harm to another, then what Elphaba is planning constitutes an evil act. They argue about whether violence against a repressive regime is ever justified. What about the potential for innocent bystanders to become victims of that violence? "What is worse?" Elphaba asks Fiyero during an argument on the topic. "Suppressing the *idea* of personhood or suppressing, through torture and incarceration and starvation, *real living persons?*" It is the thought of these real living persons, oppressed by the Wizard, that eats at Elphaba and that fuels her work. However, for all her talk, when confronted with a swarm of innocent children who surround Madame Morrible, Elphaba finds herself unable to sacrifice them to the cause. She chooses the immediate good of those children over the potential political good of ridding the world of Madame Morrible. After her failed assassination and Fiyero's subsequent death, Elphaba had a choice. She could have hardened her anger and gone further into the underground, becoming even more radicalized, but instead we see that she is brokenhearted and turns to the mauntery, turns back to the missionary work of her childhood, and works out her brokenness in service to others. Again, this is hardly the work of an evil person.

Elphaba's long period in the mauntery leaves her changed, though. She is less conscious of her own motives and has lost herself in some crucial way. Her first acts of witchcraft come almost unconsciously: the bees that attack the cook, the icicle that kills Manek; neither of these is consciously willed on Elphaba's part, and yet, could a less damaged person have prevented them? By the time Elphaba journeys to Kiamo Ko, she is a deeply wounded person, incapable of most normal human relations. She does not know whether Liir is her son, although the evidence points that way, and in her wounded state she is incapable of treating him as if he is her son, or unwilling to do so. The trauma of losing Fiyero and of failing in her role as terrorist, seems to have broken some capacity in Elphaba for kindness, empathy, and loving action. She retreats deeper and deeper into herself and into her projects, often at the expense of those around her. As Elphaba discovers her magical powers, she seems unable to use them to effect any good in the world, and she retreats deeper and deeper into paranoia and agitation. By the end of the novel, she has ironically assumed

the title "Wicked Witch of the West," and in doing so she seems to have given herself permission to act accordingly. Although her refusal of power could be seen as modesty, it could just as easily be read as a rejection of a leadership role. Maguire has drawn a portrait of a character who, for most of her life, is a virtuous person and yet allows evil to creep up on her nonetheless.

Aristocracy

Although the Wizard has deposed the Ozma, the hereditary ruler of Oz, the country is still ruled by an aristocracy, that is, a select group of people, chosen by birth, social status, and ethnicity. Elphaba is the rightful heir to the position of Eminent Thropp, complete with religious power and the mansion at Colwen Grounds. Throughout the novel, characters size up one another according to physiognomy, heredity, economic status, ethnicity, and status as Animal or human. The assignment of status according to these largely unearned categories is one of the social injustices against which Elphaba rebels. Although Elphaba inherits the status of the Eminence, her green skin and odd appearance have always made her an outcast. As such, her sympathies lie with the outcasts of society, those who do not have access to the sorts of wealth and power that Galinda aspires to and, as Glinda, achieves. Nessarose, also an outcast because of her disability, takes the opposite tack, using her beauty, invalidism, and religiosity to amass both clerical and secular power. Because Elphaba is so exquisitely aware that the possession of power necessarily means having power *over* someone else, she rejects it at every turn. When Nessarose dies, the Wizard wants to know whether she intends to take over rulership of Munchkinland, and Elphaba's natural reply is that it is time for the Munchkinlanders to rule themselves. Trapped in an aristocratic world, Elphaba rebels against the inherent unfairness of the system.

Destiny

Although Elphaba rejects the religion of her father, the very notion of religion, of God, and the idea that she possesses a soul, she cannot quite shake the idea that she, Glinda, and Nessarose are each at the mercy of a predetermined course of events that they do not entirely understand. Elphaba's birth and her bizarre appearance cause her parents to speculate about what she *means*. Frex tells her on his deathbed, "You were born to curse my life," which implies that

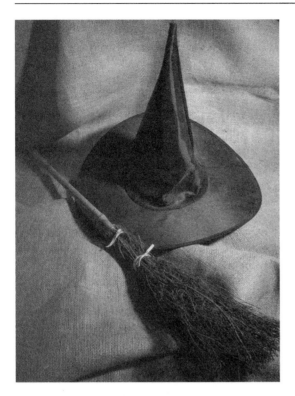

Witch's broom and hat (*Image copyright Samantha Grandy, 2010. Used under license from Shutterstock.com*)

Elphaba exists solely as a lesson to her father. To be seen by all as a signifier of something outside oneself is necessarily to demean one's own humanity and agency (that is, the power to take action), and one of the forces against which Elphaba must continually arm herself is the interpretation of her appearance by others. Even her eventual identity as Wicked Witch of the West is not something she assigns herself but a label that others place onto her. The clothing that she chooses for practicality, humility, and to protect herself from water is read as a witch's costume, and events that Elphaba may or may not have caused are attributed to her. Destiny also appears as a theme when Madame Morrible casts her binding spell on the three girls. Elphaba spends the rest of her life wondering whether it took effect and wondering whether she is the pawn that the Wizard accused her of being when she and Glinda traveled to the Emerald City. Is she the force behind her own life, or is she, as she imagines in her increasing paranoia toward the end of the story, a mere pawn, someone put on earth to act out a predetermined drama? It is a question that Maguire never entirely answers.

STYLE

Fantasy

Although fantasy novels often use elements of the world as we know it, they are distinguished by the way they create, as Roger Fowler and Peter Childs point out in *The Routledge Dictionary of Literary Terms*, "their own coherently organized worlds and myths." In *Wicked*, the use of fantasy is twofold. First, there is the fantasy world created by L. Frank Baum and imagined on screen by Victor Fleming in the 1939 film. Then there is Maguire's reimagining of those versions, both of which were meant for children, as a serious novel for adults. As such, the novel deals with all the nuances and complications of life that we often try to hide from children: sex, violence, political repression, love, death, and mourning. Elphaba is born green but apparently human, with a mouth full of razor sharp baby teeth, a fantastical occurrence that immediately places us in another world. Her father is a minister in the Unionist faith, a faith that resembles any number of Protestant religions in our world but does not match any of them. In addition, Oz comes with its own coherent mythologies, such as the story of Lurline, the Fairy Queen who founded Oz, and her matrilineal descendents, the Ozmas. There is magic still operating in this world, a magic that can be studied in college the way science or religion can be studied. Finally, there are the Animals, fully sentient animals who speak and reason and function in the world as humans do, despite their animal forms. All of these imaginings mark a world separate from our own, similar enough that we recognize the motivations and desires of its inhabitants and yet distant enough to allow us the freedom to believe that reality can unfold there in ways it cannot unfold here.

Anthropomorphism

L. Frank Baum's use of anthropomorphism, that is, the ascribing of human characteristics to animals, is one of the most commonly cited reasons why some librarians refused, for decades, to stock the Oz books on their shelves. Maguire takes literary device one step further by anthropomorphizing some Animals while others remain devoid of human characteristics. He speculates about what the real consequences would be in a world where animals could think and speak and feel as human beings do. Would we need to accord Animals the same rights as humans? What accommodations would we need to make for their physical differences? When Glinda meets Dr. Dillamond on the train, he asks her to hand his ticket to the conductor, since he has only hooves, not fingers. Anthropomorphized animals are a classic element of fantasy literature, but by taking seriously the consequences of a world shared with sentient animals, Maguire asks readers to think through the political, social, and economic ramifications of anthropomorphism. Maguire imagines Animals existing in a sort of limbo, since they are not considered quite human; they are vulnerable to persecution when the Wizard seeks to divide his people in order to keep a political grip on the realm. In this way, one could also read the fate of the Animals in *Wicked* as analogous to the manner in which African Americans were treated for the first two centuries and more of United States history. Defenders of slavery argued that blacks were subhuman, a separate species, and that they were hardly more than sentient animals. Hence, slave owners argued that the slaves could not take care of themselves and were fit only to serve white masters, who were erroneously perceived to be higher on the Great Chain of Being. Maguire alludes to this historical reality in our world by dramatizing how human beings define difference and use it for political gain, and he uses the literary convention of anthropomorphism to serve the adult ambitions of his novel.

Hero/Antihero

Elphaba is in many ways a typical antihero, that is, a flawed and problematic protagonist. Although she does not lack physical or moral courage, her position as an outsider and her refusal to accept any of the mantles of power that are offered to her mark her as antiheroic. In *Wicked*, Elphaba's antiheroic qualities, her odd color, her physical oddness, her spiky reliance on irony, and her intelligence are all contrasted with the traditional qualities of female heroes displayed by her foils (characters that serve to highlight certain qualities through contrast), Glinda and Nessarose. Whereas Elphaba is considered unattractive, Glinda relies on her physical beauty to get ahead. Where Elphaba dives into her studies and is determined to develop her intelligence as far as possible while at Shiz, Glinda often shies away from her own intelligence, content with a sort of glittery performance of charm to see her

through. If Glinda represents the qualities of a traditional female hero (often a princess) of beauty, charm, and conventional goodness, then Elphaba stands next to her as a sort of anti-princess. She is green, ungainly, not charming, and seemingly unconcerned with whether people like her or not. However, her deep concern for true moral goodness and her determination to do the virtuous thing mark her as heroic, although she does not have any of the traditional, external markers of a hero. If Glinda represents one version of female hero, the princess who gets her rich prince in the end, Nessarose represents a different version of the female hero, the religious virgin. Nessarose is also beautiful, despite her handicap. She is the brave invalid who persists in the face of her physical limitations and who turns to religion for solace. Nessarose represents the literary convention of the fierce female virgin, who takes refuge in the public perception of goodness that comes with virginity and religiosity. Maguire makes clear through her actions that these qualities do not necessarily serve Nessarose or her subjects well, that is, she might be religious and virtuous, but that does not save her from becoming a despot whose main ambition is to gain and keep power. Maguire sets up Elphaba as an antihero in order to call into question the traditional qualities of female heroism, and despite Elphaba's fall into wickedness at the novel's end, for most of the story she is the one person who acts in heroic ways, despite her antiheroic appearance.

HISTORICAL CONTEXT

In an interview for the *TheaterMania* Web site, Maguire told Erika Milvy that when he began writing *Wicked* in the early 1990s, he wanted to "explore, using fictional techniques, the nature and the range of evil—and of how we come to decide who is bad and who is good." Although he originally intended to write about Hitler, he found as he worked that his models for evil came closer to the villains of his young adulthood, particularly Richard Nixon of the Watergate scandal. For someone like Maguire, born in 1956, the political scandals of the 1970s were a loss of political innocence. Learning that President Nixon had overstepped the authority of

COMPARE
&
CONTRAST

- **1900:** L. Frank Baum publishes *The Wizard of Oz* to immediate critical acclaim and popular success. In 1902, Baum stages the first musical version of the book.

  1995: Maguire reimagines the story of the Wicked Witch of the West and publishes it as *Wicked*, his first adult novel.

  Today: Maguire continues to reimagine Baum's world of Oz, adding two sequels: *Son of a Witch* and *A Lion among Men*. Meanwhile, the Broadway musical *Wicked* breaks box-office records in cities around the world.

- **1900:** The first wave of the feminist movement is coming to a close as pioneers such as L. Frank Baum's mother-in-law, Matilda Joslyn Gage, and Elizabeth Cady Stanton begin to die. At the turn of the twentieth century, women win the vote only in Colorado and Idaho. It is not until 1920 that the Nineteenth Amendment extends the right to vote to women on a national level.

  1995: First Lady Hillary Rodham Clinton travels to Beijing and gives a forceful address to the United Nations World Women's Conference, declaring: "If there is one message that echoes forth from this conference, let it be that human rights are women's rights, and women's rights are human rights, once and for all."

  Today: After running for president, Hillary Rodham Clinton loses the nomination to Barack Obama but is appointed as his Secretary of State, continuing her lifelong commitment to the "pursuit of our human rights agenda, not compromising on our principles, but doing what is most likely to make them real."

- **1900:** Although William McKinley wins the presidential election, he is assassinated in September 1901 after serving a mere six months. Theodore Roosevelt becomes the nation's youngest president at age forty-two and institutes a number of Progressive reforms, including railroad regulation, meat and food inspection legislation, and reining in corporate wrongdoing.

  1995: While President Clinton ran for president in 1992 on a number of progressive positions, his failure to secure health-care reform combined with his support of the Welfare Reform bill in 1995 loses the support of many progressives in his own party.

  Today: Another surge of progressive political optimism accompanies President Barack Obama into office in 2009, when he begins his term by tackling health-care reform.

---

his office by authorizing unconstitutional wiretaps of his enemies, using the Central Intelligence Agency, the Federal Bureau of Investigation, the Internal Revenue Service, and even the National Security Agency to spy on his political rivals and that he had allowed supporters to break into the headquarters of the Democratic National Committee was enormously shocking, so shocking that it led the president to resign shortly before impeachment hearings were to begin. The United States had always prided itself on being a nation of laws, a nation that respected the separation of powers, and Nixon's violation of those

principles was a blow to the country. As Maguire said in the same interview with Milvy, "Nixon and Watergate was the first time I felt politically cynical."

Although it was Nixon that Maguire was thinking of when he created the Wizard, it was actually the steady erosion of constitutional rights as evidenced in scandals such as the Iran-Contra affair that Maguire saw happening in American politics throughout the 1980s and into the 1990s that inspired him. In the same interview in *TheaterMania*, Maguire noted: "Everything the Wizard says is wonderful and creepy and it could also be

Maguire's novel was adapted into a musical that went on to win a Tony Award. The Broadway, West End, and touring productions enjoyed great popularity among theater-goers.

(© Richard Levine | Alamy)

said about Nixon and to some extent, Ronald Reagan."

By the time the musical adaptation debuted in 2003, the creeping despotism of the Wizard's regime began to look to many like an allegory for the erosion of privacy protections that the Bush administration instituted after the terrorist attacks of September 11, 2001, in an effort to prevent future attacks. As Maguire told *Theater-Mania*, "None of us could know when Bush was elected that he would turn out to have such dictatorial tendencies, or that 9/11 was going to stoke up a certain kind of patriotism that would promote a blindness and muteness among citizens and members of Congress ... that we would be living under a spell for seven years."

Although Maguire has been outspoken about the specific American politicians upon whom

he based the Wizard and his tactics of fear-mongering, stoking ethnic and class divisions, and oppression of minorities, the novel is not a strict political allegory. The Wizard's tactics are representative of a set of techniques common to despots. Along the same lines, although the tactics of Elphaba's revolutionary anarchists are similar to the tactics used during the late 1980s and early 1990s by both political subversives in Latin America and ecological protest groups in the United States, those activities are not an exact allegory either. Although there are historical precedents for some of the characters and their actions, the novel remains a dramatization of how evil affects all parties: the victims, the perpetrators, and those who resist its forces.

CRITICAL OVERVIEW

When *Wicked* was published in 1995 it was Maguire's first book for adults. He had made a name for himself in the seventeen years he had been publishing children's books, so the adult themes and content of *Wicked*, as well as his audacious retelling of an American classic, came as something of a surprise to critics used to thinking of him as a children's author. Michiko Kakutani of the *New York Times* was one of Maguire's first real critics, claiming that Maguire's book was "deadly dull." Her central objection seemed to be that where Baum's original was charming because it was pure fantasy, Maguire's "insistence on politicizing Oz and injecting it with a heavy dose of moral relativism turns a wonderfully spontaneous world of fantasy into a lugubrious allegorical realm." Kakutani was in the minority, however, as novelist John Updike, quoted by Stephen Fraser in his interview with Maguire in *Writing!*, called it "an amazing novel," and Robin J. Schwartz in *Entertainment Weekly* said the book was "anything but heavy-handed ... thanks to Maguire's impish sense of humor." Robert Rodi, in the *Albany Times Union*, noted that the genius of the book lies in the way that Maguire takes a universally recognizable character and asks the reader to "accept a retrofitted history of how an otherwise well-meaning woman went so wrong."

The novel sold almost two million copies, and in 2003, it was made into an award-winning Broadway musical. The musical version has played in cities around the world and has brought millions more readers to Maguire's novel.

CRITICISM

Charlotte M. Freeman

Freeman is a freelance writer and former academic. In this essay, she addresses how Maguire mixes premodern and modern storytelling modes in order to explore the complicated question of the origin of evil in Wicked.

L. Frank Baum's original story of *The Wizard of Oz* was a fairly simplistic tale of good and evil written for children. In it, a young girl is whisked away from all that is familiar to her, and she accidentally kills a wicked witch. In the movie version, Dorothy is clearly a young woman, but in the original book she is just as clearly a small child, a girl of about eight or so, and she manages to triumph over evil through a combination of native goodness, childlike innocence, and dumb luck. In fairy tales, good and evil are binary opposites. Characters are either wholly good or wholly evil, and good usually triumphs over evil. In adult fiction, good and evil rarely appear in such a black-and-white fashion, and characters tend to demonstrate some combination of the two. The nature of evil and its manifestation in the world is one of the oldest subjects of literature. In *Wicked*, Maguire manages to combine central elements of fantasy and tragedy. By setting the novel in a fantasy world, he hearkens back to an older storytelling tradition, one in which evil is acknowledged as an independent force operating in the world, in order to explore whether evil is external to character. However, because he is also interested in how character develops, he also avails himself of the themes and techniques of the modern novel of psychological realism in order to examine how, and whether, Elphaba becomes wicked.

It is Oatsie Manglehand who articulates the external theory of evil when she notes, "To the grim poor there need be no *pour quoi* tale about where evil arises; it just arises; it always is." However, in the same speech, she also proposes the opposite theory, that evil is something that arises from within, when she asks about "how the witch became wicked, or whether that was the right choice for her—is it ever the right choice? Does the devil ever struggle to be good again, or if so is he not a devil? It is at the very least a question of definitions." In order to examine these questions, Maguire resorts to a premodern model of storytelling, the fantasy or fairy tale, in which evil, like the demonic animal in whose arms they find the baby Elphaba, can roam throughout the land. The

> ALTHOUGH LOSS OF INNOCENCE THAT ELPHABA SUFFERS IN THE WIZARD'S CHAMBERS AND HER SUBSEQUENT DISAPPEARANCE INTO THE UNDERGROUND BELONG TO THE MODERN WORLD OF PSYCHOLOGICAL REALISM RATHER THAN TO THE PREMODERN WORLD OF FAIRY TALES, HER ACT OF HUBRIS IN THE WIZARD'S CHAMBER BELONGS TO THE WORLD OF PREMODERN TRAGEDY."

modern realistic novel, relying as it does on psychological explanation, has no way of accounting for evil as an independent external force, whereas in both fantasy and tragedy, the forces of evil and anarchy are waiting to be unleashed into the world by the error of the hero. In premodern stories, from *Oedipus* to *King Lear* to the fairy tales of Grimm, evil is an animate force, always lurking on the edges of the world, or as Oatsie puts it in *Wicked*, "It always is." Whether evil is the devil, or a beast, or a mysterious gypsy maunt, or a dwarf with an enormous tiktok machine that seems to be able to see the future, in older forms of storytelling, there is room to introduce evil as something outside our control, something that can be unleashed in the world by inattention, by mistake, or by deliberate action.

It is into such a world that Elphaba is born. She appears to be sent from the devil, with skin as "green as sin," a mouth full of deadly sharp baby teeth, and had the temperament of a "little beast." Elphaba's babyhood is one long minefield. Her first word is "horror," after which she disappears, only to be found crouched in the arms of a terrifying beast, the likes of which no one has ever seen before. These are not the hallmarks of modern, realistic, psychological storytelling. Elphaba's babyhood takes place in a premodern storytelling world, one in which evil is loose in the world and characters are constantly on alert against it.

Although Elphaba's babyhood takes place in this premodern storytelling mode, her later childhood and adolescence seem to take place

WHAT DO I READ NEXT?

- *Son of a Witch* is the sequel to *Wicked*. Released in 2005, this novel follows the story of Liir, the son of Elphaba and Fiyero. Like *Wicked*, this is an adult novel and contains scenes of violence and adult sexuality. It picks up where the first novel left off and continues Maguire's quest to locate the source of evil in society.

- *A Lion among Men* completes the "Wicked Years" trilogy. Published in 2008, this book follows Brr, otherwise known as the Cowardly Lion, who does indeed turn out to be the same terrified lion club that Dr. Nikidik used in his life sciences experiment in *Wicked*. Brr, searching for information about Elphaba, seeks out the dying maunt, Yackle. As armies close in around the Emerald City, Brr and Yackle spar to obtain crucial information before it is too late. Like Maguire's other two novels in this series, this is a book for adults and contains adult scenes of violence and sexuality.

- *The Wonderful Wizard of Oz* by L. Frank Baum was published in 1900 and is the first in a series of forty books chronicling the history of Oz. Unlike *Wicked*, *The Wonderful Wizard of Oz* is indeed a story for children. The original illustrations make it clear that Dorothy was, unlike the 1939 movie, quite a young child.

- Maguire cites *The Sword in the Stone* by T. H. White as an example of the kind of book he wanted to write when he started *Wicked*. Originally published in 1938, it is the story of a young boy named Wart who befriends a magician named Merlin. Wart must undergo many trials, including transformation into several animals, and stand up to evil, before it becomes clear that he is

the future King Arthur. The first of four books that were eventually published as *The Once and Future King*, this would be suitable for readers too young for the adult themes of the Maguire novels.

- *Animal Rights: Current Debates and New Directions* (2005) is an anthology edited by Cass Sunstein and Martha Nussbaum, two law professors noted for their work on behalf of oppressed peoples. (Nussbaum is also a noted philosopher.) This is an academic anthology that brings together essays by philosophers, activists, and lawyers working on behalf of animal rights. Although not an easy read, it is a balanced introduction to all sides of these difficult issues.

- Alison Lurie writes novels for both adults and children, and she has long been interested in children's literature. In *Boys and Girls Forever: Children's Classics from Cinderella to Harry Potter*, published in 2002, she collects fourteen essays on the enduring appeal of fairy tales and children's literature. For readers interested in the way Maguire used the material of Oz, Lurie's essays should prove illuminating.

- *Daughter of the Flames*, published by Zoe Marriott in 2008, is the story of Zira, the last surviving heir to the Ruan throne. Although her surroundings are somewhat Middle Eastern, she lives in a fantasy world unique to the novel. Zira must pass through fire in order to regain her title, and she must battle her uncle Abheron, who has usurped her throne. *Daughter of the Flames* is a satisfying young-adult fantasy novel with an interesting multicultural twist.

in a sort of modern world of psychological realism. In the Quadling country, Elphaba's childhood seems to have been one of remarkable

obedience and piety. After Nessarose is born, Elphaba is largely put in charge of her care. She loves and obeys her father, and she helps him that renders Elphaba such a compelling and ultimately sympathetic character, despite her eventual disintegration. With *Wicked*, Maguire has demonstrated that one can successfully mix storytelling modes.

Source: Charlotte M. Freeman, Critical Essay on *Wicked: The Life and Times of the Wicked Witch of the West*, in *Novels for Students*, Gale, Cengage Learning, 2011.

Mal Vincent

In the following review, Vincent explains how the Broadway production of Wicked *has helped the sales of the novel.*

. . . "YOU CURSED BRAT! Look at what you've done. I'm melting. . . . Who would have thought a good little girl like you could destroy my beautiful wickedness?"

Gregory Maguire scoffs at the last gasps of the famed Wicked Witch of the West in the 1939 film *The Wizard of Oz.* There is a hint of amusement about the mischief he has caused by trying to "correct" the world's perception of one of the most evil presences in popular culture.

His book *Wicked: The Life and Times of the Wicked Witch of the West* is the source for the blockbuster Broadway musical that moves into Chrysler Hall on Wednesday for a two-and-a-half-week stay.

In it, he created an Oz before Dorothy's arrival that undercuts the characterizations of the movie.

Why is the Wicked Witch seen as pure evil, and the Wizard of Oz as kindly? Which one forced Dorothy, a homeless girl, and her ragamuffin friends to undertake an assassination?

When you read Maguire's book, it's easy to believe that the Wizard is a political tyrant who fears the Witch's opposition. And Maguire's witch is not really wicked at all. She is misunderstood and used—smart but lonely, living with the birth defect of being green. Before Dorothy Gale dropped into the Land of Oz, the green witch, Elphaba, was a social and political rebel who opposed the tyrannical Wizard.

"What I've written I regard as a homage to L. Frank Baum (author of the books about the Land of Oz upon which the movie was based) and to the mystery of what actually is evil and what is good. So often, we know only what we're told and, after all, we were only told Dorothy's side of the story."

The witch is headed for Norfolk from Omaha, Neb., where she hung out for the past few weeks of her musical tour. She's not traveling by broomstick, but in a caravan of 14 trucks that are needed to wheel in the musical *Wicked* which has a preview performance Wednesday at Chrysler Hall before a formal opening night Thursday. It will play through May 31 in a booking that is expected to sell $4 million in tickets before it leaves town.

Maguire's book was published in 1995 and had a slow start.

"I once did a reading, and there were seven people there. One of them was a homeless man who just wanted to get in out of the cold," he said, talking by phone from his home in Concord, Mass.

It was only after the musical became a hit—it's one of the biggest-selling shows in Broadway history—that book sales took off.

Maguire said he has seen the musical 37 times, and he sees something different in it every time. He doesn't mind the simplification of his book, and he loves the music.

"A book is one thing, a musical is another. A movie is another. They all have the mirror that they hold up. I got out of the way and let them make their musical. After all, L. Frank Baum didn't bother me in adding a new twist to his work, so I thought I should return the favor."

The show has music and lyrics by Stephen Schwartz as well as flying monkeys and sly, teasing references to those ruby red slippers (which were silver in the book). And did you ever wonder what the witch's dead sister, the Wicked Witch of the East, was like? The one killed when Dorothy's house fell on her. Now, thanks to Maguire, we know. Her *name* was Nessarose, and she was born with no arms, a side effect of the drug her mother took to keep her from being green, like her older sister.

Then, there is Glinda, known as the Good Witch of the North. In Maguire's version, she is a kind of sorority girl who believes "popularity is everything." She's crushed when she has to room with the green girl from Munchkinland, but they become good friends—until Glinda gives those precious slippers to Dorothy. Poor Elphaba knew that she was a loner, an outsider, and that her father would never have given her the slippers. She is an animal-rights activist, fighting the Wizard's plan to outlaw all talking animals and send them back to the farms.

Wild stuff. It was Maguire's first adult book after short-story spoofs on *Cinderella* and *Snow White*. He expanded it into a series on "the Wicked Years" that includes *Son of a Witch*, about Elphaba's purported son, and the recent best seller *A Lion Among Men*, about how the Cowardly Lion got cowardly.

But Elphaba is no doormat. She states that no wizard will bring her down. She has an affair with a prince named Fiyero.

Maguire laughs when he's asked if he's going to next make a saint out of Adolf Hitler.

"It's strange that you mention that because that is exactly the book I wanted to write. I am interested in how we see some people as so totally good or totally evil and how wrong that is. Getting into it, though, I realized that I couldn't do a fiction novel about Adolf Hitler because so much was known about him—but the Wicked Witch of the West has huge gaps in her history. No one knows what made her turn evil. I could let my imagination run wild and concoct anything about her."

To most people, it is a minor moment in the musical *Wicked*, but to Gregory Maguire there is one line that moves him tremendously each time he hears it. It is when Elphaba says, "It's my fault" in describing her sister's pale, armless state. He identifies because in 1954 in an Albany, N.Y., hospital his mother died from complications she suffered giving birth to him. He was raised by nuns who named him Gregory the Executive for his somber expression. He received his doctorate in English and American Literature from Tufts University and has championed educational charities to promote children's education.

Five years ago he married Andy Newman, a painter, in one of the first legal gay marriages in Massachusetts. They have three children: Luke, 11, and Alex, 8, adopted from Cambodia, and Helen, 7, from Guatemala. None of them has read *Wicked*.

Maguire says he has a financial piece of the play, but not a big percentage. He plans the fourth, and last, of the Wicked Years books to be called *Out of Oz*—how everyone leaves the magical country.

"I haven't started writing it yet. I'm spending too much time going to the theater."

Source: Mal Vincent, "Something *Wicked* This Way Comes," in *Virginian-Pilot*, May 11, 2009.

Kaite Mediatore

In the following review, Mediatore explains that in Wicked, *Maguire's Elphaba is a stranger and the rebel in her own land.*

Struggling to live in new worlds is no unfamiliar task to women. Historically, men have been the ones to discover new ground and convince the locals that it's in everyone's best interest to have new neighbors. Then the women are brought in to mold a society closely resembling the one everyone just left.

If men are the conqueror-explorers of unknown worlds, then, women are the shapers and builders of new societies. Sacrifice, loneliness, and despair are only some of the hardships women face while carving a place for themselves, whether in the real world, as portrayed in popular fiction, or in the thousand other worlds built in science fiction and fantasy. Just as we managed, thank you very much, to carve a place for ourselves on the desolate American prairie, so, too, can we fend off the Plutonians invading the ice-planet Zorak. Yet, for some female readers, it's difficult to suspend enough disbelief to follow the strong-willed women of sf and fantasy novels on their galactic quests to inhabit better worlds. But c'mon ladies, you can boldly go where you've never read before. Just turn the first page.

Start exploring a whole new world gradually, the way anthropologist Andrea Mitchell does in Susan Price's *The Sterkarm Handshake*, a marvelous combination of historical adventure, passionate romance, and time travel. Andrea is no beauty by contemporary standards, but as a time-traveling historical consultant for a twenty-first-century corporation, she finds herself inhabiting the sixteenth century, an era when her fleshy form is definitely in vogue. She is much admired by the Scottish tribesmen called Sterkarms and falls in love with one of their warriors. Trouble ensues, however, and Andrea faces sacrificing her lover in her century to save him in his own. Fans of Diana Gabaldon's Outlander series now have a new hero and heroine to appreciate.

Elphaba, in Gregory Maguire's *Wicked*, is a stranger in her own land, Oz, and only the appearance of another outsider will grant her the acceptance she craves. Born with a quick wit and emerald skin, Elphaba risks her place at Shiz University to fight the reigning Wizard's plan to destroy all the talking animals of Oz. But will her defense of the animals undermine her only chance at love and tear her further from society? Readers will be sucked into this fantastic secret history of Oz, which tells the story of the Wicked Witch of the West before she became wicked.

Imagine waking in a peculiar place with no memory of your arrival. That's what happens to Lilith when Earth, as she knows it, is destroyed by nuclear war. She and others are rescued by the Oankale, aliens as mysterious as they are repugnant, who plan to generate a new world using the surviving humans and members of their own species. Repulsed by her captors yet strangely drawn to them, Lilith becomes the sole human to forge a tenuous bond between the Oankale and the Earth dwellers. *Dawn*, by Octavia Butler, recounts Lilith's tenacious struggle to build a recognizable and functioning world even in the face of betrayal.

Readers who enjoy heroines who can kick cosmic butt should hop aboard the spaceship with Honor Harrington. In her debut adventure, David Weber's *On Basilisk Station*, Honor is determined to prove herself a capable leader on a remote outpost, even if her obsolete ship carries only defective weapons. Honor moves smoothly in her technical and militaristic world as she fights for acceptance from her crew and superiors. C. S. Forester meets Han Solo in this sweeping space yarn with the steady hand of a woman at the helm.

Source: Kaite Mediatore, "Mistress of Her Intergalactic Way," in *Booklist*, April 13, 2005, p. 1443.

J. Kelly Nestruck

In the following article, Nestruck claims that Maguire's success as a novelist is due mainly to the work of independent bookstores and the appeal of retelling children's stories to adults.

For Gregory Maguire, fairy tales are a serious business. The 49-year old author of *Wicked*, a revisionist version of The Wizard of Oz told from the Wicked Witch of the West's point of view, and *Mirror, Mirror*, a re-imagining of Snow White set in Renaissance Italy, has made his living retelling children's stories to adults for nearly a decade now.

"What brought me to them is a sense of how universal and accommodating the very pared down fairy-tale narrative is," Maguire explains.

"Usually it is devoid of too much culturally specific material: It's a glove that fits every hand."

In a fragmented age where niche television channels and Internet sites exist for any and every taste under the sun, the folk tales of Hans Christian Andersen and the Brothers Grimm remain one of the last universal cultural touchstones. Which goes a long way toward explaining the widespread success of Maguire's four adult novels, each of which takes the core elements of familiar tales and spins them into more complex stories: There's something for readers of all ages and all cultures to grab on to. "I drape my stories on the hangers of these old tales," says Maguire, who began his career as a professor of children's literature in Boston. "I rarely make fun of the originals; all I try to do is amplify them."

His most successful novel remains *Wicked: The Life and Times of the Wicked Witch of the West*, his 1995 apologia for Dorothy's archnemesis. *Wicked* has since morphed into a hot Broadway musical, which, it was announced last week, will play in Toronto next spring as part of the Mirvish subscription season.

In order to keep his focus on writing novels, Maguire kept his distance from the development of the musical. *Wicked*'s success on Broadway, however, has left him considering the possibility of branching out into theatre and screenplays. "That thing called the lure of the theatre, there's something genuine to it," he says.

Maguire's success as a novelist is due mainly to the work of independent bookstores, which have championed his work from the beginning. For the last eight years—with the exception of one short dip—*Wicked* has continually sold more copies every six months than it did the six months previous. To a lesser extent, his other books—*Confessions of an Ugly Sister*, a contrarian Cinderella, and *Lost*, a ghost story that combines Jack the Ripper lore with a Dickensian narrative—have followed this pattern as well.

All of which led to *Mirror, Mirror*—a return to fairy-tale form after *Lost*—spending a few weeks on *The New York Times* extended bestsellers list (which lists the Top 30 books, instead of the Top 10) last fall, his best debut yet. "My books don't age in the same way that a lot of contemporary fiction does," Maguire explains. "Cinderella's in a sense no older now than it was six years ago when I wrote *Confessions of an Ugly Stepsister*."

Maguire's attraction to fairy tales surely springs from his unusual childhood in Albany, N.Y., which sounds like a fairy tale itself. His mother died while giving birth to him and, while his father tried to pull himself together after his loss, Maguire and his three older siblings were placed in orphanages. After his father remarried—to his mother's best friend, the four children were reunited and three more children were born into the family, bringing the total of kids to the magic number seven (see the Von Trapp family, dwarves in Snow White).

Things were very strict in the reconstituted household. "Because my mother died, I think that my father, who was already a fairly nervous person anyway, was even more alarmed about losing another life on his watch," explains Maguire. The children were not allowed to ride two-wheel bicycles until they were 16 and had passed the New York driver's licence exam. They were only allowed 30 minutes of television a week and had to agree as a family what half an hour to watch.

This left only two escape routes for the Maguire children: The local library and their imaginations. It's no surprise then that five of the seven children have grown up to be writers of some sort. "It's as if we were a little Bronte family in an Irish-Catholic neighbourhood in the 1950s," jokes Maguire, who now has three children of his own, adopted with his partner from Cambodia and Guatemala. "None of us really regret our upbringing now, since we're all happy adults and pretty functioning."

While Maguire makes a fine living from his books—he has written children's literature as well—his adult versions of fairy tales have yet to garner him much in the way of serious critical praise. "Will there ever be a *New York Review of Books* article on my collected works?" he asks. "I wouldn't mind if that happened, even after I am dead. But if it doesn't happen, I'm not going to sit around and beat my head against the wall."

Source: J. Kelly Nestruck, "Telling a Familiar Tale: Maybe His Fairy-Tale Childhood Inspired Gregory Maguire to Adapt the Classics for Adults. Or Maybe It's Because They're 'a Glove That Fits Every Hand,'" in *National Post*, March 30, 2004, p. AL5.

SOURCES

Baum, L. Frank, *The Annotated Wizard of Oz*, edited by Michael Patrick Hearn, W. W. Norton, 2000, pp. 89–90.

Boyer, Paul S., *Oxford Companion to American History*, Oxford University Press, 2001, pp. 677, 819.

Childs, Peter, and Roger Fowler, "Fantastic," in *The Routledge Dictionary of Literary Terms*, Routledge, 2006, pp. 82–83.

"Father Knows Best," in *Oprah.com*, http://www.oprah.com/relationships/Incredible-Fathers-and-Their-Families/10 (accessed January 4, 2010).

Fraser, Stephen, "Wicked with Words, Gregory Maguire Reimagines Fairy Tale," in *Writing!* February-March 2006, p. 8.

Goldberg, Bev, "Gregory Maguire's Wicked Beginnings," in *AL Inside Scoop*, July 15, 2009, http://www.alx.ala.org/insidescoop/2009/07/15/gregory-maguires-wicked-beginnings/ (accessed January 3, 2010).

"Gregory Maguire Brews Another Wicked Mix of Historical Fiction and Timeless Myth," in *Bookselling This Week*, September 16, 2003, http://news.bookweb.org/m-bin/printer_friendly?article_id = 1800 (accessed January 3, 2010).

Kakutani, Michiko, "Let's Get This Straight, Glinda Was the Bad One?," in *New York Times*, October 24, 1995, http://www.nytimes.com/1995/10/24/books/books-of-the-times-let-s-get-this-straight-glinda-was-the-bad-one.html?scp = 1&sq = Gregory + Maguire&st = nyt (accessed January 3, 2010).

Landler, Mark, "Clinton Defends Human Rights Approach," in *New York Times*, December 14, 2009, http://www.nytimes.com/2009/12/15/world/15clinton.htm (accessed January 3, 2010).

Maguire, Gregory, *Wicked: The Life and Times of the Wicked Witch of the West*, HarperCollins, 1995.

Milvy, Erika, "A Wicked Writer," in *TheaterMania.com*, February 23, 2009, http://www.theatermania.com/sanfrancisco/news/02-2009/a-wicked-writer_17655.html (accessed January 3, 2010).

Minzesheimer, Bob, "'Wicked' Author Gregory Maguire Casts His Spell," in *USA Today*, October 12, 2005, http://www.usatoday.com/life/books/news/2005-10-12-gregory-maguire-interview_x.htm (accessed January 3, 2010).

Rodi, Robert, "'Wicked' a Marvelous Fantasy Novel of Ideas," in *Albany Times Union*, November 28, 1995, p. D2.

Schwartz, Robin J., "Wicked, The Life and Times of the Wicked Witch of the West," in *Entertainment Weekly*, November 17, 1995, p. 73.

Tyler, Patrick E., "Hillary Clinton, in China, Details Abuse of Women," in *New York Times*, September 6, 1995, http://www.nytimes.com/1995/09/06/world/hillary-clinton-in-china-details-abuse-of-women.html (accessed January 3, 2010).

FURTHER READING

Auxier, Randall E., and Phil Seng, eds., *The Wizard of Oz and Philosophy*, Open Court, 2008.

> This book is part of a series that examines classics of popular culture from a philosophical point of view. Many of the questions that Maguire addresses in *Wicked* are examined in this collection, including moral theories of virtue and evil.

De Giere, Carol, *Defying Gravity: The Creative Career of Stephen Schwartz from "Godspell" to "Wicked,"* Applause Books, 2008.

> This biography of Stephen Schwartz explores the creative process of this celebrated composer. De Giere reconstructs both Schwartz's hits and his flops. The book includes an appendix of "Creativity Notes" about the creative process.

Hearn, Michael Patrick, ed., *The Wizard of Oz*, Schocken Books, 1987.

> This is a collection of critical essays on L. Frank Baum's book, the MGM movie, and the historical reception of the original novels. Published before Maguire's novel, it does not contain any references to *Wicked* or to the musical.

Schiebinger, Lorna, *Nature's Body: Gender in the Making of Modern Science*, Rutgers, 2004.

> Elphaba states that after she proves Dr. Dillamond's theory that Animals and humans are fundamentally the same, she wants to extend that work to gender. In this book, Schiebinger traces the manner in which culture influenced the scientists such as Linnaeus, who did the first classification of life forms. She then goes on to trace how racism and sexism affected the so-called scientific classification of beings and how that in turn affects current scientific exploration.

Singer, Peter, *In Defense of Animals: The Second Wave*, Wiley Blackwell, 2005.

> Peter Singer is a professor of bioethics at Princeton University. His work on the nature of moral thinking, based on utilitarianism, led him in 1975 to write one of the first books on animal rights, *Animal Liberation. In Defense of Animals: The Second Wave* continues his thinking on this subject, while taking into account the significant work that has been done by others concerned with animal consciousness and animal rights since that time.

SUGGESTED SEARCH TERMS

Gregory Maguire

Gregory Maguire AND Wicked

Gregory Maguire AND interview

Wicked AND novel

Stephen Schwartz AND Wicked

L. Frank Baum

L. Frank Baum AND Oz

Wicked Witch of the West AND Maguire

Maguire AND Baum

Gregory Maguire AND evil

Gregory Maguire AND fantasy AND Wicked

Glossary of Literary Terms

A

Abstract: As an adjective applied to writing or literary works, abstract refers to words or phrases that name things not knowable through the five senses.

Aestheticism: A literary and artistic movement of the nineteenth century. Followers of the movement believed that art should not be mixed with social, political, or moral teaching. The statement "art for art's sake" is a good summary of aestheticism. The movement had its roots in France, but it gained widespread importance in England in the last half of the nineteenth century, where it helped change the Victorian practice of including moral lessons in literature.

Allegory: A narrative technique in which characters representing things or abstract ideas are used to convey a message or teach a lesson. Allegory is typically used to teach moral, ethical, or religious lessons but is sometimes used for satiric or political purposes.

Allusion: A reference to a familiar literary or historical person or event, used to make an idea more easily understood.

Analogy: A comparison of two things made to explain something unfamiliar through its similarities to something familiar, or to prove one point based on the acceptedness of another. Similes and metaphors are types of analogies.

Antagonist: The major character in a narrative or drama who works against the hero or protagonist.

Anthropomorphism: The presentation of animals or objects in human shape or with human characteristics. The term is derived from the Greek word for "human form."

Anti-hero: A central character in a work of literature who lacks traditional heroic qualities such as courage, physical prowess, and fortitude. Anti-heroes typically distrust conventional values and are unable to commit themselves to any ideals. They generally feel helpless in a world over which they have no control. Anti-heroes usually accept, and often celebrate, their positions as social outcasts.

Apprenticeship Novel: See *Bildungsroman*

Archetype: The word archetype is commonly used to describe an original pattern or model from which all other things of the same kind are made. This term was introduced to literary criticism from the psychology of Carl Jung. It expresses Jung's theory that behind every person's "unconscious," or repressed memories of the past, lies the "collective unconscious" of the human race: memories of the countless typical experiences of our ancestors. These memories are said to prompt illogical associations that trigger powerful emotions in the reader. Often, the emotional process is primitive, even primordial. Archetypes are the literary images that grow out of the "collective unconscious." They appear in literature as incidents and plots that repeat basic patterns of life. They may also appear as stereotyped characters.

Avant-garde: French term meaning "vanguard." It is used in literary criticism to describe new writing that rejects traditional approaches to literature in favor of innovations in style or content.

B

Beat Movement: A period featuring a group of American poets and novelists of the 1950s and 1960s—including Jack Kerouac, Allen Ginsberg, Gregory Corso, William S. Burroughs, and Lawrence Ferlinghetti—who rejected established social and literary values. Using such techniques as stream of consciousness writing and jazz-influenced free verse and focusing on unusual or abnormal states of mind—generated by religious ecstasy or the use of drugs—the Beat writers aimed to create works that were unconventional in both form and subject matter.

Bildungsroman: A German word meaning "novel of development." The *bildungsroman* is a study of the maturation of a youthful character, typically brought about through a series of social or sexual encounters that lead to self-awareness. *Bildungsroman* is used interchangeably with *erziehungsroman,* a novel of initiation and education. When a *bildungsroman* is concerned with the development of an artist (as in James Joyce's *A Portrait of the Artist as a Young Man*), it is often termed a *kunstlerroman.*

Black Aesthetic Movement: A period of artistic and literary development among African Americans in the 1960s and early 1970s. This was the first major African-American artistic movement since the Harlem Renaissance and was closely paralleled by the civil rights and black power movements. The black aesthetic writers attempted to produce works of art that would be meaningful to the black masses. Key figures in black aesthetics included one of its founders, poet and playwright Amiri Baraka, formerly known as LeRoi Jones; poet and essayist Haki R. Madhubuti, formerly Don L. Lee; poet and playwright Sonia Sanchez; and dramatist Ed Bullins.

Black Humor: Writing that places grotesque elements side by side with humorous ones in an attempt to shock the reader, forcing him or her to laugh at the horrifying reality of a disordered world.

Burlesque: Any literary work that uses exaggeration to make its subject appear ridiculous, either by treating a trivial subject with profound seriousness or by treating a dignified subject frivolously. The word "burlesque" may also be used as an adjective, as in "burlesque show," to mean "striptease act."

C

Character: Broadly speaking, a person in a literary work. The actions of characters are what constitute the plot of a story, novel, or poem. There are numerous types of characters, ranging from simple, stereotypical figures to intricate, multifaceted ones. In the techniques of anthropomorphism and personification, animals—and even places or things—can assume aspects of character. "Characterization" is the process by which an author creates vivid, believable characters in a work of art. This may be done in a variety of ways, including (1) direct description of the character by the narrator; (2) the direct presentation of the speech, thoughts, or actions of the character; and (3) the responses of other characters to the character. The term "character" also refers to a form originated by the ancient Greek writer Theophrastus that later became popular in the seventeenth and eighteenth centuries. It is a short essay or sketch of a person who prominently displays a specific attribute or quality, such as miserliness or ambition.

Climax: The turning point in a narrative, the moment when the conflict is at its most intense. Typically, the structure of stories, novels, and plays is one of rising action, in which tension builds to the climax, followed by falling action, in which tension lessens as the story moves to its conclusion.

Colloquialism: A word, phrase, or form of pronunciation that is acceptable in casual conversation but not in formal, written communication. It is considered more acceptable than slang.

Coming of Age Novel: See *Bildungsroman*

Concrete: Concrete is the opposite of abstract, and refers to a thing that actually exists or a description that allows the reader to experience an object or concept with the senses.

Connotation: The impression that a word gives beyond its defined meaning. Connotations may be universally understood or may be significant only to a certain group.

Convention: Any widely accepted literary device, style, or form.

D

Denotation: The definition of a word, apart from the impressions or feelings it creates (connotations) in the reader.

Denouement: A French word meaning "the unknotting." In literary criticism, it denotes the resolution of conflict in fiction or drama. The *denouement* follows the climax and provides an outcome to the primary plot situation as well as an explanation of secondary plot complications. The *denouement* often involves a character's recognition of his or her state of mind or moral condition.

Description: Descriptive writing is intended to allow a reader to picture the scene or setting in which the action of a story takes place. The form this description takes often evokes an intended emotional response—a dark, spooky graveyard will evoke fear, and a peaceful, sunny meadow will evoke calmness.

Dialogue: In its widest sense, dialogue is simply conversation between people in a literary work; in its most restricted sense, it refers specifically to the speech of characters in a drama. As a specific literary genre, a "dialogue" is a composition in which characters debate an issue or idea.

Diction: The selection and arrangement of words in a literary work. Either or both may vary depending on the desired effect. There are four general types of diction: "formal," used in scholarly or lofty writing; "informal," used in relaxed but educated conversation; "colloquial," used in everyday speech; and "slang," containing newly coined words and other terms not accepted in formal usage.

Didactic: A term used to describe works of literature that aim to teach some moral, religious, political, or practical lesson. Although didactic elements are often found in artistically pleasing works, the term "didactic" usually refers to literature in which the message is more important than the form. The term may also be used to criticize a work that the critic finds "overly didactic," that is, heavy-handed in its delivery of a lesson.

Doppelganger: A literary technique by which a character is duplicated (usually in the form of an alter ego, though sometimes as a ghostly counterpart) or divided into two distinct, usually opposite personalities. The use of this character device is widespread in nineteenth- and twentieth-century literature, and indicates a growing awareness among authors that the "self" is really a composite of many "selves."

Double Entendre: A corruption of a French phrase meaning "double meaning." The term is used to indicate a word or phrase that is deliberately ambiguous, especially when one of the meanings is risqué or improper.

Dramatic Irony: Occurs when the audience of a play or the reader of a work of literature knows something that a character in the work itself does not know. The irony is in the contrast between the intended meaning of the statements or actions of a character and the additional information understood by the audience.

Dystopia: An imaginary place in a work of fiction where the characters lead dehumanized, fearful lives.

E

Edwardian: Describes cultural conventions identified with the period of the reign of Edward VII of England (1901-1910). Writers of the Edwardian Age typically displayed a strong reaction against the propriety and conservatism of the Victorian Age. Their work often exhibits distrust of authority in religion, politics, and art and expresses strong doubts about the soundness of conventional values.

Empathy: A sense of shared experience, including emotional and physical feelings, with someone or something other than oneself. Empathy is often used to describe the response of a reader to a literary character.

Enlightenment, The: An eighteenth-century philosophical movement. It began in France but had a wide impact throughout Europe and America. Thinkers of the Enlightenment valued reason and believed that both the individual and society could achieve a state of perfection. Corresponding to this essentially humanist vision was a resistance to religious authority.

Epigram: A saying that makes the speaker's point quickly and concisely. Often used to preface a novel.

Epilogue: A concluding statement or section of a literary work. In dramas, particularly those of the seventeenth and eighteenth centuries, the epilogue is a closing speech, often in verse, delivered by an actor at the end of a play and spoken directly to the audience.

Epiphany: A sudden revelation of truth inspired by a seemingly trivial incident.

Episode: An incident that forms part of a story and is significantly related to it. Episodes may be either self-contained narratives or events that depend on a larger context for their sense and importance.

Epistolary Novel: A novel in the form of letters. The form was particularly popular in the eighteenth century.

Epithet: A word or phrase, often disparaging or abusive, that expresses a character trait of someone or something.

Existentialism: A predominantly twentieth-century philosophy concerned with the nature and perception of human existence. There are two major strains of existentialist thought: atheistic and Christian. Followers of atheistic existentialism believe that the individual is alone in a godless universe and that the basic human condition is one of suffering and loneliness. Nevertheless, because there are no fixed values, individuals can create their own characters—indeed, they can shape themselves—through the exercise of free will. The atheistic strain culminates in and is popularly associated with the works of Jean-Paul Sartre. The Christian existentialists, on the other hand, believe that only in God may people find freedom from life's anguish. The two strains hold certain beliefs in common: that existence cannot be fully understood or described through empirical effort; that anguish is a universal element of life; that individuals must bear responsibility for their actions; and that there is no common standard of behavior or perception for religious and ethical matters.

Expatriates: See *Expatriatism*

Expatriatism: The practice of leaving one's country to live for an extended period in another country.

Exposition: Writing intended to explain the nature of an idea, thing, or theme. Expository writing is often combined with description, narration, or argument. In dramatic writing, the exposition is the introductory material which presents the characters, setting, and tone of the play.

Expressionism: An indistinct literary term, originally used to describe an early twentieth-century school of German painting. The term applies to almost any mode of unconventional, highly subjective writing that distorts reality in some way.

F

Fable: A prose or verse narrative intended to convey a moral. Animals or inanimate objects with human characteristics often serve as characters in fables.

Falling Action: See *Denouement*

Fantasy: A literary form related to mythology and folklore. Fantasy literature is typically set in non-existent realms and features supernatural beings.

Farce: A type of comedy characterized by broad humor, outlandish incidents, and often vulgar subject matter.

Femme fatale: A French phrase with the literal translation "fatal woman." A *femme fatale* is a sensuous, alluring woman who often leads men into danger or trouble.

Fiction: Any story that is the product of imagination rather than a documentation of fact. characters and events in such narratives may be based in real life but their ultimate form and configuration is a creation of the author.

Figurative Language: A technique in writing in which the author temporarily interrupts the order, construction, or meaning of the writing for a particular effect. This interruption takes the form of one or more figures of speech such as hyperbole, irony, or simile. Figurative language is the opposite of literal language, in which every word is truthful, accurate, and free of exaggeration or embellishment.

Figures of Speech: Writing that differs from customary conventions for construction, meaning, order, or significance for the purpose of a special meaning or effect. There are two major types of figures of speech: rhetorical figures, which do not make changes in the meaning of the words, and tropes, which do.

Fin de siecle: A French term meaning "end of the century." The term is used to denote the last decade of the nineteenth century, a transition period when writers and other artists abandoned old conventions and looked for new techniques and objectives.

First Person: See *Point of View*

Flashback: A device used in literature to present action that occurred before the beginning of the story. Flashbacks are often introduced as the dreams or recollections of one or more characters.

Foil: A character in a work of literature whose physical or psychological qualities contrast strongly with, and therefore highlight, the corresponding qualities of another character.

Folklore: Traditions and myths preserved in a culture or group of people. Typically, these are passed on by word of mouth in various forms—such as legends, songs, and proverbs—or preserved in customs and ceremonies. This term was first used by W. J. Thoms in 1846.

Folktale: A story originating in oral tradition. Folktales fall into a variety of categories, including legends, ghost stories, fairy tales, fables, and anecdotes based on historical figures and events.

Foreshadowing: A device used in literature to create expectation or to set up an explanation of later developments.

Form: The pattern or construction of a work which identifies its genre and distinguishes it from other genres.

G

Genre: A category of literary work. In critical theory, genre may refer to both the content of a given work—tragedy, comedy, pastoral—and to its form, such as poetry, novel, or drama.

Gilded Age: A period in American history during the 1870s characterized by political corruption and materialism. A number of important novels of social and political criticism were written during this time.

Gothicism: In literary criticism, works characterized by a taste for the medieval or morbidly attractive. A gothic novel prominently features elements of horror, the supernatural, gloom, and violence: clanking chains, terror, charnel houses, ghosts, medieval castles, and mysteriously slamming doors. The term "gothic novel" is also applied to novels that lack elements of the traditional Gothic setting but that create a similar atmosphere of terror or dread.

Grotesque: In literary criticism, the subject matter of a work or a style of expression characterized by exaggeration, deformity, freakishness, and disorder. The grotesque often includes an element of comic absurdity.

H

Harlem Renaissance: The Harlem Renaissance of the 1920s is generally considered the first significant movement of black writers and artists in the United States. During this period, new and established black writers published more fiction and poetry than ever before, the first influential black literary journals were established, and black authors and artists received their first widespread recognition and serious critical appraisal. Among the major writers associated with this period are Claude McKay, Jean Toomer, Countee Cullen, Langston Hughes, Arna Bontemps, Nella Larsen, and Zora Neale Hurston.

Hero/Heroine: The principal sympathetic character (male or female) in a literary work. Heroes and heroines typically exhibit admirable traits: idealism, courage, and integrity, for example.

Holocaust Literature: Literature influenced by or written about the Holocaust of World War II. Such literature includes true stories of survival in concentration camps, escape, and life after the war, as well as fictional works and poetry.

Humanism: A philosophy that places faith in the dignity of humankind and rejects the medieval perception of the individual as a weak, fallen creature. "Humanists" typically believe in the perfectibility of human nature and view reason and education as the means to that end.

Hyperbole: In literary criticism, deliberate exaggeration used to achieve an effect.

I

Idiom: A word construction or verbal expression closely associated with a given language.

Image: A concrete representation of an object or sensory experience. Typically, such a representation helps evoke the feelings associated with the object or experience itself. Images are either "literal" or "figurative." Literal images are especially concrete and involve little or no extension of the obvious meaning of the words used to express them. Figurative images do not follow the literal meaning of the words exactly. Images in literature are usually visual, but the term "image" can also refer to the representation of any sensory experience.

Imagery: The array of images in a literary work. Also, figurative language.

In medias res: A Latin term meaning "in the middle of things." It refers to the technique of beginning a story at its midpoint and then using various flashback devices to reveal previous action.

Interior Monologue: A narrative technique in which characters' thoughts are revealed in a way that appears to be uncontrolled by the author. The interior monologue typically aims to reveal the inner self of a character. It portrays emotional experiences as they occur at both a conscious and unconscious level. images are often used to represent sensations or emotions.

Irony: In literary criticism, the effect of language in which the intended meaning is the opposite of what is stated.

J

Jargon: Language that is used or understood only by a select group of people. Jargon may refer to terminology used in a certain profession, such as computer jargon, or it may refer to any nonsensical language that is not understood by most people.

L

Leitmotiv: See *Motif*

Literal Language: An author uses literal language when he or she writes without exaggerating or embellishing the subject matter and without any tools of figurative language.

Lost Generation: A term first used by Gertrude Stein to describe the post-World War I generation of American writers: men and women haunted by a sense of betrayal and emptiness brought about by the destructiveness of the war.

M

Mannerism: Exaggerated, artificial adherence to a literary manner or style. Also, a popular style of the visual arts of late sixteenth-century Europe that was marked by elongation of

the human form and by intentional spatial distortion. Literary works that are self-consciously high-toned and artistic are often said to be "mannered."

Metaphor: A figure of speech that expresses an idea through the image of another object. Metaphors suggest the essence of the first object by identifying it with certain qualities of the second object.

Modernism: Modern literary practices. Also, the principles of a literary school that lasted from roughly the beginning of the twentieth century until the end of World War II. Modernism is defined by its rejection of the literary conventions of the nineteenth century and by its opposition to conventional morality, taste, traditions, and economic values.

Mood: The prevailing emotions of a work or of the author in his or her creation of the work. The mood of a work is not always what might be expected based on its subject matter.

Motif: A theme, character type, image, metaphor, or other verbal element that recurs throughout a single work of literature or occurs in a number of different works over a period of time.

Myth: An anonymous tale emerging from the traditional beliefs of a culture or social unit. Myths use supernatural explanations for natural phenomena. They may also explain cosmic issues like creation and death. Collections of myths, known as mythologies, are common to all cultures and nations, but the best-known myths belong to the Norse, Roman, and Greek mythologies.

N

Narration: The telling of a series of events, real or invented. A narration may be either a simple narrative, in which the events are recounted chronologically, or a narrative with a plot, in which the account is given in a style reflecting the author's artistic concept of the story. Narration is sometimes used as a synonym for "storyline."

Narrative: A verse or prose accounting of an event or sequence of events, real or invented. The term is also used as an adjective in the sense "method of narration." For example, in literary criticism, the expression "narrative technique" usually refers to the way the author structures and presents his or her story.

Narrator: The teller of a story. The narrator may be the author or a character in the story through whom the author speaks.

Naturalism: A literary movement of the late nineteenth and early twentieth centuries. The movement's major theorist, French novelist Emile Zola, envisioned a type of fiction that would examine human life with the objectivity of scientific inquiry. The Naturalists typically viewed human beings as either the products of "biological determinism," ruled by hereditary instincts and engaged in an endless struggle for survival, or as the products of "socioeconomic determinism," ruled by social and economic forces beyond their control. In their works, the Naturalists generally ignored the highest levels of society and focused on degradation: poverty, alcoholism, prostitution, insanity, and disease.

Noble Savage: The idea that primitive man is noble and good but becomes evil and corrupted as he becomes civilized. The concept of the noble savage originated in the Renaissance period but is more closely identified with such later writers as Jean-Jacques Rousseau and Aphra Behn.

Novel: A long fictional narrative written in prose, which developed from the novella and other early forms of narrative. A novel is usually organized under a plot or theme with a focus on character development and action.

Novel of Ideas: A novel in which the examination of intellectual issues and concepts takes precedence over characterization or a traditional storyline.

Novel of Manners: A novel that examines the customs and mores of a cultural group.

Novella: An Italian term meaning "story." This term has been especially used to describe fourteenth-century Italian tales, but it also refers to modern short novels.

O

Objective Correlative: An outward set of objects, a situation, or a chain of events corresponding to an inward experience and evoking this experience in the reader. The term frequently appears in modern criticism in discussions of authors' intended effects on the emotional responses of readers.

Objectivity: A quality in writing characterized by the absence of the author's opinion or feeling about the subject matter. Objectivity is an important factor in criticism.

Oedipus Complex: A son's amorous obsession with his mother. The phrase is derived from the story of the ancient Theban hero Oedipus, who unknowingly killed his father and married his mother.

Omniscience: See *Point of View*

Onomatopoeia: The use of words whose sounds express or suggest their meaning. In its simplest sense, onomatopoeia may be represented by words that mimic the sounds they denote such as "hiss" or "meow." At a more subtle level, the pattern and rhythm of sounds and rhymes of a line or poem may be onomatopoeic.

Oxymoron: A phrase combining two contradictory terms. Oxymorons may be intentional or unintentional.

P

Parable: A story intended to teach a moral lesson or answer an ethical question.

Paradox: A statement that appears illogical or contradictory at first, but may actually point to an underlying truth.

Parallelism: A method of comparison of two ideas in which each is developed in the same grammatical structure.

Parody: In literary criticism, this term refers to an imitation of a serious literary work or the signature style of a particular author in a ridiculous manner. A typical parody adopts the style of the original and applies it to an inappropriate subject for humorous effect. Parody is a form of satire and could be considered the literary equivalent of a caricature or cartoon.

Pastoral: A term derived from the Latin word "pastor," meaning shepherd. A pastoral is a literary composition on a rural theme. The conventions of the pastoral were originated by the third-century Greek poet Theocritus, who wrote about the experiences, love affairs, and pastimes of Sicilian shepherds. In a pastoral, characters and language of a courtly nature are often placed in a simple setting. The term pastoral is also used to classify dramas, elegies, and lyrics that exhibit the use of country settings and shepherd characters.

Pen Name: See *Pseudonym*

Persona: A Latin term meaning "mask." *Personae* are the characters in a fictional work of literature. The *persona* generally functions as a mask through which the author tells a story in a voice other than his or her own. A *persona* is usually either a character in a story who acts as a narrator or an "implied author," a voice created by the author to act as the narrator for himself or herself.

Personification: A figure of speech that gives human qualities to abstract ideas, animals, and inanimate objects.

Picaresque Novel: Episodic fiction depicting the adventures of a roguish central character ("picaro" is Spanish for "rogue"). The picaresque hero is commonly a low-born but clever individual who wanders into and out of various affairs of love, danger, and farcical intrigue. These involvements may take place at all social levels and typically present a humorous and wide-ranging satire of a given society.

Plagiarism: Claiming another person's written material as one's own. Plagiarism can take the form of direct, word-for-word copying or the theft of the substance or idea of the work.

Plot: In literary criticism, this term refers to the pattern of events in a narrative or drama. In its simplest sense, the plot guides the author in composing the work and helps the reader follow the work. Typically, plots exhibit causality and unity and have a beginning, a middle, and an end. Sometimes, however, a plot may consist of a series of disconnected events, in which case it is known as an "episodic plot."

Poetic Justice: An outcome in a literary work, not necessarily a poem, in which the good are rewarded and the evil are punished, especially in ways that particularly fit their virtues or crimes.

Poetic License: Distortions of fact and literary convention made by a writer—not always a poet—for the sake of the effect gained. Poetic license is closely related to the concept of "artistic freedom."

Poetics: This term has two closely related meanings. It denotes (1) an aesthetic theory in literary criticism about the essence of poetry or (2) rules prescribing the proper methods, content, style, or diction of poetry. The term poetics may also refer to theories about literature in general, not just poetry.

Point of View: The narrative perspective from which a literary work is presented to the reader. There are four traditional points of view. The

"third person omniscient" gives the reader a "godlike" perspective, unrestricted by time or place, from which to see actions and look into the minds of characters. This allows the author to comment openly on characters and events in the work. The "third person" point of view presents the events of the story from outside of any single character's perception, much like the omniscient point of view, but the reader must understand the action as it takes place and without any special insight into characters' minds or motivations. The "first person" or "personal" point of view relates events as they are perceived by a single character. The main character "tells" the story and may offer opinions about the action and characters which differ from those of the author. Much less common than omniscient, third person, and first person is the "second person" point of view, wherein the author tells the story as if it is happening to the reader.

Polemic: A work in which the author takes a stand on a controversial subject, such as abortion or religion. Such works are often extremely argumentative or provocative.

Pornography: Writing intended to provoke feelings of lust in the reader. Such works are often condemned by critics and teachers, but those which can be shown to have literary value are viewed less harshly.

Post-Aesthetic Movement: An artistic response made by African Americans to the black aesthetic movement of the 1960s and early '70s. Writers since that time have adopted a somewhat different tone in their work, with less emphasis placed on the disparity between black and white in the United States. In the words of post-aesthetic authors such as Toni Morrison, John Edgar Wideman, and Kristin Hunter, African Americans are portrayed as looking inward for answers to their own questions, rather than always looking to the outside world.

Postmodernism: Writing from the 1960s forward characterized by experimentation and continuing to apply some of the fundamentals of modernism, which included existentialism and alienation. Postmodernists have gone a step further in the rejection of tradition begun with the modernists by also rejecting traditional forms, preferring the anti-novel over the novel and the anti-hero over the hero.

Primitivism: The belief that primitive peoples were nobler and less flawed than civilized peoples because they had not been subjected to the tainting influence of society.

Prologue: An introductory section of a literary work. It often contains information establishing the situation of the characters or presents information about the setting, time period, or action. In drama, the prologue is spoken by a chorus or by one of the principal characters.

Prose: A literary medium that attempts to mirror the language of everyday speech. It is distinguished from poetry by its use of unmetered, unrhymed language consisting of logically related sentences. Prose is usually grouped into paragraphs that form a cohesive whole such as an essay or a novel.

Prosopopoeia: See *Personification*

Protagonist: The central character of a story who serves as a focus for its themes and incidents and as the principal rationale for its development. The protagonist is sometimes referred to in discussions of modern literature as the hero or anti-hero.

Protest Fiction: Protest fiction has as its primary purpose the protesting of some social injustice, such as racism or discrimination.

Proverb: A brief, sage saying that expresses a truth about life in a striking manner.

Pseudonym: A name assumed by a writer, most often intended to prevent his or her identification as the author of a work. Two or more authors may work together under one pseudonym, or an author may use a different name for each genre he or she publishes in. Some publishing companies maintain "house pseudonyms," under which any number of authors may write installations in a series. Some authors also choose a pseudonym over their real names the way an actor may use a stage name.

Pun: A play on words that have similar sounds but different meanings.

R

Realism: A nineteenth-century European literary movement that sought to portray familiar characters, situations, and settings in a realistic manner. This was done primarily by using an objective narrative point of view and through the buildup of accurate detail. The standard for success of any realistic work depends on how faithfully it transfers common experience into fictional forms. The realistic method may be altered or extended, as in stream of consciousness writing, to record highly subjective experience.

Repartee: Conversation featuring snappy retorts and witticisms.

Resolution: The portion of a story following the climax, in which the conflict is resolved.

Rhetoric: In literary criticism, this term denotes the art of ethical persuasion. In its strictest sense, rhetoric adheres to various principles developed since classical times for arranging facts and ideas in a clear, persuasive, appealing manner. The term is also used to refer to effective prose in general and theories of or methods for composing effective prose.

Rhetorical Question: A question intended to provoke thought, but not an expressed answer, in the reader. It is most commonly used in oratory and other persuasive genres.

Rising Action: The part of a drama where the plot becomes increasingly complicated. Rising action leads up to the climax, or turning point, of a drama.

Roman à clef: A French phrase meaning "novel with a key." It refers to a narrative in which real persons are portrayed under fictitious names.

Romance: A broad term, usually denoting a narrative with exotic, exaggerated, often idealized characters, scenes, and themes.

Romanticism: This term has two widely accepted meanings. In historical criticism, it refers to a European intellectual and artistic movement of the late eighteenth and early nineteenth centuries that sought greater freedom of personal expression than that allowed by the strict rules of literary form and logic of the eighteenth-century neoclassicists. The Romantics preferred emotional and imaginative expression to rational analysis. They considered the individual to be at the center of all experience and so placed him or her at the center of their art. The Romantics believed that the creative imagination reveals nobler truths—unique feelings and attitudes—than those that could be discovered by logic or by scientific examination. Both the natural world and the state of childhood were important sources for revelations of "eternal truths." "Romanticism" is also used as a general term to refer to a type of sensibility found in all periods of literary history and usually considered to be in opposition to the principles of classicism. In this sense, Romanticism signifies any work or philosophy in which the exotic or dreamlike figure strongly, or that is devoted to individualistic expression, self-analysis, or a pursuit of a higher realm of knowledge than can be discovered by human reason.

Romantics: See *Romanticism*

S

Satire: A work that uses ridicule, humor, and wit to criticize and provoke change in human nature and institutions. There are two major types of satire: "formal" or "direct" satire speaks directly to the reader or to a character in the work; "indirect" satire relies upon the ridiculous behavior of its characters to make its point. Formal satire is further divided into two manners: the "Horatian," which ridicules gently, and the "Juvenalian," which derides its subjects harshly and bitterly.

Science Fiction: A type of narrative about or based upon real or imagined scientific theories and technology. Science fiction is often peopled with alien creatures and set on other planets or in different dimensions.

Second Person: See *Point of View*

Setting: The time, place, and culture in which the action of a narrative takes place. The elements of setting may include geographic location, characters' physical and mental environments, prevailing cultural attitudes, or the historical time in which the action takes place.

Simile: A comparison, usually using "like" or "as," of two essentially dissimilar things, as in "coffee as cold as ice" or "He sounded like a broken record."

Slang: A type of informal verbal communication that is generally unacceptable for formal writing. Slang words and phrases are often colorful exaggerations used to emphasize the speaker's point; they may also be shortened versions of an often-used word or phrase.

Slave Narrative: Autobiographical accounts of American slave life as told by escaped slaves. These works first appeared during the abolition movement of the 1830s through the 1850s.

Socialist Realism: The Socialist Realism school of literary theory was proposed by Maxim Gorky and established as a dogma by the first Soviet Congress of Writers. It demanded adherence to a communist worldview in works of literature. Its doctrines required an objective viewpoint comprehensible to the working classes and themes of social struggle featuring strong proletarian heroes.

Stereotype: A stereotype was originally the name for a duplication made during the printing process; this led to its modern definition as a person or thing that is (or is assumed to be) the same as all others of its type.

Stream of Consciousness: A narrative technique for rendering the inward experience of a character. This technique is designed to give the impression of an ever-changing series of thoughts, emotions, images, and memories in the spontaneous and seemingly illogical order that they occur in life.

Structure: The form taken by a piece of literature. The structure may be made obvious for ease of understanding, as in nonfiction works, or may obscured for artistic purposes, as in some poetry or seemingly "unstructured" prose.

Sturm und Drang: A German term meaning "storm and stress." It refers to a German literary movement of the 1770s and 1780s that reacted against the order and rationalism of the enlightenment, focusing instead on the intense experience of extraordinary individuals.

Style: A writer's distinctive manner of arranging words to suit his or her ideas and purpose in writing. The unique imprint of the author's personality upon his or her writing, style is the product of an author's way of arranging ideas and his or her use of diction, different sentence structures, rhythm, figures of speech, rhetorical principles, and other elements of composition.

Subjectivity: Writing that expresses the author's personal feelings about his subject, and which may or may not include factual information about the subject.

Subplot: A secondary story in a narrative. A subplot may serve as a motivating or complicating force for the main plot of the work, or it may provide emphasis for, or relief from, the main plot.

Surrealism: A term introduced to criticism by Guillaume Apollinaire and later adopted by Andre Breton. It refers to a French literary and artistic movement founded in the 1920s. The Surrealists sought to express unconscious thoughts and feelings in their works.

The best-known technique used for achieving this aim was automatic writing—transcriptions of spontaneous outpourings from the unconscious. The Surrealists proposed to unify the contrary levels of conscious and unconscious, dream and reality, objectivity and subjectivity into a new level of "super-realism."

Suspense: A literary device in which the author maintains the audience's attention through the buildup of events, the outcome of which will soon be revealed.

Symbol: Something that suggests or stands for something else without losing its original identity. In literature, symbols combine their literal meaning with the suggestion of an abstract concept. Literary symbols are of two types: those that carry complex associations of meaning no matter what their contexts, and those that derive their suggestive meaning from their functions in specific literary works.

Symbolism: This term has two widely accepted meanings. In historical criticism, it denotes an early modernist literary movement initiated in France during the nineteenth century that reacted against the prevailing standards of realism. Writers in this movement aimed to evoke, indirectly and symbolically, an order of being beyond the material world of the five senses. Poetic expression of personal emotion figured strongly in the movement, typically by means of a private set of symbols uniquely identifiable with the individual poet. The principal aim of the Symbolists was to express in words the highly complex feelings that grew out of everyday contact with the world. In a broader sense, the term "symbolism" refers to the use of one object to represent another.

T

Tall Tale: A humorous tale told in a straightforward, credible tone but relating absolutely impossible events or feats of the characters. Such tales were commonly told of frontier adventures during the settlement of the west in the United States.

Theme: The main point of a work of literature. The term is used interchangeably with thesis.

Thesis: A thesis is both an essay and the point argued in the essay. Thesis novels and thesis plays share the quality of containing a thesis which is supported through the action of the story.

Third Person: See *Point of View*

Tone: The author's attitude toward his or her audience may be deduced from the tone of the work. A formal tone may create distance or convey politeness, while an informal tone may encourage a friendly, intimate, or intrusive feeling in the reader. The author's attitude toward his or her subject matter may also be deduced from the tone of the words he or she uses in discussing it.

Transcendentalism: An American philosophical and religious movement, based in New England from around 1835 until the Civil War. Transcendentalism was a form of American romanticism that had its roots abroad in the works of Thomas Carlyle, Samuel Coleridge, and Johann Wolfgang von Goethe. The Transcendentalists stressed the importance of intuition and subjective experience in communication with God. They rejected religious dogma and texts in favor of mysticism and scientific naturalism. They pursued truths that lie beyond the "colorless" realms perceived by reason and the senses and were active social reformers in public education, women's rights, and the abolition of slavery.

U

Urban Realism: A branch of realist writing that attempts to accurately reflect the often harsh facts of modern urban existence.

Utopia: A fictional perfect place, such as "paradise" or "heaven."

V

Verisimilitude: Literally, the appearance of truth. In literary criticism, the term refers to aspects of a work of literature that seem true to the reader.

Victorian: Refers broadly to the reign of Queen Victoria of England (1837-1901) and to anything with qualities typical of that era. For example, the qualities of smug narrowmindedness, bourgeois materialism, faith in social progress, and priggish morality are often considered Victorian. This stereotype is contradicted by such dramatic intellectual developments as the theories of Charles Darwin, Karl Marx, and Sigmund Freud (which stirred strong debates in England) and the critical attitudes of serious Victorian writers like Charles Dickens and

George Eliot. In literature, the Victorian Period was the great age of the English novel, and the latter part of the era saw the rise of movements such as decadence and symbolism.

W

Weltanschauung: A German term referring to a person's worldview or philosophy.

Weltschmerz: A German term meaning "world pain." It describes a sense of anguish about the nature of existence, usually associated with a melancholy, pessimistic attitude.

Z

Zeitgeist: A German term meaning "spirit of the time." It refers to the moral and intellectual trends of a given era.

Cumulative Author/Title Index

Cumulative
Nationality/Ethnicity Index

Potok, Chaim
The Chosen: V4
Davita's Harp: V34
Roth, Philip
American Pastoral: V25
Salinger, J. D.
The Catcher in the Rye: V1
Franny and Zooey: V30
Spiegelman, Art
Maus: A Survivor's Tale:
V35
West, Nathanael
The Day of the Locust: V16
Wiesel, Eliezer
Night: V4
Yezierska, Anzia
Bread Givers: V29
Yolen, Jane
Briar Rose: V30

Korean
Choi, Sook Nyul
Year of Impossible Goodbyes:
V29

Mexican
Esquivel, Laura
Like Water for Chocolate: V5
Fuentes, Carlos
The Old Gringo: V8

Native American
Alexie, Sherman
*The Lone Ranger and Tonto
Fistfight in Heaven:* V17
Reservation Blues: V31
Dorris, Michael
A Yellow Raft in Blue Water:
V3
Erdrich, Louise
Love Medicine: V5
Momaday, N. Scott
House Made of Dawn: V10
Silko, Leslie Marmon
Ceremony: V4
Welch, James
Winter in the Blood: V23

New Zealander
Hulme, Keri
The Bone People: V24

Nigerian
Abani, Chris
GraceLand: V35
Achebe, Chinua
No Longer at Ease: V33
Things Fall Apart: V3

Emecheta, Buchi
The Bride Price: V12
The Wrestling Match: V14

Norwegian
Rölvaag, O. E.
Giants in the Earth: V5

Polish
Conrad, Joseph
Heart of Darkness: V2
Lord Jim: V16
Kosinski, Jerzy
The Painted Bird: V12

Portuguese
Saramago, José
Blindness: V27

Romanian
Wiesel, Eliezer
Night: V4

Russian
Asimov, Isaac
I, Robot: V29
Bulgakov, Mikhail
The Master and Margarita:
V8
Dostoyevsky, Fyodor
The Brothers Karamazov: V8
Crime and Punishment: V3
Notes from Underground: V28
Nabokov, Vladimir
Lolita: V9
Pasternak, Boris
Doctor Zhivago: V26
Rand, Ayn
Anthem: V29
Atlas Shrugged: V10
The Fountainhead: V16
Solzhenitsyn, Aleksandr
*One Day in the Life of Ivan
Denisovich:* V6
Tolstoy, Leo
Anna Karenina: V28
War and Peace: V10
Turgenev, Ivan
Fathers and Sons: V16
Yezierska, Anzia
Bread Givers: V29

Scottish
Grahame, Kenneth
The Wind in the Willows: V20
Scott, Walter
Ivanhoe: V31

Spark, Muriel
The Prime of Miss Jean Brodie: V22
Stevenson, Robert Louis
Kidnapped: V33
Treasure Island: V20

South African
Coetzee, J. M.
Dusklands: V21
Courtenay, Bryce
The Power of One: V32
Gordimer, Nadine
July's People: V4
Head, Bessie
When Rain Clouds Gather: V31
Paton, Alan
Cry, the Beloved Country: V3
Too Late the Phalarope: V12

Spanish
de Cervantes Saavedra, Miguel
Don Quixote: V8

Sri Lankan
Ondaatje, Michael
The English Patient: V23

Swedish
Spiegelman, Art
Maus: A Survivor's Tale: V35

Swiss
Hesse, Hermann
Demian: V15
Siddhartha: V6
Steppenwolf: V24

Turkish
Pamuk, Orhan
My Name is Red: V27

Uruguayan
Bridal, Tessa
The Tree of Red Stars: V17

Vietnamese
Duong Thu Huong
Paradise of the Blind: V23

West Indian
Kincaid, Jamaica
Annie John: V3

Zimbabwean
Dangarembga, Tsitsi
Nervous Conditions: V28

Subject/Theme Index

Tragic heroes
  Oroonoko; or, The Royal Slave: A True History: 277
Tranquility
  Oroonoko; or, The Royal Slave: A True History: 270
Transformation
  The Contender: 30
  GraceLand: 103
  Of Human Bondage: 245
Travel
  Oroonoko; or, The Royal Slave: A True History: 276–277, 280, 287
Triumph
  The Contender: 56
Trust (Psychology)
  The Contender: 35, 36
  The Sea-Wolf: 329
Truth
  April Morning: 25–28
  The Contender: 54–55
  Of Human Bondage: 232
  Maus: A Survivor's Tale: 192, 193, 195, 196
  Oroonoko; or, The Royal Slave: A True History: 288, 289, 294
  Wicked: The Life and Times of the Wicked Witch of the West: 381, 391
Tyranny
  Wicked: The Life and Times of the Wicked Witch of the West: 373, 379, 382, 383, 386, 388

U

Understanding
  Maus: A Survivor's Tale: 196
Unity
  GraceLand: 101

Urban life
  The Contender: 39, 52–53, 57
  Fever 1793: 70–72
  GraceLand: 110–111
  See also Harlem life

V

Values (Philosophy)
  The Sea-Wolf: 322–323, 331
Vanity
  Wicked: The Life and Times of the Wicked Witch of the West: 376
Verisimilitude
  Fever 1793: 70
  Oroonoko; or, The Royal Slave: A True History: 280
  Shabanu: Daughter of the Wind: 355
Victorian values
  Of Human Bondage: 245
Victory. *See* Triumph
Vigilante justice
  GraceLand: 99
Violence
  GraceLand: 88, 91, 94, 99, 102, 107, 110, 111
  The Outsiders: 306, 309, 314, 315
  The Sea-Wolf: 323–326, 330, 337–338
  Shabanu: Daughter of the Wind: 350
  Wicked: The Life and Times of the Wicked Witch of the West: 373, 377, 384, 385, 391
Virginity
  Wicked: The Life and Times of the Wicked Witch of the West: 386
Virtue
  Wicked: The Life and Times of the Wicked Witch of the West: 373, 386

Vulnerability
  April Morning: 16
  Shabanu: Daughter of the Wind: 360

W

Warning
  Shabanu: Daughter of the Wind: 360
Wars
  April Morning: 1, 4–6, 9–12, 15, 16, 22–24
  Oroonoko; or, The Royal Slave: A True History: 283
Weakness
  The Contender: 32
  The Sea-Wolf: 342
Wealth
  Shabanu: Daughter of the Wind: 350, 352
  Wicked: The Life and Times of the Wicked Witch of the West: 380
Western culture
  GraceLand: 97, 100–102, 104, 105
Wisdom
  April Morning: 6
  Fever 1793: 66
Women's rights
  Fever 1793: 72, 73, 75, 76
Work
  Never Let Me Go: 218
World War I, 1914-1918
  Of Human Bondage: 247

Y

Youth
  The Outsiders: 310–312, 315

For Reference

Not to be taken from this room

DATE DUE

GAYLORD			PRINTED IN U.S.A.

DATE DUE

GAYLORD | | | PRINTED IN U.S.A.